The Roman Inquisition

on the Stage of Italy, c. 1590–1640

THE ROMAN INQUISITION ON THE STAGE OF ITALY, C. 1590–1640

Thomas F. Mayer

PENN

UNIVERSITY OF PENNSYLVANIA PRESS

PHILADELPHIA

A volume in the Haney Foundation Series, established in 1961
with the generous support of Dr. John Louis Haney.

Published by
University of Pennsylvania Press
Philadelphia, Pennsylvania 19104-4112
www.upenn.edu/pennpress

Printed in the United States of America on acid-free paper
2 4 6 8 10 9 7 5 3 1

Library of Congress Cataloging-in-Publication Data

Mayer, Thomas F. (Thomas Frederick), 1951–
The Roman Inquisition on the stage of Italy, c. 1590–1640 / Thomas F. Mayer. — 1st ed.
p. cm. — (Haney Foundation Series)
ISBN 978-0-8122-4573-8 (hardcover : alk. paper)
Includes bibliographical references and index.
1. Catholic Church. Congregatio Romanae et Universalis Inquisitionis. 2. Inquisition—Italy—History—16th century. 3. Inquisition—Italy—History—17th century. 4. Trials (Heresy)—Italy—History—16th century. 5. Trials (Heresy)—Italy—History—17th century. 6. Italy—Church history—16th century. 7. Italy—Church history—17th century. I. Title. II. Series
BX1723.M385 2014
272'.20945 2013020964

CONTENTS

Introduction

Heresy-hunting probably always had a political dimension. It only intensified once the popes took an increasingly active role beginning in the twelfth century.[1] Lucius III's pivotal decretal *Ad abolendam* (1184), sometimes mistakenly taken as *the* or at least *a* foundational document of the papal inquisition, called on imperial authorities to assist in the search for heretics, and may have been issued with Emperor Frederick I's tacit support.[2] It also dictated a mode of investigation containing some of the elements of the new technique of *inquisitio*.[3] Although originally intended for the investigation of abuses committed by the higher clergy, when Innocent III began to systematize it in the early thirteenth century, he did so in a similarly political context. He certainly made the attack on heresy a political question when, for example, early in his reign he aimed another key document in the development of papal efforts to suppress heresy, *Vergentis in senium*, at the commune of Viterbo at a time when he was struggling to bring it under papal obedience. By applying imperial law to heresy, the decretal made heretics' property forfeit.[4] Innocent was also responsible for one of the most notorious political heresy-hunts, the Albigensian crusade.[5]

Neither politicizing heresy nor creating a new means of seeking it out automatically entailed the creation of an institution designed to pursue it, an inquisition. Instead, thirteenth-century inquisitors often worked in quasi-independent fashion without papal authorization. The popes responded with intense efforts to bring inquisitors under their authority, quickly taking an interest in this remarkably useful tool and putting it to work, especially against forms of heresy that would eventually develop into witchcraft.[6] Thus in the mid-thirteenth century Gregory IX deputed Conrad of Marburg as his personal agent against a group of "Luciferians" in the vicinity of Cologne.[7] But even Gregory enjoyed only indifferent success in controlling local inquisitors and his efforts did not create any kind of institution, certainly not a Roman Inquisition.[8] It was not until the late fifteenth century that even local inquisitions could be spoken of as institutionalized. The popes assiduously pursued efforts similar to Gregory's in some cases, the kingdom of Aragon being one of the best illustrations. Other efforts were almost entirely abandoned, as happened in most of the Italian peninsula until 1542, when Paul III refounded the Inquisition. After several protracted struggles, those with Venice and the duke of Mantua being among the best known, by the end of the century the popes largely succeeded by in gaining theoretical control of all local inquisitions in Italy.[9] Practical dominance was another matter, with several of the most important tribunals either almost eluding papal control, as in Venice and Naples, or constantly resisting it, as in the Spanish duchy of Milan, seat of another major inquisitorial tribunal.

By the early seventeenth century when this book begins, the popes had made the nature of their ambitions clear. Urban VIII spoke only a little more bluntly than his immediate predecessors when he described his government as "absolutely monarchical."[10] As it had done from the first, the Roman Inquisition continued to provide one of the best tools for establishing such a regime. In *The Roman Inquisition: A Papal Bureaucracy and Its Laws in the Age of Galileo*, I began by endorsing the usual view that the Inquisition was the most powerful papal congregation, the only one headed directly by the pope. I went beyond that to argue that Urban VIII (reigned 1623–1645) developed an unprecedented degree of control over the institution, which he was prepared to put to nearly any end, including, as had his predecessors, the papacy's political goals. A prosopographical study of all the Inquisition's professional staff and a large sample of the Cardinals Inquisitor demonstrated the same point. Loyalty to Urban and his family became a much more important qualification than either preparation in law or theology or the on-the-job training that all members of the Holy Office, including the cardinals who directed its operations, had previously undergone. Urban's attitude also at first glance undercut the centuries-long development of the Inquisition's procedure and "style," in theory developed to protect defendants (see the end of this Introduction and in more depth *Roman Inquisition*, Chapter 5). In the Inquisition the law—civil, canon, and its own adaptation of both—and careful bureaucratic procedures stood in tension not only with constantly changing papal goals but also with that "style," designed to produce maximum flexibility and, in theory anyway, speedy justice. While the second of these often remained an ideal in direct proportion to a case's importance (see especially those of Tommaso Campanella, Cesare Cremonini, and Rodrigo Alidosi discussed below), the Inquisition's drive to innovate virtually invited Urban's use of it to new ends, or further development of it to pursue older ones. One innovative legal device in particular, the precept, will often be singled out, because it is the hinge on which Galileo's trial turned. It will be treated more fully in my final volume, where its meaning and usage will be spelled out.

In this book I detail how the Roman Inquisition operated to serve the papacy's long-standing political aims in Naples, Venice, and Florence, within the bureaucratic and legal parameters laid out in the earlier volume. The timeframes differ between the three places. In Naples the peak of papal efforts to insert an Inquisition directly answerable to Rome came under Urban VIII, who achieved a considerable degree of success. By contrast, the popes made their most intense efforts to bring the Venetians to heel in the decade or so following the interdict of 1606, and after largely suffering defeat mainly left the Serenissima alone in the future. Florence somewhat surprisingly provides a middle case. Despite the debt the grand dukes owed to the papacy for support in founding their duchy in the mid-sixteenth century, and constant protestations of their Catholic orthodoxy, the grand dukes could strongly resist papal mandates and kept almost as much control over the local inquisition as the Venetians did, albeit through less obviously institutional means. Also like the Venetians, when the grand dukes wished to protect a subject, they largely succeeded. In this respect, Galileo makes a notable exception.

A Sketch of the Book

Please note: This book began as the second half of a single volume intended as an introduction to Galileo's trial. The first half is *The Roman Inquisition: A Papal Bureaucracy and Its Laws in the Age of Galileo* (2013). While this book is designed to stand independently of the earlier volume, reading them in sequence will make understanding this one easier.

Jurisdictional squabbles were a permanent feature of relations between the papacy, the Inquisition, and Italian states.[11] The Roman Inquisition's situation was more complicated in Naples than in Venice, because it was one of two largely independent inquisitions, the archbishop's and the pope's. Papal claims resembled those in Venice, but instead of being crystallized by a particular event, they developed gradually through constant reiteration, in a series of cases concerning the extent of and boundaries between papal and lay jurisdiction. Unlike the situation in Venice, the Neapolitan viceregal authorities suffered from the disadvantage of not having representation on the Inquisition's tribunal, leaving it a much freer hand to plot and sometimes outflank the lay authorities. The body in Naples responsible for supervising the Inquisition, the Collateral Council, the highest council under the viceroy, could only act from outside the Inquisition and usually only after the fact. Nevertheless, the viceroy could intervene easily and always had the king of Spain to appeal to when necessary. Nevertheless, the Roman Inquisition in Naples successfully challenged the lay authorities, to the point of prosecuting and condemning some of them as well as a number of high-ranking nobles. But the Roman Inquisition in Naples suffered from an inherent weakness, in addition to competition from the archbishop. Its agent originally had low status, a defect Paul V remedied in part by sending out men with experience in the central tribunal. Thus several successive agents had served as commissary and several nuncios as assessor or in another Inquisition office. It was not until the 1640s that the agent managed to keep permanently the title of inquisitor. The turning point came with Urban VIII's aggressive drive to establish effective papal control through the agency of the Inquisition. Urban also achieved more success than his predecessors in the highest-profile case tried in Naples in our period, that of Tommaso Campanella. While Clement VIII (reigned 1592–1605) had initiated proceedings to condemn Campanella, it took years of complicated negotiations with the viceregal authorities before this was achieved and then only under Paul V. Urban, by contrast, accomplished Campanella's liberation in a matter of a couple of years. At least there was nothing obviously irregular about how he did so. In keeping with his marked tendency from the late 1620s when Campanella was transferred to Rome, Urban did interfere in a number of Neapolitan cases, ignoring or even subverting proper process.

Venice conceded even less than Naples to papal pretensions, including those about the Inquisition. It was a jurisdictional dispute over clerical immunities that gave rise to the interdict Paul V placed on Venice in April 1606. For a year, the Venetians bombarded the papacy and the rest of Italy with a mountain of books and pamphlets demonstrating the legitimacy of lay control of most religious matters. After Paul lifted the interdict, he resolved to use the Roman Inquisition to get revenge on the writers of those books and pamphlets, chief among them the Republic's official theologian, Paolo Sarpi, as well as a number of other authors. This struggle provides the substance of Chapter 3. Through the agency of the nuncio to Venice, who headed its Inquisition with the local inquisitor in a subordinate role, the pope tried for almost a decade to get those men into his hands for condign punishment. In the main he failed, succeeding in executing only one of them, Fulgenzio

Manfredi, after the Venetians also tired of him. The rest whom the Venetians decided to protect remained safe, even Sarpi, despite three assassination attempts, at least one of them almost certainly directed by the nuncio. The nuncio was reduced to trying to use Venetian political institutions to achieve his aims, with, unsurprisingly, next to no positive results. Nevertheless, using the Roman Inquisition in such fashion made its political nature abundantly clear. In this chapter, rather than break each of the numerous cases out into individual threads, I have chosen to follow them all at the same time in a strictly chronological narrative. This may risk a little confusion, but it has the great advantage of showing just how much the Inquisition and the nuncio—not to mention the Venetians—had on their plates at one time.

The first two of the three cases treated in Chapter 4 are less overtly political. The trial of Giordano Bruno, which lasted about eight years, and the long investigation of the Paduan philosopher Cesare Cremonini do nonetheless demonstrate that when the Venetians chose to protect a subject from the Roman Inquisition, they succeeded. Bruno, not a Venetian, was extradited and executed, while Cremonini not only remained safe in Padua, but flaunted his secure position by overt appeals to Venetian political organs, which responded through their ambassadors in Rome. The last case in the chapter points the contrast with the Venetians' solicitude for Cremonini. They quickly abandoned Marcantonio De Dominis. Although it took the Roman Inquisition a decade, it succeeded in condemning him posthumously and burning his corpse. De Dominis's trial was also at least as political as those in Chapter 1. From the first the Roman Inquisition showed an interest principally in his ideas about papal power and the structure of the Christian republic, and they figure largely in his sentence in 1624.

Urban also had a little more success bringing the Florentines to heel, and not just through silencing Galileo. After more than thirty years he accomplished the likely original aim of the papal attack on Rodrigo Alidosi, the centerpiece of Chapter 5, incorporating his tiny but strategically located fief into the papal states. Alidosi, who lived almost continuously in Florence, was not a major subject of the grand duke. His wife, on the other hand, was the sister of Concino Concini, a powerful figure in the French court through her husband, a major military commander who had the patronage of Marie de Medicis, wife of Henry IV. Almost certainly because of this connection, the grand duke determinedly protected Alidosi, eventually taking his fief of Castel del Rio under his wing. One of the grand duke's best strategies was to maintain control or at least strong influence over the Florentine Inquisition. The

Congregation demanded the replacement of at least one inquisitor because he favored Alidosi. Thus the popes could not rely on the local Inquisition to gain their ends, despite a dogged pursuit of both Rodrigo and his son Mariano lasting in total almost thirty years. Instead, Urban finally had to seize the minuscule state on a spurious charge of treason, once more resorting to means that were at least legally dubious. In these two cases and many others, the popes gradually adopted the same tool they used in Venice and Naples, going around the local inquisitor and using the nuncio as the Roman Inquisition's principal agent instead. Thus by the late 1630s the Roman Inquisition, already the most powerful papal congregation, in effect took over the next most powerful organ of papal power, its diplomatic apparatus.

The Roman Inquisition's Trial Process in Brief

The Roman Inquisition used a summary version of the procedure of *inquisitio* fleshed out by Innocent III in the early thirteenth century.[12] A summary proceeding omitted steps in order to speed up a trial, primarily the *libelli oblatione*, the presentation early on of written evidence by both parties to a suit, and the *litis contestatio*, the moment at which the suit was joined and the judge began to hear evidence. Both derived from civil pleadings and neither ever fit well into a criminal proceeding. Nevertheless, legal commentators struggled mightily to assimilate both to a criminal trial, above all the second, which had come to be regarded as the moment of pleading. In practice, despite their repeated insistence that nothing could be left out of a plenary process if the omission would harm a defendant, the assimilation of these two moments had one serious effect: it helped to delay the presentation of charges until the first phase of the trial, the investigative process (or *processo informativo*), had ended. When this was combined with a further deemphasis of *publica fama* (public report) as the ineluctable starting point of an *inquisitio*, the defendant's position had been seriously weakened.

Another alleged change in the summary version of *inquisitio* has been misunderstood and had its consequences grossly overstated. While advocates (defense attorneys) did indeed have restrictions applied to their action, which in local tribunals might be taken to mean virtually ignoring them (see, e.g., the *Malleus maleficarum*, an especially poor guide to the theory behind proper legal proceedings but just for that reason an excellent guide to practice), they were never eliminated and the Roman tribunal virtually insisted on their involvement. Following the practice in other papal courts, it also appointed what we would call a public defender to represent those too poor to afford their own counsel. As we shall see below, for example, in the Neapolitan cases of Cristovál de Figueroa and Tommaso Campanella, advocates could have a major impact on a trial's outcome. One more change from Innocent's day definitely worked against a suspect, the suppression of witnesses' names. As often the case with moves to a defendant's disadvantage, Boniface VIII introduced this modification at the beginning of the fourteenth century.

Instead of beginning with a "public report" that a particular person had committed a particular crime, the Roman Inquisition came to rely on denunciations to open proceedings. It rarely adopted the alternative of proceeding ex officio (see the case of Fabrizio Caracciolo in Chapter 1, in the course of which Urban VIII—no stickler for legal niceties—insisted that the bishop's trial had to begin with a denunciation, not the Inquisition's commissary's mere action). After a denunciation and a decision that the case belonged to the Inquisition, the investigative phase, the *processo informativo*, opened. It began with testimony from witnesses before the suspect was examined. At this point another problem arose for him or her, the oath of telling the truth. By the late fifteenth century, bowing to practice despite the theoretical prohibition against self-incrimination, it had become usual in a criminal *inquisitio* to demand such an oath from the suspect already in the investigative phase. He or she was not free to refuse it. (Some commentators, including the authoritative Francisco Peña, dean of the Rota and a long-time consultor of the Inquisition, also thought it was licit to torture a vacillating suspect at this point.) As far as one can tell, the Roman Inquisition did not follow this practice, but we have too few trial dossiers to speak with any assurance.

Once the investigative phase had ended, the suspect had to be cited to appear. It was the unanimous view that this moment could not be omitted, the principle often being rooted in either natural or divine law (God's summons to Adam in the Garden of Eden). Nevertheless, the citation was still not supposed to include the charges, although it appears that some did. It was usual to cite the suspect three times before declaring him or her contumacious (in contempt). A suspect who did not surrender could be captured and imprisoned. This was not an action to be taken lightly, since it harmed the suspect's reputation, a consequence the Inquisition insisted it wished to avoid at all costs. That principle undergirded its notorious rule of secrecy.

Once in the Roman Inquisition's hands and probably, although not necessarily, in its prison in the Palazzo del Sant'Ufficio, the governor of Rome's in Tor di Nona, or sometimes for especially favored suspects Castel Sant'Angelo, the suspect was interrogated. Many commentators discussed the kinds of questions to be asked, including the first substantive one, whether the suspect knew why he had been summoned. He or she would never be told the charges, putting the suspect at a major disadvantage. That was counterbalanced by strict prohibitions on asking leading questions, or about other offenses than the one under investigation. Despite these protections of the suspect, the interrogator, usually the Inquisition's commissary, literally the Congregation's stand-in, was allowed to engage in trickery. The notary was to record exactly everything the suspect said. The questions were often entered in more formulaic fashion.

Finally, at the moment still often identified as the *litis contestatio*, the suspect entered a plea. At that moment he or she became a defendant and, in theory anyway, the fiscal or public prosecutor took over the case. Now began the *repetitio*, the questioning of witnesses for both prosecution and defense. The defendant (and his or her advocate) had to be given a full copy of the dossier, missing only the witnesses' names, in order to prepare questions. Any witnesses who had appeared in the *processo informativo* had to be questioned again. The judge was to go out of his way to protect the defendant, including by asking questions he or she had forgotten to supply. Once the *repetitio* had ended the defense proper began, another phase rooted in natural law and therefore unavoidable. A complete copy of the *repetitio*, including the fiscal's articles, should once more go to the defendant, who was given another chance to deny the charges and to respond in detail to testimony within the term granted. This might range from a few days almost literally to years. The best defense was threefold. A defendant and his or her advocate could deny the fact, enter legitimate "exceptions" to the prosecution's witnesses, mainly to their character or to alleged mortal enmity between them and the defendant, or stress his or her own good character and enter an excuse for his or her actions, ranging from drunkenness to frivolity.

After the defense concluded came the liminal moment of the *expeditio*, literally expedition. This fleeting phase contained three elements: the writing out of the *summarium*, a résumé of the case which was the only document the Congregation saw; its consideration by the Inquisition's experts (consultors) along with submissions by the defense; and the proposal and passing of sentence, sometimes by the cardinals alone, sometimes with the pope's approval. The consultors' opinion provided the essential element of the *expeditio*, even though the Congregation was free to reject it. Once the sentence, usually containing a clause that the Congregation could change it whenever it saw fit, was handed down, there followed abjuration and punishment. The first was supposed to be public, although it seems the grace of literally "swearing off" the convict's heresy in private was granted fairly often. Punishment could range from "salutary penances" to perpetual relegation to the galleys to death. The Inquisition rarely handed down explicitly capital sentences, and executed fewer than one person a year in Rome during the period covered by this book. Nevertheless, perpetual relegation to the galleys could amount to the same thing, and those sentences were much more frequent. Finally, the sentence might be "published," but never to more than a restricted group, for two reasons. First, doing so would defame the convict; second, it might encourage others to imitate his or her heresy.

The Sources

As in *The Roman Inquisition*, my principal sources are the surviving materials generated by the Roman Inquisition's central tribunal, especially the underused decree registers.[13] These produced a wealth of new evidence, especially about the Roman Inquisition's relations with Venice, including during the trial of Marcantonio De Dominis, and the actions of the long serving inquisitor of Venice, Giovanni Domenico Vignuzzio, whose tenure has attracted little attention. The Congregation's correspondence, especially as preserved possibly complete for 1626–1628, often fleshes out the decrees. Especially in the chapters about Venice, diplomatic correspondence and records of secular governments' deliberations have been brought into evidence.[14] *Avvisi*, newsletters, although much less reliable than diplomatic dispatches, nevertheless at least provide what reasonably well-informed observers thought was happening. The lucky survival of pieces of several trial dossiers allows this volume to adopt the perspective of the big trials which is only rarely possible, given the almost complete loss of the Roman Inquisition's *processi*. Two partial dossiers prove especially valuable, that of Rodrigo and Mariano Alidosi, the backbone of the chapters about Florence, and of Tommaso Campanella's trials in Naples. The development of the Holy Office's Neapolitan branch also becomes much clearer with the help of this source. As in *Roman Inquisition*, I have emphasized the legal side of developments, while remembering that the law is a human institution and that the men who administered it might prove almost as important as the law itself. Thus where possible I continue to use the prosopographical approach adopted in the earlier book, for example, in capsule biographies of inquisitors in Naples and Florence; unfortunately, lack of evidence does not allow the same treatment of Venice.

A Note About Terminology

"Inquisition" is a confusing term because it means at least three things, only two of which are usually relevant here: (1) the corporate body of the Roman Inquisition, often officially known as the "Sacred Congregation of the Holy Office," including its satellite tribunals throughout Italy; and (2) a procedure, common to all civil law systems but developing into an increasingly distinctive form in the hands of the Sacred Congregation. A third meaning of the term, the loosest, used to describe any inquisition, perhaps especially the Spanish variant, will be avoided here. Thus "Roman Inquisition" refers to the entire apparatus of the Sacred Congregation and its satellites; "Inquisition" with a capital "I" refers to one of those satellites; and "inquisition" with a small "i" means the procedure. "The Congregation" means the corporate body that, by the beginning of the period covered here, had just recently evolved out of the cardinals originally deputed individually by Paul III and who had therefore issued decisions in all their names. "Inquisitor" with a capital "I" means one of these cardinals; "inquisitor" with a small "i" means any inquisitor not a member of the Sacred Congregation. I have not used the term to apply to Inquisition officials.

Latin *processus* and Italian *processo* mean both a trial and the resulting dossier. I have tried to stay as close to these words as possible when translating them. Thus I have sometimes written of "making process," which may sound awkward in English but is more accurate than "proceeding," for example, which need not mean the formal investigation denoted by *processus*. Similarly, a "formed process" means that a trial had reached the point at which its dossier was complete as far as the evidence went and was ready for judgment.

Two other terms need definition. Congregation with a capital "C" refers to the corporate body of the cardinals Inquisitor, while the word with a lower case "c" denotes one of its meetings.[15] "Coram" ("in the presence of") signifies the weekly Thursday meeting of the Congregation with the pope; all its other meetings are non-corams.

CHAPTER 1

Spain and Naples

Beginning no later than the mid-fifteenth century and intensifying spectacularly after the Sack of Rome followed in 1536 by Charles V's hectoring of the pope in his own palace, the papacy suffered from strained relations with the Hapsburg powers, above all Spain. This situation arose partly as a natural reaction to the preponderance that country enjoyed throughout this period, in Rome as well as over most of the rest of the Italian peninsula, including the most dangerous case, the Spanish dependency of Naples.[1] Beginning in the early seventeenth century, the popes, especially Paul V and Urban VIII, tried to escape Spanish tutelage. Urban achieved more than his predecessors, but the specter of Spain lurked constantly in the shadows behind the Roman Inquisition's operations, especially during Urban's protracted struggle with Cardinal Inquisitor (and sometime Spanish ambassador to Rome) Gaspar Borja y Velasco.

From the first, the Roman Inquisition had a peculiar status in Naples. Barely a decade after the founding of the Roman Inquisition in 1542, it appointed a commissary in Naples.[2] It arrived precociously relative to other Italian states, for example, Mantua, where it did not manage to establish its tribunal until the 1570s.[3] From the first, the nuncio was also deeply involved, a model of local inquisition tribunals eventually extended elsewhere, especially to Venice and Florence.[4] More than in Mantua or anywhere else except Venice, the Inquisition in Naples found itself hedged in by the local political authorities.[5] Thus, not until the late 1630s did its agent regularly call himself inquisitor, a signal indication of the success of Urban's pressure and of earlier failure. Even odder, there were always two inquisitions in Naples, archiepiscopal and papal, distinguished in no way as to competence or even often as to personnel since it was usual in the sixteenth century to make the archiepiscopal vicar general the Roman Inquisition's commissary. Unlike every other diocese in Italy, the archbishops succeeded in keeping their own inquisition not only in being but also healthy, handling for a long time a vastly greater volume of business than its papal counterpart.[6] Despite the Congregation's own construction in 1596 of the situation as meaning there was only one "ordinary tribunal" of the Inquisition in Naples, the archbishop's, together with a "manner of extraordinary provision for the service of this [Roman] Inquisition," the second was explicitly not a "tribunal" (the delegated papal one), reasonably quickly Rome asserted and gained ascendancy over the archbishop.[7] Luigi Amabile, whose *Santo Officio . . . in Napoli* remains the basic work, thought the corner had been turned already in 1564 when Giulio Antonio Santoro, one of the key figures in the Inquisition's history, became commissary "even though he was not the archbishopric of Naples' lieutenant" (meaning vicar general as Amabile clarified elsewhere) with the right to further subdelegate his authority.[8] Amabile also thought that Santoro's appointment began an unbroken string of officials with the same status. As Giovanni Romeo has shown, Amabile's first claim is not true—Santoro had indeed been "luogotenente" of the archdiocese—nor is the second.[9]

The process by which the Roman Inquisition established itself in Naples was much more drawn out and conflicted than Amabile thought. Romeo also, probably rightly, sees a difference in status between "minister" or commissary and inquisitor, and thinks the second may have had more power. This seems plausible, even if lack of documents makes it impossible to demonstrate the point.[10] During the tenure of the longest-serving sixteenth-century commissary, Carlo Baldino (in post, according to Romeo, from 1585 to 1598), Romeo found a number of disputes between him and the archiepiscopal court, including an effort by one archbishop to have the delegated inquisition withdrawn.[11] Instead of the the smooth arc Amabile saw, interrupted only by brave but futile local resistance, Romeo finds a contradiction internal to Rome's drive to centralization which intensified just at the time of Baldino's appointment.[12] The next fifteen years marked the period "perhaps most intense in the whole history of the Roman Inquisition," in terms of both volume of cases and effectiveness of Rome's control over both Neapolitan courts.[13] Romeo places the crucial moment in 1622, when the otherwise little-known Giovanni Girolamo Campanile asked Rome for guidance in the use of the title "inquisitor" that others had applied to him. Rome counseled caution, but allowed him to adopt the new designation.[14] In fact, the point was not yet won, and Campanile's immediate successors Giacinto Petronio and Antonio Ricciulli called themselves both "minister" and "inquisitor."[15] A better indication of the arrival of the Roman Inquisition at the height of its powers is the four executions Ricciulli was allowed to conduct.[16]

The degree to which the Roman Inquisition operated successfully in Naples is one of the best indicators both of the aggressiveness of papal policy and of its success or lack thereof. This chapter divides into three in order to demonstrate this proposition. First, it analyzes the fraught relationship between Urban VIII and Cardinal Borja as perhaps the best indication of the nearly permanent tension in the larger stand-off between the pope and the Spanish Crown in the first half of the seventeenth century, which of course directly affected what happened in Naples. Second, it details the history of the Inquisition's "minister," an official who would be called "inquisitor" in most places. Finally, it recounts a series of cases that raised political and jurisdictional issues between the Congregation, the archbishop of Naples, and the viceregal authorities in Naples. All three show a vaguely upward trajectory, ending in something resembling victory for Rome in the establishment of a dominant position for its local official, except that this official was not the "minister" but rather the nuncio.

Part I: The Specter of Spain and Cardinal Borja

As simultaneously a member of the Inquisition—from 22 August 1629 its most senior member—and Spanish ambassador to the pope, Cardinal Borja stood at center stage of the papacy's ongoing efforts to free itself of Spanish hegemony.[17] It seems likely that Urban's decision to have the Congregation hold its Wednesday meeting at the Dominican convent of Santa Maria sopra Minerva was designed to keep those sessions out of Borja's palace or that of any other Spanish or imperialist cardinal. In 1628, until Urban's order of 14 September, eleven meetings without the pope (called non-corams here; meetings with the pope are corams) had been held at Ottavio Bandini's palace, five at Secretary Gian Garzia Millini's, the same number at Borja's, but twelve at the imperialist Ludovico Madruzzo's, giving the Spanish and their allies a preponderance of the non-corams.[18] If possible, Borja's profile rose in the four years from early 1629. That year represents the apogee of his attendance at corams when he made all but nine of thirty-eight (76 percent) and in 1630–31 his record was almost as good, at 70 percent.[19] Never one to take a perceived insult lightly and therefore always a favorite of the media, Borja gave the newsletter-writers excellent copy, beginning with the furor caused when Constable Colonna, whose family had been an erstwhile pillar of the Spanish establishment in Rome, but who had gone over to Urban's party after his daughter married the pope's nephew Taddeo, turned his back on Borja during a service at the Minerva.[20] In the coram a week later and in highly irregular fashion, Borja raised the matter. Although Urban gave no more than general replies, he also did not attempt to silence Borja.[21] A week later the pope was reported to be trying to get Colonna to apologize.[22]

By the end of the year, Borja's position had slipped as Urban pursued his anti-Spanish campaign. The pope chose a symbolically clever tactic. In a coram attended by Borja, he silenced one Fra Innocenzo, a Reformed Observant Franciscan friar at S. Pietro in Montorio, and confined him to his convent.[23] Although not the Spanish national church (that was S. Giacomo degli Spagnuoli on Piazza Navona), since the late fifteenth century S. Pietro had received lavish gifts from the Spanish Crown. Borja was a strong supporter of Innocenzo, not least because his popularity brought in generous alms. When Borja tried to defend him, Urban became angry, calling it an abuse to venerate a living saint (it was) and gave Borja personally an order under pain of excommunication not to see Fra Innocenzo again.[24] Urban's action was said to be rooted in Innocenzo's prediction of the pope's death, possibly on astrological grounds.[25] It will also bear noting that Urban's action against Innocenzo left no previous trace in the decree registers.

It appears that Borja confronted Urban again a couple of weeks later.[26] This time smilingly, Urban replied to Borja's lengthy defense by saying he knew that the cardinal had often gone to hear Innocenzo's "oracles." This upset Borja, who retorted that they were "much better than the counsels and thoughts of Fr. [Tommaso] Campanella." Urban replied in kind, ordering Borja (again?) not to frequent Innocenzo under pain of excommunication, at least according to an *avviso*, a newsletter.[27] The second *avviso* also reported another disagreement with a powerful Spanish cardinal, Baldassare Moscoso y Sandoval, then temporarily in Rome.[28] He objected that Urban had overridden a unanimous decision in his favor made by the Congregation of Bishops and Regulars. Moscoso accused the papal court of having caused a scandal and declared that he would never return. The pope's brother Antonio Barberini, Sr., now secretary of the Inquisition, intervened "with the greatest modesty," saying Urban would give Moscoso more than any congregation might. The eminent canonist Prospero Fagnani, the Congregation of Bishops and Regulars secretary, tried to support Cardinal Antonio, but Moscoso told him tobe quiet. Moscoso was in Rome at all because of Inquisitor Desiderio Scaglia, who had written to Spain that Urban was dying. Scaglia was also a devotée of Fra Innocenzo, to whom he allegedly spoke after Urban's prohibition.[29]

Borja's Protest

The temper and bad manners manifested thus far fade almost to insignificance at the most notorious moment of Borja's strained relations with Urban. This is his "protest" of 8 March 1632. There is no missing its diplomatic significance. It marked the end of a Spanish attempt to secure an alliance with the papacy against France and its replacement by Urban's protracted campaign to put together a coalition against Spain to be headed by the grand duke of Tuscany. The pivotal moment actually came about a month earlier, when Borja temporarily took over as Spanish ambassador to the pope.[30] According to the most authoritative study, Borja first officially appeared as ambassador in a coram of the Holy Office, dramatically flaunting his new authority.[31] Perhaps drawing on his deep wells of obtuseness, perhaps deliberately manifesting his contempt for Urban and proper modes of doing business, Borja raised an objection about a matter which had nothing to do with the Inquisition, attacking Urban's claim to tax the Spanish clergy. As in the case of the dispute over Fra Innocenzo, the decree registers take no notice of Borja's action. The following Monday Borja took his offensive into consistory, the weekly meeting of pope and cardinals that had become an almost entirely ceremonial occasion, appearing in a body with the other nine Spanish cardinals, demanding a new subsidy for the emperor. Moscoso rather than Borja took the lead, urging Urban to set an example to Christendom, but the pope told Moscoso that he had already spoken to the Spanish cardinals about the matter and to be quiet.[32] Next, the papal master of ceremonies rebuffed an effort to secure a collective extraordinary audience, which Borja chose to interpret as Urban's refusal of any kind of audience.[33] This became the pretext for his actions in the consistory of 8 March.

The protest took the form of a Latin oration delivered by Borja complaining about how slow Urban had been to help the emperor.[34] Urban listened until Borja either called him "cunctator" (delayer) or accused him of delaying ("cunctatur," as the best text of the protest reads).[35] At that point, when Borja had come very near the end of his blast, Urban ordered him to stop speaking, according to at least one account shouting his command. Borja tried to continue, but Urban again shouted at him to be silent. Antonio Barberini, Sr., approached Borja, "a little angry," according to one version, and asked him to cease. He probably also either took Borja's hand or grabbed his sleeve, a breach of protocol that bulked large in Spanish reactions. Cardinal Moscoso intervened, told Antonio not to speak to another cardinal that way, and may have added that it was "indecent" for a Capuchin (Antonio's order) to take the pope's part in a matter of such importance to religion. Urban asked Borja in what capacity he spoke, whether as ambassador or as cardinal. Borja replied "as ambassador" and Urban told him he could not act as such in consistory. Instead, Borja should request an audience like any other ambassador. Borja retorted that he had been refused a meeting, which Urban called a lie. Then Cardinal Colonna tried to defuse the situtation by ringing the bell signaling the consistory's end. Neither Borja nor Urban paid any attention. Only when Borja got Urban's agreement to take a written copy of the protest did he agree to leave. One account has him leave three copies for the heads of religious orders before marching out in company with Scaglia.[36]

More important than the event is the sequel. Borja took his protest into that week's coram of the Inquisition, which it appears Urban had tried to prevent him from attending.[37] At any rate, Borja shouted at Commissary Ippolito Lanci accusing him of failing to send the meeting's agenda.[38] Interestingly enough, Borja allegedly tried afterward to apologize for his behavior and Urban apparently tried to mollify him.[39] By contrast, on at least one other occasion, he refused to give Borja the usual audience after a coram.[40] Both Borja and the pope set their propaganda machines to work, Borja quickly sending out copies of his protest, the pope a little more slowly through his Cardinal Nephew (secretary of state) Francesco Barberini, convening his loyalists (Laudivio Zacchia, Berlinghiero Gessi, Giulio Sacchetti, Giovanni Battista Pamphili, Fabrizio Verospi, Giovanni-Francesco Guidi di Bagno, Francesco Barberini, and Antonio Barberini, Jr.) to draw up their version of what had happened. It went at least to the nuncio in Madrid.[41] In this rendition under Cardinal Francesco's name, Urban's action was justified on the grounds that the pope did not have to follow church councils, much less cardinals, and if anyone objected that the cardinals could weigh in on matters affecting the *respublica christiana*, the nuncio was to reply that the pope's power "is absolutely monarchical."[42]

Over the next month or six weeks, Urban exacted harsh revenge on most of the Italian cardinals in Borja's party, especially Ludovisi and Roberto Ubaldini, whom he accused of being the chief conspirators. He forced them out of Rome along with Florentine cardinal Luigi Capponi.[43] More important, Urban tried to act in exactly the same a-legal fashion he had in the cases of Orazio Morandi, Fra Innocenzo, and others recently. He tried to get the fiscal general of Rome to raid Ubaldini's palace and seize his writings as well as imprison him in Castel Sant'Angelo. The fiscal refused to do so without evidence and demanded a breve authorizing him to act. The pope flatly ordered him to obey and only Cardinal Francesco's intervention saved him from the pope's anger. Nevertheless, it was thought that he had lost his chance to move up to governor and might lose office altogether.[44] Next, Urban tried to manipulate the record. He wanted Ludovisi out as vice-chancellor of the church, a highly lucrative office, and tried to intrude his favorite Inquisitor, Marzio Ginetti. Only fear of the viceroy in Naples led him to back down. Still, only Ginetti had the pope's writing on the matter, which might well not be entered into the consistorial acts because the pope wanted no trace of Borja's protest there.[45]

Urban's Revenge on Borja

It took Urban a while to execute his plot to get rid of Borja. The scheme would make him archbishop of Seville and was already in train before the protest. Borja was provided 19 January 1632 and granted the pallium on 16 February.[46] Since Urban was on record as demanding that bishops take up residence in their sees as laid down by the Council of Trent, holding a bishopric would force Borja out of Rome.[47] He did not go quietly. He accepted the pallium only on 17 June, significantly before a coram.[48] Throughout the first half of the summer, Urban and Borja brandished metaphorical swords at one another, Borja ostentatiously showing up for an audience (usually with a large number of carriages, sometimes including Scaglia's), the pope just as ostentatiously refusing to see him.[49] Even the arrival of a replacement ambassador did not help much.[50] Curiously, the tension eased for a moment when Borja secured cordial audiences following the corams of 1 and 29 July.[51]

In August things appeared headed for a full thaw.[52] Several observers thought the mover was Cardinal Francesco, perhaps because he was terrified of Spain.[53] He was said to be negotiating with the new Spanish ambassador while continuing to keep Borja at arm's length, refusing to come to any meetings which Barberini knew he would attend. Agents from Spain tried to strike a deal.[54] In early September it was thought that the matter was on the point of resolution.[55] Borja's position steadily weakened as Cardinal Francesco courted

Cardinal Scipone Borghese, Paul V's cardinal nephew.[56] When Borja had a brief audience at the end of October, both Francesco and Antonio Barberini, Jr., avoided it.[57] Nevertheless, the Venetian ambassador heard many rumors of an imminent deal.[58]

Almost as soon as Urban and Cardinal Francesco returned from Castel Gandolfo at the end of the month, a deal by which Borja would admit that he had exceeded his instructions and ask forgiveness broke down. It was announced in an *avviso* of 13 November, saying that Borja was "most disconsolate" while Urban crowed about his victory.[59] Yet on the same day the evidently better-informed Venetian ambassador announced that Borja refused to go through with it, even though it had come from him in the first place.[60] The terms concerned Urban's agreement to a general league against "the heretics" and a tax on the Spanish clergy. In return, Borja in consistory would declare him "the most zealous for the Catholic religion, the most closely tied to his king, the most deserving of the house of Austria that [any pope] ever has been" ("il più zelante della Religione Cattolica, il più congionto col suo Re, il più benemerito della Casa d'Austria, che sia mai stato") and say he had no intention to offend by his protest.[61]

Then, at what should have been one of the high points of his papacy, either intentionally or accidentally the pope committed what the Spanish chose to interpret as a major gaffe. Lutheran nemesis Gustav Adolf was killed at the battle of Lützen, leading to universal joy in Rome. While the Spanish cardinals violated protocol and wore non-Advent habits (the Venetian ambassador twice called them red or *cremesino* and once *paonazzo*, a shade of purple), Urban, in proper garb for the season, in the German national church of Santa Maria dell'Anima celebrated only a low Mass and omitted certain ceremonies usual on great occasions.[62] At the end of December, Borja's refusal to execute the deal was reported as fact.[63]

Meantime, Urban got a big break when Cardinal Ludovisi died on 18 November.[64] Almost immediately, Cardinal Francesco replaced him as vice-chancellor, Borja attending that consistory.[65] He and the other Spanish cardinals ostentatiously refused to join the chorus of praise.[66] Urban had worse luck in the case of Ludovisi's co-conspirator Ubaldini. Seizing the opportunity provided by the pope's complaint that few cardinals had attended chapels during Advent, and taking his cue from Cardinal Borghese, Ubaldini appeared on Christmas Eve, greatly annoying Urban, who took this as a sign of how sure Ubaldini was of Spanish protection.[67] Unsurprisingly, Ubaldini had trouble getting an audience.[68] Having failed to see the pope, he tried Borja's tactic by trying to speak in consistory, but was told that the question was "impertinent." He therefore decided to go back to Frascati.[69] Nevertheless, the Spanish continued to court him and persuaded him to come back to Rome for a meeting of Propaganda Fide presided over by Urban.[70] When he also succeeded in drawing a pension from Cardinal Richelieu, Urban had to admit defeat.[71]

If it is not crystal clear that the Inquisition had become (if it ever was not) politicized, the Venetian ambassador spelled out the point in the context of the marriage dispensation for the duke of Mantua, which the French and the Venetians badly wanted in order keep his fief out of Spanish or imperial hands.[72] The ambassador offered the assessment that "In this Congregation [of the Inquisition] there is good and bad, good since it includes subjects rather well inclined and authoritative, and almost all these same [men] whom Padre Bombino [the duke of Mantua's agent] wished [to have involved, in the hopes of a speedy resolution]. . . . bad, because they go with the strictest rigor in silence, and there are great excommunications for resaying anything at all of that which they consider in the said Congregation, whence one can only badly use defensive weapons, resolve doubts (*dubbii*) and difficulties; and Cardinal Borja also attends, even though he and the ambassador of Spain have made various rejoinders to Bombino."[73]

Those "rejoinders" were probably not launched in the Inquisition's meetings. Borja stayed scrupulously away, attending a grand total of only six meetings before 12 May 1633. This strategy, if such it was, of course only enhanced Urban's already impressively greater degree of control over the Congregation.[74] Even when Borja had a complaint to make that might have concerned the Inquisition, he did not so do in one of its meetings. He instead had an audience with Cardinal Francesco about his objection to an anti-Spanish book that had been printed at Bologna.[75]

Part II: The Roman Inquisition's Agents in Naples

A brief sketch of the careers of the Roman Inquisition's commissaries in Naples through Ricciulli († 1642) underscores both the lack of orthogenetic development, and the significance of Urban's actions. The first two commissaries are both well known to historians of sixteenth-century heresy: Scipione Rebiba (1553–1555) and Santoro (appointed 1564), both of whom became cardinals. Neither could have made much of an impact in Naples, since neither served as long as two years.[76] Almost more significant than their later eminence is the fact that the next commissary certainly known, Baldino, occurs in the record only in 1585 or 1583 at the earliest, when he appears as "specially delegated" for a single case.[77] Despite this gap, the Sacred Congregation, in a letter to the archbishop of Naples in 1596, claimed that Baldino had been in office for "more than twenty-five years."[78] In a document of 20 October 1585 he is called "ministro del Santo Officio dell'Inquisizione."[79] He was from Nocera in the *regno* and had been a consultor of the Neapolitan Holy Office since 1571, which seems to be the date the Congregation took as his appointment as minister.[80] Even after he certainly became "minister" he continued to be called a consultor.[81] He also continued to lecture on law until about 1591 as he had since at least 1566.[82] In the first year he was provided to the archbishopric of Sorrento, at least six years after he became minister.[83] Amabile gave him a reputation for rigor, but not enough evidence survives to say much about how he conducted his office or about his relations with the archbishop beyond one or two moments of high tension.[84]

The situation changes in the case of Baldino's successor, Benedetto Mandina. As in Baldino's case, we do not know exactly when Mandina gained appointment sometime after Baldino's death probably early in 1598.[85] Mandina was probably in Rome for much of the time until early 1601, necessitating the appointment of Alberto Tragagliolo as his substitute at least for Tommaso Campanella's trial.[86] Like Baldino, Mandina was from the kingdom of Naples, in this case Melfi. He trained as a lawyer before becoming a Theatine in 1584; he later went to the order's house at Sant'Andrea della Valle in Rome.[87] When he became commissary he was already bishop of Caserta, and it thereafter became usual for the commissaries either to hold a bishopric before or be provided to one at the time of their appointment, probably as an effort to raise their status.[88] Mandina had a higher profile than Baldino in other ways as well. In 1596 he went on a mission to the Emperor Rudolf and in 1604 he served as administrator of the archdiocese of Naples.[89] At least at the time of Giordano Bruno's sentence, which he witnessed, he served as a consultor.[90]

Tragagliolo's appearance in Naples marks a major if impermanent development, the first time the commissary in Rome moved to the same office in Naples. Tragagliolo apparently became commissary in Rome about October 1592, succeeding Vincenzo da Montesanto.[91] Also called Drago, he came from Firenzuola in the Picentino, the same city that later produced his successor Vincenzo Maculano, suggesting once again the importance of geographical ties in staffing the Holy Office. He became a Dominican in Piacenza and then served as inquisitor in Faenza, Genoa, and Milan before ascending to commissary in Rome.[92] The pope nominated him to the bishopric of Termoli 29 November 1599, the royal assent (the *exequatur*) coming on 8 March 1600.[93] Tragagliolo did not hold office in Naples long. He was assigned Campanella's case only on 22/23 April 1600 and died on 1 January 1601.[94] Mandina apparently then resumed office.

At Mandina's death in 1604 Deodato Gentile (1558–1616) succeeded him as both commissary and bishop of Caserta.[95] Gentile had also followed Tragagliolo as commissary of the Roman Inquisition.[96] Nevertheless, in 1608 he was identified only as "delegate of this Holy Congregation in the Neapolitan kingdom."[97] A Genoese, he had been prior of Santa Maria del Castello where he had entered the Dominican order in 1574, being elected provincial diffinitor in 1589 before moving again as prior to Santa Croce in Bosco (1590), San Domenico in Brescia, and Santa Sabina in Rome (1591).[98] He then took a big jump, at least as far as the record says, to inquisitor of Milan (1593). He published two books and allegedly left three manuscript treatises, still in the Biblioteca Borghese in the early eighteenth century, including "De potestate summi pontificis" and "De immunitate ecclesiastica," just the sort of work to recommend him for service in Naples.[99] His tenure there is especially important not only for his energetic prosecution of Campanella, but because he moved up from minister of the Holy Office to nuncio. Between his appointment as nuncio 29 March 1610 and sometime in early 1611 he remained minister, giving the Roman Inquisition an unprecedented stature in Naples.[100]

Gentile's replacement was once again the sitting commissary in Rome, Stefano Vicari from Garessio (province of Cuneo). He had taken the oath as commissary on 17 October 1607.[101] The plan to send him to Naples took shape in late August 1610 when he was nominated bishop of Nocera de' Pagani.[102] Like other commissaries, Vicari was a theologian who served beginning in 1600 as inquisitor in Ancona, one of the more junior posts, before moving on the usual cursus to Faenza and Milan.[103] He is the first commissary thought to have written a manual, "Praxis brevis de modo procedendi in sancto officio in causis fidei."[104] Unfortunately, except for his involvement in the trial of Giulia de Marcos (see below), we know little about Vicari's long tenure either as commissary in Rome or as minister in Naples.[105]

This lack of information together with his undistinguished replacement might lead one to think that Paul V had his attention elsewhere in the 1610s. Both facts may indicate rather that the pope had decided to raise the status of the Inquisition in Naples by attaching it more closely to the office of nuncio, as had already happened with Gentile. At any rate, Gentile's successor was

Paolo Emilio Filonardi, former assessor of the Roman Inquisition.[106] We see glimpses of him in the proceedings against Campanella, but his correspondence as nuncio remains to be systematically investigated, as does that of his successor Cesare Monti, also a former assessor.[107] One point is already abundantly clear from some of the nuncios' letters: their office not only served as an independent conduit to the Inquisition, but also exercised control over its minister, suggesting that Paul's plan worked.[108]

Still, progress was less than linear. The experience of Vicari's replacement in Naples, Giovanni Girolamo Campanile, highlights the continuing ambiguous status of the Roman Inquisition's representative. Shortly after he took office as "ministro," he forwarded to Rome a letter addressed to him as inquisitor in the kingdom of Naples, citing the dangers of using that title. The Congregation replied that he could do so "prudently." In this he had the viceroy's support. Amabile found the viceroy's action unsurprising since he was Cardinal Antonio Zapata y Cisneros (in office December 1620–December 1622), but Amabile did not know that Zapata was a member of the Congregation and might well have been acting as such in supporting Campanile's status.[109] Romeo sees Campanile's new title as the turning point in the history of the Roman Inquisition in Naples, despite acknowledging that later commissaries continued to call themselves by the lesser title.[110] Even Campanile, at his translation to Isernia in 1625, was called only "minister of the Inquisition in the Neapolitan kingdom."[111] A native Neapolitan and a lawyer, Campanile lacked his immediate predecessors' qualifications, since he seems to have been no more than a canon of the cathedral before becoming bishop of Lacedonia in 1608.[112]

At Campanile's death in June 1626 a much weightier person succeeded him, Giacinto Petronio (ca. 1580–1648).[113] As former master of the sacred palace, chief papal censor, Petronio is the most important minister in Naples in our period. Although we lack much comparative evidence, the sheer volume of letters from Rome to him for one of the three years for which these survive (1626) suggests as much, a total of 231.[114] The proportion of letters to Petronio was also high, six of thirty-four on one occasion, nine of forty on another, eight of thirty-four on a third.[115] The decree registers record what is probably at least as high a volume of letters from him, although I have not made a systematic survey.[116] The size of the territory Petronio covered—the entire kingdom of Naples—accounts for some of this scale, but it is still impossible to miss the large increase in his correspondence relative to that before 1625 (see below). A Roman by birth, he studied theology in Salamanca and held the lectorate in Avila.[117] In 1608 he gained the bachelorate of theology at Sta. Maria sopra Minerva.[118] On 11 September 1614, as master of the sacred palace, he swore his oath of secrecy as a consultor to the Inquisition.[119] He attended regularly. Undoubtedly his most notorious act as master was to sign the suspension of Copernicus's *De revolutionibus*. His was possibly the most conflicted of all the tenures of the Holy Office in Naples of interest here, as we shall see. It is also important that, despite his bravado in clashing repeatedly with royal officials, the Congregation still thought of him only as "minister of this Holy Office in Naples," not as inquisitor.[120] Like Mandina, Petronio already held a bishopric in the kingdom, Molfetta, to which he had been provided in 1622.[121] From two letters to Paul V's former cardinal nephew in 1623, reminding him of his promise to restore Petronio as master after the new pope's election, it appears that Petronio may have been exiled, perhaps forced out by the new master of the sacred palace, Niccolò Ridolfi.[122] In any case, after his ouster in August 1622 he never gained another position in Rome.[123] After a ten-year stint as minister of the Inquisition, he died fifteen years later in 1648, still bishop of Molfetta.[124]

The last of the Holy Office's representatives in Naples to be considered had, like Petronio, held an important office in Rome, although not in the Inquisition. Antonio Ricciulli (1582–1642/3) was another native of the *regno*, a member of the largest land-owning family in Rogliano, near Cosenza.[125] By far the most substantial lawyer to serve in Naples, in 1622 he published *Tractatus de jure personarum extra ecclesiae gremium existentium libris novem distinctus . . . ; annexus est alter Tractatus de neophytis* (Rome: Giovanni Angelo Ruffinelli and Angelo Manni, 1622), which described him as "jurisconsult of Rogliano, *rheginus* patrician [i.e., of Reggio Calabria?] [and] consistorial advocate," one of the body of lawyers charged with prosecuting cases of sainthood.[126] Its book V, "De haereticis," has a fair amount about inquisitors as well as a lot about heretics' property. In 1626 he succeeded a probable relative (also a lawyer and a professor at La Sapienza) in the bishopric of Belcastro, which he resigned three years later for a 300-*scudi* pension.[127] Probably about the same time he served as vicegerent of Rome. As such, he gave the first imprimatur for Galileo's *Dialogo*, in 1630. According to Amabile, the viceroy, Manuel de Acevedo y Zúñiga, count of Monterrey, suggested Ricciulli as Petronio's replacement.[128] Like his immediate predecessors, Ricciulli already held a bishopric in the *regno*, Umbriatico, to which he was provided on 16 February 1632.[129] As in Petronio's case, this appears to have been a demotion. Ricciulli was Francesco Barberini's client and had managed to annoy his patron in October 1631.[130]

Barberini used him to visit his abbey of Farfa in May 1632 before dispatching him to Umbriatico.[131] After a year there, Ricciulli was summoned back to Rome, rumored to be in line for one of three posts, including "inquisitor" in Naples.[132] He returned as such to Naples on 28 June 1633.[133] For some reason, perhaps to curry favor with the viceroy, he came without the usual breve of appointment or written instructions; Amabile says the object was to keep secret the names of those he was to imprison. It still took the Crown until the end of March 1634 to approve his appointment. Within a year, he was back in the same kind of trouble as Petronio for calling himself "general inquisitor" in a sentence.[134] In 1639 he became bishop of Caserta, before briefly serving as archbishop of Cosenza.[135] The end of his tenure of the Holy Office in Naples is as significant as the confusion over his title. When he died on 17 May 1643, the archiepiscopal vicar succeeded him.[136]

Amabile saw in Ricciulli's period in Naples the final establishment of the Roman Inquisition. He emphasized as the best evidence the four executions Ricciulli successfully carried out, all of men acting as priests without orders.[137] Romeo is more cautious, citing the title Ricciulli was given on the title pages of two of his books, published in Naples while he was in charge.[138] Both called him "formerly consistorial advocate, then bishop of Belcastro and private apostolic visitor of our most holy lord and vicegerent of Rome, now indeed archbishop of Cosenza and consultor of the Holy Universal Inquisition and minister general in the Neapolitan kingdom."[139] So far as is known, Ricciulli was never a consultor in Rome, although its governor—not vicegerent—sat ex officio. As the end of his career indicates, it would be hard to describe a trajectory in the establishment of the Roman Inquisition in Naples through the single lens of its "minister."

Nevertheless, the political and jurisdictional issues raised by Rome's assertion of its "rights" when trying to establish its local branch carried into a number of cases before the Inquisition in both Naples and Rome. These tell a clearer, if more complicated, tale. For one thing, the Congregation learned a lesson from its failure to make its minister the dominant local inquisitorial power. It turned instead to the nuncio, beginning with temporary experiments early in the century, before giving that office permanent superiority toward the middle of Urban's reign. The Congregation also flexed its muscles in these trials, even when they highlighted the problems with its minister, and won more often than it lost, thereby slowly giving it a solid record of precedent to which to appeal in constant struggles with the archiepiscopal inquisition and the viceregal authorities.

Part III. The Roman Inquisition's Trials in Naples

Giulia de Marcos

One of the most notorious trials conducted by the Roman Inquisiton in Naples took place under Paul V, that of Giulia de Marcos and her accomplices, who seem in effect to have run a well-connected brothel, that is, if we believe her sentence.[140] Opinions differ about whether the case went by the book. The most important issues are the minister's behavior, especially how he related to the viceregal authorities, and how carefully he followed procedure. On the first dimension, it makes virtually a textbook case of Roman experimentation. As for procedure, Romeo claims it was scrupulously followed precisely because the case had so much importance in Naples, while Elisa Novi Chavarria says it was not, for the same reason.[141] Romeo's assertion is not quite true, since, as he points out himself, the minister during the second phase, Stefano Vicari, was related to one of the principal defendants and tried to protect him. Novi Chavarria points out a more substantial problem: the viceroy, the count of Lemos, appointed advocates for the three principal suspects, de Marcos, Giuseppe Vicari (or de Vicariis), and Aniello Arceri, not to mention a judge recommended by him to whom the Inquisition agreed to transfer the investigation.[142] In the end, neither mattered much, since all three were condemned, but those advocates may well have helped to lighten the sentences.

After an initial investigation in 1608 that resulted in exile for both de Marcos and Arciero until 1611, the second *processo* began originally in the hands of Minister Stefano Vicari on 31 July 1614, with well-organized denunciations from the Theatine community in Naples, including Mandina's nephew of the same name.[143] The Congregation heard the accusations, which especially concerned unspecified sexual offenses, on 13 August.[144] Within a week, acting on complaints from the Theatines that Stefano Vicari was not only "suspected, but had shown himself an open defender" of the three accused ("sospetto, ma se n'era di più mostrato all'aperta difensore"), the Congregation transferred the case on 20 August to Fabio Maranta, bishop of Calvi and vicar general of Naples.[145] Much has been made of the irregularity of this move, but we will meet two similar cases below, the excommunication of the Collateral, which was transferred from the Inquisition's minister to the Congregation of Immunities, and the investigation of a bishop for extortion, which Rome moved from a special commissary of the Inquisition to the archbishop's vicar general (who may also have been special commissary).[146] A lawyer who may have at least theoretically practiced in Rome, Maranta († 1619), had been bishop of Calvi since 1582 and, more important, vicar general of Naples since at least the previous year.[147] As such, he had presided over Inquisition cases.[148] Four days after Maranta's appointment, the third principal defendant, Avvocato Vicari, was captured.[149] The transfer to Maranta turns out to be of small significance. The main charge alleged against Minister Vicari had been that he let the viceroy interfere in the case by, for example, giving Avvocato Vicari a royal counsellor as advocate and showing the viceroy the *processo*.[150] Maranta behaved in exactly the same way, giving the *processo* to the viceroy and allowing him to appoint royal advocates for all three defendants as well as—following Neapolitan but not Roman practice—immediately telling them the charges, the denunciations, and the witnesses' names.[151] The Theatines complained again, this time backed up by Archbishop Decio Carafa, and between 14 and 27 September the Congregation ordered the case given to Nuncio Gentile.[152]

This time the change of judge made a difference. On 17 September the nuncio sent Avvocato Vicari to the prisons of the Holy Office in Naples while Gentile requested testimony from Rome, apparently from the first trial he had conducted.[153] Vicari was shortly taken to Rome in chains. Arciero was also arrested. Then, most dramatic of all, in early October de Marcos was apprehended at midnight and spirited away to Rome under heavy guard.[154] By 22 October she had begun to testify, admitting that she had persuaded her codefendants not to confess sexual sins.[155] The fact of only two more *constituti* or sets of *constituti* by the principals is presently known, Arciero's from Naples, which arrived by 19 November, and Vicari's last on 17 January.[156] The case was expedited on 4 February 1615, but, as often happened, the pope delayed sentence until 25 June.[157] All three were to be tortured and to abjure *de formali*, the lowest grade of heresy.[158] The sentence was also to be read in the cathedral of Naples, as it was after negotiations with Archbishop Carafa.[159] After the sentence all three principals underwent one more *constitutus* on 8 July, in which they were asked whether they wanted to abjure.[160] They must have agreed, since the abjuration took place the following Sunday, 12 July, in Santa Maria sopra Minerva.[161] A large number of cardinals attended (Secretary Millini claimed the whole college), including some but seemingly not all Inquisitors, as well as some, but again not all, of the Inquisition's professional staff.[162] The occasion was heavily guarded by 250 *sbirri* plus the Swiss Guards and light cavalry in the piazza. For our purposes, the most important element is the reading of the *summarium* that emphasized pretense of sanctity, the claim that a living person was a saint, in this case de Marcos, and sexual offenses, and included a previously unknown charge that Vicari had contravened a precept not to interact with de Marcos. All three remained in prison three years later, when de Marcos was still pretending sanctity.[163] As often, the final outcome is unknown. What is clear is the impact on the case of relations between the Holy Office in Naples and the viceregal authorities, as well as the nuncio's importance. Under Minister Vicari and his successor, the case went nowhere, in large part because they cooperated closely with the viceroy's men. Only when Nuncio Gentile took over did matters proceed quickly to a conclusion.

Urban's Offensive: Fabrizio Caracciolo

Rome certainly tried hard to create a Neapolitan Inquisition, especially under Urban VIII. The raw numbers for the Congregation's correspondence with Naples indicate the intensity of his concern. Whereas in the years before 1625 the highest annual total is only sixty-five, for the three years 1626–1628, for which registers of the Congregation's out-letters survive, the average is at least 220.[164] That number is also at least four or five times higher than the traffic from the Congregation to Venice and Florence; the highest total for the first is sixty-four and for the second only fifty-three.

Nor was the standing tribunal outside Porta San Gennaro in Naples the Inquisition's only instrument.[165] In addition, in part because of the permanent problem of its "minister," the pope used both special deputies and apostolic vicars, as illustrated in the case of the diocese of Catanzaro and its bishop Fabrizio Caracciolo.[166] Caracciolo's troubles began with a report by Costantino Testi, probably the future *socio* of the commissary in Rome and then its commissary in Calabria, sent to the Holy Office from Cosenza in summer 1624.[167] Testi alleged that the bishop had extorted money.[168] Testi, called "deputed commissary," also reported both Judaizers and an opinion about Francisco Figueroa from Catanzaro in October.[169] In December, Testi sent evidence of the bishop's extortion at the same time as he denounced the bishop's cousin (or possibly his brother). He was ordered in January 1625 to summon Caracciolo to Rome by means of the Congregation for Bishops and Regulars, and given all necessary faculties to conduct the case.[170] After completing the informative process, Testi was ordered again in July to send Caracciolo to Rome and to take control of the diocese in his absence.[171] On 23 July 1625 the Congregation considered the case against two of Caracciolo's accomplices in the extortion, and decided to torture one and release him "cum monitione" ("with a warning"), and to dismiss the other under bond, "a precept having been made to him under pain of the galleys not to talk about the merits of the case."[172]

Then the process took a strange turn, apparently because a new man had taken over from Testi. On 1 January 1626 Benedetto Clementini came out from Rome as vicar general of the diocese, with specific powers from the Holy Office to proceed against Caracciolo.[173] Barely three weeks later, almost as soon as he arrived, he complained that the bishop had interfered in the administration of justice, and Urban ordered information collected.[174] Three months later, Urban once more considered Clementini's denunciation of the bishop for extortion. The entry is too badly damaged to tell what the pope ordered, but the Congregation's letter to Clementini survives and praised at length his actions to date and ordered him to continue to send information.[175] In July Clementini got his reward. On 2 July Urban ordered him appointed apostolic vicar in Catanzaro, in addition to vicar general, the post he already held.[176] Three weeks later, three of his letters denouncing Caracciolo were read. He was again ordered appointed apostolic vicar and told secretly to report on how the diocese was run, as well as to investigate the bishop's brother Mario's interference in Inquisition matters and form a process and send it to Rome; he was ordered to use the Congregation of Bishops and Regulars whenever the bishop's offenses belonged to it.[177] On 10 October Clementini was ordered to have the bishop exile his brother.[178] On 4 November, Caracciolo's complaint about Clementini was reported. On the 12th Clementini got a harsh rebuke for proceeding against Caracciolo ex officio and "per viam inquisitionis," as well as a warning in future not to act without a denunciation or a complaint.[179] Despite this reprimand, in the meantime the order about Mario's exile was repeated. Two weeks later Urban ordered Clementini paid an annual supplement on top of his regular salary.[180]

Urban quickly changed his mind again, repeating his original order to Clementini not to proceed without a denunciation or complaint and ordering proceedings halted.[181] On the cathedral chapter's complaint six weeks later that Clementini had imprisoned a large number of people, he was ordered to send all his *processi* to Rome.[182] After review, the Congregation commended his actions in April.[183] In its session of 8 June, first more complaints against Clementini were heard, then he was ordered to use his discretion in inducing witnesses to depose in cases of solicitation in the confessional, before two other cases he had reported were decreed not to belong to the Inquisition's jurisdiction.[184] By this time Caracciolo had been brought to Rome, which he was under a precept not to leave without Urban's permission. On

10 June he was allowed to return to Naples to feed himself, under another precept not to leave that city.[185]

And there his case sat so far as the decree registers say. A request from his diocese for his return was denied on 31 August 1628.[186] Finally, in the summer of 1629 at Caracciolo's initiative, first via the nuncio and then in his own name, negotiations were opened for either his return to Catanzaro or a move to a bishopric with "better air."[187] He did in fact receive Oppido on 28 January 1630, where he died before 19 January 1632.[188] Caracciolo's case may perhaps represent one of the rare instances in which Urban and the Congregation disagreed. It was also one in which Urban appeared in the somewhat unusual guise of stickler for the niceties of Inquisition procedure, as well as for the jurisdictional boundaries of two Roman congregations, to the Inquisition's possible disadvantage. What is not in doubt is the pope's determination to bring an erring bishop to book, including through extraordinary means, and for offenses that do not appear to belong to the Inquisition.[189]

Urban's Offensive: Cristóval de Figueroa and the Collateral of Naples

Shortly after Caracciolo's case wound down, a much more serious one arose, full of jurisdictional disputes and with major implications for the Holy Office in both Naples and Rome.[190] It began with action taken by the bishop of Nicotera, Carlo Pinti, against a royal tax collector, Francesco (or Francesco Antonio) Stanzione, whom he excommunicated for trying to collect on various kinds of theoretically exempt ecclesiastical property.[191] When the collector thumbed his nose at the excommunication(s), the bishop imprisoned him, treating the case as one of blasphemy and therefore under the the Holy Office's jurisdiction. In response, the viceroy, Antonio Álvarez de Toledo y Beaumont de Navarra, duke of Alba, dispatched a commissary, Cristóval Figueroa de Figueroa, a minor literary figure but also a royal judge, to free the tax collector. He did so by force in violation of the bull *Si de protegendis*, which among other things protected the Inquisition's personnel, and of excommunication, which put his case properly under the Inquisition's jurisdiction.[192] On the bishop's complaint, Petronio had the commissary arrested in Naples, almost literally under the viceroy's nose, and imprisoned. That gave rise to a war over jurisdiction, with the viceroy issuing a "hortatory" to Petronio demanding that he show his powers and the pope responding with thunderous breves against the viceroy. It is no surprise that the case ran for almost four years.

The moment was already fraught, the issue of the Neapolitan Holy Office's imprisonment of laymen causing some of the worst contention. As just one earlier example during Petronio's tenure, there is the case of the printer Domenico di Ferrante Maccarano, imprisoned in 1626 for surreptitiously reprinting Pedro Arias Pérez, *Primavera, y flor de los meiores romances que han salido* . . . (ed. prin. Madrid 1621), a collection of chivalric romances. Maccarano's printshop is attested from 1621 until 1653. It also brought out Guarino's *Il pastor fido* (1622) and the Lincean *Il telescopio ovvero Ispecillo celeste* by Antonio Stelliola (1627).[193] Petronio had originally alerted Antonio Barberini, Sr., about the publication, but next heard from the Inquisition's Secretary Millini writing somewhat testily on 25 April a third letter with the same order.[194] That order was to turn the investigation over to the archbishop, so it appears that at this moment the Congregation may have been trying to defuse a volatile issue.

Not for long. On 2 May Millini wrote again that the new nuncio, Antonio Diaz, was coming with a "commission" to deal with the vicreoy about his "pretensions" relating to the imprisonment of laymen and threats against Petronio by the fiscal of the Vicaria (Giulio Mastrillo, a major mover in the resistance to the Inquisition) to send Spanish soldiers to break Maccarano out of prison.[195] Petronio was told meanwhile to continue the ancient practice of jailing laymen without royal license, albeit only in serious cases and only with an express order from the Congregation. Millini also retreated on his earlier instruction and told Petronio not to give Maccarano's *processo* to the archbishop's vicar general.[196] It appears that the issue of Maccarano's imprisonment had brought Rome to regard the case more seriously. A week later Millini wrote the auditor of the nunciature that Petronio had reported his troubles with Fiscal Mastrillo, who, in addition to his threat to use force to free Maccarano, had also threatened the imprisonment of all of Petronio's servants and the sequestration of their revenues. Millini called it a "strange pretension" that the Holy Office needed permission to imprison laymen. A complaint had been made to the Spanish ambassador in Rome. Millini enclosed a copy of a breve to the viceroy, giving the auditor grounds to complain as well as various talking points, including that it was unnecessary to investigate whether clandestinely published books contained heresy, since mere publication without license was enough by the deal worked out in 1607 covering books published in both Rome and Spain.[197] This time the viceroy quickly blinked, Petronio writing on 23 May that he had allowed Maccarano's imprisonment.[198] On the basis of this agreement, Petronio was told once more to give the archbishop the case, since it was not usual for the Roman Inquisition's delegate to deal with the press.[199]

This was anything but the end of the case which had heated up considerably when last we see it in October. Then the nuncio was told the book had been prohibited for two reasons: (1) publication without license and with the false imprint of "Douai: apud Guilelmum N." contravened Index rules, and (2) its "dottrina" was very prejudicial "to ecclesiastical jurisdiction and liberty" (one example cited). The nuncio was to use this information only in talks with the viceroy. Meanwhile, efforts were under way via the nuncio in Spain to ensure the book's prohibition.[200]

The situtation had changed little a year later, the Congregation holding a long discussion on 16 December 1627 about the Holy Office's imprisonment of laymen in Naples.[201] Two weeks later, Urban ordered Zapata written about royal ministers' pretensions.[202] At this tense moment came reports of Figueroa's action from Nuncio Monti and Bishop Pinti. Worse, the viceroy had claimed cognizance of the case. In an unusual Friday meeting, the Congregation ordered Monti to complain to him in person.[203] Six days later Urban considered the situation and ordered the *processo* sent to Rome.[204] On 22 January, apparently acting on his own initiative, Petronio sent the Congregation an "Apology in favor of the absolute and independent liberty that the Holy Inquisition has and always has possessed in imprisoning laymen without informing any person whatsoever and against the unjust and strange pretension of royal ministers in the kingdom of Naples newly arisen," which succinctly sums up his position.[205] In February, first Petronio and then both he and Monti reported that Stanzione, the collector, was at liberty in Naples. Urban tried a fairly subtle approach via a Discalced Carmelite who was to show the viceroy the "inconveniences" of the situation and induce him to arrest Stanzione and surrender him to Petronio who was to proceed against both him and Figueroa. On the second occasion the negotiations were ordered to be kept secret.[206] They had enjoyed some success by 2 March, when Monti and Petronio reported the viceroy's "inclination" to reimprison Stanzione. Urban ordered Pinti to send the dossier and then come to Rome.[207] On 9 March the summary and sentence by Pinti of both *processi* was read in a coram, together with Petronio's letters of 29 February and 2 March. Urban ordered Monti "ex professo" to have the viceroy remedy the situation "and insist" that Stanzione be imprisoned in the vicar of the Holy Office's prison. Figueroa was to be shown how much better it would be if he surrendered, and "the quick and merciful expedition" he could expect.[208] At the end of March Stanzione asked his case to be heard in Rome, because he did not trust Pinti. Urban agreed, ordering him placed under the largest bond possible and brought quickly and secretly to Rome.[209] At the end of April, the same Discalced Carmelite earlier sent to the viceroy was ordered to try to persuade Figueroa to surrender, again assuring him that he would thereby avoid the law's rigors.[210] A month later Urban ordered that tactic tried again, adding that if Figueroa refused, he would feel the law's teeth.[211] In June the archbishop got involved, saying judicial action was required in Figueroa's case. Nonetheless, Urban ordered Monti and Petronio to try one more time via the friar, as well as threatening legal action, while allowing Figueroa to testify before Petronio instead of being brought to Rome.[212] Petronio does not seem entirely to have grasped the point of Urban's orders, at least at more or less the same time he drew up another hard-edged statement of the Holy Office's case.[213]

The Collateral Digs In

Meanwhile the nunciature changed hands, going to Alessandro Bichi, a diplomat without experience in the Holy Office.[214] The move seems to have helped. In his first dispatch read in a congregation, he could report that the viceroy had ordered Figueroa to give the Inquisition "satisfaction."[215] Almost a month went by before Urban ordered Petronio to have Figueroa appear.[216] Throughout September and October, the viceroy apparently pretended to try to get Figueroa to cooperate.[217] On 22 November the Congregation confronted another provocation. Two royal officials were accused of breaking the Holy Office's secrecy; this resulted in a precept to desist, and if not they were to be captured and the Congregation informed.[218] In the next day's coram, despite a report that Figueroa had still not been removed from office, Urban merely sent Bichi back to the viceroy.[219] Once again, he met with success and Petronio's report of Figueroa's dismissal was heard in the coram of 7 December. In keeping with the nuncio's superiority to the minister, Bichi was ordered to verify the news.[220]

In January 1629 the case reached a crisis, when Stanzione was cited to appear before Pinti and Figueroa was summoned to the Inquisition, both by precept.[221] Stanzione failed to turn up, and his sureties were ordered to Rome.[222] The citation of Figueroa got the Spanish authorities' attention. In a meeting of the Collateral on 30 March, he was ordered not to go to Rome on pain of death. He told the committee that he had only a small force and had not acted scandalously. Besides, as the Collateral agreed, he was only following orders. Several of its counsellors insisted that the Holy Office had never acted without viceregal license, and it was ordered that Petronio show the powers under which he had.[223] Getting slightly ahead of things, Petronio asked what to do with Figueroa, and was told on 5 April that he was to be sent to Rome. If Petronio, Bichi, and the archbishop judged him contumacious, then he was to be put into a convent "in place of prison," under bond.[224] In the midst of such a dramatic episode, it is slightly disconcerting to see the Congregation considering Bichi's report that a register for the Inquisition had just been made and its former notary arrested![225]

Two weeks later, Petronio and Bichi reported Figueroa's disobedience to the summons, resulting in an order to put him under an appearance bond.[226] Another week later, Petronio was "firmly" told that Rome would hear the case.[227] Then someone thought of trying to use the viceroy's chief chaplain, but Petronio replied that this would be difficult, since he was always surrounded by soldiers. Instead, the archbishop and Bichi were to try to sneak up on Figueroa and capture him "without shouting" ("sine strepitu").[228] On 22 May Petronio's letter saying that both the viceroy and the visitor general had ordered Figueroa to Rome was heard. The Congregation ordered another bond for him. If he refused it, the archbishop and nuncio were to execute the order of 21 April, citing that order by the date of Millini's letter transmitting it rather than by the decree's date two days earlier.[229] At the end of May, Urban ordered Figueroa imprisoned when he arrived in Rome.[230]

Once again the Holy Office got ahead of itself. A week after the pope's order, Petronio reported that Figueroa would come but not under bond, nor could he catch him because of the large numbers of soldiers around him, nor avoid raising jurisdictional issues and exacerbating complaints about the Inquisition's imprisonment of laymen.[231] A month went by, during which Stanzione finally appeared but claimed Pinti lacked faculties to try him; Petronio was ordered to supply such. Then on 4 July Pinti reported that Figueroa would go to Rome as ordered.[232] Stanzione's case concluded quickly, but the Inquisition had less luck with Figueroa. In the same session in which Stanzione's absolution was announced, Urban ordered Bichi to try again with the new viceroy, Fernando Enriquez d'Afán de Ribera y Enríquez, duke of Alcalá, about Figueroa.[233] Again Bichi seems to have succeeded; at least, later in August Petronio submitted a long report of his negotiations that resulted in an order to him not to send the *monitorium*. This is probably a reference to the document containing the precept for Figueroa's surrender.[234]

In early September, Bichi and Petronio wrote that the viceroy had ordered Figueroa to Rome, but they feared he might have gone to Spain instead.[235] The rest of September saw Urban lose his patience, the pope twice ordering both proceedings against Figueroa *in contumaciam* and the expedition of the *monitorium*. If he was really in Spain, the inquisidor mayor, Cardinal Zapata, and the nuncio were to imprison him.[236] Nothing resulted. Urban advised caution when noting, on 4 October, Petronio's report that the viceroy had ordered the nuncio not to imprison laymen without his approval.[237] A week later Petronio recounted negotiations with royal ministers about imprisonment and extradition. The Congregation praised his diligence but warned him not to enter into such negotiations without knowing its wishes.[238] On 22 October Petronio reported that Figueroa had just published a book in Naples, *Posilippo* [*Pusilipo*] *ratos de conversaciones*, dedicated to the viceroy and seeking his protection.[239] Urban kept the copy Petronio had sent and ordered another for Niccolò Riccardi, master of the sacred palace. At the same time, Petronio sent word of a *consilium* of 27 October (probably by the Collateral) that he had erected a tribunal without royal approval, that the viceroy wished to introduce the Spanish Inquisition, and finally that Figueroa was in hiding in Naples. Small wonder Urban ordered Petronio to act "with dexterity."[240]

A Blank Warrant for Figueroa and a Hortatory for Petronio

The pope's next move did not meet that standard. He ordered Petronio, if he could not capture Figueroa outside the Spanish quarter, to invoke the secular arm but without naming Figueroa.[241] This, however, suspicious it may sound, was actually standard Inquisition procedure, based on the theory that blank warrants would protect the accused.[242] Two weeks later, on Petronio's welcome news of 17 November that he had personally served the *monitorium* on Figueroa, Urban ordered Bichi to secure the viceroy's assistance in having Figueroa appear, and Petronio to give Figueroa a copy of the *monitorium* "as far as the law allows" ("prout est de jure").[243] Then things again hung fire for a month, during which Petronio asked twice whether he should imprison Figueroa.[244] Urban so ordered on 3 January 1630, and also asked Petronio for his opinion about whether to expedite the case in Naples or Rome, but he did not respond to Bichi's question whether it was permissible for the viceroy to assist in Figueroa's capture.[245] The day before, Figueroa had gained a new judicial post in Capua, and the Collateral was asked to consider the appointment on 7 January; two weeks later it decreed that Figueroa should not go to Rome, but took no position about the judgeship.[246] Three days later Urban heard the news, which "seriously annoyed his most holiness" ("valde animum

S. S.tis perturbasse"), as Bichi was to be told.[247] In response to Bichi's and Petronio's letters of 12 and 19 January saying that Figueroa had submitted, on the 24th they were sent detailed instructions about how to capture him.[248] They seem to have already acted, since Figueroa was arrested in the church (or the convent) of S. Luigi the very next day. Petronio's men failed to make the arrest stick, and Figueroa was rescued by a powerful detachment commanded by the Neapolitan sergeant major in person.[249]

The viceroy reacted in strongly negative fashion to the attempted arrest. In a meeting of the Collateral the next day he recounted a conversation that morning with Petronio in which he had complained about the proceedings. Petronio had replied that there were many Spanish cardinals on the Congregation and promised that Figueroa would be imprisoned by the nuncio and not extradited. After reviewing the case, including two *monitorii* from Rome to Figueroa, the Collateral decreed that he had only been following orders and that his matter did not belong to the Inquisition. Even if it had, the Inquisition could not imprison anyone without the viceroy's consent (*exequatur*). That and Petronio's formation, also without an *exequatur*, of a court with twelve judges (apparently meaning consultors) in addition to the archbishop's required a remedy. The hard-line position demanded Petronio's expulsion, but everyone settled instead for a "hortatory" to him, demanding that within three days he show his powers as inquisitor or merely minister, and meanwhile refrain from exercising any jurisdiction or retaining armed familiars. Figueroa was also to be freed, and some wished to send Petronio's armed men to the galleys.[250] The hortatory considerably heightened the tension. It accused Petronio of using illegally armed men to capture Figueroa in a place full of soldiers, where a "tumult" could easily have ensued. He had pretended to be "ministro del santo officio," but had given no notice of his action nor of his powers, nor asked for an *exequatur* as everybody else had always done including the Holy Office's commissaries.[251] Bichi had a long discussion with the viceroy on 19 January 1630 about the "hortatory," which he reported to Cardinal Nephew Francesco Barberini the same day. The viceroy had sweetly deflected Bichi's claim that the order was the worst abuse ever (the rhetoric ran at that level on both sides at this moment), and insisted that Naples had no inquisitor other than the archbishop. He also did not recognize Petronio as *ministro*, because he had not shown his patents and, even worse, had failed to seek the *exequatur*. Since Petronio had done neither, the viceroy could not possibly have offended the Holy Office.[252]

Rome reacted almost as quickly as the viceroy. In the secret part of the coram of 31 January, Urban ordered proceedings against the viceroy's secretary, the sergeant major, and the others who had broken Figueroa out of prison, thereby overstating Petronio's success. Then, acting on Petronio's letter of two days earlier as well as five letters from the archbishop and Bichi, Urban ordered Petronio to publish a *monitorio* against all involved, after first examining witnesses about the "unsafe" execution of the *monitorio* ordering Figueroa's arrest. He was to continue to exercise jurisdiction but "abstain from public acts which could cause disturbance." The pope further ordered two "hortatory breves" (*brevia hortatoria*) to the viceroy about Figueroa's crime which would "exhort and warn him [the viceroy] to order Figueroa restored to the said Holy Office." The viceroy was to withdraw his hortatory to Petronio, and the archbishop was to impress on him the scandal that had been caused thus far, as was Bichi. Finally, the nuncio in Spain, Monti, former holder of the same office in Naples, was to be informed and sent powers specifically to secure Figueroa's surrender, using the king's confessor, Cardinal Zapata, and chief minister the Count Duke Olivares.[253] The breves to the viceroy were drawn up on 2 February. The first called his *monitorio* to Petronio a *monstrum* and a lie, threatened him with the day of judgment, and ordered him to rescind it,"relinquishing the legitimate liberty of the Holy Office's minister" ("legitimam libertatem sanctae Inquisitionis ministris relinquens"), or face the legal consquences.[254] The second specifically criticized the rescue of Figueroa, during which the viceroy had dared to disarm *ministros* of the Holy Office and thereby committed the crime "laesis sacrae inquisitionis ministris," assimilating assaults on its officers to treason.[255] In a letter enciphered on the same day, Cardinal Francesco Barberini ordered Bichi to await the Congregation's decision, even though the second breve said Bichi had more to say to the viceroy.[256] The Collateral considered the breves in its meeting of 4 February. Its principal member insisted on the degree to which Figueroa had been mistreated, and the next speaker demanded a settlement of the Inquisition's pretensions once and for all. After lengthy discussion, the Collateral took no action.[257]

On 6 February the Spanish ambassador in Rome had an audience with Urban and Cardinal Francesco Barberini about Figueroa's case. According to an *avviso*, the ambassador did not find "great rigor" in Urban, who had entrusted the case to the datary Maraldi (apparently still Marco Aurelio, appointed in 1611) and the eminent canonist Prospero Faganani.[258] The ambassador visited both. In answer to his fears that Urban would act against "the house of Austria," the pope had reassured him that he would arm no further. (The writer also claimed that no dispatches had been sent to Naples yet except for Petronio's missing patents, but neither allegation is true.) The viceroy pressed for Figueroa's release because of the handling of another recent case, including what he considered an illegal search. The same *avviso* also reported that Cardinal Borja had refused the "voluntary contribution" the pope had sought, since it would be used against Spain.[259] Urban's alleged use of two members of the datary's staff does not accord with what we know of Inquisition procedure to this moment, although it could be a harbinger of the propensity he manifested a little later to use any means to an end. Then again, these two might have formed a particular congregation, the existence of which was reported in another *avviso* of 16 February, which said it was also considering troubles in Milan.[260] Similarly, the rest of the first newsletter does not fit terribly well with the actions taken in the coram of 7 February. Note was taken of Petronio's report that the viceroy supported his action with theologians and a hortatory against him, but also saying that he would surrender Figueroa if not sent to Rome. He was ordered to examine witnesses about whether the imprisonment was done *sine strepitu* by the "summo statore" (the viceroy?) and his men or with violence. Meanwhile he was to continue to exercise his office "cum dexteritate" and say that Figueroa would not be extradited, since he had no orders, but at the same time writing to ask for them. Bichi got the same instructions, as did Monti in Spain and Giovanni Battista Pamphili, the former nuncio in Naples, and the former viceroy (Cardinal Zapata?) was also to be informed.[261]

The Collateral's Reply

In the Collateral's meeting of 9 February the viceroy replied to both breves. The attempted arrest of Figueroa on 25 January "virtually in my presence" ("casi en mi presencia") had caused a great scandal. The Inquisition's guards had been disarmed because "they were not part of a household with recognized jurisdiction" ("no ser familia de juridicion conocida"). The pope was misinformed about the hortatory, since it did not (and could not) suspend Petronio's jurisdiction because his failure to exhibit his powers meant he had none. It was best that he show them in order to avoid further uproar and damage to the papacy and the archbishop, a point the viceroy underscored by an unsubtle reference to the near-rebellion in 1547, when Rome had first tried to introduce the Inquisition to Naples. The breve about Figueroa's crime he contemptuously dismissed.[262] Three days later another Collateral identified the heart of the matter as the papacy's claim since 1585 to "have always had an inquisitor, who had acted at the instance of his majesty's ministers on occasion when the [arch]bishops molested his majesty's vassals on account of the Inquisition" ("han siempre tenido unos Inquisidores, y ha sida á istancia de los ministros de Su Magestad con occasion que los Obispos molestavan los vasallos de Su Magestad por causa de Inquisicion"). As a convenience they had been allowed to make process, have a prison, and send reports to Rome, and the duke of Alba had always "recognized [Petronio] as inquisitor" ("conocido [Petronio] por Inquisidor"). When asked for his powers, Petronio said he had "a letter from Millini" ("una carta de Melino"). Therefore, "he should proceed at the instance of parties when notified by the bishops, and when he should have a denunciation, consult Rome" ("procediesse á instancia de partes quando se quexavan de los obispos, y quando havía alguna denuncia, se avisare a Roma"). As for Figueroa, Petronio's power had to be known, and in no case were vassals to be extradited. The archbishop was to imprison Figueroa on the Inquisition's behalf, and negotiations were to be undertaken with the nuncio about the other points.[263] A third Collateral on 14 February considered the nuncio's request to have Figueroa in his prison, since it would be hard to execute orders from Rome if he remained in the archbishop's. The hortatory to Petronio was to be sent to Urban. Meanwhile, a response was awaited to Petronio's request to Rome for a copy of the letter to the bishop of Nocera about vassals and the Inquisition. It was decided that the cardinals' familiars would get their weapons back, that Petronio would secretly absolve the sergeant major, and that the viceroy would not impede Petronio's jurisdiction provided he did not innovate.[264]

On the same day as the third Collateral, a coram heard Petronio's letter of 9 February about the first Collateral, underscoring once again how communication problems affected the exercise of the Inquisition's jurisdiction, even when a fast courrier could carry a dispatch from Rome to Naples in two days. Urban ordered Monti to approach the king about preserving the Inquisition in Naples; Petronio was not to proceed against royal officials who had "imprisoned" Figueroa; and Rome would "supersede" in the publication of a "hortatory" against the sergeant major and suspend further process. This all sounds fairly conciliatory. The further order to Bichi to spell out the lies in the Collateral's statement was not, nor was the instruction to secure the ringleaders' opinions, nor that to tell the viceroy to act without awaiting orders from Spain.[265]

Figueroa Surrenders

Two days later royal authorities surrendered Figueroa, the day after the "Secretario del Reyno" sent an unidentified correspondent the *processo* about his imprisonment and a relation of the case since Stanzione's.[266] Bichi and Petronio triumphantly reported that, in addition, the Inquisition's weapons had been returned, the "impediment" to Petronio's "free exercise of the Holy Office" had been removed, and the viceroy's hortatory withdrawn as damaging to the pope. Urban pressed his advantage by ordering that the hortatory be canceled in the registers or at least have a marginal note added that it had been intended to damage the papacy, and that the archbishop's name not be used as ordinary in Inquisition cases (effectively ending his jurisdiction over them), in which the nuncio should always be consulted. Then the pope turned magnanimous. The *monitorio* to the sergeant major was not to be published, and he was to be absolved at his request. But Urban's mood lasted only for a moment. He next ordered the collection of acts favorable to the Holy Office, authentic copies of which were to be deposited in the Inquisition's archive in Rome, in the nuncio's curia, and in the Holy Office in Naples. Bichi was to be told that nothing had been decided about imprisoning laymen, pending the Collateral's opinion and word from Spain, and if he were to assist Petronio in imprisoning suspects, the pope and the Holy Office would be "truly grateful."[267] In sum, as an *avviso* of 23 February reported, numerous breves had been sent to Naples, which had calmed the viceroy down and led him to surrender Figueroa.[268] Urban was so pleased that the same day he sent blessings to Bichi via Cardinal Francesco.[269]

This jubilation marked the end neither of the trial nor of troubles over imprisonment, two more cases being notified to Rome in February and March.[270] In fact, comparatively little had been settled to the satisfaction of the Neapolitan authorities, who proposed to send a delegation to Rome.[271] A month later the nuncio lamented that the delegation would be long delayed, and that meanwhile replies to Urban's breves would go to the viceroy's agent in Rome, insisting on a trial in Naples.[272] Even the apparently iron-clad deal about the hortatory proved difficult to execute.[273] Probably by the end of March (the date of his letter is destroyed), Petronio had to admit that the viceroy was having second thoughts about Figueroa's imprisonment. Urban refused to bend about the hortatory and ordered Petronio to keep it up "in manly fashion" (*viriliter*), in conjunction with Bichi.[274] Nor was Pamphili getting anywhere in Madrid.[275] The day this bad news was heard, Petronio reported a possibly even more worrying development: a secular court demanded cognizance of a polygamy case that had already been sentenced in his tribunal.[276] The appointment on 18 April of Inquisitors Scaglia, Antonio Barberini, Sr., Millini's replacement as secretary, and Verospi to consult on Figueroa's case underlines the situation's continuing gravity.[277] Two days later Francesco Barberini passed on orders to Bichi to tell the viceroy that the Congregation acted only according to the canons, one of the more colossal lies in the history of the institution.[278]

Movement in Spain, but Not in Naples

In the middle of May, Urban took a flurry of actions. First, he heard Petronio's report that royal ministers were taking documents about lay imprisonments out of their archives and were awaiting orders from Spain about Figueroa. In the next act, the pope granted Petronio powers to absolve in Figueroa's case; he was to report in full on how he used them. Then Urban replied simply to another letter from Petronio asking what more to do about Figueroa's imprisonment: nothing. Finally, he ordered Bichi written to get letters missive or something similar from the viceroy saying that the hortatory to Petronio had not damaged the Inquisition, since otherwise trying Figueroa in Naples would be "most difficult," before approving Bichi's opinion that Figueroa should not be surrendered to Petronio.[279] A few days later there was good news from Monti in Spain. The powers that be, including Zapata, Olivares, and the royal confessor, all favored the Inquisition in Figueroa's case.[280] This was no small matter in Olivares's case, since he had had a number of "brushes with Rome" in the 1620s and would shortly prepare a "direct challenge."[281] In the same session, the news from Naples was not as good, especially that royal ministers were again trying to extract taxes from the clergy, the origin of the Figueroa affair. Nor was it encouraging to hear from Bichi that the viceroy said the question of Figueroa's imprisonment had to be dealt with "anew" ("de novo").[282]

It quickly developed that the viceroy had decided to go on the offensive. Cardinal Francesco Barberini wrote Bichi on 25 May about a conversation the previous day with the viceroy's agent, in which he had said that the viceroy was not one to be led around by the nose. This forced Barberini to reply that this was going too far, and that it was not up to the viceroy to interpret Barberini's words, since an inferior minister could not obligate a superior.[283] Just as the viceroy rattled his sword loudly, Bichi reported the "express or virtual" ("expressa aut virtualis") revocation of the *hortatorium* and Petronio sent a public act by the Inquisition's notary testifying to Figueroa's reimprisonment.[284] A week later Bichi confirmed the viceroy's willingness to give satisfaction about the *hortatorium* leading Urban to ask that he leave a note to that effect for his successor.[285] At the end of June, Urban ordered added to Figueroa's dossier the viceroy's letter in effect withdrawing the *hortatorium* and promising not to interfere in the Inquisition's jurisdiction.[286]

Figueroa's Trial

Finally in July, Figueroa's trial began, perhaps not coincidentally shortly after the appointment of a new nuncio, who had just finished a stint as inquisitor on Malta. This was Niccolò Enriquez de Herrera.[287] As the viceroy asked, Petronio heard the case in Naples. Among its first acts was an interrogation over Figueroa's demand for a better prison.[288] On 11 July Urban told Petronio to execute the earlier orders about Figueroa's prison since the viceroy had sent a new *hortatorium* allowing him to proceed "without fear." Herrera was sent a detailed report and ordered to smooth things over, allowing the Inquisition to operate in Naples.[289] By 25 July the Congregation had Figueroa's testimony and ordered the *repetitio* and *defensiones*.[290] Figueroa apparently refused the *repetitio*, and the viceroy appointed Francisco Castaldo his advocate.[291] Petronio rejected Castaldo, an action Urban approved on 22 August, on the grounds that he was under a suspended process for Judaizing. Figueroa should pick someone else to receive his copy of the *processo*. If the viceroy proved stubborn, Petronio was to tell him about Castaldo's investigation.[292] Tommaso Imparato or Imperato took over as Figueroa's attorney by 31 August, but he also tried to secure the services of Carlo Maranta, a consultor of the Holy Office.[293] Undeterred by the pope's rejection of Maranta, the viceroy ordered the Spanish agent in Rome to handle the "despacho" of Figueroa's case carefully.[294] By 5 September the case had moved to the point of expedition. Urban decreed that Figueroa came under *Si de protegendis*. If nothing came out in his defense, the sentence (left unspecified) was to be read in the congregation of consultors, and Figueroa was to be absolved. A summary of his sentence was ordered to be sent to the nuncios in Spain and Naples, who were to emphasize how "mercifully" the case had been expedited and then immediately turn to "those more guilty."[295]

About 5 November Figueroa presented his defense, which turned on the reason for Stanzione's imprisonment.[296] At the end of the month, Imparato announced that the viceroy and other royal ministers wanted to mount a stronger defense, including informing consultors and perhaps sending an attorney to Rome. Urban replied that it was fine with him, but then the whole trial would have to be moved to Rome, which would only harm Figueroa.[297] The pope had publicly declared his intention to be master in his own house and rid himself of Spanish domination. He had deliberately picked a fight with one of the most powerful Spanish-Italian cardinals, Carlo Emmanuele Pio di Savoia, apparently over a piece of real estate.[298] While Urban did try to leave Pio a way out of his condemnation by blaming the matter on misinformation and the machinations of inferior ministers, other cardinals allegedly counselled him to flee to Naples.[299] A week later Urban supposedly went on record as saying, "although no process had been formed in this [Pio's] case, and that it could not be formed, at any rate the pope laughed at it, alleging that it was enough for him to know the truth of the matter, not caring that it should appear to be handled judicially."[300] By the end of the year, the pope had resolved to drive all Spanish cardinals out of Rome, in tandem with an attack on the grand duchy of Tuscany. Thus, he had told the Florentine Cardinal Capponi to return to his bishopric. He was also vigorously pursuing a case against Cardinal Luis de Torres in the Segnatura di grazia, acting with a little more circumspection than in Pio's case (indeed, Urban both allowed a vote on the matter, which came out favorable to Torres, and then apologized to his backer Cardinal Ludovico Ludovisi, former cardinal nephew of Gregory XV).[301] Nevertheless, Torres, Capponi, and Ludovisi all left for Naples. Furthermore, Urban was sinking large resources into rebuilding the port at Civitavecchia, in order to destroy the grand duke's trade through Livorno.[302] The pope's actions plainly worried both the Florentines and the Spanish.[303]

On 11 December the Congregation made Figueroa's legal representation into a general principle, announcing that it was against the "style of the Holy Office" to allow more than one person to take an oath to counsel him.[304] Undeterred by this rebuff, Viceroy Alcalá recommended Figueroa to his incoming replacement Monterrey and to Alvaro de Toledo, the viceroy's chief chaplain and the same man Petronio had once proposed to ask for help in capturing Figueroa. Toledo was about to leave for Rome in mid-January 1631 in company with Imparato, "to take charge of the case" ("á patrocinar la causa").[305] Petronio reported this development, noting that Imparato was coming "soliciting and defending, in voice and writing," which would only protract the case. Action was not taken until 6 February when Urban ordered Herrera "immediately" (*statim*) to assign a term for the defense and send a copy of Imparato's letter asking a *supersedeat*, while he came to Rome and negotiated with the viceroy about avoiding delay.[306] In the meantime, Petronio had tried to imprison another "doctor" in Naples and was told to seek secular aid.[307]

The next we hear is not until 6 March, when Petronio wrote that the viceregal authorities wanted to give Figueroa an honorary post once his trial had ended and that the *hortatorium* was not in the royal secretary's register.[308] The viceroy also paid Figueroa's expenses on several occasions during the trial.[309] Finally, on 3 April Urban handed down Figueroa's sentence, which he had already proposed in September 1630. He found Figueroa guilty of infringing *Si de protegendis*. His case was to be expedited in secret in the congregation of consultors and his sentence commuted.[310] The deed was done before 24 April, when Petronio sent the sentence, and Urban again ordered its commutation and Figueroa's release from the nuncio's prison. He also instructed Petronio to keep pressure on the viceroy about how his agents conducted themselves, and to keep an eye on Figueroa in particular.[311] One way of keeping pressure on was to continue to arrest polygamists, as Petronio was ordered to do on 10 April, "any and all fear put aside" ("postposito omni et quocunque metu").[312] As usually happened, Figueroa's sentence was commuted gradually. Nuncio Herrera proposed a scheme (details illegible) which Urban rejected, apparently because he was to be put in a room without a lock. The nuncio moved him to more secure lodgings, at which time Urban ordered Figueroa put under bond, while Herrera continued to negotiate with the new viceroy, Monterrey.[313] Herrera was also ordered to continue negotiating with Monterrey over freedom for Petronio to do his job.[314] On 26 June Figueroa was allowed to leave the house on feast days, under a renewed bond.[315] Figueroa continued to garner powerful backers, including Borja.[316] Then the issue of a blank warrant cropped up again, the outgoing viceroy refusing to imprison Figueroa on such a basis and the Collateral continuing adamantly to reject blank warrants. The Congregation therefore ordered the nuncio not to seek secular aid.[317]

Another Royal Attack, and the Secretary of State Takes over Figueroa's Case

The council's resistance presaged another royal attack. In the meeting of 10 July, the Congregation heard a letter from the king of Spain, forwarded by Petronio. The Crown refused to allow the exercise of Inquisition jurisdiction without royal license, nor extradition without the viceroy's agreement, as well as demanding "other things prejudicial to the jurisdiction of the Holy Office." Unsurprisingly, Urban ordered Petronio "to oppose them with all his strength."[318]

Worse soon came. A week later another coram heard Petronio's report that royal authorities had claimed cognizance of polygamy cases, one of the major areas the Inquisition tried to reserve to itself.[319] Urban also ordered the nuncio to help a royal councillor dismissed for an opinion favorable to the Holy Office. The next coram heard three letters from Petronio, including a lengthy complaint about the viceroy.[320]

These turned out to be only the preliminaries. A Collateral of 13 September in the viceroy's presence decreed Figueroa's imprisonment illegal while the hortatory to Petronio by contrast was not. More, it became a general principle to decide two other cases. "No delegate or commissary that comes from Rome exercises any jurisdiction in this kingdom if he should not first have presented his letters of commission and obtained the royal *exequatur*" ("ningun Delegado ó Comissario que venga de Roma exercite Juridicion alguna en este Reyno si no huviere primero presentado las lettras di comission y ottenido el Regio Exequatur"). The Inquisition was never to act without the viceroy's permission, none of its agents could carry prohibited arms, and Monterrey was to induce Urban to "reprehend" Petronio.[321] The last we hear of Figueroa's case and its implications comes from the nuncio in Spain's report in early October, that he had executed his orders to tell the king about the "injustice and fraud" about imprisonments committed by the viceroy's ministers.[322]

On the same day (according to an *avviso*), in a consistory Urban "shouted loudly" at Borja over the excommunication of the Collateral by the bishop of Sant'Agata de' Goti, Ettore Diotallevi, Borja saying it was null on the basis of Cardinal Egidio Albornoz's study of both case and law.[323] The case concerned a jurisdictional dispute over the fief of Bagnoli.[324] In reply Urban summoned Verospi and the dispute became heated, Urban calling a Spanish lawyer "ignorant." It was decided that the newly established Congregation of Immunities would "administer good justice," but it was known only that it had ordered the *processo* made by Diotallevi sent to the king.[325] Whether this development meant the case had become more or less serious is difficult to say, since little is known about the Congregation of Immunities, and consistories had become largely formal occasions. In any event, the matter was out of the Holy Office's hands. Cardinal Francesco Barberini personally took over the excommunication and turned it over to Pamphili and Antonio Cerri, both his trusted agents, who found Diotallevi's *processo* full of "nullities."[326] By the end of November Barberini reportedly had a deal that would allow the Collateral to be absolved by its own confessors, but the viceroy rejected it and insisted that the excommunication be voided and Diotallevi and his vicar exiled from

Naples.[327] Just a week later, the same newsletter-writer reported that Herrera was being praised for his success in securing the deal.[328] It is a fitting place to end this series of episodes, with Urban's interpretation of eruptions from Vesuvius as signs of God's anger at the viceroy and Collateral for their contempt of Diotallevi's excommunication.[329]

Conclusion

On 27 November 1631 the Congregation heard more problems about the Inquisition's powers to imprison. A week it later issued a long order about how to deal with them; at the end of the month it heard a lengthy report from the nuncio in Madrid.[330]

Thus the issue of *giurisdizionalismo* proved intractable. The Roman Inquisition's efforts to establish its tribunal in Naples seriously exacerbated an already fraught situation. Between the middle of the sixteenth century, when a revolt wrecked the Congregation's first efforts, and the middle of the following century, the Neapolitan Holy Office nevertheless became reasonably firmly established, both against secular authorities and also against the archbishop's inquisition. Its struggles with the viceroy and the supreme council of the Collateral laid bare the papacy's political ambitions, rooted ultimately in its status as feudal lord of the kingdom of Naples. The kings of Spain were naturally reluctant to admit their subordination, and their agents, especially Inquisitor Borja, did all they could to rein in the pope's pretensions. What should have been an unequal struggle, given Spanish hegemony in much of the Italian peninsula including the city of Rome, resulted in an impressive papal victory, symbolized by the transformation of its "minister" into an inquisitor and its almost complete success bringing the viceregal agent Figueroa to book. The central figure in both achievments was Urban VIII. Although the point cannot yet be conclusively demonstrated, it seems likely that his success arose in large part from his development of an unprecedented control of the Inquisition itself.

CHAPTER 2

Naples: Tommaso Campanella

The most notorious case in our period involving Rome and Naples was that of Tommaso Campanella.[1] It may have set a record for length at nearly thirty years, not counting three other trials lasting another eight years that Campanella underwent at the hands of authorities in Naples and elsewhere before his most important *processo* began. That trial raised in particularly acute form the same issues of overlapping jurisdiction between Rome and Naples and jealously guarded prerogatives between secular and religious authorities in Naples that we have already considered. Unlike those episodes, Campanella's trial is exceptionally well documented in both the decree registers and documents in Naples, allowing us to watch closely the maneuverings for advantage between the pope, the Congregation, its ministers in Naples, the nuncio, the archbishop, and royal officials there and how these affected the course of the trial, or rather trials. Part of the exceptional complexity of Campanella's troubles arose from the fact that he was charged almost simultaneously with two different but related crimes in both papal and viceregal courts. His case also allows a detailed consideration of how the Roman Inquisition slowly constituted its branch in Naples. Finally, the trials throw a great deal of light on the Inquisition's procedure, particularly how its "style" underwent almost constant innovation.

No sooner had the Congregation instructed Campanella's diocesan to bar him from preaching and hearing confessions on 16 August 1599, apparently as part of the sentence ending his second (or possibly third) trial, than Pope Clement VIII, acting on a denunciation dated two days earlier and containing a much more serious charge, fomenting a rebellion in part by prophesying the end of the world, ordered the viceroy written to imprison him.[2] Six days later Cardinal Nephew Cinzio Aldobrandini sent the nuncio powers to arrest the clergy and religious involved in the uprising.[3] On 1 September the Dominican provincial visitor opened proceedings against them, including Campanella. It is highly interesting that this official immediately drew up a document headed *Inquisitionis acta*, which ended with the claim that all the actions taken drew on "the advice of legal experts" ("iuris utriusque peritorum consilium"). It included an allegation of *fama publica praecedente* ("precedent public report"), enumerated the charges—following Neapolitan practice, but against the usual Roman view that they were not to be given to the accused until after the investigative phase had ended—and closed with a request to the secular arm, here called *litterae capturae* and a precept in another document, to arrest Campanella.[4] The charges included a number that continued to appear throughout the trial, beginning with atheism, doubts about the sacraments, miracles, and the resurrection, and a sheaf of attacks on papal and ecclesiastical authority.[5] The visitor followed canon law to the letter.

Campanella and the rest of the conspirators panicked when the viceroy moved against them, and by 6 September 1599 Campanella had been arrested.[6] Despite the antecedent request from the pope, Campanella found himself in the hands of the secular power, thus beginning a protracted jurisdictional dispute. Tricked by the local Neapolitan fiscal, on 10 September he drew up the so-called "Declaration of Castelvetre," full of incriminating evidence on the score of rebellion.[7] A week later, the Roman Inquisition first intervened directly, sending the provincial visitor orders to capture Campanella, turn him over to the nuncio, and send the information thus far collected. Secretary Giulio Antonio Santoro also ordered the visitor to cooperate with local bishops.[8] Brought to Naples, Campanella underwent his first interrogation by a royal official and the nuncio on 23 September 1599, although it is unclear on what authority they acted.[9] The case was complicated since there were two separate but overlapping investigations, one for rebellion and conspiracy nominally in the hands of viceregal agents, the other for heresy, equally nominally under the control first of the nuncio alone and then jointly with the Holy Office, which the pope wanted involved right from the first.[10] The viceroy was equally determined that the Holy Office not take a hand in the trial for rebellion, while the nuncio feared the royal authorities would engulf the heresy case as well.[11] Since Campanella was a religious, the pope had to give authority both to a viceregal appointee to assist in the trial for heresy, and also in general terms for the trial on charges of rebellion. For six weeks from late September, the nuncio negotiated with the viceroy for the surrender of the clerical prisoners, which signified only that they would be held in the same prison in his name, not the viceroy's.[12] During the same time, negotiations proceeded about the auspices under which the two trials would be conducted, the pope stubbornly insisting no royal agents should intervene "in matters touching the Holy Office."[13]

A Charge of Heresy

On 11 November 1599, we do not know on what charges save for a very late indication that they included *ateismo*, the Congregation judged Campanella *inditiatus* (approximately "giving indications") of heresy and ordered him brought "to this Holy Office."[14] "This" meant Naples, not Rome, where Campanella's case ran until he was released in 1626, but even then only into the custody of the Holy Office itself.[15] Just when the Inquisition ordered Campanella's detention, the nuncio, while perfectly happy to cooperate with the archiepiscopal vicar general, was handicapped in the jurisdictional dispute with the viceroy by the absence of the Inquisition's "minister" in Naples, Benedetto Mandina, who had gone to Rome.[16] The nuncio asked for a replacement on 16 November and again a week later; on 4 December his request was denied, although that turned out not to be Rome's final decision.[17] On 30 November the viceroy reported to the king of Spain the resolution of the prisoner problem, but went on to express his disapproval of papal orders that the nuncio always be involved. He proposed that the pope should either appoint the viceroy's nominees or give a breve allowing him to put his own men into office. He was also stalling the Inquisition until the trial for rebellion had concluded.[18] Rome flatly rejected his proposal to act alone as "apostolic delegate" and instead demanded that the nuncio conduct the trial along with an unmarried royal minister, given the first tonsure for the occasion in order to preserve the fiction that the case was strictly ecclesiastical. Nor would the pope allow the heresy trial to go forward in Naples.[19] The Spanish ambassador in Rome accepted those terms, adding only that the pope wanted to know the name of the viceregal nominee.[20] The next day the pope bent more and ordered the nuncio to proceed without tonsuring the lay deputy and using the royal fiscal and notary.[21] The matter of the first tonsure proved insignificant, since the man nominated, Pedro de Vera, already had it and it was therefore unnecessary to put the stipulation into the breve. The nuncio wished to move cautiously, preferring to await the breve's arrival to "establish the jurisdiction," instead of using Aldobrandini's letters.[22] The viceroy agreed.[23] Meanwhile, he wrote Spain that both

Campanella's offenses should be tried in Naples, that for heresy being put into the nuncio's hands.[24]

Then negotiations hit what would seem to be a serious glitch. A day after Aldobrandini promised that the breve was on the way, the nuncio wrote complaining about the speed with which the viceroy had condemned to death Cesare Pisano, since his testimony was needed in Campanella's heresy case; he may also have been a clergyman.[25] We hear nothing further of the protest at this moment. When the nuncio renewed it belatedly in the wake of the man's drawing and quartering on 16 January 1600, he was met with incomprehension.[26] The Congregation apparently did not raise the issue until 3 February (misdating the execution by a day), instructing the nuncio and vicar general to try to prevent too rapid justice by the secular court since this would impede—to put it mildly—the *repetitio* and might also prevent getting at the truth.[27] Instead, the breve of 8 January arrived and was immediately exhibited before the nuncio.[28] Five days later the royal officers were appointed and two days further on—after the rescript was exhibited to the nuncio—the court for the case of rebellion had finally been constituted.[29]

On 21 January Campanella underwent interrogation twice, denying the charges.[30] The nuncio proved far too optimistic in hoping that the weight of evidence against him would induce a confession the next day. He sounded disappointed when reporting another interrogation three days later during which five of the witnesses against Campanella had confronted him.[31] The nuncio apparently did not object to this bending of canonical procedure, which may have been adopted from Neapolitan practice, but he did when the fiscal said it was Neapolitan usage to torture during the informative phase without giving the accused a copy of the evidence against him, citing a case of rebellion in which an apostolic deputy had been involved.[32] The fiscal seems to have deferred to the nuncio; at least the next move was another confrontation between Campanella and a witness.[33] Luigi Amabile thought the pope shortly gave permission to torture Campanella, citing the nuncio's letter of 4 February 1600 referring to a missing letter from Cardinal Aldobrandini. Although the nuncio's letter does mention the question of torture, he continued that he would not repeat the problem, "remembering [reminding Aldobrandini of] only a quick resolution that I consider helpful to this same business" ("ricordando solo la presta resolutione per che così reputo servizio del medesimo negotio"), which must mean that no decision had yet been made in Rome.[34] Nevertheless, on 7 February Campanella underwent torture.[35] A missing authorization had come from Rome, as the nuncio noted on 11 February in his report of the confession that resulted. He stressed that, despite it and the consequent imminent end of Campanella's trial for rebellion, he would not proceed to Inquisition matters, "reserving it whole to the order that the pope will give about it" ("riservandola integra all'ordine che ci darà sopra N. S.re") despite Santoro's authorization to do so in company with the archiepiscopal vicar, a decision made in the coram of 3 February.[36] The nuncio thought it best to finish the case for rebellion, both so that numerous innocent prisoners could be released and also because the pope wanted the Holy Office case transferred to Rome. If it was not moved, then the nuncio demanded "experienced persons and good theologians to dispute with that Campanella" ("persone pratiche e buoni Theologhi per disputare con quel Campanella") since by his own testimony he had abjured "another time."[37] The nuncio wrote the same substance to Santoro at the same time, adding that he had renewed the protest over the witness's execution.[38]

A New Minister

A month later, when saying that the case for rebellion had still not been concluded, the nuncio acknowledged Santoro's repeated order that the Holy Office had to handle the heresy case, at the same time as he renewed his request for a theologian should it be heard in Naples.[39] In mid-April and sounding desperate, the nuncio begged for instructions about the heresy case since the royal fiscal was applying a great deal of pressure to expedite that for rebellion, which could well end in Campanella's execution.[40] Despite the nuncio's urgency, the Congregation did not consider his letter for two weeks.[41] Then on 27 April the pope ordered the heresy case committed to the nuncio and a new actor, the theologian for whom he had been begging, Tragagliolo.[42] Santoro's letter based on this decree, written the next day, said that Tragagliolo had left only three days before, increasing the likelihood that his selection was an afterthought, and also stressed his experience.[43] A letter of the same date to Tragagliolo with much the same content emphasized that the pope wanted the case expedited as soon as possible, but not before he had sent both the *summarium* and the judges' opinions about expedition. Santoro also reminded Tragagliolo that he was well informed in general and knew in particular about Campanella's abjuration *de vehementi*.[44] With a third letter on the same day, this one to the archiepiscopal vicar general, Ercole Vaccari, the panel of judges was set.[45] However belated, Tragagliolo's selection was not in the least casual.

Campanella claimed almost thirty years later that the pope had deliberately sent him to handle his trial.[46] This assertion may not be true, but Tragagliolo had certainly helped Campanella earlier. While imprisoned in Santa Sabina in 1596, Campanella had sent Tragagliolo a copy of his "Discorso politico contro i Luterani," thanking the commissary for his kindness; Tragagliolo reviewed the work before suggesting that Campanella dedicate it to Cardinal Cinzio Aldobrandini, protector of the Dominicans, and Campanella asked Tragagliolo to present the work for him.[47] Tragagliolo is alleged to have lamented on his deathbed that he had not been able to free Campanella.[48]

Tragagliolo took up his post on 5 May 1600.[49] After one interrogation five days later the nuncio promptly left for his bishopric of Troia with an almost audible sigh of relief.[50] His departure had no material effect on the case, which he expected to be protracted, since he appointed his auditor as his "general lieutenant."[51] The nuncio did not even stay for Campanella's landmark first interrogation on 17 May and thus missed him pretending to be insane.[52] Tragagliolo reported to Santoro two days later, but once again the matter did not make it to the Congregation for at least two weeks and more likely not until 8 June.[53] As usual, Santoro sent the pope's order the next day, leaving it to Tragagliolo and his team to decide whether to apply the torture of the *corda* to Campanella in order to test his madness. Whatever they decided, they were strictly enjoined not to question him about the rebellion lest that interfere with the royal fiscal's proceedings.[54]

Tragagliolo's arrival had an immediate effect, inducing another Dominican to denounce Campanella.[55] Tragagliolo kept hard at it, with an interrogation on 19 May and another a week later.[56] The second of these included another face-to-face confrontation with two witnesses.[57] Nor did Tragagliolo do all the work himself, delegating authority to unknown persons to question a Dominican in Naples.[58] Tragagliolo had one advantage denied earlier to the nuncio—the viceregal authorities left him alone. Having most of what he wanted, the condemnation of the conspiracy's other ringleaders, the viceroy did not even bother to report on Tragagliolo's arrival and the formal opening of Campanella's trial until three weeks later, although he did cast it as a victory for the Spanish since the pope had wanted the case advoked to Rome.[59] Things were not quite so simple, and the jurisdictional dispute had not entirely disappeared. On 5 June the viceroy wrote that he was proceeding against Campanella again and asking the pope not to summon the heresy trial to Rome, but rather let an unnamed bishop and the nuncio decide the case in Naples. The king should keep pressure on the pope to that end.[60] Clement refused to concede the point, ordering on 22 June that the heresy case take precedence over that for rebellion, applying one of the Inquisition's most cherished principles, that its proceedings always came first.[61]

Campanella's First Torture

The delegated court was busy on 18 July, among the more dramatic moments of the trial. First, it interrogated one of the most important witnesses against Campanella, apparently regarding his examinations in Calabria (before the rebellion) as part of the same proceedings.[62] Then it decided to torture Campanella with the *corda*. Campanella continued his mad act, the notary stressing that on the way to the torture chamber he had babbled incoherencies, that is, when he was not singing them. Under torture he shouted that he was dying and had been murdered, cursed his torturers, and insisted that the pope was coming to save him. When asked how long he had been imprisoned in Rome, he replied "always, always" ("sempre, sempre"). To the question where he was captured, he said "absolutely everybody" ("tutti quanti"). The threat of further torture brought the retort "yes, yes, do it, do it" ("si si fatelo fatelo"). But as in his first utterances, at least some of what he said seems rational, including the claim "I am not pretending anything" ("io non fici niente"). Similarly, his announcement that he had both urinated and defecated in his shoes seems only what one might expect. Then again, when asked towards the end what grace he wished from "these lords," he replied, "let me shit." Asked the name of the commissary when he was imprisoned in Rome, Tragagliolo, who was present, Campanella replied, "let me alone, fra Tommaso." Asked who that was, he replied "I am." An hour of torture in total, the usual time, having elapsed, the notary again laconically noted that after calling out to the pope and Mary, he emitted "other senseless words."[63] On balance, his judges might well have concluded that Campanella was at least close to compos mentis.

Two days later Tragagliolo tried again. Things began promisingly when Campanella swore the deponent's oath, as he had earlier refused to do. Brought to the hall of examinations, he tried to leave and began kissing pictures. Asked how many sisters he had, he answered three. Then he claimed to have preached to "Signora grande" who gave him wine and eggs and relieved the pain of torture. He also claimed to see his father (who had testified in his case) in prison all the time, the money was buried under the church, and "blacks" came to kill him every night, let in by the soldiers, and he had run twenty miles to escape them. Absent torture, Campanella's act improved.[64] Six days after Campanella's exam and on the reading of Tragagliolo's now antique letter of 7 July, the Congregation ordered him to question Campanella about "an impious epigram" that had come up in his first trial in Padua. This seems an almost trivial point in the context of events in Naples, but it well illustrates the Inquisition's obsessive attention to detail.[65] Then communication became seriously snarled. On 31 July, although not convinced that Campanella was insane, in order to err on the side of caution the Neapolitan panel had granted him a tutor (*curator*) and advocate who had been given the *capituli* (charges) against his client in order to draw up an *interrogatoria*, or list of defense questions to be asked in the *repetitio*. But three days later the pope explicitly denied Campanella a *curator*.[66] The pope did order the *repetitio* and a defense, as Tragagliolo had already done.[67] In another tangle, on 21 September Clement ordered the ex-commissary to investigate whether the archbishop's court had an *advocatus pauperum* ("advocate of the poor"), and if not to provide one.[68] Although he was acting on Tragagliolo's letter of 12 September, the point of this inquiry is obscure since Campanella already had an advocate.

On 16 August Campanella's advocate presented forty-eight questions, many of them about his preaching, designed to attack the evidence, but a number also designed to elicit information that could be used to impugn witnesses against him.[69] The first of the next two examinations on 21 August did not involve the *interrogatoria*, and the second asked (or at least the notary recorded answers to) only twenty of them.[70] The interrogators did better on the next and subsequent days, sometimes asking all forty-eight of Campanella's questions and most if not all of the twenty drawn up by the fiscal.[71] At this same moment, the fiscal of the archbishop's court—not his inquisitorial tribunal—laid the same number of charges (*positiones et articuli*) against Campanella, drawing on all formed processes, witnesses, and last, *publica fama*. They begin with allegations about his atheism and contain a number of others about miracles including the resurrection, that the Eucharist was a "bagatelle" and not instituted by Christ, that he denied heaven, hell, and purgatory, that he believed the rational soul was mortal (the principal charge against Cesare Cremonini; see Chapter 4) and that an action was a sin only if it came to public notice, that he was a necromancer (coming far down the list at number 19), and finally that Turks lived better than Christians.[72] Tragagliolo remained thorough, continuing an examination of a man who had already undergone a *repetitio*, and reexamining witnesses heard in Calabria although not formally treating these sessions as *repetitiones*.[73] Sometimes he added ex officio questions, sometimes in between the defense and prosecution questions, sometimes in the middle of one or the other.[74] He also brought in new witnesses.[75]

On 8 September 1600 the nuncio forwarded a copy of the *processo* from Tragagliolo.[76] The viceroy, while deferring to ecclesiastical jurisdiction, was becoming impatient and often asked expedition of the case for rebellion. Nevertheless, almost two months elapsed before on 26 October the pope ordered Tragagliolo to have Campanella prepare his defense, and only after the viceroy had written directly.[77] On 31 October, the defense opened with the administration of the oath to Campanella's advocate, Giovanni Battista Dello Grugno, a lecturer at the University of Naples († 1604).[78] A week later, Dello Grugno assured the court that Campanella was insane and therefore could not mount a defense, offering testimony from the prison warden and other witnesses.[79] On the 17th the nuncio forwarded the *processo difensivo* for a group of friars, without specifying whether it included Campanella.[80] Santoro acknowledged receipt only on 1 December, the day after a coram heard Tragagliolo's cover letter.[81] Finally, on 7 December after another letter from Tragagliolo, the pope ordered the case referred or reported to the Inquisitors.[82] Nothing happened, forcing the viceroy to ask again, at which time, on 23 January 1601, the Congregation ordered the case "proposed" within a fortnight.[83] Almost another two months passed before the consultors gave their (unknown) opinions.[84] Some of the delay resulted from Tragagliolo's death. The Congregation and then Santoroclaimed the nuncio did not request a replacement until 23 February (although he had immediately announced Tragagliolo's demise), and despite his constant bombardment of Rome for instructions, it appears that he did forget to ask explicitly for a new Inquisition agent. Not until two days after the consultors' opinions were heard was Mandina appointed (13 and 15 March).[85] Why Mandina, who allegedly held that post in Naples from 1598 to 1604, was not previously involved and what he was doing in Rome instead of Naples until this moment is a mystery.[86] Since he was already the "minister" in Naples, his appointment to Campanella's trial must represent a special delegation, even though the decree does not explicitly call it that, heightening the probability that Tragagliolo also held a special commission.

The *Repetitio* Ends

In the same coram of 15 March in which Mandina was appointed, the pope ordered the end of the *repetitiones* and new questioning of corroboration witnesses in Calabria.[87] He went further. His actions make clear that Pope Clement did not believe Campanella mad. He ordered both the standard medical examination in such cases and also the extremely unusual and exceedingly cruel torture of the *veglia*, which consisted of constant repetition of the *corda* interspersed with that of the *cavaletto*, in which the prisoner was tied to a chair and suspended from the walls of the torture chamber for forty hours consecutively, during all which time he remained awake.[88] Since this was the same pope who had held office from the beginning of this *processo*, that he had ever tried to protect the Dominican seems highly unlikely. Five days later Clement ordered the bishops of Gerace and Squillace together to undertake the assignment in Calabria, but eight days further on that plan had to be abandoned and the bishop of Squillace (who was then in Rome) empowered to act alone.[89]

On orders from Santoro, Tragagliolo's replacement Mandina took over the case in April 1601, sending his first report on the 13th.[90] Among his tasks was the collection of more testimony, "among [?through] which it [Campanella's defense] can be contested to the end of convincing the said Campanella" ("tra quali può essere contestura a fine di convincere il detto Campanella").[91] Giulio Monterenzi, the fiscal in Rome, sent four new questions presented on 30 March, before Mandina returned, and two days later Campanella's advocate responded to them with new ones of his own. This must mean that the nuncio, or sometimes his auditor, as he admitted, had conducted the case until Mandina arrived.[92] On 31 May Mandina was ordered to proceed, to continue to monitor Campanella for signs of feigned madness, and to see to it that his order paid Campanella's costs.[93] After an unexplained delay following the papal command of 15 March, Campanella suffered the *veglia* beginning on 4 June. The *verbale* of the torture runs for fifteen pages in Luigi Firpo's edition, with the interrogators finally giving up after thirty-six hours.[94] The Florentine ambassador thought the torture resulted only in more confusion.[95] Mandina reported on it three days later, but only three weeks after that did the Congregation order the matter referred to the pope.[96] We do not know the result. Two medical certificates came in June, neither of which drew a solid conclusion.[97] There is almost nothing about Campanella in the decrees for the rest of the year. All we have until 4 January 1602 is yet another demand that the Dominicans cover his costs.[98] Since Mandina took over the case, the nuncio's correspondence also goes silent. Who stumbled is not apparent, but the Congregation—in the secret part of the meeting before the consultors entered—blamed Mandina, claiming to have had nothing from him in the interval.[99] This may be true, given the speed with which Santoro executed the decree, writing Mandina on the very day.[100] He wanted a detailed report in order to proceed to expedition, the more so in that the bishop of Squillace's death had aborted the further investigation in Calabria, and witnesses would now be difficult to find because of the delay. Mandina got the point, writing three times before the Congregation next deliberated on 21 February, when it ordered another full report including the opinions of his "co-judges" (*coniudices*) about expedition.[101] By coincidence, a consultor in Naples had just delivered his judgment that a *scartafaccio* (notebook, to judge from the Latin equivalent *quadernus*) of Campanella's containing various medical remedies, including one for how to avoid confessing under torture (!), was not against the faith.[102]

The *Expeditio*

It is the more surprising that Rome took little action, given that under pressure from the viceroy the nuncio went back to his strident demands for expedition.[103] The new secretary of the Inquisition, Camillo Borghese, the future Paul V, took more notice than Santoro had of the nuncio's complaints, writing him just a week after the first and on the same day as the Congregation gave the order that Mandina should send the rest of the case's documents and the opinions of his "co-judges" in order to proceed to expedition of all the cases in Naples.[104] Mandina was then in Caserta. The nuncio did not expect him to return until the weather improved, despite Borghese's order to him to intervene "as inquisitor," perhaps in Campanella's case but more likely in that of another suspect, Pietro Ponzio. Nevertheless, two more months passed before the Congregation ordered its consultors to consider the case.[105] Then, before it could be expedited, news of the prison break of some of Campanella's co-conspirators distracted the Inquisitors.[106] Finally, on 13 November 1602, the Congregation without the pope decreed his imprisonment "without any hope of liberation" ("sine aliqua spe liberationis").[107] Borghese waited until three other cases had also been expedited on 28 November, this time with the pope, before ordering both Mandina and the nuncio on the 29th to expedite all of them.[108] With the usual delay, the Neapolitan judges, called "specially delegated judges of this case" ("huiusmodi causae iudicibus spetialiter delegatis"), did not promulgate Campanella's sentence until 8 January 1603, specifying both that he was a prisoner of the Holy Office *de Urbe* and that it would not interfere in his trial for rebellion.[109] After more than three years Campanella's heresy case had finally ended.

As always, Campanella's dossier remained open, and in July 1606 matters appeared to take a dramatic turn. Acting on a memorial by Campanella sent via the nuncio (dated 23 May, so despite the tone of urgency in the new minister Deodato Gentile's dispatch, he took his time sending it), Gentile wrote the new Cardinal Secretary Pompeo Arrigoni that suspicious men had visited Campanella. Gentile, although it was late at night, had immediately asked and received permission from the viceroy to take a judicial deposition from Campanella, since he thought it likely that God had finally "illuminated his spirit" and led him to confess. Early the next morning Gentile's agent and a notary went to hear Campanella, only to discover that all he had for them was an autograph appeal. More significant, the agent and other witnesses thought him no longer insane, and Gentile sniffed out traces of Campanella's former "impieties" in the document and their reports. Campanella's request came down to sufficient food and access to a confessor.[110] Although docketed as received in Rome on 7 June, Gentile's letter was not considered until the coram of 13 July.[111] The new pope, Paul V, ordered both requests granted, and on 2 August Assessor Marcello Filonardi added their fulfillment to the agenda for the next day's coram, which took the proposed action, albeit in slightly modified form, ordering negotiations with the viceroy about a confessor.[112] Meanwhile on 19 July the Congregation heard more charges against Campanella, lodged by a man on the point of execution.[113]

A week after Arrigoni's most recent order about Campanella's confessor, on 11 August Gentile reported another initiative by Campanella that had led him and the nuncio to visit the prisoner "five or six days ago."[114] Campanella again refused to divulge anything unless he were heard outside Castel Sant'Elmo, and presented an autograph page of "pretensions" which Gentile at least received judicially. The courier moved much more quickly to Rome this time, Gentile's report being received on 17 August, when it was accurately summarized, but no action taken. Acknowledging a missing letter of 30 September, Gentile wrote Arrigoni again on 6 October, muttering about all the tasks he had been assigned.[115] Finally he got around to Campanella, saying that his food had improved and that two Spanish Dominicans, approved by the viceroy, had confessed him. This time a minute of the Congregation's order was added to the foot of Gentile's letter. He was to write "more clearly" whether Campanella's confessor had actually been appointed, or the point merely conceded in principle, and whether he had to be a Spaniard. Virtually the same order appeared in the decree register under 30 October.[116] The matter of Campanella's confessor dragged on into April 1607. On the 7th, the cardinals referred to the pope Gentile's request for faculties to the confessor to absolve Campanella from the sins specifically reserved to the pope in the bull *In Coena Domini.*[117] Filonardi then added the request to the agenda of 18 April, identifying the confessor as the *socius* of the Spanish bishop of Monopoli.[118] In the following day's coram, the faculties were somewhat surprisingly granted. At the same time, the pope also ordered Gentile to send Campanella's writing "for converting heretics" ("pro convertendis haereticis") to Rome, probably "Quod reminiscentur" (see below).[119]

With the matter of his confessor settled, Campanella launched another offensive, this time asking to be transferred to a better prison and also to have his case heard in Rome. On 5 July the pope ordered Gentile to see to the first and a summary of his case to be drawn up and reported.[120] At the end of August, Gentile wrote that the viceroy had agreed to a transfer.[121] The review in Rome apparently never went ahead; at least in January 1608 Paul rejected a request from Campanella for such an action, citing a decree of 28 December 1602.[122] Yet on 19 June 1608, Paul ordered Gentile to negotiate with the viceroy for Campanella's surrender to the Inquisition's prison, and repeated this at the end of September, although adding that he should not press the matter.[123] Indeed he did not, since we next hear of it only a year later.[124] Pressure applied by Campanella's friends, especially the future Lincean Johannes Faber, had changed the pope's mind.[125] A week later, the Congregation referred to the pope the question of a replacement for the nuncio on the viceroy's commission trying Campanella for rebellion. The pope appointed the nuncio, Guglielmo Bastoni, on 9 October 1608.[126] The action came just in time. The new man announced on 22 October the case's imminent expedition.[127]

Political Pressure Is Brought to Bear

The nuncio's report gave rise to no urgency in Rome. The next known order dates from March 1609, when the pope, perhaps in response to the viceroy's move, ordered the new nuncio, Valerio Muti, to take cognizance of Campanella's case as his predecessor had.[128] Then Campanella's supporters began to cause trouble, especially Kaspar Schoppe, who engaged in an intense correspondence with Campanella while trying to get various of his works published in Venice. The nuncio in Graz reported their epistolary exchange, including copies of two works, "contra Venetos" (*Antiveneti*) and "de Monarchia Papae" (*Monarchia del Messia*), which Campanella had sent Schoppe. The pope ordered Gentile to search for Campanella's writings and to prevent him from producing any more or communicating them outside the prison, as well as to summarize his case.[129] It may have been the discovery of the writings that led the pope to renew efforts to have Campanella turned over to the Inquisition. At any rate, on 13 August 1609 he ordered negotiations on that score with the king of Spain at the same time the nuncio there was to be sent a list of Campanella's errors.[130] The nuncio in Graz, whence the archduke had attempted to secure Campanella's release, reported again in April 1610 the circulation of Campanella's works, and Gentile was again ordered to search for them, find their errors, and shut down Campanella's communication with the outside world.[131] Gentile, recently promoted to nuncio, wrote back that he could find no new errors.[132] Meanwhile, Viceroy Pedro Fernández de Castro, count of Lemos, gave way a little, first allowing and then revoking the right for Spaniards other than his confessor to visit Campanella, and, more important, on 20 May 1610 granting the nuncio's "ministers" access to him in order to pursue his case.[133]

In 1611 Campanella's confrères in Naples tried to help him, petitioning for the expedition of his case for rebellion. The pope ordered Gentile to investigate and to see whether after its conclusion Campanella could be turned over to the Holy Office.[134] On 7 April Gentile was "subrogated" as "co-judge" (i.e., put in place of the previous man, his predecessor as nuncio) in the case for rebellion.[135] In June the nuncio received a favorable reply to his request for expedition when the viceroy also ordered the case referred.[136]

Before we next hear of Campanella's case, Gentile's replacement as the Holy Office's commissary arrived, Stefano Vicari. Perhaps because Gentile had so much experience with Campanella, Vicari seems not to have taken over from the nuncio until July 1612, as long as eighteen months after his appearance in Naples.[137] Then he reported that the viceroy refused access to Campanella without his license.[138] In September, after the viceroy had allowed Vicari to see the prisoner, Pope Paul again rejected a request by the Dominican hierarchy for his release.[139] In 1614 the case heated up again. In May, on a new denunciation from a fellow Dominican forwarded by the order's vicar general (Raphael Riphoz, who sat as a consultor to the Congregation) saying that Campanella continued to write books, Vicari was ordered to investigate.[140] He examined the witness in June when it emerged that the charge came secondhand.[141] When Vicari sent the source's testimony later in June, it was ordered ignored "for now."[142] Viceroy Lemos's command that after "disorders" Campanella could no longer see his confessor and had to be transferred back to Castel Sant'Elmo left no trace in the decree registers.[143] The Congregation did not interest itself in Campanella again until April 1615, when Gentile's report about his "Ateismo trionfato" worried it.[144] When the book came in, the Dominican Inquisitor Agostino Galamini undertook its review.[145]

In November 1616 Campanella paid a visit to the viceroy, asking to be released.[146] Lemos agreed to seek such an order from the pope (meaning not liberation, of course, but transfer to the Inquisition), and then added that had Campanella been a layman he would have burned him, new Nuncio Paolo Emilio Filonardi, former assessor of the Holy Office, thought on the strength of the information he had provided, including Campanella's prophecy that the viceroy would never hold that office. Zapata also spoke against Campanella. As a result of their efforts, the outgoing viceroy ordered Campanella more strictly imprisoned and deprived of writing materials.[147] When Filonardi returned a week later to see the (unnamed) viceroy, he did so on the pretext of a development in another high-profile case, that of Marcantonio De Dominis.[148] Saying that such sad cases (meaning Campanella rather than De Dominis) should be left to the pope, Filonardi led the viceroy to say that he would surrender Campanella were it in his power. This offer was taken up in the coram of 8 December, when both Filonardi's letters and two from Zapata—one announcing his appointment to the viceroyalty—were discussed. The pope again rejected the proposal to release Campanella to the Dominicans before saying that if the viceroy, perhaps now meaning Zapata, were of himself to surrender Campanella, the offer should be taken up. Meanwhile the Congregation would consider the best way of getting Campanella to Rome.[149]

A Long Lull (1615–1626)

Despite these promising auguries, nothing further happened until 1618. In May, on Campanella's petition, he was ordered given a "more comfortable" prison and allowed to hear Mass, confess, and take the Eucharist, that is, if the pope agreed.[150] He did, and on 10 May Nuncio Filonardi was ordered to see both that Campanella's conditions were improved and that he was kept securely.[151] These two orders make it appear that the viceroy might have turned Campanella over to the Inquisition, albeit keeping him in viceregal prisons, as had happened earlier. The silence of the Inquisition's records for the next year makes it impossible to confirm this speculation; the next entry once more merely rejects Campanella's request for release.[152] In the interval all we have is Cardinal Nephew Scipione Borghese's approval of Filonardi's refusal to speak to Campanella, together with a further order to prevent him from writing or seeing anyone.[153]

In contempt of Rome's best efforts, Campanella continued to write. In 1620, on a report from a Dominican in L'Àquila sent to Giacinto Petronio as master of the sacred palace, the archbishop of Naples was ordered to gather in copies of a writing in which Campanella abused the words of Christ's passion.[154] Nine months later Campanella himself asked the Congregation of the Index to review his "Quod reminiscentur," a work intended to persuade believers in the other major world religions to become Christians. An exceptionally well-attended meeting, including Roberto Bellarmino, Secretary Gian Garzia Millini, Fabrizio Verallo, Scipione Cobelluzzi, Desiderio Scaglia, and Petronio, assigned the book to Bellarmino. The secretary added that the Congregation's registers contained nothing specific against Campanella beyond a decree of 1603 banning all his works.[155] A little more than a month later, at a meeting Bellarmino did not attend, three revisors got the case: future cardinal Ciriaco Rocci, Venetian turncoat Marcantonio Cappello (see the next chapter), and Niccolò Riccardi, the second two at some point consultors of the Inquisition.[156] On Bellarmino's negative report, another well-attended meeting, this time including Maffeo Barberini, the future Urban VIII, decided in August not only not to license the book, but also to turn it over to the Inquisition.[157] As far as the records say, the Inquisition never took action on what should have been an especially serious denunciation.

In fact, over the next four and a half years, the only thing the Holy Office did was three times to deny Campanella's request to hear Mass, on the last occasion in 1626 ordering a review of what it had against him.[158] That took until July, when in a coram attended by all but one of the cardinals (by now including Gaspar Borja y de Velasco, Scaglia, Antonio Barberini, Sr., and Zacchia), which also heard the deceased Bellarmino's views, Urban VIII ordered Campanella to remain in the Inquisition's prisons and to communicate with no one other than Holy Office personnel, but at the same time to be moved to a newly built prison and kept "kindly" (*benigne*) as well as licensed to read and write, and finally to be fed better than usual for prisoners, in fact, he was to lack for nothing in the quality of his food.[159] Urban had plans for Campanella.

Urban Takes a Hand

The pope could now begin seriously to act on those plans, since the Inquisition finally had custody of Campanella. His trial for rebellion had re-started in March 1626, simultaneously with the appointment of a new nuncio, Antonio Diaz, bishop of Caserta, and resulted in Campanella's release to a monastery in May.[160] So far as is known, Diaz had no ties to the Inquisition either in Rome or in Naples.[161] Immediately after Campanella's assignment to San Domenico, the new nuncio was instructed to get him to Rome, where his case had become number one on its agenda, a note added in another hand. The order to Diaz came not from Secretary Millini or his known deputy Cardinal Ottavio Bandini, but from Antonio Barberini, Sr., who enclosed further orders in cipher.[162] This, and his action in the prison visitation of 21 December 1627 (see below), suggest that Cardinal Antonio may have acted as deputy secretary. Diaz replied almost as soon as he got Barberini's letter saying only that the chief intermediary in Campanella's release had left for Sicily and that various cardinals had recommended him, among them Ludovico Ludovisi, but no Barberini dependents.[163] An *avviso* reporting Campanella's arrival in Rome emphasized Ludovisi's prominence.[164] A week later Diaz excused his inaction by a combination of Campanella's strong local support, lack of access to the viceroy, and the Inquisition's low standing in Naples.[165] Diaz was not in fact stalling. Three days later he adroitly tricked Campanella into requesting transfer to Rome, which the nuncio granted only too happily.[166] The weather frustrated Diaz's plans until 5 July, when he could finally smuggle Campanella, in the garb of a secular priest, onto a boat headed for Rome.[167] Two days later he reported that he did not know whether the viceroy would have approved, especially since he had demanded extradition in Naples. Diaz had excused himself saying the matter belonged to the Holy Office.[168]

From this point forward, the Congregation finally took over Campanella's case, ending the complicated interplay between Rome and at least three sets of authorities in Naples. Even before it officially concluded, Urban ordered him released from prison on 11 January 1629, immediately after the pope's ceremonial entry to the meeting.[169] He had already used Campanella to try to reason with one of the Inquisition's most recalcitrant prisoners, Girolamo Vecchietti.[170]

Conclusion

Beginning almost fifty years after it had first tried to establish its authority in Naples, the Roman Inquisition still had to struggle for almost thirty more to get Campanella away from the viceroy. In his case and those surveyed in the previous chapter, its ministers often but not invariably cooperated closely with the nuncios, although either could also act almost entirely independently of the other, Tragoglio from Aldobrandini, for example. The archbishop, by contrast, hardly appears in Campanella's case and except for the use of his prison plays only a minor role in the others. While Rome may not have made a great deal of progress in asserting its superiority to secular jurisdiction, it appears that it had done so on the score of the archbishop's. There might still have been two inquisitions in being, but the principle seems now to have been established that important cases, especially those like Campanella's or Cristóval de Figueroa's that raised implications for the boundaries between secular and ecclesiastical jurisdiction, belonged to the Holy Office in Rome. Despite Clement VIII's determination to destroy Campanella, it was not until Urban VIII's "absolutely monarchical" government that Rome finally established sway over Naples. Despite continuing the drive to link nuncio and Holy Office, often by making either the Roman commissary or assessor nuncio, Paul V had shown much less interest than Urban in bringing Naples to heel. Paul's overriding target was Venice, to which we now turn.

CHAPTER 3

Venice in the Wake of the Interdict

Although Naples and Venice were two of the most important local inquisitions, the Congregation attended to them in very different ways. While Naples drew steadily more interest in the seventeenth century, Rome expended most of its energy on Venice in one decade-long burst in the aftermath of the interdict of 1606. By the end of Paul V's reign in 1621, Rome took not much more notice of Venice than of the local inquisition in, say, Cremona, and the situation changed little under Urban VIII. For the three years during which we have a record of Rome's out-letters, 1626–1628, 300 or so per year went to Naples, but only a handful to Venice. The way Rome handled the nunciatures in the two places also indicates the status of their respective inquisitions. In Naples, several of the nuncios, beginning with Paolo Emilio Filonardi, had been members of the Congregation's staff, and the local Roman minister was almost always such a professional, the commissary, the assessor, or even the master of the sacred palace. The Venetian inquisitor never had such training, and the nuncio was always a diplomat, not an inquisitor. Two of the most important nuncios in our period, including the longest-serving one, went on to become Inquisitors, the reverse of what happened in Naples, where the nuncios rarely became cardinals and never Inquisitors. It was almost as if the Inquisition and its papal masters often went through the motions in Venice, while they paid scrupulous attention to what happened in Naples. This relative neglect may help to account for the fact that we have much less information about the inquisitors of Venice by comparison than about those in either Naples or Florence. Despite his twenty-two-year tenure, we know almost nothing about Giovanni Domenico Vignuzzio or Vinuccio, for example.[1] This lack of basic biographical information about the inquisitors in Venice suggests that they were much less substantial figures than their counterparts in either Naples or Florence.

These radically different experiences arose from both local and global geopolitical circumstances. Not that there was much difference in the attitude of the secular authorities in the two places. In both Venice and Naples, the governments regarded the Inquisition as virtually under their control. Certainly, at any moment of the frequent conflicts in both places, the final decision had to remain in lay hands, and more often than not it did. It would be hard to say which set of lay authorities showed less enthusiasm about the Inquisition. Venice had never seen the near-rebellion that broke out in Naples in 1549 when the pope tried to introduce the Roman Inquisition, but putting its institutions in place was no easier on the lagoon than on the bay. The Venetians always had more official control than the Neapolitans, because the metropolitan Venetian tribunal contained three lay members who in effect directed its business.[2] This happened despite the fact that, unlike the situation in Naples, the nuncio was a permanent, indeed the dominant, member of the Venetian tribunal. The nuncio could and often did intervene in trials in Naples, but he did not have a regular seat on the Inquisition's court nor sign its sentences as he did in Venice, along with the patriarch, the Venetian equivalent of archbishop and, even more than the archbishop of Naples, subordinate to the Inquisition.

The interdict had been a long time coming before Paul V imposed it in spring 1606.[3] The Venetians, who needed room to maneuver, later claimed that the pope had acted without consulting anyone else.[4] However that may be, among the irritants driving Paul to such an extreme measure was Venetian interference with the local Inquisition.[5] One handy summary of Venetian attitudes, arising out of the interdict and written shortly thereafter, was Paolo Sarpi's *Discorso dell'origine, forma, leggi, ed uso dell'Ufficio dell'inquisitione nella città, e dominio di venetia*.[6] Among the principles enshrined therein was that Venice never agreed to the appointment of inquisitors anywhere in its territories without its approval and more often than not on its nomination.[7] (This principle may help to explain the long tenure of inquisitor Vignuzzio, who served from 1600 to 1622, as Brian Pullan suggests.)[8] No decrees coming from outside Venice were allowed to be entered into a *processo*, and naturally no bulls nor orders from the Congregation.[9] Nor could the Inquisition issue any "precept or *monitorio*" whatsoever against secular authorities.[10] Nevertheless, Sarpi tried to make it appear that the lay consultants did not control the Venetian inquisition.[11] Bigamy and polygamy, which the Inquisition insisted belonged to it, Sarpi just as doggedly maintained had no place there without other indications of heresy.[12] A new inquisitor could publish an edict covering only six allowed cases, another principle formulated in the wake of the interdict crisis and hotly disputed during it.[13] And despite several high-profile cases to the contrary, especially perhaps that of Giordano Bruno (who was not a Venetian citizen), the Venetians—unlike everywhere else, even Naples—almost never allowed the extradition of those accused of heresy, especially if the alleged acts had been committed outside its dominion.[14] One of the best examples is the notorious case of the Paduan philosopher and friend of Galileo Cesare Cremonini whose *processo* ran throughout most of the period considered in this chapter (see the next chapter). Even in the wake of the interdict, almost none of the men on Rome's most-wanted list were allowed to leave Venice, unless the Venetians had decided for reasons of their own that they had outlived their usefulness. This is especially clear in the instance of Fulgenzio Manfredi, the only man on that list to be executed (although others may have been poisoned as contemporaries alleged). Perhaps even more serious, the Venetian authorities nearly always successfully resisted the Inquisition's efforts to control its press, one of its major industries.[15]

The Venetians made excellent use of anti-papal propaganda during the interdict crisis, much of it either written or inspired by Sarpi, their theologian consultor. The central figure as both polemicist and censor in the Roman response was Inquisitor Roberto Bellarmino, consistent with his more general status as workhorse of Roman censorship.[16] Already on 26 July 1606, the Congregation ordered one of Bellarmino's books sent to all inquisitors.[17] The Inquisition's first salvo was to prohibit Sarpi's translation of Jean Gerson's tract on excommunication and other such writings on the strength of expert theological opinions, including that of Benedetto Giustiniani.[18] Five days later Bellarmino reported his first censure on Venetian writing.[19] Still in June, the Holy Office is supposed to have prohibited Giovanni Marsilio's *Risposta d'un dottore* and any other similar works in the future.[20] Paul V took an active role from the first. On 20 July he formally began the process against Sarpi by ordering a Capuchin from Bergamo then in Ostiglia to depose about him to the inquisitor of Mantua.[21] Two days later he asked its duke whether Manfredi was preaching heretically, an approach necessitated by the papacy's loss of most of its reliable sources of information inside Venice.[22] As we shall see, despite the Venetians' best efforts, the Inquisition in both the metropolis and its satellites continued to operate throughout the interdict, albeit with drastically reduced powers. The Senate stripped the Venetian inquistor of his authority over the press on 4 August 1606, replacing him with a commission of five theologians, the most important of whom were Sarpi and Pietro Antonio Ribetti.[23] We catch just a glimpse of official concern in the report by one of the leaders of the anti-papal party about the inquisitor's continued activities, including publishing an edict from Rome in the refectory of the Dominican convent of SS. Giovanni e Paolo.[24]

Even if he never explicitly stated that he meant to claw back more control for the Roman Congregation over its Venetian branches, Paul certainly used the Inquisition as one of his principal instruments to get revenge against Venice. It therefore causes no surprise that the men who wrote its propaganda provided the Inquisition's principal target, beginning with Sarpi, Marsilio, and Manfredi, who were all condemned in less than six months.[25] The pope put the nuncio, Berlinghiero Gessi, in charge, giving him excellent experience to become an Inquisitor many years later. The nuncio had an extremely difficult, at times impossible, job, but just how "circumspect" he was in doing it is an open question.[26] Nevertheless, his experience made a profound impression on him, perhaps especially in exposing him to the widespread Venetian use of precepts; this became a common term in his vocabulary, even in his letters to Rome. It may well be that Gessi therefore served as an alembic to the Inquisition's increasing use of the device it would apply to Galileo in 1616.[27]

The Seven Theologians

Paul gave Gessi explicit instructions: Sarpi, Marsilio, and the other theologians who had written on Venice's behalf, in total at least two dozen men, were to be turned over to the Inquisition. Not all got equal attention, but none escaped notice altogether, not even a decade later, the Inquisition in this case clearly displaying its remarkable institutional memory.[28] Those in whom the Inquisition took a special interest in addition to Sarpi were Pietro Antonio Ribetti, Bernardo Giordano, Michelangelo Bonicelli (1569–1624), Marcantonio Cappello, Fra Camillo (da Venezia), O.S.A., and Sarpi's right-hand man Fulgenzio Micanzio (all of whom signed the *Trattato dell' interdetto*). Together with Fulgenzio Manfredi, these constituted the so-called "seven theologians," plus a third Fulgenzio, whose surname may have been Tomaselli and who was called Albanese. There were also Girolamo Vendramin and three Capuchins in Bergamo, Ippolito Averoldi, Bernardino da Bergamo, and Francesco Foresto (the first drew by far the most attention), the obscure Giovanni Muti, and Gasparo Ventura Lonigo (1583–1663).[29] Gessi might have been inclined to try merciful treatment first, but neither he nor his papal master had much patience. In nearly every case they quickly turned to harsher methods.

While Sarpi posed a far more serious threat than Marsilio, the papacy did not underestimate Manfredi, especially his preaching.[30] A priest from 1586, when he also took a doctorate in theology, Manfredi originally entered the Capuchin order before transferring to the Franciscan Observants. He served as a preacher from at least 1594, when the general chapter suspended him for four years. He published two books of Venetian history, a compendium of lives of the doges in 1598, and *Degnità procuratoria di s. Marco in Venetia* (Venice, 1602).[31] In 1605 his *Apologia, overo Difensione . . . sopra la riformazione dell'Ordine suo* was placed on the Index. During the interdict he preached at the Redentore and the convent of Santa Maria dell'Umiltà (taken from the expelled Jesuits), which he also governed.[32] On 3 August 1606 two depositions against Manfredi, given in the Venetian Holy Office on 29 July and reported by the inquisitor the same day, were ordered read in the next coram.[33] On that occasion a week later, in the second case considered, the pope ordered Manfredi's removal and a discussion of how to proceed.[34] Then another week later it was Sarpi's turn. The first deposition against him was read again, and the pope ordered a supersedeat in the examination of "Scaino de Salodio legum professor Paduae et Doctore Raguseo lectore philosophiae" named in it.[35]

Perhaps because Rome knew he was not a Venetian subject and might therefore be more vulnerable than the others, the first man it cited was Marsilio on 23 August 1606 despite the fact that there is no sign of process against him before then.[36] Marsilio alleged that he appeared on 9 September before Vignuzzio to explain why he could not answer the citation.[37] On the same day as Marsilio's citation, a deposition against Sarpi, taken by the inquisitor of Florence, was heard in Rome.[38] In the following day's coram, it was read again, and another witness was ordered examined by the inquisitor of Genoa.[39] Then, in an almost impossibly quick reaction, information against Manfredi sent by the inquisitor of Venice came up only two days later.[40] At the same time, Sarpi's *Considerazioni sopra il breve delle censure* and the collectively authored *Trattato dell'interdetto* were ordered censured by consultors.[41] On Wednesday and Thursday, 13 and 14 September, the minute of the edict of prohibition of Sarpi's *Considerazioni* was first read and then approved by the pope and ordered printed, as it was on 20 September.[42] Paul continued to drive the Inquisition forward, probably with the active assistance of Secretary Pompeo Arrigoni.[43] A week later Sarpi was ordered to surrender all his writings. The Venetian resident in Naples who was passing out copies of Sarpi's *Considerazioni* was to be sent the edict prohibiting it.[44] The following week it was back to Manfredi, a deposition from Cremona diocese being added to his dossier.[45]

In the second case on the agenda of 26 October, Paul ordered proceedings continued against Sarpi, Manfredi, and the printer Roberto Meietti, whose press produced much of the Venetian propaganda.[46] Four days later the first two were cited to Rome, and all of Meietti's output was prohibited.[47] Manfredi, Marsilio, and Sarpi shot back in individual writings, later collected into *Theologorum Venetorum Joan. Marsilii, Pauli Veneti, Fr. Fulgentii ad excommunicationis, citationis et monitionis Romanae sententiam in ipsos latam Responsio*, which was not certainly published until 1673 in volume 1 of *Opere del padre Paolo dell'ordine de' Servi* (Venice: Roberto Meietti).[48] Manfredi's contribution, *Frater Fulgentius . . . Reverendissimis in Christo patribus, dd. archiepiscopis . . . nec non & cuiuscumque status laicis saecularibus Christianis catholicis, gratiam Sancti Spiritus, Spiritum Christi, Zelumque Apostolorum* did appear in Venice in 1606 (dated 25 November), and is supposed to have been translated into Italian as *A tutti li reverendissimi Padri in Christo . . . La gratia dello Spirito Santo, lo Spirito di Christo, et il zelo de gli Apostoli* (Venice, 1606).[49] Manfredi attempted to make legal arguments, but they lacked much force, quibbling, for example, over the meaning of "fiscal."[50] Sarpi, as one might expect of the official Venetian canonist, did much better. His reply, also dated 25 November, alleged, among other points, that his citation did not arise from proper process, making the legally strong objections that "no order of the law had been served" ("nullo servato iuris ordine"), nor had he been cited the requisite number of times.[51] At just this time, the worrying news was reported that the extraordinary Spanish ambassador's confessor, Paolo de Sulmona, acting on the orders of Cardinal Arrigoni (as protector of the Franciscans, not as secretary of the Inquisition) and in concert with the new legate of Romagna, Cardinal Bonifacio Caetani, was trying both to browbeat and to bribe some of the propagandists, especially Manfredi.[52] The same day the doge upbraided the the ambassador over Fra Paolo's actions.[53] On 14 December the Congregation heard Vignuzzio's report that both Sapri and Manfredi had brought out *protestationes* from Meietti's press.[54] The pope left it to the inquisitor how safely to proceed.[55] Apparently Rome contemplated a reply to Manfredi, an action which the "boni" in Venice applauded.[56] On 6 December the fiscal of the Holy Office reported the citations of Sarpi and Manfredi, and the Congregation ordered the cases pursued to sentence.[57] The repetition of that action for the second time of the required three came in more formal terms on 20 December, and on 29 December at the fiscal's "instance," the Congregation pronounced sentence "as in the attachment."[58] Within a week, Paul got a splendid new year's gift in the form of excommunications of Sarpi and Manfredi.[59] Meanwhile, the Inquisition pushed for publication of more propaganda, including the agreements between Sixtus IV, Julius II, and Venice.[60]

In the coram of 4 January 1607 another of the prime suspects first came to the Inquisition's attention, when it banned a book by the Conventual Franciscan Marcantonio Cappello, public reader in metaphysics at Padua, *Controversiae tra il sommo Pontefice Paolo V.o e la serenissima Republica di Venetia*, known as *Parere*, Giustiniani again being among the consultors.[61] At the same time Vignuzzio reported the unsurprising news that none of the authors of a book called *Protestationes*, among them Sarpi, Manfredi, and Cappello, could be brought to recognize it judicially; this must mean the famous *Trattato dell' interdetto*.[62] A week later Cappello's reply to Antonio Possevino had arrived.[63] Cappello had taught at the Frari in Venice after 1581, when he had been friendly with the Jesuit Possevino.[64] For some reason, Cappello's reply to the inquisitor of Florence, Lelio Medici, escaped notice.[65] What was probably the *Trattato*, sent by Manfredi, showed up in Ancona, whose inquisitor was ordered to renew the edict against the book. Manfredi's covering letter went into his dossier.[66] Shortly thereafter, another denunciation of Sarpi, Manfredi, and Marsilio was added to their dossiers.[67]

Vignuzzio continued to try to do his job, reporting that it was impossible to examine witnesses against Sarpi and Manfredi.[68] The next week's coram at least heard his news that Manfredi and Micanzio were preaching against the interdict and that one of the recalcitrant Capuchins from Brescia had been appointed to preach Lent. This possibly was Ippolito Averoldi, whose preaching in Bergamo had been praised by its rector.[69] The next week the inquisitor forwarded a copy of Micanzio's *Confirmatione delle Considerationi del P. Mastro Paolo de Venetia con le oppositioni del R. P. Maestro Gioantonio Bovio Carmeletano*.[70] In March and April he reported, first, that both Manfredi and Micanzio had been prohibited from preaching, and then that Manfredi had been restored to preach on the Ten Commandments.[71]

Shortly before the inquisitor's March report came the shocking news that Cappello had fled to Bologna.[72] The next day the alarmed Council of Ten in Venice issued orders to various podestàs that he was to be brought back, but too late.[73] The lifting of the interdict on 21 April made it easier to pursue the *processi* in train, now with Cappello's help.[74] Three days later another denunciation was added to Manfredi's file.[75] A month later, the pope summoned a witness against Sarpi and Micanzio to Rome.[76] The same day he ordered Cappello examined.[77] Cappello's reward was the prohibition—first by the Index and then by the Inquisition—of his *Parere*.[78] On 7 June Paul ordered his case's expedition.[79] Two weeks later his deposition was read and expedition referred back to the pope.[80] The following week, after the consultors' opinions were heard, Paul ordered Cappello to abjure *de vehementi* before the commissary, retract his book, and be rehabilitated.[81] As usual, the order was not finalized until 19 July.[82] At the same time as Cappello's sentence was originally proposed, other books against the interdict also appeared on the agenda. After the news that the podestà of Padua was preventing the inquisitor from collecting them (confessors were ordered to get them instead), came the more distressing report that the archivist of the Camera Apostolica, Michele Lonigo, and his brother Gaspar had both written such books.[83] A note of their writings was ordered sent to the new nuncio Gessi.[84] From Este, Gaspar († 10 September 1667 at the age of more than eighty) had taken degrees at Bologna, Parma, and Padua before securing a chair at the last in 1609. Fiercely proud of his canonistic learning, deferring in it only to Prospero Fagnani, in 1634 he became a *consultore* of Venice, the same post Sarpi had held.[85] Among other offices, he was auditor and vicar general of the patriarch of Aquileia, one of the heads of the Venetian religious establishment. He left a manuscript edition of the works of Bartolo da Sassoferrato.[86] Michele (1572–1639) was an equally indefatigable writer with a more checkered career, in part because he chose to pursue it in Rome. He published his first book there in 1601 before becoming a client of Cardinal Bartolomeo Cesi and unofficial papal archivist.[87] His denunciation did not hurt much, since he was already a papal notary (created 3 May 1607), a post confirmed in 1610 when Paul V made him "prefect of the registers and apostolic bulls of the Vatican Library" ("praefectus registrorum et bullarum apostolicorum Bibliothecae vaticanae"). This also gave him control of the new papal archives in Castel Sant'Angelo; he also served the pope as master of ceremonies in the papal chapel.[88] After 1612 his power gradually waned, before he found himself on trial and imprisoned in 1617.[89] He later recovered and published several more books.[90] A number of his manuscripts are in the Barberiniani latini, among them a work on the conclave (MS 1272). He also left part of a treatise on the precedence of the prefect of Rome—the post Urban VIII invented for his nephew Taddeo—dedicated to Cardinal Giovanni Colonna, apparently an attempt to ingratiate himself with the Barberini at one remove.[91]

A New Nuncio

On 1 June 1607 Berlinghiero Gessi became nuncio, a post he held for eleven years. He arrived in Venice on 26 June and presented his credentials on 3 July.[92] He went to work on Inquisition business immediately, if not necessarily in the Venetian Holy Office. In fact, since one of its members (did Gessi mean a consultor or a lay asssistant?) had written against the interdict and Gessi could not see how to exclude him, he was trying to avoid meetings.[93] Part of his instructions concerned burning books against the interdict, something the Inquisition also did in Rome, including those by Meietti to the ruin of his business.[94] Four days after officially taking office, Gessi sent his first report to Cardinal Nephew Scipione Borghese, impatiently noting that he had no instructions from Commissary Agostino Galamini yet about the theologians.[95] Two weeks later he still had nothing from the commissary, nor from Arrigoni.[96] On 4 August he wrote Borghese that the "bad theologians" were making more trouble than ever. Sarpi at least lived in retirement and said Mass frequently; this was really a complaint since it added to his reputation for sanctity. Manfredi and Marsilio lived "dissolutely" "and are generally hated" ("e sono comunemente odiati"). And then Gessi ripped off the mask. "I put into consideration that one could by means of exiles or such men one evening capture at least one of these and take him quickly by boat into the ecclesiastical state. And I believe it would not be difficult in Fra Fulgenzio's case since he wanders around a lot and comes back to his convent at night and the woman whom he visits is known. In Fra Paolo's case it would be difficult, but if one were captured perhaps the others would flee, and we would gain great reputation. Cardinal Caetani [legate of Romagna] would be the best to find men and execute everything." After all, everybody expected the Holy Office to proceed against the seven theologians.[97]

Gessi elaborated on his plan in his next weekly dispatch. "The removal from here by trickery and force of one of the three excommunicates [Sarpi, Manfredi, and Marsilio] and especially Fra Fulgenzio I believe could succeed by means of Cardinal Caetani as I wrote, and from this we would gain great reputation and make clear to the world that the pope is prepared to provide for these scandals. Once the action is completed the Venetians would see that there was no remedy and I believe they would do nothing about it. One could well worry whether this would damage ecclesiastical jurisdiction and disturb especially ecclesiastical persons, but if the capture took place outside their residence as could be done since Fra Fulgenzio often goes around these nearby places and sometimes to a monastery of Reformed [Franciscans] called "il Deserto" [San Francesco del Deserto, an island in the lagoon] five miles away. One could believe that this displeasure [*disgusto*] would pass because he is commonly hated and abhorred."[98] The seven theologians could be cited to the Holy Office because the Venetians (at least the "good ones") were annoyed that such measures had not been tried, and even though the theologians could not be taken from Venice, proceedings in contumacy could be pursued just as had been done against the three excommunicates. Gessi was sure Venice would defend them, so the papal authorities would have "to go dissimulating and come to a break [with Venice] over time" ("andarli dissimulando, o col tempo arrivare a rottura"), but the Venetians would abandon the defense after "the pope's admonitions" and pressure from princes. Doing nothing was not a good idea because that would "turn the world upside down again" ("mettere di nuovo il mondo sottosopra").

Meanwhile it was the turn of one of the minority of Capuchins in Bergamo who had sided with Venice, Ippolito Averoldi.[99] On 9 August 1607 "erroneous" propositions from his "Controversia de Mahomette et Antichristo," which had begun to be printed, were read. The pope ordered printing stopped and Gessi written to be sure he could proceed against Averoldi.[100] Two days later Gessi reported that the doge and Senate were angry over Meietti's handling by the Index, but he would still use his auditor and the notary from the Torrione in Bologna (one of the principal criminal courts in the papal states) to make an informative process.[101] In his second dispatch of 18 August, Gessi reported that he had tried both to have the inquisitors of Vicenza and Brescia reinstated and to get secular aid against Averoldi.[102] Despite the fact that Antonio Querini and Niccolò Contarini, both major powers among the antipapalisti, assured him that the book was unpublished and Averoldi "not very bright" ("di poco cervello"), Gessi was not optimistic.[103] Another Venetian author had already found himself in the hands of the Inquisition, although it is not known exactly when his case began. This was Benedetto Benedetti, who asked to have his untitled book returned to him, and the pope therefore ordered a diligent search made for it.[104] The book was probably "Apologia Benedicti de Benedictis Veneti pro liberatione animae Traini Imperatoris," which was assigned to Bellarmino for censure on 20 September. His report came just a week later, when the Dominican theologian and Inquisitor Cardinal Girolamo Bernerio was asked to review it.[105]

Averoldi's case renewed one that had begun before 10 January 1602, when he had a request for the return of his writings denied.[106] Almost two years passed before Averoldi next appears in the record, on 6 November 1603 when the commissary, Deodato Gentile, reported errors in his book and was ordered to negotiate with the prior of the Capuchins and their provincial about how to get him to Mantua or Cremona and thus to prison.[107] On the following 8 January the commissary reported to the pope on his imprisonment.[108] Two weeks later the pope ordered the theologians to consult with him in order to remove his ideas about the Antichrist, and about his rehabilitation.[109] Rehabilitation came in early February, but Averoldi was not allowed to leave his convent and was prohibited from writing or talking about the Antichrist except with qualified theologians.[110] On 10 February he was allowed to write his father, provided he not mention his case.[111] By then he had been imprisoned in a monastery in Rome, whence his letter of 16 March led the pope on the 18th to order him brought to his presence to hear him; we do not know whether he this happened.[112] On 1 April he was assigned to his superiors, who were to keep him in Rome.[113] Four days later the Congregation denied his request for the "printing of a cross he made" ["impressionem crucis ab ipso factae]," but on the 22nd the pope granted it.[114] On Tuesday 27 April "heard in congregation [which may mean meeting, not necessarily of the Congregation, given the day of the week] he was given a precept not to leave Rome without license."[115] On 6 May he was ordered to repeat the *revocatio* of his book in the Holy Office. It was then to be sent to Brescia to be read in his convent, and apparently he was allowed to leave Rome for the summer.[116]

Just when it looked as if his case had ended, it started up again. On 12 May, the Congregation heard him once more when he was "seriously reproved" ("gravissime reprehensus").[117] In the next day's coram, Averoldi's situation worsened, if anything. His letter of 10 May was read along with his abjuration and the consultors' opinions, and he was ordered reimprisoned and examined "about all these propositions."[118] A week later, back in prison, he was denied the right to compose memoranda.[119] On 14 July and again on 5 August the pope heard his depositions read. On the second occasion, after the meeting had ended, Cardinal Camillo Borghese, secretary and future pope, passed on Clement VIII's order to keep Averoldi in prison.[120] At another Tuesday meeting on 17 August, his petition for release was ordered read before the pope, as it was the following Thursday, when Clement rehabilitated him to his Roman convent and prohibited him from writing or speaking about his case.[121] After a petition for release was rejected on 19 October, on 5 November his expedition was ordered proposed to the pope.[122] On 11 November, having heard the consultors' opinions, Clement ordered

Averoldi's case terminated and his memorandum and a report on his book "de Antichristo et Mahometo" heard. His superiors were then to put him in the convent they thought best, and his *revocatio* was once again to be read in Brescia.[123] Then in what had to have been a purely formal move, three days later he was assigned a term for his defense.[124] On 25 January 1609, another Tuesday, letters from Aurelio Averoldi, a theologian and lawyer who was probably a canon of the cathedral in Brescia and would later be a bishop, were read; they may have recommended Ippolito, probably a relative.[125] In the coram of the 27th, Clement ordered a supersedeat, and the inquisitor of Brescia was to collect Averoldi's writings.[126] Three months passed, before on 27 April he was allowed to visit the basilicas of Santa Maria Maggiore and San Giovanni in Laterano, but not to discuss his case nor approach the Holy Office without permission.[127] A "sententia remissionis" was read on 13 July, before on 28 September a sentence drafted by Arrigoni was approved.[128] On 5 and 6 October the question of printing his "opus de Cruce" came up again. This time both the Congregation and the pope denied a license, and on the second occasion he was sternly enjoined not to "molest" the Congregation in the future.[129] On 14 October he heard sentence and retracted the "propositions contained in the book composed by him about the Antichrist."[130] His case ended, for now, with the order five days later to have his sentence read in Brescia to ten or twelve "grave fathers" but no laymen.[131]

Books were once more on Gessi's mind in his dispatches of 25 August. Giovanni Battista Ciotti, who had been involved in Giordano Bruno's trials and who Gessi realized was acting out of animus, had told the nuncio that Meietti was planning to send two works by Sarpi to be printed in Frankfurt, and another to princes demanding a council; he could not confirm this. He could say that he had the same answer about Averoldi: the book had been printed "et la stampa guasta" (literally the print/ing destroyed), and, since he was insane, there was no point in proceeding. The Venetians would, however, allow the inquisitor of Brescia to take over the case at the right time.[132] In the coram of 30 August, Paul demanded that the inquisitor take action after seeing an *instructio*.[133] In his dispatch of the next day, the Venetian ambassador confirmed Gessi's report about Meietti, whom he had defended to the pope.[134] The same day Gessi wrote a lot of news. First, the inquisitors of Vicenza and Brescia had been allowed back. Next, the second man was being allowed to handle Averoldi, which gave Gessi a chance to launch into a long complaint about the Capuchins in Brescia, many of whom had supported the Venetians.[135] Finally, Gessi had an update about

Manfredi, who had spent almost all summer at S. Francesco della Vigna, sometimes going to the Jesuit's former church, all in the close vicinity of the Palazzo del Nunzio, through which he had even passed once, claiming public passage.[136] Needless to say, it was dangerous to let him preach where there were so many *frati*.[137]

Gessi had three pieces of good news in his next dispatch. In the matter of Averoldi, he confirmed that he had gotten the podestà of Brescia to leave the matter to its inquisitor. Next, a Servite had come to him who thought he could bring Micanzio around and was headed to Rome to talk about this with the pope, because Gessi feared neither Micanzio nor Sarpi would trust him. Last, he had spoken to the Franciscan commissary to be certain that Manfredi did not preach at the Umiltà, and he had agreed to assign the preaching to two other friars. Manfredi wished to give an account of himself in Venice, since he distrusted going to Rome.[138] The next week that last point had changed: Gessi advised Borghese that he thought it best to allow Manfredi to preach in the Umiltà, where there were fewer friars and people than in the crowded San Francesco. (Manfredi did indeed preach at the ex-Jesuit church.)[139] Gessi complained again of having to watch Manfredi strut past his house. Unless he was ordered to, Gessi would say no more and would report on Manfredi's sermons. Sarpi and Manfredi both said that they would not come to Rome and that Venice had promised to defend them. Gessi had pressed the Franciscan commissary to try again with Manfredi, and was doing what he could about postponing the Servites' general chapter, which was to be held in Sarpi's convent.[140] Gessi kept after the Franciscan commissary, Padre Brasavola, to see what he had done about Manfredi. The result was Gessi's opinion that Brasavola had to hear the case in Venice, along with the nuncio and two or three others he named. The commissary refused to have Gessi hear it alone. If the inquisitor was involved, it would appear to be in the hands of the Inquisition, which the Venetians would not allow. Manfredi had told Brasavola that he would abjure and reveal much about other false theologians. Gessi had replied that he could not move without knowing what the pope wanted. Manfredi had said many things in the pulpit that would be hard to prove in a *processo* because witnesses would not testify, fearful of angering the Venetian authorities. Manfredi admitted to no more than dissuading observance of the interdict, and denied all the rest. Gessi closed by saying that the doge and Collegio were pressuring Manfredi's order to hold its general chapter in Venice, and that Brasavola had behaved well.[141]

An Attempted Assassination of Sarpi

Before Gessi wrote again, an action remarkably like the one he had proposed back in August took place. In the early evening of 5 October persons unknown attempted to assassinate Sarpi.[142] It was 23 hours (one hour before sunset) on 5 October 1607. A big fire had broken out two days before in Venice, in Salizzada San Lio, then as now a main street leading to the Mercerie near Piazza San Marco. It was still not out. Such fires were always a threat and caused great excitement. This time one of the curious onlookers was Sarpi's bodyguard. That evening Sarpi too wanted to see the fire badly enough to leave the monastery of San Marco a Santa Fosca, in the company only of his servant Marino and an aged admirer, Alessandro Malipiero. As they crossed the Ponte Del Pugno, five assassins attacked Sarpi with daggers and struck fifteen blows, wounding him three times, twice in the neck and once in the head, the stab passing from behind his ear and out his right cheek. The weapon lodged so securely next to his nose that the would-be murderer could not pull it out. Believing he had killed Sarpi, the ringleader drew his arquebus (a firearm) and menaced the bystanders, including Sarpi's terrified servant, who fled after hearing shots. Malipiero, alerted by the cries of some women at a window, came to Sarpi's aid, pulling the dagger out of his head and giving the alarm that the assassins, pistols in hand, were escaping down Strada San Marciliano into Corte Vecchia della Misericordia, where a gondola awaited. From there they went (or at least so Sarpi's biographer Fulgenzio Micanzio believed) to the nuncio's house, before getting away to the Lido, where a veritable fleet of boats waited to take them to Ravenna or Ferrara, both in papal territory.

From his bed Sarpi laid the blame for his attack in an awful pun: "It was given 'stilo Romanae Curiae,'" "with the stylus/dagger of," with at least overtones of the sense Dante had used, "in the style of the Roman Curia." Another observer said Sarpi blamed the Jesuits.[143] It was said that letters from Bellarmino were found in the house of one of the conspirators; others thought he had tried to warn Sarpi.[144] Micanzio provided circumstantial evidence incriminating the pope (who, incredibly enough, had just issued an order that assassination was not to be used as an instrument of policy).[145] The man in charge was Ridolfo Poma, a bankrupt Venetian merchant and a client of Cardinal Borghese and his uncle Paul V. He had recruited three soldiers and paid them with money from the papal treasury at Ancona (and maybe Ravenna, too).[146] He himself was allegedly promised 10,000 *scudi*, which the pope refused to pay. The fifth conspirator was a priest, Michele Viti from Bergamo. He had spied on Sarpi for months, even going to confession with him. Naturally, all came to bad ends, Viti in the notorious prison of Tor di Nona in Rome. After having been shot with an arquebus, Poma also wound up imprisoned.

The affair hindered Gessi's action for a long time into the future. The Council of Ten immediately put his house under watch.[147] The next day he reported to Rome that "many senators have a great suspicion that the matter came from Rome" and the populace followed their lead. He was walking very carefully indeed and suggested that if the perpetrators came into papal territory and were imprisoned, that would end the murmuring.[148] Of course, this pious wish may well have been meant for Venetian eyes. Two days later he repeated the news of the attack and emphasized his new caution, a point to which he returned.[149] In his next regular weekly letter he had bad news about the Franciscans' chapter, fearing that Brasavola would receive a "precept on pain of death to hold this chapter" ("precetto sotto pena della vita di far questo Capitolo"). The only remedy was to get him out of Venice so there would be no one else to summon it. Gessi suspected that Manfredi was tricking Brasavola, in concert with Niccolò Contarini. He feared the same thing would happen in the case of the Servites, whose general he had ordered to leave in order to avoid his own *precetto*.[150] In light of all the ill feeling generated by the attack on Sarpi, Gessi thought he could no longer rely on Brasavola to restrain Manfredi, who, it was rumored, would preach Advent along with Micanzio.[151] Gessi could not corroborate that rumor, but thought he should be able to stop Manfredi as an excommunicate. He noted again the Venetians' "firm resolve to defend these writers."[152] Manfredi boasted that he would preach at the Umiltà, but well-inclined senators assured Gessi that nothing had been decided.[153] At the end of November, his letter to Arrigoni of 7 September and a deposition by the Spanish ambassador's confessor went into Manfredi's dossier.[154]

Averoldi had not been forgotten in all the uproar over Sarpi. On 24 October, when he was imprisoned in Brescia, the Congregation told its inquisitor to prevent him from writing again to the pope, to "proceed further," and to send the *processo*.[155] The pope repeated the order on 8 November.[156] Two weeks later, the day after Benedetti got a *noli proseguire*, Gessi received an order to find the copies of Averoldi's book or books (manuscript or printed) left in the house of the chancellor of the podestà of Bergamo at his death.[157]

Gessi continued to urge caution, suggesting that the Inquisition's plan to burn Marsilio in effigy was certainly reasonable. However, it would make it appear that his powerful backers supported heretics. This might lead the majority to agree to the plan to make their own "patriarch." They might choose Sarpi, who was "revered more than is credible." Such an action would also make Sarpi think he and Micanzio were shortly to undergo trial, so it would be a good idea to defer action.[158]

That last statement makes it sound as if Gessi were not very fully informed of the Congregation's earlier actions and had at least forgotten that both had been excommunicated. In a second dispatch of the same date, Manfredi was back on Gessi's mind. He had for some time been in Friuli, but would shortly return, boasting that he would preach. The question came up in the Senate, where the doge "praised and excused" Manfredi. Gessi had said he was certainly excommunicated by the Holy Office, so the doge backed down. The Senate intended to consider allowing Manfredi to preach, although Gessi thought it would deny him the license.[159]

At the same time as Gessi's next weekly letter, the Venetian ambassador in Rome reported that on 1 December 1607 Antonio Faiano, a Theatine from Padua, had abjured at the house of the most senior Inquisitor, Cardinal Pinelli, for writing against the pope, an irregular ending to an irregular proceeding that left no trace in the decree register.[160] At least one other major event was reported as occuring in the Holy Office which also does not appear in the registers. The Venetian ambassador wrote on 8 December that he had heard that it was taking over the case against Sarpi and the other theologians, a report Gessi reflected back to Cardinal Borghese two weeks later.[161] At the end of the year it looked as if ground was being lost on the score of Sarpi, Averoldi, and Manfredi. It was thought certain in Rome that Sarpi would bring out a new book.[162] The news about Averoldi was mixed. On the one hand, the inquisitor of Bergamo was ordered to collect copies of his book printed there in the previous year and burn them, after a similar order had already gone to the inquisitor of Brescia. The theologian consultors were to censure his work, and a summary of his testimony was to be drawn up.[163] On the other, Gessi reported that, although no printed sheets of Averoldi's writings were found in any officials' hands, some half-folios called "Liber Apologeticus" had been found, about which they refused to do anything. There had also been a lot of people at Manfredi's brief sermon on St. Andrew's Day (22 December) at the Umiltà, but the nuncio had been unable to learn what he had said.[164]

Henning Arnisaeus's Books

At roughly the same time, the case of a book by the Lutheran Aristotelian Henning Arnisaeus (ca. 1575–1636) came up in Venice and quickly became a flashpoint in relations between the Inquisition, the nuncio, and the Venetian authorities. It also well illustrates how much sway the lay assistants could exercise. This was his popular textbook *Doctrina politica* (Frankfurt: published by Johann Thieme, printed by Johann Eichorn, 1606). In it Arnisaeus put forward an extreme defense of princely sovereignty, which he spent the rest of his career elaborating.[165] The future Inquisitor Desiderio Scaglia, then head of the provincial tribunal in Pavia, one of the prinicipal watching posts for publications from northern Europe, had brought the book to Rome's attention in a letter of 5 November.[166] After another reading on 22 November, the book was prohibited.[167] The inquisitor in Padua, Zaccaria Orcioli, O.F.M., also banned the book, apparently independently of the Congregation's action.[168] On 11 December the Ten ordered the Savvi del Collegio and the Senate to consider the issue.[169] The podestà of Padua had already intervened, refusing to allow the inquisitor to ban the book without the doge's agreement. When his letters were read in Congregation on 20 December, an order to Gessi resulted to "remove this impediment" and prevent the inquisitor from seeking the podestà's permission.[170]

A week later Ambassador Francesco Contarini wrote that Inquisitor Pinelli had come to see him to say, first, that the new inquisitor for Capodistria had been ordered to behave himself to the Venetian authorities there, and then that the inquisitor of Padua, complaining about the podestà's interference in the banning of Arnisaeus's book, had been ordered to act more "modestly." Contarini had been suitably grateful.[171] On the same day, Gessi's weekly dispatch concerned both the book and Manfredi. The nuncio had finally learned the content of his sermon: he had said that all priests equaled the pope. The matter would be brought up again nearer Lent. As for the book, the doge had been angry about the attempts to prohibit it, since he had licensed its publication, and in any case no inquisitor could act without the local authorities' agreement. Gessi had replied that formerly the Inquisition had banned books without any secular involvement, "and that it was not proper to impede the course of the Holy Office in any manner" ("et che non conveniva in modo alcuno impedire il corso del S.to Offitio"). The Collegio stood fast and Gessi assured Borghese that so would he.[172] Probably about the same time, Vignuzzio reported reviewing the book and discussing whether to publish the edict of prohibition. Two other Venetian inquisitors, of Aquileia and Vicenza, reported the secular authorities' refusal to allow them to act.[173] In Borghese's letter of the next day to Gessi, the Cardinal Nephew wrote that Paul had told Ambassador Contarini that *Doctrina politica* must be banned and the Inquisition left to do its job freely.[174] Gessi's reply to Borghese's previous letter sent the welcome news that the prohibition had been allowed. The Venetians had objected only to the inquisitors' mode of proceeding and had not meant to defend the book. [175] Five days later his letter, summarized as about negotiations over the "impedimentum" to the Inquisition's activity, was read in Congregation.[176] And in fact the "impedimentum" remained. Despite his own apparent reservations, Contarini had given Pinelli some "capitoli" about the Venetian Inquisition's assistants' involvement in the prohibition of books.[177] The flood of reports of lay resistance continued.[178] By the middle of February some Venetian authorities had bent enough to allow prohibition of Arnisaeus's book in a manner they had approved. The Congregation wanted to compare the forms proposed in Udine and Verona.[179] This is the last we hear of this book of Arnisaeus's, but the conclusion did not become a general principle. Within a week, another book had been ordered passed through the press with a dedication to the heretical English ambassador Sir Henry Wotton, after its approval by the inquisitor. The matter was to be reported to the new Cardinal Secretary Millini, but Gessi was forced to admit that he could do little.[180]

No sooner had the issue of Arnisaeus's book been resolved than Manfredi came up again. On 26 January 1608 Gessi reported to Borghese that an Observant Franciscan had attacked Fra Paolo Zen (the name should probably be Zevio; see below), "a close friend of Fra Fulgenzio" ("intrinseco di Frate Fulgentio") and wounded him in the head, much as had happened to Sarpi. For his part, Manfredi had put the papal arms used during the interdict over the door of the Umiltà, an action the doge had excused by saying perhaps they were left over. In the same letter, the nuncio also announced another jurisdictional conflict. The inquisitor of Verona, on orders from Rome, had made an informative process against one Zaccaria da Verona, a Servite, but the doge had annulled it because the assistants had not been involved. When Gessi asked for the revocation of that order, the doge replied that the Inquisition in Venice always included three nobles, and the rector and "dottori" on the Terraferma. Gessi had tried to object that many people had told him that outside the metropolis inquisitors acted without local lay officials, but the doge replied that that was nonsense. Agostino Nani, another of the leaders of the anti-papal party, claimed that Clement VIII had allowed the assistants to intervene in

Index cases. Gessi promised to find out the truth.[181] Two weeks later he proposed that an ecclesiastical person—but not the inquisitor—in Verona handle the case.[182] In the meantime another problem arose, imprisonment by the nuncio. Gessi claimed to have documents ("molti mandati") demonstrating that his predecessors had used the captain of the Holy Office without permission. After the interdict, the Venetians decided all arrests had to go through the Collegio instead of the Capi dei Dieci, which Gessi said was intolerable. In short, the Venetians wanted him to ask for permission every time he made an arrest, an equally burning issue in Naples.[183]

All these other matters rarely caused as much trouble as did dealing with the theologians who had written against the interdict. Many people in Venice asked Gessi what had happened to Cappello. He had replied sanctimoniously but disingenuously that he did not know, because it was an Inquisition case. Manfredi, not content with abusing papal arms, had brought out a print of himself with the motto "the sharpest [or fiercest] champion of evangelical truth" ("Evangelicae veritatis propugnator accerrimus"). At least he was not preaching, as far as Gessi knew (but he had been wrong before, an interesting reflection on his intelligence-gathering apparatus). The warden of Manfredi's house, Bernardo Giordano (1538–1621), another of the seven theologians, had been quieted by proceedings Gessi had begun against him (he did not say for what).[184] In his letter of 23 February, Gessi wrote that he had asked the bishop of Mantua to have the Observant Franciscan general stop Manfredi printing his portrait, that a replacement for Giordano had been appointed, and that he had Cappello's sentence, which he would use as necessary.[185] On 8 March Gessi confidently reported the certainty of Cappello's abjuration, which must mean that he had returned to Venice.[186] On the 28th, the Congregation noted it, "to the great consolation of the good."[187] Cardinal Borghese ordered Gessi not to disseminate the abjuration, since that was against the Holy Office's style.[188] The Inquisition had less success with Manfredi's portrait, which circulated in print by late March.[189]

In early March, Gessi reported that Ventura Vicentino d'Este, a pseudonym of the ultra-cautious Gasparo Lonigo under which he had written his consilium for Venice, wanted absolution; Gessi told him to go to Rome.[190] (Two months later Lonigo made the same request, still using his pseudonym.)[191] The rest of the news was less encouraging. The Venetians had banished another religious (via a *precetto*) for advising the surrender of some Venetian fortresses, and Giordano was putting up a fight against his removal as warden.[192] The issue of control of the press remained urgent, now coupled with the question whether an incoming inquisitor could publish a general edict, in what form, and with what permission. The appearance in Frankfurt of *Decisiones novissimae Rotae Romanae sive Sacri Palatii Romani Pars quarta . . . Prosperi Farinacii . . . ex officina Patheniana* [*sic*] *anno 1608* was reported to Millini by Vignuzzio; despite its title, it contained nothing but decrees of the Congregation for the Council.[193] On 8 May 1608 on another letter from the inquisitor about plans to reprint *Declarationes Concilii Tridentini usque ad annum 1601* (Frankfurt, 1601), of which Farinacci's volume was the newest part, the pope ordered an investigation to see what Cardinal Pamphili had done, probably as prefect of the Congregation for the Council, and the inquisitor to send copies.[194] When one arrived, it went to Pamphili.[195] The Index prohibited at least Farinacci's volume on 9 August, leading to another dispute in December, when the inquisitor of Bergamo reported that a printer refused to print the edict without the rector's approval.[196] The new inquisitor found himself in trouble over his general edict. Both sides showed a little more flexibility than they sometimes did, at least at first. Although Venetian "interference" with the inquisitor as usual quickly angered Paul V, he still ordered Millini to write him not to innovate.[197] On 26 April, Gessi thanked the Collegio for resolving the problem, only to come back on 8 May and complain that they had not corrected the situation. At the end of the month it once more looked as if they had, as it did again at the end of June. Gessi gave up, but the pope ordered the same edict published at Bergamo as at Crema, ignoring Gessi's diplomacy.[198]

Gessi continued to write that many people wanted to see Cappello's abjuration but he had kept it very close, not giving a copy even to the inquisitor.[199] No sooner had the Inquisition scored one success against the Venetian Franciscans with Cappello than it and Gessi turned back to Manfredi. The nuncio complained to the doge according to his letter of 29 March 1608, the same day on which Borghese wrote that Manfredi's "foolhardiness" ("temerità") passed all boundaries in printing his "pittura."[200] The following week he reported that the new warden had taken office at San Francesco della Vigna, but also perhaps that Manfredi had preached Lent (the text may be corrupt).[201]

Inquisition business almost entirely took up the nuncio's next bulletin of 19 April, beginning with a doubtful report that the Servite general had written Sarpi to surrender himself. The nuncio continued to cooperate with Vignuzzio in the campaign against prohibited books, but there was little they could do about those arriving in nobles' or ambassadors' baggage. Trying to raise the issue in the Collegio had served only to anger its members. Then followed a long briefing about the inquisitor of Brescia's edict, over which he was also having trouble. Gessi asssured Borghese that he would follow orders about Cappello's sentence. The long-running case of Marcantonio Brandolini, abbot of Nervesa, one of the two triggers of the interdict, had progressed to the defense stage; he had retained of counsel none other than Farinacci.[202] Gessi feared the defendant would try to intimidate witnesses, so he would attempt to depose them himself.[203]

Two more law books needed attention in April and May, both signalled by Vignuzzio. The first was a planned reprint of *Declarationes Concilii Tridentini usque ad annum 1601* (Frankfurt, 1601).[204] Paul ordered Cardinal Pamphili asked how he had handled the first printing, and the inquisitor to send copies.[205] When a copy arrived, it went to Pamphili.[206] At the same time, the inquisitor was ordered to make the corrections thus far agreed to Arismino Tepato (or Teppato), *Variarum Iuris Sententiarum [perutile compendium]* (Turin, 1598).[207] I have located about twenty copies of the first edition of 1597, making it a reasonably popular book, but only a couple of any subsequent editions, none by a Venetian publisher.[208]

On 10 May Gessi had important news. Although Manfredi considered it too dangerous to deal directly with the nuncio, one of his friends had seen Gessi twice. He had tried to convince Manfredi to go to Rome, and he had agreed on two conditions: there could be no trouble over his opposition to the interdict and he wanted absolution from excommunication. Gessi was prepared to grant the safe-conduct he also asked, but had refused to consider either of the other concessions until Manfredi went to Rome. Gessi had a low opinion of him. "This man is ambitious, vain, and not devout such that he cannot be won over with reasons that aim only at the soul and the spirit but one needs to bring in worldly reputation and honor and put up with and condone certain things after his humor."[209] Borghese agreed to a safe-conduct on 17 May, telling Gessi to assure Manfredi that he would be treated "with all paternal love" and not imprisoned, even if his abjuration had to take place in Rome.[210] A week later in the midst of a letter about books, Gessi recommended Paolo Zeni [Zevio], O.F.M.Obs. going to Rome, "sent by his friend" Manfredi. Gessi could see no possible harm in bringing Manfredi to Rome, and had licensed both him and his companion to go. He asked Borghese to protect Manfredi from his superiors and allow him to stay in the convent at the Araceli; Borghese agreed.[211] Perhaps it was only coincidence, but a week later Ambassador Contarini wrote that Cappello had been made provost of Constantinople in order to give him a (meaningless) title; in mid-July he received a stipend of 200 *scudi*.[212] At the same time, Gessi emphasized that

Manfredi wanted to be absolved in Venice, but he would settle for Rome, with absolution from the pope or his deputy but not from the Holy Office. Gessi had told him it was unusual and against the canons, because the official or institution that had issued the excommunication had to absolve from it. Manfredi expressed the wish to send Zevio ahead to talk to Borghese, and perhaps to the pope.[213] Gessi therefore forwarded Manfredi's credential letter for Zevio.[214] He arrived in Rome by 21 June.[215] By the same token, Gessi heaped scorn on a plan to convert Sarpi, using one of the men he had spying on Manfredi, while reporting trouble over the edict for Crema which was missing "the precepts it was usual to make about prohibited books" ("precetti soliti farsi per i libri prohibiti").[216]

It was only a matter of time before the Inquisition received a denunciation of a noble or nobles. That happened in the course of a rather scattershot deposition to the legate in Ravenna from Antonio Mazzalorsi, a Venetian deacon. He admitted to having given a "secret" reading to a dozen Venetian nobles three years earlier, during which he claimed the soul was mortal. He also denounced Girolamo Cicogna, Marcantonio Bracchi, and Sebastiano Rossi, priest, who had planned to go to Geneva and Margarita, "in a matter of sorcery."[217] Vignuzzio followed up the delation, and on 9 August sent information against Cicogna, Lucrezia Mazzalorsa (perhaps a relative of Antonio), and others, among them Cremonini.[218] And there matters sat until May the following year, as we shall see.

More Trouble over Control of the Press

Cardinal Borghese had handled much of Gessi's recent business, even when it concerned the Inquisition. But the coram of 12 June dealt with a number of Venetian matters, especially consideration of a report from Vignuzzio that Venice had deputed a lay official with "Agentis Inquisitorum status" to review books, which could not be published without his license. This was bad enough, but the man chosen, G. B. Leone, had written against the interdict. The pope ordered the inquisitor and nuncio written to prevent innovation.[219] That was the substance of a long oration Gessi delivered to the Collegio on 20 June about the powers of the Inquisition in Venice.[220] In his dispatch of the following day, Gessi already had a list of other problems to confront, beginning with another inquisitor, this time of Udine (properly of Concordia and Aquileia), faced with a *precetto* of banishment, whom Arrigoni had ordered him to protect.[221] The man was going to Rome to try to avoid it.[222] He ended with a report on the inquisitor of Bergamo. Gessi continued to gather information about Sarpi, including some from a bishop who was an old friend of his. The Servite was working on a chronology of the popes to show when they got jurisdiction in various cases. Gessi also had more evidence against Micanzio, but had little to report; both he and Sarpi lived a Christian life, except that Sarpi refused to confess in public. Sarpi continued to be active as a consultor and to frequent Flemish merchants. Whenever he went out he wore protective clothing, carried weapons, and was escorted by three well-armed friars. Marsilio, on the other hand, stayed near the monks of Santa Caterina with a woman named Cecilia (leaving the clear implication that he was not merely lodging with her). Although he was not in good odor, the Venetians continued to protect him.[223]

The next week Gessi had to report that Ambassador Contarini had learned of the plan to send Manfredi to Rome.[224] Niccolò Contarini, one of the leaders of the anti-papal party, had been ordered to dissuade him (as others had already done) and to offer money for his convent. Gessi had sent his secretary to Manfredi, who remained determined to go. His agent Zevio should not return to Venice, because he would face imprisonment. On Arrigoni's orders, Gessi had held a session of the Inquisition to deal with those who believed that the soul was mortal, and the assistants had made some trouble because Cremonini had been named, one "whom they hold in great esteem."[225] Among the cases Gessi had in mind was one that had come up in March, which had contributed to the inquisitor of Udine's difficulties. He had sent writings about the soul's mortality found in the hands of Gaspar a Monte Regali, a physician of Terrae Venzoni. Tomás de Lemos, one of the consultors at the time of Copernicus's suspension, was assigned to review them.[226] On 30 May Gaspar and two others, a painter and an Augustinian hermit, were sentenced to abjure *de vehementi*.[227] For some reason, on 1 October after Lemos's opinions were heard, he was again ordered to abjure *de vehementi* in the presence of the patriarch of Aquileia, the Inquisition's vicar, and consultors there, and put under house arrest.[228]

The Congregation's agenda on 5 July 1608 contained three books either from Venetian territory or to be published there. The first two were political works by German authors. The inquisitor of Vicenza had sent a report on the errors in Arnoldus Clapmarius [Arnold Klapmar or Klapmeier] (1574–1604), *De Arcanis Rerumpublicarum Libri Sex* (Bremen: Johann Wessel, 1605).[229] He was ordered to send a copy.[230] On the same day the inquisitor of Treviso was asked to send a similar work by the much less distinguished Gregor Richter, published in Görlitz by Hans Rambau in 1604, which apparently the inquisitor had given the incorrect title *Axiomatum politicorum, et Axiomatum oeconomicorum*. Meanwhile it was to be suspended.[231] This was a new edition of Richter's *Axiomata Historica, eaque Politica, Hoc est: Regulae de Eventibus Negociorum Politicorum*.[232] Apparently the inquisitor either did not really have a copy (which could explain the mistaken title) or could not find it. A copy the inquisitor of Verona reported as sold in Venice, together with a report on it from Gessi, led to an order for its examination on 20 December 1608, with what result is unknown.[233] The third book was an unnamed publication by Marcatonio Pellegrini (1530–1616), perhaps the most famous law professor at Padua, which Vignuzzio was allowed to licence.[234] This action was part of the carrot the papacy extended to Venice, since Pellegrini had been one of three legists from Padua (Gioacchino Scaino was one of the others) elected to write a consilium in defense of the republic.[235] The book in question was probably the first volume of a new edition of his *Consilia*, parts of which had been reprinted in Venice in 1606 and 1607 after the editio princeps of 1600.[236] And while thinking of books, as the Congregation obviously was, it also ordered the inquisitor of Brescia to keep Averoldi in prison until further orders.[237]

Another Plan to Assassinate Sarpi

Sarpi and Manfredi never wandered far from Gessi's and the Holy Office's minds. On 12 July the nuncio reported that Sarpi was busy as a consultor, probably about a Spanish fleet, against the rumor that he was concerned with the "false theologians" (including himself). He doubted that Sarpi would have the nerve to publish his papal chronology, since the Inquisition would never license it. Gessi's secretary had talked again to Manfredi, who still intended to go to Rome, promising revelations about not only Sarpi but also the English ambassador, Sir Henry Wotton.[238] Borghese was not entirely cooperative about Manfredi, whose writings he thought possibly worse than Sarpi's and who deserved to be declared at least a formal heretic.[239] Gessi still thought going ahead a good idea, if Paul decided to proceed against "falsi theologi" and Venice would still not abandon them. If they could win Manfredi with money, "if that appears honest to the pope" ("se cosi pare honesto a N.ro Sig.re"), they could also tempt Marsilio, since he was a foreigner and "venal and corruptible" ("venale e corruttibile"). All the others were Venetian subjects who would never be allowed to go to Rome. Some will still come, he thought, but it would have to be in secret. Demanding that the penitents proceed via breve would only lead "to greater contumacy but I do not believe it will have any effect whatsover" ("in maggior contumacia, ma non credo che facesse effetto alcuno"). The nuncio had only one other plan: "take cognizance of the case" ("conoscere la causa") before the Holy Office in Venice or another judge delegate, but he could not tell whether the Venetians would accept either without putting the matter to the Senate. Gessi foresaw "difficoltà grandissima," especially over the condemnation of their false propositions.[240] Besides, there was a more radical solution, even if it had failed once already. Somebody could assassinate Sarpi. One Jacques Giaffer from Avignon had offered himself to that end, both to his secretary and to Gessi himself, but Gessi had paid no attention, not because he found the idea repugnant, but because he thought the Frenchman "not up to it" ("non fosse atto a tal impresa"). And there was the pope's decree of the previous April that assassination was not to be used as an instrument of policy. Giaffer had persisted, coming back to the secretary to say that he was expecting a letter from Cardinal Orazio Spinola, the legate of Ferrara. Gessi had no such letter, but thought it best to inform Borghese, since Giaffer was so persistent. The nuncio underscored the difficulty the pope's edict posed, as well as the danger to himself, since Giaffer had been seen entering his residence.[241]

Manfredi Goes to Rome

Vignuzzio continued to spy on Manfredi, independently of Gessi. On 31 July the Congregation heard his report that Manfredi was teaching bad doctrine privately, but a week later decided not to pursue the matter.[242] On that very day Gessi issued a safe-conduct for the friar.[243] (The same day, the Congregation ordered the inquisitor of Brescia to proceed against Averoldi and two other Capuchins and report where he was imprisoned.)[244] Two days later Manfredi left for Rimini with his safe-conduct and 100 *scudi* from Gessi. That was the good news. Gasparo Lonigo constantly changed his mind about going to Rome, despite Gessi's assurances that everything would be kept secret to prevent trouble in Venice. Otherwise, Gessi had heard that both Micanzio and another of the seven theologians, Michelangelo Bonicelli, might preach.[245]

Once he reached Bologna, Manfredi wrote an autograph letter to the doge and Senate dated 15 August, saying they could not accuse him of ingratitude, since he was not a theologian and had written for the republic only out of the goodness of his heart, not duty.[246] In another letter, Manfredi claimed he had been better treated in two days in papal territory than he had been in two years in Venice.[247] The doge told Gessi that Venice did not care about Manfredi's flight.[248] Marsilio nevertheless had seen fit to defend him in the Collegio.[249] Perhaps stimulated by the occasion, the French ambassador had advised Sarpi to be reconciled either in Rome or in Venice, but Gessi had told him that the pope did not wish to absolve the friar.[250] The Capi dei dieci had sequestered four boxes of Manfredi's books and a letter in the hand of a friend who had been examined for not revealing his departure, along with some other friars from the Umiltà. Manfredi's letter to the doge from Bologna was read in the Pregadi. Gessi added that he would do what he could to prevent Micanzio and Bonicelli from preaching.[251]

Toward the end of August Manfredi was expected in Rome. Borghese assured Gessi that he would treat Manfredi well despite doubts about his intentions. Ambassador Contarini sent rumored details bearing Borghese out, including a provision like Cappello's and a secret abjuration; he reported the rumor that Manfredi would be executed but thought that Paul would for now keep his word.[252] Contarini added the interesting comment that since the Congregation was meeting unusually on Saturday, it would be easy to learn what was happening. At the same time as he awaited Manfredi, Borghese instructed Gessi to make life as difficult as possible for Marsilio.[253] Manfredi made slower progress than expected, no doubt reveling in his reception.[254] So did Lonigo. He had come to see Gessi again and insisted that he could not go to Rome because of his family. Instead, he would accept abjuration and absolution in Ferrara, as well as censures of his book, which should go to the inquisitor there. Lonigo demanded absolute secrecy and "to be expedited immediately" ("essere spedito incontinenti"), in order not to arouse suspicion. The nuncio also had an incriminating manuscript by Marsilio.[255]

On 31 August the much awaited Manfredi and his companion Zevio entered the convent at Araceli. They disliked their rooms, and went instead to the Reformed Franciscan house at San Pietro in Montorio, where they were given a suite which belonged to the titular cardinal, Maffeo Barberini, the future Urban VIII. The pope had received both well (this displeased many, including some cardinals), and Ambassador Contarini expected Zevio to return to Venice to try to bring other friars around.[256] During the next week Manfredi had a second papal audience, but his manner did not go over well.[257] According to Borghese, he had managed to see the pope five times by 13 September.[258] By 20

September Contarini was certain that the Holy Office would force Manfredi to abjure, especially over his printed reply to his citation.[259] On 30 September he celebrated Mass at Santa Maria Maggiore, Paul V's favorite basilica, as Pinelli reported in the Inquisition meeting the next day.[260]

More Troublesome Books

In the coram of 4 September Paul handled three Venetian cases when three letters from Gessi were read a total of six times, well indicating the Inquisitors' scholastic training in *divisio*. Then again, their skill in dialectic could have unfortunate effects, as when two decrees on exactly the same topic—Benedetti's book—were separated by three pages of other actions. The pope first heard all of Gessi's dispatches from the month of August, and then ordered Arrigoni to make a summary of Manfredi's misdeeds "to the recognizing of his and [ill.] actions" ("ad recognoscendam suas et [ill.] operationes.")[261] In the same meeting, Benedetti's case came up again.[262] Bellarmino reported on his "Iacula catholicae Christi ecclesiae," sent by Vignuzzio,who was ordered to inspect it carefully before publication and send a copy, in order to see what it said about papal authority. Benedetti wrote on 16 August from Bologna to Cardinal Pinelli, sending a copy of his *Iacula* (Venice: Evangelista Deuchino and Giovanni Battista Pulciano, 1608).[263] Finally, Lonigo was considered, as if for the first time, beginning from the publication of his book. The pope endorsed Lonigo's plan to have matters, including the censure of that book, handled in Ferrara.[264] Further action was taken in the next meeting, before Borghese wrote Gessi that Arrigoni would do whatever was necessary.[265]

Gessi made less progress with Marsilio, in part because he was associated closely with the most strongly anti-papal nobles. The nuncio thought his brother might make the best agent. He had more hope with Micanzio, who had shown some confidence in him before pulling back, perhaps on Sarpi's advice.[266] In another letter of the same day, Gessi reported that Abbot Brandolini had produced a huge defense document, including 140–160 witnesses, not a few of them his dependents. Gessi was trying to get rid of the irrelevant and to frame narrower questions than Brandolini wanted. At least he saw that recommendations and political maneuvering would not work, a sign that Gessi was current on at least some Inquisition jurisprudence. Vignuzzio reported a long talk with Archdeacon Ribetti, another encouraging sign.[267]

Lonigo continued to worry the nuncio, who wrote on 11 October that he was anxiously waiting for Arrigoni to send the censures on his book (an apparent violation of the deal by which those censures would be made in Ferrara).[268] The delay may be a sign of divided counsels in the Congregation, which noted Gessi's request on 23 October but took no action on it.[269] If there had been any such over Manfredi, they ended that same day, when Paul endorsed the Congregation's order to its commissary to collect "everything" against him.[270] In the second meeting yet another Venetian subject found himself in trouble. Vignuzzio reported that Fulgenzio Albanese (whose surname was Tomaselli or Tomacelli) refused "reconciliation" in Ferrara because he feared the Venetians would find out. The pope ordered him to the Holy Office in Rome instead.[271] There has been considerable confusion over Tomaselli († 1624), which his Inquisition trial resolves.[272] It makes it certain that he, and not Cappello, wrote the violent reply to Antonio Possevino, *Le mentite filoteane*, which then caused his trouble (see below).[273]

Gessi had his own ideas about how to handle Manfredi, a copy of whose letter to the doge he sent Borghese on 25 October. Given Manfredi's behavior, it would be well to get him out of public view in Rome and send him to some city of the papal states, where he could preach, be well treated, and be kept under surveillance by the legate or the governor. That would mean less chance of scandal, since even in Venice it was known that he was not behaving with proper humility.[274] Gessi was relieved to have the censures on Lonigo's book, and would send him to Ferrara without showing them to him. Gessi added news about Ribetti. Giordano, too, wanted reconciliation by means of a secret abjuration before Gessi. The nuncio passed the plan to Rome.[275] There was also progress about the inquisitor of Udine. Ambassador Contarini managed to keep him in Rome, where he was made a bishop. The ambassador then entered into negotiations with Pinelli about a replacement.[276] He was named before 13 November, when he was ordered to come to Rome "in order to give him instruction in how he ought to exercise his office" ("ut veniat ad Urbem pro danda ei instructione quomodo se gerere debeat in officio exercendo"), an unusually explicit statement of the Inquisition's on-the-job training program.[277] His appointment seems to be another illustration of how patronage affected the Inquisition's operations, since he was from Cagli (PS), the same place as Serafino Montini, who had just been hand picked by the Dominican general Galamini to become inquisitor of Faenza.[278] When the new man took office, Gessi advised him to be "circumspect" ("circonspetto") in the publication of his edict of entry; the nuncio did not want a repetition of the trouble in Bergamo caused by the publication of a similar edict.[279]

Manfredi's Case Approaches Resolution

Rome's principal interest at this moment was Manfredi, and his case moved fast. On 6 November the pope ordered him examined in the Holy Office.[280] A week later, in the first item of business, his *constituti* of 10 and 12 November were considered, before Paul ordered expedition.[281] On the 19th the theologian consultors were ordered to give their opinions.[282]

The speed with which Manfredi's case progressed is probably a function of the mercy the Inquisition was prepared to show to Venetian subjects who behaved themselves. Thus Arrigoni passed orders to Gessi allowing Tomaselli's abjuration to the nuncio, but he would not see the censures on his book beforehand.[283] On 17 November Tomaselli appeared before Gessi, "a notary and three witnesses and abjured *de vehementi* for the bad propositions of his book of *Mentite filotiane* [*sic*] after having been examined and I having condemned him by sentence in the manner and form that was written to me by the order of his holiness and the most illustrious Cardinal Arrigoni." Gessi had a little trouble controlling "his [Tomaselli's] humors and extravagances," before he could draw up the act in the authentic form he had sent Arrigoni.[284] After his abjuration, Tomaselli brought books against the interdict.[285] At the same time as his trial concluded successfully, Gessi tried to spur Rome to move on Lonigo, who had come from Este, terrified that he would be imprisoned in Ferrara, where he insisted he would not go.[286] Meanwhile, Ribetti was sticking to his good intention, while Giordano backslid.[287]

In early December Manfredi's trial hit an obstacle, when his testimony revealed that he possessed a copy of *Defensorii Guilelmi Ockami*.[288] Given the importance of this book to Manfredi's condemnation, it is worth identifying it more carefully than usual. Richard Gibbings, following Edward Brown, said Manfredi's copy had to have been a manuscript of a work published in Brown's edition of *Fasciculus Rerum expetendarum et fugiendarum*, the first part of which Brown thought summarized Ockham's *Opus nonaginta dierum*.[289] Brown had titled it "Defensorium venerabilis inceptoris magistri Guilelmi Okam et fratrum suorum ordinis minorum de paupertate Christi et fratrum minorum ac statu evangelico contra multifarios et varios errores Johannis pape XXII. ad universos Christi fideles in subsidium & defensionem oppressae veritatis authenticissimae & catholicae descriptum." He could not trace its source behind a manuscript a friend had given him but speculated that its original had been printed. Brown was right. His title turns out to have been that of two books published in 1512 and 1513 containing a collection of documents about the Franciscan order. Sigmund Riezler identified the second of these, *Singulare opus ordinis Seraphici Francisci . . . fratribus minoribus eorumque devotis perutile . . . (Quod Speculum Minorum seu Firmamentum trium ordinum intitulatur) tripartitum.*[290] Ten years later Karl Müller located its editio princeps in the form of *Firmamentum trium ordinum beatiss. patris nostri Francisci.*[291] Müller also found an edition of the work in an incunable of 1495, Ockham's *Opus XC dierum etc* [*sic*].[292] The opusculum interested Müller because it was also included in Niccolò Minorita's fourteenth-century "Chronica."[293] He demonstrated that the work could not be by Ockham, but probably did come from his circle in Munich.[294] Like Manfredi and his Inquisitors, those who had banned the book first in 1559 and then at least twice more in the sixteenth century thought it by the heresiarch Ockham.[295] It was certainly a dangerous item to have in one's possession.

Paul V may have found even more threatening Manfredi's seventh censured proposition, "omnipotent God does not order the impossible and in these which he orders a man to do that are naturally and civilly [politically] impossible, he pushes him only minimally, etc." ("Deus omnipotens impossibilium non praecipit et in his quae praecipit hominem ad ea, quae sibi naturaliter et civiliter impossibilia sunt, minime impellit etc."). He ordered another examination over this, as well as over prohibited books, before the case could go to expedition.[296] A week later, on the strength of that final examination, the pope ordered commissary Stefano Vicari, whom we have met as minister of the Holy Office in Naples, to make Manfredi abjure *de vehementi.*[297]

On 13 December 1608 Vicari sentenced Manfredi, signing the document in his name alone.[298] The narration (the list of charges) contained the following propositions that Manfredi held: that (1) the interdict was void; (2) confession, going to the "Dottrina christiana" (a new catechistic initiative that caused a lot of trouble in Venice) was for children;[299] (3) he had no superior except the doge and God; (4) he had praised England; (5) popes had asked permission from emperors to declare holidays, etc.; (6) the pope had no temporal authority; and (7) Christ was not of the house of David. Then followed the citation by *monitorium,* which led to Manfredi's excommunication when he failed to appear. The narration continued that Manfredi had appeared in Rome a few months earlier and undergone interrogation. He deposed that he had preached that the interdict was not to be observed, but not because the doge said so which he did not have the power to do, nor had he faulted the "Dottrina christiana" or the use of sacraments, but only their abuses. From his printed reply to his citation, the Congregation drew the proposition that

God "did not command a man [to do] a naturally or civilly impossible thing," the point which Paul had particularly wanted investigated. In an autograph private letter he had called the church a "wicked court" ("corte iniqua"). He had been denounced for having "Difensorio di Guglielmo Okam, contra Papa Giovanni 22.o" which he lent to a fellow friar to copy, saying he would resist Paul V as Ockham had John XXII. Interrogated about these points, Manfredi replied that the first did not apply to matters of faith, he had written the letter out of excessive zeal in order to criticize the clergy's scandalous lives, he admitted having Ockham's book, lending it and knowing it was prohibited, and that he wished to resist as Ockham had out of concern for souls. Manfredi further confessed that he had read other prohibited books, including Jean Calvin's *Institutio* (which he had thumbed through out of curiosity before being "disgusted" by it), [Bishop John Jewel's] *Ecclesiae Anglicanae Apologia*, and a Calvinist *Catechismo* he had gotten from Wotton's house in Venice, but not out of evil intention.[300] On this evidence, expedition was ordered in the coram of 11 December, together with a definitive sentence as "vehemently suspected," especially because of the prohibited books (made plural, even though only one was in evidence). Although forced to abjure *de vehementi*, Manfredi was treated as a *sponte comparens*, leading to a much lighter punishment. The act took place in Vicari's room, in the presence of Assessor Marcello Filonardi and Santo di Santi, a sub-notary of the Inquisition. Manfredi's recantation did not correspond very closely to his sentence, instead following the narration almost point for point, albeit in a somewhat different order, beginning with the prohibited books stressed in the sentence and adding one more charge at the end not in either sentence or narration.[301]

Pietro Antonio Ribetti Between Venice and Rome

The outcome of Manfredi's trial did not help Gessi. Its turn against him had led Manfredi to write a letter "of great complaint," and the nuncio feared that it would greatly damage his efforts to "bring the others to obedience" ("et temo, che mi noccino in estremo nel disporre gli altri a venire all'ubbidienza"). He was also losing ground with Lonigo, who had left, saying he could not return until after Christmas. By then Lonigo might also have known that his case had been expedited on 26 November.[302] Lonigo refused the deal when the pope ordered him to be forced to abjure.[303] At least Ribetti would shortly leave for Rome.[304] He must have done just that, since he had arrived by 20

December. As he left his papal audience, he met Manfredi but refused to speak to him. Ribetti was given 500 *scudi* and well treated, in hopes of winning others, significantly over resistance from the Inquisition. Manfredi was no longer receiving quite the same generous treatment. He had been stopped from saying Mass again in S.ta Maria Maggiore, as its archpriest Cardinal Pinelli told Ambassador Contarini, and the matter had gone to the Inquisition, which decided that he was still suspect.[305] It may be that Contarini's report refers to the period immediately before Manfredi's sentence, since it continued that he had been interrogated many times by Vicari with an eye to a sentence. In any case, Manfredi was unhappy, since this result differed greatly from what he had been promised in Venice. Cappello got similarly shabby treatment, including the nonpayment of his promised Spanish pension.[306] Nor, as it turned out, had Manfredi's case really concluded. A week after his sentence, Gessi wrote that, since the matter of his writings held so much importance, he would defer a report on them until the next courier, but did say, in contradiction to Contarini, that Manfredi had written to Venice that he had been greatly "consoled by the expedition of his case."[307]

Despite what Contarini considered the exceptionally good treatment given Ribetti, he, too, had to face the Inquisition. Vicari interrogated him, especially about the orders he had given others, but when he professed ignorance the pope stopped any further investigation, ordering the commissary "to move on the slow road, and very dexterously" in the hope of bringing others over.[308] Early in the next year, Paul ordered a lenient sentence for Ribetti.[309] Even Lonigo had come around. Gessi had persuaded him to abjure fully, as per Arrigoni's orders, and sent the authentic instrument.[310] And Manfredi had indeed written of his consolation, even if it appeared that he had sent other letters bemoaning his treatment.[311] Borghese congratulated Gessi on both successes in a letter of 3 January 1609.[312] Nevertheless, complaint seemed to be Manfredi's dominant mood, and it had infected Ribetti. By the end of the year, Manfredi was talking of returning to Venice with Zevio, and about the same time Contarini reported that he had seen the Venetian Cardinal Giovanni Delfin, complaining that promises had not been kept (including, horrors, being forced to eat in the refectory with the other friars).[313] Gessi had his writings, which Manfredi apparently wanted permission to publish. Gessi thought them Calvinist, just like those of "Fra Fulgenzio," meaning Micanzio, which Borghese reported were not as dangerous as feared, although Gessi should still try to depose someone about their "Calvinist conceits."[314] The nuncio still had spies on Marsilio, from whom he had precise details of where he was living, except that he moved every month. There might be a little hope with Bonicelli if the pope would agree to a secret abjuration. And a new suspect had come onto Gessi's radar, Giacomo Castelvetro, nephew of the more famous Ludovico. Gessi thought him nothing like as dangerous, but he might still try to distribute books.[315] On Manfredi's evidence, sent, according to him, with the pope's knowledge (this was sometimes true), Borghese ordered Gessi to keep working on Giordano and on Bonicelli.[316] Gessi also tried to complain to the secretary of the Collegio, but was told that the theologians were under Venetian protection, leaving him no reply but to shrug his shoulders and leave.[317] Meanwhile, the Dieci retaliated with *processi* of their own against Ribetti and other theologians who had gone to Rome.[318] The priest who had persuaded Ribetti to leave was imprisoned.[319]

The English Ambassador and New Evidence Against Sarpi

Back in November, Benedetti had complained from Bologna that Vignuzzio had banned his book "in defense of the apostolic see," but the Congregation only got around to considering the matter on 7 January 1609.[320] It had probably become more urgent since Gessi had written to the Inquisition that Wotton had a copy of *Antithesis qua, tam falsum esse, quod vicarius Dei sit antichristus, quam falsum est, quod Christus sit antichristus, demonstratur*, and had sent one to England.[321] Benedetti had also offered to revise and add "multa." He was ordered first to send the "compositio," apparently meaning the book.[322] In the same meeting the master of the sacred palace, the chief papal censor for Rome, reported Bernerio's and Bellarmino's censures.[323] On 24 January the Congregation heard from Benedetti, perhaps promising not to reprint without license.[324] Borghese could only write Gessi in frustration that he wished the book had not appeared.[325] At least Benedetti was not in the hands of the Inquisition as was Averoldi, whose petition for mercy it denied five days later.[326]

Gessi submitted an almost entirely pessimistic report at the end of January. He began that there was no hope for Sarpi's or Marsilio's "conversion," and they were collecting more "enemies [of Rome]" every day.[327] Since they were making so much trouble, the Inquisition should proceed against them, even though the nuncio knew they would be protected. His chancellor's coadjutor had been arrested, but not Gessi's familiar, probably the priest serving as his fiscal, whom the Venetians had tried to arrest earlier.[328] Manfredi's suggestions about how to deal with Venice Gessi thought mostly impracticable, especially trying to deny Sarpi the Mass.[329] The patriarch, according to Gessi, had always said he was not prepared to try to silence Micanzio, and there was nothing to be done about prohibited books.[330] He did finally attend an Inquisition session in early February.[331]

Fulgenzio Micanzio's Preaching

A few days later, the Congregation considered a fresh deposition by a Somascan Father against Sarpi and "Fra Fulgenzio" (probably Micanzio).[332] The Venetian Alvise Valeriano had appeared spontaneously before Archbishop Federico Borromeo in Milan. His testimony led to his abjuration *de vehementi*, and a particular congregation was set up to investigate. Manfredi was to be asked whether the French ambassador to Venice's physician was a heretic and had heretical books. Sarpi's and Micanzio's dealings with Wotton were to be looked into, as well as whether the English ambassador had images of Luther, Calvin, and Sarpi, and Micanzio's sermons were to be observed to see whether they were Calvinist.[333] Some time before 4 March, probably about 19 February, Arrigoni wrote Gessi to make process against Sarpi.[334] A month later the Congregation heard Gessi's letter confirming that Valeriano could have useful information.[335] The very next day that promising report was overtaken by another letter from Gessi, saying it was hard to investigate Valeriano, not least because he had fled prison, to which he was ordered returned.[336] Valeriano was eventually brought to Rome, where the Congregation put him under its protection.[337]

Despite pressure from Borghese to use Manfredi, Gessi once more gave his opinion that the remedies he proposed for the Observant Franciscan province including Venice would not solve the problem.[338] What was needed was better leaders and breaking the power of Giordano and Bonicelli. Sarpi contemned prohibitions of books, leaving Gessi again helpless. Manfredi himself, along with Ribetti, sounded more disgruntled all the time.[339] There was a little movement by the Venetian authorities, along with a little pettiness by Gessi. Although it was scandalous that they gave preachers "ammonitioni," as Borghese wrote Gessi, Gessi wrote back that he had insulted Micanzio by refusing the customary Lent blessing in the Holy Office.[340] The Venetians, for their part, had forbidden Lent preachers to talk about the interdict. The inquisitor in Venice reported the same good news.[341] Micanzio, however, drew big crowds, leading Gessi to appear in the Collegio twice to complain.[342] When that produced the usual non-result, Gessi set spies on Micanzio and sent Borghese résumés of his sermons, including attacks on papal *precetti*, on miracles, and on penance, and the claim that Venice had preserved true Christianity.[343] The Congregation heard his letter on 19 March.[344] Gessi reported his lack of success in trying to prevent Micanzio's sermons, and Borghese said that the pope would talk to Contarini, and that Arrigoni would write in more detail.[345] On 26 March the inquisitor of Venice was ordered to send particular points against Micanzio.[346] A week later, he was to keep Micanzio under surveillance, and Borghese sent the pope's praise of Gessi's efforts.[347]

Just when the Inquisition began to move against Sarpi for the second time came news of another assassination attempt, by two members of his own order.[348] This was actually the third attempt on Sarpi's life, the second following in fairly quick succession on the first.[349]

The nuncio now had his hands full. In addition to Micanzio's preaching and the two Servite assassins, he had the case of the bishop of Capodistria to worry about. All three came up in his letter of 4 April.[350] He had heard that one of the two friars had been secretly executed. At least, Micanzio was preaching a little more "circumspectly." Finally, the nuncio had Arrigoni's orders about the bishop, Girolamo Contarini, and had "secretly and extrajudicially" investigated, finding the accusations partially true.[351] Nevertheless, it would be hard to make process. Despite that, Paul V again praised Gessi's report.[352] Vignuzzio, too, kept Micanzio under observation and was ordered on 9 April to examine witnesses about his sermons.[353] Naturally, ambassador Contarini defended the Servite's preaching.[354] Gessi, equally naturally, stressed that the preacher tried to reduce papal authority as much as possible, although he had praised confession the previous Thursday. Nor had he preached much in the previous week.[355] Borghese ordered Gessi to continue to collect evidence about Micanzio and have witnesses examined in papal territory. The pope also ordered him to continue to try to help the two Servite assassins, evidently hoping the news false that one had died.[356] A week later, Rome showed palpable relief that Micanzio had finished preaching.[357] That did not lessen the Inquisition's interest. On 23 April the Congregation considered both Vignuzzio's report on two of Micanzio's sermons and probably Gessi's letter of 11 April.[358] At nearly every meeting thereafter Gessi reported another move, for instance, 7 and 14 May, when the depositions he had sent arrived, along with a report from legate Caetani.[359]

Two Assassins in Venetian Hands

The case of the two Servites had reached a more disquieting stage. Gessi sent a long update, the result of his efforts "by every good means to try secretly to learn what had happened." It turned out his earlier report that one had been executed was wrong. The rest of his news caused much more worry. One of the two friars, Gianfrancesco da Perugia, who was studying in Padua, had been written by another Perugian friar from Rome, with the knowledge of "great personages and cardinals" who had been charged to manage the assassination. He had recruited Antonio da Viterbo, a young friar and Sarpi's "most loved" familiar. The two had plotted in Antonio's room in Venice, Gianfrancesco hiding in it for some days awaiting the proper moment. He had finally given up and left, writing Antonio to keep his courage up, putting the letters into the hands of a Jew. Antonio replied that he could not actually attack Sarpi, but if Gianfrancesco could get poison, he would use it. Gianfrancesco procured some from Rome.[360] The two continued to communicate in a secret language, until one day the usual Jew gave a letter for Antonio to another Jew, who left it with the *socio* of San Giacomo instead of delivering it to Antonio's room. The *socio* had become suspicious while questioning the bearer and came to think that the letter had a false address. Its content increased his reservations, and he told Sarpi, who summoned Fra Antonio. After protesting his innocence, he eventually confessed everything. Sarpi had Antonio write Gianfrancesco to say that he would take an impression of the key to Sarpi's room and would enter one night and kill him. For that he needed wax from Gianfrancesco. Gianfrancesco thus came to Venice with the proper material wrapped up in a piece of paper, which accidentally contained three or four letters about the plot, one of them discussing the poison. The Dieci set the trap, and Gianfrancesco fell into it. He had been examined at length and condemned to die unless he revealed his accomplices. Gianfrancesco therefore revealed all the arrangements with Rome and Antonio, who was immediately imprisoned but had not yet been examined. Gessi thought it likely that Sarpi's favor would protect him. The nuncio added anticlimactically that Sarpi had written a book about papal authority.[361]

As if all this were not enough, Marcantonio De Dominis appeared on the scene. First, Gessi was ordered to prevent his plan for a Venetian synod.[362] Then, his Serbo-Croatian missal led Gessi to comment that he now saw the same thing he had earlier as secretary of the Congregation for the Council, "he truly acts with greater audacity and less reverence towards the apostolic see than one ought" ("egli veramente tratta con maggiore audacia, e manco riverenza verso la Sede Ap.ca di quello che dovria"). Gessi therefore advised ignoring De Dominis's wish to have the book printed. The nuncio was still finding it difficult to investigate Micanzio's sermons. An Augustinian had given him some notes, but Gessi had not wanted formally to examine the man. He did send two interrogations taken in Ferrara. As for the Servite assassins, Gessi had learned that Antonio da Viterbo would have been executed, but Sarpi had gotten the sentence commuted to ten years in prison or for life. The doge had pushed for publication of the *processo*, but the majority (Gessi did not say of what) had opposed him, news Gessi could not confirm. Once again, the affair had made the nuncio's job harder. All the Venetian nobles avoided him in order not to fall under suspicion.[363]

Among the nobles who would have been especially happy to avoid Gessi was Girolamo Cicogna, whose case, begun a year earlier, now began to move ahead again. On 7 May the pope ordered the nuncio to examine witnesses.[364] Borghese wrote Gessi on the following Saturday, almost as if he were secretary of the Inquisition, about a number of its matters, most of which are too opaque to make sense, except for an order diligently to pursue Cicogna, "imprisoned (*confinato*) in Ossero [modern Osor, Croatia]."[365]

Books were never far from Gessi's mind. He complained to Borghese about "perverse theologians" who were making trouble by demanding censures of books from the Holy Office and then reporting them to the Venetian authorities. *Dottrina christiana* also encountered difficulties, the Venetians wanting changes in the sections Bellarmino had written about papal obedience. They had asked Vignuzzio to stop publication, but he had said he could not prevent the reprinting of licensed books.[366] Gessi tried to get help from the patriarchal vicar, the office Ribetti had held. At the same time, Borghese told him that the situation represented a dangerous novelty and that he should continued to cooperate with Vignuzzio, who should report to the nuncio as to the pope. He was also to press on examining witnesses in Cicogna's case.[367]

June and July 1609 were rather slow, for a change. Aside from an order to Gessi to keep after Cicogna, the high point came in the sentencing of Vincenzo Valentini, *philosophiae doctor*, on 6 June.[368] His is a mysterious case, not helped by the state of the decree register for 1608. Gessi had apparently begun proceedings against him in the previous October, including collecting evidence in Ferrara; the matter somehow overlapped with Cremonini's trial.[369] By January 1609 he was imprisoned by the Inquisition, when he was to be brought to Venice to tell everything he knew about the plots against Sarpi and Marsilio.[370] The Venetians agreed to his imprisonment in early June; he stayed in the Inquisition's hands until he was released, at the intercession of the king of Poland, in 1610.[371] In July, Gessi had to write that the Capuchins in Brescia who had written against the interdict complained of persecution from their brethren who supported it, and asked "a more effective order . . . one of my precepts or edicts" ("un ordine più gagliardo . . . un mio Precetto, o Editto").[372] Sarpi wrote constantly to northern European heretics and met them in "bottega Zecchinelli," as did Micanzio. Gessi hoped that Micanzio would continue to refrain from preaching. The nuncio thought his motive was to avoid wrecking the reputation he had established during Lent. There were more difficulties over *Dottrina christiana*, but before Gessi had a chance to respond, two more serious problems arose.[373]

A Prison Break and a King's Book

The first was Guglielmo [*sic*; his name was Alvise] Maffei's escape from the Inquisition's prison in Padua, about which he complained on 31 July. At the same time, Gessi initially broached the second, his orders to deal with King James I's book in the Inquisition.[374] The Venetians were more prepared to cooperate on the second point, the new ambassador in Rome, Giovanni Mocenigo, telling the pope that Venice would act as if the book were prohibited, but the pope demanded its complete banning.[375] Borghese passed the order to Gessi to proceed against the book in the Inquisition, but the assistants, although agreeing that the book was bad, said they could not act unless Gessi raised the matter in the Collegio. He therefore asked Arrigoni to write the doge for help. The escaped prisoner Maffei had fled to Venice, where he had been imprisoned until the jurisdictional problem could be sorted out. The inquisitor and his vicar in Padua wanted to pursue a case against those who had helped Maffei, but the secular authorities refused their assistance. Gessi had asked in the Collegio, but got no useful response.[376] One can almost feel Gessi's surprise when both matters seemed to be cleared up by the time of his next dispatch.[377]

In fact, they were not. The king's book took another month, when the Venetians agreed to let the Inquisition ban it.[378] The prison break proved much more difficult. The problem was that Maffei's helpers were "Greeks," and Gessi could not find any local precedents for prosecuting them. He could only suggest that Paul speak to Mocenigo.[379] It may be, too, that Gessi was not entirely au courant. The inquisitor of Padua, Orcioli, had written Rome on 21 August that the podestà had sent an armed familiar to the notary of the Holy Office's house "with a precept that he hand over the formed process about the prison-break and flight of Alvise Maffei, otherwise the notary would be imprisoned" ("cum praecepto ut consignare processum formatum super effractura carcerum et fuga Alvisii Maffei, alioquin notarium ducerit ad carceros"). Paul ordered the bishop of Padua, Marco Corner, then in Rome, to say where its Inquisition kept its records and Gessi written "not [*sic*] to be given an example that the Inquisition should proceed against prison-breakers" ("non [*sic*] dari exemplum, quod Inquisitione processerit contra effractores carcerum"), although in fact he was supposed to make forceful representations about the Inquisition's rigor against such men.[380] Even before he got these orders, Gessi demanded that the Inquisition take cognizance of the case concerning Maffei's helpers.[381] Probably with his new instructions in hand, he reappeared before the Dieci the next week to the same effect.[382] It causes no surprise that the pope ordered Orcioli to keep the *processi* in question, but it does that nothing seems ever to have been said about the podestà's use of force majeur.[383] Despite finding two precedents, at the end of September Gessi was still pessimistic about his "Greek" prison-breakers.[384]

Meantime another mysterious case had taken a promising turn. Gessi took satisfaction in telling Borghese, that after long efforts, he had induced the man who had published against the interdict under the name of Giovanni Muti to go to Rome to abjure. The process, which was well advanced by January 1609, had been protracted by the man's imprisonment and fear of coming to Venice.[385] Gessi and his confessor both recommended him to Arrigoni and left the censure of his book to the pope.[386] Gessi's recommendation gave the man's name as alias "Giovanni Muti de' Benti della Terra di Pare nel Bergamasco."[387] Paul obliged by decreeing on 24 September that the man, now called Giovanni Pietro Morana, who had published under the name of Muti, be treated as a *sponte comparens* and abjure *de vehementi*.[388] I have been unable to track him further.

On 10 November, Congregation ordered the case of a man who had certainly written against the interdict—Averoldi—to proceed on the grounds that his writings were heretical and that he had refused to abjure.[389] The Venetians were about as happy with Bellarmino's reply to James I, *Apologia Roberti S.R.E. cardinalis Bellarmini, pro responsione sua ad librum Iacobi magnae Britanniae regis, cuius titulus est, Triplici nodo triplex cuneus*.[390] Gessi received a copy by 21 November, probably about a week after publication, and the Venetians banned it by 12 December.[391] Or at least so Gessi initially reported.

A week later he had to admit that he was not sure what was happening. He had several times praised the book in the Inquisition as if it needed defense, and the assistants had always reacted blankly. Booksellers told him there was no ban, so either there was not or the booksellers had a *precetto* not to talk about it.[392] This impressive piece of self-defense was undercut by the news the next week that a bookseller had sold two copies.[393] Mocenigo insisted it was not banned and had himself sent copies to Venice.[394] Gessi had to admit on 9 January 1610 that he had made a mistake.[395]

Manfredi's Case Takes Two Odd Turns: A Pardon Followed by His Execution

This controversy overshadowed a legally more significant event, a pardon for Manfredi in the form of a breve issued on 17 November. The text is highly interesting. It has the usual note at the end, "it can be expedited if it pleases his holiness" ("Si S.mo placuit potest expediri"), and is signed by both Cardinals Aldobrandini (as cardinal chamberlain) and Arrigoni (as datary, both also Inquisitors) on 17 October, but *not* by the pope, as are other documents in the same volume, e.g., fos. 462v or 530v, and farther down by Scipione Cobelluzzi (as secretary of breves). It is docketed on fo. 488v "Pro Fulgentio Veneto ord[ini]s minorum de observan[ti]a S[ancti] Franc[is]ci," and then "Declaration that he should not incur disability [from holding ecclesiastical office] nor the stain of infamy on account of the sentence with restitution handed down against him by the Congregation of the Universal Inquisition" ("Declaratio quod non in curreit inhabilitatem, nec infamiae maculam ob sententiam contra eum per congregationem S. Universalis Inquis[ition]is latam cum restititutione"), then "His most holiness ordered it seen by your most illustrious and reverend lordship ("S[anctissi]mus mandavit videri ab Ill[ustrissi]ma et R[everendissi]ma D[ominatione] V[estra]"), probably meaning Aldobrandini or Arrigoni, which may explain why Paul did not sign it. A draft of part of the text on fo. 479r is headed "the lord assessor of the Holy Office gave this to me 10 [or 11] October 1609" ("D. Assessoris S.ti Off.ci tradita mihi 10/11 octobris 1609").[396] Whether this means the document came out of the Holy Office, as a similar document for De Dominis did (see the next chapter), or whether Assessor Filonardi was acting as the pope's messenger is unclear. The text is straightforward.[397]

In Manfredi's eyes, the pardon was too little, too late. At the end of January 1609 Gessi discovered that Manfredi had written to Venice, apparently to the powerful Niccolò Contarini, asking to be taken back. Contarini had not wished to raise the matter in public, and had tried to give Manfredi's letter to the Inquisitori di Stato, who had refused it as coming from a rebel who would expect a reward if he returned, when he would have to be allowed to preach. Gessi's source could not absolutely confirm the story, but Gessi thought it worth keeping an eye on Manfredi.[398] The Roman authorities did more than that. Probably on 5 February, twenty *sbirri* arrested him at the Araceli.[399] Mocenigo put the cause down to speaking too freely of the pope and others. Borghese did not give a reason, but blamed the decision to arrest the friar on the pope. Implicitly the motive was his wish to return to Venice. When he was seized, he was found to have a portrait of a woman "dressed alla venetiana," which served as evidence of his intention, along with items for a woman's use and letters manifesting his evil intent.[400] Gessi was to emphasize Manfredi's ingratitude and the pope's generosity, who continued his twenty-five *scudi* per month.[401] A week after the arrest, Mocenigo had not been able to learn the reason for it, except his scandalous behavior and the portrait.[402] Mocenigo knew that Manfredi had been imprisoned in Tor di Nona with one of the original conspirators against Sarpi, the priest Michele Viti. According to the "Relazione," Viti had delated Manfredi to Cardinal Pamphili, the vicar of Rome, as preparing to flee, not to Venice but to England, where he would write against the Jesuits, and in particular Bellarmino.[403] It also alleged that Gessi had interecepted Manfredi's letter to the Senate.[404] After a search turned up autograph writings and letters indicating that Manfredi did indeed plan to go to England, he was put into "the most secret" Inquisition prison.[405] Gessi assured Borghese that Manfredi was in such ill odor in Venice that his imprisonment had caused no trouble.[406] In the same letter Gessi reported that Fra Antonio, who had tried to poison Sarpi and had wound up exiled, had returned to Venice and been imprisoned.[407]

Beginning in late February, Manfredi underwent a total of nine interrogations. On 3 March the Congregation discussed his first examinations on 23 and 25 February, along with the heretical propositions in his works. The next day, Paul V having heard "the more principal points" ("in punctis magis principalibus"), he was ordered examined again about an English pilgrim he had seen at San Pietro in Montorio and about a friar who wanted to go to England with him, as well as to be visited frequently in prison to prevent his flight.[408] A week later the pope ordered another interrogation, after reading that of (probably) 28 February.[409] The same thing happened the next week.[410] The Congregation alone considered his next three depositions, including one in an unusual Saturday meeting.[411] Paul V intervened on 1 April, ordering Manfredi's defense and a *summarium* drawn up for the case's expedition.[412] Four days later, at the Easter prison visitation, Manfredi "asked indulgence," because his sin was only attempted, not completed, and was hidden.[413]

As usual, there was a delay before Manfredi's case went ahead, as it did toward the end of May, at the same time as Averoldi's once again became active. On 18 May the second friar's propositions were referred to the consultors, and two days later Paul V ordered Manfredi's case considered at the next congregation.[414] A week after that, Averoldi's sentence was proposed, abjuration *de vehementi* and continued imprisonment.[415] In the same session, after Manfredi's *processo* was read along with the consultors' opinions, the pope ordered him tortured about his accomplices ("but without prejudice to those who had confessed and given evidence" ["tamen sine praeiudicio confessatorum et probatorum"]), assigned a defense, and then relaxed to the secular arm, his sentence to be read in S. Pietro.[416] Although there is some reason to think that this whole passage is a formula which does not necessarily indicate that torture was actually used, according to the "Relazione" it was.[417] That text also claimed that he said nothing more, greatly annoying his "tormentatori." A month later the minute of his sentence was read again, and again ordered to be pronounced in S. Pietro before the consultors, officials, "and some members of religious orders" ("ac convocavit aliquot religiosos singulorum ordinum").[418]

On 1 July 1610 the sentence—which we are lucky to have—was handed down at the Quirinal Palace.[419] It was given in the names of and signed by all ten Inquisitors.[420] The narration began with a brief summary of his abjuration in 1608. In 1610 he had originally been imprisoned by the vicar of Rome in Tor di Nona. When a search turned up "many prohibited books and pernicious writings," Manfredi was moved to the Inquisition's prison. Examined, Manfredi had acknowledged the books and writings. They contained these errors: (1) the pope was not head of the church; (2) it was blasphemy to say the apostles were subject to Peter; (3) the pope and his successors did not have power over all churches; (4) he "did not have authority to institute bishops;" (5) it was not necessary to salvation that all Christians be subject to the pope (Boniface VIII's notorious claim in *Unam sanctam*); (6) the church militant had no visible head; (7) the Roman church was not holy except in vows ("se non di voti"), nor was it catholic, apostolic, or Christian, but heretical, and spread heresies; (8) it was not head of all others; (9) there were no canonically chosen bishops; (10) it bound in things Christ left free (introducing the hotly contested topic of adiaphora); (11) the Council of Trent was neither universal nor legitimate; (12) the "papisti" could not prove Peter's supremacy from the gospel; (13) all popes and papists were heretics; 14) the pope erred in defining the faith; and so on.

In his interrogations, Manfredi had claimed that he did not know some of his books were prohibited. Having talked to an English pilgrim in his cell, Manfredi had planned to go to England. Interrogated about his writings, he said he intended them to confute heretics, but admitted that he had held some of their ideas, which were once more listed. They began with propositions like those above about papal primacy before adding others, including an attack on celibacy, and that temporal property had been held in common in the time of the apostles (a Spiritual Franciscan theme declared heretical by John XXII). The recital ended with Manfredi's contention that he had been wrongly judged in his first trial. Manfredi had renounced a defense and admitted that he meant to write against the pope, but still did not consider his ideas heretical, adding that he wanted to go to Germany or England, and that he had written but not sent a letter to James I. When interrogated, Manfredi had claimed he meant to live in England under Roman obedience, and when told these two were contradictory, Manfredi had agreed. Three minutes of letters to heretics had been found, along with a letter from an English heretic, all full of "evil will" ("mala volontà"). Manfredi acknowledged the letters but said that he had never meant to write against Catholics.[421] Again having refused a defense, he was ordered tortured about his accomplices. He was sentenced as relapsed, and ordered degraded from his orders and relaxed to the governor of Rome.

The following Sunday, 4 July, the sentence was read according to the authentic act attached to it, witnessed by two canons of San Pietro and Giovanni Antonio Tommasi, then a substitute notary of the Inquisition.[422] The "Relazione" put the audience at 20,000 and added that since it appeared that Manfredi wanted to speak, his tongue was secured, perhaps in the same way Bruno's had been; whether this was true or not, the "Relazione" required the impediment to prove that Manfredi had not abjured.[423] The text gives a highly circumstantial account of Manfredi's execution the following day.[424] After the reading of the sentence, Manfredi was taken as usual to the church of S. Salvatore in Lauro, where he was degraded, and then put into the governor of Rome's prison and not allowed to speak to anyone. Dominicans came to confess him. Early the following morning he was taken to Campo de' Fiori, and "strangled and half-alive he was thrown into the flames ("appiccato e semivivo [semivivio TC, R.3.42] buttato alle fiamme").[425] It was not true that he was allowed to speak.[426] He had said a couple of indistinct words when the executioner strangled him. There was thus no authentic proof that he had abjured, the anonymous author insisted again.[427] The Trinity College, Cambridge, version of the "Relazione" adds that Viti said he had a promise that if Manfredi became a secular priest, he (Viti) would get a fat benefice in the Ferrarese.[428] Viti was the only one of the "conspirators" to escape divine retribution. Pamphili died a month later, shouting that he was being strangled and burned from inside.[429] Another of the witnesses against Manfredi also died shortly thereafter.[430] On 21 July the Congregation ordered Orcioli, then in Rome, to be read the sentence but not given a copy of it.[431] When word came from Venice that "disputations were being held there every day between 'Fulgentians' on the one side and 'papists' or Jesuits on the other, the first putting forward that Fra Fulgenzio Manfredi was not a heretic but had been betrayed and some friars of the order of minor obervants assert that he was a martyr" ("disputationes ibi quotidie haberi inter Fulgentianos ex una et Papistas, seu Jesuitas partibus ex altra, pretentes ostendere Fratrem Fulgentium Manfredum non fuisse hareticum, sed proditum, ac quosdam fratres ordinis minorum observantium asserere illum fuisse martirem"), the pope ordered Gessi to publish his sentence.[432] There was a scramble for Manfredi's books that began even before his trial concluded, with the Observant provincial (or minister) asking for those at San Pietro in Montorio. On a second occasion, shortly after his execution, the Inquisition's commissary was told to return those thought safe.[433] The claims were still in dispute in September, when Gessi and Vignuzzio were to see whether those left in Venice included any prohibited volumes.[434] At the end of the month, on news from the nuncio in Cologne that a "libellum" had appeared defending Manfredi as "a martyr, because he denied the pope's authority," Paul ordered an investigation into whether he had recanted before he died.[435]

The Interdict Begins to Blow Over

The cases of other anti-interdict authors received action of one kind or another about the time of Manfredi's execution, as things calmed down considerably thereafter. Cappello was the luckiest. On 8 July the pope gave him a license to print his *Adversus praetensum primatum ecclesiasticum regis Angliae liber in quo Iacobi Regis, & eius eleemosynarij confutantur scripta de captioso iuramento proposito Anglis catholicis* (Bologna: Bartolomeo Cocchi).[436] This was a reply to royal almoner Lancelot Andrewes's *Tortura torti*, itself a reply to Bellarmino's attack on James's *Triplici nodo, triplex cuneus. Sive Apologia pro iuramento fidelitatis* (London: Robert Barker, 1607) in his pseudonymous *Responsio Matthaei Torti presbyteri, et theologi papiensis, ad librum inscriptum, triplici nodo triplex cuneus* (Cologne: Bernard Walter, 1608). Averoldi was also luckier than Manfredi, by a little. On 1 July he was ordered imprisoned at will, but on 9 September, after letters from the inquisitors of Venice and Brescia and the nuncio, this became perpetual imprisonment, if he sought abjuration.[437] At the end of September Gessi was asked whether his case could be expedited without difficulty, and that is the last we hear for quite some time.[438] Averoldi refused to abjure as had been agreed, unless the Inquisition passed judgment on his "de Mahometto et Antichristo."[439] On 16 June 1611 the inquisitor of Brescia reported that the Venetian rectors had visited Averoldi in prison and would report to the doge.[440] And the indefatigable Benedetti wrote again about his *Antithesis*, offering to bring it to Rome for revision. He wrote again a year later, asking for the return of his "Apologia pro anima Traiani," when it and any other writings of interest to the Holy Office were to be sought from Cardinal Bernerio's heirs.[441]

The interdict continued to leave fallout, but this gradually became less frequent. One of the handful of cases concerned Lucio Turchatto from Vicenza, denounced from Padua on 11 May 1612.[442] On 27 June witnesses were ordered examined there.[443] After a sheaf of letters against him from the inquisitors of Vicenza, Modena, and Reggio, on 21 August Turchatto was ordered imprisoned.[444] Ambassador Mocenigo reported the arrest of "one Father Master Lucio," a Franciscan tertiary, on charges of preaching during the interdict.[445] Two weeks later he was trying to help by talking to members of the Inquisition. The charge had developed into preaching that the pope was bishop of St. John Lateran, that is, not pope, and refusing to post the interdict in Vicenza.[446] On 22 November, by which time Turchatto had been imprisoned in Rome, after the consultors were heard, another witness was ordered examined in Vicenza.[447] Turchatto last appears in the prison visitation of 22 December 1612.[448] The Inquisition never specified the charges against him.

Among the handful of other significant Inquisition business in 1612 was Inquisitor Felice Centini's report on Benedetti's "Antilogia . . . contra Guilelmum Vichenum," leading to the denial of a license for it, the issuing of a precept to a Servite who taught mathematics in Pavia not under any circumstances to print additions to Cesare Baronio's martyrology, and at the very end of the year the appearance of two new books by Arnisaeus, reported by

Vignuzzio as in the hands of Bortolo Rodella, bookseller.[449] They were called *De subjectione et exemptione clericorum, item de potestate temporali Pontificis in Principes*, and *De auctoritate Principum in populum semper inviolabili etc.*[450] The subtitle of the second indicates the source of the Inquisition's concern, in addition to its earlier—and therefore permanent—interest in Arnisaeus: *Opposita Scriptis eorum, qui in his controversiis contra Sereniss. Regem M. Britanniae, & Florentiss. Rempubl. Venetorum disputarunt, potissimum vero libris Robert. Bellarmini.* The same information was reported to the pope on 3 January 1613, before on 22 February the inquisitor was ordered to get a copy.[451]

Cherubino da Udine

Although Micanzio continued to concern the Inquisitors, and Gessi regularly if impotently reported on Sarpi, neither received anything like the amount of attention he once had.[452] Indeed, in 1613 the Inquisition's activity in Venice of interest to Rome came down almost to a single book by the Capuchin Cherubino da Udine, which was adjudged to contain Sarpi's ideas. I have first found the case on 7 February 1613, when it was deferred.[453] Three weeks later it was reported that the book had been printed. Gessi was ordered to prevent its circulation, and the Capuchin general who had approved it was to be roundly upbraided.[454] A month later Vignuzzio reported that the book had not been circulated and that Gessi was negotiating with the printer to get copies. He did this before 17 April, when he sought reimbursment.[455] He had gathered up a total of 744 exemplars. These had come from the printer Rampazetto, and must be nearly the whole print run, since no trace of it remains.[456] Cherubino was thought to have a few others.[457] The book had been burnt by 7 June, when proceedings were declared closed.[458] The printer was probably Francesco Rampazetto, who probably shortly thereafter became the ducal printer and had earlier handled much official printing.[459]

This did not turn out to be the end. In July, at Cherubino's request, Bellarmino was assigned to censure the book.[460] Working with his customary speed, by the end of the month the cardinal could say that the book would receive "neither correction nor emendation."[461] Two weeks later the rejection was repeated, this time spelling out that Cherubino's printed *Speccio di Confessori e penitenti* "will not receive correction and contains the the erroneous doctrine of Master Paul of Venice, Servite" ("non recipere correctionem, et continere doctrinam erroneam Mr. Pauli de Venetiis Ord. servorum.")[462]

After eighteen months' silence, Averoldi came back to notice in July 1613, when worries arose that he might break prison.[463] On Gessi's recommendation, Averoldi was brought to Rome and process ordered made.[464] This order was reconsidered when the inquisitor of Brescia said the prisoner stood ready to abjure, and asked where he should expedite the case. The pope ordered a delay until the rectors could weigh in.[465] Two weeks later the inquisitor reported that there would be no trouble sending Averoldi to Rome.[466] On 26 September the pope ordered no expedition in Brescia, and Averoldi brought to Rome.[467] Two months later it appears that the rectors forced the inquisitor to expedite the case after all, so Paul ordered abjuration *de vehementi* and permanent imprisonment. He still wanted Averoldi in Rome, to be sent via Cremona.[468]

The Appointment of Local Inquisitors, and Meietti Redivivus

At the end of the year a permanent problem that had lain dormant for a couple of years surfaced again: the appointment of local inquisitors. The trouble spot was, as often, Udine, but there had also been difficulties over Belluno.[469] On the Senate's rejection of the appointee for the second, Gessi (still under surveillance) had intervened, and had secured the Venetians' acquiescence. This result emboldened Paul to order further consideration of Udine.[470] As this decree indicates, Mocenigo was right that the the difficulty came from the pope.[471] The ambassador responded by submitting the names of five nominees for Udine. Two weeks later he had changed his tune a little, saying the pope did not want to make the choice without the Congregation.[472] In March the rub was Crema, which Paul put into Millini's hands.[473] Millini, as smooth as ever, promised to favor the Venetians, and Mocenigo accepted the result. The inquisitor of Treviso would move to Udine, being replaced by the inquisitor of Capodistria, and a Trevisan going to Dalmatia.[474] In fact, Capodistria went to Udine, and Treviso stayed put.

A big case broke in April 1614, involving Roberto Meietti, one of the most important Venetian printers. Vignuzzio, acting on his own, had allowed Meietti secretly to "lacerate" all the books he had printed against papal authority during the interdict, and absolved him. When the news reached Rome, Paul ordered a supersedeat and then rejected the absolution. Unfortunately the rest of this decree is illegible, but on 19 June he ordered earlier decrees to remain in force unless Meietti promised never to publish prohibited books.[475] Meietti insisted on absolution; on the inquisitor's letter of 5 July the pope blinked, while refusing to give the testimonial Meietti wanted, "the Sacred Congregation not having been consulted" ("inconsulta sacra congregatione").[476] On 24 July 1614 the pope was still worried that Meietti would sell illegal books through others.[477] Vignuzzio re-absolved Meietti (even though he thought it unnecessary), and Meietti still insisted he wanted an affidavit. The pope bent a little again, ordering him treated as a *sponte comparens*, a supersedeat in any further action "for now," but no affidavit. Meietti was to be notified somehow of his absolution.[478] When Vignuzzio sought permission to inform other inquisitors of Meietti's absolution, he was ordered to send a copy of it.[479] Several months passed before on 11 December Paul refused to grant an affidavit, "but he [or it] will be notified what has been done" ("sed notificetur quibus opus fuerit"), almost the same language as that used in September.[480] When Meietti continued to demand an affidavit for business reasons ("quae sibi valde sunt necessariae in suis negotiis peragendis"), on 22 January 1615 the pope allowed no more than notification via other inquisitors.[481] Unlike Galileo, Meietti never did get his affidavit.

Then it was back to conflict over inquisitorial appointments, especially for Ceneda, about which the Venetians were especially sensitive. Mocenigo had at least secured the concession that the inquisitor of the border town of Crema would be a Venetian subject.[482] Gessi reported in August that the inquisitor of Ceneda had refused to come to Venice to hear confessions (as the Venetians apparently wanted) when he was ordered to stay put and do his job.[483] In November, the new Venetian ambassador, Simeon Contarini, reported that the pope was angry over Ceneda.[484] At the end of the month, the ambassador complained that the Inquisition's "rigorosa segretezza" was making it impossible for him to learn or do much.[485] (Like clockwork, on 5 November Benedetti's request to have his *Antithesis* taken off the Index was ignored.)[486]

Whether the change of ambassador contributed to the situation is difficult to say, but in early 1615 relations between Rome and Venice became much more tense than they had been for several years. In Contarini's second letter of 3 January, he reported that an influential cardinal had spoken to him about the interdict crisis, emphasizing that Venice should not interfere with its clergy. Contarini offered his opinion that Gessi was behind the warning.[487] Two weeks later, in the middle of another long letter about problems with the patriarch, Contarini reported the possibility that Paul would set up a special congregation for jurisdictional disputes with Venice, like the one he had just established for Milan.[488] Contarini proved too pessimistic. The crisis blew over by mid-year, when it looked as if an agreement had been reached about the sore point of the form of imprimaturs for books printed in Venice.[489]

Rome and Venice even managed to cooperate in the trial of the Brescian noble Annibale Soncini. Paul ordered him to Rome on 27 May 1615, when the inquisitor of Cremona [*sic*] was ordered to send his *processo*, an order repeated on 25 November.[490] There may have been some local resistance, since, although the *processo* made it to Rome, Soncini did not.[491] In July 1616 he was given an "attestation" that he was in "these prisons" [of the Inquisition in Rome], in order to protect himself from Venetian officials.[492] On 29 September 1616 he was condemned to prison for three years.[493] Three months later he was rehabilitated under bond, a sign that his case could not have been too serious.[494] It took a while for the bond to be put together, and only on 19 April 1617 was Fiscal Carlo Sincero ordered to check it and, if it was in order, to release Soncini.[495] On 28 September 1617 he was finally allowed to go home.[496]

After all the negotiations over the new inquisitor for Crema, when he arrived, the podestà refused to let him exercise his office.[497] Two weeks later, he was ordered to Venice to negotiate with the doge.[498] The same thing happened in "Cladium" (possibly Ceneda) in early 1616, but the Venetian Senate quickly ordered the podestà to cooperate.[499] Secular authorities resisted more successfully when it came to the Inquisition's attempt to extend its jurisdiction over polygamy cases. At the end of 1615 the podestà of Vicenza refused to allow Inquisition proceedings against a man from Como diocese.[500] In February 1616 the podestà of Verona took a turn.[501] The two problems overlapped once more in Crema in late 1617 and early 1618.[502]

With ritual precision, on 9 September 1615, Benedetti's request that Galamini (Centini's name was deleted) review his *Antithesis* was denied.[503]

More Compromise over the Interdict, and the Case of Guilio Pace

The shadow of the interdict gradually shortened. On 10 March 1616, Averoldi's confessor was allowed to absolve him *in foro conscientiae*.[504] Two weeks later, Vignuzzio was allowed to do the same thing for other, unnamed, writers against the interdict.[505] At the end of the year, Giordano died and Gessi prohibited a funeral, apparently without objection from the Venetians. At the same time, a Capuchin appointed to preach Lent would do so with ecclesiastical authority.[506] Rome had clawed back a considerable amount of ground, and also gained new territory. Unlike the case of Naples, where the secular authorities never relinquished their claim to cognizance of polygamy cases, in early 1618 Gessi and Vignuzzio reported that meetings of the Inquisition, including assistants, would "satisfy" the Holy Office in cases of witchcraft, *maleficii*, and polygamy.[507]

Paul doggedly stayed on the offensive. Given the degree of concern the Inquisition showed with law books, it is not surprising that it would worry about law professors. At the end of 1618, just before Gessi left office as nuncio, he wrote that "Giulio Pacio [Pace]" of Vicenza was being appointed "primarius lector legum" at Padua. He had gone to France years before and had become a heretic. Paul ordered the nuncio to interfere.[508] The case especially galled the Inquisition because the man Pace was replacing, Jacopo Gallo († ca. 1618), had been a fairly docile lawyer. In 1608 he had sought and received a license to read all the prohibited books he listed except those of Bernardo Telesio.[509] Given how much trouble Telesio's ideas got Tommaso Campanella into, it causes some surprise that the mere mention of his name did not draw unwelcome attention to Gallo. When Gallo died and Pace was proposed for appointment, Galileo's friend Paolo Gualdo reported the news (somewhat belatedly, since he put Gallo's death two years earlier!), praising Pace for his publications in both law and philosophy.[510] By contrast to Gallo, Pace, who had studied law in Padua under Giacomo Menochio and Guido Panziroli, had been in the Inquisition's bad books since at least 1609, when his offer to convert if he were given a lectureship in Avignon "in locum Doctoris Baldeschi" was rejected.[511] On 30 November the inquisitor of Vicenza forwarded the news from the archpriest of Padua and others that Pace would gain appointment, and Venice was arranging a complicated way around his inconvenient heresy. The response was dry: "non placet."[512] Had Rome known of Sarpi's praise for Pace's treatise *De dominio maris Hadriatici disceptatio*, the response would no doubt have been more pointed.[513] The same inquisitor reported in early 1620 that Pace had returned to France, and the inquisitor of Avignon was ordered to check.[514] A few weeks later the inquisitor of Vicenza wrote that Pace lived a Catholic life, but had not been able to bring his family from France.[515] Pace seems to have been working through the inquisitor, who wrote again on 27 March that the jurist had been absolved by a Jesuit and the archbishop of "Aquen" (this would probably be Dax in France rather than either Aix or Acqui in Italy, except that the inquisitor was mistaken). The pope ordered both written for confirmation.[516] On 23 April Paul ordered a copy of Pace's reconciliation sent to Rome and to his son, who had recently abjured in Padua.[517] The coram a week later heard a report from the vicar of the Holy Office in Padua that Pace had abjured to the bishop of Valence and lived openly as a Catholic in Padua. This elicited the order to send a copy of the document and keep a sharp eye on him and his son.[518] Finally, on 1 October 1620 the inquisitor of Vicenza was asked to send what he had against Pace; the information was to be kept in Rome.[519] By then the eminent jurist and scholar of Aristotle's logic—his edition of the *Organon* remained standard, especially in northern Europe, until almost the end of the century—had probably returned to Valence or was about to do so.[520]

With the end of Gessi's tenure as nuncio, some of the conflicts thrown up by the interdict had been superficially resolved. As a quick survey of the next fifteen or twenty years of Holy Office activity shows, the underlying issues remained largely unchanged, even if the frequency with which they caused trouble declined considerably: control of the press, appointments of local inquisitors, the role of the lay assistants, and in general relations between secular and ecclesiastical authorities as mediated through the Inquisition. Each of Gessi's two immediate successors held the post for less than three years. The second was Laudivio Zacchia, like Gessi a future Inquisitor.[521]

CHAPTER 4

Venice: Giordano Bruno, Cesare Cremonini, and Marcantonio De Dominis

Three Venetian cases deserve separate treatment, both for their political, religious, and philosophical importance and the copiousness of their documentation, and for the tenacity with which the Inquisition pursued them, albeit with markedly different results. These are the trials of Giordano Bruno, apostate Dominican and natural philosopher; Cesare Cremonini, long-time professor of philosophy at Padua and denier of the soul's immortality; and Marcantonio de Dominis, whose unquiet career began in Croatia, took him to England and then back to Rome, before it ended in the burning of his corpse.

Giordano Bruno

Giordano Bruno's case has given anticlerical historians almost as much ammunition as Galileo's.[1] After wandering over much of Europe for a decade, Bruno returned to Venice in 1591, when his troubles with the Inquisition began in earnest. The first denunciation came in a letter from his host, Giovanni Mocenigo, on 23 May 1592.[2] Mocenigo lodged a long list of accusations that began with Bruno having said that transubstantiation was blasphemy and included perhaps his most famous claims, that the universe was eternal and infinite and that he was a species of magus. One of the charges that interested his judges most concerned the assertion that Christ was a "tristo," in part because he had tried to avoid death, as well as a magus, and Bruno further raised doubts about the virgin birth, together with launching a number of anti-clerical sallies. Mocenigo offered the names of two witnesses, both booksellers, "Ciotto" and

Giacomo Bertano, especially the second, and also handed in three unnamed books by Bruno.[3] Two days later Mocenigo wrote again, perhaps inadvertently revealing one of his motives, that Bruno had refused to teach him the secrets (of the *ars memoriae*) as promised. Mocenigo had tasked Bruno with some of his accusations and duly reported his failure to reply to all but the charge that he was an apostate religious.[4] That same day Mocenigo appeared before the inquisitor, Giovanni Vincenzo Arrigoni, to authenticate his denunciations; both letters were registered the next day.[5] Again that same day both the witnesses Mocenigo named were examined and Bruno—by then imprisoned—also underwent his first interrogation.[6] The Sienese Giovanni Battista Ciotti, whose shop was "at the sign of the Minerva" near the church of San Zulian, had recently been in a little trouble with the Inquisition in Rome and would be again.[7] Ciotti did not do Bruno much damage while throwing a good deal of light on Mocenigo's sour grapes. Ciotti had introduced the two. The only substance of his interrogation was the titles of three of Bruno's books. He ended first with a character reference and then with negative gossip drawn from his acquaintance with Bruno in Frankfurt. He confirmed but did not sign his deposition.[8] The Antwerper Bertano (Jakob van Brecht), like Ciotti, had first known Bruno in Frankfurt, but, unlike his fellow printer, van Brecht emphasized that everyone in the German city was a heretic and that Bruno had read heretical books there. Then he, too, offered the same kind of character witness as Ciotti had.[9] Again, the only substance to his examination was the titles of three other of Bruno's books. Neither printer did much damage.[10] Bruno's first interrogation contained mostly biographical information, together with an account of how he had met Mocenigo.[11]

Three days later Mocenigo returned to the attack. Now he remembered other of Bruno's criticisms of the church, especially for its departure from the apostolic model in both government and wealth. He also alleged that Bruno believed in universal salvation and in living according to nature.[12] Bruno's second *constitutus* on 30 May, once again, contained mostly biographical information, as well as the startling revelation that he had meant to present himself and some of his works to the pope.[13] This resolution was supported by the examination of a Neapolitan Dominican who had attended the order's general chapter in Venice and spoken to Bruno.[14] No time was lost in examining the suspect again twice on 2 June. The first time the topic was his books and teaching. In both cases, Bruno launched what would be his steady defense.[15] Both concerned "materia filosofica," which by implication did not properly belong to the Inquisition's jurisdiction.[16] He had never "directly" taught anything against Christianity, but only "indirectly."[17] Then he summarized his views about the universe. It was ruled by "providenza universale," the action of which he explained in two technical fashions. He explicated his notion of the godhead as composed of three attributes (power, wisdom [*sapientia*], and goodness), before defending himself on the grounds that he held a view of "creation" identical to that of both Aristotle and Thomas Aquinas. He admitted that his philosophical ideas had implications for the faith, especially his ideas about God's nature. He put much more stress than usual on the Spirit, at the same time as he admitted that he had doubts about calling either it or the Son "persons." Still, he insisted, "I have believed and held undoubtedly everything that any faithful Christian ought to believe and hold about the first person," before spelling out in more detail his heterodox beliefs about the other two.[18] Unlike Galileo, Bruno did not need accusers. He was perfectly happy to incriminate himself. The second examination on 2 June began with what else he had written or said against the faith, taking off from his own declarations in the morning session. No doubt one can find many such, said Bruno, but never expressed *ex professo*.[19] Bruno then repeated what he had said in the morning about the divinity. Next, the witness maintained that he had always taken miracles as "divine, true, real, and not apparent."[20] He denied ever saying anything about the Mass, which he had not attended since he apostasized (he had left the Dominican order in 1576). In the rest of this very long session, the interrogators went over virtually everything alleged against Bruno. They concluded by reciting the charges against him, almost as if defending themselves. He had been in many heretical places, making it plausible that he would have said Christ was not God's son nor born of a virgin but a magus who produced false miracles, that religious orders should be abolished, that transubstantiation was false, that penance was "superfluous," that prohibiting anything natural was bad, in short, that he believed everything he had been asked about. Nevertheless, if he came to his senses, Bruno could be assured that he would be treated as lovingly as possible for the good of his soul. He promised to reflect further, and the interrogation ended.[21]

The authorities gave him little time to reflect. They called him back the next day for another long session, when, as often, they read him his previous day's testimony and asked for his reaction to it. The length of Bruno's depositions nicely illustrates how much pressure the Inquisition put on defendants' memories, as well as how much of its work it did orally in the course of generating its voluminous records. Now the interrogator resorted to one of the favorite modes of questioning a suspect, objecting to Bruno that something or other "is not verisimilar" ("non è verisimile").[22] The inquisitor took Bruno through many but scarcely all of his previous admissions before inducing him to confess, "I now detest and abhor" all the errors previously committed ("hora io le [the errors] detesto et abhorrisco"), before throwing himself on the court's mercy.[23] The tribunal could only allow that once it knew whether other *processi* had been formed against Bruno in the past. He admitted only to a disciplinary one while a novice. Other than that, he could think only that he might have been tried for defending the heretics' learning to a fellow Dominican, but so far as he knew none of these proceedings had ever been concluded. In order to track them down, the inquisitor ended the interrogation by asking Bruno what his name was before he entered the order.[24] A request to Rome for a search of its archives went off a week later. Nothing was found.[25]

Bruno went through one more grueling examination on 4 June, when all his previous testimony was again read to him. Afterward he was specifically asked about magical writings. He would admit only to having transcribed one in Padua. Then, a little belatedly but better late than never, the inquisitor asked the obligatory question if Bruno had any enemies in Venice. He named only Mocenigo.[26]

It is likely that the lack of a second witness to confirm Mocenigo's delation left the Inquisition in a difficult position.[27] According to the Holy Office's style, one witness was no witness.[28] Thus, on 23 June Andrea Morosini, mentioned at the end of Mocenigo's first attack as patron of the famous *ridotto*, appeared under citation to testify that he had never heard Bruno say anything incriminating and regarded him as a good Catholic.[29] On the same day Ciotti was summoned for a second time and asked whether he remembered his previous examination and had anything to add to it. He could only note Bruno's plan to approach the pope.[30] More than a month passed before Bruno was brought from prison again on 30 July. After this further time to reflect, did he have anything more to say? No, he did not. So the inquisitor put a series of propositions to Bruno, beginning with the accusation that his long apostasy "makes you very suspect of the holy faith."[31] Bruno agreed, but insisted his conscience had always troubled him until he decided to talk to the pope, apparently now not in the hopes of bringing him around to Bruno's reform plans, but about a dispensation to leave his order. Then it was a pair of questions of the verisimilar variety, both of which Bruno denied.[32] Next, the inquisitor alleged that witnesses had contradicted Bruno's claim never to have taught heresy, to which Bruno replied with a contradiction of his own, that only Mocenigo could have so testified.[33] Finally, Bruno again asked pardon and for private punishment in order not to dishonor his habit. Rather than object to this really inverisimilar assertion, the inquisitor simply asked whether he had anything more to say. Again, no.[34]

Rome Takes a Direct Hand

Some of the changed rhythm was probably due to Rome's involvement; it slowed things down considerably. Secretary Santoro's relatively advanced age may have had something to do with the slow pace of the trial, although the volume and complexity of Bruno's output were probably more important causes. A copy of Bruno's dossier had been sent to the Inquisition's secretary, perhaps already before his examination of 30 July.[35] Neither the letter, Cardinal Santoro's reply of 9 January 1593, nor the Congregation's decree before 12 September 1592 that Bruno be sent to Rome are found in the *decreta*.[36] From the end of September until early January 1593 the record, such as it is, consists of negotiations for Bruno's extradition.[37] The Venetians at first resisted the request from Rome, but not strenuously. In fact, when the nuncio alleged that he had more than two dozen precedents, the Venetians capitulated almost immediately. Nevertheless, the only two certainly then known appear in Santoro's instructions to the nuncio, the case of Bartolomeo Spadafora, a Sicilian, extradited in the reign of Paul IV, and Guido da Fano, under Pius V.[38] Once again, the decree registers contain no reference to a search for precedents, neither an order to undertake it nor its results. None is documented until Francesco degli Albizzi, long-time assessor, then cardinal and author of probably the most authoritative seventeenth-century manual on Inquisition practice, set out to write a reply to Paolo Sarpi's history of the Venetian inquisition and could find only eight instances.[39]

It is of great importance that Bruno's case did not begin anew in Rome but rather was thought of as being continued in a different venue. This point shows that the Congregation regarded its satellite tribunals as extensions of itself.[40] Bruno first comes up in the Inquisition's central records when ordered on 12 April 1593 to surrender all his books and manuscripts. Otherwise he appears during his first year in Rome only at prison visitations on 22 December 1593 and 4 April 1594. On the first occasion, he was not only visited but heard in "the hall of the said Congregation" about his necessities. On the second, he asked for a copy of his *processo*.[41] The request was granted "as quickly as possible" ("quanto citius") on 31 May 1594.[42] In the meantime another event of tremendous, even determinative significance, to Bruno's trial happened.[43] His fellow prisoner in Venice, Fra Celestino da Verona, lodged a second denunciation.[44] The mere denunciation was bad enough, since in and of itself it fulfilled a prime requisite of proper procedure thus far absent, but its content was worse. It probably fell in autumn 1593, which is probably also when the witnesses Celestino named were examined. In any case, their interrogations must have been over before Bruno could have expected to receive a copy of his dossier. His request means that the trial had moved into the *repetitio*, or examination of all witnesses, for which the defendant would need a copy of the dossier in order to prepare questions to be put to them.[45] Accordingly, the Venetian inquisitor was ordered to reexamine some (but not all) of the witnesses over the list of questions drawn up by the fiscal procurator with input from Bruno. Apparently, since Rome had taken charge of the case, the records were sent straight there from Venice and were lost along with the rest of Bruno's dossier.[46] Their content must therefore be reconstructed from the document misleadingly labeled the "Sommario" by its first editor, Angelo Mercati.[47] Mocenigo's reexamination extended to at least two sessions spread over five days.[48] Among three new witnesses was Fra Celestino, whose testimony doomed Bruno, since it not only finally confirmed Mocenigo's charges but added new ones, which other of Bruno's fellow prisoners in Venice in turn supported. Their appearance indicates that this phase, although intended as part of the defense, actually better served the fiscal, who could put any questions he wished, apparently to any witnesses he wished, at the same time as he asked those suggested by the defendant.[49] Among the accusations proved or raised by Fra Celestino were Christ's desire to avoid death, the infinity of worlds, sharp criticism of Moses and the prophets as liars and cheats, and more implausibly that were he forced to return to his order, Bruno would blow up the house in which he was confined.[50]

This testimony was probably among the targets of a document Bruno submitted at the prison visitation of 20 December 1594, intended "to reject [or rebut] the witnesses' testimony" ("ad repellendum dicta [none named nor previously referred to] testium").[51] It may be that Bruno's counter-charges had some effect; at least, on 12 January 1595 Mocenigo's depositions were read, again a week later, as well as on 9 and 16 February, all three being corams.[52] The Congregation took such an action only rarely, although it frequently considered a key move several times.[53] It is at least clear that the Inquisition was moving cautiously, so much so that it appears to have decided that the evidence really was inadequate and ordered a new step, the censure of Bruno's books.[54] It is equally clear that the pope had taken charge of the case. Then, for another year, Bruno shows up only at prison visitations.[55] At the second of these, more than a year after censure of his books had been ordered, the theologian consultors were ordered to review his books and draw up propositions for censure.[56] Such a delay was not unusual, however disconcerting the prisoner might have found it. In September 1596 those propositions were turned over to three reviewers, Master [Garcia?] Guerra, Fra Pedro Juan Zaragoza, *socio* of the master of the sacred palace, both Dominicans, and a Jesuit named Gallo.[57] On 10 October, in the context of a review of prisoners, they were ordered to continue their work.[58] By this time, both Camillo Borghese and Pompeo Arrigoni had joined the Congregation, both future secretaries. Finally, by March 1597 the censures were ready, and the trial lurched back into the defensive phase. The order at the prison visitation of 24 March 1597 contains the usual oddities, especially the sequence of actions which makes it appear that Bruno would be given the censures only after he had been examined over them.[59] This examination *stricte* did not include torture, but rather a close questioning over particular propositions.[60] The decree registers say nothing about it having been executed. This decree is significant for another reason. It represents the first time the man who finally pushed the case to its conclusion appears in Bruno's record, Roberto Bellarmino, at this time still a consultor but to become a cardinal Inquisitor before Bruno's condemnation. Another year passed before on 16 March 1598 it was reported that the *summarium* of the case was done and ready to go to the consultors.[61] They would then decide which of its propositions were heretical, but we do not know their opinions nor even certainly the propositions. Nor do we know why Bruno wanted paper at the prison visitation in December, and his wish was only granted if he gave a reason.[62]

Condemned Propositions Put to Bruno

Matters were coming to a head. On 12 January 1599, an unusual Tuesday meeting, the Congregation without the pope ordered propositions put to Bruno "in order that he should consider and weigh them" ("ut illas consideret et ponderet"), and in another meeting "it should be proposed that he revoke them" ("proponatur ut illas revocet").[63] The possibility that he would refuse was raised, but no consequence decided upon. All this apparently was " Propositae per patrem Bellarminum." The act ends, "license conceded" ("concessa licentia").[64] This gnomic syntax leaves obscure exactly what happened. Was this all Bellarmino's plan? Was Bruno really to be given the propositions first and only afterward told which he had to revoke? And to whom was "license" conceded? To Bellarmino to act as he proposed? A marginal note "have a word with the assessor" ("Fiat verbum cum assessore") does not help much, except to underscore that whatever was being done, it was serious. The note of the coram on Thursday sheds a little light. Then eight propositions drawn from Bruno's "books and *processo*" by Bellarmino and the commissary, Alberto Tragagliolo, were read, and it was specified that they were to be shown to Bruno to see whether he would abjure them. But matters were still in train, since the entry ends with an order to look for other heretical propositions "from the *processo* and books."[65] Finally, in the coram of 4 February, the same order in substantially the same words was considered for the third and final time. We have three records of the meeting, a minute in ACDFSO, Decreta 1599–1600, together with an incomplete fair copy, both by the sloppy notary Flaminio Adriani as well as a summary fair copy by his replacement Quintiliano Adriani in ACDFSO, Decreta 1597–1599.[66] In all of them, Clement VIII ordered Bruno to see the propositions that Bellarmino and Tragagliolo deemed heretical. If he refused to acknowledge them, he would once and forever be given his defense of forty days. The only novelty from the previous meeting was the claim that the propositions had been condemned "by the most ancient fathers, the church and apostolic see" ("ab antiquissimis Patribus, ab Ecclesia et Sede apostolica").[67] The truncated fair copy refers both to the "formed process" and to the consultors' opinions (which it fails to give). This explicit reference changes the context slightly, since it means the case had entered the *expeditio*, the final phase before sentence. Quintiliano Adriani's fair copy departs from his uncle's (or father's) two notes by adding the Dominican general to the deputation sent to Bruno, and adds formulaic language about penance and the term of the defense absent in the first two. A marginal note says that Santoro revised the entry.[68] It will bear pointing out that the original plan for Bruno's abjuration went up in smoke. Beethoven, who loved to mock composers who did not know when to end a piece, would have had great fun with the difficulties the Inquisition sometimes encountered in concluding its most important trials.

It was probably in Bruno's last *constitutus* of 15 February 1599 that he saw the propositions, at which time he handed in another memorial. Both were reported on 18 February, when the pope once more ordered other errors collected.[69] According to the record of the prison visitation on 5 April 1599,

Bruno's entire case was reviewed in the Congregation's meeting hall.[70] According to a copy made for Cardinal Borghese, "his case was to be proposed" ("Si ha da proporre la sua causa"), language equivalent to moving the case into the *expeditio*.[71] In fact, this is inexact, since the case was not ordered "proposed" until 24 August, on Bellarmino's report that Bruno had "clearly" revoked six of the eight propositions in a writing submitted on 1 April, "at the time of visitation [of the prison]." About two points only did Bruno demur, the first, "about the Novatian heresy," and no. 7, about the soul being in the body like "a sailor in a ship" ("nauta in navi").[72] At the same time, Bruno was ordered to be given glasses (*perspicilia*) and writing materials.[73] After the usual delay of two weeks but on an unusual day of the week, Monday 6 September, Bruno's case was ordered proposed at the next coram, as indeed it was on 9 September.[74] On that day the consultors gave their opinions, as usual in reverse status order, beginning with Fiscal Giulio Monterenzi. Both he and Assessor Marcello Filonardi did not think Bruno "convicted" on all counts, but thought he should be tortured over those on which he was. Commissary Tragagliolo, by contrast, thought he should be tortured over those on which he had *not* been convicted and given a term to reply to the others, an opinion in which Pietro Millini (probably a relative of the later secretary of the Inquisition, Gian Garzia Millini) concurred. The last two consultors, the Dominican general Ippolito Beccaria and Anselmo Dandini, were more hard-nosed, Beccaria wanting Bruno tortured twice and Dandini proposing that if he could not sustain torture over his anti-Trinitarianism, he should be executed. The pope was more lenient, ordering a term assigned for Bruno to "come to his senses" about the articles he had confessed, and further examination of his testimony and confessions; meanwhile, the case was to be proposed.[75] In the next coram, a statement of Bruno's intention to acknowledge his errors and "do all that had been enjoined on him by the holy Roman church," and also yet another memorial were read, but no further action taken.[76] Two months passed before the cardinal theologians were ordered to consider the *expeditio*.[77]

Sentence

Bruno refused to cooperate. At the prison visitation he flatly declared that he had nothing to think about nor did he know how he might do that even if he had. The response ordered was almost identical to that proposed in February, with a slightly different cast. Now the Dominican general and vicar general were to induce Bruno to see his errors.[78] Q. Adriani's revision says nothing of Bruno's defiance, while emphasizing the necessity of the general and vicar general's action in order to move the case to expedition.[79] On 20 January 1600 the Congregation meeting with the pope decreed Bruno's sentence and execution.[80] And there the case would end, in the current state of the record, since Bruno's sentence is lost. We have only a partial copy, sent to the governor of Rome to justify his execution.[81] This version sneaks up on but never spells out the propositions for which Bruno was condemned. The simple fact is that we do not know why he was executed.[82] Nevertheless, Francesco Beretta must be right that the articles could not have included any Copernican charges, because they were all specified in the sentence as heretical.[83] The only other point of interest is that all nine cardinals signed the document. On 8 February, in a non-coram in the palace of the most senior inquisitor Ludovico Madruzzo, Bruno was ordered "relaxed to the secular court," and on the 17th he was burned alive.[84]

Cesare Cremonini

So far as is now known, the Paduan Aristotelian Cesare Cremonini (1550–1631) first came to the Inquisition's attention in 1598, when the inquisitor of Venice reported his lectures on *De anima*, following the opinion of Alexander Aphrodisias. The inquisitor of Padua was ordered to investigate.[85] That is all to be found in the decree registers or the Venetian ambassador to Rome's correspondence for 1598.[86] In 1604 the rectors of Padua had more detail about what had happened, although they were vague about the date, whether 1598 or 1599. Their source was a decree of the Holy Office, dated only "1599," that the vicar of the Paduan Holy Office had sent to Rome in response to an order from the pope to the inquisitor and the bishop of Padua to search for correspondence from Rome "and also find the *processo* and *monitio* [warning] made to Doctor Cremonini about the mode prescribed to him of reading the matter of the soul's immortality."[87] The decree reported an order to the inquisitor "seriously to warn" (*graviter monendum esse*) Cremonini not to interpret *De anima* in any way contrary to the decrees of church councils.[88] Cremonini was said to have accepted the *monitio* "reverently."[89] That the Congregation could not find this evidence in its own files is not particularly odd, but it is strange that six years later, without, as far as the decree registers say, any further correspondence with Padua on the subject, the Inquisition insisted that it had given Cremonini a precept in 1598, which it now renewed. The context had changed. Cremonini and Galileo were jointly under investigation in Padua, and on 5 May 1604 the Serenissima had summarily ordered its rectors to quash proceedings.[90] Nevertheless, a week later the Inquisition heard a denunciation sent by the vicar of the Paduan Holy Office on 16 April,[91] and later identified as by Cremonini's colleague Camillo Belloni. In the next day's coram, on the strength of the denunciation, a familiar of ambassador (and future patriarch) Francesco Vendramin was ordered examined. Simultaneously, Cremonini was taxed with "inobservance" of the precept.[92] The following Saturday Secretary Camillo Borghese transmitted the orders to Padua (his letter is missing), adding that the pope had commanded a search for former Secretary Santoro's letters from 1598.[93] It appears they were never found, either. On 4 June the inquisitor of Padua was sent a copy of testimony taken in Rome, probably from Vendramin's servant.[94] In response, the rectors dug in their heels harder and flatly told the inquisitor, "information is not to be collected against Cesare Tremonini [*sic*], public professor of philosopy, about the contravention of a precept not to lecture [that] the soul is mortal according to Aristotle's opinion." The Congregation then turned to the bishop of Padua, asking him to investigate extrajudicially—that is, outside the normal course of the law—at the same time as the abbot of San Paolo was to be examined in Rome.[95] The bishop sent two letters, content unknown.[96] In September, Cremonini's old enemies the Jesuits first took a hand in the person of Stefano Del Bufalo, probably a member of the prominent Roman family, who offered information and was examined along with some non-Jesuits.[97] Again, we do not know what he or they said.[98]

For a time, Cremonini's case overlapped that of another Paduan professor, Antonio Vendramin, also suspected of believing the soul mortal. Unfortunately, the decree for the disposition of his case later in 1604 is illegible.[99]

The Jesuits Intervene

Then for two years nothing happened until early 1607, when the Jesuits went back on the attack. They gave Secretary Arrigoni an anonymous denunciation, and the Congregation ordered him to find the author in order to examine him *formiter* [*sic*; probably a mistake for *formaliter*] along with other witnesses in Rome.[100] In mid-year more disquieting news arrived from the inquisitor of Udine. He reported that a local physician had many manuscripts by Cremonini and others that he claimed had been printed in Padua by Paolo Meietti, and that Cremonini's "disciples avidly disseminated this opinion."[101] Naturally, the Congregation wanted the physician examined and the writings forwarded to Rome.[102] So far as the decree registers say, nothing happened. Instead, we get a bizarre twist, when in January 1608 the Congregation told Cardinal Nephew Scipione Borghese that Cremonini was not suitable to enter his service! Almost as odd, the evidence supporting the judgment came from a single letter from a man in Cremonini's home town of Cento. The Congregation also ordered the usual search of its registers, but only after communicating with Borghese.[103] A week later, the Inquisitors heard the *summarium* from the files, and in the next day's coram, Paul V ordered Secretary Millini once more to use the bishop of Padua extrajudicially.[104] Its inquisitor also belatedly took a hand, saying in a letter of 29 February (read 13 March) that Cremonini took the sacraments and heard Mass, and that he would keep an eye on his views about the soul. The pope instead ordered the bishop to do that.[105]

Cremonini went on the offensive, approaching the Dieci on 8 May for help. They reacted quickly, resolving on 11 May that his defense against the "perturbationi" newly moved pertained to the Senate, and forwarded the matter for their consideration of "however much might be considered convenient and necessary."[106] Unfortunately, we do not know what the Senate decided at this point.

Rome remained intensely interested. The agenda for the coram of 22 May contained the reading of evidence from Antonio Mazzalorsi, a Venetian deacon, given to Cardinal Aldobrandini and the vicar of the Holy Office in Ravenna. He deposed in early April that three years earlier Cremonini had given a "secret" reading to a dozen nobles, in which he claimed the soul was mortal. Mazzalorsi also denounced Girolamo Cicogna, Marcantonio Bracchi, and an unnamed priest of Verona, apparently in connection with Cremonini.[107] The pope ordered a copy of Mazzalorsi's testimony sent to the inquisitor of Venice, Giovanni Domenico Vignuzzio, who was secretly to depose witnesses and give their evidence to Nuncio Berlinghiero Gessi. Gessi would then report to the Congregation, making crystal clear the hiearchy of authority in the process.[108] Despite an entry in the agenda of 11 June saying that Gessi and Vignuzzio had collected Mazzalorsi's evidence, there is nothing in the decrees for either 12 or 18 June.[109] While not making much progress against Cremonini himself, the Holy Office did do so against at least one of his followers, even if the assistants only reluctantly gave approval and would not allow testimony against Cremonini to be taken.[110] The lay members of the Venetian tribunal otherwise caused as much obstruction as possible. On Gessi's complaint of 12 July that they were intimidating witnesses named by Mazzalorsi (their names are missing from the decree), Paul ordered the nuncio written to send a copy of the information.[111]

In August Borghese wrote Gessi that the bishop of Padua had depositions that Cremonini "held the soul's mortality." When following them up, Gessi was to take testimony carefully so that no one could say that procedure had not been followed.[112] To Borghese's further order to have witnesses examined in Venice, Gessi objected that Padua was better, where the assistants were not required. He also noted that no deponents had come from Padua, but if there really were any, he would depose them carefully and encourage them not to be afraid. Nevertheless, the matter would be "most difficult" because the assistants would certainly punish the notary and possibly even the inquisitors if matters were handled otherwise. He feared that the assistants would quibble over words, as they had just done over Mazzalorsi's testimony, saying that his evidence constituted the same old "malignity" that had been cleared up with proof that Cremonini had been expounding Aristotle's opinion. The assistants had therefore allowed the witnesses to be examined only in order to make sure they were not trying to stir up trouble for Cremonini. He had hopes that one of the three assistants would be "reasonable," but none for the other two.[113]

Gessi proved too pessimistic. On 9 August the inquisitor of Venice sent evidence against Cicogna, Cremonini, Bracchi, Lucrezia Mazzalorsa (Mazzalorsi's wife?), and others.[114] The same day as the Congregation received this welcome news, Borghese wrote Gessi that the bishop of Padua, by contrast, said it was more dangerous to examine witnesses there and that they would not depose anywhere the assistants took a hand, making it hopeless to proceed in the Holy Office.[115] Gessi corroborated this report a week later, suggesting that witnesses might be taken to Ferrara.[116] The pope stipulated that the Inquisition's usual secrecy still had to be maintained, before ordering such a course on 11 September.[117] Ferrara was not the only alternative locus. On 23 August, Filippo Fabbri, one of Cremonini's professorial colleagues in Padua, deposed against him in Faenza, Fabbri's home town. Although the decree says nothing about what Fabbri said, the agenda describes his testimony as based solely on *fama* (public report, or in this case, rumor).[118] Gessi made further progress before the end of the month, although Cardinal Borghese got the news faster than the Holy Office did.[119] The same ten-day lag occurred in early November.[120] Just about the same time the inquistor of Ferrara sent two more depositions.[121] Then Cremonini discovered the scheme and got the Venetians to prevent any further testimony in Ferrara.[122] On the strength of two Ferrarese depositions, on 18 December Paul ordered the examinations of three witnesses, including a Franciscan at the Collegio Bonaventura in Rome.[123] Two days later Gessi wrote Borghese, apparently giving up.[124]

Gessi's pessimism proved justified. Over the next five years, almost nothing happened beyond trivial events. In 1609 one Fra Giovanni Battista Aiata denounced Cremonini in Parma, together with the poet Giovanni Battista Marini. Marini was to be imprisoned and his poetry sought, while Aiata's denunciation of Cremonini merely went into the file.[125] In April 1610 Cremonini's rather brazen petition to continue his lectures to the Benedictines of Santa Giustina in Padua was rejected.[126] On 17 May 1611 came the notorious but mysterious order, well known to Galileo scholars, to see whether Cremonini's dossier mentioned the astronomer.[127] In an even more inexplicable development, on 3 July 1612 Vignuzzio licensed Cremonini's *De coelo* for publication even before the Venetian senate did.[128] The assistants must have done very good work. To continue the oddities, the Inquisition took no notice until late the following year, when Bellarmino brought the book to its attention. The Congregation ordered Vignuzzio to send a copy.[129] I am mystified what to make of the announcement in a letter of 3 May 1613 that Cremonini had been absolved.[130]

De coelo and the Inquisition's Revived Interest

The publication of Cremonini's book, even if not the one that really interested the Congregation, nonetheless revived his case. On 16 January 1614 it wanted to know whether Vignuzzio had approved the book; he replied before the following week's coram that a committee had revised it. The pope wanted the manuscript and the printed book compared.[131] It was a near certainty that Bellarmino would be assigned to censure the book, as he was on 5 March.[132] Whether he did not or asked help in the effort, the theologian consultors reported as a body on 15 May, when the pope ordered the inquisitor of Padua "of himself" (*ex se*) to induce Cremonini to admit his errors.[133] A week later a spontaneous denunciation of a former student of Cremonini, Carlo Giostreri, came in, when the pope is also supposed to have ordered negotiations with Cremonini about corrections. At the same time the inquisitor of Padua was to collect copies without banning the book.[134]

In June it appears that Fabbri had substituted for the bishop in warning

Cremonini about correcting his errors, or perhaps Fabbri had acted for the inquisitor of Padua, as he was explicitly ordered to do now.[135] The fresh censures the pope ordered were ready by 7 July to be given to Fabbri to use on Cremonini.[136] Two days later the Venetian ambassador reported that he had been slipped a note from "one who serves in the Congregation of the Holy Office," favorable to Cremonini, telling the ambassador that the morning's congregation had considered banning *De coelo*.[137] Five days later, on 10 July, Giostreri's claim that Cremonini had taught the soul's mortality during his student days came from the inquisitor of Adria.[138] Apparently the Venetians ordered their ambassador to intervene; at least, on 2 August he defended himself for not having reported, even though he had done with the Holy Office what he thought "convenient;" he expected a reply the following week.[139] Whether he received one does not emerge, but the pope did then order Cremonini's response to the censures taken into account.[140] A week later, according to the agenda, Cremonini's replies, now together with his request to be treated like Pietro Pomponazzi, his notorious sixteenth-century predecessor, led to a proposed order to the theologians to draft solutions that would allow the book's printing, but Paul denied the parallel to Pomponazzi and decreed further corrections.[141] Could the assessor have been the Inquisition servant trying to help Cremonini?

In a preemptive move, on 11 September the Congregation ordered its censures sent to nuncios in France, Spain, and Belgium.[142] The record of the coram of 18 September is confusing. The agenda correctly said Cremonini would not correct his errors and would instead reply to the censures, while the decree quotes the same source as saying Cremonini stood ready to correct his errors, resulting in the pope's order to Cremonini to correct or see his book prohibited.[143]

Just when Cremonini most needed his help, Venetian Ambassador Tommaso Contarini died. The legation's secretary, Cristoforo Surian, filled in as best he could. In a letter of 27 September in response to a question about the status of *De coelo* sent on 12 July, he said he knew the ambassador had not had a chance to talk to Borghese, so he had done so. The cardinal told Surian that the book would remain permanently suspended, "because it needed great correction." He complained that Vignuzzio had let it out despite its being full of "bad doctrine and particularly that the soul is mortal." That was certainly Borghese's own opinion. Nevertheless, the cardinal nephew then offered to ask the pope and the Inquisitors what had happened, an egregious breach of the Inquisition's secrecy. He thought that Cremonini had failed to discuss the counter-arguments to mortality, thereby meriting "suspension and correction." Borghese also objected to other points, among them Cremonini's treatment of free will.[144] On 4 October Surian reported several more conversations with Borghese, containing mainly the same substance, but also two new points. The cardinal nephew told the secretary to talk to Cardinal Millini and emphasized the special treatment the Inquisition had given Cremonini in the form of the unusual grace of prepublication censorship, intended to help him "accommodate" the book to its wishes.[145]

The Apology for *De coelo*

The Inquisition's attention then shifted to Cremonini's apology for *De coelo*, which it expected to appear soon.[146] On 23 October Paul ordered Gessi not to negotiate about it in the Collegio and Venetian Inquisition and instead simply to report.[147] A week later Paul directed the inquisitor of Padua, who had sent the first part of the apology, to send the rest.[148] After this flurry of activity, the pace slowed considerably. Not until 23 July 1615 did the Inquisition take any further note of the apology—at the same time as it noted Cremonini's plans to correct the original—when Paul V ordered it to await the Franciscan regent of Padua's review of the first.[149] Nine months went by, before the Inquisition heard the news in early March 1616 that the apology was about to come out.[150] A further three months passed before the pope ordered a copy of the apology, again on the point of appearance, sent to Rome.[151] Two weeks later the first folio came from Vignuzzio, and the Inquisition responded quickly in an unusual Saturday meeting, ordering its review.[152] The reviewer turned out to be Agostino Galamini, although he did not receive the assignment until 13 July.[153] Now the thread becomes tangled. The next we know, a half-year later on 28 January 1617 the Index, not the Inquisition, refused to license a possibly new book under the title "De mortalitate animae."[154] But the Inquisition had not finished with *De coelo*. In July 1617 its congregation of theologians handed in a set of censures on it, now in BAV, Vat. lat. 6539, fos. 79r–85r, which are unfortunately nearly illegible. Another set of censures follows, including one addressed to the inquisitor of Padua (fos. 90r–92r, largely illegible), most of which must be earlier in date, including one by Luis Ystella (fos. 93r, signed jointly by Fra Agostino, proctor general of the Conventual Franciscans), former master of the sacred palace, who died 5 September 1614, as well as another addressed to Andrea Giustiniani as commissary, an office he held from 1612 to early 1615.[155] Perhaps all extant censures were collected together in 1617. However that may be, the next information about Cremonini does not concern either *De coelo* or its apology, but rather *De anima*, which the Index again prohibited in October 1618. At the same time Bellarmino was directed, rather belatedly, to ask Galamini whether he had a copy and whether it was corrected.[156] For some reason, the Inquisition seems to have shared responsibility for Cremonini's books with its junior partner, in an odd way. While the Inquisition continued to interest itself in two published books, usually the Index's domain, it left the Index to deal, most unusually, with an unpublished—indeed, never published—book.

The Inquisition had not lost interest in *De coelo* and Cremonini's apology for it. In its first meeting of 1619 it asked the master of the sacred palace whether he had a copy of the first and, if not, to write the inquisitor of Venice for a copy.[157] Three months later Bellarmino's and Desiderio Scaglia's censures on the apology were reported. They judged that it did not take enough account of the Fifth Lateran Council nor confute Aristotle "according to the form prescribed to him in the year 1614." Paul ordered the censures sent to Galamini and the inquisitors of Venice and Padua for their reactions.[158] On 10 May the inquisitor of Padua reported Cremonini's response, that the refutation of Aristotle "does not pertain to a philosopher but to a theologian to whom he himself would promptly subscribe," and if that were not acceptable, he would write more in the future. When the letter was finally read on 13 June, Paul directed the inquisitor *ex se* to persuade Cremonini to correct and "dissolve" Aristotle's argument, or "at least refer to the Lateran Council."[159] The next item of business was Galamini's letter of 5 May saying he had read the apology and wondered whether it should be prohibited, but not because of the "precept" given him to correct *De coelo* and confute Aristotle.[160] A week later he listed "the errors reported" in the book, which now had the title "De quinta coeli substantia." The inquisitor of Padua was to have them corrected.[161]

Cremonini's response came a month later. He proposed to write a third book after *De coelo* and *De quinta coeli substantia*. In response, Paul demanded that the inquisitor "enjoin" him at all costs (*omnino*) to provide "satisfaction" in writing within three months.[162] He complied with intended corrections about the soul's mortality and the world's eternity. Their review was assigned to Commissary Scaglia on 18 September.[163] In November, Cremonini's "promise" to make corrections "as soon as he could" led Paul to order the inquisitor of Padua to "take care of its execution with effect."[164] The pope conceded some delay on 19 December, while insisting that Cremonini "satisfy."[165]

Cremonini still had not done so by 1621 and, worse, was not following the proper form. As a result the Inquisition suspended the book, apparently now *De coelo*, not the apology, "until corrected," and if it were not, "from now as if from then prohibited."[166] Two weeks later, possibly on a second reading of the same report from Padua, the pope ordered propositions in the book "qualified."[167] Whether that happened is unknown. In December the pope again considered whether to suspend *De coelo* if not corrected, giving Cremonini a year to complete the task.[168] Curiously, the Index meeting on 3 January 1622 claimed that the assessor had told it the book was suspended "until corrected," a decision it endorsed.[169] Two years later, first the Index, and only then the pope and the Inquisition, flatly prohibited the book.[170]

Cremonini's Case Revived Again

Another two years later and without explanation, the Inquisition ordered Cremonini's case resumed.[171] On 26 June Urban VIII, pope since 1623, having heard a summary of it, ordered the inquisitor of Padua extrajudicially to investigate whether Cremonini continued "to teach and publicly lecture [on] the soul's mortality." He also ordered a circular letter to all inquisitors in Italy, ordering them to check their files for information against Cremonini, which Secretary Millini duly produced the following Saturday.[172] The inquisitor of Padua reported in the negative before 24 July, but did add that Cremonini was lecturing in Santa Giustina, leading to another papal order to cease and desist.[173] The circular produced only the stale self-accusation from Genoa of Paolo Andrea Doria that had first surfaced in 1614 and a second from the inquisitor of Ceneda of another ex-student.[174] The stern injunction about Santa Giustina had little more effect, Cremonini brazenly asking in December for a license to teach there.[175]

1626 brought a fresh denunciation in Rome from a Minim, Angelo Castellani.[176] On 30 July Urban directed the nuncio to decide, with the inquisitor of Venice, Girolamo Zappetti da Guinzano, how best to depose the physician Marco Antonio Della Rovere.[177] The next day Secretary Millini sent a copy of Castellani's deposition, probably to Zappetti, ordering him and the nuncio, Giovanni Battista Agucchi, to examine Della Rovere on the strength of Castellani's testimony. This was that on 1 August 1625 Della Rovere told him that as a student in Padua he had gone to Cremonini's house where he had heard things. Della Rovere's undated deposition (but taken on 19 August) did not contain a great deal of useful information.[178] The first substantive question concerned the soul's immortality, even though that had not come up in Castellani's deposition. Della Rovere claimed never to have heard Cremonini say the soul was mortal, although he did have it in his teacher Mazzoleni's writings and had heard many students over the space of fourteen years say that. Pressed on the point whether Cremonini had said it, including an alleged written claim that he had heard him express that belief many times, Della Rovere again denied that he had. The interrogators then introduced another, apparently missing deposition referring to Cremonini's writing on the subject, asking Della Rovere if he knew where it was. He said not, but admitted to knowing that Cremonini was writing on the subject. Then the question became the world's eternity. Again, Della Rovere had heard nothing. Taxed with Castellani's very precise claim that Cremonini had denied it, Della Rovere backtracked a little, saying he might have heard it from others. The interrogators next brought up the subject of miracles, again drawing on Castellani's deposition, which claimed Della Rovere had said that Cremonini thought miracles were only for the uneducated (*idioti*). No, he had not, replied Della Rovere. Della Rovere further answered in the negative a number of other questions about Cremonini's beliefs, for example, whether he had taught against ecclesiastical authority. Even after a warning (*monitus*), he maintained that he had said "the true truth." It causes little surprise that Urban decided on 3 September that Della Rovere had given the Congregation nothing to go on.[179]

De membrorum principatu and "De anima"

In mid-1627 came news from the vicar of the Holy Office in Padua that Cremonini was about to publish a book. The nuncio and inquisitor of Venice were to send a copy and keep their eyes open.[180] They did so, reporting on 1 July that it had passed muster. Urban was not convinced and ordered them to try again, threatening prohibition.[181] It seems they managed to find problems; at least, a "note of the pretensed errors in Cesare Cremonini's book called Apology of Aristotle's opinions about the origin and primacy of the members," sent with the inquisitor's letter of 7 July, led Urban to order on 19 August that a copy be sent to Rome.[182] Nothing more is heard of the book. A roughly contemporary denunciation from a Carthusian led Cremonini to threaten further recourse to the Venetian senate.[183]

The Congregation also tried sanctioning, unofficially of course, at least one work against Cremonini and rewarding its author, with unknown results both as to publication and effects. In early 1628 a Dominican, Camillo da Soresina, asked permission both to publish against Cremonini and to be created master of his province. Urban conceded both. I have not been able to find that Camillo ever published anything against Cremonini.

When Cremonini died in 1631, Urban ordered the inquisitor of Padua, working with the nuncio, secretly to investigate his papers for "false and heretical doctrine."[184] The inquisitor acted quickly, contacting Cremonini's executor, who told him the doge had prohibited him from saying anything about the writings left to the Venetian republic. Nevertheless, the executor, an abbot, "on account of his observance to the holy office," had secretly given the inquisitor three quarto volumes "of writings and lectures on three books *de anima*" for review. Urban ordered such seeking "false and heretical propositions" with the aid of a notary.[185] The investigation took until January 1632, when the inquisitor sent the results to Rome. The pope ordered them given to the qualifiers.[186] On 16 July they delivered their judgment that Cremonini's books contained "erroneous and indeed absolutely heretical propositions, which not only from Aristotle's texts, but absolutely and simply he tries to prove," denying divine omniscence, the soul's immortality, and the intellective will.[187] On 28 July the Congregation ordered the qualifiers' opinions referred to the pope, who the next day apparently (the entry is damaged) ordered the assessor to confer about the censures with a theologian, whose name is missing.[188] And there the matter ends. "De anima" was never published.

Marcantonio De Dominis

While Cremonini's case concluded quietly in the hands of Urban VIII, a second high-profile investigation of a Venetian subject ended spectacularly under the same pope, that of Marcantonio De Dominis (1560–1624), archbishop of Split (Spalato) in Croatia and perhaps the most important ecumenist of the early seventeenth century.[189] An ex-Jesuit, he was also an associate of Galileo in Padua who published scientific writings especially on optics and held a theory of the tides more accurate than Galileo's.[190] He seems to have been cantankerous, and frequently found himself in trouble with his flock and his Venetian lords. Despite writing in their favor during the interdict crisis in 1606–1607, he largely escaped Gessi's subsequent efforts to recuperate or punish Venice's other prominent defenders, because neither of his anonymous treatises had been published.[191] They certainly contained views the papacy would not have liked, any more than it did his close association with Paolo Sarpi.[192] Nevertheless, not until early 1614 did De Dominis come to the Roman Inquisition's attention. Then the bishop of Šibenik (Sebenico), Vincenzo Arrigoni, O.P., De Dominis's major delator, suffragan of his archenemy the bishop of Traù (Trogir, Croatia in the province of Split), Marzio Andreucci, and future inquisitor of Venice, was ordered to investigate whether De Dominis had authored the heretical propositions contained in a letter he wrote to the clergy of his diocese.[193] At least in this instance, we have some idea of the in-letter's content. Often we do not, as in the next one in De Dominis's case. On 10 April, after a letter from Andreucci himself, the nuncio in Venice, Gessi, was ordered to persuade De Dominis to come to Rome, the same basic initial approach used on other Venetian theologians.[194] After another letter from Arrigoni, on 26 June Gessi was to investigate in "secret and extrajudicial" fashion (*secreto et extraiudicali*) and see whether there was any hope that De Dominis would resign.[195] Gessi had already reported in April both De Dominis's wish so to do and his refusal to come to Rome, for lack of money. There may have been some miscommunication between nuncio and Congregation, or perhaps Gessi reported the proposed resignation only to the secretary of state and not the Holy Office.[196] The next week, acting on another denunciation by Andreucci, the Congregation ordered Gessi to examine a witness from Split, now a curate in the diocese of Padua, and—unusually—forward a copy of his deposition to Rome.[197] De Dominis certainly worried the Congregation. Just two days later it fired off another order via Gessi to Arrigoni to see if he could secretly and "without scandal" sum up the information against De Dominis.[198] Gessi, who was nothing if not efficient, sent the requested deposition on 17 July.[199] Probably the same letter was read again about a month later, when Pope Paul ordered 1) a delay until Arrigoni's report arrived with its *summarium* (in a non-technical sense) and 2) the Congregation to deliberate whether to proceed.[200] Arrigoni delivered his evidence in a letter of 8 September that was not read until 15 October, perhaps because it offered no more than propositions which "it is said he [De Dominis] spread" and the names of witnesses who knew about them.[201] And there for the moment the matter rested. On 27 November Paul ordered a supersedeat, the removal of a case to a higher jurisdiction, because De Dominis was finally resigning.[202]

Flight to England

By this time De Dominis had opened negotiations to flee to England.[203] Already in January 1616, long before he left on 20 September, the Inquisition had again interested itself in him. Acting on a letter from the inquisitor of Padua of 30 December 1615, on 14 January the Congregation ordered the examination in Rome of Pietro Gaudenzio, canon of Split; the inquisitor was to summarize the information he had.[204] Andreucci seems once again to have been the motive force; at least he sent in another denunciation of De Dominis and the archpriest of Split, on the strength of which Gaudenzio was to be examined again.[205] A month later on 17 March probably this deposition, perhaps of 20 February, was read along with other evidence in the Holy Office, and Paul ordered Gessi and the inquisitor in Venice to be asked how best to proceed in examining one Pietro Zindro or Zinder and the archpriest while meanwhile observing De Dominis.[206] The two wrote back almost immediately, saying Gaudenzio should try to persuade Zinder and the archpriest to testify either in Rome or to Gessi or Arrigoni, following a tactic often used earlier on the interdict theologians.[207] On 3 June De Dominis's letter to his clergy, sent by the inquisitor of Padua, was added to his *processo*.[208] Twelve days later, acting on an anonymous delation and thereby contravening the Inquisition's rules, Gessi was ordered once more to examine "Slenda" (perhaps Zinder) and the inquisitor of Venice, both to report on De Dominis's books and also continue to keep an eye on him.[209]

The inquisitor failed in the second task. At least, he seems never to have reported De Dominis's departure to England on 20 September, leaving that job to Gessi, who passed the news to Rome only on 5 November.[210] His letter triggered a flurry of activity, Assessor Mario Filonardi adding it to the top of his agenda for the coram five days later.[211] The situation did not at all please the pope, especially not the failure of the Venetian Inquisition to prevent De Dominis's escape.[212] Rome's entire apparatus was moving with extraordinary dispatch: the first action the Congregation took was to hear a reading of De Dominis's ten-sheet pamphlet explaining why he fled. As *Consilium profectionis* it had first appeared at Venice on 20 September and then been republished at Heidelberg.[213] It and his yet unpublished *De republica ecclesiastica* were to be prohibited and all copies of the first collected, if need be at papal expense (an extraordinary concession), but without mentioning this clause, no doubt in order to avoid driving up the price; all nuncios were to be alerted to his flight; Cardinal Ludovico Madruzzo, prince-bishop of Trent and an Inquisitor, was to see that no copies were brought into Italy; and Gessi and Vignuzzio were to guard their copies carefully. Finally, the Spanish ambassador in London was to be notified of both De Dominis's flight and his books.[214]

More Trouble over Split

On 12 November the Index, under Cardinal Paolo Emilio Sfondrato's presidency, duly prohibited *De republica*, whether published or yet to be.[215] Cardinal Millini passed on at least part of this order to Venice, where Gessi and Vignuzzio opened a case on 17 November by taking a deposition from De Dominis's relative Sforza Ponzone, who had replaced him as archbishop, and his brother Matteo, who had accompanied De Dominis as far as Chur.[216] Among the complaints justifying this action was De Dominis's *Consilium* or *Manifesto*.[217] The same day, on the strength of their letter of 12 November, Gessi and Vignuzzio were encouraged to keep up the good work, Filonardi once more adding this item to the top of his agenda.[218] On 18 November Gessi and the inquisitor searched Giovanni Bartoli's house in Venice, where they found a number of De Dominis's books, including a catechism in Serbo-Croatian and many banned volumes.[219] The following day they took a deposition from another of De Dominis's nephews, Melchior (to whom De Dominis had also sent a copy of his manifesto from Heidelberg), and then from the Tuscan lawyer Bartoli, who practiced in the ducal palace in Venice and De Dominis's in-law, and yet another to receive his manifesto which Bartoli had turned over to Gessi, plus three other unbound copies that he had given to the designated recipients.[220]

In the next week's coram Paul issued more orders, including one to the inquisitor of Bergamo to be on the lookout for the books and to warn nuncios lest De Dominis change his name on them, and also acted on an apparently lengthy report from Gessi and Vignuzzio of 19 November. They had forwarded a letter from Arrigoni of 10 October in which the bishop seems to have enclosed more writings about De Dominis; if Gessi got other such from the archbishop of Rab (De Dominis's birthplace) or his vicar, these too were to be sent to Rome.[221] (Gessi did indeed receive a letter from the archbishop, but it contained the innocuous news that there was a portrait of De Dominis in a nearby monastery. Nevertheless, he was ordered to hide it.[222]) Meantime, they were to continue investigating, especially via Bartoli.[223] This they did by taking another deposition on 24 November from Matteo Alberti, who gave an enormously detailed account of jurisdictional disputes in Split at the beginning of De Dominis's archiepiscopate, a heretical sermon by him, and other complaints (finally admitting that his brother had been a candidate for archbishop whom De Dominis had then dispossessed) and cited Archpriest De Fransiscis, Pietro Gaudenzio, the archdeacon of Split, Girolamo Allegreti, Canon Marino of Split, and a priest from there serving in Padua diocese.[224] Allegreti was heard on 26 November.[225] That same day Gessi and the inquisitor sent Rome De Dominis's letter to the doge from Chur on 8 October and a censure on the breviary he had begun to revise. On 1 December Paul thereupon allowed proceedings in contumacy and further deliberations.[226] An announcment that the process had been formed should have preceded this action; Paul later implicitly admitted his error when properly citing De Dominis to appear (see below). The next deponent in Venice, on the 29th, candidly admitted to being De Dominis's enemy, but was allowed to testify anyway.[227] Similarly, another witness heard on 3 December testified to Alberti's hostility to De Dominis; the investigation was beginning to lose headway, as the second witness that day said he had heard De Dominis preach but remembered nothing about his sermons.[228] Much the same happened in Rome, as the best Paul could do on 15 December was order a watch kept on the diocese of Split to see whether it was Catholic.[229] A week later he had more circumstantial evidence from Venice that De Dominis had gone to s'Gravenhage in the garb of a secular priest, an item Filonardi again added at the head of his agenda.[230]

Proposed Attacks on De republica

By January 1617 De Dominis's apostasy had given rise to proposals to refute his still unpublished *De republica*. The nuncio in Brussels had demanded the right to license replies to the *Manifesto* in December 1616 and was told that Millini would answer on behalf of the pope.[231] We do not know what he said, but the nuncio in Cologne was to tell those wishing to respond to *De republica* to await its appearance; in the meantime they could send their criticisms to Rome.[232] The coram of 19 January heard De Dominis's letter to Bartoli from s'Gravenhage on 23 November, forwarded by Gessi. It announced that "he had been received with great applause by the heretics" ("cum magna applausa receptus fuit ab hereticis"), and again merited first place on Filonardi's agenda.[233] On 1 February the inquisitor of Padua was ordered to allow "Slenda" to read De Dominis's *manifestum* and letters before his flight, for what reason not said. This may mean the investigation in Venice was still in being, even though there are no more documents from it extant.[234] By this time plans to reply to De Dominis had reached a fever pitch. The pope always responded saying to wait until *De republica* came out. This was the answer sent to the German convert Kaspar Schoppe, friend of Tommaso Campanella and indefatigable propagandist, and to the Capuchin Giacinto da Casale, apparently in Faenza, where he was already preaching against De Dominis.[235] Bellarmino and Scaglia undertook a detailed censure of *De republica*, an action which had been meant to lead to an official reply.[236]

De Dominis's First Citation to Rome

Although the intensity of interest in De Dominis diminished for a time, Rome did not cease to observe him by proxy. On 16 March the Congregation heard a letter of 18 February from the nuncio (of Cologne, confirmed from Filonardi's agenda), reporting that De Dominis was not entirely happy in England, and Paul ordered a *monitorium* (damage to the text makes it hard to say precisely why; it turns out to be the first citation to appear—see below). In the same session the Index was ordered to prohibit De Dominis's book, sent by the nuncio in Flanders. It was also to be translated into Italian, the language in which the Inquisition did a surprising amount of business, and censured. [237] The prohibition by the Index of this unidentified book and others in English was to be discussed again on 30 March, according to Filonardi's agenda, but the decree register instead notes Gessi's report on De Dominis's manner of life and his question whether he should send a copy to the nuncio in Flanders. Paul thought it would be better to work up a catalogue of De Dominis's vices, apparently for publication.[238] On 6 April two copies of De Dominis's book were ordered burnt, one noted in the decree register, the other scribbled into Filonardi's agenda "before [the pope's] entry."[239] Similarly, on 13 April Filonardi's agenda contained a long report on De Dominis's treatment in England which appears only in summary in the decree register.[240] On the 20th the form of the *monitorium* ordered a little more than a month earlier was read, and Paul ordered it published in manuscript.[241] The citation gave De Dominis a term of six months to appear.[242] While Rome moved ahead, so did Vignuzzio, at the same time as he continued to gather in De Dominis's "apologia" (the *Manifesto*) in Italian.[243] It was unusual, but not unheard of, for cases to proceed in two of the Inquisition's tribunals at once. Proposed replies to De Dominis continued to pour in, including one by the archdeacon of Cambrai, assigned on 26 May 1617 to Inquisitor Felice Centini for censure.[244] Shortly thereafter Paul ordered all such sent to Rome.[245] In June Arrigoni's proposed mission to Split, perhaps intended to execute the pope's order to see whether the diocese was Catholic, had to be abandoned after it became known.[246] Elsewhere the news was better, including that from the nuncio in Cologne, who thought in a letter of 2 July, read on the 20th, that it would be "easy" to bring De Dominis back to Catholic territory if the pope and the king of Spain agreed not to punish him.[247] Efforts to control the printing of replies to De Dominis met with only indifferent success, as illustrated by the book written by the archpriest of Antwerp, Laurens Beyerlinck, that had to be taken away from the inquisitor of Verona.[248]

Despite the Inquisition's best efforts, its meeting of 3 November 1617 learned that the nuncio in Flanders reported the appearance of *De republica christiana*; Gessi and Vignuzzio were to be notified.[249] In the coram a week later, Millini reported that the Jesuit general had gotten "Andreae Graeci" to reply, his book to be reviewed before printing.[250] This was the Cypriot [Andreas] Eudaemon-Johannes, Bellarmino's collaborator.[251] At the same time, Paul ordered Cardinal Madruzzo thanked for his assurance that he was trying hard to keep the book out of Italy.[252]

More Citations

On 6 December De Dominis's first *processo* moved into a crucial phase with a fresh set of citations to appear, the previous one apparently being forgotten. "Next" (*successive*), Fiscal Carlo Sincero declared De Dominis contumacious and ordered him cited again "by monitorial and citational letters" ("literis monitorialibus et citationalibus").[253] Six days later the papal cursitor duly reported the second citation, Sincero again asking a declaration of contumacy before ordering the third citation.[254] Although the Inquisition's short break for Christmas did not materially affect De Dominis's trial, one of Sincero's periodic bouts of ill health did cause delay while Camillo Giudici, the long-serving *summista*, took over for him as special deputy.[255] Not until 17 January 1618, the same day "the Sorbonne's" censure on *De republica* was read, that is, the work of the faculty of theology of the University of Paris, was the third citation formally noted.[256] Giudici again asked for a declaration of contumacy, and then a highly unusual fourth citation was ordered.[257] Perhaps someone realized the mistake, because two days later Giudici requested and got a citation to hear sentence for contumacy.[258] A separate citation to hear definitive sentence followed on 14 March. Sincero had a signed copy from the pope that the cursitor read to the assembly before publishing it. The next day Pope Paul pronounced sentence.[259] On 4 July 1619, after one of those normal but nonetheless inexplicable delays in which the Holy Office specialized, when considering whether to execute the sentence and "his [De Dominis's] effigy relaxed to the secular court" ("relaxanda [esse] eius statua curie seculari"), the pope ordered "let the usual serve" ("servit solitum") followed by an illegible word, possibly "stylum," but nothing further happened, as far as the registers say.[260]

More Refutations

At the same time as De Dominis's final citation, Centini wrote from his diocese of Macerata that the theologians of the University of Padua—so noted in the decree register without saying which of the several bodies which might have been called that was meant—had joined the crowd clamoring to refute De Dominis's *De republica*, and had already published a rebuttal to his *Consilium profectionis*.[261] One of those theologians, Cremonini's antagonist Filippo Fabbri, had drafted "De primatu pontificis romani" against De Dominis.[262] Its censure went to Bellarmino, whom Paul ordered on 26 April 1618 to tell Fabbri the "shape" his book would take and report before it was published; meantime Fabbri's request for a license to read heretical books was put on hold.[263] More than two years later Fabbri's proposed reply was rejected, although the inquisitor of Padua was told to try to keep him happy.[264] Fabbri could persist with the best of them, and in August his request to send the *capitula* of his reply *Anglis* (whether to England or perhaps to the English Jesuits organizing various attacks from the Low Countries is unclear) was denied.[265] In mid-1621 the Congregation bent a little and assigned censure of his book to the new Cardinal Scipione Cobelluzzi, formerly librarian of the Vatican Library.[266] In August Fabbri won an order to Vignuzzio not to impede printing of his book.[267] In the interval between De Dominis's death and his sentence, Scaglia reviewed another request for a license to print.[268] Four years later Fabbri was still seeking permission to publish against De Dominis, and the inquisitor of Venice was once more ordered to license the book, as his predecessor had also been.[269]

Fabbri's fellow Paduans were nothing if not eager, and had to be told again on 26 April 1618 to be patient until the censures by the universities of

Paris and Louvain had been approved.[270] On 25 May the inquisitor of Padua forwarded the censures anyway, and Paul ordered them considered. At the same time Schoppe's apparently much cruder sketch of De Dominis's work as nothing but lies was flatly rejected.[271] In June the review of the theologians' work was delegated to the inquisitor of Padua, who was to tell them via third-party theologians the "shape" of their publication and find out secretly whether they would agree, and if he found something unacceptable, to fix it before publication.[272] On 3 August the inquisitor, acting with the bishop of Padua, sent the theologians' censures, which were assigned to Bellarmino and Scaglia for review.[273] On 5 September, after the inquisitor sent another censure or set of censures, permission was granted to publish both.[274] The Venetian authorities did not agree as quickly. On 14 September the inquisitor of Padua reported that the *riformatori* of the university, who had control over publication in the Venetian republic, had dismissed a deputation of theologians sent to get their imprimatur, saying the matter needed deep consideration.[275] Bellarmino remained in loose charge of such censures, including those from Louvain, assigned to him on 18 September 1619 (they had arrived on 31 August), as well as another batch in November, and Scaglia eventually joined him, both of them objecting sufficiently for Paul to threaten a supersedeat if the nuncio in Cologne could not persuade the theologians to accept the revisions.[276] Both were ordered on 4 November 1620 to respond to the reply from Louvain.[277] Millini sent orders, probably based on these censures, to Jan Janssens, the author of Louvain's refutation.[278] Scaglia, the number two reviewer, also went over some replies by himself, including the work of the former Servite prior general Lelio Baglioni.[279] Fra Zaccharia da Saluzzo complained from Milan in 1620 that its inquisitor was not allowing him to publish his "Censura Parenetica ad libros Marci Antonii De dominis," and the Congregation ordered it sent to Rome.[280] Others were recruited to reply, including Domenico da Gravina, O.P. (1573–1643), who was licensed to read *De republica* to that end.[281] He eventually produced *Pro Sacro deposito fidei catholico et apostolico . . . apologeticus. Adversus novatorum calumnias, et praesertim noviss. M. Antonii de Dominis* (1629), published by the same man who had been hotly pursued by the Inquisition for publishing Paolo Antonio Foscarini's Copernican *Lettera* in 1615, Lorenzo Scorrigio.[282]

The effort to gather in De Dominis's works scored a signal success when the nuncio in Cologne reported on 1 June that he had managed to collect at the Frankfurt book fair all copies of a sermon De Dominis had preached in England.[283] A little later, at the nuncio's request, thanks were ordered via

Cardinal Nephew Borghese to the University of Cologne for its censures, and to its archbishop and Graf Zollern.[284] On 13 September 1618 Paul ordered the inquisitor of Padua to send *Sorex primus Oras Chartarum primi libri De Republica Ecclesiastica* [. . . *Archiepiscopi Spalatensis corrodens Leonardus Marius Theologaster Coloniensis*], which the Congregation thought might be by De Dominis, and the inquisitor of Venice was ordered to watch for other copies.[285] The same kind of scrupulous vigilance was maintained for several years, if at more sporadic intervals.[286] When Sarpi's *Istoria del Concilio di Trento* appeared in London, thought to be De Dominis's work, it too was carefully sought.[287]

The Banning of De republica

Then, just as abruptly, as De Dominis's first *processo* failed to end, at least so far as the decree registers say, on 30 April 1620 *De republica* was ordered sent to the Index for prohibition.[288] This action was taken despite the fact that the Index had already proleptically banned the book in late 1616 and had for some time been enforcing that prohibition. De Dominis definitely had the Congregation's undivided attention. The next entry in the decree register ordered Scaglia to check over the anonymously published *Hypochrisis Marci Antonii De Dominis*, that the Inquisition thought the English Jesuit Joseph Creswell had written.[289] This seems to be a case of one Roman hand not knowing what another was doing; Creswell had sent his manuscript to Cardinal Borghese on 31 May 1619. He in turn had asked Paul to allow its publication, and the pope agreed.[290] Someone forgot to tell the Inquisition, even though Paul may well have used it to issue the license in the first place.[291] On 11 June Scaglia's *observatione* was ordered used to correct the book before it was reprinted, and a copy was to be collected.[292] There is no sign that this ever happened, although Creswell was ordered on 6 August to send "the leaves of the index that are to be printed next" ("folia quae successive indici imprimentur").[293]

The Return to Rome

There had been rumors that De Dominis was unhappy in England almost from the first, but in 1621 the Spanish ambassador undertook serious efforts to recuperate him.[294] On 12 January 1622 a draft breve in his favor was read and the ambassador was ordered notified about it, but it was not to be sent until after De Dominis's absolution.[295] By 6 May he had left England, in company with an apostate Benedictine, and reached Brussels, whence he wrote on 14 May.[296] The nuncio, Giovanni-Francesco Guidi di Bagno, later an Inquisitor, reported to Millini De Dominis's arrival on the previous day and promised that he would abjure the following week.[297] Acting on orders from the pope transmitted by Millini, allegedly on 25 December 1621, on 17 May the nuncio subjected De Dominis to a judicial interrogation after which he abjured a number of heresies before being absolved. Millini's letter gave the nuncio carte blanche to decide whether De Dominis had actually confessed any heresies and nothing was said about their degree either in the letter or in the record of his abjuration and absolution.[298] Perhaps while De Dominis was still in Flanders, Guidi di Bagno reported the printing of the last four books of *De republica*.[299] He alerted Millini to De Dominis's departure on 24 August.[300] In the coram of 3 November the Congregation heard that he had arrived in Rome. De Dominis was ordered to appear before it and be "diligently judicially" examined "for further truth" ("pro ulteriori veritate") and about his intention, absolved from censures by Commissary Ippolito Lanci, and assigned penance.[301] A week later his examination by the most senior Inquisitor, Ottavio Bandini, and other officials was reported, along with his abjuration *de formali* and his sentence for contumacy in 1618. Pope Gregory XV ordered full rehabilitation. Once the Inquisition had considered how to do that, a breve was to be drawn up.[302]

This second phase of De Dominis's trial continued to move quickly, the pope remaining in charge. The minute of the breve of absolution was approved a week later, when the summary of his *processo* for contumacy was read. "Literae monitoriales," this time apparently meaning the breve, were to be issued within six months and were to include many penalty clauses, including those of a *relapsus*. De Dominis was to appear before the Congregation, to respond "de fide," and to be cleared of heresy and other crimes "as in the acts" ("prout in actis," his now missing dossier), which he had incurred by failing to appear within the term set by Paul V. At his humble if staged request, he was then to be rehabilitated fully.[303] Putting somebody else's money where its mouth was, the Inquisition ordered the Venetian inquisitor to see whether he could get De Dominis's pension on his former archbishopric restored, and the inquisitor succeeded.[304] In return, De Dominis wrote *Sui reditus ex Anglia consilium*, dated 24 November 1622 and printed by the Apostolic Chamber; it was republished numerous times and translated into English and other languages.[305] He drafted at least five versions.[306] Six weeks later (not six months as the pope had feared), on 8 January 1623, the breve docketed as "for Marco Antonio once archbishop of Split, pardon [*condonatio*] of all and whatever sentences and punishments incurred by him after his flight to England, with [his] dignities (?) and honors" ("Pro Marco Antonio Archiepiscopo olim Spalaten., Condonatio sententiarum, et poenarum quarumcumque per eum incursarum post fugam in Angliam, cum dignitatibus [?] ac honoribus") was issued.[307] It incorporated the official copy of the Holy Office's decree of 17 November, signed by Andrea Pettini, its notary, and still bears the Inquisition's damaged seal.[308] On 2 March 1623 De Dominis received the bonus of an apparently unrestricted license to read heretical books, part of the usual mass batch of such things at Easter time.[309] De Dominis remained in the Inquisition's good graces in January 1624, when it ordered an investigation of Jesuit attacks on him.[310] These marks of favor did not mean the Inquisition had become less interested in *De republica*; the nuncio in Cologne was twice ordered to send a copy of book 3.[311]

Condemnation

On 17 April the roof fell in.[312] De Dominis was arrested and imprisoned in Rome. On the 25th, acting on a denunciation to Secretary Millini (of unknown content, but see the narration in his sentence below) and a search of De Dominis's house—not previously ordered in the decree register—the new pope, Urban VIII, "deputed in commission of this case with the assistance then offered by officials the cardinal of Cremona [Scaglia], and gave him all authority and power necessary and opportune of creating a notary at his pleasure and examining witnesses, and taking depositions from the said archbishop's other accomplices, and in this case or cases which depend, emerge from, are annexed and connected to [it], both against the same archbishop and against anyone else whatsoever, of forming process and informations all the way to definitive sentence."[313] All four narrative accounts of De Dominis's last trial correctly put Scaglia in charge.[314] Between Scaglia's commission and the reading of De Dominis's interrogations on 6 June the decree register is almost silent about his case.[315] It notes the order on 2 May for the extradition from Spain (after the reading of an interrogation done there) of one of De Dominis's most important servants.[316] The only other entry is an order to Eliseo Masini, inquisitor in Genoa, to examine one Marco

Garzoni, S.J., on the strength of two letters from a Capuchin to Fra Zaccaria da Saluzzo.[317] Sarpi's close collaborator Fulgenzio Micanzio reported that De Dominis underwent fifteen examinations.[318] At the time his testimony was first reviewed, nuncios were also ordered to be informed about the the matter's gravity. In the next coram a week later, on a second reading, De Dominis's evidence against Micanzio was ordered sent to the nuncio and inquisitor in Venice, who were to learn secretly and extrajudicially what the Senate thought of him.[319] Again moving steadily forward, a week later, after Urban solicitiously ordered the payment of De Dominis's pension, more ominously he demanded the "qualification" of his interrogations "and the content of his 'book' [really a letter] to Joseph Hall and advisory opinion about the marriage between Prince Vincenzo and Lady Isabella Gonzaga."[320] The discovery of the opinion was noted in the "Relazione," not as itself a cause of trouble but because "in it were contained many heretical propositions" ("in qua complures propositiones haereticae continebantur") which the "Relazione" hurried on to list, none of them at first having to do with De Dominis's views about marriage. When the document came up later it did mention as heretical or erroneous his idea that a marriage could be dissolved for various reasons, but again, the real target was his criticism of Trent, against Pietro Redondi's interpretation that this opinion served only as a pretext for De Dominis's trial.[321] The next week De Dominis's pension may have been back on the agenda (the entry is almost illegible).[322] In the last coram of June, on the 27th, Urban renewed his order for qualification this time specifically by Scaglia, his judgment then to go to the theologian qualifiers.[323] It was bad enough that De Dominis had associated with English heretics in an increasingly dangerous political situation, but, when Urban learned of a letter De Dominis had sent to the king of Spain via one Vittorio Pianigrani, he ordered both De Dominis's interrogation and the inquisidador mayor of Spain to capture Pianigrani.[324] Three weeks later, with Scaglia still in charge, Pianigrani was ordered to Rome.[325] Continuing its usual solicitude for the economic affairs of a prisoner, the Congregation ordered the treasurer of the Apostolic Chamber to pay the costs of printing De Dominis's "De fluxu et refluxu Maris."[326] (The book had been approved for printing by none other than Galileo's target in *Il saggiatore*, Orazio Grassi, as he told Galileo's friend Mario Guiducci, mentioning Galileo's draft book of the same title.)[327] On 22 August De Dominis's last, undated, examination was read, "in which he acknowledged [his] heretical assertions . . . and is also ready to detest them." The *censura* on his opinion about the Gonzaga annulment was to go to the nuncio in Florence, who was to deal directly with the duke, then in residence there, and get the original.[328]

In September 1624 the trial moved to the stage of forming process, but not until Urban issued a questionable order to De Dominis's confessor to talk to Lanci after consultation with Scaglia. We do not know the subject of this discussion, but in this context it could have come perilously close to breaching the seal of the confessional, even if the intention was to use the confessor to induce De Dominis further to incriminate himself or simply to admit his guilt.[329] And then on 9 September De Dominis died of a fever. Given the suspicions his death immediately raised, his corpse was carefully autopsied by several prominent physicians, including the pope's own private doctor, Giulio Mancini and the Lincean Johnnes Faber.[330]

Scaglia's discovery underpinned the decision to move against De Dominis's memory. His corpse was therefore carefully preserved, and four relatives were summoned to stand in as his defenders. All refused.[331] As a result, on either 8 or 9 October two advocates were appointed for him, Bonaventura Passero of Nola, a Conventual Franciscan and regent of the Collegio Bonaventura in Rome, and Teodosio Rossi of Priverno (province of Latina), who held degrees in both theology and law and was an advocate in Rome, as he was described in the decree.[332] Rossi (ca. 1565–after 1637) was indeed an advocate, practicing before the Roman Rota and publishing two large collections of its decrees.[333] He was also a student of Christopher Clavius at the Collegio Romano, and a mathematician and astronomer who designed the sundial, executed by Francesco Borromini, that still stands in the Quirinal garden.[334] Even if his role was purely pro forma, he had excellent qualifications to play it. Passero, although lacking either legal or scientific credentials, published at least two books and approved two other important publications as regent of his Collegio.[335] A month later, on 7 November, the day after De Dominis's former servant extradited from Spain was suspiciously released on bond, after the usual formula "the case proposed, the summary reported, and opinions [of the consultors] heard" ("proposita causa, relato summario processus, et auditis votis"), Urban ordered De Dominis declared a relapsed heretic.[336] Two weeks later, someone raised the question whether De Dominis's body should be burned as a *relapsus* or conceded ecclesiastical burial, but Urban would have none of the second option. He ordered it, his effigy, and his books turned over to the secular court "in order to be burned."[337] On 18 December a layman from Milan who had celebrated Mass, as well as De Dominis's proctors, were summoned to hear sentence as in the *schedulis* with the cardinals' autograph signatures. Then "word was passed" to the Swiss Guard to draw weapons from the armory in preparation for the sentence's execution at Santa Maria sopra Minerva on the 21st.[338] The sentence, which survives in two copies in the Inquisition's archive, was signed by all nine Inquisitors, beginning with Bandini, the most senior, through to Francesco Barberini, the newest.[339]

Interestingly enough, the recital of the facts of the case began with De Dominis's departure for England, not with the opening of the Inquisition's dossier in 1614. The first tangible act of heresy noted was the publication of *Consilium profectionis*, followed closely by *De republica ecclesiastica*. Formal proceedings were regarded as having commenced with his citation to Rome on 20 April 1617. Instead, "taking no care to appear," De Dominis continued spitting out "pestilential" books in various languages, sometimes under false names (a reference to the *Istoria del concilio di Trento*, even though the Inquisition knew by now its true authorship, thanks to De Dominis). Paul V had then pronounced sentence, on a date not given. In 1622 De Dominis had judicially abjured a long list of heresies. Nevertheless, he went back to his bad habits and in 1624 had been denounced for 1) questioning indulgences in conversation with a "heretical prince" (James I?), which led to statements about councils defining too many articles of faith; 2) faulting Trent in particular on that score; and 3) saying all heretics could come back to the church if it would relax its rigor, particularly about transubstantiation.[340] After imprisonment and judicial examinations De Dominis was judged guilty of a much longer string of propositions, beginning with his proposals for Christian reunion and extending to ideas about marriage. All this made manifest that he had falsely abjured, and he was therefore interrogated "diligently" about his action, before being assigned a term for defense and given a copy of his dossier.[341] While preparing a defense with his proctor, De Dominis died. As he was a *relapsus*, however, his *processo* did not end, and the cardinals stood ready to expedite it. The sentence itself was brief: De Dominis was a relapsed heretic and would receive all the appropriate punishments. The only oddities were those arising from the fact that these would be executed on a memory and a corpse. As usual, the final clause reserved to the Inquisitors the right to change or improve the sentence as they saw fit. There followed first Pettini's note that the sentence had been issued in Bandini's palace on 18 December in the presence of Giudici and future assessor Alessandro Vittrici, still a consultor, and then another of its execution on Saturday 21 December, with Francesco Maddaleni Capiferreo as one of the two witnesses, although he was not identified as secretary of the Index.[342] As these exceptionally high-powered observers indicate, to the last, De Dominis got special treatment.

The burning of books and body was not quite the end. Only two days later the inquisidador mayor reported from Spain that "Acta concilii tridentini cum dedicatoria," still thought to be De Dominis's work, had been found in the Venetian ambassador's baggage.[343] More seriously, Urban ordered on 2 January 1625 that nuncios in France and Spain were to read the sentence to two or three principal men, for example cardinals, and the main heads of it were to be communicated to others, but under no circumstances was anyone to be given a copy, and the nuncios were to return theirs within a fortnight.[344] Evidently other nuncios (perhaps all?) also received the sentence; the papal diplomat in Venice acknowledged his on 29 April 1625.[345] Even as late as December 1625 the Inquisition was still after De Dominis's baggage.[346]

Conclusion

One obvious conclusion arises. When the Venetians wished to protect a subject from the Roman Inquisition, they succeeded, whether that subject was a political figure like Sarpi or a philosopher like Cremonini. Subjects who either rejected Venetian protection or managed to make themselves *personae non gratae* with the Serenissima might well find themselves executed for heresy, either in person or in effigy, as befell Fulgenzio Manfredi, Bruno, and De Dominis. So little did the Venetians care about De Dominis, a troublemaker from the provinces, that there is no sign of the lay assistants raising any objections to Gessi taking testimony in Venice against him. Even more, Bruno underwent most of his trial in Venice before being extradited quite easily to Rome. By contrast, the Venetians never agreed to the extradition of any of the theologians the Inquisition sought in the wake of the interdict, including Manfredi. Indeed, when one of them, Giovanni Ribetti, fled to Rome, the Venetians tried to stop him. In all other cases, Rome instead had to resort to subterfuge, including assassination plots. Although none of those ever succeeded, more subtle blandishments did work on most of those theologians, who slowly made their way to Rome for absolution. These successes were largely a function of the changed political climate in Venice, as pro-papal factions came to power once the hostilities over the interdict gradually faded. At the center of all Roman activity in Venice, including the Inquisition's, stood the nuncio. For more than ten years after the interdict he was Berlinghiero Gessi, who accomplished much in a politically difficult role. His constant negotiations with Venetian power structures, the Senate, the Collegio, and the lay assistants in the Venetian Inquistion, not to mention the similarly long-serving inquisitor of Venice Vignuzzio, make manifest the degree to which the Inquisition operated as a political institution, as well as the powerful constraints on how much success it could enjoy when faced with the resolute opposition of a state like Venice.

While Cremonini largely escaped the Inquisition, its reach finally ensnared even him, as it forced the suppression of "De anima," after it managed to purloin his papers following his death, even though the doge had forbidden anyone from breathing a word of their contents. This instance highlights several major conclusions about the Inquisition and censorship. First, it repeatedly engaged in pre-publication censorship of Cremonini's work, usually without success, again because the Venetians refused to bend. His case and De Dominis's both support another conclusion about censorship, the sheer scale of the Inquisition's interest in the press. It devoted enormous resources, both its own and those borrowed from the papal diplomatic apparatus, to reining in publications it deemed heretical. Sometimes it enjoyed unreserved success, as in the case of Cherubino da Udine discussed in the last chapter, who saw a book printed in at least 744 copies disappear without a trace before publication. Cherubino had especially bad luck. More often, the Inquisition achieved more limited success, or sometimes none, as in the case of De Dominis's writings, all of them published outside areas of direct Roman control. The same holds true of the numerous refutations of De Dominis, which the Inquisition nevertheless tried to orchestrate minutely. The points it found most objectionable in both De Dominis and his attackers concerned papal power. As that topic indicates, at its heart, the Roman Inquisition always remained a political institution, exactly like the papacy that spawned it and tried to use it as its most effective means of projecting power.

These three cases highlight the role of politics in the Inquisition's operations in another way. Their outcomes turned on Venetian calculation of advantage. Interestingly enough, questions of allegiance did not enter in. It made no difference to the result of his trial that De Dominis was a Venetian subject, the only one of the three to have that status. It may have mattered a little to the Venetians' half-hearted defense of Bruno that he was not, but neither was Cremonini, whom they protected to the uttermost. The fact that Bruno had no official post in Venetian territory probably mattered more. Cremonini, unlike Bruno, deserved protection as a professor at their flagship university of

Padua and as a philosopher with a European reputation as a "libertine," both demonstrating the Venetians' vaunted liberty of thought. It was De Dominis's bad luck to get into trouble long after the interdict crisis had blown over and anti-papal political ideas no longer had much utility. Like Bruno, De Dominis had also long since become a major irritant, with ideas that not even the Venetians were prepared to foster. Both could safely be sacrificed in order to gain the Venetians a little political currency in Rome.

CHAPTER 5

Florence I

Unlike many of their peers, the grand dukes fairly quickly accepted the new Roman Inquisition, as indicated by the execution in Rome in 1567 of Pietro Carnesecchi, a scion of the Florentine establishment. Carnesecchi would have done well to stay in Venice (as many friends advised him to do); the Venetians, even after they reluctantly allowed the Inquisition to operate in their territory, almost always succeeded in keeping it under their control, especially when it came to extraditions, the most notorious exception perhaps being the case of Giordano Bruno. Still, if the matter were politically important, the grand dukes could put up impressive resistance to the Inquisition. They always tried at least to influence the appointment of the inquisitor of Florence, if not more actively to circumscribe his and his masters' activity.[1] The loss of most of the Florentine Inquisition's archive makes it harder to discuss it than in the case of Venice or Naples, but a fair amount can be said about its inquisitors. The chance survival of part of one enormous *processo*, as well as pieces of others, allows us to get some idea of how the tribunal operated and related to the Congregation.[2]

Although there were inquisitors in Siena and Pisa, the tribunal in Florence took precedence already at the time of Cosimo I.[3] Against the norm, its inquisitors were Conventual Franciscans instead of the more usual Dominicans.[4] The first inquisitor of Florence in our period, Dionigi Sammattei da Costacciaro, also held office for by far the longest time, more than twenty-three years, before his death on 7 July 1603. He first appears in June 1566 as theologian of Michele Della Torre, bishop of Ceneda and future cardinal.[5] He was allegedly a famous preacher, but none of his sermons survive. Within his order he served as provincial of Umbria (1574) and helped to lead its 1577 general chapter. Immediately thereafter he became inquisitor of Siena, before moving to Florence in late 1578 or early 1579.[6] Sixtus V nominated him (along with Lelio Medici; see below) as general of the Conventuals in 1590.[7] He is best known for his exoneration of Monna Gostanza at San Miniato in 1600 in a witchcraft case.[8] A severe rebuke about his handling of another case the year before, which the Congregation dismissed, may have taught him a lesson.[9] His vicar during much of his tenure was his relative Matteo Sammattei, who was ordered to inventory his property after his death.[10]

Costacciaro's successor was one of the most distinguished men to hold the post of inquisitor, Lelio Medici (or Medici Bitturica) da Piacenza. Nevertheless, his tenure did not enjoy success. The Congregation never held its hand about criticizing inquisitors in Florence, but they kept an especially tight rein on Medici. By the early 1570s, when he was already pursuing a distinguished career as a teacher (bachelor of Bologna 1569, regent of Venice 1571), Medici preached widely. He became regent of Bologna in 1578 before becoming its provincial the following year, when he also took a doctorate in theology. With Costacciaro, he was one of Sixtus V's four nominees for general of his order in 1590.[11] By then he had been inquisitor of Pisa, whence he moved to Florence on 18 September 1603.[12] His breve of appointment is dated 9 September.[13] At first he did well, being praised for his diligence in February 1604.[14] His vicar also performed well.[15] Within a couple of months, the worm turned and both were in trouble, the vicar first being denounced for having books of astrology.[16] While his case was quickly dismissed, Medici, despite his experience and stature, found himself in almost constant trouble with the Congregation from this moment forward. In an unusual move, in a case close to the grand duke's heart, that of Jacopo Isparielli, Medici was summoned to Rome, where he sat in on at least two Inquisition meetings, on the second occasion facing a list of "defects" in his handling of the case. These were referred to the pope, who a week later ordered Medici to be "sharply faulted for this sort of defects" by Secretary Camillo Borghese, the future Paul V.[17] A year later, reflecting its obsession with finances, the Congregation ordered him to send annual accounts and not to spend money except on inquisitorial business.[18] Medici may have recouped some of his standing with a strongly pro-papal pamphlet, that he belatedly contributed to the interdict crisis of 1606.[19] If so, he had lost his gains by early 1609, when, on the report of a special commissary sent out from Rome, he was ordered given a precept to observe the Holy Office's secrecy by not revealing witnesses' names. This time the case was even more important than Isparielli's and will be the subject of most of this chapter, that of Rodrigo Alidosi.[20] After a delation for favoring Alidosi, which he seems likely enough to have done, Medici was unceremoniously removed from office about a month later.[21]

The man who replaced him offers an excellent example of the tensions appointments of inquisitors and their staff could cause between Florence and the Congregation. Cornelio Priatoni, from Monza in Lombardy, lacked the stature of either of his predecessors. Nothing is known of him before 1604, when he went as an apostolic commissary to Aosta to prove the Inquisition's jurisdiction in Savoy. He found early sixteenth-century records demonstrating the point, as well as two witnesses who named an earlier inquisitor. From this evidence Priatoni drew up a *processo* dated 9 February 1604 that he gave the nuncio in Turin.[22] The following year he was elected provincial of Lombardy.[23] At some point he took a master's degree in theology, but nothing is known of a teaching career.[24] On 8 August 1607 he became inquisitor of Pisa.[25] By 7 April 1609 he had certainly moved to Florence, when he was specially deputized by Paul V to intervene in Alidosi's case.[26] An elaborate act survives of his swearing the oath of secrecy on 19 January 1612 ordered by the pope on 7 October 1611, but there is no reason to think he had violated it, unlike Medici's case.[27] Shortly thereafter he gave the imprimatur for Galileo's *Discorso sulle cose che stanno in su l'acqua* (Florence: Cosimo Giunti, 1612). Probably for political reasons, Grand Duke Cosimo II had tried to get rid of him at least by 2 November 1613, identifying him as a partisan of Inquisitor (and fellow Northerner) Ferdinando Taverna. The Tuscan ambassador called him better suited to service with the French queen.[28] Priatoni was prepared to play along, trying to resign on 31 December. The Congregation ordered him to continue in office.[29] On 29 August 1614 Cosimo proposed a replacement, Francesco da Piombino, inquisitor of Siena.[30] The ambassador, who himself was not happy about the grand duke's intervention, tried to persuade Taverna and the Spanish cardinal Inquisitor Antonio Zapata y Cisneros to put forward candidates "as if from themselves," but Taverna resisted, insisting that the usual course from Siena to Pisa and then Florence had to be followed, as well as doubting da Piombino's competence.[31] Once again Priatoni tried to resign, claiming that poor health made it impossible to do his job. The Congregation ignored him.[32] Only on 4 June 1615 did it finally give in.[33] The ambassador's sources must not have been as good as he thought, since he was still writing a week later that he hoped Lelio Marzari would get the post.[34]

Priatoni's messy end had an impact on the early stages of the investigation of Galileo. On 4 April 1615 the Congregation sent him a copy of Tommaso Caccini's deposition, taken in Rome, and ordered him to depose a key witness named therein, Ferdinando Ximenes.[35] The inquisitor reported only six weeks later, on 11 May, that he could not, since Ximenes had gone to Milan at the end of March.[36] And there things stalled until November, when Marzari finally took a hand.

Marzari had followed the path Taverna wished, serving as inquisitor in Siena and Pisa. His profile more nearly resembled Medici's than Priatoni's. After taking his M.A. in Bologna (1588), he held a chair at Cremona (1591), served as regent of Brescia, and had another chair in Milan before becoming regent of Cracow (1596), where he was also theologian to the nuncio. He remained in Poland until 1609, being elected its provincial in 1606.[37] Then, on 10 November 1609, his fellow Franciscan and Inquisitor Felice Centini was ordered to investigate his suitability as inquisitor of Siena; he was appointed 30 December.[38] He stayed there for less than two years, being deputed inquisitor of Pisa 22 September 1611.[39] On 2 November he received an appointment as reader in theology in its university, probably a courtesy post, also held by other inquisitors.[40] Soon afterward his vicar (also called chancellor) came under suspicion on unknown grounds, of which Marzari cleared him.[41] In an unusually smooth transaction, three years later Marzari was allowed to replace him with his first choice.[42] At the same time, the inquisitor became involved in the censoring of the Huguenot Hugues Doncau's legal work. After being sent the errors found in it, he replied that he could not act, and the case was referred to the Congregation of the Index. It banned the book at the same time as it suspended Copernicus's *De revolutionibus* on 3 March 1616.[43] He also received his first assignment concerning Galileo, reporting on 7 March 1615 that he was trying to find the original of his "Letter to Castelli." He failed.[44]

Once Marzari moved to Florence, the Congregation continued to keep its customary close eye on the Florentine inquisitor, ordering him in September 1615 to get evidence in writing before imprisoning an accused.[45] He also became directly involved in Galileo's trial. Marzari was finally ordered to depose Ferdinando Ximenes on 7 November and quickly did so a week later—after retrieving Caccini's deposition from the archives—at the same time as he heard the testimony of the man who probably did most to clear Galileo temporarily, Giannozzo Attavanti. He forwarded copies immediately and the Congregation read them almost on receipt.[46] And that ended Marzari's role.

A number of missteps marked the rest of his tenure as inquisitor. On 16 February 1616 the Congregation denied him a new vicar.[47] A week later it referred his request for two licenses to read prohibited books for medical professors at Pisa to the master of the sacred palace.[48] For unknown reasons he seized Savonarola's works from the Dominicans of Florence, who complained to Rome.[49] On 9 August he was ordered to rebuild his office's rooms.[50] Matters did not improve in 1617. The Congregation warned him on 7 February not to torture without consulting it "when time allows," because it had found "in some processes sent by him" that he had failed to do so. In the same meeting the Inquisitors dismissed a Florentine case and warned Marzari about defects in its dossier.[51] A few months later it brusquely rejected his nominee for inquisitor of Pisa in unusually blunt language, perhaps because he had overstepped his bounds.[52] In July he was once more in trouble over his handling of *sponte comparentes*, people who turned themselves in, and had another case dismissed because the Holy Office did not proceed against *insordescentes* (excommunicates who had not sought absolution after a year) without first citing them as such, a crucial mistake.[53] In yet a third case, he was warned not to interrogate a suspect without first collecting evidence (the first phase of the *processo informativo*).[54] The usual August lull had barely passed when Marzari was replaced on 5 September, his successor swearing his oath on 19 September.[55]

The new inquisitor, whose tenure lasted barely three years, left little trace in the decree registers and I have found nothing else about him. Fra Giovanni Paolo a San Giovanni (Giovanni Paolo Panzarasa da S. Giovanni in Persiceto) did start with a success, having his nominee for vicar accepted without demur.[56] Unlike Marzari, Panzarasa consulted the Congregation not only about when to torture but also about which to use.[57] Yet both he and his vicar were denounced for unknown reasons, and both were investigated, the inquisitor by the Franciscan general. The results came in quickly, but with what effect is not known.[58] As obscure as Fra Giovanni Paolo was, his immediate successor might almost not have existed as far as the decree registers say. Although the man next in line is at least better known, the exact dates of neither man's tenure have been found in the decree registers. First came Michele da Bologna (appointed 21 October 1621), followed after barely eighteen months by Ludovico da Montone in Umbria, whose surname was Corbuzio (Corbucci, Corbuzzi, Corbuccio, Carboccio; ca. 1585–22 July 1637).[59] Michele Masserotti or Misserotti da Bologna (ca. 1576–1630) was actually a Franciscan of consequence, more so after his tenure than before. On 2 June 1623 the pope intruded him, via the agency of Cardinal Gian Garzia Millini, vice-protector of the order but also secretary of the Inquisition, as general in the course of a hotly disputed election. Almost as quickly as Urban VIII replaced Gregory XV, he forced Masserotti out as general by making him bishop of Bitetto on 26 February 1624.[60] As inquisitor of Florence he had personnel problems. He was told almost immediately that he had too many consultors, and a year later the Congregation demanded a list of all his vicars.[61] In between he was questioned about the sale of Holy Office property and why he had failed to pursue a denunciation for solicitation in the confessional, a serious matter.[62] He did, though, take an interest in the Holy Office's record-keeping, opening a new register of out-going correspondence (a *copialettere*) shortly after his appointment.[63] Corbuzio must have taken office shortly after Masserotti became general, and we have a *terminus ante quem* for the end of his tenure, probably immediately before his appointment as a consultor of the Holy Office in Rome in 1626.[64] This unusual mark of favor probably means he had done his job better than his predecessors, a contention which the virtual absence of complaints in the decree registers may support. His standing in his order was at least as high as that of most previous inquisitors, too. He taught in Perugia, the Veneto, Naples, and Assisi, as well as serving as provincial of Hungary; after his time as inquisitor he became proctor of the Conventuals from 1631 to 1635.[65] As did several other inquisitors of Florence, he served first in Siena. As a consultor he took part in some of the interminable censures of Tommaso Campanella's works.[66] A famous preacher, he wrote many sermons as proctor, especially for Lent, but died before he could publish them.[67]

Corbuzio's appointment as consultor probably coincides exactly with the beginning of the tenure of his replacement as inquisitor. An undated letter covering Clemente Egidi's breve comes in the midst of a run of the Congregation's correspondence dated 26 December 1626.[68] He may have owed his appointment in part to his fellow Umbrian Corbuzio.[69] He was still in office in October 1635, and had left it before December 1636.[70] In 1588 he was in Rome, where he dedicated "Vita della B. Chiara di Montefalco ridotta in breve compendio" to the convent of S.ta Chiara.[71] When he was commissary of the Franciscan province of San Francesco, Urban VIII promoted him to be inquisitor of Siena, an office he still held as of August 1625.[72] He apparently died in the Franciscan house in Montefalco in 1639; according to a memorial plaque he had a master's of sacred theology and was "an outstanding preacher."[73] Egidi played a central role in the last phase of Galileo's trial, and in Mariano Alidosi's (see below). Otherwise, he did not leave many traces in the decree registers.[74] By 29 July, 1632, he had finished the Inquisition prison and was allowed to go home.[75] Less than a year, later in May 1633, Urban denied another request to go home "for domestic matters," and in September he accepted a reprimand from the Congregation "with all greater humility" for having licensed Galileo's *Dialogo* for publication.[76]

In general, the inquisitors of Florence fit a fairly standard pattern, except that their length of time in office shows no clear regularity: reasonably well-educated Conventual Franciscans, most with teaching, preaching, and administrative experience in their order, nearly all also with training as inquisitors, usually in Siena and Pisa, some with publication credentials. One or two went on to grander things, but for most their stint as inquisitor marked the summit of their careers. Another commonality runs through the tenures of these eight men. The Congregation at least thought it kept them reasonably tightly in check. On a few occasions, the grand duke successfully, if at length, forced a nominee on the Inquisitors. In several cases they handled, he also managed to have his political ends served, and tried hard to protect his officials and clients.[77]

One of the best instances concerns a case that got Inquisitor Medici in trouble, that of Jacopo Isparielli, an alleged Judaizer.[78] It began before 1602 and ended only in March 1606. When I first picked it up, the grand duke's commissioner in Pisa, Baccio (or Bartolomeo) Valori the younger (1535–1606), was in trouble for refusing a precept from the Congregation of 13 October 1602 to pay Isparielli's debts, a point to which the Inquisition paid close attention.[79] Valori had claimed that he was impeded, apparently by the inquisitor of Pisa's commissary.[80] Rome did not accept his excuse, and in January 1603 the grand duke had to ask absolution for Valori, then perhaps imprisoned in Pisa. Although the cardinals were inclined to grant his request, the pope ordered them to wait for a report from Pisa.[81] The outcome is not recorded.

Meanwhile the grand duke had more success helping Isparielli. After a personal appeal from the pope in September 1602, Isparielli, *pretenso Marrano*, was imprisoned in Pisa, where he confessed a year later. On the basis of that confession, the Congregation ordered further investigations in Lyon, where Isparielli had been baptized, Bordeaux, and Portugal. His wife and son were cautioned not to leave Pisa, and he himself was released under caution, a common practice by the Inquisition.[82] Despite this, on 1 April 1604 the inquisitor of Florence, Medici, reported difficulty trying to imprison Isparielli and his family.[83] Part of the trouble stemmed from the grand duke's resistance, and a breve was ordered sent to him. Isparielli was to be treated as contumacious, and Medici was to proceed against his guarantors, including Giuseppe Israele. (In the last part of the order, Medici was ordered to Rome, where he received the reprimand discussed earlier.)[84] Medici reported the arrests of Isparielli's wife and daughter on 2 June.[85] Despite further intervention by the grand duke, Isaprielli's wife and two daughters, Rosa wife of Moses Corduere [*sic*], and Ester wife of Ioseffe Israeli, were to be proceeded against.[86] In August both were "rehabilitated" (released from prison) under caution.[87] Isparielli seems to have fled to Venice with his son; its inquisitor was ordered to investigate his sons.[88] Rosa and Ester, far from being in the clear, were given their defense on 19 October 1605.[89] Shortly thereafter Jacopo was ordered sentenced, but his process did not finally conclude until after 18 March 1606.[90]

Thus the grand duke ultimately met with only limited success protecting Isparielli. Nor were others of his own servants, like Valori, immune from the Inquisition. Proceedings moved with extraordinary speed against Pandolfo Petrucci, a knight of Santo Stefano and descendant of the former lord of Siena. The inquisitor reported him in late 1602; by 21 February 1603 he had been imprisoned and assigned a defense. Then on 21 May the case was referred to the pope, who ordered the case to Rome and an examination, specifically over Petrucci's allegation that demons do not exist. In September the case concluded with torture, "and if nothing should result, he will abjure *de levi* [the lightest degree of heresy], heavy salutary penances will be imposed on him, and the bull *Si de protegendis* [about assaults on the Inquisition's ministers, among other points] be intimated to him."[91] Throughout, the pope controlled events. Petrucci's case overlapped that of Antonio Cepparelli, a major benefactor of the hospital attached to the Florentine national church in Rome.[92] The inquisitor reported him in February 1603. In March the pope again took control, ordering interrogatories sent to Florence and Cepparelli's release on a caution of 1000 *scudi*. In addition, the evidence given to the nuncio to France (Maffeo Barberini, the future Urban VIII) was to be reheard. The testimony of Fra Angelo Massei, given to the nuncio, was sent off to Florence, and Cepparelli was re-imprisoned and assigned a defense. Like Petrucci, he was tortured, but this time "sharply, and if nothing should result he shall be dismissed and diligently observed." Three weeks later, the inquisitor reported no results and that he had therefore dismissed Cepparelli.[93]

The grand duke could not prevent another of his men from being tortured, but he did manage to have him only lightly punished, and in a much more serious case. Pietro Vitale or Vitalbo, a Bergomasque captain, had been accused of murdering a consultor, apparently of Bergamo's Inquisition. After the Florentine inquisitor examined him in September 1617, the nuncio to Florence was ordered to ask the grand duke for extradition, which he granted. After being tortured twice in April 1618, Vitale was released and returned to Florence. The grand duke rendered due thanks. Vitale's final sentence was exile from papal territory, which he had in any case already left.[94]

One other constant in Florentine relations with the Congregation concerned licenses to read prohibited books. The results are mixed. A lawyer might be allowed to read the work of the Lutheran Ulrich Zasius. Alessandro Venturi, another lawyer, auditor of Siena, archdeacon of Florence, and a consultor of the Florentine Inquisition might get permission for a long list of books, but he might also find himself in serious trouble over his own book about the apostasy of Turkish captives.[95] Similarly, the grand duke's librarian might be allowed to read many condemned books at the pope's pleasure, but not even he could have access to Machiavelli.[96] The grand duke's physician, Jacopo Nardi, could read some books, but not those he listed about astrology.[97] Pietro Antonio Guadagni received the extraordinary privilege of being allowed both to own and to read prohibited books and, even more, was given a year to draw up an inventory for the Congregation's consideration. Three years later he was given an extension of six months.[98] Guadagni, member of the Accademia fiorentina (1595) and della Crusca (1610), who helped to finance its first *Vocabulario* in 1612, was also nephew of Cardinal Ottavio Bandini,who was on the point of becoming an Inquisitor when Guadagni got his extension.[99] Another similarly important member of the Florentine literary establishment, if not its political one, Raffaele Gualterotti (1543–1638), got a somewhat unusual license to read both the *Decameron* and Juan Luis Vives's annotations on Augustine.[100] One of the grand duke's principal secretaries, Andrea Cioli, probably along with his physician Nardi (mistakenly called Giovanni) got a license to read the books they listed for three years.[101]

The Cases of Rodrigo and Mariano Alidosi

One of the best windows into the operations of the Roman Inquisition as political institution in Tuscany—even though most of the case did not take place within its confines—is the enormously protracted investigation of two Alidosi lords of Castel del Rio, feudatories of the grand duke.[102] The trials of father and son, Rodrigo and Mariano, rivaled Tommaso Campanella's for length.[103] The grand dukes protected their vassals for thirty years, until Urban VIII succeeded in almost literally ripping the Alidosi fief away from the Florentines, but only after the Inquisition had failed to achieve that effect. When the grand dukes wanted to protect an important client, they did.

The Processo *as Physical Object*

We are exceptionally lucky that a big chunk of the two Alidosis' once massive dossier survives in the Biblioteca Estense Universitaria in Modena, Raccolta Campori, MS 'Y.O.4.21–27. Seven volumes remain, totaling 1030 folios, all donated by the nineteenth-century collector Giuseppe Campori. Except for that containing the transcript of Alidosi's interrogation in Florence in April and May 1609 (BEM:RC, MS 'Y.O.4.26), the volumes were bound in almost entirely random order, after they came into his possession, and after he had removed a number of items and put them in his Autografoteca, which is also in the BEM. Unfortunately, many of the extracted pieces cannot now be traced. The contents of these seven volumes probably came from the Holy Office in Faenza, which conducted the trials, and may have been assembled in their present form in the middle or late eighteenth century.[104] The Florentine Inquisition was also involved, and at one point a commissary sent out from Rome took a hand, both drawing up the *summarium* and also forming the whole *processo*, in cooperation with the inquisitors of Faenza and Florence.[105] Although only about half of it survives, the *summarium* was carefully done, no doubt because it was meant for Rome.[106] It is keyed to other surviving pieces, especially BEM:RC, MS 'Y.O.4.22, as well as to others no longer extant. It is therefore possible to estimate the scale of losses from vol. 22 on the basis of a key to it in part of the *summarium* (BEM:RC, MS 'Y.O.4.25, fos. 36rff.) as well as to show that the present numbering of the volumes does not reflect the original. Volume 22 originally had at least 491 folios, of which only 138 survive, making a loss of about 72 percent. It is also now the second, instead of the seventh, volume, dated 1608–1617.[107] Even the reconstructed original *summarium* itself must be incomplete since it lacks any reference to Rodrigo's extensive testimony, preserved in a fair copy in BEM:RC, MS 'Y.O.4.26, signed at the end of each *constitutus* by the notary, Luca Antonio Martinelli, "citizen of Faenza, notary by apostolic authority and chancellor of the most holy Inquisition of Faenza, and also delegated and deputed in this case by the most illustrious lord cardinals supreme Inquisitors in the whole Christian republic" (fo. 1v).[108] The present copy of the *summarium* almost certainly came from Florence, where many of the depositions were taken, including all of Alidosi's, and whence a copy was sent to the inquisitor of Faenza on 25 July 1609.[109] It was then described as "entirely complete with the letters and other appurtenances as it was left to me by Sig. Camillo Giudici" and contained 255 *carte*, probably meaning leaves, interrogations of forty people as well as the forty-nine affidavits (*fedi*)

Alidosi requested together with correspondence from the inquisitor of Faenza, physicians, the archbishop of Prague, Alidosi's allegations (*capitoli*), and other acts. The scale of loss can be estimated from the fact that less than half the *fedi* mentioned survive. Similarly, of the Inquisition's vicar in Imola's three letters marked as exhibits "A" through "C," only the first is now in the file. Of other exhibits marked as high as "R" and inserted in the *processo* all the rest have disappeared. (Contrariwise, the vast majority of the correspondence in the dossier was apparently never entered into evidence, at least it has no such markings.) The presence, especially in volume 23, of items which must be extraneous, for example, the deposition of the Englishman Toby Matthew taken in Florence on 20 February 1608, or a letter of 1617 to the vicar of Firenzuola, reinforces the likelihood that at least part of the present *processo* originated in Florence.[110]

The *summarium* is by far the most valuable volume, drawn up or at least supervised by Giudici, *summista* of the Holy Office, specially sent out from Rome for that purpose, and therefore a specimen of what should have been best practice.[111] Drawing up the *summarium* took about seven or eight months, with Giudici present for about half that time.[112] He also did not carry out all his instructions.[113] Thus, despite three orders to him, it was the new inquisitor of Florence and not he who interrogated Alidosi.[114] The *summarium* opens with a fascicle of twenty folios on smaller paper, all in the same hand, headed "Copia." It begins with the governor of Imola's *processo* over an incident at the Porta dell'Osservanza in Imola, which became one of the central charges against Alidosi.[115] The rest consists of depositions taken in Rome as well as "information for the Holy Office against Sig. Roderico," which probably came from Imola or Faenza, and ends with a decretum ordering Giudici to go to Florence to assist its inquisitor in making process against Alidosi.[116] Giudici must therefore have brought these documents with him from Rome. The rest of the volume contains pieces numbered 1, 3, 5, 9, 11, 14, 15, 17, 18, 19, 20 (the present sequence is 9, 14, 1, 20, 3, 5, 15, 11, 17, 18, 19). If the total of 123 folios is really just over half the *summarium*, as the eleven surviving numbers of an original twenty suggest, that bulk is just about half of what Giudici left for the inquisitor of Florence, making the *summarium* the copy he was ordered to send to Faenza. The numbers usually appear in the upper left throughout each section, including on versi, e.g., the first charge, "That he procured the flight of Hans Christoph from the prisons of Bologna" on fos. 21r–28v (the first sheet of which is blank), headed "9."[117] All the sections of the *corpora* include references to the precise folios of the original *processo* and usually transcribe the witnesses' testimony *in extenso*. When these can be checked, they are found to be scrupulously accurate. Contrariwise, only once is a quinternus of interrogations marked as *Somariatus* [*sic*], but it is not now found in the *Summarium*.[118] A number of pieces of evidence are also found in the seven volumes which came from the Apostolic Chamber, probably the Consulta, and perhaps the Congregation for Frontiers (dei Confini), now in the ASV, Arm. 36:28, 29, 30, 31, 32, 32A and 37:14, some of which concern the Alidosi cases before the Inquisition, at least indirectly.

While too much is missing from the *processo* to allow its use as a guide to procedure, undoubtedly the most interesting point to emerge from it is that Giudici's summary did not represent the penultimate stage of proceedings, but rather a preparatory phase leading to Alidosi's interrogation. As such, it both represents massive over-kill and manifests how carefully the Inquisition could do its work, thereby throwing into sharper contrast the more usual and sloppier situation.[119]

The Alidosi and Castel del Rio

The small Alidosi fief lay on the frontier between Tuscany and the papal states in the hills between Firenzuola and Imola, of which the Alidosi had once been rulers, and where Rodrigo still claimed to own a palace (the present Palazzo Monsignani), as well as maintaining a large clientage; it also bordered a property of the Roman grandee the duke of Altemps. The holding was ideally placed, not so much for border defense, as to function as a haven for exiles and bandits who could come in useful in harrying the papal authorities. As Rodrigo bragged, "I am the sole and absolute lord of Castel del Rio, which is a free state, nor subjected to any prince, and therefore I keep bandits of the grand duke my lord and of the Church and of any other state [literally men banned from those places], of which I am rather proud, since I can be useful to friends and relatives when for some murder or other excess they cannot stay elsewhere."[120] Naturally, the presence of such bandits also made the tiny, not very wealthy, fief an ideal recruiting ground for soldiers.[121] Perhaps the most famous exile hosted in Castel del Rio was Cornelio Malvasia, later Urban's general of cavalry, who was sent there in 1631 after a dispute with his fellow Bolognese Virgilio Malvezzi, the famous writer, could not be resolved.[122] Malvezzi will play a subsidiary but important role in Mariano's downfall.

The Alidosi first achieved prominence in Castel del Rio at the beginning of the sixteenth century when Cardinal Francesco, a favorite of Julius II, began building a grand palace.[123] As legate of Romagna, he was murdered in Ravenna by the duke of Urbino.[124] Rodrigo, his great-nephew, was born in Florence about 1564 to Ciro Alidosi and Elena di Rodrigo de Mendoza, about whom not much is known.[125] His marriage to Lucrezia Concini signalled his high standing in the Florentine court. Her brother, Concino, was a successful general in French service and a favorite of Marie de Medicis and Henry IV. According to the biography Alidosi offered in his first deposition, he was intended for the priesthood and therefore studied law in Siena and Pisa, where he took his degree about 1587.[126] Although he became lord of Castel del Rio in about 1590 on the death of his older brother, he spent nearly all his time in Florence[127] when he was not on diplomatic missions for the grand duke. These began in 1590 (Munich), followed by others to Spain (1602), Warsaw (1605), and the Emperor Rudolf II in Prague (1605–1607). The last of these gave rise to his first trouble with the Inquisition.

Feud and Faction

As we might expect in a place as small as Castel del Rio, cross-currents of feud and faction figured in Alidosi's case.Trying to sort out the large cast of characters on the basis of family and allegiance can present challenges.[128] Many of Alidosi's enemies thought they saw their chance in 1607–1608, including one Affricano Ravaglia, who had almost nothing to say but said it vociferously nonetheless. A few figures played a disproportionately large role, especially both of the Inquisition's functionaries in Castel del Rio. Alidosi's principal local antagonist was its vicar and also *parrochiano* of Sant'Andrea for fifty-three years, Andrea Mazzoni.[129] He would later be shot, allegedly on Alidosi's orders. Annibale Della Vigna, once called "ministro del S. Officio" and its notary, was rumored to be behind Alidosi's arrest. After those two, matters become less clear-cut. Many of Mazzoni's relatives were Alidosi's dependents. The same held true for the family of the Carmelite Alberto Tossani, possibly the first to denounce Alidosi, at least one of whose probable relatives (Domenico) was certainly in Alidosi's service. There were also those of Antonio Del Monte, rector of San Miniato barely a kilometer south of the town, another leader of the opposition to Alidosi (one of his relatives would also try to assassinate Alidosi), and Domenico Domenici, an important witness against

Alidosi, whose likely relative Giovanni Battista Domenici was one of the two attempted assassins of Andrea Tedeschi, warden of the Holy Office's prison in Imola. Most of the rest of the local clergy also opposed Alidosi, especially the local man Bartolomeo (alias Meo) Vanti da Sassoleone, curate of S.ta Margherita, Carseggio, an impoverished hamlet just north of Castel del Rio.[130] In Imola, Alidosi's most determined enemy was Tedeschi. Tedeschi, a tailor by trade, was another local man, coming from Osta, just across the Ponte Alidosi over the Santerno from Castel del Rio. Alidosi had much more powerful supporters than enemies in Imola, including apparently in the Inquisition. A number of his backers were his relatives and not only citizens of Imola but also servants of the grand duke, chief among them Giovanni Battista Baffadi and Ciro Pantaleone, who married Alidosi's sister, together possibly with his nephew (Alidosi called both him and Baffadi his *nipoti*) and another nephew, Francesco Feraldi. Their retinues, together with Alidosi's own retainers, figured prominently in the affray at the Porta dell'Osservanza. Chief among his local men were the Suzzi or Sozzi, especially Battista Suzzi, who often served as his commissioner.

The First Denunciations and the Affray at the Porta dell'Osservanza

While Alidosi was still at the emperor's court, Tossani, from the tiny Carmelite house at Montefune in the territory of Castel del Rio, wrote Mazzoni in Imola that "we are desperate" over Alidosi's actions, and complained both to the order's vicar and to Cardinal Millini; whether as bishop of Imola or as an Inquisitor is not said.[131] Another scribbled denunciation, possibly from October 1607, concerns a forced marriage and violence at least threatened on Alidosi's orders.[132] In May 1608 the Inquisition first took an interest, acting, as it was not supposed to do, on an anonymous denunciation of Alidosi. The Congregation ordered the inquisitors of Florence and Faenza (officially, of Romagna) to investigate whether he had a Bohemian hanging around him.[133] A week later the vicar of Imola reported what may be the same denunciation in more detail to the inquisitor of Romagna, Pietro Maria da Urgnano (or Pietro Martire Fatigati or Faticati), but he also included the damning note of the *publica voce* (reputation) that Alidosi was not a good Catholic.[134] That, combined with the specific denunciations, was enough to open a file, even without orders from Rome. On Fatigati's report of 25 May that Alidosi did indeed have in his household a Bohemian, whose name, Hans Christoph Berbistorff, gave the Italians fits, the inquisitor was ordered to investigate secretly and then have Alidosi arrested, with the help of the legate in Ravenna, Cardinal Bonifacio Caetani.[135] On 31 May the inquisitor of Florence reported that Alidosi had Hans Christoph constantly with him.[136] A week later the first interrogation took place before the Inquisition's vicar in Imola (who was also the prior of its Dominican convent), Ippolito Maria d'Alba. A "Hungarian," Cosmo Schell, appeared "spontaneously" (at Tedeschi's suggestion) to denounce Alidosi's guest as a Lutheran, naming two other witnesses.[137] Five days later he was examined again and named two more witnesses.[138]

A month into the investigation, the vicar of Imola himself appeared before Fatigati, to whom he had written, forwarding information from Mazzoni—some of which Mazzoni claimed to have from Alidosi himself—but also reporting his own interrogations taken in Castel del Rio. He testified on the strength of one or both sources that Alidosi (1) had eaten meat on a fast day, (2) had Hans Christoph about him and allowed him to follow his own religious observances, including taking all images out of his room, (3) had read a prohibited book, and (4) laughed at excommunications. The vicar urged Mazzoni to testify, but Alidosi frightened him too much. Finally, Alba added that Alidosi had imprisoned and fined two witnesses in a blasphemy case.[139] In the usual tangle of correspondence, on 3 July the Congregation acted on a outdated report of 2 June from Fatigati, that it was hard to collect evidence, and enclosing a copy of Rodrigo's secretary's letter threatening Mazzoni, who had denounced him at Imola. The Congregation ordered the inquisitor to depose Mazzoni in Bologna and then arrest Hans Christoph.[140] Mazzoni did not testify until 15 July. Much of what he said, although circumstantially detailed, including a physical description of the suspect book (of which he had forgotten the title, despite having checked it in the Index) about "all the sects of heretics," the author of which was a "a canon of those parts of Germany [Todescaria]," added nothing new. He did name more names, including witnesses and two Carmelites Alidosi had allegedly imprisoned, as well as testifying that Hans Christoph had a printed but possibly altered affidavit from the nuncio, apparently to the emperor. Finally, he added that Alidosi practiced usury.[141] Mazzoni came back a week later to say he had made a mistake in the day of the week on which Alidosi ate meat (!) and to name yet more witnesses. Antonio Del Monte appeared on the same day in Bologna.[142] At this time, Alidosi still thought Mazzoni was helping him.[143]

Before Mazzoni testified and the Congregation's order of 3 July arrived in Imola, the most dramatic episode in the whole affair took place, the affray at the Porta dell'Osservanza.[144] On the morning of 4 July, when Alidosi and his party tried to leave via that narrow gate leading out of Imola to the south, Alba (or someone; Alidosi's deponents chose to blame the order on Tedeschi, perhaps in an attempt to lessen the offense, but the vicar took responsibility in his own testimony) ordered the gatekeepers to close it.[145] The bargello of the Holy Office appeared with armed *sbirri* (police), seven men in total, to enforce the order. Alidosi's party, including Hans Christoph and numbering perhaps fifteen or twenty men (Alba said fifty, and Tedeschi, who admitted to being terrified, made it forty), of whom probably about an equal number to the bargello's carried arms, some arquebuses, an illegal weapon for Inquisition familiars, threatened the bargello. Alidosi objected to the vicar at such treatment, at which point Alba (or someone) ordered the gate unbarred. According to most witnesses, violence was narrowly averted.

Just then the grand duke did not need another subject in trouble with Paul V. The pope had thrown into Castel Sant'Angelo the Marchese Riano, Paolo Emilio Cesi, seventy years old and a dependent of the grand duke, charging him with one of the implicit complaints against Alidosi, harboring a bandit.[146] The popes had been campaigning against banditry in the papal states for years.[147] Cesi's was not an Inquisition case, but it provides context for Alidosi's. He had been immediately examined for two hours, and four more on the next day. It was said that the pope had a vendetta against him from the time the marchese had refused to observe a sentence Paul had passed down as auditor of the Chamber. Many cardinals had tried to intercede for him, but Paul rebuffed them all.[148] The grand duke, by means of a gentleman sent express, tried and failed to get the marchese released to house arrest, Paul saying Castel Sant'Angelo was for quality prisoners (it was) and had enough "comfort [commodità]."[149] Recommendations poured in, including ones from the Spanish and French ambassadors and the dean of the College of Cardinals. The Florentine ambassador took the grand duke's gentleman with him to his audience every week, and the pope promised to do what he could, but the process continued to be formed. The pope also refused to grant house arrest, even though Virginio Orsini had offered security of 10,000 *scudi*. Other similarly highly placed barons had also been cited over banditry, including Orsini and Duke Cesarini, but their cases were not going ahead.[150] A week later the process had been formed, and a copy had gone to Cardinal Domenico Toschi, a lawyer and Cesi's friend, who said it contained no evidence.[151] Cardinal Montalto, Sixtus V's former cardinal nephew, spoke warmly on behalf of the prisoner in late August, and it was therefore thought the marchese's life was no longer in danger.[152] And that is the last we hear. Whatever the outcome, it does look as if Paul was manifesting a degree of animus against Florence that would not have helped Alidosi.

After the near-miss at the Porta, the investigation into which began that very day and continued in the hands of the Inquisition well into 1609, proceedings against Alidosi moved faster.[153] At successive meetings of the Congregation on 16 and 17 July, the second a coram, after the reading of an anonymous denunciation and letters from Alba and Fatigati of 5, 6, and 10 July, the last of which reported that Alidosi had told Fra Vincenzo Mordano, O.P., that he had a license from the inquisitor of Florence to convert Hans Christoph. Paul V then ordered the Bohemian imprisoned, through negotiations with Alidosi if possible, and then the Congregation was to decide what to do about Alidosi himself.[154] In the next entry, Mordano, who had leaked word of the Inquisition's moves against Alidosi, was ordered jailed.[155] Alba, perhaps acting on this order, tried to arrest Mordano at their convent, after visiting him the day before at Pantaleone's house in Imola, but Mordano fled.[156] On 20 July Alba once again appeared before Fatigati to testify about the events of 4 July, explaining that he had mistakenly thought he saw Hans Christoph in Alidosi's room in Imola instead of his brother Rudolf, which led him to give the order to close the gate.[157] Four days later in a coram, after hearing a sheaf of correspondence from Fatigati, the otherwise unknown Alessandro Antonio Vaglia of Castel del Rio, and Alidosi, the pope ordered the grand duke written, via the inquisitor of Florence and the legates of Bologna, Ferrara, and Romagna, to imprison Alidosi, and a supersedeat if he was not caught, followed by proceedings for contumacy. The next three decrees all concern Alidosi as his case rapidly expanded. Berbistorff, captured in Bologna, was to be brought to Rome, the governor of Imola was to be written about the gatekeeper there, and, finally, Caetani was to imprison Giovanni Baffadi and Ciro Pantaleone,[158] who had allegedly been sent to capture Alidosi.[159]

The grand duke stood solidly if perhaps coincidentally behind Alidosi. On 26 July the Venetian ambassador in Florence reported that Alidosi had been assigned a mission to Lorraine.[160] In September the Venetian ambassador in Rome informed the doge that the Holy Office was trying to find a way to keep the duke and the French ambassador happy about Alidosi coming to Rome, but the grand duke absolutely refused to allow the trip and was dealing with Cardinal Anne d'Escars de Givry, who was an Inquisitor and was putting off his trip home (as he told the ambassador in person). Florentine soldiers had also occupied Alidosi's "castle," meaning the whole fief, an inconvenient fact which Paul V tried to ignore.[161] As the ambassador explained three days later, the grand duke's men rebuffed the pope's effort to occupy Alidosi's territory—which he mistakenly thought was in Siena. The French ambassador had intervened for Alidosi on the queen's orders, moved by a female relative of Alidosi, "the queen's most favorite," and had begun to try to persuade the Congregation to let the trial proceed in Florence instead of Rome.[162] Once again, Ambassador Tommaso Contarini got things a little garbled. Alidosi's backer in the French court was his wife's brother, Concino Concini, one of the most successful French generals and indeed a favorite of the Florentine queen, Marie de Medicis.[163] Her husband Henry IV would also strongly recommend Alidosi. The Venetian resident in Florence also did not quite understand what was going on. In his *relazione* (report to the Senate after his return to Venice), Francesco Morosini, in the course of describing the close relationship between the grand duke and Paul V, touched on the allegations against Alidosi (all false) and thought they would be handled by the inquisitor of Florence and a commissary sent from Rome, since the grand duke's policy was to "flee conflicts [*incontri*]."[164] The reference to a commissary must mean Giudici's mission, but its object was never to settle the case in Florence. Nevertheless, Morosini did not miss the degree of the grand duke's support for Alidosi.

Rodrigo Alidosi's Arrest

In one of the most bizarre coincidences in any of the cases I have studied, on 9 August 1608 Alidosi was 1) confirmed as ambassador to Lorraine and 2) arrested by the Inquisition in Florence.[165] That second action made it as unnecessary for Fatigati to act on Alba's news he sent from Imola the next day that Alidosi was headed north by an unknown route, as it did for the Congregation to act on Legate of Romagna Domenico Rivarola's suggestion that the grand duke's name be added to Alidosi's citation.[166] Nevertheless, the pope, ignorant of the arrest, ordered a species of citation *ad domum* ("at the house") instead of in person, a tactic Rivarola would adopt ten years later.[167] A week after Alidosi's capture, Tedeschi appeared again before Niccolò da Bologna, the Inquisition's vicar in Faenza, to testify about Pantaleone's plot to kill him.[168] The same day another of the conspirators in the Porta affair, an organist in the cathedral of Imola, was deposed.[169] (Alidosi rewarded him by making him commissioner of Castel del Rio in 1611.)[170] Mazzoni was also busy, going back to Castel del Rio—once Alidosi was safely imprisoned—to collect depositions (and ignore orders from Alidosi's wife, as he usually did).[171] It appears he was right to worry about his safety. On 22 August Giuseppe Rosa, a young soldier under Pantaleone's command who had been at the Porta, deposed in detail about efforts to harm Tedeschi.[172]

At the same time as Alidosi's arrest, efforts failed to round up his co-conspirators, Caetani reporting that Baffadi had gone to Florence and Pantaleone could not be found. An order therefore went out to Fatigati to cite both and proceed against them.[173] Holding Alidosi proved difficult, too. He escaped at least once, and even when imprisoned in Florence, Inquisitor Medici allowed him to talk freely to visitors.[174] Medici somewhat obtusely insisted that he had allowed only a physician and Alidosi's cousin (or his wife's) Bartolomeo Concini, ambassador-designate to France, to see the prisoner.[175] Perhaps encouraged by the news of Alidosi's good treatment, Baffadi quickly turned himself in and got similarly gentle treatment, being put under an appearance bond for only 1000 *scudi* and confined to his surety's house![176] Two weeks later the Inquisition imprisoned him.[177] The news that Pantaleone had also surrendered proved false. He had already fled an attempt by the bargello of the Campagna to arrest him in August.[178] Alidosi, by contrast, although ordered on 15 October released to house arrest because of illness, was slapped with a bond of 10,000 *scudi*.[179] Fatigati stayed busy, making a special trip to interview a thirteen-year-old witness. The boy, duly if doubtfully sworn after a long exhortation about the seriousness of the matter, denied stoutly that he had witnessed any of the suspect actions another witness alleged the boy had seen in Alidosi's house in Florence. Even when quoted that witness's deposition and warned repeatedly, the youth still refused to confirm the allegations. His exculpatory evidence did not make it into the *Summarium*.[180] This was apparently because his testimony was adjudged to have been coerced, although he was never called to confirm the allegation, nor was this instance added to the charge of witness intimidation lodged against Alidosi.[181] The boy's evidence just disappeared.

Vincenzo Mordano Testifies

On 30 September the Congregation got its first direct information about the events in Imola and its surroundings when its assessor and fiscal, joined part way through by the commissary, interrogated Mordano. He gave nicely circumstantial evidence. His involvement began when he went to Imola to preach Lent and told someone in the convent of San Domenico there that he hoped to do the same in Castel del Rio. His unnamed interlocutor objected that Alidosi was a "terrible man" and had a non-Catholic German in his house. Alba added that Alidosi "never lived a very good life" ("non faceva troppo bona vita"). On another occasion, Mordano asked the notary of the Holy Office why "Andrea del hoste [Osta]," meaning Tedeschi, was around the convent so much, since Mordano knew Andrea was "referendario" of the Inquisition. The notary replied that he was expecting to capture an important gentleman coming to Imola soon. Mordano deduced that he meant Alidosi.[182] He therefore went to see Cavaliere Baffadi, asking a recommendation to preach in Castel del Rio and warning him to tell Alidosi not to come to Imola. He also told Cesare Cirone, the curate of Valsalva, a few kilometers south of Castel del Rio but still in its territory, the same thing.

While Mordano was arranging his transfer to Argenta (province of Ferrara), Alidosi arrived in Imola. Mordano immediately went to Baffadi's house to talk to him again about preaching in Castel del Rio. Alidosi summoned the Dominican and asked him why he had warned him not to come; Mordano replied, because of danger from the Holy Office.[183] Alidosi professed his intention to convert the two Germans who were causing the trouble. That was the only time Mordano saw him. As he left he ran into Alba, to whom Alidosi also talked. The next morning, as Mordano was leaving for Argenta, Alba appeared in his room and ordered him not to leave. Since the vicar had stated no penalty, Mordano thought he was free to ignore the command, even though he recognized it as "a simple precept," an admission he made worse by claiming he had no experience in any court, a context that made it clear he considered Alba's order a legal act ("non credendo d'essere obligato a non partire per un precetto semplice, non havendo sin qui mai pratticato in alcun Tribunale"). When he arrived in Lugo, its Dominican prior and Inquisition vicar (possibly the same person, as in Imola) with other friars said they had an order from the inquisitor of Faenza to bring him there "without giving me another precept" ("senza farmi altro precetto"). Mordano graciously agreed to go, even after the insult of being arrested in his home territory (Mordano is close to Lugo), but instead asked various people to intervene for him and wrote the Dominican vicar in Rome for permission to plead his case there.[184]

When no license arrived, he went to Rome anyway and somehow contrived to appear before unnamed cardinals, who told him to go to the Inquisition. Shown his memorial by his interrogators, Mordano acknowledged it as written in his brother's hand. Apparently it narrated the case, since they then began to question him about his earlier assertions. Did he give Alidosi a reason not to come to Imola? No, Mordano told him about the Inquisition's interest only after he arrived and only because of its notary's passing remark, which Mordano doubted he would remember. Had he told Baffadi the reason? Not at first, answered Mordano.[185] That answer was judged "inverisimilar," and Mordano was urged to try again. He changed his testimony a little, saying he had only been speculating and trying to secure Baffadi's good will. His questioners pressed him on the point of whom he had warned and in what order, first Alidosi or the curate of Valsalva? Mordano thought there might have been a week between the time he had alerted the curate and Alidosi's coming to Imola.[186] He had met the priest fourteen years earlier, when he had preached Holy Week at Valsalva and confessed him. Later Mordano claimed to have seen the priest in Prague, when serving as prior of a Dominican house there, and had talked to him on one other occasion on convent business.[187] Then it was back to Mordano's attempt to preach in Castel del Rio, at which point the Inquisition's commissary arrived.[188] Now he thought he remembered having told either the priest or Alidosi that the Inquisition's vicar might have gone to Castel del Rio to take action against Alidosi.

By this point, the Congregation had other information against Alidosi, although it is not clear how it got it. His interrogators read Mordano a section of a *processo* against Alidosi incriminating him. Mordano insisted that he had not told Alidosi why the vicar had gone to Castel del Rio, although admitting that he might have mentioned the trip. Maybe Alidosi deduced his motive? After more inconsequential questions about Alidosi's German, the interrogation ended with the demand to say why Mordano had not obeyed "the precepts" (*praeceptis*). Answer: to avoid embarassment, and in the hopes of better treatment in Rome. Finally Mordano was asked whether he thought it was a good idea to violate the Holy Office's secrecy. He admitted it was not, blaming his action on imprudence, and there his interrogation ended.[189] Two days later he was assigned a defense, and on 8 October his case was suspended, pending testimony from Alidosi and Baffadi.[190] On 28 January 1609 he was sentenced, unfortunately on unknown grounds, to exile and loss of voting rights in his order. He was still trying in 1612 to have his punishment canceled.[191]

At this moment, who had charge in Imola becomes murky. Alba was still in office as of 13 October, but before the 25th one Vincenzo da Cotignola had replaced him.[192] Virginio da Modena took over before 14 November.[193] Since the inquisitorship of Faenza also changed hands, it looks as if a house-cleaning in the offices handling Alidosi's case was under way. The same day as the soon-to-be-former inquisitor Fatigati reported that he was still looking for Pantaleone, the pope ordered the inquisitor of Reggio, Serafino Montini da Cagli (province of Pesaro), to move to Faenza (also called Romagna).[194] He had been hand-picked by Dominican General Agostino Galamini, later one of Paul's most favored Inquisitors.[195] He may have brought a notary with him; at least, another friar from Cagli appears as notary of the Inquisition in Imola in November.[196] The only post which seems not to have turned over was that of vicar of the Inquisition in Faenza, but the next holder known does not appear until 1610; there may be a gap in our information.[197] Even more significant, at more or less the same time as these other moves, on 15 and 16 October, a coram, Giudici was ordered north to assist the inquisitor of Florence.[198] For some reason, Giudici did not leave at once. In November his orders were changed, first to cooperating with the inquisitor of Faenza, not Florence, possibly because the Congregation did not trust a man so close to the grand duke, and then to working with both.[199] He had made it only as far as Perugia by 15 November, where he was stopped in order to work on another case.[200] He did not certainly arrive in Imola before 20 December.[201]

The Bohemians Testify

Shortly before Alba lost office, he reported on 9 October the good news that the prisoners bound for Rome would leave shortly for Faenza, where they were delivered that evening.[202] (Since his letter went to the vicar-general of Romagna, Caetani apparently had taken charge of their transit.) They arrived in Rome on 22 or 23 October.[203] Their number included Hans Christoph, but not his fellow Bohemian Lorenz, to be one of the most damaging witnesses against Alidosi; he was not arrested until the 17th. Lorenz had been reported by Mazzoni and Antonio Del Monte as having said the pope had no more power than any other prince and having called Alidosi "the greatest Lutheran and heretic."[204] At the time of Lorenz's arrest by Tedeschi, a summary of the evidence against Alidosi by Mazzoni (with Tedeschi's collaboration) was also handed in.[205] A very similar text was among the documents Giudici carried.[206] The next day, Niccolò da Bologna, the vicar of the Inquisition of Faenza, came to Imola to examine Lorenz. He testified that he had returned from Prague with Alidosi, for whom he waited at table, and then lived with Baffadi before Baffadi's arrest. He denied having done anything un-Catholic or eaten meat on prohibited days. After "being benignly admonished," he still refused to admit any wrongdoing. His post in Alidosi's service made him ideally placed to know whether Alidosi, who always had Hans Christoph with him, had committed dietary infractions. After another general warning, he still insisted that the charges were false. Since he remained pig-headed despite the warnings, Lorenz was sent back to prison "to every good end and effect."[207]

While Lorenz reflected on his testimony, ten days later Mazzoni was summoned to testify, on the strength of the evidence presented in his name at Lorenz's arrest. After Mazzoni acknowledged the text, it was accepted into evidence. Then the inquisitor (it is unclear whether Montini had taken up office yet) took one of those actions which seem superficially meaningless, but which testify to how much the Inquisition preferred to work orally. He asked Mazzoni if he remembered what the writing said, and Mazzoni replied that he could recall its main points. Rather than letting him go, the inquisitor instead gave him his document, and he apparently read from it during the rest of his interrogation. First, he testified that Alidosi had tried to get Hans Christoph to Bologna and had refused to give Mazzoni or any other priests access to him. Second, he reported being told that Alidosi said he wanted to kill the inquisitor (of Faenza) and his vicar (probably of Imola), as well as Mazzoni and any priests or friars mixed up in his case. Alidosi's commissioner got a testimonial from the comune of Castel del Rio denying the charge, but Mazzoni cited witnesses saying it had been coerced. Mazzoni noted various other threats, before deposing that Alidosi had made the clergy of his small state subject to the same decrees (bandi) as the rest of his subjects, refused to allow them to celebrate funerals without his license, demanded a fee from any priest seeking a benefice, and alienated the property of the only hospital in Castel del Rio. Finally, he denounced Lorenz and reported hearsay testimony that Hans Christoph shared the views about papal power he and Tedeschi had attributed to Lorenz.[208]

In early November, Hans Christoph underwent interrogation in Rome for the first time. He was asked mainly about his family and religious practices while in Bohemia. He said the Jesuits in Prague had educated him for a year when he was thirteen, but that was the extent of his formal religious schooling. Nevertheless, they and their Dominican counterparts had trained him well in the Mass. This deposition makes Hans appear completely innocent.[209] Six days later he was examined again, first about his religious practice in Castel del Rio and then about his brother Rudolf.[210]

Tedeschi Intervenes

The changing of the guard in Imola coincided with a big increase in the amount of evidence collected, even if the new vicar, Virginio da Modena, had to share duties with Niccolò da Bologna.[211] First, Tedeschi appeared spontaneously with much of the same information he had given numerous times before, but adding a number of details about the plot to assassinate him in Castel del Rio. He especially feared Feraldi.[212] Four days later and a month after his first appearance, Lorenz was interrogated for the second time, again by Fra Niccolò, who also brought his own notary with him. He began by following the rules and asked Lorenz what else he had to say, before quickly firing off a strictly forbidden leading question: what more do you remember about the incident at the Porta? I saw Alidosi's men on the point of committing "un atto di violenza," said Lorenz. He described the ringleader as a tall man from Imola with a black beard and a pistol, who shouted that it was wrong to close the gate. On 19 November, apparently once more Fra Niccolò (the occasion is identified only as "in the presence of the aforesaid father vicar") examined two participants in the incident at the Porta. Both agreed tolerably well about what had happened, increasing the evidence that Alidosi had known that the Inquisition was involved and that his men had threatened violence.[213] On 20 November Montini first certainly took a hand, when the twenty-year-old Baffadi underwent interrogation for the first time.[214] He described a dinner at his house in Imola the previous July which Alidosi attended. Pressed, he produced the whole list of guests, which included both Lorenz and Rudolf Berbistorff, the second of whom ate by himself. He had no idea whether Rudolf was a Catholic since that was the only time he had seen the man. Baffadi knew his brother ate with Alidosi, but knew nothing of his religion, either. Then the interrogator turned to events at the Porta. Baffadi provided more details of his actions, as well as testifying that Alidosi knew from Alba before leaving Baffadi's house that the Inquisition was after Hans Christoph. His evidence about what happened at the gate was of a piece with that of earlier witnesses.[215]

Then it was back to Fra Niccolò. The next day he first heard Mazzoni again and then Antonio Del Monte, the first *sponte comparens*, the second cited. Since both men's evidence concerned events exactly a week old, Fra Niccolò was working fast, taking the situation in Castel del Rio seriously. To judge from the arrangement of the texts in the *processo*, Del Monte was heard twice, before and after Mazzoni. Initially he was asked about his and Mazzoni's joint written denunciation, which he acknowledged. Otherwise he had little to add, except that everyone in Castel del Rio was under orders not to talk to Mazzoni. His fellow priest brought news of another attempt to kill him which resulted in an evidently small wound to a finger, which he exhibited. He had more information that Alidosi was out to have him murdered, some of it firsthand. Summoned again, Del Monte largely supported Mazzoni's story. Then he dropped a bombshell. A month ago, he said, he and Mazzoni had visited Cardinal Millini in Carseggio. Alas, he did not say what they discussed, but did say he was threatened again on the return trip.[216]

Tedeschi stayed busy, denouncing more participants in the Porta incident, who underwent examination almost immediately. On 24 November he confirmed his written delation of three men as having been present and having seen Feraldi threaten the bargello. Later that day two of the three were summoned.[217] The first repeated the now agreed-upon version from Alidosi's side, that Tedeschi was to blame for the gate's closing and that only he had been threatened by the armed men in Alidosi's party, but the second denied—loudly—having heard any threats uttered.[218] The third had to be captured, which also happened immediately, and almost as quickly he complained of his treatment.[219] Tedeschi's superiors kept an eye on him and intercepted the letter in which he had forwarded the complaint to Montini. The next day Fra Niccolò examined Tedeschi over it. Tedeschi admitted he had written the letter the previous evening, adding the prisoner's claim that if he had money like the other accused, he would not have been imprisoned.[220] His deposition is not only signed but authenticated twice by the notary.

By 27 November, Fra Niccolò had gathered a large number of men from Castel del Rio about the attempted assassination of Tedeschi.[221] On that day he interrogated three of them, Domenico Domenici, his father, and Vincenzo Beccari, called Filetti from his profession of butcher.[222] Domenici admitted he knew Tedeschi, as he told Beccari/Filetti, one of the more unsavory characters in the story, whose brother was a musketeer in Imola. Battista Suzzi, the commissioner of Castel del Rio, asked Domenici to confirm his identification, which he did, but Domenici had no idea why he wanted to know. Then he was asked about his dealings with Lorenz, confirming only that he had said Hans Christoph was a heretic but nothing about Alidosi, nor Lorenz's alleged claim about papal power. Finally, he testified to being present at the Porta and confirmed in broad outline what Niccolò already knew, adding a few details about the foot soldiers, among whom he had been. He added at the end that both he and his father had been imprisoned in Castel del Rio, he for having said that he preferred the grand duke's rule to Alidosi's and for having carried letters for the Holy Office.[223] Looking suspiciously pre-arranged, the next witness was Domenici's father, Alessandro, who blamed his imprisonment on his son's having acted as a messenger for the Holy Office.[224] Then it was Beccari's turn. He admitted knowing Pantaleone and Feraldi, with the second of whom he had associated after being exiled from Imola, but nothing more. He had certainly never threatened to stick a knife in Tedeschi.[225] Finally, that evening Niccolò and Montini interrogated Lorenz for the third time. He refused to confess.[226]

Two days later Domenico was re-examined and mainly corroborated his testimony about Tedeschi, highlighting the degree of Beccari's involvement. Now he remembered spontaneously that Lorenz had belittled papal power, and added piously that Beccari was a terrible blasphemer, as was one Miano, probably Damiano Domenici, yet another *bravo* in Castel del Rio, who may have been Domenici's relative.[227] Wandering slightly off track in the course of pursuing Lorenz's statement about the papacy, but in keeping with the vicariate in Imola's concern with blasphemy, Niccolò asked another witness about Filetti's swearing; he did not support Domenici.[228] Throughout December the Holy Office continued to interrogate new and old witnesses and suspects about the assassination plot, the affair at the Porta, and Alidosi's evil deeds in Castel del Rio. Unfortunately, included in these, the originals of which are mostly missing, were three interrogations of Lorenz on three successive days.[229] Meanwhile, Hans Christoph remained in prison in Rome.[230] Giudici, in Imola, claimed to have had less success than his predecessors, reporting to Rome on 20 December that he could "hardly" (*vix*) find any witnesses because they were all frightened, but at least Mazzoni had testified that the inquisitor of Florence (Medici) favored Alidosi. Giudici was ordered to find a trustworthy notary—the Dominican vicar general was to be asked whether someone could be found in S. Marco or S.ta Maria Novella—and examine Alidosi.[231] In the following coram of 1 January 1609, the order became to go with an assistant and "give the Inquisitor of Florence a precept to observe the secrecy [of the Holy Office] under pain of excommunication *latae sententiae*," and especially not to reveal witnesses' names.[232] Whatever trouble Giudici may have been having, it was allegedly not for lack of cooperation by Lucrezia Concini, acting in her husband's stead. In a later affidavit, the lawyer Alessandro Machiavelli claimed that she had sent him to Castel del Rio in January specially, to make sure that anyone summoned by the inquisitor of Faenza appeared, giving them a "penal precept" if necessary, but he had not needed to do anything to ensure the denizens' compliance with the Inquisition's citations.[233] To judge from the number of interrogations Fra Niccolò and the inquisitors had managed to conduct, Giudici may well have been making excuses, or perhaps jockeying for position relative to the local authorities, or he may not yet have been shown the masses of testimony after his recent arrival. In mid-March Giudici was ordered not to examine Alidosi's wife, to send the names of witnesses, and to return "him" to prison after his interrogations.[234] Whoever was meant, it cannot have been Alidosi, whose examination did not happen until after Giudici had left Florence, as he shortly and unexpectedly did, apparently without incurring any consequences. Why he never executed the order to examine Alidosi is unknown.

Ciro Pantaleone and His Men

Nevertheless, Giudici's arrival in Romagna coincided with a yet more vigorous burst of activity than Fra Niccolò and Montini had already shown and the scene of operations almost certainly shifted to Faenza, whence Giudici wrote on 28 December.[235] In addition to Lorenz's three interrogations on successive days at the end of December, in early January 1609, interrogations of the principals in the Porta incident began and the vicar of the Holy Office in neighboring Casola was sent to interview witnesses in Castel del Rio. (The Inquisition had established a system of local vicars overlapping the rural deans [*vicarii foranei*] set up by the Council of Trent.)[236] On the 2nd, Pantaleone appeared for the first time.[237] He began at the beginning of the episode that led to the Porta dell'Osservanza, giving the most detailed account yet, but varying in no significant detail from that already known. In his interrogation the next day, he emphasized that he had not known Mordano nor what he was doing in Pantaleone's house. He did think that Alidosi had sent Alba money. Then Pantaleone admitted that he himself might have been the source of all the trouble, since he had told Alba about both Hans Christoph and Rudolf.[238] Although in his fourth interrogation on 4 January he gave a precise list of the armed men (including himself, with *two* loaded arquebuses), he claimed to know neither the Inquisition's bargello nor Tedeschi before he was imprisoned. He blamed the threats on Feraldi.[239] In yet another interrogation the next day he admitted that he had known both the bargello and Tedeschi and the offices they held, and was sure that Alidosi and Feraldi also both knew what was afoot.[240] On 6 January another of the gunmen at the gate was interrogated for the first time. He, too, began at the beginning, spinning a narrative much like Pantaleone's, while adding that Tedeschi had told the witness he held a patent from the Holy Office, but he did not know that the bargello (who also worked for the bishop) was in its employ.[241] The Inquisition's vicar in neighboring Casola, Paolo Maria Vecchi from Bologna, went on Montini's orders to Castel del Rio three days later, with the Dominican notary Jacopo Zucchella da Imola. He collected a few details about Hans Christoph from a serving girl but, aside from an appearance by the irrepressible Mazzoni, once more accusing Beccari of attacking him, got little more.[242] He returned on 12 March, again mainly to interview women, but could not avoid Mazzoni once again.[243]

A much more important interrogation took place the same day, the first appearance by Francesco Feraldi. He claimed to have done nothing at the gate other than ask Alidosi whether he believed Alba when he claimed not to have ordered the closure. Alidosi obviously relied on Feraldi, whom he asked to complain to both the governor of Imola and the inquisitor of Faenza. He had also returned with Alba to the gate to ask Tedeschi and the bargello (who Feraldi insisted he did not know worked for the Inquisition) what had happened. The inquisitor ordered Alba to go to the governor of Imola and secure the release of the gate-keepers whom he had arrested.[244] In a second interrogation the next day he added a few details about Camillo Zampieri's (the organist's) and Rosa's involvement and claimed never to have touched the bargello.[245] In the midst of all this trouble and mounting evidence, Alidosi still regarded Mazzoni as his servant, ordering him in mid-January to stop the new commissioner—the old one having been murdered—from doing damage to him![246] Despite Alidosi's suspicions of the new commissioner, on 2 March he wrote a strongly worded commendation of Alidosi's behavior since 1593, which became part of the defense documents exhibited in the Holy Office in Florence on 23 May 1609.[247]

The Inquisition's satellite tribunal in Faenza could have as long a memory as the main office. On 22 January 1609 the inquisitor of Modena interrogated a Carmelite there about an insult to a member of his order in Castel del Rio committed in 1591.[248] It could also be extremely thorough. When Beccari claimed he had no money to pay his expenses, Montini ordered a search of his cell, which resulted in a detailed list of the coins found.[249]

More Damaging Testimony

Throughout January, interrogations of figures both major and minor continued. In early February one of the most damaging witnesses testified, a man who had been with Alidosi in Prague as a secretary. Galeazzo Giuntini stressed the prohibited books Alidosi owned and had shown around in Castel del Rio, as he did Alidosi's solicitude for Hans Christoph's practice of his own religion.[250] At the same time Giudici was ordered to proceed, and the fiscal to make a summary of the case thus far.[251] On 25 February Giudici, then still in Faenza, was ordered to examine Alidosi in Florence; three days earlier, in a letter the Congregation had yet to receive, he had professed his eagerness to do so.[252] The inquisitor of Florence's excuse that he could not do so because of "infirmity" led to an order the next day to turn the examination over to his vicar (apparently along with Giudici).[253]

Still the evidence against Alidosi mounted, even if it was often buried in testimony more harmful to others. That was the case with Cesare Cirone, the curate of Valsalva, who began testifying in January, at first giving evidence mainly against Mordano. He confirmed some of Mordano's own testimony of 30 September, as he did again probably on 1 March.[254] At the end of the month he claimed to have warned Alidosi not to bring Hans Christoph with him.[255] Tasked then, and again on 13 February, with having seen the letter in which Alidosi promised Hans Christoph's mother that he would allow the youth to remain a Lutheran, Cirone insisted he had not.[256] In his fifth deposition on 5 March Cirone got around to Alidosi and to Alba. When he had been cited to appear in Imola, he met Alidosi on the road, who asked him to show him "the precept [to testify]." Having seen it, Alidosi recommended that Cirone reflect on what he meant to say. He also told Cirone that Alba was his married sister's "great friend," and she would recommend Cirone to him. When he saw Mordano in Imola, whom he had first met in Valsalva years earlier, the Dominican (to whom Cirone referred by the diminuitive "Mordanino") told him that Alidosi was in trouble. A few days later Alba summoned him and asked him what he had talked to Mordano about; Cirone replied, about "the precept" Alba had given him.[257]

On 6 March Tedeschi was back at it, reporting to Rome an attack on him at Alidosi's behest. He was ordered committed to Legate Caetani's protection.[258] No such episode is otherwise documented until early 1611 (see below).[259] Three days later Alba, former Inquisition vicar, signed a lengthy account of what he had done in Alidosi's case, as it appears the Inquisition had begun to take an interest in him.[260] His involvement began in May 1608, when the rector of Valsalva told him Alidosi had brought a Lutheran home with him. Alba went to Castel del Rio on a market day and got confirmation from "Domenico son of Alessandro" whose surname he did not know (it was probably Domenici). In a subsequent meeting of rural deans he spoke to his close friend Mazzoni, for whom he had once preached Lent and lived in his house.[261] He said the report was "most true," and that he would denounce Alidosi judicially, including about eating meat, except he did not dare. Alba gave "my inquisitor [of Faenza]" a detailed report, and he in turn reported to Rome, which ordered Alidosi captured. Meantime a Hungarian servant of the Alidosi family in Imola [Cosmo Schell] denounced Alidosi and Hans Christoph. Alba was ordered to find a stealthy way to depose Mazzoni, but, almost crying, he said that was impossible. The inquisitor therefore told Alba to tell him that he could go to Bologna or Casola, "and gave me a precept to take to him." As he was getting ready to go, Pantaleone came with a letter from Alidosi, saying a friar in Imola had told Alidosi that an Inquisition vicar was coming. Alidosi cared not, but apparently Pantaleone was to find out what was going on in the Holy Office. He read Alba the letter to see what he could learn. The friar was Mordano, as Alba later discovered, but he did not know how Mordano knew. He had been with Alidosi in Prague and also knew that Alba had been spying in Castel del Rio. He asked Alba's notary what he was doing there, but he refused to say anything. Mordano said he did not want Alba to cause trouble for Alidosi, because he wanted to preach Lent in Castel del Rio. This annoyed his fellow friars and Alba thought that was why he told Alidosi what was happening. Then Alba tried again with Mazzoni. He managed to get permission to stay in Castel del Rio in order to observe the young Lutheran and gave the inquisitor a report, so that he could inform the inquisitor of Bologna to capture the heretic. Alba went to see Alidosi again and found Mordano there, who left immediately. Alidosi told Alba he could not believe that Alba would betray him, because Mordano told him that a servant of the Inquisition had come with letters. Alba was proud of having tricked Alidosi by saying it was all about the case against Mordano. Alba was expecting the inquisitor, but when he failed to arrive, Alba sent the Inquisition's bargello to fetch him and then Tedeschi. The vicar had posted guards in Imola, but Alidosi had been spying on him and therefore knew all about it when he arrived. Alba therefore told Alidosi that a true Christian knight would surrender a heretic. Alidosi said he would, if he had him, and offered to pay for a messenger to Castel del Rio to see whether he was there. He told Alba he would be embarrassed if the heretic turned out to be in Imola. He took offense when Alba said he, Alba, should pay the messenger, and immediately paid one of "our" servants to go. Alba then warned the *sbirri* to be ready. Alidosi came with three carriages, holding all those named in the *processo* with guns, some armed men on foot, and Rudolf on a white horse. All were searched, but nothing was found. The *sbirri* then closed the gates without Alba's order. Seeing the danger, he shouted "open, open!" Alidosi became angry, but Alba insisted that the closure was not his idea. Ciro shouted that Mazzoni was responsible. Alba tried to reply, but tumult supervened. The vicar returned to his convent and, meeting Mordano, "gave him a precept in the presence of the present prior and sub-prior of Imola that he should not leave the house," but Mordano immediately fled.[262] Toward the end of his text, Alba added a significant detail: the inquisitor arrived right after Alidosi left and was angry with Alba, whom he told to write to Rome recounting his mistake. Alba therefore wrote Secretary Pompeo Arrigoni excusing his conduct.

Mordano, even though he had already been sentenced, remained of interest. In another of his numerous interrogations, this one on 13 March, Pantaleone was asked whether he knew a friar from Mordano. He said no, but then immediately continued that three or four years ago a Dominican had come to him saying he was the son of Credo da Mordano, whose family were servants of Pantaleone's family. Despite all this detail, Pantaleone had failed to get his name. The same friar had returned a year ago, but only to exchange compliments, and, oh yes, asking Pantaleone to favor his preaching with Alidosi, whom he had written about ten months ago asking for the post. Thereafter Pantaleone had seen the friar many times, and he always asked about preaching. He came again to see Pantaleone (but failed to do so) shortly after he returned from a visit to Castel del Rio and shortly before the Porta incident, while Alidosi was in Pantaleone's house. Pantaleone saw him come out of Alidosi's room and reminded him about preaching, which he said he would on the way to Tossignano.[263]

Alidosi's Interrogations

At the end of March, after one more distraction in the form of the prison break of Giovanni Battista Domenici, Alidosi's case apparently came to the point of expedition.[264] The grand duke "warmly" recommended that step on 13 March, and two weeks later the pope and Cardinal Nephew Scipione Borghese allegedly agreed.[265] Just at this moment, Giudici unexpectedly left Florence, as the nuncio, who seems to have taken over the case by default, reported on 23 March.[266] In the coram of 2 April Paul ordered the new inquisitor of Florence, Cornelio Priatoni, to imprison and examine Alidosi (he was to receive an "instruction" about how to do that), using Martinelli, who had written the informative process, as notary. The *constituti* were to be sent to Rome, not merely a summary of them.[267] The ongoing use of Martinelli highlights the notary's importance in a *processo*. The "instruction," really a special commission, was dated 7 April and written by Arrigoni.[268] That this step was regarded, most unusually, as ushering in the *expeditio* is further suggested by the order of 22 April, that two witnesses complaining of threats from Alidosi were to be protected in the *expeditio*, as often happened.[269]

Between 28 April and 14 May 1609, Alidosi testified fifteen times.[270] Proceedings began in scrupulously correct fashion, with Alidosi's guarantors (*fideiussores*) producing him. Immediately (*incontinenti*), by Priatoni's mandate, in the presence of Jacopo Monticelli, fiscal of the Florentine Holy Office, and two named witnesses, Giovanni Battista, *capitano di piazza* of the city of Florence, was ordered to imprison Alidosi and keep him incommunicado.[271] It appears that the Florentine Inquisition lacked its own prison until 1632.[272] Alidosi's imprisonment was in part a ceremonial act, since he was soon brought from it for his first examination. In response to the standard opening question, whether he knew why he was there, Alidosi began with a complaint about the manner of his arrest by fifty *sbirri*, one of whom waved an arquebus in his wife's face.[273] The next day the fiscal told him he had been imprisoned for heresy and demanded his credentials as ambassador, meaning that Alidosi really had been on the point of leaving for Lorraine. He remained in prison for eighty days without hearing more. His questioner (probably Priatoni) asked again why he was there.[274] Alidosi said the only thing he could think of was because of Hans Christoph's arrest in Bologna. Pressed on the significance of that event, Alidosi admitted he had kept the Bohemian in his house. Was there a problem about the faith? Alidosi knew only that the church prohibited contact with heretics. The interrogator pursued the matter of Hans Christoph's arrest, which led Alidosi to blame it on Mazzoni (BEM:RC, MS 'Y.O.4.26, fos. 3v–4r). Alidosi brashly testified that if Mazzoni had not been a priest, he would have strangled him ten times. He had also written Millini (no doubt as bishop of Imola) that he wanted "hard priests," meaning Mazzoni and Del Monte, out of his state (fo. 4v). Alidosi went on at length about his hostility to Mazzoni, insisting that he had always treated the priest with the deepest respect notwithstanding (fo. 5r–v). Then Alidosi attacked his own secretary Giuntini. Asked whether he knew reproving Inquisition witnesses was an offense, Alidosi replied that they deserved upbraiding. Did Alidosi know that Mazzoni had gone to the inquisitor in Faenza? No, because on the day of their conflict Alidosi had received his orders as ambassador and left for Florence (fo. 6v). Had Alidosi written anything about Mazzoni? He thought he had, but could not remember what. The interrogator lodged one of the favorite objections, that this reply was "inversimilar." That led Alidosi to admit that he had asked for Hans Christoph's *expeditio*, which must mean that he was treating Mazzoni as the Inquisition's vicar (fo. 7r). The rest of the interrogation concerned details of Alidosi's embassy to Prague, including his small household, how he had met Hans Christoph, and what kind of heretics were in that city. Lutherans, naturally. The protocol closed with Alidosi's signature and those of two witnesses (fos. 7v–9v).[275]

The next day Alidosi was heard twice, probably in the morning and afternoon. The first session began with the order to recount his life. Born in Florence, as the second son he had studied law in Siena and Pisa, where he took his degree, intending to enter the church. Then he spent three years in Rome with Cardinal Altemps, whose family owned a territory neighboring Castel del Rio, and studied "through the means" of Cardinal Castagna with an auditor of the Rota. His brother's death meant he had to marry, so he began a new career as privy chamberlain of the grand duke and ambassador for twenty years: to Archduke Karl II of Austria on the death of his brother Ernst, the duke of Mantua, Archduke Ferdinand the old in Innsbruck, Wilhelm of Bavaria in Munich, Archduke Ferdinand (of Styria) in Ingolstadt, Duke Maximilian of Bavaria in Ingolstadt, the archbishop of Salzburg, twice more to Mantua, once each to Ferrara and Spain, and finally in Poland as extraordinary ambassador to the emperor (fo. 10v). About forty-six years of age, he had lived in Florence for forty-three years. Then he was asked about enemies. He said he had such only in Romagna, first singling out Affricano Ravaglia.[276] Then he named at least one member of nearly every family in Castel del Rio, claiming that at least half a dozen of them had tried to kill him or have him killed.[277] Mazzoni he denounced as both a sodomite who had attacked one of Alidosi's servants, whom he named, and a rapist. The next interrogator wanted to know about Alidosi's servants on his embassy and about the heretics in Prague in general before narrowing the focus to Hans Christoph (fos. 13v–15r). Alidosi gave a detailed account of his efforts to convert the young man, supported by at least one Jesuit and a number of Dominicans in Prague (fos. 15r–17r and 27r). When two of his servants including Giuntini warned Alidosi not to bring Hans Christoph back with him, the second in part because he was too good-looking and would make Alidosi's mistress jealous, Alidosi blithely said he had beaten Giuntini, "as it was usual for me to do often." Alidosi also accused him of stealing and trying to poison him (fos. 17v–18r). The interview ended with a long account of the letter Alidosi had written Hans Christoph's mother, allegedly promising her that he could remain Lutheran. Alidosi read his testimony and signed it, again in the presence of two witnesses and the notary, and was returned to prison.

In the afternoon, asked as usual what he had to add, Alidosi said there was more about his enemies, which he would save for his defense. The interrogator returned to Alidosi's letter to Hans Christoph's mother, this time citing other testimony that copies had been sent to Italy. Alidosi insisted he had given it only to "this Biagio," probably Neri, his maestro di camera, deeply involved with his master (fos. 21v–22r). Had he talked to Hans Christoph about it? No. The interrogator thought this "inverisimilar." Alidosi replied that disseminating or discussing the document went against his plan. Otherwise, he had sent only diplomatic correspondence to Italy (fos. 22r–23r). Had he burned any of it? Yes, a good deal of diplomatic material on two occasions in Castel del Rio, about which he gave a circumstantial account, including making a list of it in case he had to go into quarantine in Florence, as in fact he had done (fos. 23r–24v). Then the interrogator asked Alidosi whether he had read any books in Prague. Yes, the nuncio or Spanish ambassador had given him one confuting all heresies, which he had brought home with him, since the Jesuits had vouched for it. This was the work of Gabriel du Préau (Prateolus; 1511–1588), *De vitis, sectis et dogmatibus omnium haereticorum qui ab orbe condito ad nostra usque tempora . . . proditi sunt, elenchus alphabeticus* (Cologne: Heinrich Colenius and Heirs of Johannes Quentel, 1569, reprinted in 1581 and 1583) (fo. 25r). He had lent it to various people including Mazzoni, and thought it would be easy to find his copy since he did not have many books. Alidosi thought he had checked whether the book was on the Index, and in any case Mazzoni should have warned him if it were (fo. 25v). Then the interrogator wandered through a series of questions about Alidosi's household in Prague, including whether it contained any women and if there had ever been any mention of sorcery in it. Alidosi innocently answered in the affirmative to both (fo. 26r–v). Back to the Germans in Italy, which led to the interesting detail that Hans Christoph had been forced to leave Florence because he was having intercourse with a married woman (fo. 27v). Nevertheless, he always behaved in a Catholic fashion, as did his brother Rudolf, who had converted in Turin and had a writing to prove it (the interrogator wanted to know whether it had been altered). He had also gone to confession to the prior of the Carmine in Florence, later one of Alidosi's character witnesses (fos. 28r–30r).

30 April saw another pair of depositions. Again prompted to add anything that had occurred to him, Alidosi refused. The questions resumed with Rudolf's affidavit. As often happened, the interrogator referred to the original elsewhere in the *processo* (now lost) to contradict Alidosi's testimony. Alidosi maintained that he knew nothing of any changes in it and named two witnesses (fo. 31r). What about blank sheets with signatures? The only ones Alidosi knew about concerned the grand duke's business (something to do with Pitigliano), and although he had ordered his wife and Giuntini to search high and low, they could not be found (fos. 31v–32r). Did the Germans have any writings? Alidosi did not know, a response judged "inverisimilar" (fo. 32r). Did Alidosi ever check his books? He had no reason. What about translations? Alidosi professed not to understand the question (fos. 32v–33r). Then back to Rudolf and how much time he spent with Alidosi. Were he and Hans Christoph always with Alidosi? Yes, except for a week. Alidosi had prevented them from talking to anyone else because he was especially worried about that sodomite Mazzoni and even more about Giuntini (fo. 33r–v). Asked about the young men's reputation and their Catholic behavior, Alidosi assured his interrogator that they were taken as "the very best catholics" and always behaved accordingly. The interrogator shot back with contradictory evidence from Hans Christoph's testimony. Alidosi said he was lying and added one of his favorite rejoinders, that he would have killed them had he thought them heretics (fos. 34r–35r). To whom had he talked in Florence about Hans Christoph's conversion? A Carmelite who said Hans Christoph should go to the inquisitor. Alidosi objected that he had come from Prague, where there was no inquisitor. Two weeks later the Carmelite returned and said he had talked to [Claudio] Seripando, S.J., and the inquisitor. The second said that since Hans Christoph had confessed and communicated all was well, but that it would still be good to send Hans Christoph to him (fo. 37v). Alidosi knew Hans Christoph would be terrified, but asked Seripando to prepare him, anyway. In the meantime came the grand duke's order to bring both him and Rudolf back to Seripando. Alidosi scrupulously told Alba about the doubt the Carmelite had raised. The then-vicar agreed with the Carmelite and thought an abjuration a good idea. He suggested Imola, but Alidosi wanted it done in Florence (yet more evidence that at least its inquisitor did indeed favor him) (fo. 38r). Shortly afterward, Alidosi had learned from the curate of Valsalva that something was afoot against him among the Dominicans of Imola and had written Pantaleone to find out what was happening (fo. 38v). The interrogator wanted to know if there were any witnesses to Alidosi's talk with Alba, but he said he had sent everyone away, as

he usually did when talking to strangers, nor had he ever talked to Alba again. Alidosi retorted that evidence from Hans Christoph's *processo* that Alidosi had advised him to refuse abjuration and flee was 30,000 times false (fo. 39r). Had Alidosi said Hans Christoph is a heretic? No, said Alidosi, correcting the verb to the past tense (fo. 39v). In answer to another question Alidosi said that he had complained to the inquisitor, being surprised by Hans Christoph's arrest, since the inquisitor had told Alidosi that all was well (fo. 40r). Acting on the inquisitor's orders, Alidosi had Rudolf abjure, twice, since his attestation from Turin was invalid in Florence (fos. 40v–41r).

In the afternoon session, after the usual encouragement to blurt out an incriminating admission, all the interrogator could get was Alidosi's complaint that the proceedings were dragging on. This elicited from the inquisitor the adjuration that Alidosi tell the truth about harboring heretics (fo. 41v). The inquisitor prodded, Alidosi denied, before he added that he thought maybe Baffadi had told him about the Dominicans in Imola (fo. 42r). That line of questioning quickly ended, and another about Alidosi and Hans Christoph's eating habits began. Asked if he observed Lenten dietary restrictions, Alidosi said he had not for years and had a license to eat meat and dairy products then (one such from 1607 is in the *processo*) (fos. 6r–7v). This led into a detailed discussion of Alidosi's medical history, including a ten-year-old "fistola nel sesso" (a syphilitic ulcer?), a back problem that prevented violent movements (leaving open how he managed all those beatings in which he took such pride), palsy, difficulty breathing, etc., etc., such that he had to travel everywhere in a litter or a boat lying down, since he could sit only with difficulty (except, apparently, when leaving Imola in a carriage stopped at the Porta) (fos. 43–45r). Warned again on the strength of Hans Christoph's *processo*, Alidosi asked God to strike him dead if he were lying (fo. 46r). Next came a detailed account of his eating on the vigil of the last Christmas (fo. 46v). This was followed by a long excerpt from Hans Christoph's *processo*. Alidosi contemptuously answered the questions arising from it (fos. 47v–49r).

Next, in one of those sometimes dizzying changes of direction possibly intended to catch the witness off guard, the inquisitor asked Alidosi if he had ever dealt with cases of conscience. This set up a series of questions about usury (which had been mentioned in Mazzoni's deposition of 15 July 1608). These Alidosi brushed aside, saying he had no *quattrini* to lend in any case (fo. 49r). Showing the effects of a scholastic education more than following a possibly productive line of questioning, the inquisitor asked whether Alidosi had ever discussed prices with anyone. Grain, he said. At what price? Alidosi had left that to his factor (fo. 50r). Had anyone said the contract was illicit? Alidosi answered that this was all idle chit-chat (fo. 50v). Taxed with having denigrated confession in front of many witnesses, Alidosi airily waved the charge aside (fo. 51r). Had he taken any trips with Hans Christoph and Rudolf? Only to Imola to see his sister. Naturally that led to a discussion of his armed escort, where the interrogation ended (fo. 51v).

The sole session the next day, 1 May, picked up where the previous day's had ended, with a detailed discussion of Alidosi's trip to Imola. Alidosi said he had taken many guards out of fear of Ravaglia, not the Inquisition (fo. 53r–v). While he was having lunch with Pantaleone and his sister, Mordano came to see Alidosi, saying he had met him in Prague along with "Padre Gonzaga," which Alidosi thought was a good joke, since the two had not gotten along. When Mordano reported that Alba had written the inquisitor of Faenza, Alidosi did not believe him, the more so in that Alba came to lunch later (fo. 54v). Afterward, two other priests, one of them Alidosi's "domestico amico" (both of whom had already written affidavits about Alidosi's generosity to their establishments, which had not yet been entered into evidence) came to see him before he went to Baffadi's house for the night.[278] First thing the next morning Alba came with orders to examine Hans Christoph. Alidosi gave an account of the negotiations over a messenger to Castel del Rio like Alba's earlier one, even though Pantaleone had warned him that Alba wanted security that Hans Christoph was not in Imola (fo. 55r–v). When Alidosi heard that the *sbirri*, whom he took as Caetani's men, were at the Porta, he was annoyed, since he had just talked to the legate in Florence and the Consulta had not yet heard his side of the case. Unfortunately, he did not say what the case concerned, and no other testimony corroborates that any such was running (fo. 56r). Alidosi had sent his nephews to the governor to ask whether he had any orders about him, and when told no, Alidosi and his party left (fo. 56v). His account of the incident at the Porta differed from all the others, in saying that he still thought Caetani was behind the closure, and from most others in praising Alba for not only punching one of the *sbirri* but coming to breakfast in Tossignano.[279]

Then it was on to Mordano, whom Alidosi called by the diminuitive Mordanino throughout. Alidosi alleged he had not said anything more about the danger Alidosi and Hans Christoph were in, except that Alba was proceeding against him, as Alidosi claimed he had already said (fos. 59r–60r). With some reason the interrogator objected that it was "inverisimilar" that Mordano did not know the Holy Office was after Alidosi (whatever this might say about the inquisitor's expectation that its secrecy would be observed) (fos. 60v–61r). Had anyone else warned him? Monsignor Baffadi, on a trip to Florence last April, had said his brother had written to Castel del Rio to alert Alidosi, but he claimed not to have heard anything from Cavaliere Baffadi.[280] Alidosi appeared to contradict himself by saying that Monsignor Baffadi had spoken to him only about Mordano's preaching in Castel del Rio, which the monsignor had not wished to allow. The inquisitor next gave a lot of attention to the circumstances under which Alidosi had seen Alba and Mordano in Imola. He slipped in a question about why Alidosi had given Alba money, and Alidosi replied that Alba had asked for it "for my case."[281] Alidosi said again that Alba had treated him with great courtesy, calling out loudly "buon viaggio" at the Porta, and that he had feared only Caetani (fos. 61r–62r). Finally, the inquisitor, explicitly and unusually identified, once more said it was "inverisimilar" that Alidosi had no other fear, to which Alidosi replied that he did not, because Hans Christoph was in Castel del Rio and Alba had said he was not after Alidosi (fos. 63v–64r).

On this day there was only one *constitutus* since the afternoon was apparently devoted to a search of Alidosi's house for books, especially the 1581 edition of Du Préau's precisely described *De vitis* (see above). This means that Alidosi or someone must have given a fuller desciption of the book than that in his earlier deposition (fo. 64v). The search was made over protests by Lattanzio Seculo or Seculi, probably still commissioner of Castel del Rio, and the otherwise unknown Francesco Valdabano, apparently acting as Alidosi's proctors. Notary Martinelli conducted the search and signed the protocol (fo. 65r).[282]

The next three interrogations, one per day, mainly concerned the affair at the Porta. On 6 May Alidosi repeated his earlier testimony and added another long list of enemies whom he had not mentioned before, in order to justify the size of his escort. At the end of the session, he testified that Mazzoni had talked to the inquisitor of Faenza about Hans Christoph, but Alidosi had never dealt with either of them, especially not the contemptible Mazzoni (fos. 65r–73r). On the 7th the inquisitor began with a long list of specific questions about the events in Imola, to which he wanted more truthful answers. Once again, Alidosi mainly repeated his earlier answers. The interrogator zeroed in on Alidosi's use of messengers. The questioning wandered a little off topic when Alidosi complained that "Ardoino" (probably Suzzi) had failed to teach Alidosi's son, and the inquisitor wanted to know about payments to him, too. Alidosi admitted that he could not have paid him anything, since his wife kept all his cash (fo. 74v). Switching gears, the questioner wanted to know about Alidosi and the curate of Valsalva, and whether Alidosi had tried to help him in his case before the Inquisition (fo. 76r). Changing tack yet again, the questions turned to Hans Christoph's imprisonment in Bologna, the interrogator raising doubts about Alidosi's excuse that he had sent the youth to Bologna to get clothes. Could he not have gotten them in Florence? He pressed the point repeatedly, and Alidosi answered almost in monosyllables (fos. 76v–78v). Why did Alidosi not realize something was wrong once Hans Christoph came under investigation (fo. 79r–v)? What did he know about the Bohemian's intention to return to Prague (fos. 79v–80r)? Again confronted with evidence from Hans Christoph's *processo*, Alidosi insisted all his testimony was false. When he claimed that he never thought the Inquisition of Faenza was involved in Hans Christoph's capture, the interrogator contradicted him with his own words, to which Alidosi replied that he had never said them (fos. 80v–81r). And at that impasse, the interrogation ended in the usual way.

Alidosi's ninth deposition, on 8 May, returned to Imola. The record immediately contains a discontinuity between question and answer, suggesting that Martinelli was not paying scrupulous attention (fo. 81v).[283] Alidosi wound up talking about Rudolf on his white horse, leading to questions as to whether he looked scared and where he was now. Alidosi claimed ignorance on both scores. He knew only that Rudolf had left while he was in prison, according to his wife (fos. 82r–83r). It was "inverisimilar" that he would do that once his brother was imprisoned, and that he would go to Rome, suggested the questioner. He could only have left out of fear. Alidosi rebutted that contention, saying there was nothing against him in the Holy Office in Imola and therefore no reason for him to be afraid (fo. 83r–v). The interrogator objected that it could not be a coincidence that Rudolf and Biagio (Neri) left Florence at the same time, after Alidosi testified that none of his servants had accompanied Rudolf. Alidosi said they left together only because his wife did not like either (fo. 84r–v). In a tale reminiscent of Martin Guerre, Alidosi observed that once upon a time, Biagio had disappeared for two years and had wound up fighting in Flanders. He had come home covered with scars. He might have done something similar this time. A baker by trade, he was a big liar, which mightily annoyed Lucrezia Concini (fo. 85r). Fine, said the interrogator, what about Hans Christoph's capture in Bologna? Alidosi said he knew only the one hosteria where he had sent the youth. He did not remember whether Hans Christoph's single escort told him that either had resisted, but he thought it unlikely that two "foreigners" could defend themselves in the big city. The questioner demanded that Alidosi stop lying and Alidosi replied in equally huffy fashion (fos. 85v–86r). Yes, he had made efforts on Hans Christoph's behalf, including sending Mazzoni to Faenza, Imola, and Bologna, where he had also sent Giuntini, as well as writing his nephews and various other people (fos. 86v–87r). Yet he had never known the cause of Hans Christoph's imprisonment. Warned repeatedly to tell the truth, Alidosi claimed he knew next to nothing about either Bologna or the Holy Office (fo. 88r–v). The examination ended with brief attention to money Hans Christoph might have gotten from Alidosi's wife (fo. 89r–v).

The tenth interrogation, of 9 May, picked up where the ninth had ended, evidently drawing once more on information from Hans Christoph's *processo*. Alidosi was asked a number of questions about servants he had not mentioned, for example (fo. 91r–v). The charges that he had plotted to break Hans Christoph out of prison in Bologna were lies; when warned to watch how he answered, Alidosi spat out an insult (fo. 92v). He had dealt with the inquisitor in Faenza only as far as was legal in order to help a dependent (fo. 93r). Before the next question on the same track, the questioner slipped in an innocent-sounding query, whether Alidosi had ever confessed to an unauthorized priest. No, nor had he interfered in any investigation by the Holy Office; indeed, he had sent Alessandro Machiavelli to Castel del Rio to enforce compliance with its orders (fo. 94r–v). If any prohibited cases were transferred thence, it was because the Florentine law that governed his fief had demanded that (fo. 95r). After another insistence that he had never interfered in any Inquisition case, Alidosi was told to examine his conscience in the light of information from other investigations (fo. 97r). Then apparently in somewhat random order, the interrogator asked about any rings Alidosi had given as tokens (none), and again about blank, signed sheets of paper (fo. 97v). Finally, Alidosi called God to witness that he had never hidden anything of interest to the Inquisition. Warned, he said his enemies had invented the charge (fo. 98r–v).

On 10 May it was back to two sessions. In the morning Alidosi was asked about prisoners in Castel del Rio, his execution of justice there, and interference in the Inquisition's and bishop's jurisdiction. Naturally, he denied all the accusations and explained most of the imprisonments as arising out of attacks on him or failure to execute his orders reinforcing the bishop's authority (fos. 99r–105r). After lunch, Alidosi was immediately invited to take back any lies. He could not, he replied, since he had never told any (fo. 105v). Faced with Alidosi's obstinacy, the interrogator resorted to showing him documents, beginning with a letter from Hans Christoph, numbered 35.[284] Why had he not mentioned it before? I forgot, said Alidosi, although once shown it he remembered well enough that it had stressed his responsibility for the young Bohemian (fos. 106r–107v). Most of the rest of the afternoon was devoted to the same subjects as the morning session, with Alidosi offering many more details to prove how he not only had never obstructed the Inquisition and the bishop, but had also always tried to help them. Had he ever complained about the Holy Office to a long list of witnesses? Of course, under the circumstances (fo. 108v) Alidosi could not say whether anyone in Castel del Rio had interfered in depositions since he had been imprisoned, but it was likely that its residents had talked about his case, since the place was small and there was not much to do (fo. 109r). He knew nothing of any threats and had never told Giuntini he would refuse the Inquisition's jurisdiction (fo. 109v). Urged to confess that he had tried to break the Inquisition's secrecy, Alidosi refused (fo. 110r). Again accused of lying about his attitude, he stubbornly insisted that he had never obstructed it (fo. 111r). Asked a number of specifics about escaped suspects and plots against him, he deflected the charge that he had asked a couple of men to attack Mazzoni by asserting that they were the priest's friends and his enemies (fos. 111v–113r). Besides, he had never learned the details of how he had been delated, so how could he try to exact revenge (fo. 113v)?

At the beginning of the next morning's session, the first of another two that day, Alidosi said he had remembered something about the questioning of the previous day. He had indeed dealt with an old Venetian servant, but only about innocuous matters, not Hans Christoph (fo. 114v). Whether Neri and Domenico Tossani had ever been in Venice, he had no idea, as he scrambled to distance himself from Tossani, whom other testimony had identified as at the Porta and an attempted assassin of Mazzoni. Alidosi certainly knew this, saying that Mazzoni had hurt himself and tried to blame the injury on Tossani (fos. 115r–116r). He further admitted that his wife had used Tossani about some Inquisition bulls (fo. 117r). Enjoined to tell the truth, Alidosi huffily said he had never been called a liar, had never heard anything about the attack on Mazzoni, and could not remember having prohibited communication with him (fo. 118r–v). Then Alidosi adverted to his letter to Millini about "hard priests," this time in the context of a request from the priest of Valsalva for Mazzoni's benefice (fo. 119r–v). He admitted that he had once complained to Mazzoni's relative Ardoino about Mazzoni, and Ardoino had written Mazzoni a letter, claiming to act for Alidosi. He added that just to give the letter more weight, alleged Alidosi (fo. 120r). Although he said he had not seen the letter, Alidosi accepted the invitation to try to recognize it, dated 13 June 1608, when shown him. The interrogator launched a long discussion of the letter, Alidosi insisting that he had no reason to write or dictate it, since he was not then in trouble, and throwing in a good deal of abuse of Mazzoni in passing (fos. 121v–125r). He said again that he had asked Millini to eject Mazzoni (fo. 125v). Nearing the end of the interrogation, the questioner shifted gears to questions about Alidosi's alleged interference in investigations, which he again denied. Warned about the *publica fama* against him and the inverisimilitude of his answers, Alidosi refused to budge (fo. 126r–v).

In the afternoon, asked as usual if he had remembered anything relevant, Alidosi noted the case of two legacies for pious uses that he had allowed and somewhat testily answered the question (which does appear a little out of the way) whether he impeded them, no, of course not. Why, his own ancestors had built a chapel (in Florence) and spent more than 500 *scudi* on the church of San Francesco di Paola (fo. 127v). As for the legacy for pious uses that he had allegedly stolen, that was nonsense, nor had he required licenses for such bequests (fo. 128r–v). He had also never interfered in the hospital in Castel del Rio (fo. 129r–v). Asked whether he had ordered the clergy to announce anything in church, Alidosi denied that he had, unless perhaps alms (fo. 130r). It was ridiculous to suggest that he had ordered priests to procure from the altar women to dance for him (it was, after all, impious to dance in church), although he admitted that he might have asked about some of those priests' relatives; the questioning turned back toward the original denunciation against him, which might seem to have little to do with the Inquisition (fo. 130v). A series of questions about marriages in Castel del Rio pursued the same tack, before the interrogator turned back to the accusation that Alidosi had subjected his clergy to secular legislation (fos. 131r–134r). The ritual warning at the end of the session produced the usual response: lies, all lies (fo. 134v).

In his fifteenth and final deposition, on 14 May, Alidosi was immediately asked whether he was finally ready to tell the truth (fo. 135v). As we might expect, he replied that he had told no lies (fo. 136r). Confronted with evidence from the record that he had ordered no priest to seek a benefice without his license, Alidosi dismissed the charge as Mazzoni and Della Vigna's invention (fo. 138r). Asked whether he had ever prevented any religious person from attending a funeral, he said no. The record says otherwise, rejoindered the interrogator. This led Alidosi to burst out that the proceedings demanded him "to remember not only all my actions but also all the words that I have said in the entire span of my life" (fo. 138v).[285] It would appear that he was not too far off the mark. He insisted that he had never ordered process against any religious except two rapists, one of whom had married after taking minor orders, the other a Carmelite. Yes, Mazzoni might have threatened an excommunication in the first case, but Alidosi had consulted theologians in Florence and demonstrated Mazzoni's ignorance (fos. 139r–140v). As for the Carmelite, he had never been imprisoned, merely held in a room until Alidosi returned from hunting (fo. 141r). The record says otherwise, the interrogator objected. Alidosi predictably called that evidence a lie (fo. 142r). Then he was asked whether he remembered any sermons in Castel del Rio, which served as a lead-in to the charge that he had upbraided a preacher. That, too, was one of Mazzoni's lies (fos. 142r–143r). As a good Christian he could never have ejected any religious from Castel del Rio, as the *processo* alleged (fo. 143v). Asked about the beating of the curate Scipione, Alidosi at first could not remember, but then recalled having heard about the instance when he, Alidosi, was twelve (fo. 144r). Alidosi admitted he might have become angry at Mazzoni and the prior of the Carmelite house at Montefune because of their ignorance, but he had never prevented them from absolving anyone, whatever the *processo* might say (fos. 145r–146v). He had neither threatened nor banished either, again, no matter what the record might indicate (fo. 146v). After the usual formalities, Alidosi's interrogations ended.

The repetitio

After this two-week span of lengthy interrogations, the trial shifted into the *repetitio* (while Fra Niccolò continued to take depositions), as Alidosi's proctor, Filippo Valentini, submitted forty-nine affidavits on his behalf on 22 and 23 May 1609, some as old as the end of the previous year, some collected in the week since his examination ended.[286] According to the Inquisition's rules developed later, Alidosi should have had only one proctor (see the case of Christóval Suárez de Figueroa in Chapter 1 above), but Seculo and Valdabano may also have continued to act, given the amount of evidence collected, most of it in the space of only two days. Among the most important of the second sort was that from Claudio Seripando, S.J., confirming in all details Alidosi's account of the license he had secured from Inquisitor Medici for Seripando to do whatever he thought best with Hans Christoph.[287] Nor could it have hurt to have the undated testimonial from the grandduchess mother Christina of Lorraine's confessor that Alidosi had always been "a very good Catholic" ("molto buon Catholico").[288] This was one of a number of such given by other religious figures, including two submitted by the prior of the Carmine in Florence who had been with Alidosi in Prague, along with another by the sub-prior, the Carmelite who had dealt with Seripando, confirming his story, and adding that Alidosi was "the very best Catholic," through to one by a canon of Florence, to another from Galileo's antagonist Tommaso Caccini.[289] In fact, nearly the whole of the Florentine hierarchy of the Carmelites lined up behind Alidosi and against their fellows at Montefune, including their provincial vicar and the man who had confessed Rudolf, the last affidavit submitted at the end of the *repetitio* on 26 May.[290] There were also four or five certificates from prominent religious in Prague, one of them attested by the signature and seal of its archbishop.[291] A number of what must have been Alidosi's defense witnesses also gave depositions at this time.[292] We have only a few of Alidosi's defense questions.[293] They were to be put by his proctor Valentini. The general defense was in keeping with all those affidavits from religious, that Alidosi was a good Catholic and a victim of his enemies.

Sentence

On 28 May Priatoni reported that the *repetitio* had been completed and Alidosi had renounced a defense.[294] Martinelli, the notary, thought his job done and asked the large sum of fifty *scudi* in compensation; eventually he got it (paid from Pantaleone's fine), with the strict injunction that he would see not a sou more.[295] The same day, the Congregation, acting on Priatoni's letter of 18 May and a request from Alidosi, ordered the *expeditio*, which had already occurred.[296] On 2 July, Paul V put the case on the docket for the next meeting, the expedition of Baffadi and Pantaleone having been postponed the previous day until Alidosi was finished.[297] A week later he was ordered to abjure *de vehementi* as per the enclosed formula (missing), in the presence of the nuncio, archbishop, and inquisitor of Florence and deputies of the bishop of Imola and inquisitor of Faenza, to be imprisoned at the Congregation's discretion, given serious penances, and put under a bond "for a notable sum not to insult (or hurt) witnesses in any manner whatsoever" ("pro summa notabili de non offendendo aliquo modo testes"). The grand duke was to be notified and both he and Alidosi intimated the contents of *Si de protegendis*, the bull protecting the Inquisition's familiars, among other points.[298] A week later, after a protest by the French ambassador, the pope changed the order to abjuration in the presence only of Priatoni and the punishment to house arrest.[299] Thus Alidosi got the biggest piece of his proposed penance, house arrest.[300] The grand duke might not have particularly worried Paul, but Henry IV did. At the same meeting Hans Christoph was ordered to abjure *de levi*, be assigned a confessor, stay in Rome "for some time," and report to the Holy Office every month.[301] A week later Pantaleone, Feraldi, and Baffadi were to undergo the same kind of abjuration, pay a 500 *scudi* fine, enter house arrest, and then come to Rome under bonds like Alidosi's not to "insult" witnesses and to appear before the Inquisition "as often as" required, and to lose their licenses to bear arms.[302] Case closed. On 18 July Arrigoni ordered Priatoni to send the whole of the *processo* to Montini, which he did a week later.[303]

Bonds

Even before Priatoni could act and five days before Alidosi's abjuration on 27 July, Tedeschi announced his imminent danger at the hands of Alidosi, Feraldi, and Panataleone, all of whom were ordered on 6 August to take out protection bonds.[304] Alidosi showed more inclination to play by the rules than his co-defendants. Thus, on the same day as Montini learned of Baffadi's escape from Imola to Florence, Alidosi had his petition for release from house arrest denied for the time being. Priatoni was to send the names proposed as his sureties for 12,000 *scudi*. Without them, he would be re-imprisoned.[305] Alidosi's, Baffadi's, and Pantaleone's cases continued to intertwine, especially when the bonds of the second two were used to pay the costs of Alidosi's trial (the rest went for the free food Hans Christoph was given in prison, as well as the payment he received to cover his return home—he had asked for the whole fine!), but I shall confine most of the rest of this discussion to Alidosi's alone.[306] The negotiations for his bond dragged on for quite some time. On 21 August Inquisitor Ferdinando Taverna was assigned to check it; on his report, it was accepted on 9 September.[307] On Priatoni's letter of 24 August naming Alidosi's surety as Francesco Avogli, the son of a *cavaliere* from Massa Lombarda, the legates of Ferrara and Romagna, Rivarola, and Caetani were ordered to investigate whether he had that much wealth, at the same time as another request for release from house arrest was denied.[308] When Rivarola wrote on 12 September that Avogli had sufficient resources but was a minor, Alidosi was ordered to find somebody else.[309] When the grand duke bitterly complained about Alidosi's "retention," Paul ordered him told that he was "ill informed about the seriousness of the case," and that without a suitable surety Alidosi could not be released.[310] Meanwhile, the grand duke kept Alidosi afloat with a loan of 2,000 *scudi.*[311] Caetani apparently had better sources than Rivarola, and reported that Avogli's resources were *intricatas* (encumbered) and most of them tied up in inheritances subject to *fideicomissi.*[312] Then Alidosi had an idea. What if Avogli were to ask "habilitation" for being under age? Paul agreed to dispense him for the "defect" and take him as surety.[313] On 3 November, Avogli's petition and a letter from the French ambassador about Alidosi's surety were ordered read in the next coram.[314] In fact, the matter did not come up until 24 November, after a letter from Alidosi and possibly another from the ambassador, when Alidosi was ordered released on bond and his penance commuted to visiting holy places in Rome.[315] The day before Priatoni wrote that Alidosi was already using Avogli as surety in Ferrara or Faenza, and on 16 December, the minute of his bond in Ferrara having been read, the Congregation ordered the whole thing to be sent.[316] Finally, after seeing Avogli's *fideiussio* of 5 January, on the 14th Alidosi was ordered released.[317] Avogli eventually married Alidosi's daughter, making his surety a weird kind of bride price.[318]

On 28 January 1609 the Congregation heard Priatoni's letter of nine days earlier, announcing that Alidosi took his "rehabilitation" "humbly" and would come to Rome within a month.[319] Two weeks later the Venetian ambassador in Florence reported that Alidosi would return to his post as "receiver of foreigners."[320] Shortly thereafter, Baffadi and Pantaleone were allowed to go home, after a personal warning from Millini.[321] As often happened, Alidosi quickly went on the offensive to have his sentence reduced, as well as complaining about his enemies' renewed attacks. His request was denied on 3 March, the same day as Mazzoni's attempted murder came onto the front burner.[322] We do not know the disposition of the case.

CHAPTER 6

Florence II

Another Attempted Murder

The latest murder case against Rodrigo Alidosi could scarcely have ended before Annibale Della Vigna, "ministro del S. Officio," its notary, was attacked in April 1610, and yet another set of *processi* began. They posed much more danger to Alidosi than his first trial, since after his abjuration he stood to be condemned as a *relapsus*, which would have meant a death sentence. For some reason, this possibility never arose. The news of the assault on Della Vigna reached Rome in the form of letters from the commissioner of Castel del Rio and Alidosi himself of 16 and 17 April.[1] The assailants were Alidosi's nephew Gianfranceso Albizzi da Montefalco (Villa Montefalco; see below)[2] and Domenico S.to Brigo, usually called just Brigo, from Casal Fiumanese, the next comune north of Castel del Rio, both of them banned from the papal states, along with Antonio Manbieni.[3] For some reason Andrea Mazzoni waited to send the horrifying news to Serafino Montini, inquisitor of Faenza, until the 23rd.[4] Thus began an investigation and trial that lasted for two years.[5] Before anything could be done, Rome needed to know whether the alleged assault had taken place, and on 1 May Secretary Gian Garzia Millini ordered Montini to investigate.[6] On 19 April the curate of Carseggio, Alidosi's old enemy Bartolomeo Vanti, sent the news to Rome that Della Vigna had been shot three times. When his letter was read on 4 May, Montini, now together with Millini's episcopal vicar general, was ordered to collect information.[7] Acting faster than usual, Millini wrote up the order the next day, a Wednesday, emphasizing that the Congregation needed to know the motive behind the wounding.[8] In the coram the next day, the pope further ordered Montini and Millini's vicar to have the attackers brought to Imola if they were in prison.[9] Montini moved rather slowly, his letters of 15 and 16 May apparently containing little information, leading Millini to urge him on in his reply of 29 May.[10] On Montini's letter of 3 June with some unidentified information, he was ordered secretly to examine Della Vigna and other witnesses, Millini adding in his letter that these were not to include Alidosi's defense witnesses.[11] By 17 June Manbieni had been captured and interrogated, but progress otherwise was slow.[12]

Finally on 25 July, just after Alidosi made a flying visit to Castel del Rio, Della Vigna testified as well as handing in written evidence. According to him, Alidosi had vowed revenge through Giovanni Squarcioni or Squarzoni, and was trying to get Della Vigna and Mazzoni to Florence. "Bambano," apparently Manbieni, whose name also comes out something like Dimambino, had returned thence and talked secretly to the two would-be assassins and G. B. di Miano, probably a variant of Manbieni's name. The first two had been back to Castel del Rio twice since they had wounded Della Vigna. Alidosi himself had appeared on 22 July, calling himself "the most desperate man in the world" ("il più disperato uomo del mondo") because he feared being summoned by the Inquisition over the attack. He had begged Della Vigna to write Rome together with Mazzoni that he was innocent.[13] Squarcioni, "summoned with a precept," testified on 30 July that Brigo had told him that he had been asked to attack Della Vigna, but did not say by whom.[14] The Congregation considered Della Vigna's evidence, along with more from Mazzoni and Andrea Tedeschi, on 4 August, but took no action.[15] (By then, Tedeschi found himself in trouble, a case probably for false witness having been expedited with an unknown result the previous October. The matter cannot have been taken seriously, since Tedeschi also asked for and received compensation—with interest (!)—from one of the Alidosi conspirators on 8 July 1610.)[16] In the next day's coram, Paul V ordered Squarcioni, living at Imola, to be asked from which papal territories "Bigi" and Albizzi had been exiled. Those two were to be captured when they came to Florence and sent to Castel del Rio.[17]

Paul's order was superseded by another to the legate of Bologna on 24 August to capture Brigo.[18] Two weeks later the legate said he was trying.[19] He did not have much luck. Instead, Mazzoni reported to Montini the hearsay that Alidosi had killed someone.[20] Perhaps this rumor made it to Rome before the evidence against Alidosi was discussed on 3 December (a Friday) and referred to the next coram, but in the event nothing happened until 26 January 1611.[21] Then, still as part of proceedings against Alidosi and on the strength of Squarcioni's then six-month-old deposition, Cornelio Priatoni, inquisitor of Florence, was ordered to capture Albizzi and Brigo "as present agents of Alidosi" ("uti presentos mandatarios Alidosi") in Della Vigna's wounding if they were in Florence. The next day's coram was to discuss Alidosi and his bond. Paul approved the decree.[22] One reason for the slow pace of action against Alidosi may have been the uproar caused when the agents of Cardinal Caetani, legate of Romagna, broke into Montini's rooms and arrested his vicar.[23] Nor could the denunciation for adultery by Millini's vicar of Montini's vicar in Imola and his removal from office have helped.[24]

In response to Priatoni's letter of 15 February saying that, although Albizzi was at Villa "Montisfalconis" (Montefalco) twenty-five miles from Florence, and that Brigo often visited him, the inquisitor did not think he could capture them, because he could not rely on Archbishop Alessandro Marzi Medici's officers ("ob infidelitatem executorum Curiae")," on 3 March the grand duke was asked to use his men in the arrest.[25] On 14 March, the grand duke's "superintendent of justice" ("superintendens negotiis iustitiae apud Magnum Ducem") replied that his officers could not usually be used to make arrests for the Inquisition, but if he received a specific request from Priatoni, he would extend all possible aid. Paul V refused the offer and instead ordered the usual blank warrants to be issued and executed by the archbishop's officers.[26] Three days after the superintendent's letter, Priatoni reported that Albizzi could not be caught. He also said that Alidosi had a letter from the queen of France asking the cancellation of his bond. Paul instead ordered proceedings against his surety, Francesco Avogli.[27] Even after letters from the French ambassador, the queen, and the nuncio in France, together with a memorandum from Alidosi, on 14 April after hearing the consultors, Paul ordered proceedings against Albizzi and Brigo and refused to cancel Alidosi's bond.[28]

Another *Processo* Opens

A week later, on 21 April, on another denunciation of Alidosi to Montini from the previous November and correspondence from Mazzoni, the pope ordered Montini to make a case.[29] The next week's coram heard a report of the sentence of contumacy against Albizzi and Brigo.[30] On 12 May, after the French ambassador again interceded for Alidosi, he was ordered to be told that Alidosi would receive a safe-conduct to come to Rome, but not about his case. Yet a week later the ambassador got the news that Alidosi was coming "in order to inform the Sacred Congregation of his innocence."[31] At the end of the month and beginning of June, Della Vigna's role came up again, first with a letter that was ordered added to Alidosi's dossier and then with the troubling report that Montini had asked him to depose that Alidosi was not involved in his wounding, but he had refused.[32] (Montini was also denounced for interfering in the elections of superiors of religious houses, but allowed to proceed when legitimately acting with the brothers.)[33] At the same time, a letter from Montini announced that Alidosi had made Camillo Zampieri, the organist involved in the run-up to the Porta dell'Osservanza incident (see the previous chapter), commissioner of Castel del Rio and proposed Alberto da Lugo, prior of the Dominican house in Ravenna, as its Inquisition vicar.[34] A man of the same name had earlier been inquisitor of Verona, where, at least according to Paolo Sarpi, in 1590 he had tried to make process against Venice for favoring heretics. He had been disgraced by the Venetians in 1591, and had been transferred to Cesena, whence it appears he moved to Cremona.[35] He was removed from that post late in 1603, when Michelangelo Seghizzi, later to become commissary in Rome, replaced him and began to investigate a long series of complaints from serious financial improprieties to womanizing and weapons violations.[36] Almost certainly the same man as Alidosi's appointee was in 1610 prior of Forlì, becoming its Inquisition vicar in 1619, at the same time as Niccolò da Bologna returned to office in Faenza.[37] If this is all the same man, he had the kind of checkered record that would have appealed to Alidosi, if even some of the crimes alleged against him were true. It is therefore a little surprising to find his appointment approved on 15 June, a sign that even the Inquisition's long arm could not reach everywhere.[38]

A week after Alberto got his new post he lost it. Alidosi was then in Rome, staying with the French ambassador "in order to expedite his rather well-known business with the Holy Office."[39] The ambassador got right to work. On 30 June the Congregation read his memorandum in the queen's name, asking the cancellation of Alidosi's bond and no delay in the case against Albizzi for the alleged wounding of Della Vigna, along with four letters from Mazzoni and one Gabriele Franctini (?). The cardinals gave Alidosi almost none of what he wanted. Not only was Alberto to be removed (granted, along with Mazzoni, a small victory), but Albizzi was also summoned to Rome immediately, the "aforesaid letters" were to be compared by experts to those in the Inquisition's hands ("fieri comparationem per peritos praedictarum literarum cum aliis eorundem literis existentibus in officio"), and the Inquisitors postponed deliberations about cancelling his bond.[40] As the lack of the referent for those letters indicates, this is a typically sloppy *decretum*. It also makes a mistake in the ambassador's second request. He had not sought "no delay" but exactly the opposite, as emerges from another decree a week later granting such. From this entry it also develops that the letters were Mazzoni's. Apparently a suspicion of forgery had arisen. Alidosi was also allowed to deal with Albizzi, presumably over his surrender, and Priatoni was to be sent the results of the examination of the letters.[41] Probably about the same time, Alidosi thanked the emperor for help from his ambassador in Rome, even though he had been prevented from delivering the emperor's recommendation.[42] Alidosi left Rome by mid-July.[43]

Neither Alberto nor Mazzoni went quietly. Alberto remained in office long enough to file a complaint about Caetani's criminal auditor, heard on 13 July.[44] Mazzoni, as we might expect, proved an even tougher nut. Montini reported on 24 July that he had failed to eject him as well as to find a suitable replacement. On 4 August he was ordered to consult the new bishop of Imola and to continue to work on Mazzoni.[45] Millini, who had wanted to leave the bishopric since he became vicar of Rome in August 1610, resigned on 27 June to Rodolfo Paleotti, archdeacon of Bologna.[46] The next entry for the Congregation's meeting of 4 August concerned a 27 July letter from Alidosi's ally Giovanni Battista Baffadi from Imola, saying Mazzoni had induced the podestà of Castel del Rio to depose before witnesses that Alidosi was trying to force him out, and many other contumelies against Alidosi, along with details of Mazzoni's evil life.[47] While there was progress a week later on Albizzi's coming to Rome (he wrote that he would be there at the end of September, after the French king's intervention), the demilitarization of Castel del Rio ran into Mazzoni's refusal to publish Montini's edict to that effect. The Congregation could do no more on either that score or Mazzoni's removal than once more ask the diocesan to intervene.[48]

As far as the pope was concerned, Mazzoni was out, but not even a letter against him from the French ambassador could get him to leave office.[49] The ambassador kept at it, trying to broker the sale of Mazzoni's property at the same time Pope Paul licensed him to appoint a substitute at Sant'Andrea, while allowing him to keep most of its revenues.[50] Della Vigna, meanwhile, continued to press for damages from Alidosi, but the pope ordered him to wait until the case for his wounding had been concluded.[51] We have to take the pope's word for it that it was still in progress, since the register says little about it now. The ambassador kept pressing for a resolution. On 29 September his request for the expedition of the case was heard, as well, apparently, as another memorandum against Mazzoni and Della Vigna. Paul ordered cognizance of the case, which should mean that it had moved into the hands of another tribunal, probably to the Holy Office in Faenza, where most of the evidence had been taken in its opening stages.[52] But the move to seek a peaceful resolution also gathered headway. In response to Mazzoni's and Della Vigna's request for redress, the Congregation in its next Wednesday meeting ordered a negotiated settlement.[53] It may be that there was some difference of opinion between the Congregation and the pope. In the next week's coram, he ordered compensation to Della Vigna (the relatively nominal sum of 10 *scudi*), and Priatoni to demand that Alidosi produce Albizzi and find out where Brigo was. The next entry was a decree to find out whether another witness against Alidosi had been examined and what Montini reported "about the injuries suffered by [the witness]."[54] If there were disagreements between pope and cardinals, they may have arisen in part from the confusing evidence coming from Castel del Rio. Thus, Battista Suzzi, probably then commissioner, in August gave extrajudicial testimony against Alidosi (not considered until Wednesday 26 October), but in the coram of 27 October a petition in his name and "the men of Castel del Rio" was heard asking that Mazzoni not be allowed to return.[55] Paul ignored Mazzoni's position altogether and ordered Alidosi to produce Albizzi within an unspecified term.

The next non-coram featured Priatoni's letter saying that Alidosi was making every effort to produce Albizzi, and asked a guarantee that Brigo would not be sent to the galleys. The next entry reported the bishop of Imola's order to Alidosi to take care of church property. The Congregation ordered witnesses examined in his case.[56] By the end of November, Albizzi was finally in prison.[57] He petitioned for expedition almost immediately, and in a *constitutus* of 10 and 16 December blamed Brigo for the attack on Della Vigna.[58] In the next entry, after his request for expedition heard on 14 December, on memos from Della Vigna and Mazzoni, Inquisitors Taverna and Rochefoucauld were asked to negotiate with the French ambassador about their dispute with Alidosi, Della Vigna was ordered given 6 *scudi* for the expenses of his return home, and Caetani and Montini were to be written to imprison Brigo. In early January 1612 the ambassador was back at it, asking Albizzi's expedition. His pressure worked, so well that Paul ordered Albizzi's release under caution and the suspension of his process.[59] In the next entry,of 4 January, on Taverna's report the bishop of Imola was ordered to find somebody to value Mazzoni's "and the brothers' of Castel del Rio" property which Alidosi intended to sell.[60]

The disposition of Mazzoni's property was the last obstacle to his removal, and the negotiations proved protracted, the French ambassador again being centrally involved in the initial stages.[61] The same process had to be gone through in Della Vigna's case until in late summer 1613 he finally got the vastly better post of fiscal of Faenza.[62] In early April the French ambassador reported Mazzoni's and Della Vigna's reconciliation with Alidosi, but the bishop of Imola was still ordered to estimate their property for sale. In the next two entries Mazzoni was allowed to return, and in the second we finally learn that the false letters were allegedly his against Galeazzo Giuntini (who had returned to Alidosi's side). Mazzoni asked experts to prove that they were not in fact by him.[63] When others in Castel del Rio, including the former Carmelite prior, tried to lodge or revive serious charges against Alidosi, including that he had castrated another Carmelite, they were brusquely told the matters did not pertain to the Inquisition and it had absolutely no interest in them.[64] Paul agreed that the Inquisition lacked jurisdiction, and instead he referred the Carmelite's complaint first to the order's vicar and then to the auditor of the Chamber.[65]

The reconciliation evidently did not go smoothly. First in May and then again in August, Della Vigna still sought compensation and objected to the cancellation of Alidosi's bond.[66] On the second occasion, the pope ordered Alidosi to find "some prince" as guarantee or his bond had to remain in force. On the ambassador's assurance that the queen of France would stand surety, in the non-coram on 6 September "it was taken as resolved" that his bond was canceled.[67] Commissary Andrea Giustiniani on 21 December formally canceled it, in a document bearing both his autograph attestation and notary Andrea Pettini's authentication and seal.[68]

Meanwhile, Brigo in mid-January was still with Alidosi in Castel del Rio, where neither Caetani nor the bishop of Imola could catch him. Paul ordered the bishop to find someone to do so and to serve as Inquisition vicar in the commune.[69] Evidently, the bishop succeeded. On 3 May Montini reported Brigo's imprisonment and was ordered to make process, to send a copy, and to check whether there was any evidence against him in Albizzi's dossier.[70] And then the same thing happened to him that had befallen Albizzi, the suspension of his process. True, he was ordered exiled from Castel del Rio and explicitly left open to prosecution in other courts, but he could have received much worse treatment.[71] Alidosi and his satellites had gained powerful protection. That protection cut both ways. Since the French had provided security for Alidosi, they were also required to keep him in line. Thus Rochefoucauld was ordered to warn Alidosi in January 1613, on Alberto Tossani's complaint.[72] However much backing Alidosi had in France, his standing in Florence had been seriously damaged. In late 1613 the nuncio reported that the whole court laughed at him.[73] Two years later, he was reported to have lost the grand duke's pension and had to leave Florence.[74] At least Montini's replacement in Faenza was in his corner.[75]

More Trouble

In summer 1616 Alidosi found himself back in trouble, although equally back in the grand duke's favor. Initially the Inquisition passed the case to the legate of Romagna, Domenico Rivarola.[76] Although the denunciation by Antonio di Luca Del Monte was answered with an order to the new inquisitor of Faenza, Paolo Delli Franci, O.P., to investigate, it never made it into the decree registers.[77] Instead Rivarola wrote Alidosi warning him about Del Monte's case (which involved a large fine levied by Alidosi the year before) as well as Mazzoni's report that, although he had returned to Castel del Rio under Delli Franci's protection, he had fled to Imola on word that Alidosi wanted to kill him, and that Alidosi had told Mazzoni's host in Imola not to receive him since he was Alidosi's enemy. Rivarola told Alidosi to fix matters, or he would send a commissioner.[78] Alidosi promptly brought Rivarola's letter to the grand duke's attention and he just as promptly wrote Rivarola a strongly worded letter telling him not to interfere as his predecessors had tried to do.[79] The grand duke also reinforced his claim to protect Castel del Rio, including symbolically by the grant of a standard to the territory.[80] About the same time, Della Vigna, perhaps still fiscal in Faenza, complained to Rivarola about Alidosi's commissioner.[81] Rivarola reported to Cardinal Scipione Borghese, including the grand duke's letter, and the cardinal nephew ordered him to find out where Castel del Rio was (!) and the extent of its jurisdiction, and to see whether Andrea di Luca had any writings.[82] Then Tossani weighed in again, and this time the Congregation agreed to intervene, albeit with an extrajudicial investigation.[83] As usual, Alidosi's enemies concerted their efforts, several Suzzi joining Tossani in complaining to Rivarola.[84] At first some of these complaints went to the Consulta, but by November the Inquisition had probably once more taken an interest, including apparently in Alidosi's fief.[85]

The Congregation proceeded cautiously.[86] On more complaints from Tossani and his brother, on 9 February 1617 it ordered Delli Franci once more to investigate extrajudicially.[87] When the inquisitor certified the accusations as true, he was ordered to warn Alidosi, but again extrajudicially.[88] In November a garbled entry at least records an order to see what the Inquisition had against

Alidosi.[89] On 4 December 1617, a Monday, Millini wrote the new inquisitor of Faenza, Girolamo Maria (or Girolamo) Zambeccari, about complaints of mistreatment by Alidosi, including threats to kill various people, adding that the inquisitor's reports about Andrea di Luca had been read in the pope's presence and had led to orders for a secret investigation, especially into how witnesses knew what they knew and about hatred of Alidosi.[90] This action does not appear in the decree register, unless it is misdated and should follow the similar decree of three days later (but that was not a coram).[91] It appears once again that the pope and the Congregation might have been acting in part independently of one another.

While Del Monte's and Tossani's complaints continued to be investigated, more dramatic events transpired.[92] After a report to the grand duke in January 1618 about Alidosi's treatment of his fief, and Rivarola's letter announcing his switch from the statutes of Imola to those of Florence, came Annibale Della Vigna's letter of 12 May 1618, probably to Rivarola, reporting his inspection of Castel del Rio.[93] Alidosi had complained to the grand duke that his vassals refused to obey him and ran to the Inquisition for "every little thing" ("ogni minima cosa"). He could not stay in his fief because of his distrust of his neighbor Affricano Ravaglia. Combined with his large debt, this led him to decide to rent the fief to the grand duke, and the deal had been completed. Della Vigna enclosed notarial evidence that the fief had always belonged to the church. A week later Cardinal Borghese told Rivarola that the pope had no interest in buying Castel del Rio, since it was too far away.[94] Rivarola replied that Alidosi was trying to sell to the Pepoli of Bologna.[95]

A Precept to Alidosi?

The same day as Rivarola's letter, Borghese replied. His order has great importance. The cardinal nephew informed the legate that Pope Paul did not want the sale to go through. In order to prevent it, Rivarola was to get Alidosi to Ravenna or another papal territory and "in person give him a precept not to sell" ("ella di faccia fare un precetto che non venga a venditione") without papal license. He also gave Rivarola instructions about how to administer the precept by "affixing" (in certain public locations, usually ecclesiastical) or "personally," but that he was not to give it unless he was certain that the sale was proceeding. If not, the precept would be superseded ("che il precetto eseguito per affixionem afficiat ac si personaliter fuisset intimatum al qual precetto V.

S. Illma non verrà, se non quando sia certa che la vendita al Gran Duca vada avanti, et sia per effetuarsi, perche quando il negotio fusse sospeso, restarà servita anche elle soprassedere in detto precetto").[96] It appears the effort to inhibit Alidosi from selling his fief took on even larger proportions. In Felice Contelori's narrative account drawn up to justify Urban VIII's later seizure of the fief from Alidosi's son Mariano, the nuncio in Florence was also ordered to act on the strength of two breves, as was Rivarola, one of 26 May, the other of 31 June 1618.[97] Contelori's version calls the orders "mandates."[98] The breve of 16 [*sic*] June 1618 to Rivarola reads that "we [the pope] enjoin you through these presents that by our authority you order [*praecipias, et mandes*] [Alidosi] under [threat of] our wrath and that of the holy see and incurring ipso facto the penalties in the said constitutions [of Sixtus V and Clement VIII]" not to sell without permission, "giving you full and free faculty to warn [*monendi*] the aforesaid Rodrigo" by affixing "the warning or precept" [*monitionis seu praecepti*] on the doors of the palace of the Curia in Ravenna or elsewhere.[99] Four days after his last letter, on 30 May 1618 Borghese wrote Rivarola emphasizing that he should give the *precetto* only when the sale was certain. If he had no time to consult, he should use the breve "and issue the said precept acting according to the writing in the said letter of 26 May ("et faccia fare il precetto suddetto regolandosi nel resto con lo scritto in dette lettere").[100] On 2 June Rivarola acknowledged receipt of the "contingent breve to give the precept to Alidosi" ("breve facoltativo per fare il precetto all'Alidosio"). This makes it sound as if he already knew about the precept, which could only mean he already had Borghese's letter of 26 May.[101] That is also supposed to be the date of one of his two breves, which must be the one referred to on 2 June. It thus appears that Borghese's letter and the breve of 26 May traveled separately, despite their identical dates. If so, the pope and his nephew were both intensely interested and as inefficient as usual.

A week later Borghese acknowledged Rivarola's of 2 June with the news that he had the breve "to precept" (*precettare*) Alidosi, and told the legate that the nuncio in Florence was investigating secretly.[102] The procedure of giving a precept was evidently common enough for a neologistic verb to have been invented to describe it.[103] On 4 July Borghese wrote that Paul wanted to strengthen the penalties in the breve about the *precetto*, but still left it up to Rivarola whether to administer it.[104] A week later Rivarola acknowledged the new, beefed-up breve.[105] On 21 July Borghese wrote that the nuncio would keep Rivarola informed and meanwhile "supercede in the execution of the precept . . . pending new advice" ("soprasedere nell'essecutione del precetto . . .

sino a nuovo aviso."[106] Rivarola announced his compliance on 29 July.[107] Then until March 1619 all goes quiet, except for a report of 21 July 1618 from Della Vigna, probably to Rivarola, that a contract for the rental of Castel del Rio to the grand duke had been completed, together with news of agreements between Alidosi and the Mazzoni clan.[108] Apparently Della Vigna wrote prematurely. Rivarola did not report the deal with the grand duke until 24 March 1619.[109] In response, Borghese asked the legate's opinion about the *precetto*.[110] What Rivarola may have thought we do not know, since his next letter replied to Borghese's of 10 April (missing) about having copies made of all documents about Castel del Rio.[111] The last we know, Borghese (and the pope) decided not to proceed to *precettare*.[112]

The Inquisition's Renewed Interest

Dodging the precept did not put Alidosi in the clear. Instead, in late summer 1619 the Inquisition displayed renewed interest. On 24 August Zambeccari reported that he had interrogated Galeazzo Giuntini and had asked "Andrea" (probably Mazzoni) to come back with Giuntini.[113] On 18 September, Zambeccari was ordered to find out what his vassals had against Alidosi.[114] On 22 September Alidosi defended his treatment of Antonio Del Monte, probably directly to Millini.[115] Three days later Zambeccari ordered the Inquisition's vicar in Castel del Rio, Ventura Morara, to order Alidosi not to molest "Dreino Del Monte," on the strength of the *processo* Alidosi had given Zambeccari, "made by the commissary" ("fatto dal d.o Commessario"), but none was named.[116] Morara administered the order on 29 September. In the sixth item of the coram of 10 October, on Zambeccari's letter of 28 September covering Andrea Luca Del Monte's complaint of 7 September, Zambeccari was warned to be certain a case belonged to the Inquisition before proceeding.[117] A month later he got the same order.[118] On 11 December the inquisitor was ordered to say whether and by what right he gave licenses to carry arms in Castel del Rio.[119]

Perhaps drawing encouragement from Zambeccari's troubles, Alidosi went on the offensive. His agent Domenico Tossani first gave a testimonial on 12 December 1619, written by Annibale Giuntini, that he had carried letters to Ciro Pantaleone and Zambeccari, apparently asking the fiscal of Florence to pay to send a man to Rome to Millini and to Ottaviano Di Letto, agent and secretary of Cardinal Carlo de' Medici, apparently about Alidosi's claim to Castel del Rio.[120] Then in June 1620 Bartolomeo Vanti with a number of other witnesses handed in a "Writing against the Mazzoni."[121] Also in June, Rivarola got a complaint that Tossani, called Alidosi's factor, had been imprisoned in Ravenna through the evil-inclined Ravaglia clan's action, all of whom had been banned from the ecclesiastical states for "most enormous crimes and homicides." Alidosi had kept order, but in his absence the situation was deteriorating, as evidenced by two recent killings. Tossani's scrawled *constitutus* of 20 July, saying he had been imprisoned the day before, is attached to the complaint.[122] Rivarola replied by accusing Tossani to Alidosi of aiding bandits in Castel del Rio.[123] Alidosi agreed, turning his patronage of bandits into the second selling point, when in October he drew up a document probably intended to persuade the unknown recipient to marry one of his daughters to Mariano.[124] Mariano eventually married Margherita Tonti, grand-niece of Cardinal Michelangelo Tonti, a high flyer in the papal curia before his disgrace and retirement to his bishopric of Cesena in 1612.[125]

And there the Inquisition's sometimes minute attention to Rodrigo Alidosi ended. He is supposed to have died in Rome in 1623, but also to have been buried in the Carmine in Florence. The second seems more likely.[126]

Mariano Alidosi's Troubles Begin

Until 1629 the Inquisition left Castel del Rio alone. In August of that year the comune, probably egged on by the Suzzi, filed a familiar-looking complaint against Rodrigo's son Mariano. Three points were underlined, including the first, that he never confessed (and lived like a heretic).[127] As in the past, Alidosi's enemies also approached the Inquisition. On 13 September the inquisitor of Faenza was ordered to examine Giacomo Suzzi judicially and send the results to Rome.[128] At the end of October he was to send the whole *processo*.[129] Probably the same man then filed a more detailed complaint, possibly with the legate of Romagna, saying that his family and a number of others, including the Mazzoni, were "persecuted" by Alidosi.[130] Among the complainants was the redoubtable Carmelite Alberto Tossani. The Suzzi kept the pressure on when Battista deposed to Clemente Egidi, inquisitor of Florence, that Mariano had asked him to kill Mazzoni for acting against his father.[131]

The next entry in the decree registers about Mariano, of 20 March 1631, is badly damaged, but it appears to reflect Urban's order to capture him, either in the papal states or by sending an armed Inquisition familiar to Castel del Rio.[132] When the inquisitor of Faenza reported that catching Alidosi would be difficult, Urban ordered it done "without shouting" ("sine strepitu") and asked the inquisitor whether he needed soldiers. Once captured, Alidosi was to be taken to Ferrara or somewhere in Romagna and the inquisitor was to say whether delay would hurt the case.[133] The situation in Romagna had turned against Alidosi. On 9 July, Della Vigna became the fiscal of its Inquisition.[134] Or maybe not, since in September he sought a recommendation to Cardinal Giovanni Battista Pallotta, legate of Ferrara, to be made fiscal in Imola.[135] The Inquisition's vicar in Castel del Rio reported himself ready to imprison Alidosi, but Urban wanted to know about the enmity between him and Mariano, and the pope still hoped Alidosi would go elsewhere where he could be seized.[136] On 23 October the inquisitor of Faenza reported Alidosi's imprisonment and rendition to Florence. Urban wanted to know whether a search had been made.[137] The first entry in the coram of 27 November reported that Egidi had been written to capture and search Alidosi.[138] This he had done by 11 December.[139] Nor could Alidosi be put in a less strict prison, no matter how ill he might be.[140]

Rome was still not happy about the conditions of Alidosi's confinement. In January 1632, Cardinal Nephew Francesco Barberini tried to improve the situation through the nuncio. As reported by Secretary Antonio Barberini, Sr., although in prison, Alidosi had too much freedom and opportunity to escape, and therefore the nuncio, Giorgio Bolognetti, was to keep an eye on him and think about how to get him safely to Rome.[141] A. Barberini thought it safest to bring him via Livorno and the sea route to Civitavecchia, where he would be consigned to the castellan of its Rocca. Bolognetti was to act secretly, especially because of the Holy Office's secrecy.[142] On 7 January, the Congregation, considering Egidi's letter of 7 December covering Mariano's writings, told the inquisitor that if he found any more to use them to make process, and to think about whether to try Alidosi in Florence or Rome.[143] On 15 January, the Congregation learned from the inquisitor of Faenza (who wanted to go to Castel del Rio to collect evidence) that the Florentine Inquisition had not imprisoned Alidosi, but rather the bargello, in his unsafe prison. Urban ordered that, if this was true, Egidi be reprimanded via the nuncio, who was to summon the inquisitor and warn him to keep Alidosi locked up and preserve secrecy.[144] A week later, Alidosi's mother's request for quick expedition was noted, before a reading of the inquisitor of Faenza's report that one of Alidosi's associates had been arrested. Urban apparently ordered the man sent to Florence; an (illegible) cardinal was to assist.[145] Against orders, Egidi wrote on 17 and 24 January that he had moved Alidosi to an easier prison, and that the

Inquisition always used the bargello's facility, since it lacked its own.[146] Urban snapped off an order for a new prison.[147] He peevishly demanded, on 4 March, that Egidi get on with it and build it out of his own revenues. Another letter from Alidosi's mother, Lucrezia Concini, brought debate about whether to haul him to Rome.[148]

On possibly 20 April, Urban ordered Alidosi brought to Rome, with the aid of secular authorities.[149] Four days later, the nuncio sent Francesco Barberini an unsealed copy of a letter to Antonio Barberini, Sr., in case the Tuscan ambassador [Francesco] Niccolini spoke to him.[150] Cardinal Francesco's letter, enciphered on the same day, responded to the nuncio's report that Alidosi wanted to sell Castel del Rio to the pope. Bolognetti was to assure Alidosi that the Inquisition's process was not a land grab and—this time as if from the nuncio himself—that he would be kindly treated, but nevertheless was to come with security and bond and be kept incommunicado.[151] Egidi had little success, and was ordered on (probably) 6 May to press the matter with the grand duke, in tandem with Bolognetti.[152] The nuncio, by contrast, seems to have had much better sources, enough so that he accused the Tuscan authorities of interfering with his packet for Rome, going after a letter to Antonio Barberini, Sr., in particular, perhaps because they feared that Alidosi's case would wreck their efforts to buy his fief.[153] In his reply, Francesco Barberini referred to a letter, unfortunately now missing, from the Congregation about the proposed sale.[154] In a cross of letters, Bolognetti also noted that he had not received the letter (about which he knew from a letter to Egidi, also missing), thinking it stolen, for the same reason he had already given. The nuncio also reported that artillery was being moved into Castel del Rio.[155]

A week later, Bolognetti reported that Alidosi had repeatedly told the Florentine Inquisition's vicar that he wanted to sell Castel del Rio to the grand duke, but he would also sell to the pope in order to clear his debts and live in Rome, if he were guaranteed no trouble with the Inquisition. The nuncio could learn no more, since only the grand duke, his principal secretary Andrea Cioli, and chief advisor Orso d'Elci were involved.[156] Cardinal Francesco replied that before proceeding, Bolognetti should find out whether Alidosi was trying to sell only to escape his *processo*.[157] On 5 June Bolognetti wrote that he had the duplicate of the Congregation's letter of 8 May ordering good treatment for Alidosi and continued negotiations for his transmission to Rome.[158] The nuncio had seen the grand duke, who agreed to order Niccolini to talk to Urban, despite wanting the case heard in Florence. Bolognetti thought he could persuade Cosimo II, if not the stubborn Cioli. He added that he wrote everything in cipher and only to the cardinal nephew, because he did not think the Congregation should know in detail about the plans ("Significo tutto ciò in Cifera a V. Em.za, senza scriverne cosi distintamente alla Sac. Congrge.ne, parendomi, che il negotio non meriti esser confidato in piano"). As Bolognetti was sealing the letter, Cioli had come with more reasons to keep the case in Florence.[159] On 12 June Cardinal Francesco sent word that a deal had been struck, but not concluded, because Niccolini had not been able to see the indisposed pope.[160]

Meanwhile, there was also movement in the north. On the same day as Cardinal Francesco's letter, one Martino Tondo wrote from Lugo that he had gone to execute the order, with a patent making him commissioner of archives through the chancellery of Imola.[161] He had seen Alberto Tossani, then living in Sabiosa (unidentifed), four miles from Imola. Although he had pursued a vendetta against the Alidosi under Paul V, was badly educated, and never finished anything he proposed, no one knew more about the situation. He told Tondo that all the notarial records were in Fontana[nelice], a "castle" of the duke of Altemps. Tondo had not been able to get anything out of Galeazzo Giuntini, the commissioner, especially the volume of *bandi* Tondo hoped he had, despite Giuntini's hostility to Mariano and reputation as a member of the papal faction. The other party, headed by Mariano's cousin Niccolò, supported the grand duke. Niccolò had everyone intimidated and fearful that Mariano would govern like his father, and seek revenge once his trial was over. Tondo reported at length about who had which documents, including the Mazzoni, and what they were trying to do, before concluding that he would have to go to Castel del Rio. This worried him, since he was banned from Florence.

A month later, Francesco Barberini again wrote to Bolognetti. He sent word that Urban had brought up Alidosi's case since Niccolini had not, insisting on his transmission to Rome. Niccolini replied that the grand duke had captured Alidosi on the understanding that that would not happen. Urban contemptuously dismissed the objection, saying that not only was it invalid, but that the Inquisition could always force him to come under *Si de protegendis*. Niccolini said he would send a full report to Florence and Barberini would inform Bolognetti, so as not to damage his relations with Cioli. Bolognetti was to waste no time arguing with Cioli.[162] Bolognetti had somehow heard that Niccolini was spreading the word that he had agreed to keep the case in Florence, which he protested on 17 July was a lie.[163] At the end of the month Cioli told the nuncio that it had turned out that the case did not concern heresy, but a homicide against one of those who had attacked Alidosi's father. Therefore, the grand duke wished Urban to distinguish that case from any charges about heresy and put the point in writing. Bolognetti had said he could not do that, since waiting for the writing would only delay the deal already worked out. It was also not true that secular assistance had been promised on condition that the case stay in Florence. Grand Duke Ferdinando, however, insisted that if the case did not involve heresy it should be heard in Florence, by the inquisitor and the nuncio. Bolognetti did think that if he were given the heresy case, that would make things easier.[164]

In another cross of letters on 7 August, Cardinal Francesco insisted the grand duke had no need of consultations and should immediately execute the deal. Urban had said that the Inquisition never accounted to anyone for the charges it laid, saying no more than that they were "most sufficient" ("sufficientissimo") to justify proceedings. It had condemned lots of "principal persons," including some under *Si de protegendis*, and the Inquisition never gave princes reasons for requesting their help. Bolognetti was to tell the grand duke of the matter's gravity.[165] For his part, Bolognetti wrote that he had tried again to get Ferdinando to concede the *braccio* (secular aid) for "transmission" of Alidosi as agreed, telling him as ordered that ministers' arguments did not enter in. The grand duke insisted on having Niccolini talked to again, but assured Bolognetti that he would not drag things out.[166] Ten days later the nuncio said he had talked to Ferdinando again "with the greatest care" and had seen Cioli several times at length, telling him especially about *Si de protegendis*. After their "lying interpretations and frivolous replies" there was nothing to say except to wait for Niccolini's dispatch.[167]

But then in a surprise move Alidosi asked to be transferred to Rome under bond, and Urban ordered Mariano's agent, Monsignor Francesco Baffadi, probably the same man formerly in his father's service, to be asked about the quality of Alidosi's bond.[168] This gave Urban just what he needed to close Niccolini's mouth when he asked again to have the case heard in Florence, as Cardinal Francesco wrote Bolognetti two days later.[169] When Bolognetti got Francesco's letter, he went immediately to the grand duke and told him he should be completely satisfied, not only over negotiations with Niccolini, but because the Sacred Congregation had much more against Alidosi. Bolognetti had reminded Ferdinando of the censures he ran the risk of incurring by delay. When the grand duke said he was doing no such thing, Bolognetti told him that "delay" meant "impediment."[170] On 11 September, after having written that Urban and Niccolini had made an arrangement for Alidosi's imprisonment in Rome, the cardinal nephew had received a letter from the grand duke "a little annoyed." He had therefore given the pope the gist rather than showing it to him. Eventually, after a long discussion, Francesco "gathered" that Urban would "allow" Alidosi to come with proper security and on the grand duke's word, but this plan had to appear to come from the Florentines. If they proposed to send Alidosi on the duke's word alone, the pope would reject the offer.[171] The same day, Bolognetti reported another conversation with the grand duke, who ordered a consultation for Thursday morning.[172] He told the nuncio that Alidosi wanted guarantees of his safety and that someone had written his mother that he would get them. Bolognetti could only say he had no orders.

In his next weekly dispatch, Bolognetti reported that Ferdinando, when given Francesco Barberini's last letter, had said that he wished nothing more than to have the accused in Rome, but that was a question of security. The nuncio answered that Urban would certainly take care of that "for the case's seriousness," and the grand duke could give his word. So could Alidosi, rejoindered Ferdinando. Bolognetti worried that the grand duke would leave before giving orders for Alidosi's transmission.[173] Three days later, Bolognetti wrote the Congregation, but not Francesco Barberini, "through hidden notes," saying that the grand duke would back Alidosi's bond "verbally" (*verbo*).[174] On the 23rd, unmoved by Ferdinando's objections, Urban laid out its requisites.[175] Two days later, in the second of the two letters in which Cardinal Francesco ordered Galileo summoned to Rome, he added that Egidi had been written that evening that Urban wanted both security from Alidosi *and* the grand duke's word.[176] In the next coram, Urban ordered the same thing, adding that the nuncio should propose *ex se* that the duke commit the giving of his word to Niccolini, but he still had to send the names of Alidosi's sureties in Rome.[177]

Urban spent from 30 September to 30 November at Castel Gandolfo, slowing the pace a little. Finally, on 18 November in what would have been a coram, Bolognetti reported that Alidosi's bond was in place.[178] Two days later, Baffadi (who had done a masterful job of stalling) came to the nuncio.[179] In light of Alidosi's *speditione*, Baffadi wanted to know what would happen to the jurisdiction of Castel del Rio.[180] Baffadi alleged that the order that Alidosi would have to enter the Inquisition's prison once he got to Rome violated the negotiations, and he would not agree to that stipulation. Bolognetti, realizing that Baffadi was after more delay, had replied that he could say nothing about jurisdiction, and as for the further request for the freedom of Rome, Alidosi had already been granted the privilege of coming under parole (which Baffadi sought from the Congregation on the same day as Bolognetti's dispatch, so something is a little confused here). Meanwhile Egidi told Bolognetti what Baffadi was up to and his intention to "muddy things up as much as he could." Baffadi said he was going to join the government of Alidosi's fief, and his mother had assigned the management of the whole affair to him. Accordingly he had complained to Cioli, d'Elci, and the grand duke that they had favored Niccolò Alidosi taking charge of Castel del Rio.[181] Much more clearly than in Rodrigo's case, the fief had come front and center in Mariano's.

No sooner had Urban returned from Castel Gandolfo than he denied Baffadi's request for Alidosi to come to Rome on parole only.[182] Baffadi certainly had a talent for spinning things out. Cardinal Francesco warned Bolognetti in cipher to keep an eye on him on 11 December. Two weeks later Bolognetti could only report that Baffadi remained hard at it to have the case heard in Florence. Bolognetti could only warn him not to abuse the Congregation's clemency.[183] Acting on Egidi's letter of 18 December (to which Bolognetti had probably also referred) enclosing an undated letter from Alidosi, on 30 December Urban ordered Egidi, if Alidosi did not immediately execute the order about his bond, to send him in chains to Rome with the assistance of the grand duke's armed servants.[184] Baffadi remained unimpressed. Bolognetti reported in early January that he was still working to have the case heard in Florence, showing no concern for the censures with which he had been threatened. In order to secure his end, he had proposed selling Castel del Rio to the grand duke. Bolognetti, with nothing more to say, could only tell Baffadi that the case was Egidi's business.[185] This letter or another of the same date was read in Congregation on 13 January, but no action was taken.[186] In his next letter, Bolognetti announced that he was keeping the pressure on Alidosi and his mother, thus far without result.[187]

On 22 January Cardinal Francesco told Bolognetti that he had asked the nuncio to the emperor to see whether Castel del Rio was really for sale, at the same time as Bolognetti reported another talk with Baffadi, with whom he had used the example of Galileo's compliance. He also had more news about the disposition of the fief, which Baffadi claimed Niccolò Alidosi had given to a relative's husband.[188] By early February, Alidosi's case was taking precedence over Galileo's, when Urban ordered an immediate answer from Egidi as to why Alidosi had not been sent to Rome under bond.[189] All the rest of the month and the following March were taken up with negotiations about the bond. A wealthy Florentine merchant, Angelo Galli, offered to put up 10 or 12,000 *scudi,* which Baffadi proposed to secure by the grand duke's word.[190] In the event, the bond was for 2,000 *scudi mon. rom.*, which led Urban to release Alidosi from the Inquisition's prison.[191] Baffadi made as much trouble as possible over passports for Alidosi's escort; Cardinal Francesco gave Bolognetti latitude about them because of the plague, for measures against which Francesco had responsibility as prefect of the Congregation for Health.[192] Only after more difficulties was the bond finally drawn up, probably on 22 March, and Alidosi and his mother left for Rome on the 24th.[193] Bolognetti sent the instruments on 2 April, five days before Urban ordered their transmission. Cardinal Francesco acknowledged receipt on 9 April.[194] The outcome so pleased Urban that he ordered Cardinal Francesco to send Bolognetti his blessing.[195]

Trouble in Castel del Rio, and the End of Alidosi's *Processo*

No sooner was Alidosi dispatched to Rome than trouble flared up in Castel del Rio. On 8 May 1633 Arduino Suzzi, "vicario del S.to Off.o" wrote a letter, perhaps to the inquisitor of Romagna, complaining that Baffadi and Alidosi's mother were working through Galeazzo Giuntini, and that Baffadi had ordered Suzzi's patent ignored and that of Luigi Vetolani published.[196] (In the postscript, Suzzi added that Virgilio Malvezzi, the Bolognese political writer, was his patron.) Exactly a month later, after Commissary Vincenzo Maculano had reported, the Congregation ordered Egidi to send the "formed processes" against Giacomo and Battista Suzzi, whose cases were to be expedited as soon as possible, as well as an investigation into the firing of an arquebus by Battista, including once at a window in Alidosi's house.[197] Three weeks later, the Congregation considered a letter from either Egidi or possibly the inquisitor of Faenza (the entry is again badly damaged) of 19 June, saying he would get the process formed in Imola against Fabriano or Fabiano Galeazzi of Castel del Rio and have him examined by local commissary, Luigi Pala, over the evidence that emerged in Alidosi's dossier.[198] On 29 June Suzzi complained to the same addressee as that of his earlier letter that the case against the other two Suzzi for an attack on Alidosi was invented.[199] Nevertheless, Galeazzo Giuntini would send their dossiers. There is apparently some confusion here, since on 2 July Antonio Barberini, Sr., still acting as secretary of the Inquisition, wrote the inquisitor of Faenza to work with Egidi to get the *processo* Giuntini had made against Alidosi; the Congregation already had the file from Imola.[200] On 14 and 20 July, first Urban ordered the usual payment to Egidi for a copy of the *processo* against Alidosi in an unidentified secular court, and then the

Congregation ordered the inquisitor of Faenza to get possibly the same dossier, which it thought might have been compiled in Castel del Rio.[201]

On 8 September, Alidosi's *processo* was referred. In the coram of 16 September (incorrectly called *feria sexta*), when it was the only case on the docket, it was suspended and Alidosi ordered released under caution.[202] What should have been a week later but is incorrectly dated 22 September, Urban approved Alidosi's "sentence," even though none had been so much as proposed, and ordered Bolognetti to complain to the grand duke about the "serious prejudice" the Holy Office suffered because of the delay in Alidosi's imprisonment and sending to Rome. This had led to the deaths of many witnesses, who therefore unsurprisingly could not be found.[203] And there the case almost rested, except for a mysterious letter of 9 October from Maculano addressed to his "patron," possibly but not certainly Francesco Barberini. It read that three days after being freed, Alidosi had come to Maculano and told him some matters of "more serious interest," especially about losing his *stato* and therefore transferring himself to Rome instead. Maculano had told no one and awaited the addressee's return to Rome from the Quirinal, an interesting commentary on the military engineer Maculano's grasp of geography.[204] The last we hear of poor Alidosi before his death in 1645 is the loss of his fief for *lèse majesté*, in a case beginning in 1636 when he had tried to sell it. On 19 January 1638 Monsignor Terzaghi, governor of Imola, took possession of Castel del Rio.[205]

The long travails of the Alidosi produced one positive result. On 28 January 1640, the Congregation decreed that no parish priest could serve as the Inquisition's vicar, or at least must have its license.[206]

Conclusion

Thus did a pair of cases lasting in total almost thirty years end. In addition to adroit maneuvering by some Alidosi agents, especially Francesco Baffadi, the principal element protracting things was the role of the grand duke and of politics more generally. Not only did the grand duke often at least hem in the Florentine inquisitor's powers, but he also exercised his protection more directly over the Alidosi and their fief. Other European monarchs also intervened, including the emperor and the king and queen of France. In the first two cases, these monarchs acted to defend a diplomat; in the case of the French, it was a question of patronage within the royal court. It is worth emphasizing the contrasting styles of the two popes involved in the two Alidosi cases. Paul V, former secretary of the Inquisition, took a reasonably careful, legalistic line, including obsessing over the precept to Rodrigo about the sale of his fief. Urban VIII, by contrast, would use any means to achieve his ends, including what looks very much like prevarication when he told Mariano that the issue was not his fief. When balked by Florentine resistance, including from its inquisitor, Urban responded by working around him and using the nuncio instead. The situation in Florence thereby came to approximate the normal state of affairs in Venice, where the nuncio always had the upper hand in the Inquisition's operations.

Castel del Rio was a small, nearly impoverished fief. True, it had a strategic position on the frontier between Tuscany and the papal states, but there were other such territories. Its value as a haven for bandits, of which Rodrigo Alidosi made so much, must have been fairly limited and in any case would not have interested the grand duke, nor have presented much of a threat to the popes. In the whole time covered by these cases, Castel del Rio certainly attracted only two Bolognese exiles, albeit an important military leader and a political writer. Perhaps the frequency with which Pius V's bull *Si de protegendis* was invoked offers a clue to the popes' motivations. Rather than being concerned about the fief as property, although that certainly entered into both Paul's and Urban's thinking, the issue was the insults, including physical attacks, both Alidosi had offered to the Inquisition, especially to Annibale Della Vigna.[207] The disproportionate attention given to the minor affray at the Porta dell'Osservanza, which even the Inquisition's local officials in Imola tried to downplay, supports the same possibility. Rodrigo Alidosi had dared to defy the Inquisition's vicar's order to close the gate. His sentence points in the same direction. Unfortunately, the content of his abjuration is unknown, but the sentence's other two elements both involve "insulting" witnesses or the Inquisition's functionaries. Rodrigo's real crime was to hold the Inquisition in contempt, as he often did in the course of his testimony. However thin the evidence of heresy that may have been alleged against him—one condemned book, a couple of heretics whom he may well have had proper authority to convert, a handful of rude remarks that could be stretched only with difficulty into the outer boundaries of blasphemy—Alidosi made a big mistake in manifesting his attitude to the institution, if not to the faith it was supposed to defend.

Conclusion

In this book I have taken a somewhat unusual angle of vision and emphasized the degree to which politics affected the Roman Inquisition's development, sometimes almost to the exclusion of other factors. The big trials covered—of Tommaso Campanella, Giordano Bruno, Cesare Cremonini, Marcantonio De Dominis and the two Alidosi—have almost nothing in common except the degree to which politics determined the outcome. Thus the nearly permanent jurisdictional disputes in Naples between the Roman Inquisition, the archbishop's Inquisition and the viceregal authorities almost by themselves account for the length of Campanella's nearly thirty-year *processo*. Similarly, Venetian subject De Dominis's ideas on the limited nature of papal power would have suited the Venetians nicely during the interdict crisis in 1606–1607, but they came to public notice more than a decade too late, when the Venetians no longer needed them (or him). While nearly all those who had written in defense of Venice remained safe within its borders, two who left, De Dominis and Fulgenzio Manfredi, were also the only two to be executed, albeit De Dominis only symbolically. Likewise, Giordano Bruno, who might have hoped for protection from the Venetians when he chose the republic as his point of reentry to Italy in 1591, had insufficient standing in it to merit such protection and wound up relatively easily extradited to Rome, where he too would be executed. Finally, the Alidosi. Their interlinked trials lasted nearly as long as Campanella's, as the grand dukes successfully protected one of their symbolically more important vassals—who also attracted strong backing from France and the Empire—and his son. In order to achieve his goal of dispossessing the son, Urban VIII had to abandon the Inquisition and use other papal bureaucracies. Despite Urban's marked propensity to use the Inquisition for any and all purposes, it failed him in the case of Castel del Rio, as it had Paul V against Venice.

When their beautiful new instrument turned under their hands, the popes had little choice but to revert to one of their oldest tools, diplomacy. The papal diplomatic apparatus had undergone an evolution similar to the Inquisition's, if longer, becoming steadily both more subordinate to the pope and also more bureaucratized. Until the late sixteenth century, the popes had relied on direct personal representatives, legates, to stand in for them on important missions. Most were designated *a latere*, literally "from [the pope's] side," and thereby became for all practical purposes the pope himself. For example, Reginald Pole (1500–1558), during his final legation for the reconciliation of England (1553–57), *was* another pope and could do whatever Julius III might have done, with Julius's full backing.[1] While legates did hold an office in the sense of a formalized post, it retained important overtones of the classical sense of *officium*, an obligation incumbent on a particular individual, rather than the modern one of a post that anyone might occupy. Their appointments were never permanent, and their legatine staff, as in Pole's case, were almost indistinguishable from the members of their households. In short, the institution of legate was never fully bureaucratized, and a powerful legate could challenge the pope, as Paul IV, the moving force behind the establishment of the Roman Inquisition, feared Pole intended to do. It was not until the early seventeenth century that the office of legate fell increasingly into desuetude, replaced by that of nuncio, a lower-ranking but permanent representative, entirely beholden to the pope and to the rules of his office, by then highly routinized.[2] It is a tell-tale coincidence that Giovanni Garzia Millini, later the Inquisition's secretary, early in his career exercised one of the last legations.[3] His junior status clearly indicates how the position had declined in importance. When the pope used diplomacy in preference to the Inquisition, he exercised his will through one bureaucracy at the expense of another.

As in Florence, so in Venice and Naples. Despite the best efforts of the popes and the Roman Inquisition to build out to the localities its fully bureaucratized and professionalized institution, thereby creating a unified tool for an "absolutely monarchical" papacy. But local forces put up enough obstacles that the Roman Inquisition was often forced to go around its own local agents and deploy papal diplomats instead.[4] This pattern manifests itself clearly in Galileo's case, the subject of my next book, but this one has already demonstrated that there is nothing whatever peculiar or unique about it. After all, the pressures to which the men on the ground were subjected almost inevitably forced them out of the tracks laid down for them by the Congregation, as Christopher Black has shown in his study of the long-serving inquisitor of Modena, Giacomo Tinti (also tangentially involved in the first phase of Galileo's trial as the commissary's *socio*).[5] Nevertheless, at first sight this is curious, since both institutions used men appointed by Rome in a deliberate effort to obviate local resistance. In fact, as the case of Venice makes clearest, there could be much more local input into the choice (or dismissal) of an inquisitor than into the selection of a nuncio.[6] Thus, despite the power of the Congregation in Rome, it had difficulty projecting that power into the localities. As a result, the Congregation turned to the nuncios. This situation resulted in an apparently bicephalic system, the Congregation and the papal secretariat of state competing to control heresy, and in the process producing two streams of information coming to Rome and two channels for the dissemination of orders thence, seemingly a recipe for confusion. In fact, things were less complex, as the cardinal nephew often, if not always, cooperated in passing on the Congregation's orders and seeing to their execution. Cardinal Nephew Scipione Borghese's huge reserves of patronage helped him retain a measure of sway over both his own diplomatic agents and the Congregation's men and at least attentuate the potential for conflict between the two agencies.[7] It took Urban VIII's cardinal nephew Francesco Barberini longer to realize the potential of linking the office of secretary of state to that of secretary of the Inquisition, but it seems plausible to suggest that during the more than forty years that he held both offices diplomats and Inquisitors came almost to coalesce into a single institution.

There is no doubt that the nuncios in all three places, Venice, Naples, and Florence, came by the early 1630s to dominate the local inquisitorial apparatus to a greater or lesser degree. The situation is clearest in Venice in the decade after 1607, when Nuncio Berlinghiero Gessi dictated policy to the Venetian inquisitor at the same time as he plotted to find ways around both him and the Venetians, who were trying to control their own Inquisition. Lest there be any doubt, Cardinal Borghese on one occasion told Inquisitor Giovanni Domenico Vignuzzio that he should report to the nuncio as to the pope. It is highly significant that the order went via the nuncio.[8] In Naples, the picture is a little different, as the Roman Inquisition's minister more often cooperated with the nuncio, probably as a function of deliberate papal policy to reinforce the local Inquisition, a situation rooted in the original if temporary fusion of nuncio and commissary. The routinized interchange of Inquisition personnel with the offices of both nuncio and "minister" in Naples served the same end even more effectively. Florence offers an even more pronounced instance of the popes resorting to the nuncio in the face of the Congregation's local agents' failure to carry out its bidding.

Nevertheless, as had been true almost from the beginnings of a papal inquisition in the twelfth and thirteenth centuries, questions of papal power and thus of politics provided much of the Roman Inquisition's agenda for all three tribunals. The heart of the papal response to Venetian writers against the interdict lay in questions of papal power, including over the Roman Inquisition, target of one of Paolo Sarpi's numerous writings. The same holds true for De Dominis. Nearly every article alleged against him concerned his claim that Christendom was a republic, a direct challenge to papal monarchy. Similarly in Naples, where questions of jurisdiction formed the carrier wave of the often fraught relations between the Inquisition and viceregal authorities. And although this study's attention to Florence rests mainly on two exceptionally well documented cases, they could not be more political, at least in subtext, if not always in manifest content. Indeed, since they concerned the popes' efforts to dispossess a subject of the grand duke, they make clearest the way in which the Roman Inquisition could easily be put to political ends.

The Roman Inquisition thus ran true to both its earliest and its most highly developed uses as a political institution put to political ends; changes in its procedures of *inquisitio* did not necessarily represent abuses. As I demonstrated in *The Roman Inquisition: A Papal Bureaucracy and Its Laws in the Age of Galileo*, the institution served as the most direct expression of papal power. Since the exercise of power unavoidably leads into a political context, the political developments outlined in this second volume fit neatly into the structures described in the first volume. These are not the only points of contact between the two books. The professionalized bureaucracy discussed in the previous volume also appears here in the use of *Si de protegendis*, Pius V's bull issued on 1 April 1569 against those who would interfere with the Inquisition's agents. Without such acts becoming heresy, those who committed them were nonetheless treated as heretics. However elastic its concept of heresy might be and however many crimes it defined as falling under that rubric despite the lack of any obvious justification (polygamy is one of the best instances), the Inquisition increasingly used heresy proceedings as a means to defend its own bureaucracy. While there was never any concept of "jurisprudential" heresy, as Leon Garzend once argued, or better yet "administrative" heresy, interfering with the Inquisition's ministers in the course of executing their duty became a recognized offense, as the attachment of the bull and its punishments to sentences for heresy indicates.[9] Violation of the bull could even be treated as grounds for an investigation, as it was in the cases of Cristóval Figueroa de Figueroa (see Chapter 1) and Rodrigo Alidosi (see Chapter 5). *Si de protegendis* proclaimed that the pope had a special care for the Inquisition and would strike down anyone who might attack its officials or premises, coming down especially hard on prison-breakers or those who aided or abetted them, one of the charges against Figueroa. They and their descendants were to be condemned as heretics and to lose all their property and inheritances.[10] Pius ordered the bull published, and the Holy Office followed his lead in, for example, a circular letter of 14 July 1607. It seems that the bull was republished regularly.[11]

Another point of contact between this book and *The Roman Inquisition* is that in the main the trials discussed in this volume followed the constantly evolving procedure of *inquisitio*, further underlining its flexibility. Even if its object might not have been pure heresy—as a liberal admixture of politics found its way into all the cases considered here—the procedure could still be put to political ends without deforming it in any obvious way. Setting *processi* like Campanella's or Rodrigo Alidosi's in a clearer legal context not only helps to make the popes' objects stand out, it also shows how *inquisitio* could easily be adapted to serve political objects without seriously damaging the safeguards built in to protect defendants.

Finally, this book does not bear out particularly well one of the major conclusions of *The Roman Inquisition*, Urban VIII's unprecedented dominance of the institution, which he filled with loyalists whom he expected to do his bidding, whatever the rules might say. The pope's successful intrusion of the Roman Inquisition into the kingdom of Naples might superficially support that point, except that Urban carefully played by the rules, especially stipulating that a *processo* could not start ex officio and had to arise from at least two denunciations. Thus he harshly rebuked Benedetto Clementini, the man he had originally sent as the Holy Office's special deputy against Bishop Fabrizio Caracciolo, for not observing that rule.

Nevertheless, the Inquisition's role in building Urban's "absolutely monarchical" state appears not only in Naples but literally in the case of the Alidosi and their small fief of Castel del Rio. Of next to no economic or military value, it represented an anomaly intruded into the fabric of the papal states, the haven for bandits which made Rodrigo Alidosi so proud. The popes spent the better part of thirty years trying to clear up this anomaly by way of the Inquisition. They were wrong that this would prove their best weapon, and thereby learned one of the most serious limits to the Inquisition's reach. While it might convict rulers of heresy, as it did both the Alidosi, that by itself did not suffice to deprive them of their state, at least not when another political power intervened to defend them. A direct confrontation between the pope and the grand duke of Florence was dangerous, a point that would arise throughout Galileo's trial. A conflict mediated through a tiny fief could be much safer and achieve the same end. Ultimately, all those testimonials to his good character and right Catholic belief that Rodrigo collected signified nothing, any more than the minor heresies alleged against him, such as eating meat on prohibited days. It was the affront he presented to the Inquisition as an institution when he defied its local agents at the Porta dell'Osservanza in Imola that made the worst trouble. That gate also represented a political boundary between papal territory and the grand duke's. By demanding that it be opened to him and riding through it Alidosi simultaneously showed his contempt for the papal state, the Inquisition, and the pope. While the last could easily be construed as heresy as it was in the papal offensive against Venice during and after the interdict, it was the second that was held against Alidosi. His heresy did not consist of belief, but rather of action, and a manifestly political action at that. Alidosi's case brings out a foundational element of the Roman Inquisition together with it limits.

Thus this book demonstrates the value in an approach to the Roman Inquisition like that suggested by Paolo Prodi.[12] He thought its activity should be located between the papal state and Italian politics, and illustrated the "angle of vision" he meant by pointing to *Si de protegendis*. Although its language was still "universalist" and therefore "medieval," Prodi saw it as representing a "symbiosis between inquisitors and political-juridical authorities," which precipitated three political areas: the papal state, Italy, and Ultramontane Europe. I have worked at the interface of the first two to show how the Inquisition, perhaps inevitably, came to serve the popes as a legal and political institution.

NOTES

INTRODUCTION

1. Scott L. Waugh and Peter D. Diehl, eds., *Christendom and Its Discontents: Exclusion, Persecution, and Rebellion, 1000–1500* (Cambridge: Cambridge University Press, 1996); and Andrea Del Col, *L'inquisizione in Italia* (Milan: Mondadori, 2006), 29–138.

2. X.5.7.9; Emil Friedberg, ed., *Corpus iuris canonici*, 2 vols. (Leipzig: Bernhard Tauchnitz, 1879), 2, cc. 780–82.

3. See *RI*, Chapter 5.

4. X.5.7.10; Friedberg, ed., *Corpus*, 2, cc. 782–83; August Potthast, *Regesta pontificum Romanorum 1198–1304*, 2 vols. (Berlin: Rudolf von Decker, 1871), no. 643.

5. Of the enormous bibliography, see most recently Mark Gregory Pegg, *A Most Holy War: The Albigensian Crusade and the Battle for Christendom* (Oxford: Oxford University Press, 2008).

6. Edward Peters, *The Magician, the Witch and the Law* (Philadelphia: University of Pennsylvania Press, 1982).

7. Gregory IX–Conrad of Marburg, 11 October 1231; Dietrich Kurze, "Anfänge der Inquisition in Deutschland," in *Die Anfänge der Inquisition im Mittelalter: Mit einem Ausblick auf das 20. Jahrhundert und einem Beitrag über religiöse Intoleranz im nichtchristlichen Bereich*, ed. Peter Segl, Bayreuther Historische Kolloquien 7 (Cologne: Böhlau, 1993), 131–94, 190–91; Alexander Patschovsky, "Zur Ketzerverfolgung Konrads von Marburg," *Deutsches Archiv für Erforschung des Mittelalters* 37 (1981): 641–93, 643n; Gregory IX–Conrad of Marburg, 10 June 1233; Karl Rodenberg, ed., *Epistolae saeculi XIII e regestis pontificum Romanorum selectae*, 1 (Berlin: Weidmann, 1883), no. 533, 429–30; Potthast, *Regesta* no. 9226. See also Balthasar Kaltner, *Konrad von Marburg und die Inquisition in Deutschland* (Prague: Tempsky, 1882); Ludwig Förg, *Die Ketzerverfolgung in Deutschland unter Gregor IX. Ihr Herkunft, Bedeutung und ihre rechtliche Grundlagen* (Berlin: Emil Ebering, 1932); and Karen Sullivan, *The Inner Lives of Medieval Inquisitors* (Chicago: University of Chicago Press, 2011), chap. 3.

8. Richard Kieckhefer, "The Office of Inquisition and Medieval Heresy: The Transition from Personal to Institutional Jurisdiction," *Journal of Ecclesiastical History* 46 (1995): 36–61.

9. Paul F. Grendler, *The Roman Inquisition and the Venetian Press (1540–1605)* (Princeton,

N.J.: Princeton University Press, 1977); and Sergio M. Pagano, ed., *Il processo di Endimio Calandra e l'inquisizione a Mantova nel 1567–1568* (Vatican City: Biblioteca Apostolica Vaticana, 1991). See most recently, Christopher F. Black, *The Italian Inquisition* (New Haven, Conn.: Yale University Press, 2009), chap. 2.

10. BAV, Barb. lat. 8376, fos. 87r and 89v, a dispatch of probably 16 March 1632.

11. See the fundamental sketch in Adriano Prosperi, *Tribunali della coscienza: inquisitori, confessori, missionari* (Turin: Einaudi, 1996), chap. 3.

12. The following summary is based on *RI*, chap. 5.

13. For them, see *RI*, 26–37.

14. It has not been possible to delve as deeply into either papal or secular diplomatic correspondence in the case of Naples (which has not been much used despite intensive attention to the Neapolitan inquisition over the last twenty years), nor into viceregal governmental records. Fortunately, the work of Luigi Amabile and others supplies a great deal of the lack. I have also not been able to work in Florence as much as in Rome or Venice. This deficiency is offset by intensive study of the rich Alidosi *processo* in Modena and local records concerning the case in Imola and elsewhere.

15. See *RI*, 11.

CHAPTER 1. SPAIN AND NAPLES

1. See Thomas Dandelet, *Spanish Rome, 1500–1700* (New Haven, Conn.: Yale University Press, 2001). The similarly important—and similarly three-headed—tribunal in Milan is nearly impossible to treat for lack of records. For one key moment in its history, see Cesare Beretta, "Jacopo Menochio e la controversia giurisdizionale milanese degli anni 1596–1600," *Archivio Storico Lombardo* 3 (1977): 47–128 and "Jacopo Menochio giurista e politico," *Bollettino della Società Pavese di Storia Patria* 91 (1991): 245–77.

2. Amabile, *Santo Officio*: 1, 214, calling Scipione Rebiba "delegato della Congregazione" and "vicario di Napoli e Commissario della SS.ma Inquisizione di Roma," but he does not cite the original language or its source. Giovanni Romeo, "Per la storia del 'Sant'Ufficio a Napoli tra '500 e '600: Documenti e problemi," *Campania sacra* 7 (1976): 5–119, 19 quotes Amabile. Amabile's book goes into much more detail about the sixteenth century than later developments, and Romeo's work also largely concerns the earlier period. The following offers a partial response to his call for more work on the seventeenth century.

3. Sergio Pagano, ed., *Il processo di Endimio Calandro e l'Inquisizione a Mantova* (Vatican City: Archivio Segreto Vaticano, 1991).

4. *DSI* 2: 1122. This article covers only the sixteenth century and while its claim that the fusion of commissary and nuncio did not persist, it gives the misleading impression that the nunciature and the Congregation did not continue to have an unusually close relationship.

5. Giovanni Romeo, "Una città, due Inquisizioni: l'anomalia del Sant'Ufficio a Napoli nel tardo '500," *Rivista di storia e letteratura religiosa* 24 (1988): 42–67, 60–65, especially

for his study of developments in Pisa. See also Agostino Borromeo, "Contributo allo studio dell'inquisizione e dei suoi rapporti con il potere episcopale nell'Italia spagnola del Cinquecento," *Annuario dell'Istituto Storico Italiano per l'Età moderna e contemporanea* 29–30 (1977–1978): 219–76.

6. 345/393 surviving *processi* 1585–1607 come from the archiepiscopal court. Romeo, "Documenti e problemi," 18.

7. " talche non per questo si puo dire, che siano doi [*sic*] Tribunali d'Inquisitione, perche uno di V. S. Ill.ma è il Tribunale ordinario et l'altro non è Tribunale ma è (?) modo di provisione (?) straordinario per servitio di questa S.ta Inq.ne, et per rimediarci alla salute dell'anime di quelli [Neapolitans]." The Congregation to Archbishop Gesualdo 22 November 1596. BAV, Barb. lat. 1369, fo. 95r–v, a copy taken from "tom. 8 [?] fo. 182," presumably a lost Inquisition correspondence register. Nevertheless, the letter concluded by telling Cardinal Gesualdo that, while the Congregation was "sodisfatissimo" with his handling of the Holy Office, he was nevertheless to accept whatever Carlo Baldino had done or would do.

8. Amabile, *Santo Officio*, 1: 284, again without a source, making it impossible to say whether the quotation is Amabile's paraphrase or translation of the original, and his further statement "con la nomina stabile del Commissario specialmente delegato, distinto dal Vicario arcivescovile, si ebbe il coronamento dell'edifizio dell'Inquisizione romana tra noi" (1: 332).

9. Romeo, "Due Inquisizioni," 44.

10. It is possible that breves of appointment may turn up, although at least one of these commissaries, Antonio Ricciulli, was deliberately sent without one. Amabile, *Santo Officio*, 2: 37.

11. Romeo, "Documenti e problemi," 22–25 and "Due Inquisizioni," passim.

12. Romeo, "Due Inquisizioni," 56.

13. Ibid., 58.

14. Ibid., 66 and "Documenti e problemi," 19.

15. Whatever Petronio may have tried to call himself, the Congregation called him minister, e.g., "Ministrum huius S. Officii Neapoli" in the session of 5 December 1630. ACDFSO:DSO 1630, fo. 196v. As Romeo, "Documenti e problemi," 19 points out against Amabile, although Ricciulli labeled himself "Inquisitore generale" (citing Amabile, *Santo Officio*, 2: 37), in two of his books published in the early 1640s he appears only as "olim in Aula romana advocato, deinde Episcopo Bellicastrense, & Sanctissimi Domini Nostri D. Urbani Papae VIII. in Apostolica Visitatione a secretis, Urbisque Vicesgerente, nunc vero Archiepiscopo Consentino, ac Sanctae Universalis Inquisitionis Consultore, & in Regno Neapolitano Ministro Generali" on frontispiece of *Tractatus de personis quae in statu reprobo versantur* (Naples: Roberto Mollo for Giovanni Domenico Montanari, 1641), again on frontispiece of *Lucubrationum ecclesiasticarum libri sex* (Naples: Camillo Cavalli, 1643), which makes against Romeo's own suggestion about the significance of 1622. Ricciulli was still called minister as late as early 1634. 1634, Copia, p. 92, session of 11 January.

16. Romeo, "Due Inquisizioni," 67.

17. For Borja as Inquisitor, see also *RI*, 89–91.

18. Statistics from the decree register for 1628. See also Pierre-Noël Mayaud, "Les 'Fuit Congregatio Sancti Officii in . . . coram . . . ' de 1611 à 1642: 32 ans de vie de la Congrégation du Saint Office," *Archivum Historiae Pontificiae* 30 (1992): 231–89, 250–51. For Urban's decree, see ACDFSO:DSO 1628, fo. 156v; and cf. BAV, Urb. lat. 1098 II, fo. 510r.

19. See *RI*, Table 6, 225.

20. *Avviso* of 15 March 1630 in ASMod:AE, 138, fasc. March 1631, unfoliated.

21. *Avviso* of 22 March 1630, in ibid.

22. *Avviso* of 29 March 1630, in ibid.

23. The pope had ordered "fieri praeceptum fratri Innocentio Min: Obs. Ref: existenti in conventu S. Petri in Monteaureo, ne sub gravissimis poenis arbitrio S.tis Suae loquatur cum aliqua persona etiam quacumque Dignitate fulgente, exceptis tamen fratribus suae propriae religionis, et non exeat a Conventu, et Ecclesia supradicta. Petri absque licentia Suae S.tis sub eisdem poenis." ACDFSO:DSO 1630, fo. 191v, 28 November. As usual, the reticence of the decree registers means they contain no sign of Borja's discussion with Urban, but they also do not contain the "decree" directed at him, as the *avviso* called it, unless it is hidden under "etiam quacumque Dignitate."

24. *Avviso* of 14 December 1630 in ASMod:AE, 137, fasc. December 1630, unfoliated.

25. ASVe:SDR, f. 103, fo. 262r–v, 14 December; and *avviso* of the same date in ASMod:AE, 137, fasc. December 1630, unfoliated. If astrology was behind Innocenzo's problems, then Borja's protection counted for something.

26. There is often a time-lag in the *avvisi*, making it hard to tell how fresh their news was. It is possible that the second *avviso* refers to the same event as the first. Borja attended the corams of 12 and 19 December, both of which predate the second *avviso*.

27. *Avviso* of 21 December in BAV, Urb. lat. 1101, fo. 12r. The letter of the same date from Camillo Molza to the duke of Modena reports the episode in almost exactly the same words, as does the Modenese *avviso*. ASMod, Cancelleria ducale, Ambasciatori Italia Roma, 227, fo. 451r, printed in Amabile, *Congiura*, 2: 154; and Amabile, "L'Andata di Campanella," no. 15, 44; and ASMod:AE, 137, fasc. Dec 1630, unfoliated.

28. *HC* 4: 13.

29. *Avviso* of 22 February 1631 in ASMod:AE, 138, fasc. February 1631, unfoliated. Aside from this report, the next we hear about Innocenzo is the announcement of his death. *Avviso* of 17 December 1631 in ASMod:AE, 137, fasc. December 1631, unfoliated.

30. Auguste Leman, *Urbain VIII et la rivalité de la France et de la maison d'Austriche de 1631 à 1635*, Mémoires et Travaux publiés per des professeurs des facultés catholiques de Lille 16 (Lille and Paris: R. Giard and É. Champion, 1920), 119.

31. Ibid., 127. Leman's study, well grounded in archival sources, is nonetheless strongly biased in Urban's favor and his incessantly reiterated claim to act only as *pater communis* of all of Christendom. See, e.g, Leman's assertion on 11 that Urban never tired of trying to reconcile the Catholic powers or on 29 that he never abandoned strict neutrality.

32. Ibid., 130.

33. Ibid., 132. See the testimonial of 10 March 1632 by Francesco Adriano Ceva. BAV, Barb. lat. 8376, fo. 99r–v.

34. There are a number of accounts that agree tolerably well in details. They include the official papal version in a dispatch to Nuncio Cesare Monti in BAV, Barb. lat. 8376, fos. 85r–95r, printed in Ludwig von Pastor, *The History of the Popes from the Close of the Middle Ages*, 29, trans. and ed. Ernest Graf (London: Kegan Paul, Trench, Trübner, 1938), 560–64, and dated 8 March although it seems rather to be dated the 16th, together with a Latin account, on fos. 96r–98v, signed by Guido Bentivoglio, Scaglia, Zacchia, Berlinghiero Gessi, Giovanni Francesco Guidi di Bagno, Fabrizio Verospi, and Marzio Ginetti (all either then or later Inquisitors); a "Relatione" enclosed in an undated *avviso* and another account in an *avviso* of 13 March (which may well be the date of the "Relatione"), both in ASMod:AE, 138, fasc. March 1632, unfoliated, both printed in Ferdinand Gregorovius, *Urban VIII. im Widerspruch zu Spanien und dem Kaiser: eine Episode des dreissig-jährigen Kriegs* (Stuttgart: J.G. Cotta, 1879), 135–38, 132–34; a very similar report in Vienna printed in ibid., 124–27; and an exceedingly anodyne Spanish account printed in Leman, *Urbain*, 560–63, followed by a text of the protest on 563–64, the nearest to the original that Leman could find in Simancas. Unfortunately, the Venetians had no representation in Rome at this time, having withdrawn their ambassador in the dispute over precedence occasioned by both the title of *eminenza* for cardinals and Taddeo Barberini's newly exalted status as prefect of Rome. Among many accounts in other European archives, there are supposed to be eight copies in The National Archives in London, Public Record Office, SP For 85/7, fos. 51–55 and 270–76. R. A. Stradling, *Philip IV and the Government of Spain, 1621–1665* (Cambridge: Cambridge University Press, 1988), 140.

35. Leman, *Urbain*, 564. The text in Gregorovius, *Urban VIII*, 123–24 has the same reading.

36. "Relatione" in ASMod:AE, 138, fasc. March 1632, unfoliated.

37. "Relatione" and *avviso* of 13 March 1632, both in ibid. From the location of this information in the first text, it seems likely it came from Scaglia.

38. *Avviso* of 13 March 1632 in ASMod:AE, 138, fasc. March 1632, unfoliated.

39. "Relatione" and *avviso* of 13 March 1632, both in ibid.

40. *Avviso* of 6 June 1632 in ibid., fasc. June 1632, unfoliated.

41. For Borja's dissemination of his version, see the dispatch of 17 March 1632 in BAV, Barb. lat. 7306, fo. 18r; same content in ASV, Seg. Stato, Nunz. Firenze 20, fo. 26v.

42. BAV, Barb. lat. 8376, fos. 87r and 89v. The dispatch is probably dated 16 March, although it may be as late as the 18th, when the Latin version of the consistory was signed. The *congregazione* that debated the pope's diplomatic response met at Cardinal Spada's palace on 12 March. Leman, *Urbain*, 565–68.

43. *Avviso* of 20 March 1632 in ASMod:AE, 138, fasc. March 1632, unfoliated; and nuncio in Florence–F. Barberini, 5 June 1632. BAV, Barb. lat. 7306, fos. 56r and 61r and ASV, Seg. Stato, Nunz. Firenze 20, fos. 41r and 43v.

44. *Avviso* of 27 March 1632 in ASMod:AE, 138, fasc. March 1632, unfoliated.

45. And in fact it was not. See *RI*, 33.

46. *HC* 4: 204.

47. *Avviso* of 15 April 1628 in BAV, Urb. lat. 1098 I, fo. 191r.

48. *Avviso* of 19 June in ASMod:AE, 138, fasc. June 1632, unfoliated. See also another *avviso* of 6 June in the same volume saying that Urban thought of nothing but getting rid of Borja by using residence.

49. *Avvisi* of 17 and 24 July and 14 Augusta in ASMod:AE, 138, fasc. July and August 1632, unfoliated. The Venetian ambassador once made the number of carriages fifty. Dispatch of 14 August 1632 in ASVe:SDR, f. 105, fo. 93r.

50. *Avviso* of 13 June 1632 in ASMod:AE, 138, fasc. June 1632, unfoliated; and see the Venetian ambassador's dispatches of 24 July 1632 II and 31 July 1632 in ASVe:SDR, f. 105, fos. 41r and 58r.

51. *Avviso* of 3 July 1632 in ASMod:AE, 138, fasc. July 1632, unfoliated, and ASVe:SDR, f. 105, fo. 74r, 31 July. The attendance list for the first meeting is destroyed in ACDFSO:DSO 1632. Borja certainly attended the second.

52. *Avviso* of 14 August 1632 in ASMod:AE, 138, fasc. August 1632, unfoliated.

53. See the Venetian ambassador's dispatch of 14 August 1632 in ASVe:SDR, f. 105, fo. 120r–v.

54. See the Venetian ambassador's dispatch of 14 August 1632 in ibid., fo. 139r–v.

55. *Avviso* of 4 September 1632 in ASMod:AE, 138, fasc. September 1632, unfoliated.

56. See the Venetian ambassador's dispatches of 10 and 25 September in ASVe:SDR, f. 105, fos. 192r and 237r, and the *avviso* of 28 September about a banquet Borghese hosted for the Barberini nephews in ASMod:AE, 138, fasc. September 1632, unfoliated.

57. ASVe:SDR, f. 105, fo. 309r, dispatch of 23 October 1632.

58. Ibid., fo. 329r, dispatch of 30 October 1632.

59. ASMod:AE, 138, fasc. November 1632, unfoliated.

60. ASVe:SDR, f. 105, fo. 402v. It had been planned for the consistory of the following Monday, 16 November. *Avviso* of 20 November 1632 in ASMod:AE, 138, fasc. November 1632, unfoliated.

61. ASVe:SDR, f. 106, fo. 28r, dispatch of 4 December 1632.

62. Ibid., fos. 60r–61r and 76r–v, dispatches of 11 and 18 December 1632. For more on this notorious episode, see Stephan Ehses, "Papst Urban VIII und Gustav-Adolf," *Historisches Jahrbuch* 16 (1895): 336–41, and Joseph Schnitzer, "Urbans VIII Verhalten bei der Nachricht vom Tode des Schwedenkönigs," in *Festschrift zum elfhundertjährigen Jubiläum des deutschen Campo Santo in Rom*, ed. Stephan Ehses (Frieburg/Br: Herder, 1897), 280–84.

63. *Avviso* of 25 December 1632 in ASMod:AE, 138, fasc. December 1632, unfoliated.

64. *DBI.*

65. BAV, Barb. lat. 6352, fo. 183r.

66. ASVe:SDR, f. 106, fo. 3v, dispatch of 27 November 1632.

67. *Avviso* of 1 January 1633 in ASMod:AE, 139, fasc. January 1633, unfoliated. For the pope's complaints about thin attendance, see also ASVe:SDR, f. 106, fo. 133r, dispatch of the same date.

68. *Avviso* of 8 January 1633 in ASMod:AE, 139, fasc. January 1633, unfoliated.

69. *Avviso* of 15 January 1633 in ibid.

70. *Avviso* of 29 January 1633 in ibid. This was apparently a meeting held in place of a Monday consistory. ASVe:SDR, f. 106, fo. 214v, dispatch of the same date.

71. *Avviso* of 30 April 1633 in ASMod:AE, 139, fasc. April 1633, unfoliated.

72. This episode deserves a full study to itself.

73. "In questa Congregatione vi è del bene, e del mali, del bene, perchè vi sono inclusi soggetti assai inclinati, e d'auttorità, et quasi tutti quei medesimi chi desiderava il Padre Bombino, oltre chi ridducendosi infallibilmente due volte la settimana se ne può sperare pur cellere rissolutione: Del mali, perchè si camina con sommo rigore nel silentio, et vi sono scomunichi grandi a redire cosa alcuna di quello, che in essa Congregatione si tratta, onde si potrà mallamente usar l'armi da diffesa, rissolver i dubbij, e li difficoltà; v'intervenne anche il Card. Borgia, sebene egli et l'Amb.r di Spagna hanno fatto dei repplicamente al Padre Bombino." Dispatch of 5 February 1633 in ASVe:SDR, f. 106, fo. 231r–v.

74. See *RI*, chapter 3.

75. *RI*, 91.

76. Rebiba became a cardinal in May 1555 (*HC* 3: 35) and appeared in an Inquisition meeting as governor of Rome on 1 October (Ludwig von Pastor, "Allgemeine Dekrete der römischen Inquisition aus den Jahren 1555–1597," *Historisches Jahrbuch* 33 (1912): 479–549; reprinted as extract paginated 1–71, 14). Santoro was summoned back to Rome by 5 February 1566. He also spent at least part of 1564 in Rome, where he took his law degree on 14 September. Massimo Firpo and Dario Marcatto, eds., *Il processo inquisitoriale del cardinal Giovanni Morone*, 6 vols. (Rome: Istituto italiano per l'età moderna e contemporanea, 1981–1995), 1: 45; see 39–49 for a capsule biography of Santoro. The gap between Rebiba and Santoro proves Amabile wrong in his contention that Rebiba's appointment began an "uninterrupted series of commissaries." Amabile, *Santo Officio*, 1, 214.

77. Romeo, "Documenti e problemi," 58–59. This lacuna is in part—but only in part—a function of the loss of records. Amabile, *Santo Officio*, 1: 328.

78. BAV, Barb. lat. 1369, fo. 95r–v.

79. Romeo, "Documenti e problemi," 59.

80. Amabile, *Santo Officio*, 1: 331.

81. Romeo, "Documenti e problemi," 59.

82. Amabile, *Santo Officio*, 1: 331.

83. *HC* 3: 306.

84. Romeo, "Documenti e problemi," 25. His successor in Sorrento was provided 1 January 1598. *HC* 3: 306.

85. Amabile, *Santo Officio*, 1: 345.

86. See below.

87. Antonio Francesco Vezzosi, *I scrittori de' cherici regolari*, 2 vols. (Rome: Sacra Congregazione di Propaganda Fide, 1780), 2: 27–29; Giuseppe Silos, *Historiarum clericorum regularium* [*libri duo*], 2 vols. (Rome: Mascardi, 1650), 2: 156–58.

88. From 1594. *HC* 3: 156.

89. Vezzosi, *Scrittori*, 2: 27–29; Silos, *Historiarum . . . [libri]*, 2: 156–58, both incorrectly

dating his tenure as administrator to 1601. In fact, he held the post for less than a month in 1604 before he died. *HC* 4: 138.

90. Luigi Firpo, *Il processo di Giordano Bruno*, ed. Diego Quaglioni (Rome: Salerno, 1993), 344 and 346.

91. Amabile, *Congiura*, 1: 51 and 2: 119.

92. *QE* 2:1: 343, incorrectly saying he was from Florence.

93. *HC* 4: 334 and Amabile, *Congiura* 2: 120. *HC* 4: 334, for example, calls him Drago, but also identifies him as commissary at the time of his provision. Baldini and Spruit, eds., *CCMS* 1:2: 979 miss the identification with Tragagliolo, who they mistakenly say was then no more than Mandina's vicar.

94. He arrived in Naples by 27 April. ACDFSO:DSO 1599–1600, fo. 20v, copy in 1600–1601, fo. 60v, 23 April 1600, printed in Enrico Carusi, "Nuovi documenti sui processi di Tommaso Campanella," *Giornale Critico della Filosofia Italiana* 8 (1927): 321–59, no. 15; Baldini and Spruit, *CCMS* 1:2: no. 45; and Santoro–Nuncio Jacopo Aldobrandini, 28 April in Amabile, *Congiura*, 3: no. 308a, 256–57. The date of 1 January for his death is in Luigi Firpo, *I processi di Tommaso Campanella*, ed. Eugenio Canone (Rome: Salerno, 1998), 224n, without a source. He was buried on 3 January, as the nuncio reported the same day to Cardinal Cinzio Aldobrandini. Amabile, *Congiura*, 3: no. 108, 68.

95. Vezzosi and Silos both give the date of Mandina's death as 2 July 1604, but Romeo, "Documenti e problemi," 14, cites a document putting it before 26 June. Gentile was provided to Caserta on 9 July 1604, when he was called "S. Officii inquisitor et commiss. gen.," *HC* 4: 138 and note. Information about Gentile not otherwise attributed is from *DBI*. See also *DSI* 2: 648–49, which does not use the registers of the Inquisition's correspondence with him. See below.

96. He was certainly in post as of 4 January 1602. ACDFSO:DSO 1602, pp. 3–4, printed in Baldini and Spruit, eds., *CCMS* 2: no. 10. He was appointed 25 November 1599. Innocenzo Taurisano, *Hierarchia ordinis praedicatorum* (Rome: Manuzio, 1916), 56.

97. BC, MS 2653, fo. 534v, 28 December 1608, original not traced.

98. *DBI* does not include San Domenico in Brescia.

99. *QE* 2:1: 403, drawing on Fontana. His two short printed books are apparently more devotional in nature: *Aurea catena in novem annulos distincta hieroglyphice perquisita* (Bologna: Giovanni Rosci, 1583) and *Almae urbis mystica descriptio* (Genoa: Girolamo Bartoli, 1589).

100. *HC* 4: 138 and Amabile, *Santo Officio*, 2: 22. The royal assent came on 24 July 1604. Ibid., 21.

101. ACDFSO:DSO 1607, fo. 230r–v.

102. *Avviso* of 10 November 1610 in BAV, Barb. lat. 6344, fo. 140r. He was provided by the pope 24 November 1610, with the royal assent coming after 28 January 1611. *HC* 4: 263; BAV, Barb. lat. 6344, fo. 200r; and Amabile, *Santo Officio* 2: 22, incorrectly dating his nomination or provision 2 October 1610.

103. *QE* 2: 424. His appointment to Ancona was approved by the Dominican general chapter of 1600. *MOPH* 10: 402.

104. *QE* 2: 424, citing Andrea Rovetta, *Bibliotheca chronologica illustrium virorum provinciae Lombardiae Sacri Ordinis Praedicatorum* (Bologna: Longi, 1691). Vicari's work has not been found.

105. He seems to have remained in office to his death in 1621. Amabile, *Santo Officio* 2: 34. His replacement took office in Nocera on 29 March 1621. *HC* 4: 263. Other than the beginning and ending of his tenure, Amabile does not say much about Vicari and Romeo does not mention him.

106. See *RI*, 130–31.

107. Filonardi's diplomatic correspondence is in ASV, Nunziatura di Napoli, 20, 20E, 22, 23, and 326. His instructions are in BAV, Chigi Q. I. 24 (*DBI* 47: 829–30). Out-letters are in ASV, Fondo Borghese I 900 and II 488 and probably elsewhere. Unfortunately, Amabile did not thoroughly investigate the *fondo* Nunziatura di Napoli. Monti was assessor from 2 October 1624 until 8 April 1627, when he became nuncio, although he continued to attend congregations for a while longer. ACDFSO:DSO 1624, fo. 152r and 1627, fo. 64r.

108. See especially Nuncio Niccolò Herrera's letters to Francesco Barberini in BAV, Barb. lat. 7494 from 7 September 1630 to 27 April 1632. For letters to the Congregation forwarded by the nuncio, see., e.g., fos. 115r–116v,120r, 124r, and 125r. See also many of Herrera's dispatches enclosing information for the Congregation from the bishop of Pozzuolo, e.g., one of 21 February 1632, both cipher and decipher in BAV, Barb. lat. 7504, fos. 33r–v and 34r–v. For the office's superiority to the minister, see, e.g., Herrera–F. Barberini, Naples, 3 January 1632, saying he would ensure that Petronio followed orders. BAV, Barb. lat. 7504, fos. 1r and 2r–v (cipher).

109. Amabile, *Santo Officio*, 2: 34. In *RI*, 64, I mistakenly made Zapata viceroy already in late 1616, misreading an entry in ACDFSO:DSO 1616, p. 494. The entry says "Illustrissimi cardinalis Zapatae lectis litteris datis Neapoli die 26 novembris, et nunzii apostolici datis die 29 eiusdem, in quibus petitur nomine proregis previdere ne laici graventur ab ordinationibus. . . . Sancti Officii, Sanctissimus dixit, quod in accesus dicti domini cardinalis ad urbem, deliberabitur." I am grateful to Giorgio Caravale for checking this text. Zapata was named viceroy 5 September 1620 (Juan Ramírez or Remírez de Arellano, "Relazíon de la Jornada desde Madrid a Nápoles hizo el Illmo. y Rvdmo Sr. Don Antonio Zapata," fo. 3r cited in Eduard Escartín, "Virrey y virreinato: La jornada del Cardenal Zapata, de Madrid a Napoles," http://www.raco.cat/index.php/Pedralbes/article/viewFile/101405/152216, accessed 19 January 2013, 234); he took possession 16 December 1620. Jose Raneo, "Libro donde se trata de los virreyes del reino de Nápoles (1634)," in *Colección de documentos inéditos para la historia de España*, 23, ed. Miguel Salvá (Madrid: Imprenta de la Vieda de Calero, 1853), 408–16, 408, and Escartín, "Virrey," 239). He left for Spain 22 December 1622 (Raneo, "Libro," 412 and Escartín, "Virrey," 240). His tenure was meant from the first to last only two years instead of the usual three.

110. Romeo, "Documenti e problemi," 19n.

111. *HC* 4: 211. He was never bishop of Molfetta as Romeo, "Documenti e problemi," 19 says.

112. *HC* 4: 215.

113. Amabile, *Santo Officio* 2: 35. See *HC* 4: 211n for the month of Campanile's death.

114. BAV, Barb. lat. 6334, fos. 2r (2), 8r, 13r–v, 14v (3), 15r–v, 19r, 19r–v, 20v, 24v–25r, 25r–v, 29v, 30r (2), 33v, 39r, 40r–v, 40v, 42r, 48r–v, 48v, 49r, 49v–50r, 50r, 52v, 54r, 59v–60r, 60v–61r, 61r–v, 61v–62r, 62r, 71r–72r, 73v, 74v, 76v, 78v–79r, 81r, 81v, 81v–82r, 83r, 83v, 85r, 86v, 87r, 88v, 89r, 90r (2), 90v–91r, 91r–v, 96r (2), 97r–v, 98v, 99r, 102r, 103r, 107v, 107v–108r, 108r (2), 108v, 115r (2), 116v–117r, 117v (2), 121r, 122r–v, 125v (2), 126r, 127v (2), 129r, 131r, 132r, 134r–v, 136r, 137r, 141v, 141v–142r, 143r (2), 146v (2), 147v–148r, 148r, 149r–v, 149v, 150r, 150r–v, 154r, 154v, 156r, 156v, 159r–v, 160r (2), 162r, 165r (2), 165v–166r, 166v, 168r, 168r–v, 169r, 169v, 173v, 179v, 183r–v, 184v, 186v–187r, (4), 198v (2), 199r, 205r–v, 208v, 208v–209r, 209r, 209v, 217v–218r, 219r–v, 219v (2), 221r (2), 222r (2), 222r–v, 222v, 224r, (2), 225v, 226v, 229v, 235r, 235v (2), 236r–v, 236v, 236v–237r, 240r–v, 242r, 245r, 248v, 250r, 254r, 255r (2), 255v, 255v–256r, 256v, 257r (2), 257v, 258r (2), 263r, 266r, 266r–v, 270v–271r, 272v–273r, 273r, 273 (2), 273r–v, 273v, 277r, 277r–v, 279r, 279v, 279v–280r, 286r–v, 287v, 289v, 289v–290r, 294v, 297v, 298v–299r, 301r (2), 303r, 305r (2), 305v, 310r–v, 312r, 312v, 313r, 320r, 320r–v, 320v–321r, 322v, 326v, 337r, 337v, 338r, 338r–v, 338v, 338v–339r, 340r, 341r, 342r, 342r–v, 342v, 343r, 344r (2), 346r, 346v–347r, 347r (2), 347v, 350v, 351r–v, 352r (2), 352v, 353r (3), 354r–v, 355v, 357v, and 359v. The contemporary index at the head of the volume is as defective as usual; it missed forty-six letters.

115. BAV, Barb. lat. 6334, fos. 107v–108r and 108v–109r; 106v–115r; and 125r–132v.

116. For example, the meeting of 5 April 1629 considered at least two or three separate letters from Petronio reporting at least a half-dozen cases (ACDFSO:DSO 1629, fo. 67r–v), as did the session of 5 September (ibid., fos. 153v–154r, 7 November (ibid., fo. 188v), 16 January 1630 (1630, fos. 12v–15r), 2 January 1631 (1631, fos. 4r–5r), and 22 July 1632 (1632, fo. 113r).

117. Giuseppe Catalano, *De magistro Sacri Palatii Apostolici libri duo* (Rome: Antonio Fulgoni, 1751), 149–50.

118. 18 July 1608 lecturer and bachelor of Minerva, S.T.M. 1609. S. L. Forte, "I Domenicani nel carteggio del card. Scipione Borghese, protettore dell'Ordine (1606–1633)," *Archivum fratrum praedicatorum* 30 (1960): 351–416, 360.

119. ACDFSO:DSO 1614, p. 446. His predecessor as master died 5 September and Petronio immediately replaced him. Ibid., p. 436.

120. ACDFSO:DSO 1630, fo. 196v, 5 December 1630.

121. He was provided 5 September, when he was still called master of the sacred palace. *HC* 4: 238.

122. See the minutes of his letters of 10 July and 2 September 1623. Forte, "Domenicani," 415, no. 149 and 416, no. 150. Petronio was probably a Borghese client; at least, Cardinal Scipione recommended him for his S.T.M. and had another Petronio as his maggiordomo until 1630. Forte, "Domenicani," 360 and *avviso* of 14 November 1630 in BAV, Urb. Lat. 1100, fo. 704v.

123. Ridolfi replaced him between 18 and 24 August 1622. ACDFSO:DSO 1622, pp. 245 and 249.

124. *HC* 4: 238. He was in residence at least in 1646, when he held a synod. http://

www.webdiocesi.chiesacattolica.it/pls/cci_dioc_new/consultazione.mostra_pagina?id_pagina=25178, accessed 12 July 2009.

125. http://www.comune.rogliano.cs.it/portal/index.php?option=com_content&task=view&id=28&Itemid=46, accessed 12 July 2009, and Rudolf Bell, *Fate, Honor, Family and Village: Demographic and Cultural Change in Rural Italy Since 1800* (Chicago: University of Chicago Press, 1979), 16 and 27.

126. "[I]urisconsulto roblanense patritio rhegino, in Aula romana advocato." The book appeared in another edition in 1622, "sumptibus I.A. Ruffinelli & A. Manni, typis A. Phei," and there were others.

127. *HC* 4: 112.

128. Amabile, *Santo Officio*, 2: 36 and note.

129. *HC* 4: 352.

130. *Avviso* of 13 October in ASMod:AE, 138, fasc. October 1631, unfoliated.

131. *Avvisi* of 1 and 29 May 1632 in ibid., fasc. May 1632, unfoliated.

132. *Avviso* of 2 July 1633 in ASMod:AE, 139, fasc. July 1633, unfoliated.

133. Amabile, *Santo Officio* 2: 36 and note citing the Venetian resident's dispatch of that date.

134. Ibid., 2: 37.

135. *HC* 4: 138 and 171.

136. Amabile, *Santo Officio* 2: 38, incorrectly giving the year as 1642, but see *HC* 4: 171 for May 1643.

137. Amabile, *Santo Officio* 2: 37.

138. Romeo, "Documenti e problemi," 19.

139. See note 15.

140. Her name is variously spelled: Julia de Marchiis in Latin; Giulia di Marco (Amabile); Giulia de Marcos (Romeo); Giulia de Marco (Novi Chavarria).

141. Giovanni Romeo, *Amori proibiti: I concubini tra Chiesa e inquisizione* (Bari: Laterza, 2008), 180–90, 189. Elisa Novi Chavarria, "Un'eretica alla corte del conte di Lemos. Il caso di suor Giulia De Marco," in *Archivio storico per le province napoletane* 116 (1998): 77–118, 103. John A. Marino, *Becoming Neapolitan: Citizen Culture in Baroque Naples* (Baltimore: Johns Hopkins University Press, 2011), 128–38, closely follows Chavarria. The article in *DBI* contains mistakes about the trial. http://www.treccani.it/enciclopedia/giulia-di-marco_%28Dizionario-Biografico%29/, accessed 11 October 2012. See also the older treatment in Amabile, *Santo Uffizio* 2: 22–29, and the brief article in *DSI* 1: 482–84.

142. The other objections Novi Chavarria raises, including the transfer of the case from one judge to another, the conduct of interrogations without drawing up an *interrogatorio*, and even the heavy pressure brought to bear against the defendants by the Theatines of Naples, are probably not serious, if any kind of, deviations from the Inquisition's usual "style." The second of them certainly is not, since the *interrogatorio* came only once the *processo informativo* had ended and was often skipped even then. *RI*, 189–90.

143 Romeo, *Amori*, 187 for the first trial. Novi Chavarria, "De Marco," 77. The case is in part an *Ordensstreit* between the Theatines and Giulia's Jesuit protectors.

144. Pierroberto Scaramella, *Le lettere della Congregazione del Sant'Ufficio ai tribunali di fede di Napoli 1563–1625* (Trieste: Edizione Università di Trieste, 2001), 437n. The Theatines claimed that de Marcos had intercourse with Giuseppe Vicari. Novi Chavarria, "De Marco," 99.

145. Novi Chavarria, "De Marco," 100–101. She asserts, as do most other authorities, that the two Vicari were related, but it is not known how.

146. See below, XXX and XXX.

147. *HC* 3: 147, *HC* 4: 130 and Antonio Martone, "L'Archivio vescovile della diocesi di Calvi in Pignataro Maggiore," *Raccolta Rassegna Storica dei Comuni* 9 (1983): 153; for his tenure as vicar general, see Matteo Camera, *Memorie storico-diplomatiche dell'antica città e ducato di Amalfi*, 2 (Salerno: Stabilimento tipografico nazionale, 1881), 453 and Pierroberto Scaramella, *Le Madonne del Purgatorio* (Genoa: Marietti, 1991), 5. He may also have earlier been a patron of the Jesuits. Saverio Santagata, *Istoria della compagnia di Giesu, appartenente al regno di Napoli*, 3 (Naples: Vincenzo Mazzola, 1756), 318.

148. Pasquale Lopez, *Inquisizione, stampa e censura nel Regno di Napoli tra '500 e '600* (Naples: Edizioni del Delfino, 1974), 280 and 303.

149. Amabile, *Santo Officio* 2: 25.

150. Ibid., 2: 26. It is possible that Amabile confused Vicari's alleged actions with Maranta's. Novi Chavarria makes much of the role played by the viceroy, the conde de Lemos.

151. Novi Chavarria, "De Marco," 101.

152. Ibid., 102. Scaramella, *Lettere*, 437n says the Congregation on 27 August heard that the notary's prejudice made witnesses reluctant to testify.

153. Scaramella, *Lettere*, 437n.

154. Novi Chavarria, "De Marco," 102. The Congregation heard of de Marcos's dispatch to Rome on 8 October. Scaramella, *Lettere*, 437n.

155. Scaramella, *Lettere*, 437n.

156. Scaramella, *Lettere*, 437n and ACDFSO:DSO 1615, p. 46.

157. ACDFSO:DSO 1615, pp. 97, 314. The information from the decree register for 1615 is new.

158. Novi Chavarria, "De Marco," 102 is certain torture was applied, but the clause in the sentence is formulaic and there is no indication in the *decreta* that it was applied.

159. Scaramella, *Lettere*, no. 868. The sentence was ordered dispatched on 30 July and sent the next day. ACDFSO:DSO 1615, p. 366 and Scaramella, *Lettere* no. 870.

160. ACDFSO:DSO 1615, p. 324.

161. I have used "Relacion de lo que sucede an l'Auto dela S.ta Inquisicion en Roma presentes veynte y cinco cardenales," docketed as "Sentencia dada por el consistorio de Su S.ta y dela S.ta Ynquiss.on [*sic*] a la madre Julia Demarcos y al p.e Anilo Acieri, y a Jusepe de Vicariis napolitano en 12 de Julio 1615." BC, MS 2417 (già X.VI.41), fos. 176/177r–183/184v, fo. 176/177r. There are other related texts, among them "Relazione dell'eresie di Suor Giulia" in Bibliothèque Nationale de France, MS Italien 733, pp. 49–62. Secretary Millini confirmed the date in a letter of 18 July to Archbishop Carafa. Scaramella, *Lettere* no. 868.

162. BC, MS 2417, fo. 176/177v gives Inquisitors [Ottavio] Bandini, [Ferdinando]

Taverna, [Roberto] Bellarmino, "Cardinal Borghese," Millini, [Filippo] Filonardi, [Agostiono] Galamini, [Gaspar] Borja, and [Giovanni Battista] Bonsi. As usual with such lists, this one has a number of mistakes, both of commission and of omission. Bandini did not become an Inquisitor until 1621, and Bonsi did not take his oath until 21 July 1615. Borghese and Filonardi were never Inquisitors; Filonardi might have arisen out of confusion with his nephew Paolo Emilio, the assessor, except that he is named among the professional staff. Fabrizio Verallo, sub-secretary, was left out as more glaringly was Pietro Aldobrandini.

163. ACDFSO:DSO 1615, pp. 138 and 448.

164. This number is derived from the indices to the three volumes, BAV, Barb. lat. 6334–36, and includes letters to the minister, the nuncio, and the archbishop. It is certainly low, since an actual count for 1626 yields 231 letters to the minister alone, as against 195 according to the index. Numbers before 1625 are derived from Scaramella, *Lettere*, CXXIII–IV, who hypothesizes losses of various sizes depending on the year.

165. Heinrich Bach with Cesare d'Eugenio Carraciolo, *Nuova, e perfettissima descrittione del regno di Napoli* (Naples: Scorrigio, 1629), 269.

166. Caracciolo was bishop of Catanzaro from 1619 to 1629, when he resigned (*HC* 4: 141); he was possibly also bishop of Tropea 1615–1633 (†) (*HC* 4: 347), where his name is given as Caracciolo Pisquizi, one of the three branches of the noble family of Naples. http://www.tropeamagazine.it/vescovivicarigeneralifrancescoadilardi/, accessed 12 July 2009.

167. For his office of commissary, see BAV, Barb. lat., fo. 1r–v, a letter from the Congregation of 2 January 1626.

168. ACDFSO:DSO 1624, fo. 146r–v, session of 18 September discussing his letter of 21 August.

169. Ibid., fos. 165v–166r, 166r and 168r. Whether Francisco was a relative of Cristóval de Figueroa (see below) is not known.

170. ACDFSO:DSO 1625, fo. 22v, 30 January.

171. Ibid., fo. 124r, 16 July.

172. "facto ei praecepto sub poena triremium ne loquatur de meritis causae." Ibid., fo. 126v, approved by Urban the next day (fo. 127v).

173. See the Congregation's delegation to him of 2 January 1626 in BAV, Barb. lat. 6334, fo. 1r–v and for his departure from Rome, its letter to the bishop of Squillace—where Clementini was ordered to investigate a case of pretended sanctity—of the same date on fo. 2r. In addition on 20 January he was assigned the case of a Carmelite who had preached about the immaculate conception of Mary. His report (of 11 February, acknowledged 14 March [BAV, Barb. lat. 6334, fo. 61v]) led to the friar's silencing on 14 May, which Clementini was ordered to execute in a letter of 16 May. Ibid., fos. 8r and 126r and ACDFSO:DSO 1626, fo. 80v. Among other cases he reported was one of "superstitious experiments." BAV, Barb. lat. 6334, fo. 102r–v.

174. ACDFSO:DSO 1626, fo. 39v, letter of 27 January 1626 and decree of 5 March. See the resulting letter to Clementini of 7 March in BAV, Barb. lat. 6334, fos. 54v–55r.

175. ACDFSO:DSO 1626, fo. 63v, decree of 16 April and letter of 18 April 1626 in BAV, Barb. lat. 6334, fo. 95v.

176. ACDFSO:DSO 1626, fo. 113r. The breve is in ASV, Sec. Brev. Reg. 715, fo. 301, according to ASV, Indice 767 II, fo. 299r. Evidently the breve was expedited indeed, since an error in its preface necessitated its recall on 12 September. Clementini was sent the corrected form on 5 December. BAV, Barb. lat. 6334, fos. 257v and 342r.

177. ACDFSO:DSO 1626, fo. 126v, decree of 23 July 1626 and letter of 25 July in BAV, Barb. lat. 6334, fo. 204r–v.

178. BAV, Barb. lat. 6334, fo. 286v.

179. ACDFSO:DSO 1626, fos. 207r and 214v, decrees of 4 and 12 November 1626, and letter to Clementini of 14 November. BAV, Barb. lat. 6334, fo. 321r.

180. BAV, Barb. lat. 6334, fo. 312r–v, letter of 7 November 1626; and ACDFSO:DSO 1626, fo. 222v, decree of 22 November. The decree may be misdated, since the letter incorporating the order about Clementini's stipend is dated 21 November. BAV, Barb. lat. 6334, fos. 327v–328r.

181. ACDFSO:DSO 1626, fos. 239v–240r, 10 December 1626 and BAV, Barb. lat. 6334, fo. 349v, letter of 12 December.

182. ACDFSO:DSO 1627, fo. 16r, 20 January 1627.

183. Ibid., fo. 64v, 8 April 1627.

184. Ibid., fos. 96v and 98v.

185. Ibid., fo. 99r. Unlike many precepts, neither of Caracciolo's specified the consequences in case of contravention.

186. ACDFSO:DSO 1628, fo. 146v.

187. ACDFSO:DSO 1629, fos. 127v and 138r. The nuncio's letter is not in BAV, Barb. lat. 7490.

188. *HC* 4: 264.

189. See *RI*, chapter 3 for the usual degree of Urban's dominance.

190. The case is mentioned in Pietro Giannone, *Istoria civile del regno di Napoli*, 4 vols. (s'Gravenhage: E. A. Gosse, 1753), 4: 348–49, Amabile, *Congiura* 2: 35, and in garbled fashion in Henry Charles Lea, *The Inquisition in the Spanish Dependencies* (New York: Macmillan, 1908), 95. The most detailed study is J. P. Wickersham Crawford, "The Life and Works of Christóbal Suárez de Figueroa, "A Dissertation Presented to the Faculty of the Department of Philosophy of the University of Pennsylvania," 1907, 81–91.

191. Wickersham Crawford, *Life*, 81–83. *HC* 4: 260.

192. ACDFSO:DSO 1628, fos. 13r (7 January), out of order, and 9v–10r (13 January). For *Si de protegendis*, see *RI*, 114 and the Conclusion below.

193. http://opac.bncf.firenze.sbn.it/opac/controller.jsp?action=search_byauto research &query_fieldname_1=vidtutti&query_querystring_1=BVEV057397 accessed 19 September 2010; Rachel Bindman, "A Hitherto Neglected Aspect of the Pedagogical Program of the Accademia dei Lincei (1605–1624 ca.)," in *Les académies dans l'Europe humaniste: Idéaux et pratiques. Actes . . . du colloque international sur les Académies humanistes que nous avions organisé du 10 au 13 juin, 2003 dans les locaux de l'Institut universitaire de France et de l'Université de Paris-Sorbonne*, ed. Marc Deramaix, Perrine Galand-Hallyn, Ginette Vagenheim, and Jean Vignes (Geneva: Droz, 2008), 75–98, 95n.

194. BAV, Barb. lat. 6334, fo. 99r. Petronio's dealing with Cardinal Antonio Barberini, Sr., may be further evidence that Barberini acted as sub-secretary.

195. Diaz had replaced Gentile as bishop of Caserta but does not seem to have been active in the *regno*. *HC* 4: 138. He served as nuncio for just under a year, until 17 April 1627. Christoph Weber, *Die Päpstlichen Referendare 1566–1809. Chronologie und Prosopographie*, 3 vols. (Stuttgart: Anton Hiersemann, 2003), 2: 586.

196. BAV, Barb. lat. 6334, fos. 108v–109r.

197. The deal arose out of the apparently attempted publication of *De legitimis remediis regibus, principibusque liberis competentibus adversus archiepiscopos, episcopos, caeterosque temporalem jurisdictionem et bona usurpantes*, which I have not been able to identify. BAV, Barb. lat. 6334, fos. 123v–124r.

198. Ibid., fo. 43r.

199. Ibid., fos. 161r–162r, letter of 26 June 1626.

200. Ibid., fos. 282v–283r, letter of 3 October 1626.

201. ACDFSO:DSO 1627, fo. 219r–v. The issue came up again on 4 January 1628. 1628, fo. 11r.

202. ACDFSO:DSO 1628, fo. 5v.

203. Ibid., fo. 13r. The act is out of order and is missing the date of Monti's and the bishop's letters.

204. Ibid., fos. 9v–10r.

205. "Apologia in favore dell'assoluta et indipendente libertà che ha e sempre ha posseduto la Santa Inquisitione in carcerare laici senza farne consapevole persona alcuna contro l'ingiusta e strana pretensione de' Ministri Regii nel Regno di Napoli nuovamente suscitata," addressed to Urban VIII and the Congregation. It arose from the case of Tommaso Calandrino and is covered by a letter from Petronio to his patron, Francesco Barberini, dated 22 January 1628. BAV, Barb. lat. 5650, fos. 73v–89r. See Agostino Lauro, *Il Giurisdizionalismo pregiannoniano nel Regno di Napoli. Problema e bibliografia (1563–1723)* (Rome: Storia e Letteratura, 1974), 174–75.

206. ACDFSO:DSO 1628, fos. 25r and 34v.

207. Ibid., fo. 43r–v.

208. Ibid., fo. 46r.

209. Ibid., fo. 60r.

210. Ibid., fo. 77v.

211. Ibid., fos. 91v –92r.

212. Ibid., fo. 103r–v.

213. "Origine et continuatione delli Inquisitori et Ministri della Santa Inquisitione nel Regno di Napoli per lo spatio di più di 400 anni et risposta alli capi della lettera che si dice che scrivono li Ministri Regii a S. M.ta Cattolica in Spagna con occasione che la medesima Maestà non voglia che il Ministro della Sacra Inquisitione residente in Napoli venga impedito nelle carcerationi de' Laici, sempre liberamente possedute da' Ministri del Sant'Officio." BAV, Barb. lat. 5265, fos. 102r–130r, addressed "Alla Santità di N. S. Papa Urbano Ottavo, & all'Ill.mi, & RR.mi Card.li Generali Inquis.ri contro l'heretica pravità in

tutta la Republica Christiana," note on fo. 131v; "Recepi cum litteris Rev.di Epi. Melphiten., die 28 junii 1628." See Lauro, *Giurisdizionalismo*, 174–75.

214. Bichi was officially appointed 24 May 1628, but the nomination was in the works for almost two months before that. Monti thanked Barberini for his new post on 10 April, his temporary replacement sent word of taking up office on 22 April, and news of Bichi's appointment went out on 29 April. He arrived in Naples on 3 June. BAV, Barb. lat. 7481, fos. 78r, 87r, 93r and 107r. See also Andreas Kraus, *Das päpstliche Staatssekretariat unter Urban VIII 1623–1644*, *Römischer Quartalschrift für christliche Altertumskunde and Kirchengeschichte*, Supplementheft 29 (Rome: Herder, 1964), 286, and BAV, Urb. lat. 1098 I, fos. 201r–v, 204r and 213r, *avvisi* of 22 and 29 April 1628.

215. ACDFSO:DSO 1628, fo. 132r.

216. Ibid., fo. 147v.

217. Ibid., fos. 156r and 164v.

218. Ibid., fo. 194r.

219. Ibid., fo. 196r.

220. Ibid., fo. 205r.

221. ACDFSO:DSO 1629, fo. 26v.

222. Ibid., fos. 42v, 50v, and 63r, 27 February, 13 March, and 29 March 1629, the last a coram.

223. Crawford, *Figueroa*, 102–6.

224. ACDFSO:DSO 1629, fo. 67r.

225. Ibid.

226. Ibid., fo. 75r.

227. Ibid., fo. 80r.

228. Ibid., fos. 85v–86r.

229. Ibid., fo. 92r–v.

230. Ibid., fo. 98r.

231. Ibid., fo. 102r.

232. Ibid., fo. 115v. Was the bishop substituting for Petronio in a temporary absence?

233. Ibid., fos. 134r and 134v.

234. Ibid., fo. 146v.

235. Ibid., fo. 155r, session of 6 September 1629.

236. Ibid., fos. 160r and 169r, 13 and 27 September 1629.

237. Ibid., fo. 173v.

238. Ibid., fo. 178v–179r, 11 October; the copy reads "Regibus."

239. Crawford, *Figueroa*, 92, 98, and 84.

240. ACDFSO:DSO 1629, fo. 191v.

241. Ibid., fo. 196r, 15 November 1629.

242. See ACDFSO:DSO 1631, fo. 23v, 5 February 1631.

243. ACDFSO:DSO 1629, fo. 203r, 29 December 1629.

244. There is also the intriguing order to the nuncio and archbishop to undertake an

extrajudicial investigation of Petronio, about which we hear nothing more. Ibid., fo. 211v, 13 December 1629.

245. ACDFSO:DSO 1630, fo. 7r.

246. Crawford, *Figueroa*, 106–7.

247. ACDFSO:DSO 1630, fo. 11v, 10 January 1630.

248. Ibid., fo. 21r.

249. Crawford, *Figueroa*, 85.

250. Ibid., 107–21 and, from another MS in Hugo A. Rennert, "Some Documents in the Life of Christoval Suárez de Figueroa," *Modern Language Notes* 7, 7 (1892): 199–205, 203–4.

251. Crawford, *Figueroa*, 121–22.

252. Bichi–Francesco Barberini, 29 January. BAV, Barb. lat. 7488, fos. 22r–23r; printed in Crawford, *Figueroa*, 101–2 from ASV, Nunz. di Napoli, f. 27.

253. ACDFSO:DSO 1630, fo. 25r–v

254. Crawford, *Figueroa*, 122–23.

255. Printed in Rennert, "Suárez," 204–5 dated 2 February and in Crawford, *Figueroa*, 123–25 from another MS.

256. F. Barberini–nuncio, n.d. BAV, Barb. lat. 7493, fo. 52r.

257. Crawford, *Figueroa*, 125–26.

258. *Avviso* of 3 December 1611 in BAV, Urb. lat. 1079, fo. 831r and Kraus, *Staatssekretäriat*, 39. Maraldi, Francesco Barberini's majordomo, became a secretary of breves in 1627. ASVe:SDR, f. 97, fo. 24r, 4 September 1627. He later exercised Fagnani's office in the Datary, explaining both his mistaken identification and his link to Fagnani. He also acted as Fagnani's stand-in as auditor of the Rota as Fagnani went blind. *Avviso* of 28 July 1632 in ASMod:AE, 138, fasc. July 1632, unfoliated. See also Kraus, *Staatssekretäriat*, 41n23, who says Maraldi was datary only until 1622 and Weber, *Referendare*, 3. 715 only until 1621. Fagnani was also still secretary of the Congregation for Bishops and Regulars as well as Corrector Poenitentiarlae. Kraus, *Staatssekretäriat*, 39.

259. *Avviso* of 9 February 1630 in ASMod:AE, 137, fasc. February 1630, unfoliated.

260. Ibid. For particular congregations, see *RI*, 22–26.

261. ACDFSO:DSO 1630, fos., 28v–29r, 7 February 1630.

262. Crawford, *Figueroa*, 126–31.

263. Ibid., 131–33.

264. Ibid., 133–34.

265. ACDFSO:DSO 1630, fo. 32r.

266. Crawford, *Figueroa*, 135.

267. ACDFSO:DSO 1630, fo. 36v.

268. ASMod:AE, 137, fasc. February 1630, unfoliated.

269. F. Barberini–nuncio, 23 February 1630, cipher. BAV, Barb. lat. 7493, fo. 53r.

270. ACDFSO:DSO 1630, fos. 38v–39r, 27 February 1630 and fo. 58v (Copia, p. 211), 4 April.

271. Ibid., fo. 39v.

272. Ibid., fo. 51v, 21 March 1630.

273. Ibid., fo. 47r, 14 March 1630.

274. Ibid., Copia, pp. 211–12.

275. Ibid., Copia, pp. 225–26, 11 April based on Pamphili's letter of 31 January.

276. Ibid., Copia, pp. 227–28, 11 April. In September Petronio was ordered to use "praeceptis poenalibus" to get the case away from the secular court. Ibid., fo. 146v.

277. Ibid., fo. 67r.

278. F. Barberini–nuncio, 20 April 1630, cipher. BAV, Barb. lat. 7493, fo. 58v.

279. ACDFSO:DSO 1630, fo. 79r.

280. Ibid., fo. 83r.

281. J. H. Elliott, *The Count-Duke of Olivares* (New Haven, Conn.: Yale University Press, 1986), 427.

282. ACDFSO:DSO 1630, fo. 83v.

283. F. Barberini–nuncio, cipher. BAV, Barb. lat. 7493, fo. 62r.

284. ACDFSO:DSO 1630, fo. 90r.

285. Ibid., fo. 94v, 13 June.

286. Ibid., fo. 104r, 27 June.

287. Weber, *Referendare*, 2: 595 and Alessandro Bonnici, "Due secoli di storia politico-religiosa di Malta nel fondo Barberini latino della Biblioteca Vaticana," *Melita Historica: Journal of the Malta Historical Society* 4 (1967): 229–56, 243. It seems likely that Herrera was related to the wealthy Roman banker of Spanish origin Juan Enríquez de Herrera. If so, his appointment may have been a sop to the Spanish in both Rome and Naples. Dandelet, *Spanish Rome*, 152–53.

288. ACDFSO:DSO 1630, fo. 107v and Copia, p. 394.

289. Ibid., fos. 112v–113r, 11 July 1630.

290. Ibid., fo. 121v and Copia, p. 443. For these phases of an Inquisition trial, see *RI*, 188–91 and 194–96.

291. Crawford, *Figueroa*, 136–43 prints a document headed "Causas de Inquisicion," which is apparently a transcript of some of Figueroa's testimony. It ends with the refusal of the *repetitio*; very partially printed in Rennert, "Suarez," 205. For Castaldo, see Crawford, *Figueroa*, 135–36, an act of 7 August 1630.

292. ACDFSO:DSO 1630, fos. 136v–137r.

293. Ibid., fo. 148v, 12 September and fo. 173v, Urban's decree of 31 October rejecting Maranta. It may be that Imparato was a former consultor of the Holy Office; at least, a man of that name stepped down in 1626. BAV, Barb. lat. 6334, fo. 313r.

294. Crawford, *Figueroa*, 150, letter of 18 November 1630.

295. ACDFSO:DSO 1630, fo. 146r.

296. Crawford, *Figueroa*, 143–50, 150 for the date.

297. ACDFSO:DSO 1630, fo. 191r–v, 28 November.

298. *Avviso* of 28 December. ASMod, Cancelleria ducale, Avvisi dall'Estero, 137, fasc.

December 1630, unfoliated. An earlier report said the cause of Urban's attack was the cardinal's possession of writings about papal acts. *Avviso* of 23 November. ASMod, Cancelleria ducale, Avvisi dall'Estero, 137, fasc. November 1630, unfoliated.

299. *Avviso* of 16 November 1630 in ASMod:AE, 137, fasc. November 1630, unfoliated. For the matter in dispute, see the *avviso* of 28 December 1630 in ibid., fasc. December 1630, unfoliated.

300. "Ancorche non si sia formato processo alcuno in questa Causa, et che non si potesse formare, ad ogni modo il Papa se ne rideva, allegando, che a lui bastava di sapere la verità del fatto, non si curando, che apparisca giuditialmente." *Avviso* of 23 November I in ASMod:AE, 137, fasc. November 1630, unfoliated.

301. *Avvisi* of 11 January II, 25 January and 1 February 1631 in ASMod:AE, 138, fasc. January and February 1631, unfoliated.

302. *Avviso* of 28 December 1630 in ASMod:AE, 137, fasc. December 1630, unfoliated. The case concerned a pension and a disputed inheritance. Torres won on the strength of a grace from Gregory XV, which Urban was forced to accept.

303. See the Venetian ambassador in Rome's dispatch of 18 January 1631 in ASVe:SDR, f. 103, fo. 334v.

304. ACDFSO:DSO 1630, fo. 198r.

305. Crawford, *Figueroa*, 151–52.

306. ACDFSO:DSO 1631, fos. 25v–26r.

307. Ibid., fos. 4r–5r, 2 January 1631; copy in ACDFSO, St.st.H 6-f, fos. 307r–311r.

308. ACDFSO:DSO 1631, fo. 43r.

309. Crawford, *Figueroa*, 152 and 153.

310. ACDFSO:DSO 1631, fo. 60v.

311. Ibid., fos. 72v–73r.

312. Ibid., fo. 65r.

313. Ibid., fos. 77v and 82v, 1 and 8 May.

314. Ibid., fos. 71v–72r, 24 April. Petronio reported a friendly meeting with the new viceroy a week later. Ibid., fo. 77v.

315. ACDFSO:DSO 1631, fo. 109v.

316. See Monterey's letter to the viceroy of 20 May 1631, enclosing a copy of his to Borja in Crawford, *Figueroa*, 152–53.

317. ACDFSO:DSO 1631, fos. 88v–89r and 84r.

318. "et alia preiudicialia jurisdictioni S. Officii." Ibid., fo. 121r.

319. Ibid., fos. 124v–125r. For polygamy, see Scaramella, *Lettere*, XCIX–CVI.

320. ACDFSO:DSO 1631, fo. 128v.

321. Crawford, *Figueroa*, 154–55.

322. ACDFSO:DSO 1631, fo. 173v, 2 October.

323. Diotallevi had been inquisitor of Malta and a referendary. *HC* 4: 71 and Alexander Bonnici, "Malta dai manoscritti della Stanza storica dell'Archivio della Congregazione della Fede," *Melita Historica: Journal of the Maltese Historical Society* 13, 3 (2002): 229–38, 230.

324. Marcella Campanelli, *Centralismo romano e "policentrismo" periferico: chiesa e religiosità nella diocesi di Sant'Alfonso Maria de Liguori secoli XVI–XVIII* (Milan: Franco Angeli, 2003), 46ff.

325. *Avviso* of 11 October in ASMod:AE, 138, fasc. October 1631, unfoliated.

326. *Avvisi* of 25 October and 1 November II 1631 in ibid.

327. *Avvisi* of 22 and 29 November 1631 in ibid.

328. *Avviso* of 6 December 1631 in ASMod:AE, 138, fasc. December 1631, unfoliated.

329. *Avviso* of 27 December 1631 in ASMod:AE, 138, fasc. December 1631, unfoliated.

330. ACDFSO:DSO 1631, fos. 203r and 208r, 4 December and 1632, fo. 2v, 30 December 1631.

CHAPTER 2. NAPLES: TOMMASO CAMPANELLA

1. See the brief survey in *DSI* 1: 250–52, which says little about his trials.

2. ACDFSO:DSO 1599–1600, fo. 106br, copy in 1597–1598–1599, p. 787, printed in Carusi, "Nuovi documenti," no. 12 and Baldini and Spruit, eds., *CCMS* 1:2: no. 41.

3. Amabile, *Congiura*, 3: no. 44, 47. The nuncio was Giacomo Aldobrandini. I shall call him simply "the nuncio" in order to avoid confusion with Cardinal Nephew Aldobrandini.

4. For the importance of *fama* in opening an Inquisition proceeding, see *RI*, 155–56.

5. Amabile, *Congiura*, 3: no. 269, 194–96.

6. The Turkish fleet appeared a week after Campanella's arrest; ibid., 3: no. 23, 35.

7. Luigi Firpo, "La Congiura di Calabria. Narrazioni, documenti, verbali delle torture. I. Dichiarazione di Castelvetre," in Luigi Firpo, *I processi di Tommaso Campanella* (Rome: Salerno, 1998), 99–113, 100. The text follows on 102–13. Calling the declaration "la cabeça de toda esta maquina," the viceroy sent a copy to Spain on 20 September. Amabile, *Congiura*, 3: no. 17, 25.

8. Santoro–Cornelio Del Monte, 17 September 1599. Amabile, *Congiura*, 3: no. 293, 224. The visitor would later be accused of procedural abuses in defense documents of Campanella's co-conspirators. Ibid., no. 394, 446–57.

9. Amabile, *Congiura*, 3: no. 304, 246–47.

10. Throughout, the nuncio corresponded with both his masters, e.g., on 19 November 1599. Ibid., 3: no. 58, 52–53 (to Aldobrandini) and no. 59, 53 (to Santoro).

11. 23 November 1599, nuncio–Cinzio Aldobrandini. Ibid., 3: no. 64, 54.

12. Ibid., 3: no. 48, 48–49; no. 49, 49; no. 50, 49; no. 51, 49–50; and no. 53, 50–51. Even after the viceroy's order to hold the prisoners in the nuncio's name, the castellan refused to execute it unless the nuncio asked in person. Ibid., no. 54, 51–52.

13. 17 November 1599, C. Aldobrandini–nuncio. Ibid., 3: no. 56, 52.

14. ACDFSO:DSO 1599–1600, fo. 142v, copy in 1597–1598–1599, p. 834; printed in Carusi, "Nuovi documenti," no. 13 and Baldini and Spruit, eds., *CCMS* 1:2: no. 43. The claim about atheism is found in a note drawn up after 1690 in ACDFSO, St. st., Q.3.d, fo.

110r, printed in Baldini and Spruit, eds., *CCMS* 1:2: no. 48 and Amabile, Spruit, and Preti, *Campanella*, no. 47*.

15. Amabile, *Campanella nei Castelli di Napoli*, 2, "Documenti:" no. 90, 20, nos. 102–107 (24–25) and see below.

16. Amabile, *Congiura*, 3: no. 54, 51–52.

17. Ibid., 3: no. 64, 54 and no. 72, 57.

18. Ibid., 3: no. 37, 42–43.

19. 4 December 1599, C. Aldobrandini–nuncio. Ibid., 3: no. 72, 57.

20. 4 December 1599, Alonso Manrique–viceroy. Ibid., 3: no. 39, 43–44.

21. 5 December 1599, C. Aldobrandini–nuncio. Ibid., 3: no. 73, 57.

22. 10 December 1599, Nuncio–C. Aldobrandini. Ibid., 3: no. 74, 58.

23. 24 December 1599, C. Aldobrandini–nuncio. Ibid., 3: no. 80, 59.

24. 13 December 1599, viceroy–king of Spain. Ibid., 3: no. 48, 43.

25. 18 December 1599, C. Aldobrandini–nuncio and 19 December 1599, Nuncio–C. Aldobrandini. Ibid., 3: nos. 77 and 78, 58–59. Pisano's status is obscure. In his protest, the nuncio noted that Pisano had never been put to his proof of clergy, and the only evidence he could cite that Pisano was in orders was the fact that he appeared on the list of "carcerati ecclesiastici." He signed both one of his depositions in the Calabrian investigation and also his final depositions as if he had orders of some kind (243 and 252–53), and some testimony makes it appear that he was a friar (e.g., 158). Another witness called him a *seculare* in a context that seems to mean "not a clergyman" rather than a secular priest (230), while a hostile relative, a friar, said he was a deacon (267). Finally, Amabile (644) included him in a list of previously unknown laymen involved in the conspiracy.

26. 28 January 1600, Nuncio–C. Aldobrandini. Ibid., 3: no. 85, 62. For the execution, see ibid., no. 238.

27. ACDFSO:DSO 1599–1600, fo. 14av, printed in Baldini and Spruit, eds., *CCMS* 1:2 no. 45n. Unlike Campanella's heresy case, the archiepiscopal authorities handled this one, which saw him tortured and sentenced on the very day of his execution, a Sunday. To judge from Amabile's headnote, the record of this act is found among the Neapolitan Inquisition's records, but it was done in the secular Audientia Criminali and the clergymen present were identified only as "officialibus curiae Archiepiscopalis neapolitanae," not agents of the Holy Office. Amabile, *Congiura*, 3: no. 306, 248–53.

28. Amabile, *Congiura*, 3: no. 242, 128–29 from AdS Florence, Carte Strozziane, 338, fo. 160r. Amabile theorized that this and other documents in Florence belonged to the nuncio who brought them home with him before they passed into the hands of Tommaso Strozzi ca. 1670 (Amabile, *Congiura*, 1, x) where he also mentioned but did not further identify a second papal breve. Both had been found and published in summary form by Francesco Palermo in *Archivio Storico italiano* in 1846 and then in full by Alessandro D'Ancona, "Della vita e delle dottrine di Tommaso Campanella" in D'Ancona, ed., *Opere di Tommaso Campanella*, 2 vols. (Turin: Pomba, 1854), 1, i–cccxliii, cccxxv–vii (to nuncio and De Vera) and cccxxvii–xxix (to Juan Ruiz, substituting for De Vera in 1604). The minute of either in Rome has yet to be found. Since the text Amabile printed from D'Ancona's book may well

be corrupt, it is impossible to say whether the Venetian ambassador in Naples was correct that the breve to the nuncio and De Vera demanded the first tonsure. Amabile, *Congiura*, 3: no. 188, 96. At least, the only text thus far known said nothing explicit of anyone but the nuncio's involvement, save for the address to "Venerabilis Frater [a solecism; it should read 'Venerabili fratri'] et dilecte fili" (in the proper grammatical form; a similar conjoined mistake occurs in the body of the letter, referring to "fraternitati tuae frater Episcope," the first two and last word of which are in the proper case) and once the single word "conjunctim."

29. Ibid., 3: no. 243, 129, a note by the viceregal *mastrodatti* (notary).

30. Amabile, *Congiura*, 3: no. 83, 60–61.

31. 21 January 1600, Nuncio–C. Aldobrandini. Ibid., 3: no. 83, 60–61.

32. 24 January 1600, Nuncio–C. Aldobrandini. Ibid., 3: no. 84, 61; noted on 618 as part of an ecclesiastical trial where other such "confrontations" are observed.

33. 29 January 1600, interrogation of Giovanni Battista Pizzon. Ibid., 3: no. 379, 390.

34. 4 February 1600, Nuncio–Aldobrandini. Ibid., 3: no. 86, 62.

35. A note of two letters found on Campanella when tortured on that date. Ibid., 3: no. 381, 394.

36. ACDFSO:DSO 1599–1600, fo. 14av, printed in Baldini and Spruit, eds., *CCMS* 1:2 note to no. 44, a damaged note of the same act in 1600, fo. 25r.

37. 11 February 1600, Nuncio–C. Aldobrandini. Amabile, *Congiura* , 3: no. 87, 62–63.

38. 11 February 1600, Nuncio–Santoro. Ibid., 3: no. 88, 63. Santoro's letter has not been found.

39. 3 March 1600, Nuncio–Santoro. Ibid., 3: no. 92, 64–65. On the same day the nuncio assured Cardinal Aldobrandini that the Holy Office case was "integro." Ibid., 3: no. 91, 64.

40. 14 April 1600, Nuncio–Santoro. Ibid., 3: no. 95, 65–66. The undated defense of Campanella by the *advocatus pauperum* on the count of rebellion may come from about this time. Ibid., 3: no. 245, 144–49.

41. 22 April 1600, Aldobrandini–Nuncio. Ibid., 3: no. 97, 66.

42. ACDFSO:DSO 1599–1600, fo. 20v, copy in 1600–1601, fo. 60v, printed in Carusi, "Nuovi documenti," no. 15 and Baldini and Spruit, eds., *CCMS* 1:2: no. 45.

43. 28 April 1600, Santoro–Nuncio. Amabile, *Congiura*, 3: no. 308a, 256–57.

44. This passage is the source of the erroneous date of that abjuration to 1591, but Firpo (see above) is certainly right to move it to 1596 since Tragagliolo only became commissary in late 1592. Ibid., 1: 51 and 2: 119. Santoro slightly violated his orders, since instead of sending Tragagliolo a copy of the evidence found in the Roman archives, he merely told Tragagliolo to ask if he wanted it.

45. Ibid., 3: no. 308b, 257 and no. 308c, printed from the originals in the Inquisition archives now in the Archivio storico diocesano in Naples, in Scaramella, *Lettere*, nos. 568–70. Amabile gave no source for any of these three letters.

46. Firpo, *Processi di Campanella*, 312. On 224n he says that Tragagliolo died on 1 January 1601, without citing a source, but see below for his replacement in Campanella's trial. His successor as bishop was provided on 14 January 1602. *HC* 4: 334.

47. Campanella–Tragagliolo, Santa Sabina (Rome), 21 December 1595, printed in Amabile, *Congiura*, 3: doc. 4, 13. See also Amabile, *Campanella nei Castelli di Napoli*, 1: 85–86. Campanella later remembered having given Aldobrandini his "Poetica secondo i proprii principii," published in 1638 as an appendix to *Philosophiae rationalis pars. 4.a*, saying nothing of the "Discorso." Ibid., 1: 77 and 79.

48. Gerardo Cioffari, "La Provincia Calabriae: Strutture e fermenti nell'ordine domenicano al tempo di Tommaso Campanella," in Germana Ernst, ed., *Tommaso Campanella e la Congiura di Calabria. Atti del Convegno di Stilo (18–19 novembre 1999) in occasione del IV Centenario della Congiura* (Stilo: Comune di Stilo, 2000), 121–44, 129 without a source.

49. Amabile, *Congiura*, 3: no. 100, 66–77.

50. Nuncio–Santoro, 5 May 1600 (ibid., 3: no. 101, 67), first interrogation on 10 May (ibid., no. 309, 258–60), Nuncio–Aldobrandini, 12 May 1600 (ibid., no. 102, 67), and interrogation 15 May (ibid., no. 310, 260). There is some question about the nuncio's departure, since in his letter of 5 May to Santoro saying he might be absent from Naples he appeared to give as his reason a papal grace to go to his diocese for "la prossima Pasqua," but Easter fell on 2 April and was therefore long past.

51. Interrogation of 19 May. Ibid., 3: no. 317, 268.

52. Ibid., 3: no. 312, 263. For the question of Campanella's madness, see Joseph Scalzo, "Campanella, Foucault, and Madness in Late-Sixteenth Century Italy," *Sixteenth Century Journal* 21 (1990): 359–72, and most recently Vittorio Frajese, *Profezia e machiavellismo: Il giovane Campanella* (Rome: Carocci, 2002), 17, who has no doubt that it was feigned. Campanella had adopted that strategy early on. The fiscal set spies on him during the night in the first half of April to see whether he was pretending. Amabile, *Congiura*, 3: no. 350, 327–19, reprinted in Firpo, *Processi di Campanella*, 216–21 with translation.

53. ACDFSO:DSO 1600–1601, fo. 78v, copy in 1599–1600, fo. 25r–v, printed in Carusi, "Nuovi documenti," no. 16 and Baldini and Spruit, eds., *CCMS* 1:2: no. 46.

54. Santoro–Tragagliolo, 11 June 1600. Amabile, *Congiura*, 3: no. 330, 284.

55. Denunciation and deposition of 17–18 May 1600. Ibid., 3: no. 328, 281–82.

56. Ibid., 3: no. 317, 268 and no. 323, 275. Interrogations were fairly regularly spaced throughout the trial, e.g., those on 21, 26, and 28 June. Ibid., 3: no. 332, 284.

57. Ibid., 278.

58. Interrogation of 1 June, 1600. Ibid., 3: no. 329, 282–83.

59. 26 May 1600, viceroy–king of Spain. Ibid., 3: no. 41, 45.

60. Ibid., 3: no. 42, 45–46.

61. Decree of 22 June 1600 in ACDFSO:DSO 1599–1600, fo. 29r, draft on fo. 31v, printed in Carusi, "Nuovi documenti," no. 17 and Baldini and Spruit, eds., *CCMS* 1:2: no. 47.

62. Amabile, *Congiura*, 3: no. 334, 296–98.

63. Ibid., 3: no. 335, 298–300; Firpo, *Processi di Campanella*, 231–39 with translation into modern Italian, and 247 for the usual duration of the *corda*.

64. Ibid., 3: no. 338, 301–2; reprinted with Italian translation in Firpo, *Processi di Campanella*, 241–45.

65. ACDFSO:DSO 1599–1600, fo. 35r–v, not now in 1600, fo. 121v nor 1600–1601, fo. 105r (printed in Carusi, "Nuovi documenti," no. 18 and Baldini and Spruit, eds., *CCMS* 1:2: no. 49), but the entry in the first of these is badly damaged. A truncated note in it referring to Campanella's case (a request from a prisoner involved in his attempted prison-break in Padua) can still be read and is found in full in 1599–1600, fo. 35r–v, printed in Baldini and Spruit, eds., *CCMS* 1:2: 1029n.

66. Amabile, *Congiura*, 3: no. 341, 306.

67. ACDFSO:DSO 1600–1601, fo. 110v and copy in 1599–1600, fo. 36v, printed in Carusi, "Nuovi documenti," no. 19 and Baldini and Spruit, eds., *CCMS* 1:2: no. 50.

68. ACDFSO:DSO 1600–1601, fo. 139v, printed in Carusi, "Nuovi documenti," no. 20 and Baldini and Spruit, eds., *CCMS* 1:2: no. 51.

69. Amabile, *Congiura*, 3: no. 342, 306–9.

70. Ibid., 3: no. 340, 303–5 and no. 344, 311–13.

71. *Repetitiones* of 22 and 23 August. Ibid., 3: no. 345, 313–20 and no. 347, 320–24.

72. Ibid., 3: no. 343, 309–11.

73. Ibid., 3: nos. 349, 326–27, 351, 329–31 and 352, 331–32.

74. *Repetitiones* of 2 September 1600. Ibid., 3: nos. 353, 332–35 and 354, 335–37.

75. 5 September 1600. Ibid., 3: no. 355, 337–39. An undated note of the principal points in various examinations in Tragagliolo's hand does not amount to much. Ibid., 3: no. 358, 340–41.

76. Ibid., 3: no. 105, 68.

77. ACDFSO:DSO 1600–1601, fo. 160r, printed in Carusi, "Nuovi documenti," no. 22 and Baldini and Spruit, eds., *CCMS* 2: no. 53.

78. Amabile, *Congiura*, 3: no. 357, 339–40, with the day inverted in the headnote, and ibid., 1, 168 for Dello Grugno, who did not impress Amabile.

79. Statement of 6 November 1600. Ibid., 3: no. 392, 415–21.

80. Ibid., 3: no. 106, 68.

81. 16 December 1600, Nuncio–Santoro. Ibid., 3: no. 107, 68. ACDFSO:DSO 1600–1601 Copia, p. 374, printed in Carusi, "Nuovi documenti," no. 24 and Baldini and Spruit, eds., *CCMS* 1:2: no. 55n; the original in ACDFSO:DSO 1600–1601, fo. 182v is illegible.

82. ACDFSO:DSO 1600–1601, fo. 182v, printed in Carusi, "Nuovi documenti," no. 24 (from the modern copy) and Baldini and Spruit, eds., *CCMS* 2: no. 55.

83. ACDFSO:DSO 1600–1601, fo. 205r and copy in ACDFSO:DSO 1601, fo. 51v, printed in Carusi, "Nuovi documenti," no. 25 and Baldini and Spruit, eds., *CCMS* 2: no. 1. Under pressure from the viceroy the nuncio badgered Rome for orders. 19 and 26 January 1601, 2 and 16 February (plus a missing letter), 23 February (to Santoro), 15 March. Amabile, *Congiura*, 3, nos. 109–14, 68–69.

84. ACDFSO:DSO 1600–1601, fo. 225r–v and copy in ACDFSO:DSO 1601, fo. 77v, printed in Carusi, "Nuovi documenti," no. 26 and Baldini and Spruit, eds., *CCMS* 2: no. 2.

85. ACDFSO:DSO 1600–1601, fo. 225v, printed in Carusi, "Nuovi documenti," no.

26 and Baldini and Spruit, eds., *CCMS* 2: no. 2 and ACDFSO:DSO 1600–1601, fo. 226v, and copy in ACDFSO:DSO 1601, fo. 78v, partially printed in Carusi, "Nuovi documenti," no. 27 and in full in Amabile, *Congiura*, 3: no. 396, 470–71 and Baldini and Spruit, eds., *CCMS* 2: no. 3.

86. Romeo, "Sant'Ufficio," 25–26, both putting Mandina in office from some time in 1598 and also saying that he may have exercised not only complete control over the inquisition in Naples but archiepiscopal jurisdiction as well. Amabile, *Santo Officio*, 1: 346 says he was "chiamato spesso a Roma per consigli legali," but cites no evidence, nor for his presence at Giordano Bruno's execution. Mandina was certainly a witness to Bruno's sentence, when he is listed as a consultor. Firpo, *Bruno*, 344 and 346.

87. ACDFSO:DSO 1600–1601, fo. 226v and copy in 1601, fo. 78v, partially printed in Carusi, "Nuovi documenti," no. 27 and in full in Amabile, *Congiura*, 3: no. 396, 470–71 and Baldini and Spruit, eds., *CCMS* 2: no. 3. The first of these spoke of witnesses "in contestes," the second "altri testimoni allegati per contesti," the same phrase used in Santoro's letter to the nuncio of the same date (ibid., no. 116, 70). It is worth noting that the letter to Mandina speaks only of corroboration witnesses, while that to the nuncio distinguished them from others to be re-examined. New points to investigate are listed in no. 397, while new questions drawn up by the fiscal in Rome are in no. 398a.

88. Ibid., 3: no. 396, 470–71. For the *veglia*, see Firpo, *Processi di Campanella*, 247. His description does not accord precisely with that in Giovanni Battista Scanaroli, *De visitatione carceratorum libri tres* (Rome: Reverenda Camera Apostolica, 1655), "De tormento Vigiliae," 290–93, including an illustration facing 290. I am grateful to Adriano Prosperi for bringing this reference to my attention.

89. ACDFSO:DSO 1600–1601, fo. 228r and copy in 1601, fo. 80r, printed in Carusi, "Nuovi documenti," no. 28 and Baldini and Spruit, eds., *CCMS* 2: no. 4 and 1600–1601, fo. 231r and copy in 1601, fo. 84r, printed in Carusi, "Nuovi documenti," no. 29 and Baldini and Spruit, eds., *CCMS* 2: no. 5. Santoro reported the presence in Rome on 24 March 1601 of the bishop of Squillace, Tommaso Sirleto. Amabile, *Congiura*, 3: no. 396, 470. He died before 13 August 1601. *HC* 4: 321. The other bishop, Orazio Mattei, *clericus Romanus*, may well have belonged to the wealthy and powerful Roman family of that name; he may therefore also well not have been in his see, explaining his removal from the commission. *HC* 4: 202. As he almost always did, Santoro must have passed on the new order almost immediately. 30 March 1601, Santoro–nuncio, noting that he had already informed Mandina by the last ordinary courier. Amabile, *Congiura*, 3: no. 118, 70.

90. ACDFSO:DSO 1600–1601, fo. 242v and copy in 1601, fo. 99r, printed in Carusi, "Nuovi documenti," no. 30 and Baldini and Spruit, eds., *CCMS* 2: no. 6 and 24 March 1601 Santoro–Mandina and Santoro–nuncio in Amabile, *Congiura* 3: no. 396, 470–71 and no. 116, 70. Mandina had been visiting his see, whence he had not returned as of 6 April. 30 March and 6 April 1601, Nuncio–Santoro. Amabile, *Congiura* 3: nos. 117 and 120, 70 and 71.

91. Santoro–Mandina, 24 March 1601. Ibid., 3: no. 396, 470.

92. Ibid., 3: no. 398a and b, 473–44. See also 6 April 1601, Nuncio–Santoro. Ibid., 3: no. 120, 71.

93. ACDFSO:DSO 1600–1601, fo. 260r and copy in 1601, fo. 124r, printed in Carusi, "Nuovi documenti," no. 31 and Baldini and Spruit, eds., *CCMS* 2: no. 7.

94. Amabile, *Congiura*, 3: no. 402, 498–501; Firpo, *Processi di Campanella*, 248–63 with Italian translation.

95. 12 June 1601, Alessandro Turaminis–Lorenzo Usimbardi. Ibid., 3: no. 169, 86.

96. ACDFSO:DSO 1600–1601, fo. 278v and copy in 1601, fo. 148v, printed in Carusi, "Nuovi documenti," no. 32 and Baldini and Spruit, eds., *CCMS* 2: no. 8.

97. 7 and 15 June 1601. Amabile, *Congiura* 3: no. 403, 502–3.

98. 9 August 1601. ACDFSO:DSO 1600–1601, fo. 299v and copy in 1601, fo. 174v, printed in Carusi, "Nuovi documenti," no. 33 and Baldini and Spruit, eds., *CCMS* 2: no. 9.

99. ACDFSO:DSO 1602, 3–4 (fo. 269v, continuous foliation from *Decreta* 1601), printed in Carusi, "Nuovi documenti," no. 34 and Baldini and Spruit, eds., *CCMS* 2: no. 10.

100. 4 January 1602, Santoro–Mandina. Amabile, *Congiura* 3: no. 407, 507 reprinted in Firpo, *Processi di Campanella*, 270–71.

101. ACDFSO:DSO 1602, p. 69 (fo. 302r), printed in Carusi, "Nuovi documenti," no. 35 and Baldini and Spruit, eds., *CCMS* 2: no. 11.

102. 20 February 1602. Amabile, *Congiura* 3: no. 289, 221, a brief note by the Augustinian Cherubino da Verona, theologian of the archiepiscopal court.

103. 2 and 9 August 1602, Nuncio–Borghese. Ibid., 3, nos. 124 and 125, 72–73.

104. 9 August 1602, Borghese–nuncio. Ibid., 3: no. 126, 73. ACDFSO:DSO 1602, 408, printed in Amabile, Spruit, and Preti, *Campanella*, no. 66* and in Baldini and Spruit, eds., *CCMS* 2: no. 12; not in Carusi.

105. Decree of 9 October 1602, ACDFSO:DSO 1602, 528, printed in Carusi, "Nuovi documenti," no. 36 and Baldini and Spruit, eds., *CCMS* 2: no. 13.

106. 18 October 1602, Nuncio–Borghese and 31 October 1602, Borghese–nuncio. Amabile, *Congiura* 3, nos. 130–31, 74–75.

107. ACDFSO:DSO 1602, 598, printed in Carusi, "Nuovi documenti," no. 37 and Baldini and Spruit, eds., *CCMS* 2: no. 14.

108. Decree of 28 November 1602. ACDFSO:DSO 1602, 620–21, printed in Amabile, *Congiura* 3: no. 134, 75–76; Carusi, "Nuovi documenti," no. 38 and Baldini and Spruit, eds., *CCMS* 2: no. 16. Aldobrandini also sent the news on the same day. Ibid., 3: no. 135, 76.

109. Ibid., 3: no. 427, 532–53. All three judges, the nuncio, Mandina, and the archiepiscopal vicar, signed as *commissarius*. After all the pressure the viceroy had applied, once given the all-clear to condemn Campanella for rebellion, he decided to take his time and the nuncio had to play turn-about and press for expedition. 15 August 1603, Nuncio–Aldobrandini. Ibid., 3: no. 140, 78. De Vera's marriage further hindered expedition since the pope demanded his removal. 19 September 1603, Borghese–nuncio. Ibid., 3: no. 143, 78. The nuncio acknowledged executing the order a week later. Ibid., 3: no. 145, 79. Acting by himself, the nuncio pushed Secretary Salazar to move the case into the Collateral Council

on 23 September 1603. Amabile, *Campanella nei Castelli di Napoli*, 2, "Documenti," no. 9, 2. The viceroy ignored pope and nuncio and gave De Vera a fresh commission. 3 October 1603, Nuncio–Aldobrandini. Amabile, *Congiura* 3: no. 148, 80. He did not announce his intention to return to court for another two weeks. 17 October, Nuncio–Aldobrandini. Ibid., 3: no. 152, 81. A week later Borghese wrote the nuncio that his letters had been read in a coram. 24 October 1603, Borghese–nuncio. Ibid., 3: no. 153, 81. The loss of the nuncio's out-letters leaves us without further information from Naples until 23 July 1604, when he told Borghese that another attempted prison break had led to the suspension of Campanella's case. De Vera further delayed proceedings by insisting on being named first in court documents. Ibid., 3: no. 155, 81–82. Finally in October 1604, more than a year after the way had been cleared to Campanella's sentencing for rebellion, a new royal official was appointed to replace De Vera. Breve of 27 October 1604, noted in ibid., 3: no. 267, 186–87, no. 212, 112 and Amabile, *Campanella nei Castelli di Napoli* 2: "Documenti," no. 29, 6, printed in D'Ancona, "Della vita," cccxxvii–xxix.

110. Gentile–Arrigoni, Naples, 2 June 1606. ACDFSO, St. st., HH.1.e, fos. 81r–82v, 80v, printed in Amabile, Spruit, and Preti, *Campanella*, no. 84* and Baldini and Spruit, eds., *CCMS* 2: no. 30.

111. ACDFSO:DSO 1606, fo. 158r, printed in Carusi, "Nuovi documenti," no. 41 and Baldini and Spruit, eds., *CCMS* 2: no. 31. There had been four other corams since Gentile's letter arrived. Arrigoni passed on the pope's order in a missing letter of 15 July. ACDFSO, St. st., HH.1.e, fos. 29r–v, 34r–v, printed in Amabile, Spruit, and Preti, *Campanella*, no. 90* and Baldini and Spruit, eds., *CCMS* 2: no. 36.

112. ACDFSO, St. st., L.3.e, fo. 178r, printed in Baldini and Spruit, eds., *CCMS* 2: no. 33 and ACDFSO:DSO 1606, fo. 175r, copy in 1606–1607, fo. 136r, printed in ibid., no. 34. Arrigoni passed on the pope's order the next day in another letter. ACDFSO, St. st., HH.1.e, fos. 29r–v, 34r–v, printed in Amabile, Spruit, and Preti, *Campanella*, no. 90* and Baldini and Spruit, eds., *CCMS* 2: no. 36.

113. ACDFSO:DSO 1606, fo. 160v, contemporary copy in 1606–1607, fo. 126v, printed in Carusi, "Nuovi documenti," no. 42 and Baldini and Spruit, eds., *CCMS* 2: no. 32.

114. ACDFSO, St. st., HH.1.e, fos. 83r–84v, printed in Frajese, *Profezia*, 87, Amabile, Spruit, and Preti, *Campanella*, no. 89 and Baldini and Spruit, eds., *CCMS* 2: no. 35.

115. ACDFSO, St. st., HH.1.e, fos. 29r–v and 34r–v, printed in Amabile, Spruit, and Preti, *Campanella*, no. 90* and Baldini and Spruit, eds., *CCMS* 2: no. 36. Received in Rome 12 October.

116. ACDFSO:DSO 1606, fo. 240v, contemporary copy in 1606–1607, fo. 185v, printed in Carusi, "Nuovi documenti," no. 44, Amabile, Spruit, and Preti, *Campanella*, no. 91 and Baldini and Spruit, eds., *CCMS* 2: no. 37. The principal difference is the correction of the minute's singular "frater" to "fratres," as in Gentile's letter.

117. ACDFSO:DSO 1606, fo. 87r, contemporary copy in 1606–1607, fo. 288v, printed in Amabile, Spruit, and Preti, *Campanella*, no. 92* and Baldini and Spruit, eds., *CCMS* 2: no. 38.

118. ACDFSO, St. st., L.3.e., fo. 205r, printed in Amabile, Spruit, and Preti,

Campanella, no. 93* and Baldini and Spruit, eds., *CCMS* 2: no. 39. The bishop was Juan Lopez, O.P. *HC* 4: 246.

119. ACDFSO:DSO 1607, fos. 96v and 97v, contemporary copy in 1606–1607, fos. 297r and 298r, printed in Carusi, "Nuovi documenti," no. 45, Amabile, Spruit, and Preti, *Campanella*, no. 94 and Baldini and Spruit, eds., *CCMS* 2: no. 40.

120. ACDFSO:DSO 1607, fo. 155v, contemporary copy in 1606–1607, fo. 348v, printed in Carusi, "Nuovi documenti," no. 46, Amabile, Spruit, and Preti, *Campanella*, no. 95* and Baldini and Spruit, eds., *CCMS* 2: no. 41.

121. ACDFSO:DSO 1607, fo. 198r, printed in Baldini and Spruit, eds., *CCMS* 2: no. 42, 30 August. The date of Gentile's letter is missing.

122. ACDFSO:DSO 1608–1609, fo. 22r, printed in Carusi, "Nuovi documenti," no. 47 (from copy), Amabile, Spruit, and Preti, *Campanella*, no. 96 and Baldini and Spruit, eds., *CCMS* 2: no. 43. Neither Spruit nor I have found this decree. There may be an error of date for that of 13 November condemning Campanella to perpetual imprisonment.

123. ACDFSO:DSO 1608–1609, fo. 124r, printed in Carusi, "Nuovi documenti," no. 48 (from copy), Amabile, Spruit, and Preti, *Campanella*, no. 98* and Baldini and Spruit, eds., *CCMS* 2: no. 45 and 1608–1609, fo. 201v, printed in Amabile, Spruit, and Preti, *Campanella*, no. 99 and Baldini and Spruit, eds., *CCMS* 2: no. 46. In mid-1608 the Congregation also decided that the matter of resistance to preachers assigned to counteract Campanella's heresies did not concern it, even though the order to deploy them had come from the Inquisition. Fabrizio Sirleto, bishop of Squillace–Arrigoni, Squillace, 25 February 1608, note of impertinence dated 8 May 1608. ACDFSO, St. st., LL.3.c, fos. 928r–v and 933v, printed in Amabile, Spruit, and Preti, *Campanella*, no. 97* and Baldini and Spruit, eds., *CCMS* 2: no. 44.

124. ACDFSO:DSO 1608–1609, fo. 396r, 16 July 1609, printed in Carusi, "Nuovi documenti," no. 54, Amabile, Spruit, and Preti, *Campanella*, no. 105, and Baldini and Spruit, eds., *CCMS* 2: no. 52.

125. Mark Welser–Faber, Augsburg, 9 May 1608. Amabile, *Campanella nei Castelli di Napoli* 2: "Documenti," 38.

126. ACDFSO:DSO 1608–1609, fo. 207r, 2 October 1608, printed in Carusi, "Nuovi documenti," no. 49, Amabile, Spruit, and Preti, *Campanella*, no. 100* and Baldini and Spruit, eds., *CCMS* 2: no. 47 and 1608–1609, fo. 213r, 9 October 1608, printed in Carusi, "Nuovi documenti," no. 50, Amabile, Spruit, and Preti, *Campanella*, no. 101*, and Baldini and Spruit, eds., *CCMS* 2: no. 48. Bastoni served only a short time, since he died before 19 January 1609. *HC* 4:273n.

127. ACDFSO:DSO 1608–1609, fo. 229r, contemporary copy in 1608, p. 470, printed in Carusi, "Nuovi documenti," no. 51 (from copy), Amabile, Spruit, and Preti, *Campanella*, no. 102* and Baldini and Spruit, eds., *CCMS* 2: no. 49. The records of this phase of Campanella's secular trial appear to be lost.

128. ACDFSO:DSO 1608–1609, fo. 321r, 26 March 1609, printed in Carusi, "Nuovi documenti," no. 52, Amabile, Spruit, and Preti, *Campanella*, no. 103* and Baldini and Spruit, eds., *CCMS* 2: no. 50. Muti was deputed nuncio 18 November 1608. *HC* 4:152.

129. ACDFSO:DSO 1608–1609, fo. 381r, 25 June 1609, printed in Carusi, "Nuovi documenti," no. 53, Amabile, Spruit, and Preti, *Campanella*, no. 104*, and Baldini and Spruit, eds., *CCMS* 2: no. 51. For Schoppe's efforts, see Amabile, *Campanella nei Castelli di Napoli* 2: "Documenti," 39, 40, 45, and especially no. 153, a letter of 17 March 1609 saying that the witness against Bruno, Giovanni Battista Ciotti, was refusing either to print or to return Campanella's manuscript.

130. ACDFSO:DSO 1608–1609, fo. 414v, printed in Carusi, "Nuovi documenti," no. 55, Amabile, Spruit, and Preti, *Campanella*, no. 106*, and Baldini and Spruit, eds., *CCMS* 2: no. 53.

131. ACDFSO:DSO 1610, p. 179, contemporary copy in 1610–1611, fo. 73v, 29 April 1610, printed in Carusi, "Nuovi documenti," no. 56, Amabile, Spruit, and Preti, *Campanella*, no. 107* and Baldini and Spruit, eds., *CCMS* 2: no. 54. For Archduke Ferdinand's intervention, see Amabile, *Campanella nei Castelli di Napoli* 2: "Documenti," no. 141, 40.

132. ACDFSO:DSO 1610, p. 214, contemporary copy in 1610–1611, fos. 87v–88r, 20 May 1610, printed in Carusi, "Nuovi documenti," no. 57, Amabile, Spruit, and Preti, *Campanella*, no. 108* and Baldini and Spruit, eds., *CCMS* 2: no. 55. The pope made Gentile nuncio on 29 March 1610. *HC* 4: 138n.

133. Amabile, *Campanella nei Castelli di Napoli* 2: "Documenti," 9, nos. 40–42.

134. ACDFSO:DSO 1610–1611, fo. 280v, decree of 17 March 1611, printed in Carusi, "Nuovi documenti," no. 58, Amabile, Spruit, and Preti, *Campanella*, no. 109*, and Baldini and Spruit, eds., *CCMS* 2: no. 56.

135. ACDFSO:DSO 1610–1611, fo. 292r, printed in Carusi, "Nuovi documenti," no. 59, Amabile, Spruit, and Preti, *Campanella*, no. 110* and Baldini and Spruit, eds., *CCMS* 2: no. 57. Gentile must have replaced former Nuncio Muti who died in January 1610, which must mean there had been another long hiatus in the case.

136. Amabile, *Campanella nei Castelli di Napoli* 2: "Documenti," 2, 10, nos. 49 and 48.

137. He took the commissary's oath 17 October 1607 (ACDFSO:DSO 1607, fo. 230r–v), and was named bishop of Nocera de' Pagani before 4 September 1610, when it was announced that he was to be sent to Naples. He was examined for the bishopric 10 November (BAV, Barb. lat. 6344, fo. 140r) and provided by the pope 24 November 1610 (BAV, Barb. lat. 6344, fo. 200r and *HC* 4: 263). He is supposed to have written "Praxis brevis de modo procedendi in sancto officio in causis fidei." *QE* 2: 424.

138. ACDFSO:DSO 1612, p. 328, 19 July 1612 responding to Vicari's letter of 6 July, printed in Carusi, "Nuovi documenti," no. 62, Amabile, Spruit, and Preti, *Campanella*, no. 113* and Baldini and Spruit, eds., *CCMS* 2: no. 60.

139. ACDFSO:DSO 1612, p. 458, 27 September 1612, printed in Carusi, "Nuovi documenti," no. 63, Amabile, Spruit, and Preti, *Campanella*, no. 114* and Baldini and Spruit, eds., *CCMS* 2: no. 61. For the viceroy's action of 1 September 1612, see Amabile, *Campanella nei Castelli di Napoli* 2: "Documenti," 11, no. 55.

140. ACDFSO:DSO 1614, p. 230, decree of 9 May 1614, printed in Carusi, "Nuovi documenti," no. 64, Amabile, Spruit, and Preti, *Campanella*, no. 115* and Baldini and Spruit, eds., *CCMS* 2: no. 62.

141. ACDFSO:DSO 1614, pp. 294–95, 18 June 1614, responding to Vicari's letter of 6 June, printed in Carusi, "Nuovi documenti," no. 65, Amabile, Spruit, and Preti, *Campanella*, no. 116 and Baldini and Spruit, eds., *CCMS* 2: no. 63. The original witness's name was first given as Angelo "Panormitanus" and then as "Romanus."

142. ACDFSO:DSO 1614, p. 329, 8 July 1614, responding to a deposition of 20 June, printed in Carusi, "Nuovi documenti," no. 66, Amabile, Spruit, and Preti, *Campanella*, no. 117* and Baldini and Spruit, eds., *CCMS* 2: no. 64.

143. 21 October 1614 in Amabile, *Campanella nei Castelli di Napoli* 2: "Documenti," 12, no. 60, with an apparent typo of "Castel dell'Ovo" for Castello Nuovo.

144. ACDFSO:DSO 1615, p. 200, 23 April 1615, printed in Carusi, "Nuovi documenti," no. 67, Amabile, Spruit, and Preti, *Campanella*, no. 118* and Baldini and Spruit, eds., *CCMS* 2: no. 65.

145. ACDFSO:DSO 1615, p. 230, 7 May 1615, printed in Amabile, Spruit, and Preti, *Campanella*, no. 119* and Baldini and Spruit, eds., *CCMS* 2: no. 66.

146. ACDFSO:DSO 1616, p. 494, 8 December.

147. Filonardi–Borghese, 22 November 1616 in ASV, Nunz. Napoli, 20E, fo. 435r, printed in Amabile, *Campanella nei Castelli di Napoli* 2: "Documenti," 22, no. 96.

148. Filonardi–Borghese, 29 November 1616 in ASV, Nunz. Napoli, 20E, fo. 464r, printed in Amabile, *Campanella nei Castelli di Napoli* 2: "Documenti," 22–23: no. 97.

149. ACDFSO:DSO 1616, pp. 494–95, printed in Carusi, "Nuovi documenti," no. 68, Amabile, Spruit, and Preti, *Campanella*, no. 120* and Baldini and Spruit, eds., *CCMS* 2: no. 67.

150. ACDFSO:DSO 1618, p. 150, 2 May 1618, printed in Carusi, "Nuovi documenti," no. 69, Amabile, Spruit, and Preti, *Campanella*, no. 121* and Baldini and Spruit, eds., *CCMS* 2: no. 68.

151. ACDFSO:DSO 1618, p. 160, 10 May 1618, printed in Carusi, "Nuovi documenti," no. 70, Amabile, Spruit, and Preti, *Campanella*, no. 122* and Baldini and Spruit, eds., *CCMS* 2: no. 69.

152. ACDFSO:DSO 1619, p. 188, 31 May 1619, printed in Carusi, "Nuovi documenti," no. 71, Amabile, Spruit, and Preti, *Campanella*, no. 123* and Baldini and Spruit, eds., *CCMS* 2: no. 70. The nuncio's correspondence is lost until 1626 and Amabile found nothing else in Neapolitan archives.

153. 28 October 1618 in ASV, Nunz. Napoli, 326 (*sic* and *recte*; the next document gives the incorrect 26), fo. 309, printed in Amabile, *Campanella nei Castelli di Napoli* 2: "Documenti," 23: no. 98.

154. Ignazio Terracci[ani] to Giacinto Petroni, L'Àquila, 4 September 1620, note of order 14 October 1620 at foot of dorse, printed in Amabile, Spruit, and Preti, *Campanella*, no. 124* and Baldini and Spruit, eds., *CCMS* 2: no. 71.

155. ACDF, Index, *Diarii*, 3, fos. 54v and 55r, meeting of 22 May 1621, printed in Amabile, Spruit, and Preti, *Campanella*, no. 125* and Baldini and Spruit, eds., *CCMS* 2: no. 72, summary copy in ACDF, Index, *Protocolli*, AA (II.a.23), fo. 103r, printed in Carusi, "Nuovi documenti," no. 72.

156. ACDF, Index, *Diarii*, 3, fo. 58r, 30 June 1621, printed in Amabile, Spruit, and Preti, *Campanella*, no. 126* and Baldini and Spruit, eds., *CCMS* 2: no. 73, summary copy in ACDF, Index, *Protocolli*, AA (II.a.23), fo. 103r, printed in Carusi, "Nuovi documenti," no. 72. Filonardi's uncle Cardinal Filippo had just been added to the Congregation.

157. ACDF, Index, *Diarii*, 3, fo. 59r–v, decree of 28 August 1621, printed in Amabile, Spruit, and Preti, *Campanella*, no. 127* and Baldini and Spruit, eds., *CCMS* 2: no. 74, summary copy in ACDF, Index, *Protocolli*, AA (II.a.23), fo. 103r, printed in Carusi, "Nuovi documenti," no. 72.

158. ACDFSO:DSO 1623, p. 48, 1 February 1623, printed in Carusi, "Nuovi documenti," no. 73, Amabile, Spruit, and Preti, *Campanella*, no. 128* and Baldini and Spruit, eds., *CCMS* 2: no. 75; 1625, fo. 173r, 8 October 1625, printed in Carusi, "Nuovi documenti," no. 74, Amabile, Spruit, and Preti, *Campanella*, no. 129* and Baldini and Spruit, eds., *CCMS* 2: no. 76; and 1626, fo. 4r, 2 January 1626, printed in Carusi, "Nuovi documenti," no. 75, Amabile, Spruit, and Preti, *Campanella*, no. 130* and Baldini and Spruit, eds., *CCMS* 2: no. 77.

159. ACDFSO:DSO 1626, fo. 121r, 16 July 1626, printed in Carusi, "Nuovi documenti," no. 76, Amabile, Spruit, and Preti, *Campanella*, no. 131* and Baldini and Spruit, eds., *CCMS* 2: no. 78. The censures have not been found.

160. Amabile, *Campanella nei Castelli di Napoli* 2: "Documenti," 20, no. 88, royal order of 26 March, appointing judges, and another of 15 May in ibid., 20, no. 90. Two weeks later the pro-nuncio was informed that the house was San Domenico in Naples; ibid., 20, no. 91.

161. *HC* 4: 138. He was appointed nuncio on 21 March 1626.

162. Antonio Barberini, Sr.–Nuncio Antonio Diaz, 4 June 1626. Amabile, *Campanella nei Castelli di Napoli* 2: "Documenti," 23 and Amabile, "L'Andata," no. 1, 33–34, incorrectly giving the source (without folio reference) as ASV, Nunz. Napoli, 26, instead of 326. Amabile apparently could not find the enclosure.

163. Diaz–A. Barberini, Sr., Naples, 13 June 1626. Amabile, *Campanella nei Castelli di Napoli* 2: "Documenti," 24, no. 100 and Amabile, "L'Andata," no. 2, 34–35.

164. Amabile, *Campanella nei Castelli di Napoli* 2: "Documenti," 148, no. 202.

165. Diaz–A. Barberini, Sr., Naples, 20 June 1626. Ibid., 24, no. 101 and Amabile, "L'Andata," no. 3, 35.

166. Diaz–A. Barberini, Sr., Naples, 23 June 1626. Amabile, *Campanella nei Castelli di Napoli* 2: 24, no. 102 and Amabile, "L'Andata," no. 4, 35.

167. Diaz–A. Barberini, Sr., Naples, 27 June 1626 and 4 and 5 July 1626. Amabile, *Campanella nei Castelli di Napoli* 2: nos. 103–105 and Amabile, "L'Andata," nos. 5–7, 35–36.

168. Diaz–A. Barberini, Sr., Naples, 7 July 1626. Amabile, *Campanella nei Castelli di Napoli* 2: 24–25 and Amabile, "L'Andata," no. 8, 36–37.

169. ACDFSO:DSO 1629, fo. 14r, printed in Carusi, "Nuovi documenti," no. 97, Amabile, Spruit, and Preti, *Campanella*, no. 155* and Baldini and Spruit, eds., *CCMS* 2: no. 102.

170. 25 May ACDFSO:DSO 1628, fo. 91r; not in Baldini and Spruit, eds., *CCMS* 2. For Vecchietti, see *RI*, 210–13.

CHAPTER 3. VENICE IN THE WAKE OF THE INTERDICT

1. He seems never to have written anything; at least, there is no entry in *QE*.

2. Anne Jacobsen Schutte, *Aspiring Saints: Pretense of Holiness, Inquisition, and Gender in the Republic of Venice 1618–1750* (Baltimore: Johns Hopkins University Press, 2001), 26–41. This survey concentrates on the nunciature of Berlinghiero Gessi from 1607–1618, in part because it is the best documented, in part because it naturally defines the period of reactions to the interdict. For an overview of the Inquisition in Venice, see Adriano Prosperi, *Tribunali della coscienza: inquisitori, confessori, missionari* (Turin: Einaudi, 1996), 83–103, *DSI* 3: 1657–60, for the interdict crisis 2: 847–49, and for the nuncio's role 2: 1121.

3. See the excellent treatment in William J. Bouwsma, *Venice and the Defense of Republican Liberty: Renaissance Values in the Age of the Counter Reformation* (Berkeley and Los Angeles: University of California Press, 1968), especially 339–50; Francis Oakley, "Complexities of Context: Gerson, Bellarmine, Sarpi, Richer, and the Venetian Interdict of 1606–1607," *Catholic Historical Review* 82 (1996): 369–96; and A. D. Wright, "Why the Venetian Interdict?" *English Historical Review* 89 (July, 1974): 536–50. Bouwsma emphasizes Paul's autocratic and narrowly legal view of his office. The breve declaring the interdict is dated 17 April 1606. Arabella Georgina Campbell, *La vita di fra Paolo Sarpi* (Florence: Loescher, 1875), 132.

4. Contarini said the interdict "venne dal pontefice medesimo, senza previa consultatione di Cardinali, nè di alcuno altro. Non ne havendo detto parola in consistoro se non dopo fatta l'estesa del Breve e dell'interdetto." "Relazione di Francesco Contarini," Nicolò Barozzi and Guglielmo Berchet, *Relazioni degli stati europei lette al Senato dagli ambasciatori veneti, ser. 3, Italia; Relazioni di Roma* (Venice: Naratovich, 1877), 3:1, 88, a contention repeated by Renier Zen, ordinary ambassador from 1621–23 ("Relazione," 157).

5. Wright, "Interdict," 544.

6. The book was drawn up in 1613 and used by the *consultori in iure*. It was published only later. Schutte, *Pretense*, 33.

7. A principle formalized—after long previous use—in a decree of 18 October 1612. Paolo Sarpi, *Discorso dell'origine, forma, leggi, ed uso dell'Ufficio dell'inquisitione nella città, e dominio di venetia* (N.p.: N.p., 1638), 5.

8. Bartolomeo Cecchetti, *La republica di Venezia e la corte di Roma nei rapporti della religione*, 2 vols. (Venice: P. Naratovich, 1874, 2 vols.), 2, 10; and Brian Pullan, *The Jews of Europe and the Inquisition of Venice* (Oxford: Blackwell, 1983), 31–32.

9. Sarpi, *Discorso*, 8, decrees of 1580 and 1590, and 13, a decree promulgated during the interdict crisis.

10. Ibid., 4–15.

11. Ibid., 4–5, 7–8, 9, etc.

12. Ibid., 11.

13. Ibid., 15.

14. Ibid., 8–9.

15. Paul F. Grendler, *The Roman Inquisition and the Venetian Press (1540–1605)* (Princeton, N.J.: Princeton University Press, 1977).

16. *RI*, 72–75.

17. ACDFSO:DSO 1606–1607, fo. 131r. The book was probably *Risposta del card. Bellarmino a due libretti uno de' quali s'intitola Risposta di un dottore di teologia, ad una lettera scrittagli da un reverendo suo amico, sopra il Breve di censure dalla santita di Paolo 5. publicate contra li signori venetiani. Et l'altro, Trattato, & resolutione sopra la validita delle scommuniche di Gio. Gersone* (Rome: Guglielmo Facciotto and Ferrara: Vittorio Baldini, 1606; another edition Florence: Volcmar Timan, 1606; Latin translation Mainz: Balthasar Lipp & Nicolaus Stein, 1606) or possibly *Risposta del card. Bellarmino al trattato de i sette theologi di Venetia, sopra l'interdetto della Santita di n. Signore Papa Paolo quinto* (Rome: Guglielmo Faciotto and Naples: Giovanni Battista Sottile, 1606). It was probably not the more narrowly focused *Risposta alle oppositioni di fra Paolo Servita contra la scrittura del cardinale Bellarmino* (Rome: Guglielmo Facciotto and Ferrara: Vittorio Baldini, 1606).

18. ACDFSO:DSO 1606–1607, fo. 102v; 1606, fo. 126r, decree of 9 June 1606.

19. Ibid., fo. 107r, decree of 14 June 1606.

20. Aurelio Bianchi-Giovini, *Biografia di Frà Paolo Sarpi: teologo e consultore di stato della repubblica Veneta* (Basel: D.G. Bellini, 1847; second ed.), 156, but see below for at least a mistake in the date of the prohibition of Sarpi's *Considerazioni*.

21. ACDFSO:DSO 1606–1607, fo. 129r. According to the Jesuit general, proceedings had begun by 1 April, but there is nothing in the register to support this claim. Bouwsma, *Venice*, 369n.

22. R. Putelli, "Il duca Vincenzo I Gonzaga e l'interdetto di Paolo V a Venezia, II" *Nuovo Archivio Veneto* n.s. 22 (1911): 5–280, 184. Manfredi had been in contact with the duke since 1602. The Mantuan resident did what he could to collect information for the pope. Ibid., 187.

23. Enrico Cornet, *Paolo V e la Republica Veneta* (Venice: Marco Visentini, 1873), 123.

24. Niccolò Contarini, 26 November 1606. Cornet, *Paolo V*, 276–77.

25. Francesco Scaduto, *Stato e chiesa secondo fra Paolo Sarpi e la coscienza pubblica durante l'Interdetto di Venezia del 1606–1607* (Florence: C. Ademollo, 1885), and Gino Benzoni, "I 'teologi' minori dell'interdetto," *Archivio veneto* 101 (5th ser. No. 126) (1970): 31–108, passim.

26. See the summary judgment of Pietro Savio, "Il nunzio a Venezia dopo l'interdetto," *Archivio Veneto* 85 (1955): 55–110, 100.

27. See below and my forthcoming study of Galileo's trial.

28. On 28 April 1617 Secretary Millini was ordered to tell the Augustinians' general not to use Fra Camillo on their business, since he had written against the interdict. ACDFSO:DSO 1617, pp. 158–59.

29. Benzoni, "I 'teologi,'" 47. For Sarpi, see *DSI* 3: 1380–82, which lacks entries for the

others. Benzoni's list, long as it is, is not comprehensive; see below for the case of Antonio Faiano.

30. Unless otherwise noted, this sketch biography is drawn from that in *DBI*, 68, 683–86 as corrected. Manfredi was the only preacher singled out by name in "Relatione politica delle differenze nate tra Papa Paolo V.o e li SS.ri Venetiani l'anno 1605 . . . ," which called him "empio persecutore non solo della authorità apostolica e pontificia, ma vi e più in dispreggio, e schermo delle Censure e dell'interdetto." BAV, Barb. lat. 4932, fo. 82r–v.

31. There is also a manuscript copy in the Biblioteca Marciana, Venice, MS Ital. VII. 1723 (8598) (Giuseppe Mazzatinti, et al., *Inventari dei Manoscritti delle Biblioteche d'Italia* [Florence: Olschki et al., 1890–], 89, 26). See the summary in Benzoni, "I 'teologi,'" 68n–69, who judges Manfredi's preaching much more important than his publication.

32. Emmanuele Antonio Cicogna, *Delle inscrizioni veneziane*, 8 vols. (Venice: Orlandelli, 1824–53), 5, 582; for the now destroyed convent, which was just east of the Salute, see http://venicexplorer.net/tradizione/topos/uuu.html, accessed 9 July 2008.

33. ACDFSO:DSO 1606–1607, fo. 137v. This meeting should have been a coram, but is not so indicated.

34. Ibid., fo. 139r, 10 August 1606.

35. Ibid., fo. 145r, 17 August 1606. Gioacchino Scaino (1535–1608) was a reader in law at the University of Padua and, with Galileo, a member of the Academy of the Ricovrati. Antonio Favaro, *Galileo Galilei e lo Studio di Padova*, 2 vols. (Florence: Le Monnier, 1888), 2, 26 and 80. He had joined Marcantonio Pellegrini and Marcantonio Ottellio in writing a consilium in favor of Venice. *Responsa clarissimorum Iur. consultorum D. M. Antonii Peregrini Equitis, D. M. Antonii Othelii, [et] D. Ioachimi Scayni . . . reddita pro Decretis Serenissimi Principis Veneti* (Venice: Deuchino, 1606). "Doctore Raguseo" has not been identified.

36. See his printed citation in the name of all Inquisitors, signed by Pompeo Arrigoni, counter-signed by Quintiliano Adriani, notary, with note of affiction by G. B. Menochio, cursitor, on 26 August. ASV, Fondo Borghese III 42b, fo. 145r. See the two printed, undated copies of Marsilio's citation in the same form as Manfredi's, no note of execution on either. ASV, Fondo Borghese III 42b, fos. 148v and 149r. Part of the citation is printed in Marsilio's reply in *Opere del Padre Paolo dell'ordine de' Servi*, 5 vols. (Venice: Roberto Meietti, 1677), 1, 11–12.

37. Marsilio's appearance in Venice is set out in the reprint of his *Exceptio* in Melchior Goldast, ed., *Monarchia S. Romani Imperii*, 3 vols. (Frankfurt: Conrad Biermann, 1611–1614), 2: 477–80, 479–80; see also the further reprint in *Theologorum Venetorum Joan. Marsilii, Pauli Veneti, Fr. Fulgentii ad excommunicationis, citationis et monitionis Romanae sententiam in ipsos latam Responsio* in *Opere del padre Paolo*, 1, separately paginated, 16–22, set out in the proper form of an authentic document.

38. ACDFSO:DSO 1606–1607, fo. 146r, 23 August 1606.

39. Ibid., fo. 147v, 24 August 1606.

40. Ibid., fo. 150v, 31 August, in response to letter of 29 August.

41. Ibid., fo. 150v.

42. Ibid., fos. 156v and 158r. Rather unusually, the full text is on fos. 161v–162r. Sarpi refers to an edict against his book dated 20 September in his *Exceptio* (Goldast, *Monarchia*, 2, 481–82, 481; see also *Theologorum . . . Responsio* in *Opere del Padre Paolo*, 1, 27). This must be the action Bianchi-Giovini, *Biografia,*162 dated 30 September as the prohibition of the *Trattato*, Sarpi's *Considerazioni* and Antonio Querini's *Avviso delle Ragioni della repubblica di Venezia*.

43. Cardinal Giovanni Delfino wrote on 26 August that Paul listened to no one but Arrigoni. Enrico Cornet, ed., *La repubblica veneta. Giornale dal 22. ottobre 1608–9. giugno 1607* (Vienna: Tendler, 1859), 326.

44. ACDFSO:DSO 1606–1607, fo. 162r.

45. Ibid., fo. 167r; 1606, fos. 216r and 218r–v, 27 and 28 September.

46. Ibid., fo. 182v.

47. ASV, Fondo Borghese III 42b, fo. 146r, printed citation for Sarpi (cf. Bianchi-Giovini, *Biografia*, 169 and Campbell, *Sarpi*, 155, quoting Micanzio), fo. 147r for Manfredi, and 141r for Meietti, all dated 30 October 1606. Sarpi refers to his citation in Goldast, *Monarchia*, 2, 481 and *Theologorum . . . Responsio*, 28–29, calling it a *praeceptum*. See also "Relazione della morte di F. Fulgenzio Manfredi Veneziano" (BCV, MS Cicogna 1382, p. 13; TCC, MS R.3.42, fo. 144v). The "Relazione" survives in four copies, three of which I have collated: BCV, MS Cicogna 1382, the last piece in the volume, separately paginated; MS Correr 1051, fos. 210r–235v, used in the *DBI* article on Manfredi but probably less accurate than Cicogna 1382, e.g., fo. 223v, where it apparently calls Michele Vitio Truio, but it also has text not in 1382, e.g., fo. 224r where it adds "et in particolare contro il Cardinale Bellarminio;" TCC, R.3.42, fos. 139v–165r, "Relatione della morte di Fra Fulgentio Manfredi Vinitiano, seguita in Roma l'anno 1610 a v. Luglio," in "Libritto di varie scritture Politiche," "Continenza" on dorse, the whole volume in the same hand, fair copy, dated at end 23 April 1615 (last digit uncertain), no marks of ownership, second last piece, said to have belonged to Giacomo Castelvetro, according to Chiara Franceschini, "Nostalgie di un esule. Note su Giacomo Castelvetro (1546–1616)," *Cromohs* 8 (2003): 1–13, at note 24 (http://www.cromohs.unifi.it/8_2003/franceschini.html); and Osimo, Biblioteca del Collegio, 25 (Mazzatinti et al., *Manoscritti*, 6, 10) which may perhaps have come from its bishop, Agostino Galamini, who was commissary during Manfredi's first trial and master of the sacred palace, and therefore consultor of the Inquisition, during the second. Cornet, *Paolo V*, 278 said he intended to publish the "Relazione," but he seems never to have done so.

48. According to Cicogna, *Iscrizioni*, 2, 296–99 it was reprinted in Melchior Goldast, ed., *Collectio constitutionum imperialium*, 3 vols. (Frankfurt/Main: Zunner, 1673). Johannes Albertus Fabricius, *Bibliotheca latina mediae et infimae aetatis . . .* , 5 (Padua: Giovanni Manfrè, 1754), 13 refers to the same collection as containing Manfredi's "Exceptionem per edictum Cardinalium in causa Veneta." Cicogna cites a very similar title,

Exceptio contra citationem per edictum cardinalium Romanorum in causa Veneta, as published in quarto and as a loose sheet in 1606 and at Paris in 1607, which he further appears to identify with Manfredi's otherwise unconfirmed *Manifesto al documento della sacra Inquisizione di Roma che lo cita ad apparire davanti ad essa* (Venice, 1606). Cicogna also claimed that Manfredi further wrote an "Apologia" once in the "Biblioteca Barberina T. II, pp. 16–17." See below.

49. Both are also in *Opuscoli sull'interdetto* (Paris, 1607), of which there is a copy in the Marciana. *DBI.*

50. *Theologorum . . . Responsio*, 41–57, 46.

51. Ibid., 30 and 34.

52. Report from Giordano, warden of the Franciscan convent at San Francesco della Vigna, 21 November 1606 (Cornet, *Giornale*, 170n from [ASVe] "Esposizioni–Roma"), two others of the next day (Cornet, *Paolo V*, 263–65 and 165–70), and Niccolò Contarini's of 24 November (ibid., 276–77). Contarini was one of the leaders of the anti-papal party.

53. Cornet, *Giornale*, 170n1.

54. ACDFSO:DSO 1606, fo. 268r. See the agenda for this coram in Vincenzo Spampanato, "Nuovi documenti intorno a negozii e processi dell'Inquisizione (1603–1624)," *Giornale critico della filosofia italiana* 5 (1924): 97–137, 216–61 and 346–401, 247. The works in question must be those in *Theologorum . . . Responsio.* Fulgenzio Micanzio (followed by Bianchi-Giovini, *Biografia*, 169) called Sarpi's reply, like Manfredi's, *Manifesto*, which should be interepreted as a generic title. *Vita del padre Paolo, dell'ordine dei Servi, e theologo della Serenissima Republ. di Venetia* (Leiden [probably false imprint]: no publisher, 1646), 139–40.

55. ACDFSO:DSO 1606–1607, fos. 208v–209r.

56. Ibid., fo. 201r, 30 November 1606. Although replies to both Sarpi (although not to his *Exceptio*) and Marsilio were published, there seems never to have been one to Manfredi.

57. Ibid. fo. 203r.

58. Ibid., fos. 216r and 220r, 20 and 29 December 1606.

59. Sarpi's excommunication by Vignuzzio was ordered entered into the record and printed on 3 January. ACDFSO:DSO 1607, fo. 7v. It is dated 5 January by Bouwsma, *Venice*, 401, citing Vincenzo M. Buffon, *Chiesa di Cristo e Chiesa romana nelle opere e nelle lettere di fra Paolo Sarpi* (Louvain, 1941), 7n, as is Manfredi's by Achille De Rubertis, *Ferdinando I de' Medici e la contesa fra Paolo V e la Repubblica veneta*, Reale Deputazione di Storia Patria per le Venezie: Miscellanea di studi e memorie, 2 (1933), 266. His undated, printed excommunication, done in the name of Luigi Boido, fiscal, signed by Notary Quintiliano Adriani with note of its execution 5 January 1607 by G. B. Mennochio, cursitor, by posting on San Pietro, the palazzo del Sant'Uffizio, and Campo de' Fiori is in ASV, Fondo Borghese III 42b, fo. 134r.

60. Abbot Gradenigo to his brother, 9 December 1606. Cornet, *Giornale*, 330.

61. Characteristically, the notary got the title a little wrong. It should be *Delle controversie tra il sommo pontefice Paolo quinto, et la serenissima republica di Venetia. Il parere di*

frate Marc'Antonio Capello minor conventuale, dottore di teologia, metafisico publico di Padova (Venice: Alessandro Cavalcalupo, 1606). Benzoni, "I 'teologi,'" 93 calls it one of the most important defenses of Venice.

62. ACDFSO:DSO 1607, fo. 9r, two separate decrees. *Trattato dell'interdetto della santita di papa Paulo 5. nel quale si dimostra, che egli non e legitimamente publicato, & che per molte ragioni non sono obligati gli ecclesiastici all'essecutione di esso, ne possono senza peccato osservarlo. Composto dalli sottoscritti theologhi. Pietr'Antonio archidiacono, & vicario general di Venetia. F. Paulo dell'Ord. de' Servi . . .* (Venice: Roberto Meietti, 1606).

63. Ibid., fo. 14v. The book was *Lettera del Padre Antonio Possevino, Giesuita al Padre Maestro Marc'antonio Capello, minor conventuale: con la risposta di detto padre* (Venice: Alessandro Cavalcalupo, 1607).

64. This biography is largely drawn from Benzoni, "'Teologi,'" 88–108, as emended.

65. *Risposta del P. maestro Marc'Antonio Capello . . . al discorso del P. M. Lelio piacentino . . . & inquisitor di Fiorenza, sopra i fondamenti, & le ragioni delli ss. venitiani intorno all'Interdetto & censure della santita di papa Paolo quinto* (Venice: Alessandro Cavalcalupo, 1606). Medici's work was *Discorso . . . sopra i fondamenti, e le ragioni delli ss. veneziani, per le quali pensano di essere scusati della disubbidienza, che fanno alle censure, & interdetto della Santita di Nostro Signor Papa Paolo quinto* (Bologna: Giovanni Battista Bellagamba, 1606).

66. ACDFSO:DSO 1606–1607, fos. 232v–233r, 18 January 1607.

67. Ibid., fo. 243r–v, 6 February 1607.

68. Ibid., fo. 241v; Copia 1607, unfoliated, 1 February.

69. Ibid., fo. 245v, 8 February, and see http://www.bibliotecamai.org/editoria/edizioni/bergamo_interdetto_paolov/fedeli_alla_chiesa_e_allo_stato.html, accessed 9 July 2008.

70. Ibid., fo. 255v, decree of 15 February; Fulgenzio Micanzio, *Confirmatione delle Considerationi del P. Mastro Paolo de Venetia con le oppositioni del R. P. Maestro Gioantonio Bovio Carmeletano* (Venice: Roberto Meietti, 1606).

71. Ibid., fos. 283r and 294v, 29 March and 18 April 1607.

72. Cappello announced the news on 25 March 1607. Pietro Pirri, *L'interdetto di Venezia del 1606 e i gesuiti* (Rome: Institutum Historicum S.I., 1959), 318; and Benzoni, "I 'teologi,'" 98–99.

73. ASVe, Consiglio dei Dieci, Parti Roma, registro 1607, fos. 54v–55r; cf. Cornet, *Paolo V*, 111–12.

74. Bianchi-Giovini, *Biografia*, 183, and Bouwsma, *Venice*, 374.

75. ACDFSO:DSO 1606–1607, fo. 298v, 24 April 1607.

76. Ibid., fo. 322r and ACDFSO:DSO 1607, fo. 127r, 31 May 1607.

77. ACDFSO:DSO 1607, fo. 127v.

78. Benzoni, "I 'teologi,'" 94, citing a copy of the censurae of 19 May 1607 in BCV, Cod. Cicogna 3287/XII. The Index acted on 9 May. There is nothing in the Inquisition's decree register.

79. ACDFSO:DSO 1607, fo. 135v.

80. Ibid., fo. 140v, 20 June 1607.

81. ACDFSO:DSO 1606–1607, fo. 343r; ACDFSO:DSO 1607, fo. 151r, 28 June 1607.

82. ACDFSO:DSO 1607, fo. 165r.

83. Only Gaspar's has been identified, *Consilium super controversia vertente inter beatissimum Paulum papam 5. Ac serenissimam rempublicam Venetam* (Venice: Roberto Meietti, 1606). According to Giuseppe Vedova, *Biografia degli scrittori padovani*, 2 vols. (Padua: Minerva, 1831–36), 1, 531, there is a manuscript of it in the Marciana. One such confessor, Bernardino Venetiano, a monk of San Sebastiano, was banished from Venice under precept for trying to execute this order. ASVe, Consiglio dei Dieci, Parti Roma, registro 1607, fo. 89vff, 16 September and later. Paul gave the Venetian ambassador at least one long complaint as a result. Francesco Contarini–doge, 11 October in ASVe:SDR, f. 60, fos. 47v–52r.

84. ACDFSO:DSO 1607, fo. 150r; ACDFSO:DSO 1606–1607, fo. 344v, 28 June 1607.

85. Many of his consilia survive. ASVe, Consultori in iure (Inventario 102), filze 27a, 37–38, and 52–73.

86. Biography drawn from Vedova, *Biografia*, 1, 528–34, which is largely based on Cicogna, *Iscrizioni*, 3, 129–33. For the edition of Bartolo, see 531–32, and for the rest of his works 530–34. Cf. Benzoni, "I 'teologi,'" 50–51.

87. *Delle corone de prencipi christiani di D. Michel Lonigo de Este. Libro primo, nel quale si descrivono gl'arbori delle regale case di Francia, Navarra, Napoli, Sicilia, Gierusalemme, Ungaria, Polonia & Boemi* (Rome: G. Facciotto, 1601).

88. Vedova, *Biografia*, 1, 534, and Jeanne Bignami-Odier, *La Bibliothèque Vaticane de Sixte IV à Pie XI* (Città del Vaticano: Biblioteca Apostolica Vaticana, 1973; Studi e Testi, 272), 103 and 122, who refers to Leopoldo Sandri, "Un prefetto dell'Archivio Vaticano, Michele Lonigo, 1572–1639, e il suo processo," in *Studi in onore di Riccardo Filangeri* (Naples, 1959), 2, 503–23, which I have not been able to see. His *processo* is in the ASR with a copy in ASV, Misc. Arm. IX:65.

89. http://ASV.vatican.va/en/pers/prefetti.htm, accessed 9 March 2009; and Orietta Filippini, "'Per la fuga non disinteressata di notizie.' Michele Lonigo dall'Archivio Vaticano alle prigioni di Castel Sant'Angelo (1617): i costi dell'informazione," in Armand Jamme and Olivier Poncet, eds., *Offices, écrit et Papauté (XIIIe–XVIIe siècle)*, Collection de l'École Française de Rome, 386 (Rome: École Française de Rome, 2007), 705–36.

90. Among them are *Consilium Gregorio XV. Pontifici Maximo: . . . De adhortando Serenissimum Maximilianum Bavariae Ducem ad petendam dignitatis Electoralis nuper obtentae confirmationem a Sede Apostolica* (N. p.: n. p., 1623) and *Aphorismi de statu ecclesiae restaurando* (Louvain: N.p., 1623). There is a manuscript in BAV, Barb. lat. 5944.

91. Among the others are 1234–36 (notes on law), 1263, 2962–82ff. (mostly works about ceremony), 4774, and 4813 (a historical miscellany). The treatise on the prefect is ASR, Archivio Cartari–Febei, 136, fos. 232r–303r, probably autograph; there is another copy in BAV, Barb. lat. 2971. Vedova, *Biografia*, 1, 535, notes a MS treatise on precedence addressed to doge Francesco Erizzi.

92. Silvano Giordano, ed., *Le istruzioni generali di Paolo V ai diplomatici pontifici 1605-1621*, 3 vols. (Tübingen: Niemeyer, 2003), 191, citing his breve of appointment in ASV, Sec. Brev. Reg. 420, fos. 17r–23v.

93. Dispatches to Scipione Borghese of 14 and 21 July. ASV:SSV, 38, fos. 13r and 27v.

94. ACDFSO:DSO 1607, fo. 165r, 19 July 1607, and Gessi–Borghese, 14 July 1607 in ASV:SSV, 38, fo. 23r–v.

95. Dispatch of 7 July 1607 in ASV:SSV, 38, fo. 9r.

96. Gessi–Borghese, 21 July 1607 in ASV:SSV, 38, fo. 37r.

97. "Metto in consideratione che si potria per via di fuorusciti, o Huomini tali una sera fare pigliar almeno uno di questi, e condurlo all'improviso per barca nello stato Ecc.co e credo che non saria difficil cosa in fra Fulg.o che vaga assai, e torna di notte al convento e si sa la femina ove prattica. In fra Paolo saria cosa difficile, ma s'uno si pigliassae forse gli altri fuggiriano, e se n'haveria gran riputatione. L'Ill.mo Caetani saria ottimo a trovar gli huomini, e far esseguir il tutto." ASV:SSV, 41, fos. 115v–116r. This and the following citations may not prove Gessi's complicity in the attempted assassination of Sarpi on 5 October 1607, but they come close.

98. Gessi–Borghese, 18 Aug 1607 in ASV:SSV, 41, fo. 117v: "Il levare con inganno, e forza di qua per condurre nello stato Ecc.co uno de tre scommunicati, e specialmente fr. Fulgentio, credo che riusciria per via dell'Illmo Caetano come scrissi, e da ciò s'acquistaria grande reputatione e si chiariria il Mondo che N. S. è disposto di provedere a questi scandali. Quando l'attione fosse seguita li venitiani vedendo non vi essere rimedio credo ch'intorno ad essa non fariano altro. Si può ben dubitare che se havessero a portar peggio de la giurisditione ecclesiastica e travagliare maggiormente le persone ecclesiastiche pure se la cattura seguisse fuor dell'habitato come potria procurarsi poi che fra fulgentio va spesso quando intorno a questi Luoghi vicini, e qualche volta a un Monasterio de Reformati detto il Deserto lontano cinque miglia. Si potria credere che questo disgusto passasse per esser egli communemente odiato, et abhorrito."

99. His case was important enough for Sarpi to have written two opinions about it. ASV, Consultori in iure (Inventario 102), no. 16, "Sulla causa del padre Averoldo cappuccino imprigionato in Brescia per ordine dell'Inquisizione di Roma (pp. 41–44) and no. 19, "Scrittura seconda sopra il padre Averoldo" (pp. 53–54). See also Benzoni, "I 'teologi,'" 49.

100. ACDFSO:DSO 1606–1607, fo. 368v; 1607, fo. 180r.

101. Gessi–Borghese, 11 August 1607 in ASV:SSV, 38, fos. 65v–66r.

102. The inquisitor of Brescia had been banished on 14 June 1606. Cornet, *Giornale*, 110n2.

103. Gessi–Borghese, 18 Aug 1607 in ASV:SSV, 38, fos. 69v–70r.

104. ACDFSO:DSO 1607, fo. 194v, decree of 23 August 1607. Benedetti may have been the man aged 54 and a priest for twenty-five years made bishop of Caorle in Dalmatia 18 August 1610, which he resigned before 17 September 1629 (*HC* 4: 133), but probably not, since this man was described as "curato della Compagnia della Merle (?) di Roma" when provided to the bishopric worth only 200 *scudi*. Avviso of 17 August 1610 in BAV, Barb. lat. 6344, fo. 132r. Benedetti certainly published *Trattato del timor di Dio* (Bologna: Giovanni Battista Bellagamba, 1609).

105. ACDFSO:DSO 1607, fos. 214v and 218v. The book appears never to have been published.

106. ACDFSO:DSO 1602, fo. 277r–v.

107. ACDFSO:DSO 1603 Copia, fo. 249r.

108. ACDFSO, Copia 1604–1605, p. 14.

109. ACDFSO:DSO Copia 1604–1605, p. 27, 22 January 1604.

110. Ibid., p. 48.

111. Ibid., p. 54.

112. Ibid., p. 112.

113. Ibid., p. 128.

114. Ibid., pp. 130 and 154. I have not been able to find that Averoldi ever published anything. Pier Maria Soglian refers to two pamphlets of his during the interdict crisis, both published in Brescia and both supporting Venice. http://www.bibliotecamai.org/editoria/edizioni/bergamo_interdetto_paolov/fedeli_alla_chiesa_e_allo_stato.html, accessed 29 June 2009.

115. "[A]udito in congregatione, fuit praeceptum ne discedat ab Urbe sine licentia." ACDFSO:DSO Copia 1604–1605, p. 167.

116. Ibid., p. 183. The copyist could not read the original, either.

117. Ibid., p. 188.

118. Ibid., p. 196, 13 May 1604. The rest of the entry is illegible.

119. Ibid., p. 207, 20 May 1604.

120. Ibid., pp. 285 and 320.

121. Ibid., pp. 340 and 345.

122. Ibid., pp. 439 and 458; ibid., p. 468.

123. "et revocet in congregatione Ill.morum D.norum memoriale per ipsum porrectum, ac doctrinam contentam in eius libro, quem scripsit de Antichristo et Mahometo." Ibid., p. 468.

124. Ibid., p. 508, 14 December 1604.

125. Ibid., p. 557. He became bishop of Castellaneta on 5 November 1607. *HC* 4: 139, and see two dispatches from Francesco Contarini to the doge in ASVe:SDR, f. 58, fos. 185v and 237v. His appointment may have been part of the accomodation after the interdict, since during it he had been banned from Venice and its dominions for celebrating pontifical Mass, but it also appears that he may have been imprisoned, perhaps by the Inquisition. Federigo Odorici, review of Enrico Cornet, *Paolo V e la terraferma*, *Archivio storico italiano* 10:2 (1859): 171–80, 179, and see Contarini's dispatch of 29 September 1607 in ASVe:SDR, f. 58, fo. 132r.

126. ACDFSO:DSO Copia 1604–1605, p. 561; orig. fo. 242r ill. The Congregation met three times in this week, on Monday, Tuesday, and Thursday.

127. Ibid., p. 649.

128. Ibid., pp. 739 and 869.

129. Ibid., pp. 879 and 884.

130. Ibid., p. 901.

131. Ibid., p. 904.

132. Gessi–Borghese, 25 August 1607 in ASV:SSV, 38, fos. 81r and 82v–83r.

133. ACDFSO:DSO 1606–1607, fo. 387r.

134. Francesco Contarini–doge, 1 September 1607 in ASVe:SDR, f. 58, fos. 5v–6r. See further fos. 64v–66v, 92r–94r, including a parallel to Ciotti and others who had been cleared, and fo. 115v, where the pope said the case had been assigned to the Inquisition. Contarini gave it a lot of attention, e.g., on fos. 142r ff., 181rff. (where the Inquisition complained that Meietti ignored its orders), and 220vff., 242rff., 276rff., and 291vf.

135. This report, misdated 28 August, was acknowledged on 5 September. ACDFSO:DSO 1607, fo. 200v. Sarpi praised the constancy of the Capuchins in the provinces of both Brescia and Bergamo, explaining it by the lack of Jesuits to subvert them. Paolo Sarpi, *Historia particolare delle cose passate tra il Sommo Pontefice Paolo V. e la Serenissima Republica [sic] di Venetia* (Mirandola: n.p., 1687), 100–101.

136. The nuncio's residence is on the same small campo as San Francesco della Vigna, almost directly across from the main entrace to the cloister.

137. Gessi–Borghese, 1 September 1607 in ASV:SSV, 38, fos. 89v, 91r, 92v and 93r–v. This letter may include the passage cited by Benzoni, "I 'teologi,'" 305 as coming shortly after Gessi's arrival and saying "se ne proverano poche" in Manfredi's *processo*, because there were no witnesses, and Manfredi claimed to have preached only against the observance of the interdict.

138. Gessi–Borghese, 8 September 1607 in ASV:SSV, 38, fos. 101r, 108r and 108v.

139. ACDFSO:DSO 1606–1607, fo. 402v, 20 September 1607.

140. Gessi–Borghese, 15 September 1607 in ASV:SSV, 38, fos. 111v, 116r–118r, 120r, 122r and 122v.

141. Gessi–Borghese, 29 September 1607 in ibid., fos. 134v, 135r–136r and 136v.

142. Most reports give the time as "23 hours." ACDFSO:DSO 1621, p. 43, note of 28 January 1621. This was probably just before dusk, using "Italian time." Fulgenzio Micanzio, *Vita del Padre Paolo* (Leiden, 1646) is the principal source. For the time see the Florentine ambassador's dispatch of 7 October (de Rubertis, *Ferdinando I*, 356); another source says "about 24 hours," while counting only two assassins, but they wounded Sarpi four times (!). Alessandro Luzio, ed., "Fra Paolo Sarpi, documenti inediti dell'Archivio di Stato di Torino," *Atti della R. Accademia delle Scienze di Torino* 63 (1927–28): 24–60, 37. The Florentine ambassador especially emphasized the anger among the Venetians at the deed as well as their treatment of Sarpi as a saint who had miraculously escaped death; Sarpi agreed with the second point. De Rubertis, *Ferdinando I*, 359; Luzio, "Sarpi," 38; Paolo Sarpi, *Lettere ai protestanti*, ed. Manlio Diulio Busnelli, 2 vols. (Bari: Laterza, 1931), 1, 6.

143. De Rubertis, *Ferdinando I*, 358. He calls Poma "a creature of the Jesuits" (362n).

144. Luzio, "Sarpi," 38 and note. For other warnings see de Rubertis, *Ferdinando I*, 362n.

145. The Florentine ambassador in Rome reported on 2 November that the pope had forbidden the assassins to enter papal territory (de Rubertis, *Ferdinando I*, p. 362), but in fact they seem to have been received in Rome the same day. Pietro Savio, "Per l'epistolario di Paolo Sarpi," *Aevum* 13 (1939): 558–622, 590.

146. Cf. de Rubertis, *Ferdinando I*, 356.

147. Decree of 5 October 1607. ASVe, Consiglio dei Dieci, Parti Roma, registro 1607, fo. 67r–v.

148. Gessi–Borghese, 6 October 1607 in ASV:SSV, 41, fo. 122r, no. 9, the next letter in this volume after 1 September.

149. Gessi–Borghese, 8 and 20 October 1607 in ASV:SSV, 38, fos. 145r and 148r.

150. Gessi–Borghese, 13 [*sic*] October 1607 in ibid., fos. 147v and 148r.

151. Gessi–Borghese, 27 October 1607 in ibid., fo. 157v. He also noted that the Servites had put the dagger used on Sarpi on the altar, probably of the chapel of the Volto Santo at their house of San Giacomo, under a banner reading "Dei filio liberatori."

152. Gessi–Borghese, 10 November 1607 in ibid., fo. 165v.

153. Gessi–Borghese, 17 November 1607 in ibid., fo. 166r.

154. ACDFSO:DSO 1606–1607, fo. 442v, 21 November 1607.

155. Ibid., fo. 422r.

156. Ibid., fo. 431r.

157. Ibid., fo. 443r, 21 November and 1607, fo. 256r–v, 22 November.

158. Gessi–Borghese, 24 Nov 1607 in ASV:SSV, 41, fos. 122v–123v.

159. Gessi–Borghese, 24 Nov 1607 in ASV:SSV, 38, fos. 175r–176v.

160. Francesco Contarini–doge, 1 December 1607 in ASVe:SDR, f. 58, fo. 296v. Faiano does not appear in Antonio Francesco Vezzosi, *I scrittori de' cherici regolari*, 2 vols. (Rome: Sacra Congregazione di Propaganda Fide, 1780).

161. Francesco Contarini–doge in ASVe: SDR, f. 58, fo. 320v and Gessi–Borghese, 22 December 1607 in ASV:SSV, 41, fo. 129v.

162. Francesco Contarini–doge, 29 December 1607, reporting a conversation with Bellarmino, in ASVe:SDR, f. 58, fo. 395r.

163. ACDFSO:DSO 1608, p. 8, 28 December 1607 and Gessi–Borghese, 1 December 1607 in ASV:SSV, 38, fo. 187v.

164. Gessi–Borghese, 29 Dec 1607 in ibid., fos. 206r, 207v and 210v. Manfredi's sermon proved Gessi partially wrong in his earlier prediction that the friar would preach neither Advent nor Lent. Gessi–Borghese, 1 December 1607 in ibid., fos. 181r–182r.

165. Wolfgang Weber, "'What a Good Ruler Should Not Do': Theoretical Limits of Royal Power in European Theories of Absolutism, 1500–1700," *Sixteenth Century Journal* 26 (1995): 897–915, 900–901. His most important work was *De Jure Majestatis* (1610), which also encountered the Inquisition in 1622. The title and, even better the subtitle, of another best summarizes his absolutist views: *De Autoritate Principum In Populum Semper Inviolabili, seu quod nulla ex causa subditis fas sit contra legitimum principem arma movere Commentatio politica* (Frankfurt/O: Thieme, 1612), a stout defense of the usual Lutheran principle of nonresistance. See further Horst Dreitzel, *Protestantischer Aristotelismus und absoluter Staat. Die "Politica" des Henning Arnisaeus (ca. 1575–1636)* (Wiesbaden: F. Steiner, 1970; Veröffentlichungen des Instituts für Europäische Geschichte Mainz, 55). For the later difficulties of *De Jure Maeiestatis*, see the order of 7 January 1622 to the inquisitor of Venice to send *Arnesi Alberstadtiensis de iure maiestatis, de republica seu relectionis politici, de auctoritate principis in populum inviolabilem et de iure conubiorum* (ACDFSO:DSO 1622, p.

14), and Archbishop Carafa's report of 20 October that he had found the book headed for a Neapolitan bookseller (ACDFSO:DSO 1621–1622, fo. 251v).

166. ACDFSO:DSO 1606–1607, fo. 443r. The book had later editions in 1622, 1623, 1643 (2), 1648, and 1651.

167. Ibid., fo. 256r.

168. Antonino Poppi, *Cremonini, Galilei e gli Inquisitori del Santo a Padova* (Padua: Centro Studi Antoniani, 1993), 90.

169. ASVe, Consiglio dei Dieci, Parti Roma, registro 1607, fo. 75v.

170. ACDFSO:DSO 1607, fo. 277r. The inquisitor's letters were of 5 and 6 December.

171. Francesco Contarini–doge, 12 January 1608 in ASVe:SDR, f. 58, fo. 426v.

172. Gessi–Borghese, 12 January 1608 in ASV:SSV, 38, fos. 221v and 223v–224r.

173. ACDFSO:DSO 1608, p. 41, 17 January 1608.

174. Borghese–Gessi, 18 January 1608 in ASV:SSV, 39, fos. 11v–12r. Borghese wrote again the next day approving Gessi's plan to wait to bring up Manfredi. Ibid., fo. 14r.

175. Gessi–Borghese, 19 January 1608 in ASV:SSV, 38, fo. 229r.

176. ACDFSO:DSO 1608, fo. 20v, 24 January 1608.

177. Francesco Contarini–doge, 2 February 1608 in ASVe:SDR, f. 58, fo. 484r–v.

178. Reports came from Gessi and the inquisitors of Venice, Vicenza, Padua, and Treviso. ACDFSO:DSO 1608, p. 60, 31 January 1608.

179. ACDFSO:DSO 1608, p. 72, 13 February 1608.

180. Gessi–Borghese, 16 February 1608 in ASV:SSV, 38, fos. 260r–v and 274r. See also Gessi's letters cited in Savio, "Nunzio," 85 from ASV, Fondo Borghese II 274, fos. 141r and 177v.

181. Gessi–Borghese, 26 January 1608 in ASV:SSV, 38, fos. 234r, 235v–236r, and 238r–239r.

182. Gessi–Borghese, 9 February 1608 in ibid., fo. 248v.

183. Gessi–Borghese, 2 February 1608 in ibid., fos. 241r–243r.

184. Gessi–Borghese, 9 February 1608 in ibid., fos. 249r, 251v–252r and 252v. There is not much more in Benzoni, "I 'teologi,'" 60–64 about Giordano (whom he treats along with Michelangelo Bonicelli) than is contained in Gessi's dispatches.

185. ASV:SSV, 38, fo. 266r.

186. Ibid., fo. 279v.

187. ACDFSO:DSO 1608, p. 131.

188. Borghese–Gessi, 12 April 1608 in ASV:SSV, 39, fo. 61r. Benzoni, "I 'teologi,'" 98–99 garbles this moment by saying that when Borghese had proposed to circulate the sentence more widely, it was objected that this was against the Holy Office's style, which Benzoni characterizes as "garbato cinismo."

189. ACDFSO:DSO 1608, p. 153 (ill. in 1608–1609, fo. 72r), 10 April 1608 in response to the Venetian inquisitor's letters of 22 and 29 March. He gave Manfredi's motto in a form slightly different from the one Gessi reports, as "evangelicae veritatis praedicator, et propugnator accerrimus." According to the "Relazione," there were many copies of the image. BCV, MS 1382, p. 10/TCC, MS R.3.42, fo. 142v. Another print circulated with his

image and the inscription "Si fulmen fulgens fulgur, FULGENTIUS ergo/Fulgidius emisso fulmine fulgur erit." It was picked up in Ancona, brought by Venetian bookseller Trivisano Bertolotti. A copy is in ACDFSO, St. st. DD 2–b, fo. 157r; Christopher F. Black, *The Italian Inquisition* (New Haven, Conn.: Yale University Press, 2009), 107 and 280.

190. The *Consilium* is in Goldast, *Monarchia*, 2, 486–57.

191. See Gessi–Borghese, 3 May 1608 in ASV:SSV, 38, fo. 342r.

192. Gessi–Borghese, 15 March 1608 in ibid., fos. 287v, 288v, 289v, and 291v.

193. "Capitolo di lettere scritta all'Ill.mo et R.mo Sig. Card.li Millino dal Pre. Inquisitore di Venetia li 26 d'Aprile 1608" in BAV, Vat. lat. 6539, fo. 171r. The book appeared in two or three versions that year by the legal publisher Zacharias Palthenius and was frequently reprinted. See VD17 75:704816L, 12:199010K, 1:010209Q, and passim for other editions.

194. Judging from its connection to Farinacci's volume, *Declarationes* was probably the first volume of *Decisionum Novissimarum Diversorum Sacri Palatii Apostolici Auditorum Volumen* (Frankfurt: Palthenius, 1601–1608; VD17 1:010209Q).

195. ACDFSO:DSO 1608, pp. 196–97 and 249, 12 June 1608.

196. BAV, Vat. lat. 6539, fo. 171v and ACDFSO:DSO 1608, p. 519, 9 December 1608.

197. Francesco Contarini–doge, 22 March 1608 in ASVe:SDR, f. 59, fos. 42r–43v and ASVe, Collegio, Esposizioni Roma, reg. 16, fos. 11r–v, 12r–v, and 13r–v.

198. ASVe, Collegio, Esposizioni Roma, reg. 16, fos. 19r, 25v–27r, 28rff., 30r–v and 30v–31r, 34r, and 45vff and ACDFSO:DSO 1608, pp. 280 and 281. See Savio, "Nunzio," 78. For the Venetian side, see Francesco Contarini's dispatches of 12 and 19 April, 3, 17, 24, and 31 May in ASVe:SDR, f. 59, fos. 90r–91r, 113v–116r, 160r–v and 168r, 211v, 219v and 235rff.

199. Gessi–Borghese, 5 April 1608 in ASV:SSV, 38, fo. 331r.

200. Gessi–Borghese, 29 March 1608 in ibid., fo. 303v, and a second letter of same date in ASV:SSV, 39, fos. 51v–52r.

201. Gessi–Borghese, 29 March 1608 in ASV:SSV, 38, fos. 311r and 313r.

202. Gessi had Farinacci's *consilium* by 22 March. Ibid., fo. 292v. Bouwsma, *Venice*, 346 says the charges against Brandolini included sorcery, incest, and murder.

203. Gessi–Borghese, 19 April 1608 in ASV:SSV, 38, fos. 323v, 325v, 326r, 328v–329r, 329v, 330r, 330v and 331r.

204. I have found no edition of the council's and its congregation's decrees earlier than Frankfurt, 1608, and none in Venice.

205. ACDFSO:DSO 1608, pp. 196–97, 8 May 1608.

206. Ibid., p. 249, 12 June 1608.

207. Ibid., p. 197, 8 May 1608. I read the author's name as Anselmo Lepati and have not had a chance to verify that. The date of the edition is apparently an error. The editio princeps is by the Fratelli Cavallieri in Turin, 1597. Beyond the information on the title page that he was from Lanzo (province of Turin) nothing is known of the author.

208. Subsequent printings are attested in Turin in 1602, 1613 (both unconfirmed; Onorato Derossi, ed., *Scrittori piemontesi, savoiardi, nizzardi registrati nei catalogi del vescovo Francesco Agostino della Chiesa, e del monaco Andrea Rossotto* [Turin: Stamperia Reale, 1790], 16) and 1620 and Bratislava 1682, both from ICCU. The nearest copy to Venice

(of the Bratislava edition) is in the Biblioteca civica Bertoliana in Vicenza (IT\ICCU\UBOE\013551).

209. "Quest'huomo è ambitioso, e vano, et poco devoto, si che non si può acquistare con le ragioni, che mirano solo all'anima, et allo spirito, ma bisogna che vi concorra anco la reputatione et honore mondano, et mette conto a compatire, et condonare qualche cosa al suo humore." Gessi–Borghese, 10 May 1608 in ASV:SSV, 38, fos. 349r–350r.

210. ASV:SSV, 39, fo. 87r.

211. Gessi–Borghese, 24 May 1608 in ASV:SSV, 38, fo. 364r–v and Borghese–Gessi, 5 June 1608 in ASV:SSV, 39, fo. 98v.

212. Francesco Contarini–doge, 31 May and 19 July 1608 in ASVe:SDR, f. 59, fos. 242v and 359v.

213. Gessi–Borghese, 31 May 1608 in ASV:SSV, 38, fo. 370v.

214. Gessi–Borghese, 31 May 1608, quoted in Savio, "Nunzio," 60–61n from ASV, Fondo Borg. II 66, fo. 323r, Gessi's covering letter on fo. 322r.

215. Borghese–Gessi, 21 June 1608 in ASV:SSV, 39, fo. 107r.

216. Ibid., fo. 375r. The man proposed to convert Sarpi, Alessandro Bon, was an apostate Capuchin. BCV, MS 1382, p. 19; this passage is not in TCC, MS R.3.42, fo. 148r–v.

217. Francisco Peña's agenda of 21 May 1608. Spampanato, "Nuovi documenti," p. 225.

218. ACDFSO:DSO 1608, pp. 362–63, 23 August (misdated 21 August in Leen Spruit, "Cremonini, nelle carte del Sant'Uffizio romano," in *Cesare Cremonini: Aspetti del pensiero e scritti*, ed. E. Riondato and Antonino Poppi [Padua: Academia Galileiana, 2000], 196 because he missed misplaced pp. 358–59).

219. ACDFSO, S. O. Decreta 1608, pp. 249–50. No such book has been identified. The censor may perhaps be the same as Giovanni Francesco Leone, whose *Thesaurus fori ecclesiastici, in quo de quibuscunque ad forum ecclesiasticum spectantibus & stylum romanae curiae concernentibus . . . tractatur* (ed. prin. probably Vercelli: Girolamo Allari and Giuseppe Ferreri, 1602; IT\ICCU\TO0E\060347) was frequently reprinted and contains the sort of material that could well be recycled in a discussion of the interdict.

220. ASVe, Collegio, Esposizioni Roma, reg. 16, fos. 42r–43r.

221. The letter is not otherwise known.

222. And he did, where he was invited to sit in on Congregation meetings. ACDFSO:DSO 1608, p. 295, 9 July 1608.

223. Gessi–Borghese, 21 June 1608 in ASV:SSV, 38, fos. 394v, 395r, 398v, 401r–v, and 402r.

224. Part of his dispatch of 28 June about the affair was ordered read 4 July 1608 to the Savii del Collegio and then the Senate. ASVe, Consiglio dei Dieci, Parti Roma, registro 1607, fo. 87r.

225. Gessi–Borghese, 28 June 1608 in ASV:SSV, 38, fos. 415r–416v and 417v.

226. ACDFSO:DSO 1608, p. 109, 12 March 1608.

227. Ibid., p. 232.

228. Ibid., p. 421.

229. Subsequent editions of Frankfurt 1611 and 1624, Amsterdam 1641, Amsterdam

and Louvain 1644, Jena 1665 and 1673, and Frankfurt/O 1668 and 1672. Klapmeier was Professor of History and Politics at the University of Altdorf and a follower of Justus Lipsius. *De arcanis* was the first work of its type, drawing a distinction between good and bad reason of state. Michael Philipp, "Biobibliographie deutscher Politologen des späten 16. bis frühen 18. Jahrhunderts" (http://www.philso.uni-augsburg.de/web2/Politik1/clapmar.html accessed 3 March 2009), with bibiliography.

230. ACDFSO:DSO 1608, p. 291.

231. Ibid., p. 291 and 1608–1609, fo. 139r.

232. Gregor Richter, *Axiomata Historica, eaque Politica, Hoc est: Regulae de Eventibus Negociorum Politicorum* (Görlitz: Rambau, 1599–1602; VD17 001427Z). Richter (1560–1624) was a native of Görlitz, a pastor first in Rauscha and then dean of St. Nicolaus in Görlitz (VD17).

233. ACDFSO:DSO 1608, pp. 501–2, 507, and 555, 26 and 28 November and 20 December.

234. ACDFSO:DSO 1608–1609, fo. 139v and 1608, p. 292.

235. See above, p. XX.

236. *Consiliorum sive Responsorum clarissimi viri Marci Antonij Peregrini Serenissimae reipublicae Venetae iurisconsulti . . . [libri]*, 6 vols. (Venice: Deuchino and Pulciani, 1608–1623), 1, *In quo materiae iudiciorum, testamentorum, feudorum, patronalium, fideicommissorum, ac vltimarum voluntatum variae, aliarumque causarum quae in vtroque foro saepe saepius discutiendae proponuntur* (ICCU IT\ICCU\MILE\000070 and IT\ICCU\MILE\000071); ed. prin. *Consilia sive responsa iuris Marci Antonii Peregrini Patavini, sereniss.mae Reipublicae Venetae iurisconsulti, et equitis* (Venice: Paolo Meietti, 1600). There were also editions in Frankfurt: Schönwetter and Latomus in 1603 (VD17 14:663853B) and 1607 (VD17 7:697537E).

237. ACDFSO:DSO 1608, p. 292 and 1608–1609, fo. 139v.

238. Gessi–Borghese, 12 July 1608 in ASV:SSV, 38, fos. 435v–437r.

239. Borghese–Gessi, 12 July 1608 in ASV:SSV, 39, fo. 116v.

240. Gessi–Borghese, 19 July 1608 in ASV:SSV, 41, fos. 138r–139r.

241. Gessi–Borghese, 26 July 1608 in ibid., fo. 140r–v. "Ho parlato il mese passato con il Secretario, e poi meco un franzese d'Avignone detto Giacomo Giaffer già stipendiato da questa Repubblica dicendo voler amazzar fra Paolo Servita[,] ne li diedi orecchio parendomi che non fosse atto a tal impresa, e più per l'ordine di N. S. d'Aprile passato che in modo alcuno non si attenda ad occisioni. Disse costui di nuovo al Seg.rio che vuole esseguire il suo pensiero e che ne aspetta lettere dall'Ill.mo Card.le Spinola da darseli per mano mia. Non ho havuto tali lettere, ma vedendo costui cosi risoluto ho voluto darne conto. Non credo come ho detto che sia huomo a proposito per far tal fatto il quale se succedesse porteria seco l'inconvenienti che havera considerati la prudenza di N.ro Sign.re quando fece scrivere che non vuole condescendere ad occisioni non tacero che saria grande il pericolo mio e di miei per lo sdegno che tutti qui riceveriano, e massime essendosi visto costui venire in casa, e ciò cresceria quando egli ad altri dicesse d'haverlo communicato."

242. ACDFSO:DSO 1608, pp. 331 and 334; 1608–1609, fos. 159v and 161r.

243. BCV, MS 1382, pp. 21–23; the writer of TCC, MS R.3.42 said on fo. 149r that he would do it "parola per parola" and put it at the end, fos. 164r–165r; ASVe:SDR, f. 59, fo. 410r; Biblioteca Universitaria di Bologna, 8 (5), no. 4; Mazzatinti, et al., *Manoscritti*, 15, 16, and many other copies.

244. ACDFSO:DSO 1608, p. 334.

245. Gessi–Borghese, 9 August 1608 in ASV:SSV, 38, fo. 468v; and see R. Taucci, *Intorno alle lettere di fra Paolo Sarpi ad Antonio Foscarini* (Florence: Sansoni, 1939), 76; ASV:SSV, 38, fos. 469r, 469v, 470r, and 470v.

246. ASVe:SDR, f. 59, fo. 410r–v. This, the copy of Manfredi's safe-conduct, and an autograph letter of 15 August to Marco Galbano (fo. 413r) in Venice were apparently originally enclosed in dispatches from Contarini but are now in the middle of documents about a jurisdictional dispute in Ravenna and are never referred to in the dispatches. The letters are docketed as 20 August, but the docketing is crossed out. For Manfredi's vaunting his good treatment, see also "Relazione" (BCV, MS 1382, p. 25; TCC, MS R.3.42, fo. 151r–v).

247. ASVe:SDR, f. 59, fo. 413r (see previous note).

248. Gessi–Borghese, 16 August 1608 in ASV:SSV, 38, fo. 474v.

249. Gessi–Borghese, 23 August 1608 in ibid., fo. 486r.

250. Gessi–Borghese, 16 August 1608 in ibid., fos. 474v and 479r.

251. Gessi–Borghese, 23 August 1608 in ibid., fos. 486v, 487r, and 489r.

252. Borghese–Gessi, 23 August 1608 in ASV:SSV, 39, fo. 142v; Francesco Contarini–doge, 23 and 30 August 1608 in ASVe:SDR, f. 59, fos. 431r–v and 436v.

253. Borghese–Gessi, 30 August 1608 in ASV:SSV, 39, fo. 144v.

254. Francesco Contarini–doge, 30 August in ASVe:SDR, f. 59, fo. 436v, saying he had a letter from Foligno. Borghese's intelligence was better, since he knew Manfredi had been in Spoleto on the same day Contarini wrote. Borghese–Gessi, 30 August 1608 in ASV:SSV, 39, fo. 145r.

255. Gessi–Borghese, 30 August 1608 in ASV:SSV, 38, fos. 489v and 491v.

256. Francesco Contarini–doge, 6 September 1608 in ASVe:SDR, f. 60, fos. 2v–3v.

257. Francesco Contarini–doge, 13 September 1608 in ibid., fo. 15v. According to Benzoni, "I 'teologi,'" 74 Contarini also said that Manfredi, if allowed to preach, threatened to say worse about the Jesuits than he had in Venice.

258. Borghese–Gessi, 13 September 1608 in ASV:SSV, 39, fo. 147r. In the same letter Borghese sent a third censure on Sarpi's apologia against Bellarmino (fo. 147v). This is the last out-letter from Borghese in this volume until 1609.

259. Francesco Contarini–doge, 20 September 1608 II in ASVe:SDR, f. 60, fo. 29r–v.

260. ACDFSO:DSO 1608–1609, fo. 204r and 1608, p. 418, 1 October.

261. Ibid., fo. 185r and 1608, p. 378.

262. Two days earlier the inquisitor of Venice had been ordered not to let his work circulate. ACDFSO:DSO 1608, p. 374, 2 September.

263. Ibid., p. 381 (title from 1608–1609, fo. 575r) and p. 384, two widely separated entries from the same session about the same topic.

264. Ibid., p. 379.

265. Borghese–Gessi, 8 September 1608 in ASV:SSV, 39, fo. 146r.

266. Gessi–Borghese, 27 September 1608 in ASV:SSV, 41, fos. 141r–142r.

267. Gessi–Borghese, 27 September 1608 in ASV:SSV, 38, fos. 524v, 525r, and 526r.

268. Gessi–Borghese, 11 October 1608 in ibid., fo. 542v.

269. ACDFSO:DSO 1608, pp. 453–54. The notary left Gessi's letter undated.

270. Ibid., pp. 449 and 454 and 1608–1609, fos. 219r and 221r, 22 and 23 October.

271. Ibid., p. 453, 23 October 1608.

272. Tomaselli also wrote *De natura originalis peccati ac poena in illo morientes ex Dei iustitia concomitante . . . .explanatio* (Padua: Lorenzo Pasquato, 1599; ICCU IT\ICCU\BVEE\021833, the only entry under his name in ICCU that contains nothing for *Le mentite*; and "De mare venetorum increpatoria Epistula . . . ad Laurentium Mottinum I.U.Doctorem" in Bib. Marciana, Cod. Ital. VII, 2296 (7383), fos. 137r–159r, another letter on the same subject on fos. 161r–172r; printed (perhaps without Tomaselli's knowledge) as *De mare venetorum ad Laurentium Motinum romanum epistola increpatoria et monitoria* (n.p. 1619; Marc. Misc. 1311 [2]), and *De mare venetorum ad Laurentium Motinum romanum epistola increpatoria et monitoria Iteneu Ichamom Itnegluf* (a not quite accurate anagram of "Fulgenti monachi veneti") (n.p., 1620; Marc 209.d.135). Ingrid A. R. De Smet, *Menippean Satire and the Republic of Letters, 1581–1655* (Geneva: Droz, 1996), 207–8.

273. *Le mentite filoteane* (Padua: Niccolò Padovano, 1607; OCLC 20470128 and 57291592). Vedova, *Biografia*, 2, 333–34 assigns the book to him without argument (as does Bouwsma, *Venice*, 430n). Cecchetti, *Venezia*, 2, 477 (in an entry criticizing "Vedura" [Vedova]) thought it by Cappello, although he knew of the real Abbot Tomaselli, as did Benzoni, "I 'teologi,'" 94 (without reference to the earlier writer) on the thin grounds that he had been Possevino's friend and had submitted to the Church. Giacomo Pietrogrande, *Biografie estensi* (Padua: Fratelli Salmin, 1881), 70 dismissed Cecchetti's attribution without argument (other than the fact that Fulgenzio Tomaselli was real). The work's subtitle seems partly responsible for uncertainty over its authorship. It gave Tomaselli's alias as Capelletto: *Invettiva di Giovanni Filoteo d'Asti contra la Republica serenissima di Venetia, confutata da Fulgentio Tomaselli, filosofo Albanese chiamato aliàs Capelletto, à favore della istessa Serenissima Republica.*

274. "Considerando bene quello che V.S.Ill.ma mi scrive de' spiriti vivi di Fr.e Fulgentio [Manfredi] Zoccolante in Rome, ho pensato di aggiongere a quello che io risposi, che fosse a proposito levarlo di Roma, accioche non dimorasse così in cospetto de' tutti con quella prontezza, et ardire, che mostra, et mentre che si collocasse in una Città dello stato ecc.co ove fosse trattato bene, et potesse predicare, e nondimeno dal legato, o Gov.re gli fosse havuto l'occhio sopra, ci saria manco pericolo, che da lui si ricevesse scandalo . . . poiche veramente anco qui si intende che non si mostra mortificato, et humile quanto dovria." Gessi–Borghese, 25 October 1608 in ASV:SSV, 38, fo. 558r–v. For Manfredi's letter, see fo. 556r, for Lonigo 560v, and 556v for Ribetti.

275. Gessi–Borghese, 8 November 1608 in ibid., fo. 567r–v.

276. Francesco Contarini–doge, 1 November 1608 in ASVe:SDR, f. 60, fos. 75v–76r.

277. ACDFSO:DSO 1608, p. 489. He was in Rome by 3 December, when he was called inquisitor of Udine. Ibid., p. 513.

278. Ibid., pp. 430 and 436, and 1608–1609, fo. 213r, 15 October 1608. As in Montini's case, "De Callio" is the Latin form of his name, which should mean Cagli rather than Caglio (province of Como). http://www.columbia.edu/acis/ets/Graesse/orblatc.html#Calium accessed 9 March 2009. His given name was Ignazio.

279. Gessi–Borghese, 18 Apr 1609 in ASV:SSV, 40, fo. 120r–v.

280. ACDFSO:DSO 1608, p. 481.

281. Ibid., p. 489, decree of 13 November.

282. ACDFSO:DSO 1608–1609, fo. 238r and ACDFSO:DSO 1608, p. 493.

283. Gessi–Borghese, 15 November 1608 in ASV:SSV, 38, fo. 569r.

284. Gessi–Borghese, 22 November 1608 in ibid., fo. 570r–v. "Lunedì innanzi a me in presenza d'un Notaro, e tre testimonii D. Fulgentio Albanese Monaco Camaldolense abiurò de vehementi per le propositioni cattive del libro suo della mentite filotiane doppo essere stato essaminato, et haverlo io per sentenza a ciò condennato nel modo, et forma, che mi fu scritto, d'ordine di N. s.re dall'Ill.mo S. Card.le Arigone . . . mi bisognò travagliare un pezzo in reprimere i suoi humori, e stravaganze, ma all'ultimo si remise et ubbidì, come si contiene nelle scritture, che di questi atti mando authentiche al med.o S. Card. le Arigone."

285. Gessi–Borghese, 29 Nov 1608 in ASV:SSV, 38, fo. 576r.

286. Gessi–Borghese, 15 and 22 November 1608 in ibid., fos. 569v and 570v. The end of his trial did not mean that Gessi lost interest in Tomaselli. Gessi objected violently when the Venetians tried to give him the abbey of Vangadizza in early 1609. See, e.g., his dispatch of 17 January, saying that he had criticized "Fr[atr]e Fulgentio" for accepting the abbey, "ma egli è huomo audacissimo, et difficile da correggere." ASV:SSV, 40, fos. 22v–23r. Gessi gave an inordinate amount of attention to the abbey, which Paul had given to Cardinal Borghese. Virtually the whole letter in ASV:SSV, 39, fos. 186r–191r concerns it.

287. 22 November 1608 Gessi–Borghese, in ASV:SSV, 38, fo. 571r.

288. Richard Gibbings, *Were "Heretics" ever burned alive at Rome? A report of the proceedings in the Roman Inquisition against Fulgentio Manfredi. Taken from the original manuscript brought from Italy by a French officer, and edited, with a parallel English version and illustrative additions* (London: Petheram, 1852; Dublin: University Press, 1853), 13n.

289. *Fasciculus Rerum expetendarum et fugiendarum* (London: [Richard Chiswell], 1690), [2,] 436–65. He thought the second and third parts not by Ockham, the last having been added by another Franciscan sometime after 1500. Brown also noted the edition by Melchior Goldast (see below). Volume 2 of Brown's work was an *Appendix . . . scriptorum veterum* that Brown added to Ortwin Gratius's original.

290. Sigmund Riezler, *Die literarischen Widersacher der Päpste zur Zeit Ludwig des Baiers; ein Beitrag zur Geschichte der Kämpfe zwischen Staat und Kirche* (Leipzig: Duncker & Humblot, 1874), 246n; *Singulare opus ordinis Seraphici Francisci . . . fratribus minoribus eorumque devotis perutile . . . (Quod Speculum Minorum seu Firmamentum trium ordinum intitulatur) tripartitum* (Venice: Lazzaro de Soardis, 1513).

291. *Firmamentum trium ordinum beatiss. patris nostri Francisci* (Paris, 1512), fos. SS6–UU1; Karl Müller, "Einige Aktenstücke und Schriften zur Geschichte der Streitigkeiten unter den Minoriten in der ersten Hälfte des 14. Jahrhunderts," *Zeitschrift für Kirchengeschichte* 6 (1884): 63–112, 80. See also August Potthast, ed., *Bibliotheca historica medii aevi: Wegweiser durch die Geschichtswerke des europäischen Mittelalters bis 1500. Vollständiges Inhaltsverzeichniss zu "Acta sanctorum," etc.*, 4 vols. (Berlin: W. Weber, 1896), 2, 871, probably drawing on Müller. I have not been able to locate a copy.

292. *Opus XC dierum etc* [*sic*] (Lyon, Johannes Trechsel). This is probably *Opus nonaginta dierum: Litterae fratris Michaelis de Cesena* (Lyon: Johannes Trechsel, 1495; Hain, 11935f. according to Müller "Einige Aktenstücke;" OCLC:68991042 and 64705051), but it might also be *Sum[m]aria seu epitomata cxxiiii capituloru[m] op[er]is xc dierum M. Guilhelmi de ocka[m] dilige[n]ter collecta* (Lyon: Trechsel, 1495; OCLC: 45569920, 182000174, and 49042349).

293. The original MS is BAV, Vat. lat. 4009–4010, but Müller, "Einige Aktenstücke," cited from a MS in Paris and did not in any case give a reference to the location of this work in the chronicle. Müller did identify the printed version in Etienne Baluze, ed. Giovanni Domenico Mansi, *Miscellanea novo ordine digesta et non paucis ineditis monumentis opportunisque animadversionibus aucta*, 4 vols. (Lucca: Giuntini, 1761–1764), 206–358, 356–58, where the work was assigned to Michele da Cesena, and an earlier version yet in Goldast, ed., *Monarchia*, 2, 1238ff. Müller proved Baluze's attribution false (pp. 78–79).

294. Müller, "Einige Aktenstücke," 80.

295. Jesús Martínez de Bujanda, Claude Sutto, René Davignon, Ela Stanek, and Marcella Richter, eds., *Index de Rome 1590, 1593, 1596: avec étude des index de Parme 1580 et Munich 1582* (Geneva: Droz, 1994), 127, no. 502.

296. ACDFSO:DSO 1608–1609, fo. 249r and 1608, p. 515, 4 December. The quotation was almost exact, according to the text in *Theologorum . . . responsio*, 50. Its meaning in context might be another matter, since Manfredi had applied that principle narrowly to question the justice of answering his citation.

297. ACDFSO:DSO 1608–1609, fo. 253r and 1608, p. 523, 11 December.

298. It is printed from Trinity College Dublin, MS 1238, fo. 574 with a parallel English translation in Gibbings, *"Heretics"*, 7–27.

299. Gibbings misunderstood this charge (despite suggesting its meaning in the previous note) and added a reference to Bellarmino's book of that title. The Venetians did raise various objections to that book, as we shall see, but only later.

300. Gibbings thought the catechism was probably the Genevan, and that Wotton's chaplain William Bedell was also involved.

301. Gibbings, *"Heretics"*, 23–27, with a facsimile of Manfredi's signature at the end. The new charge was "Esser vano il timore di coloro ch'havevano paura di violare l'Interdetto," which was at least related to an earlier accusation.

302. ACDFSO:DSO 1608, pp. 384 and 502.

303. Ibid., p. 516, 4 December.

304. Gessi–Borghese, 13 Dec 1608 in ASV:SSV, 38, fo. 594r.

305. There is nothing of this in the decree register.

306. Francesco Contarini–doge, 20 December 1608 in ASVe:SDR, f. 60, fos. 130r–133r.

307. Gessi–Borghese, 20 December 1608 in ASV:SSV, 38, fo. 597r.

308. Francesco Contarini–doge, 27 December 1608 in ASVe:SDR, f. 60, fos. 143r–145r.

309. Francesco Contarini–doge, 10 January 1609 in ibid., fo. 179r.

310. Lonigo was pleased by the outcome, as he wrote Cardinal Borghese, who ordered Gessi to tell him that the pope was also pleased. Borghese–Gessi, 17 Jan 1609 in ASV:SSV, 39, fos. 203v–204r.

311. Gessi–Borghese, 27 December 1608 in ASV:SSV, 38, fos. 600v–601r and 602r. The reference to Manfredi is not in Benzoni, "I 'teologi.'"

312. ASV:SSV, 39, fos. 155r and 156v. He also referred to another, missing, letter to Gessi from Arrigoni.

313. Francesco Contarini–doge, 3 and 15 January 1609 in ASVe:SDR, f. 60, fos. 167r, 167v–168r, and 195v–196r.

314. Borghese–Gessi, 10 January 1609 in ASV:SSV, 39, fo. 160r–v.

315. Gessi–Borghese, 3 January 1609 in ASV:SSV, 41, fo. 142r and a second letter of the same date in ASV:SSV, 40, fos. 10r–v, 10v, and 11v. Gessi added a note (fo. 16v) that the Venetians claimed they could not stop Micanzio from preaching.

316. Borghese–Gessi, 10 January 1609 in ASV:SSV, 39, fos. 161v–162r.

317. ASVe, Collegio, Esposizioni Roma, reg. 16, fo. 97r, 11 January 1609.

318. ASVe, Consiglio dei Dieci, Parti Roma, registro 1607, fos. 92v and 93v, 12 and 16 January 1609.

319. Gessi–Borghese, 17 January 1609 in ASV:SSV, 41, fo. 142v.

320. ACDFSO:DSO 1609, p. 17.

321.

322. Ibid., pp. 26–67 and 1608–1609, fo. 275v, 15 January 1609. Gessi's letter has not been found. According to Savio, "Nunzio," 82–83, Gessi thought Benedetti's *Antithesis* contained much good material but "habbia scritto molto goffamente." Others thought Benedetti not very well educated.

323. ACDFSO:DSO 1608–1609, fo. 276r and 1609, p. 28.

324. ACDFSO:DSO 1609, p. 58 and 1608–1609, fo. 288r. The entry is damaged.

325. Borghese–Gessi, 24 January 1609 in ASV:SSV, 39, fo. 204v.

326. ACDFSO:DSO 1608–1609, fos. 287v–288r, 29 January 1609.

327. Gessi–Borghese, 31 January 1609 I in ASV:SSV, 41, fos. 142v–143r.

328. Gessi–Borghese, 24 January 1609 in ASV:SSV, 40, fo. 31v.

329. Cicogna, *Iscrizioni*, 5, 583, citing this passage, mistakenly dated 1610.

330. Gessi–Borghese, 31 January 1609 II in ASV:SSV, 40, fos. 35v, 38r–39r. See also Savio, "Nunzio," 84 from ASV, Fondo Borg. II 275, fos. 75v–76r, which is probably a version of this letter.

331. Gessi–Borghese, 7 February 1609 in ASV:SSV, 40, fo. 43r.

332. Whoever he was, he was in Rome by 1 August. Francesco Contarini–doge, 1 August 1609 II in ASVe:SDR, f. 61, fo. 256r–v.

333. ACDFSO:DSO 1608–1609, fo. 287r, 5 February 1609.

334. Gessi–Borghese, 4 March 1609 in ASV:SSV, 40, fo. 70v. Borghese wrote the nuncio in Spain on 19 February that the pope had ordered a trial for Sarpi "et contra gli altri seduttori." Savio, "Nunzio," 92 citing ASV, Fondo Borg. II 400, fo. 147r.

335. ACDFSO:DSO 1608–1609, fo. 312r; letter in ASV:SSV, 40, fo. 70r–v.

336. Ibid., fo. 303v and 304r, 1 March.

337. See ibid., fo. 361v, an order of 28 May to Borromeo to send Valeriano to Rome and 1609, p. 321, a decree in the coram of 6 August.

338. Borghese–Gessi, 7 and 21 February 1609 in ASV:SSV, 39, fos. 167r and 173v, and Gessi–Borghese,14 Febrary 1609 in ASV:SSV, 40, fo. 48r–v.

339. Francesco Contarini–doge, 7 and 14 February 1609 in ASVe:SDR, f. 60, fos. 216r and 226r, saying Manfredi wanted a bishopric in order to escape his fellow friars, and that Ribetti had complained to the pope that promises had not been kept.

340. Borghese–Gessi, 28 February 1609 in Savio, "Nunzio," 93n from ASV, Fondo Borg. II 400, fo. 96r; and Gessi–Borghese of the same date in ASV:SSV, 40, fo. 67r–v.

341. ACDFSO:DSO 1608–1609, fos. 305v and 312r, 6 and 12 March.

342. Gessi–Borghese, 7 March 1609 in ASV:SSV, 40, fo. 72v; and ASVe, Consiglio dei Dieci, Parti Roma, registro 1607, fos. 117r–118r and 120v–123r, sessions of 13 and 20 March.

343. Gessi–Borghese, 14 March 1609 in ASV:SSV, 40, fos. 79r–80v.

344. ACDFSO:DSO 1608–1609, fo. 316v.

345. Gessi–Borghese, 21 March 1609 in ASV:SSV, 40, fos. 91rff. and Borghese–Gessi, 21 March 1609 in ASV:SSV, 39, fos. 196v–198v.

346. ACDFSO:DSO 1608–1609, fo. 320v.

347. Ibid., fo. 325r, 2 April 1609, and Borghese–Gessi, 28 March 1609 in ASV:SSV, 39, fo. 215r.

348. Gessi–Borghese, 21 February 1609 in ASV:SSV, 40, fo. 58v. See also Gessi–Borghese, 7 March 1609 in ASV:SSV, 40, fo. 72r; there is no cipher about this in vol. 41.

349. Ambassador Contarini learned of it in late May 1608, and the Dieci ordered the news given to Sarpi on 4 June. ASVe, Consiglio dei Dieci, Parti Roma, registro 1607, fo. 84v. The Dieci wrote back to Contarini three weeks later that the new scheme had grown out of the first one and involved at least one of the same conspirators, the man who had owned the get-away boat used in 1607. He was instructed to string the man along in the hopes of learning more. Ibid., fo. 85v–86r, 26 June. In July the Dieci expected to be able to intercept the conspirators, perhaps in Ancona. Ibid., fos. 87r–v and 88r–v, decrees of 11 and 24 July.

350. ASV:SSV, 40, fos. 100r, 100v, and 104v.

351. Contarini was bishop from 1600 to 1620. *HC* 4: 212.

352. Borghese–Gessi, 11 April 1609 in ASV:SSV, 39, fo. 224r.

353. ACDFSO:DSO 1608–1609, fo. 329v.

354. Francesco Contarini–doge, 11 April 1609 in ASVe:SDR, f. 61, fos. 57v–60r.

355. Gessi–Borghese, 11 April 1609 in ASV:SSV, 40, fos. 106v–117r. From the length of the dispatch, Micanzio clearly worried Gessi.

356. Borghese–Gessi, 11 April 1609 in ASV:SSV, 39, fos. 225r–226v and 224v.

357. Borghese–Gessi, 18 April 1609 in ibid., fo. 231r.

358. ACDFSO:DSO 1608–1609, fo. 335r–v.

359. Ibid., fos. 343r and 349r. On the last occasion, Borghese, again acting almost as the cardinal secretary, wrote back to Gessi that he had the depositions against Micanzio which had gone to the Holy Office. Borghese–Gessi, 16 May 1609. ASV:SSV, 39, fo. 246r–v.

360. Gessi's highly circumstantial report deserves quotation at length. "Non manco con ogni buon modo di cercare secretam.te di sapere quel, che passa nella causa de' frati serviti prigioni, i quali non obstante quello, che di già mi fu riferto, hora intendo, che ambidue sono vivi, et che contra di loro in processo si ha, che fra Gio. Fran.co Perugino Bacelliero, che stava in Padova per lettere, che gli scriveva un'altra Frate Perugino da Roma con participatione di persone grandi, et Card.li s'era indotta di procurare di dar morte a fr.e Paulo [*sic*] di Venetia, et confidato il negotio con un Frate Antonio di Viterbo giovane amatissimo di d.o Fr.e Paolo, et suo intrinseco, e famigliare, l'indusse con promesse d'esser largamente premiato a dargli parola, che l'haverebbe ammazzato al sicuro, et fatto insieme questo concerto secretamente in Venetia nella Camera propria di Fr. Antonio, dove Fr.e Gio. Franc.co fu ricercato di nascosto, e trattenuto alcuni pochi giorni, non s'aspettava altro per dargli compimento, che l'opportunità; ma passando molto tempo, e non vedendosi effetto alcuno, fr.e Gio. Fran.co non mancava di tener sollecitato con lettere fr.e Antonio, et di fargli animo, servendosi del mezo d'un hebreo, che ricapitava le lettere in mano propria, senza però esser consapevole del fatto; finalmente Fr.e Antonio gli scrisse liberamente che non gli bastava l'animo di mettergli le mani addosso, et assalirlo co'l ferro, ma che se gli havesse mandato qualche veleno buono, che più tosto havria cercato di darglilo, et di privarlo di vita con esso. Così applicatoli il pensiero a questa via, Frate Gio. Fran.co procurava da Roma il veleno, e di mano in mano teneva avvisato Frate Antonio di quello, che passava, scrivendo, se non in modo, che altri non potessero intendere il loro Gergo, finche una volta, come la disgratia volle, l'hebreo mezano portava secondo il solito una lettera di Fr.e Gio. Francesco alla Chiesa de' Servi per darla in mano a fr.e Antonio, benche il soprascritto dicesse ad un hebreo, non ritrovò in Casa Fr.e Ant.o et la lasciò in mano al P. Socio, che promise di recapitarla, ma perche nell'interrogare, che fece il portatore, esso venne in sospetto, et tanto più, che la lettera haveva un soprascritto finto, et mentito; si risolvè d'aprirla, et apertala, se gli accrebbe maggiormente il sospetto dal contenuto d'essa, di maniera che conferì il tutto con fr.e Paolo, et fr.e Paolo chiamò poi a se Fr.e Antonio il quale titubando, e variando assai nel dire, scoperse poi il trattato, affermando, che fr.e Gio. Fran.co lo stimolava continuamente a conspirare contra la sua persona, et gli narrò tutto il fatto, fuorche quello, che poteva pregiudicare a lui: Sbigottito fre Paolo del pericolo, in che si trovava incorso, pensando subito al rimedio, et alla punitione di chi gli machinava contro, fece, che fr.e Antonio scrivesse a Fr.e Gio. Fran.co ch'egli era preparata, e risoluto per effettuare, quanto sapeva in questo modo, cioè che pigliarebbe l'impronto della chiave della Cam.a di Fr.e Paolo, et che una notte entrarebbe dentro, et l'ammazzarebbe, ma che bisognava, ch'esso Fr.e Gio. Fran.co venisse a Venetia, et che portasse qualche materia atta a pigliare d.o impronto, e facesse fare la chiave egli stesso; Così fr.e Gio: Fran.co se ne venne

a Venetia, et portò una cera attissima per quello, che si cercava, et la diede a fr.e Antonio dentro ad un'invoglio di carte, fra le quali per errore erano tre, o quattro lettere scritte sopra q.to trattato, una delle quali diceva, che se gli manderia la tonica fina, e benissimo cuscita (cioè il veleno) et un'altra diceva, che si procuraria havere quel Quadragesimale, segli sarebbero dati tanti denari, cioè s'havesse procurata la morte di fr.e Paolo. Di esse lettere dicono, che alcune erano scritte dal Fr.e Perugino, che stà in Roma, et furono consegnate subito da fr.e Ant.o in mano di fr.e Paolo, et con un startagemma fr.e Gio. Fran.co fu trattenuto tanto, che i Sig.i Capi di X. lo mandorno a pigliare, et fu fatto prig.e et condennato doppo molti essamini, et constituti alla forca, con conditione però, che se egli rivelava i complici, et tutto il fatto, come stava, gli fosse commutata la forca in 4. anni di galera prigionia, Onde il Perugino accettò quest'ultimo partito, et rivelò l'intendim.to che haveva in Roma, e tutto quello, che era passato poi con Fr.e Antonio, et immediatam.te fu fatto prigione d.o fr.e Antonio, il quale non è anco sententiato, ma si dubita assai, che sia per essere impiccato, o annegato, se bene Fr.e Paolo lo favorisce, et protegge gagliardamente per l'affettione più che ord.ria che gli porta." Gessi–Borghese, 18 April 1609 in ASV:SSV, 40, fos. 122v–124v.

361. Ibid., fo. 125r.

362. Borghese–Gessi, 25 April 1609 in ASV:SSV, 39, fo. 235v.

363. Gessi–Borghese, 2 May 1609 in ASV:SSV, 40, fos. 137v–138r, 140r, and 141r–v (the Servites).

364. ACDFSO:DSO 1608–1609, fo. 344v.

365. Borghese–Gessi, 9 May 1609 in ASV:SSV, 39, fo. 242r–v.

366. Gessi–Borghese, 16 May 1609 in ASV:SSV, 40, fos. 150r–v and 151r.

367. Gessi–Borghese, 23 May 1609 in ibid., fo. 162r, and Borghese–Gessi, 23 May 1609 in ASV:SSV, 39, fo. 252r–v.

368. Gessi–Borghese, 6 June 1609 in ASV:SSV, 40, fo. 167r, one of only two points in the letter.

369. Gessi–Borghese, 11 October 1608 in Savio, "Nunzio," 71 from ASV, Fondo Borg. II, 279, fo. 105r. Peña's agenda of 22 October 1608 for the next day's coram includes an entry of a report from Gessi (Spampanato, "Nuovi documenti," 227). There is nothing of this in ACDFSO:DSO 1608, pp. 448–63, nor is Vincenzo in the volume's index, but cf. Spruit, "Cremonini," p. 196, who says Gessi reported in the session of 23 October that he would send witnesses as soon as possible to Ferrara.

370. ASVe, Consiglio dei Dieci, Parti Roma, registro 1607, fo. 93r.

371. Ibid., fo. 98v, 3 June and ACDFSO:DSO 1610–1611, fo. 122r, 8 July 1610.

372. Gessi–Borghese, 11 July 1609 in ASV:SSV, 40, fos. 198r, 198v and 199r–v.

373. ASVe, Consiglio dei Dieci, Parti Roma, registro 1607, fos. 102r–v and fo. 117v–118r, 29 July.

374. Ibid., fo. 146r–v. The book was *An apologie for the Oath of allegiance* (London: Robert Barker, 1609; *STC*[2] 14402), published before 7 April. See the proclamation of that date: "By the King. Whereas there is lately published in print our apologie heretofore made for the oath of allegiance," "Given at our Palace of Westminster the seventh day of April, in the seventh year of our Reign of Great Britain, France and Ireland" (*STC*[2] 8431).

375. Giovanni Mocenigo–doge, 1 August 1609 in ASVe:SDR, f. 61, fos. 249r, 252r, and 266v.

376. Gessi–Borghese, 1 August 1609 in ASV:SSV, 40, fos. 217v–118r (40A, fos. 14r–15v), 218v, 219v, 220r, and 220v (40A, fos. 8r–9r).

377. Gessi–Borghese, 8 August 1609 in ASV:SSV, 40, fo. 225r; 40A, fo. 32r–v.

378. ASVe, Consiglio dei Dieci, Parti Roma, registro 1607, fo. 152r, Gessi's appearance of 14 August, his letter to Borghese the next day (ASV:SSV, 40, fos. 230v–231r; 40A, fos. 36r–37r) and 22 August (ASV:SSV, 40A, fo. 73r) and ASVe, Collegio, Esposizioni Roma, reg. 16, fo. 161v–162v, 10 September.

379. Gessi–Borghese, 29 August 1609 in ASV:SSV, 40, fo. 251r–v; 40A, fo. 57r–v.

380. ACDFSO:DSO 1608–1609, fo. 432v, 3 September 1609 and 1609, p. 378, 4 September. The notary was Gaspar Gratiani. ACDFSO:DSO 1609, p. 372, 9 September.

381. ASVe, Consiglio dei Dieci, Parti Roma, registro 1607, fos. 159r–160r, 4 September.

382. Ibid., fo. 165r, 11 September.

383. ACDFSO:DSO 1609, p. 405, decree of 24 September. Maffei eventually abjured *de vehementi* in Venice in early 1611. 1610–1611, fo. 285v.

384. The first he found came from 1594 (Gessi–Borghese, 5 September 1609 in ASV:SSV, 40, fo. 256v), together with another a week later from 1573 of two Greeks from Candia tried by the Inquisition in Padua, but their sentence was missing (Gessi–Borghese, 12 September 1609 in ASV:SSV, 40, fo. 260v).

385. On 24 January 1609 Borghese sent Gessi censures on Muti's book. ASV:SSV, 39, fo. 207v.

386. Gessi–Borghese, 5 September 1609 in ASV:SSV, 40, fo. 255r–v. All of September is missing in vol. 40A.

387. ASV:SSV, 40, fos. 259v–60r. The book is *Persuasione brevissima di Zuane Mutti, detto di Benti, della terra di Par, nella Valseriana di sopra, nel territorio di Bergamo. Alli fedeli sudditi del serenissimo Dominio veneto* (1607) according to the Marciana catalogue, which also says Muti is a pseudonym; there are two copies at Rari Veneti 311.2. The place should be Parre in the Val Seriana. I am grateful to Piero Soglian for both pieces of information.

388. ACDFSO:DSO 1608–1609, fo. 445r.

389. Ibid., fo. 482r.

390. *Apologia Roberti S.R.E. cardinalis Bellarmini, pro responsione sua ad librum Iacobi magnae Britanniae regis, cuius titulus est, Triplici nodo triplex cuneus* (Rome: Bartolomeo Zanetti, 1609; reprinted in 1610 at Cremona and Cologne [two editions]).

391. Gessi–Borghese, 21 November 1609 in ASV:SSV, 40A, fo. 172r–v. Ambassador Mocenigo had his copy by 14 November. Mocenigo–doge in ASVe:SDR, f. 62, fo. 114r. Gessi reported its prohibition almost exactly a month later. Gessi–Borghese, 12 December 1609 in ASV:SSV, 40, fo. 329r; perhaps also in 40A, fo. 253r–v, underlined.

392. Gessi–Borghese, 19 December 1609 in ASV:SSV, 40, fo. 333v; 40A, fo. 268r–v.

393. Gessi–Borghese, 26 December 1609 in ibid., fo. 337r; 40A, fo. 280r.

394. Giovanni Mocenigo–doge, 19 December 1609 in ASVe:SDR, f. 62, fos. 151r–152r.

395. Gessi–Borghese, 9 January 1610 in ASV:SSV, 40, fo. 348r.

396. ASV, Sec. Brev. Reg. 596, fos. 477r–478v (see ASV, Indice 761, fo. 45r): "tu quidem in S. universalis Inquisitionis S. Off.o in Urbe fueris denuntiatus, in concionibus, et sermonibus habitis ad populum in civitate Venetiarum de anno 1606, nonullas propositiones haereticales, erroneas, et scandalosas protulisse, et asseruisse; Ac ex decreto [Venerabilium fratrum nostrorum; fo. 477r] S. R. E. Cardinalium contra haereticam pravitatem Generalium Inquisitorum, monitus, et citatus per edictum, ad comparendum personaliter, et respondendum de fide coram ipsis, seu eorum commissario, non par[a]veris, ac successive declaratus incurrisse in excommunicationem maiorem latae sententiae, et caeteras penas [*sic*] in literis monitorialibus contentas, in eadem excommunicatione per annum, et ultra perseveraveris; Postea vero Dei misericordia erroribus cognitis, sponte coram Commissario S. Inq.ni Romanae compar[a]veris, a quo pluries examinatus, errores confessus, paenitentiam, et remissionem humiliter postulaveris etc."

397. This is apparently the last act relative to Manfredi by the Holy Office until his arrest in 1610. There is nothing for him in the indices to either ACDFSO, Decreta 1608–1609 or 1609.

398. Gessi–Borghese, 30 January 1610 in ASV:SSV, 40, fo. 372r-v; partially quoted in Benzoni, "I 'teologi,'" 75. "Ho penetrato, che fr.e Fulgentio Zoccolante [Manfredi] ha mandata qua una supplica di sua mano, dimandando d'esser ricevuto, et ammesso in Venetia, et che Nicolò Contarini non l'ha voluta presentare in Pregadi, o in Collegio, o per non publicare la cosa, o perche habbia creduto di non ottenere ma l'ha presentata a gl'Inquisitori di Stato i quali non hanno voluto accettarla, allegando ragioni, che se venisse qua, bisogneria premiarlo, il che non gli pare bene, essendoli lui, come essi dicono, ribellato alla Rep.ca et oltre a cio quando fosse tornato, bisogneria dargli sodisfattione di lasciarlo predicare, e per essere huomo impertinente, potria causare nuovi romori. Questo mi è riferto da persona, che è di buona mente, ma non mette tutta la relatione per sicura, et potria essere, che d.o Contarini con l'auttorità sua trovasse modo di convertire gli altri, talche saria bene, che s'havesse l'occhio al frate, perche tornando qua senza dubio faria molti mali effetti."

399. Giovanni Mocenigo–doge, 6 February 1610 in ASVe:SDR, f. 62, fo. 257r, 257v. A letter of Borghese's dated 9 February by Savio gives the date as 8 February. Savio, "Nunzio," 104–5n from ASV, Nunz. Venezia, 269, fos. 96v–97r.

400. Borghese–Gessi, 9 February 1610 in Savio, "Nunzio," 104–5n from ASV, Nunz. Venezia, 269, fos. 96v–97r.

401. Gessi acknowledged the order on 13 February, in ASV:SSV, 40, fo. 396r.

402. Giovanni Mocenigo–doge, 13 February 1609 in ASVe:SDR, f. 62, fo. 268r–v.

403. See also the "Relazione" in BCV, MS 1382, p. 30; TCC, MS R.3.42, fo. 154r–v; and BCV, MS 1051, fo. 224r.

404. BCV, MS 1382, p. 31; not in TCC, MS, R.3.42.

405. Giovanni Mocenigo–doge, 20 February 1610 in ASVe:SDR, f. 62, fo. 273r–v. See also the account of Manfredi's end in a letter of Sarpi's of 3 August 1610 in Gibbings, *"Heretics,"* 28– 32, in translation.

406. Gessi–Borghese, 20 February 1610 in ASV:SSV, 40, fo. 403r–v; misdated 27 February in Cicogna, *Iscrizioni*, 5, p. 584.

407. ASV:SSV, 40, fo. 401r.

408. ACDFSO:DSO 1610–1611, fos. 35v and 38r, 4 March 1610.

409. Ibid., fo. 41r, 11 March 1610.

410. Ibid., fo. 48r, 18 March 1610. The date of the *constitutum* is left blank.

411. Ibid., fos. 50v, 52v–53r, and 55r, 24, 27 and 31 March 1610.

412. Ibid., fo. 57r.

413. Manfredi "petiit veniam, atto (dato?) quod eius peccatum fuit attentatum (?), et non consumatum, et est occultum." Ibid., fo. 59v, 5 April 1610 prison visitation.

414. Ibid., fos. 87r and 88v.

415. Ibid., fo. 93v, 27 May 1610.

416. Ibid., fo. 94r.

417. BCV, MS 1382, p. 35. The "Relazione" makes mistakes about the Inquisition and its procedure, including calling its fiscal a Dominican. BCV, MS 1382, p. 36 and TCC, MS R.3.42, fo. 157r ("Fiscale dell'Inquisitione, che è con [*sic*] domenicano").

418. ACDFSO:DSO 1610–1611, fo. 111r, 23 June 1610.

419. Gibbings, *"Heretics,"* 32–54 from Trinity College Dublin, MS 1239, fo. 260, called "Registered memorial of the final proceedings against Manfredi."

420. See their facsimile signatures in Gibbings, *"Heretics"*, 51–53.

421. The "Relazione" said this all boiled down to two main charges, prohibited books and the capital charge of an autograph writing against papal primacy. BCV, MS 1382, p. 34; TCC, R.3.42, fo. 156r–v. It added in Manfredi's defense that the works were obviously unfinished and no one had thought them criminal, contradicting the official record.

422. Gibbings, *"Heretics"*, 55–56.

423. BCV, MS 1382, p. 37; TCC, R.3.42, fo. 158r.

424. BCV, MS 1382, pp. 39–41; TCC, R.3.42, fos. 158r–160r. See also the *avviso* in BAV, Barb. lat. 6344, fo. 108r, and the synthetic account in Cicogna, *Iscrizioni*, 5, 584–85, misdated 10 July.

425. TCC, R.3.42, fo. 159v.

426. Sarpi's letter said he was gagged. Gibbings, *"Heretics"*, 31.

427. TCC, R.3.42, fo. 160r. Sarpi agreed. Gibbings, *"Heretics"*, 31.

428. TCC, R.3.42, fo. 162v.

429. BCV, MS 1382, p. 44; TCC, R.3.42, fo. 162v. Pamphili died 11 August 1610 according to Alfonso Chacón, *Vitae et Res Gestae Pontificum Romanorum et S. R. E. Cardinalium*, ed. Agostino Oldoino, 4 vols. (Rome: Filippo and Antonio De Rubeis, 1677–1678), 4, col. 361; the monument quoted gives only the year.

430. BCV, MS 1382, p. 45; not in TCC, R.3.42; cf. Benzoni, "I 'teologi,'" 78n giving the date as 13 October 1610 from a MS record.

431. ACDFSO:DSO 1610–1611, fo. 129v.

432. Ibid., fo. 146v, 12 August 1610.

433. Ibid., fos. 95r and 124v, 4 June and 14 July 1610.

434. Ibid., fo. 158r, 1 September.

435. Ibid., fo. 177r, 30 September. I have not been able to identify the *libellum*.

436. Ibid., fo. 121v.

437. Ibid., fo. 116v.

438. Ibid., fo. 177r, 30 September 1610.

439. Ibid., fo. 245r, 19 January 1611; cf. Spampanato, "Nuovi documenti," 365.

440. Ibid., fo. 335v.

441. Ibid., fo. 131r, 22 July and 1610–1611, fo. 391v, decree of 14 September 1611.

442. ACDFSO:DSO 1612, p. 209.

443. Ibid., p. 275.

444. Ibid., p. 351.

445. ASVe:SDR, f. 67, fo. 316r, 11 August 1612.

446. Ibid., fo. 346r–v, 25 August 1612.

447. ACDFSO:DSO 1612, p. 553.

448. Ibid., p. 601 and 1613, pp. 154–56.

449. Ibid., pp. 384–85 and 491, 22 August and 17 October.

450. ACDFSO:DSO 1613, p. 3, 28 December 1612. They were printed together in Frankfurt/O by Thieme and in Frankfurt/M by Eichorn. The second also appeared separately.

451. Ibid., pp. 19 and 96.

452. For Micanazio, see, e.g., the absolution of two deponents for not having come forward sooner to delate him. Ibid., pp. 16–17, 3 January.

453. Ibid., p. 68. I am tempted to identify Cherubino with Cherubino Sandolino da Udine, a mathematician and the author of two books printed by Meietti in Venice at the turn of the seventeenth century, except that he is supposed to have been born in 1530. EDIT16 s.n. Cherubinus Sandolinus. One source, however, gives his death date as 1635. Barnabas Hughes, "Friars, hourglasses, sundials and clocks," *Collectanea Franciscana* 53 (1983): 265–79, 272. This man's books are *Thaumalemma cherubicum catholicum, universalia, et particularia continens instrumenta, ad omnes arcus, & horas Italicas, Bohemicas & Gallicas diurnas, atque nocturnas dignoscendas, & ad componenda per universum orbem earum multiformia horologia praesertim Italica exquisitissimum* (Venice: R. Meietti, 1598; EDIT16 CNCE 30970) and *Nova Horologiorum Inventio* (Venice: R. Meietti, 1600; OCLC 254429978), dedicated to long-time cardinal Secretary Giulio Antonio Santoro as an Inquisitor (fo. 2r–v). It also contains a laudatory poem to Cherubino from the inquisitor of Mantua; according to Hughes, "Friars," 272, Sandolino had served as censor there. The entry for him in *Bibliotheca scriptorum ordinis Minorum s. Francisci Capucinorum . . . retexta a Bernardo a Boninia . . . quae prius fuerit A. P. Dionysio Genuensi* [*facta*] (Venice: Sebastiano Coleti, 1747), 63 adds only that he edited Alessandro Fioravianti, *De modo practicandi retorarum mathematicum* (Venice: R. Meietti, 1585).

454. ACDFSO:DSO 1613, p. 107, 28 February.

455. Ibid., pp. 140 and 172–73, 21 March and 17 April.

456. Ibid., p. 204, 8 May.

457. Ibid., p. 221, 16 May.

458. Ibid., pp. 258 and 289 (second reading of the report on 20 June).

459. The first title I have found as *stampator ducale* is *Parte presa nell'eccellentiss. Conseglio di Pregadi. a 13. Luglio. 1613. Che statuisce le pene a i contrafattori delle parti del medesimo Conseglio, in materia di legitimationi, e del crear nodari, & dottori* (IT\ICCU\RMLE\053188, "Probabile luogo e data di pubbl. dalle indicazioni di affissione in calce: 'Adi 15. Luglio 1613. Publicata sopra le Scale di San Marco, & di Rialto'").

460. ACDFSO:DSO 1613, pp. 340 and 346, entered twice in the same session.

461. Ibid., p. 364, 31 July.

462. Ibid., pp. 391–92, 14 August.

463. Ibid., p. 359, 5 July.

464. Ibid., p. 383, 8 August, based on the same letter from Gessi of 3 August.

465. Ibid., p. 414, 22 August.

466. Ibid., p. 440, 5 September.

467. Ibid., p. 475.

468. Ibid., p. 584, 28 November.

469. Giovanni Mocenigo–doge, 28 December 1613 in ASVe:SDR, f. 70, fo. 244r.

470. ACDFSO:DSO 1614, p. 9 and 44, 2 and 16 January.

471. Giovanni Mocenigo–doge, 11 January 1614 in ASVe:SDR, f. 70, fo. 265v.

472. Giovanni Mocenigo–doge, 25 January 1614 in ibid., f. 70, fo. 304v.

473. Giovanni Mocenigo–doge, 15 and 22 March 1614 in ibid., f. 71, fos. 17v–18r, 20r, and 40r.

474. For some reason, the Spanish ambassador to Venice had involved himself in trying to get a new inquisitor for Capodistria in 1612. ASVe, Consiglio dei Dieci, Parti Roma, registro 1607, fo. 154v, 12 September 1612.

475. ACDFSO:DSO 1614, pp. 206, 232, 258, 300, 24 April, 4 and 28 May and 12 June.

476. Ibid., p. 336.

477. Ibid., p. 360.

478. Ibid., pp. 409–10.

479. Ibid., p. 432, 4 September in response to the inquisitor's letter of 30 August.

480. Ibid., p. 591.

481. ACDFSO:DSO 1615, p. 47.

482. Dispatches of 21 June and 12 July 1614 in ASVe:SDR, f. 71, fos. 173v and 181v.

483. ACDFSO:DSO 1614, pp. 415–16, 26 August.

484. Simeon Contarini–doge, 8 November 1614 in ASVe:SDR, f. 72, fos. 83r–85r and 87r–88v; see also his dispatch of 25 November.

485. Simeon Contarini–doge, 25 November 1614 in ibid., f. 72, fo. 120v.

486. ACDFSO:DSO 1614, p. 531.

487. Simeon Contarini–doge, 3 January 1615 in ASVe:SDR, f. 72, fo. 201r–v.

488. Simeon Contarini–doge, 17 January 1615 in ibid., fos. 231r and 236r.

489. The inquisitor of Venice reported the deal as done in March, but Gessi was still negotiating over it in June. ACDFSO:DSO 1615, pp. 137, 164–65, and 281, decrees of 19 March, 2 April and 4 June.

490. Ibid., pp. 258–59 and 544.

491. ACDFSO:DSO 1616, p. 30, decree of 14 January.

492. Ibid., p. 273, decree of 6 July.

493. Ibid., p. 406.

494. Ibid., p. [515], 22 December 1616.

495. ACDFSO:DSO 1617, p. 144.

496. Ibid., p. 384.

497. ACDFSO:DSO 1615, p. 320, 2 July 1615.

498. Ibid., p. 339, 16 July 1615.

499. ACDFSO:DSO 1616, pp. 62 and 110, 10 February and 10 March 1616.

500. Ibid., p. 8, 31 December 1615.

501. Ibid., pp. 65–66, 11 February 1616.

502. ACDFSO:DSO 1618, pp. 5 and 87, 28 December 1617 and 8 March 1618.

503. ACDFSO:DSO 1615, p. 428.

504. ACDFSO:DSO 1616, p. 110.

505. Ibid., pp. 129–30, 24 March 1616.

506. Ibid., p. 505, 15 December 1616.

507. ACDFSO:DSO 1618, p. 50, 1 February 1618.

508. Ibid., p. 365, 18 October 1618.

509. ACDFSO:DSO 1608, p. 555, 20 December 1608.

510. Paolo Gualdo–Galileo, Padua, 3 April 1618 (*EN*, 12, no. 1311) and 26 March 1620 (*EN*, 13, no. 1453). See also Fortunio Liceti–Galileo, Venice, 26 January 1620 (*EN*, 13, no. 1438).

511. ACDFSO:DSO 1608–1609, fo. 483r and ACDFSO:DSO 1609, p. 477, 12 November 1609. For his study in Padua, see A. Dufour, "Un adepte italien de l'humanisme juridique a Genève: Julius Pacius de Beriga (1550–1635) et son *De juris methodo* (1597)," in *Genève et Italie, études publiées à l'occasion du 50 anniversaire de la Société Genevoise d'Études Italiennes par Luc Monnier* (Geneva: Droz, 1969), 113–47, 140, citing one of Pace's works and Antonio Franceschini, "Giulio Pace da Beriga e la Giurisprudenza dei suoi tempi," *Istituto veneto di scienze, lettere ed arti, Memorie* 27, 2 (1903): 21.

512. ACDFSO:DSO 1618, p. 435, 13 December 1618.

513. Filippo de Vivo, "Historical Justifications of Venetian Power in the Adriatic," *Journal of the History of Ideas* 64 (2003): 159–76, 174. The book's full title is *Iulii Pacii A Beriga I.C. Regii Consiliarii, Et Iuris Ex Prima sede in illustri Valentina Academia Professoris De dominio maris Hadriatici disceptatio, inter Sereniss. Regem Hispaniarum ob regnum Neapolitanum, & Sereniss. Rempublicam Venetam* (Lyon: Vincent, 1619) (OCLC 258606718). Worldcat contains no fewer than 211 records for Pace.

514. ACDFSO:DSO 1620, p. 95, 12 March 1620.

515. Ibid., p. 123, 2 April 1620.

516. Ibid., p. 133, 9 April 1620.

517. Ibid., p. 149.

518. Ibid., p. 156, 30 April 1620.

519. Ibid., p. 358.

520. Dufour, "Un adepte italien," 139, citing Franceschini, "Giulio Pace," 17ff.

521. Salvator Miranda gives the dates as 12 May 1621 to 16 December 1623, http://www.fiu.edu/~mirandas/bios1626.htm#Zacchia. Requiem cites Henri Biaudet, *Les nonciatures apostoliques permanentes jusqu'en 1648*, Annales Academiae Scientiarum Finnicae Ser. B, 2, 1 (Helsinki: Suomalainen Tiedeakatemia, 1910), 292.

CHAPTER 4. VENICE: GIORDANO BRUNO, CESARE CREMONINI, AND MARCANTONIO DE DOMINIS

1. Michele Ciliberto, *Giordano Bruno: il teatro della vita* (Milan: Mondadori, 2007). For the trial, in addition to Francesco Beretta, "Giordano Bruno e l'Inquisizione romana. Considerazioni sul processo," *Bruniana & Campanelliana* 7 (2001): 15–49, see especially Saverio Ricci, *Giordano Bruno nell'Europa del Cinquecento* (Rome: Salerno, 2000), 488–549, and "Da Santori a Bellarmino. La politica romana e il processo di Giordano Bruno," in *Giordano Bruno oltre il mito e le opposte passione*, ed. Pasquale Giustiniani et al. (Naples: Facoltà teologica dell'Italia meridionale, Sezione S. Tommaso d'Aquino, 2002), 235–66; Michele Ciliberto, *Pensare per contrari: disincanto e utopia nel Rinascimento* (Rome: Edizioni di Storia e Letteratura, 2005), 325–64; and the updated bibliography in Michele Ciliberto, *Giordano Bruno* (Rome: Laterza, 2005), 290–91. Still the standard biography, replete with many extracts from the sources, is Vincenzo Spampanato, *Vita di Giordano Bruno*, ed. Giovanni Gentile, Studi filosofici, 10 (Messina: G. Principato, 1921). It is of great interest that one of the best historians to work on both Bruno's and Galileo's cases (as well as Tommaso Campanella's), Luigi Firpo, could deliver himself of an intemperate attack on the Inquisition, in defense of Galileo, on a par with those of any of his nineteenth-century predecessors, but by the time he finished studying Bruno's case, he had come to a much more balanced, even in some respects positive, view of the institution. Compare Luigi Firpo, "Il processo di Galileo," in *Pubblicazioni del Comitato nazionale per le manifestazioni celebrative del IV centenario della nascita di Galileo Galilei, Saggi su Galileo Galilei*, ed. Carlo Maccagni, 3 vols. (Florence: G. Barbèra, 1972), 3:2, 152–73 with Luigi Firpo, *Il processo di Giordano Bruno*, ed. Diego Quaglioni (Rome: Salerno, 1993). The rhetorical bombast of the first piece is entirely absent in the edition. See also the corrections to Firpo's interpretation in Beretta, "Processo Bruno," passim. Among the most important of Beretta's criticisms is Firpo's failure to take adequate account of the status of his texts (24–25). This is not entirely fair (nor does Beretta make anything of his own point), since Firpo did note carefully not only their source, but at least some of the differences between them arising from their locations. One of the cases alleged by Beretta Firpo did not in fact mishandle, at least not in any significant way. See the two versions of the pivotal decree of 4 February 1599, numbers 56a and 56c on 313–14 and 315. Firpo did apparently manufacture a problem about their dating, saying that one was dated only "feria quinta" (93 and 136n22), but in his transcription both are fully dated both 4 February and "feria quinta." Citations to Firpo are to document/s or particular page/s when more precision is needed.

2. Firpo, *Processo Bruno*, 17 identifies this moment as the beginning of the *processo offensivo*. Beretta defines this phase somewhat differently, citing Francisco Peña's scholia to Nicholas Eymeric's *Directorium inquisitorum*. He says it meant interrogations of the suspect over propositions deemed suspicious. Francesco Beretta, "Galilée devant le Tribunal de l'Inquisition" (Th.D. thesis, Universitè de Fribourg, 1997), 180. In Bruno's case, the opening phase included both witness testimony and his interrogations. This combination was usual.

3. Firpo, *Processo Bruno*, 14–15.

4. Ibid., 145–47.

5. Ibid., 147–48. Bartolomeo Cecchetti, *La republica di Venezia e la corte di Roma nei rapporti della religione*, 2 vols. (Venice: P. Naratovich, 1874, 2 vols.), 2, 10. Arrigoni was a theologian from Brescia, made bishop of Šibenik (Sebenico) 18 July 1599. He died in October 1626. *HC* 4: 314.

6. Imprisonment at this phase was unusual, but justified by the risk of flight. Beretta, "Processo Bruno," 31. Beretta claims that Bruno was arrested at Mocenigo's behest, which would have been highly irregular, but in fact, as Captain Matteo d'Avanzo attested, he had acted on the Inquisition's orders when capturing Bruno. Firpo, *Processo Bruno*, 148.

7. Whether the inquisitor in Venice knew Ciotti's history is unclear; it did not come up in his deposition. In 1598 he had been ordered not to print Giacomo Menochio's works. ACDFSO:DSO 1597–1598–1599, p. 523. Further proceedings began in 1606. ACDFSO:DSO 1606–1607, fo. 154v. Cleared in 1607, he was back in trouble in 1610. AsVe:SDR, f. 58, fo. 115v and ACDFSO:DSO 1610–1611, fo. 410v. For a beginning on his output, see Dennis E. Rhodes, "Some Neglected Aspects of the Career of Giovanni Battista Ciotti," *The Library* 6th ser. 9 (1987): 225-39.

8. Firpo, *Processo Bruno*, 149–52. Beretta, "Processo Bruno," 31 cites only the second of these, making Ciotti's testimony look more damaging than it was.

9. Firpo, *Processo Bruno*, 152–54.

10. Beretta, "Processo Bruno," 33 raises the apposite but unanswerable question of the degree to which the booksellers might have been hiding their own complicity in Bruno's ideas.

11. Firpo, *Processo Bruno*, no. 9.

12. Ibid., no. 10.

13. Ibid., no. 11.

14. Ibid., no. 12.

15. Beretta, "Processo Bruno," 31 points out that the certainty that this defense would fail raises the question of how much an accused might have known of the Inquisition's "style."

16. Firpo, *Processo Bruno*, 166.

17. Ibid., 167.

18. Ibid., 168–71.

19. Ibid., 172.

20. Ibid., 174.

21. Ibid., 182–83.

22. Ibid., 185.

23. Ibid., 190.

24. Ibid., 191–92.

25. Decree of 11 June in Baldini and Spruit, eds., *CCMS*, 1, "Giordano Bruno," no. 1, not in Firpo. Baldini and Spruit arrange their documents by name of accused with new numbering for each.

26. Firpo, *Processo Bruno*, no. 16.

27. Beretta, "Processo Bruno," 31.

28. Firpo, *Processo Bruno*, 19 quotes the maxim "Unus testis, nullus testis" without a reference. Canon law more generally accepted the testimony of a single witness only reluctantly.

29. Ibid., no. 17.

30. Ibid., no. 18.

31. Ibid., 196.

32. Ibid., 197.

33. Ibid., 198.

34. Ibid., 199.

35. The acknowledgment from Rome is dated 8 August, but a note on it says it was received in Venice on the 13th (and the same five-day interval for correspondence from Rome occurs on at least one other occasion), so the entirety of Bruno's *processo* through the end of July might have been included. Ibid., no. 20.

36. Ibid., 201 and 212. Santoro's two letters are known from BAV, Barb. lat. 1369, as well as a decree of 7 November 1592 and a copy in ACDFSO, St. st., M.3.g, p. 108 cited in Baldini and Spruit, eds., *CCMS*, 867. Barb. lat. 1369 is a heterogeneous collection of Inquisition documents. See the description in P. H. Jobe, "Inquisitorial Manuscripts in the Biblioteca Apostolica Vaticana: A Preliminary Handlist," in *The Inquisition in Early Modern Europe: Studies on Sources and Methods*, ed. Gustav Henningsen and John A. Tedeschi (DeKalb: Northern Illinois University Press, 1986), 33–53, 40. The codex came from Francesco Barberini. Cf. Beretta, "Processo Bruno," 25–26

37. See the summary in Beretta, "Processo Bruno," 36–40 and Spampanato, *Bruno*, 509–43. The documents are in Firpo, *Processo Bruno*, 201–14. See also Carlo De Frede, "L'estradizione di Giordano Bruno da Venezia [1594]," in *Religiosità e cultura nel Cinquecento italiano* (Bologna: Il Mulino, 1999), 379–424, especially 420, where he concludes that Nunzio Taverna's count of extraditions granted was close to correct. Two of the documents were included in the inquisitorial manual in BAV, Barb. lat. 1369, an order of 7 (?) September 1592 (cited as from "tomo 5, fol. 86") to the inquisitor of Venice to have Bruno extradited as was always easily done in the past, e.g., with Bartolomeo Spadafora, and another of 9 January 1593 telling him to use the example of Guido da Fano. BAV, Barb. lat. 1369, fos. 130r and 94r. The decree leading to the second is in Firpo and Baldini and Spruit, eds., *CCMS*, 868.

38. Salvatore Caponetto, "Bartolomeo Spadafora e la riforma protestante in Sicilia nel sec. XVI," *Rinascimento* 7 (1956): 219–341, and Aldo Stella, "Guido da Fano eretico del sec.

XVI al servizio dei re d'Inghilterra," *Rivista di storia della chiesa in Italia* 13 (1959): 196–238. Santoro referred vaguely to other cases in his letter of 9 January 1593. Firpo, *Processo Bruno*, 213.

39. Spampanato, *Bruno*, 536–37, and Firpo, *Processo Bruno*, 38–39.

40. Cf. Beretta, "Processo Bruno," 38.

41. Firpo, *Processo Bruno*, nos. 34–35, and Baldini and Spruit, eds., *CCMS*, nos. 5–6. It is of some interest that seven and six cardinals respectively attended, along with the entire staff. Later, many cardinals failed to appear, and it became customary for the commissary to skip the visitation. Both points suggest that the visits tended to become pro forma, a point reinforced by the numerous decrees ordering them to be taken seriously.

42. Firpo, *Processo Bruno*, no. 36; Baldini and Spruit, eds., *CCMS*, no. 7. Baldini and Spruit often silently amend Firpo's readings and frequently give less text.

43. As Beretta well brings out, the incompleteness of the decree registers does not signify that nothing of substance had been decided since such action might have been recorded only in the dossier or not at all. Beretta, "Processo Bruno," 26.

44. Firpo, *Processo Bruno*, chapter VI. Celestino himself underwent a speedy trial by the Roman Inquisition which lasted in total from 3 June to 16 September 1599, including summary judgment by the pope in just twenty days after a purely formal grant of a defense followed by a highly unusual nocturnal execution. Ibid., 45 and 126–27.

45. Ibid., 62–64 and 69. For the *repetitio*, see *RI*, 188–91.

46. Firpo, *Processo Bruno*, 63–64. Since the original *processo* is missing, we do not have the correspondence with Venice. Ibid., 129. Three earlier witnesses were not recalled (van Brecht, Morosini, and Domenico da Nocera), and neither were two other earlier witnesses whose testimony does not survive, one of whom had died. The "Sommario" does not distinguish carefully between witnesses examined in the first Venetian phase of the trial and in the *repetitio*, e.g., Fra Celestino is treated as if he had testified in both phases, although Firpo thinks he entered into only the second. Ibid., 260.

47. See the demonstration in Beretta, "Processo Bruno," 26–28. Beretta could not precisely determine the document's status, and neither can I. He thinks it likely to have been drawn up by the fiscal (28). Firpo, *Processo Bruno*, 87–88 drew a nearly identical conclusion, that the document was for the consultors' use, without being able to distinguish it from a true *summarium*. For that pivotal document on which the sentence was based, see *RI*, 196.

48. Firpo, *Processo Bruno*, 129.

49. Ibid., 63–64.

50. Ibid., 47–48, a list drawn from the so-called "Sommario," since Fra Celestino's testimony is lost.

51. Ibid. , no. 38; Baldini and Spruit, eds., *CCMS*, no. 9.

52. Firpo, *Processo Bruno*, nos. 39–42; Baldini and Spruit, eds., *CCMS*, nos. 10–13. On the last occasion someone noticed that the Holy Office lacked a list of Bruno's works, which he was duly ordered to produce.

53. Beretta, "Processo Bruno," 42. Beretta thinks that the insufficient proof offered for all the articles in the first part of the so-called "Sommario," reflecting the state of the case

in early 1595, gave rise to the reading. Firpo thought more or less the same thing, except that he did not fully understand why Bruno's books needed to be examined. Firpo, *Processo Bruno*, 74.

54. Firpo, *Processo Bruno*, no. 41; Baldini and Spruit, eds., *CCMS*, no. 12, the coram of 9 February 1595.

55. Firpo, *Processo Bruno*, nos. 43–44; Baldini and Spruit, eds., *CCMS*, nos. 14–15.

56. Firpo, *Processo Bruno*, 232; not in Baldini and Spruit, eds., *CCMS*.

57. Firpo, *Processo Bruno*, 235; ;Baldini and Spruit, eds., *CCMS*, no. 16. The transcription of Gallo's name caused problems before Firpo corrected it (ibid., 77 and 132; the index guesses that his given name was Alessandro, despite Firpo's demonstration that this is a mistake). Zaragoza or Saragoza (ca. 1546–after October 1623) is the only one of the three about whom anything certain is known. He was appointed consultor of the Index in 1592 and censored Francesco Patrizi's *Nova de universis philosophia* and Antonio Possevino's *Bibliotheca selecta* for the Master of the Sacred Palace. Baldini and Spruit, eds., *CCMS*, 357, 2931 and 2202–23.

58. Firpo, *Processo Bruno*, no. 46; Baldini and Spruit, eds., *CCMS*, no. 17.

59. Firpo, *Processo Bruno*, no. 49; Baldini and Spruit, eds., *CCMS*, no. 19. "Deinde fuit admonitus ad relinquendum huiusmodi eius vanitates diversorum mundorum, atque ordinatum quod interrogetur stricte. Postea detur ei censura."

60. Beretta, "Processo Bruno," 42.

61. Firpo, *Processo Bruno*, no. 52; Baldini and Spruit, eds., *CCMS*, no. 22, truncated. Again, this was not the so-called "Sommario," but the *summarium* properly so called.

62. Firpo, *Processo Bruno*, no. 53; Baldini and Spruit, eds., *CCMS*, no. 23.

63. There seems to have been no reason to avoid a meeting on 13 January; in 1600 a coram fell on that date.

64. "Ordinatum quod proponantur ei propositiones ut illas consideret et ponderet; et in alia congregatione proponatur ut illas revocet; et si noluerit revocare . . . [lacuna in original]. Propositae per patrem Bellarminum. Concessa licentia." Firpo, *Processo Bruno*, no. 54a; Baldini and Spruit, eds., *CCMS*, no. 24.

65. Firpo, *Processo Bruno*, no. 55a; Baldini and Spruit, eds., *CCMS*, no. 25. A fair copy in another volume of decreta reads almost identically. Firpo, *Processo Bruno*, no. 55b; not in Baldini and Spruit, eds., *CCMS*.

66. Firpo, *Processo Bruno*, no. 56; Baldini and Spruit, eds., *CCMS*, no. 26, again without the second two texts in Firpo. His handling of these texts is the object of Beretta's sharpest criticism. Beretta, "Processo Bruno," 25.

67. Firpo, *Processo Bruno*, no. 56a; Baldini and Spruit, eds., *CCMS*, no. 27.

68. Cf. Beretta's commentary in "Processo Bruno," 25.

69. Firpo, *Processo Bruno*, no. 57; Baldini and Spruit, eds., *CCMS*, no. 28.

70. Firpo, *Processo Bruno*, 319; Baldini and Spruit, eds., *CCMS*, no. 29. Firpo prints the text in full, Baldini and Spruit only the section about Bruno.

71. Firpo, *Processo Bruno*, 320; not in Baldini and Spruit, eds., *CCMS*.

72. Ibid. , no. 59, F. Adriani's minute and Q. Adriani's fair copy of it. Beretta, "Processo

Bruno," 45 notes only the second, and Baldini and Spruit, eds., *CCMS*, doc. 31, print only the first. The most important difference between them is the second's correction of "prima aprilis" to "v[a] aprilis." Firpo, *Processo Bruno*, 95 and 137 explicates the "Novatian heresy" as referring to Bruno's doubts about penance but not his anti-Trinitarianism, as Angelo Mercati thought. Baldini and Spruit, eds., *CCMS*, 955n quote Eymeric as saying Novatian was an anabaptist.

73. Firpo, *Processo Bruno*, 325n humorously notes Enrico Carusi's mistranscription of *perspicilia* as *pennicilia*, saying Bruno needed glasses not feathers ("occhiali e non pennelli").

74. Ibid. , no. 60; Baldini and Spruit, eds., *CCMS*, no. 32.

75. Firpo, *Processo Bruno*, no. 61; Baldini and Spruit, eds., *CCMS*, no. 33.

76. Firpo, *Processo Bruno*, no. 62; Baldini and Spruit, eds., *CCMS*, no. 34, again only the portion directly relevant to Bruno.

77. Firpo, *Processo Bruno*, no. 63; Baldini and Spruit, eds., *CCMS*, no. 35.

78. Firpo, *Processo Bruno*, no. 64a; Baldini and Spruit, eds., *CCMS*, no. 37.

79. Firpo, *Processo Bruno*, 335; Firpo, *Processo Bruno*, 335; Baldini and Spruit, eds., *CCMS*, 963.

80. Firpo, *Processo Bruno*, no. 65; Baldini and Spruit, eds., *CCMS*, no. 38.

81. Firpo, *Processo Bruno*, 99 points out its defective state.

82. Ibid., no. 66; Baldini and Spruit, eds., *CCMS*, no. 40.

83. Beretta, "Processo Bruno," 45.

84. Firpo, *Processo Bruno*, nos. 67 and 72; only the first in Baldini and Spruit, eds., *CCMS*, no. 39, in very abbreviated form. According to the decree registers, Madruzzo's palace was in Piazza Navona (e.g., ACDFSO:DSO 1596, fo. 201v), that is, Palazzo Simone Cybo Malaspina di Massa, between the old church of Sant'Agnese in Agone and Palazzo Millini, the present site of Palazzo Pamphili. The Congregation met there rather than in the family's palace, now the so-called Palazzo dei Penitenzieri, in via della Conciliazione near the Tiber. For both, see Pia Kehl, "Il palazzo dei Penitenzieri in Borgo," in Laura Dal Prà, ed., *I Madruzzo e l'Europa 1539–1658. I principi vescovi di Trento tra Papato e Impero* (Trent: Provincia Autonoma and Milan: Charta, 1993), 705–9, 709.

85. 25 June 1598. ADCFSO: DSO 1597–1598–1599, fo. 381r; 1598, fo. 296v; Spruit, "Cremonini," 194. These reports are summarized in BAV, Vat. lat. 10945, fo. 115v, adding that the bishop was to take a hand and correct Cremonini according to the decree about the soul's immortality laid down by the 5th Lateran Council in 1515. This report must be a little confused, for at least two reasons. First, Cremonini's only known lectures *de anima* followed Aristotle's own opinion, not that of his interpreter Alexander, and second, in the 1598–1599 academic year Cremonini lectured on *De generatione et corruptione.* Antonino Poppi, *Cremonini, Galilei e gli Inquisitori del Santo a Padova* (Padua: Centro Studi Antoniani, 1993), 60n. For a beginning on Cremonini, see especially Léopold Mabilleau, *Étude historique sur la philosophie de la Renaissance en Italie (Cesare Cremonini)* (Paris: Hachette, 1881); Heinrich C. Kuhn, "Cesare Cremonini: Volti e maschere di un filosofo scomodo per tre secoli e mezzo," in *Cesare Cremonini: Aspetti del pensiero e scritti*, ed. E. Riondato and Antonino Poppi (Padua: Academia Galileiana,

2000), 1, 153–68; Kuhn, *Venetischer Aristotelismus im Ende der aristotelischen Welt: Aspekte der Welt und des Denkens des Cesare Cremonini (1550–1631)*, Europäische Hochschulschriften, Philosophie, 490 (Frankfurt am Main: Peter Lang, 1996); Edward Muir, *Culture Wars of the Late Renaissance: Skeptics, Libertines and Opera* (Cambridge, Mass.: Harvard University Press, 2007), chap. 1; and the entry in *DSI* 1: 430. The evidence presented here supports Muir's thesis that Cremonini's religious views posed more dangers than his philosophical ones.

86. There is no mention of Cremonini in ASVe:SDR, f. 41 or 42. There is also nothing in the ASVe, Sant'Ufficio *fondo* nor in the AdS Padua.

87. Poppi, *Cremonini*, no. VIII.

88. The doge's response of 29 May called the warning a *precetto*. Poppi, *Cremonini*, no. X.

89. Poppi, *Cremonini*, no. IX.

90. Rectors of Padua–doge, 24 May 1604 in Poppi, *Cremonini*, no. VI.

91. Poppi, *Cremonini*, 58.

92. Vincenzo Spampanato, "Nuovi documenti intorno a negozii e processi dell'Inquisizione (1603–1624)," *Giornale critico della filosofia italiana* 5 (1924): 97–137, 216–61, and 346–401, 223, 12 May 1604 and ADCFSO, Decreta, Copia 1604–1605, p. 194, 13 May 1604; only the second in Spruit, "Cremonini," 194–95; Poppi, *Cremonini*, 45–46n. Belloni's denunciation is on 45–50. The corraborating witness he named was Giovanni Battista Boni or Bon. Ibid., 46.

93. Poppi, *Cremonini*, 58.

94. ACDFSO:DSO 1604 Copia, p. 228, 4 June 1604; Spruit, "Cremonini," 195.

95. The inquisitor's letters of 10 and 18 June "significant clarissimos rectores censere non esse capiendas informationes contra Caesarem Tremoninum [*sic*] publicum professorem Philosophiae super contraventione praecepti de non legendo: animum esse mortalem iuxta mentis Aristotelis: Ill.mus mandavit scribi Episcopo, ut extraiudicialiter se informet de veritate super contraventione praecepti, et hic in Urbe examinetur Abbas Sancti Pauli. ACDFSO:DSO 1604–1605 Copia, p. 256; orig. fo. 113r–v completely ill., 24 June 1604; Spruit, "Cremonini," 195. The abbot has not been identified. There was no such house in Padua.

96. ACDFSO:DSO 1604 Copia, pp. 275 and 299, 8 and 22 July; Spruit, "Cremonini," 195.

97. In 1591 Cremonini led the charge in trying to close the Jesuit school in Padua. Paul Grendler, *The Universities of the Italian Renaissance* (Baltimore: Johns Hopkins University Press, 2002), 479–82.

98. ACDFSO:DSO 1604–1605 Copia, pp. 370 and 404, 7 and 23 September; Spruit, "Cremonini," 195, missing the second.

99. ACDFSO:DSO 1604–1605 Copia, pp. 253–44 and 440, 22 June and 19 October. On the first occasion the Congregation ordered the torture of a prostitute, seeking evidence of Vendramin's views. 1604 Copia, p. 253; Spruit, "Cremonini," 195.

100. ACDFSO:DSO 1606–1607, fo. 239v, 31 January 1607; Spruit, "Cremonini," 195.

101. Meietti was from Padua or may have had a shop there, but he never seems to have printed any books in the city.

102. ACDFSO:DSO 1607, fo. 146r; 1606–1607, fo. 341v, 27 June 1607; Spruit, "Cremonini," 195.

103. ACDFSO:DSO 1608, p. 44, 22 January 1608, an unusual Tuesday meeting; cf. volume index, fo. 556v; Spruit, "Cremonini," 196. The volume index contains other references to Cremonini, but they all either are defective or refer to another Cesare.

104. ACDFSO:DSO 1608, p. 55, 22 January 1608; Spruit, "Cremonini," 196; Spampanato, "Nuovi documenti," 224; and 1608, p. 60; Spruit, "Cremonini," 196, separating Millini section from last entry.

105. ACDFSO:DSO 1608, p. 113 and 1608–1609, fo. 51v, 13 March 1608; Spruit, "Cremonini," 196.

106. ASVe, Consiglio dei Dieci, Parti Roma, registro 1607, fo. 83v.

107. Spampanato, "Nuovi documenti," 225.

108. ACDFSO:DSO 1608, pp. 217–18; Spruit, "Cremonini," 196.

109. Spampanato, "Nuovi documenti," 225.

110. Pietro Savio, "Il nunzio a Venezia dopo l'interdetto," *Archivio veneto* 85 (1955): 55–110, 67, citing ASV, Fondo Borg. II 283, fo. 191, orig. and the register copy of this dispatch in ASV, Seg. Stato, Venezia, 38, fo. 417v, which varies slightly.

111. Spampanato, "Nuovi documenti," 225; and ACDFSO:DSO 1608, p. 320, 24 July; Spruit, "Cremonini," 196. On 226 is printed another undated document saying Gessi had reported that Mazzalorsi's denunications had not been pursued, since the assistants complained that Cremonini was undergoing "persecution," but I have been unable to find either the original or any reference to such a complaint in the decree registers.

112. ASV, Seg. Stato, Venezia, 39, fos. 137r and 137v.

113. Savio, "Nunzio," 69, citing ASV, Fondo Borg. I 908, fo. 458 and 68, citing Fondo Borg. 283, fos. 324–25 and ASV, Seg. Stato, Venezia, 38, fos. 481r–482r.

114. ACDFSO:DSO 1608, pp. 362–63, 23 August; Spruit, "Cremonini," 196, misdated 21 Aug., because he missed misplaced pp. 358–59.

115. Savio, "Nunzio," 69, citing ASV, Fondo Borg. I 908, fo. 466.

116. ASV, Seg. Stato, Venezia, 38, fo. 495v; and Savio, "Nunzio," 70 citing ASV, Fondo Borg. II 283, fo. 367.

117. ACDFSO:DSO 1608, p. 393 and 1608–1609, fo. 191v; Spruit, "Cremonini," 196.

118. ACDFSO:DSO 1608, p. 378 and 1608–1609, fo. 185r, 4 September; Spruit, "Cremonini," 196, running this and last entry together; and Spampanato, "Nuovi documenti," 226. For the importance of *fama* to an Inquisition trial, see *RI*, 155 and 166–68.

119. ASV, Seg. Stato, Venezia, 38, fo. 560r, 25 October 1608, compared to the entry for 29 October; Spampanato, "Nuovi documenti," 227, saying that Gessi's letter of 18 October would be considered the following day; and the decree of that date in ACDFSO:DSO 1608, p. 470; Spruit, "Cremonini," 196.

120. Gessi–Borghese, 1 November 1608 (Savio, "Nunzio," 70 citing ASV, Fondo

Borghese II 279, fo. 155) and entry for 12 November in Spampanato, "Nuovi documenti," 227.

121. ACDFSO:DSO 1608, p. 489, 13 November; Spruit, "Cremonini," 196.

122. Gessi–Borghese, 29 November 1608. Savio, "Nunzio," 70 from Fondo Borghese II 279, fo. 223r.

123. ACDFSO:DSO 1608, p. 530 and 1608–1609, fo. 256v; Spruit, "Cremonini," 197 misses all names after Fabbri, saying "i nomi dei censori risultano quasi illeggibili" (!).

124. Savio, "Nunzio," 71 from Fondo Borghese II 279, fo. 273.

125. ACDFSO:DSO 1609, pp. 166 and 170–71 and 1608–1609, fos. 341r and 343r–v; Spruit, "Cremonini," 197.

126. ACDFSO:DSO 1610–1611, fo. 68v, 22 April 1610; Spruit, "Cremonini," 197.

127. ACDFSO:DSO 1610–1611, fo. 313v, 17 May 1611; *EN*, 19, 275; Sergio M. Pagano, ed., *I documenti vaticani del processo di Galileo Galilei (1611–1741): Nuova edizione accresciuta, rivista e annotata*, Collectanea Archivi Vaticani 69 (Città del Vaticano: Archivio Vaticano, 2009), no. 118; Spruit, "Cremonini," 197.

128. Poppi, *Cremonini*, docs. XX and XXI.

129. ACDFSO:DSO 1613, p. 598, 11 December; Spruit, "Cremonini," 197.

130. "Voglia Iddio che l'assolutione dell'Ecc.mo Cremonini li giovi più all'anima di quello che fa la mathematica alle anime delli professori di essa, allontanati assai dal spirituale." Bernardo Pisenti–Ingolfo de' Conti in Padua, Venice, 3 May 1613; *EN*, 11, no. 871.

131. ACDFSO:DSO 1614, pp. 44–45 and 52, 16 and 23 January 1614; Spruit, "Cremonini," 197.

132. ACDFSO:DSO 1614, p. 124; Spruit, "Cremonini," 198.

133. ACDFSO:DSO 1614, p. 245; Spruit, "Cremonini," 198; and Spampanato, "Nuovi documenti," 227, for the agenda entry.

134. Spampanato, "Nuovi documenti," 228. Only an action arising from the denunciation appears in the decree register. ACDFSO:DSO 1614, p. 254; Spruit, "Cremonini," 198.

135. ACDFSO:DSO 1614, p. 310; Spruit, "Cremonini," 198.

136. ACDFSO:DSO 1614, p. 322; Spruit, "Cremonini," 198. The censures are printed in Mabilleau, *Étude*, 349–55.

137. ASVe:SDR, f. 71, fo. 178r–v; excerpt in Poppi, *Cremonini*, no. XXV.

138. ACDFSO:DSO 1614, pp. 336–37; Spruit, "Cremonini," 198.

139. ASVe:SDR, f. 71, fo. 225r.

140. ACDFSO:DSO 1614, pp. 386–87, 7 August; Spruit, "Cremonini," 198–99. There is slippage between the decree and the agenda, which says that Cremonini was prepared to make corrections. Spampanato, "Nuovi documenti," 229, 6 August 1614.

141. Spampanato, "Nuovi documenti," 229; and ACDFSO:DSO 1614, p. 398, 14 August; Spruit, "Cremonini," 199.

142. ACDFSO:DSO 1614, p. 445; Spruit, "Cremonini," 199.

143. Spampanato, "Nuovi documenti," 229–30; and ACDFSO:DSO 1614, p. 454, 18 September; Spruit, "Cremonini," 199, missing last two words. He also says the orders were

sent on 24 September and are printed in Mabilleau. The date, a Wednesday, is unlikely, and I cannot find the text cited in Mabilleau.

144. ASVe:SDR, f. 71, fos. 227r–228v; excerpt in Poppi, *Cremonini*, no. XXVIII.

145. ASVe:SDR, f. 72, fos. 8v–9v; excerpt in Poppi, *Cremonini*, no. XXIX.

146. ACDFSO:DSO 1614, p. 490, 9 October, reading the inquistor of Padua's letter of the 3rd; Spruit, "Cremonini," 199.

147. ACDFSO:DSO 1614, p. 514; Spruit, "Cremonini," 199.

148. ACDFSO:DSO 1614pp. 524–25; Spruit, "Cremonini," 199.

149. ACDFSO:DSO 1615, p. 355, 23 July 1615; Spruit, "Cremonini," 200, without distinguishing clearly between the two books.

150. ACDFSO:DSO 1616, p. 93, 2 March; Spruit, "Cremonini," 200.

151. Ibid., p. 245, 15 June; Spruit, "Cremonini," 200.

152. Ibid., p. 269; Spruit, "Cremonini," 200.

153. Ibid., p. 283; Spruit, "Cremonini," 200.

154. Spruit, "Cremonini," 200.

155. For the date of Ystella's death, see ACDFSO:DSO 1614, p. 436; for Giustiniani's tenure 1610–1611, fo. 212v, and his last sentence 20 February 1615 in Trinity College Dublin, MS 1230, fos. 109r–110r.

156. Spruit, "Cremonini," 200.

157. ACDFSO:DSO 1619, p. 7, 2 January; not in Spruit, "Cremonini."

158. ACDFSO:DSO 1619, p. 147, 25 April; Spruit, "Cremonini," 201, reading *postscriptam* instead of *praescriptam*.

159. ACDFSO:DSO 1619, p. 206; Spruit, "Cremonini," 201.

160. ACDFSO:DSO 1619, pp. 206 and 207; Spruit, "Cremonini," 201. The inquisitor's letter to Cremonini of 3 July is in Poppi, *Cremonini*, no. XXXIII.

161. ACDFSO:DSO 1619, p. 218, 20 June; Spruit, "Cremonini," 201.

162. ACDFSO:DSO 1619, p. 255, 18 July; Spruit, "Cremonini," 201.

163. ACDFSO:DSO 1619, p. 334; Spruit, 201–2, without identification of Scaglia.

164. "ut curet essequtionem [Spruit: executionem] cum effectu." ACDFSO:DSO 1619, p. 420, 21 November; Spruit, "Cremonini," 202.

165. ACDFSO:DSO 1619, pp. 456–47; Spruit, 202. According to Spruit, on 12 March the Congregation noted the inquisitor of Padua's report that "Cremoninum velle post Pascha plene satisfacere," but I have not been able to confirm this text on a reading of about half the decree register line by line. On that date a letter from the inquisitor was read, but it does not concern Cremonini, nor does the next, read 2 April. 1620, pp. 95 and 124.

166. ACDFSO:DSO 1621, p. 167, 3 June; Spruit, "Cremonini," 202.

167. ACDFSO:DSO 1621, p. 177, 16 June; Spruit, "Cremonini," 202. Spruit prints another text from 17 June saying that Cremonini was standing more on his dignity than on the faith. The date must be a reconstruction from the location of the badly damaged entry between 16 and 18 June, but it certainly does not contain this text. 1621, pp. 183–86.

168. ACDFSO:DSO 1621, p. 395; Spruit, "Cremonini," 202. It could be that some of these delays arose from Venetian pressure, but I cannot say because I was several times

denied permission to see the files of the Roman ambassadors' correspondence for this period in the ASVe.

169. Spruit, "Cremonini," 202.

170. Index decree of 2 June in Spruit, "Cremonini," 202 and ACDFSO:DSO 1623, p. 206, 8 June; Spruit, "Cremonini," 203.

171. ACDFSO:DSO 1625, fo. 80v, 6 May; Spruit, "Cremonini," 203.

172. Ibid., fo. 112r–v; Spruit, "Cremonini," 203. Millini's letter is printed in Antonio Rotondò, "Nuovi documenti per la storia dell''Indice dei libri proibiti' (1572–1638)," *Rinascimento* 3 (1963): 145–211, 205.

173. ACDFSO:DSO 1625, fo. 128r; Spruit, "Cremonini," 203.

174. ACDFSO:DSO 1625., fos. 128r, 14 August and 197v–198r, 27 November; Spruit, "Cremonini," 203.

175. ACDFSO:DSO 1625, fo. 199v, 2 December; Spruit, "Cremonini," 203.

176. Spruit (in his only entry for 1626) following Domenico Berti makes his name Castellari. Domenico Berti, "Di Cesare Cremonini e della sua controversia con l'Inquisizione di Padova e di Roma," *Atti della R. Accademia dei Lincei, Memorie della classe di scienze morali, storiche e filosofiche* ser. 3, 2 (1877–1878): 273–99. Costantino Testi, the Roman commissary's *socio*, took Castellani's deposition on either 19 or 26 June; it is recorded in a hand found in the central records. ASVe, Sant'Ufficio, b. 82, fasc. 6. In addition to the denunciation, on 10 January 1626 the Congregation sounded the alarm that Cremonini's doctrine was being taught in "the schools and academies" of Venice. In May it denied Fabbri a license to read him along with various other authors, among them Pomponazzi and Calvin. BAV, Vat. lat. 10945, fos. 109v–110r and ACDFSO:DSO 1626, fo. 78v.

177. ACDFSO:DSO 1626, fo. 131r; Cecchetti, *Venezia*, 10.

178. ASVe, Sant'Ufficio, b. 82, fasc. 6. For its date, see ACDFSO:DSO 1626, fo. 157r–v.

179. ACDFSO:DSO 1626, fo. 157r–v.

180. ACDFSO:DSO 1627, fo. 99r–v; Spruit, "Cremonini," 204.

181. Ibid., fo. 117v; Spruit, "Cremonini," 204.

182. Ibid., fo. 150v; not in Spruit, "Cremonini." The book is *Apologia dictorum Aristotelis de origine, et principatu membrorum adversus Galenum* (Venice: Girolamo Piuti, 1627).

183. ACDFSO:DSO 1627, fo. 163r, 16 September; Spruit, "Cremonini," 204, dated 6 September.

184. ACDFSO:DSO 1631, fo. 157r; not in Spruit, "Cremonini."

185. Ibid., fo. 174r; not in Spruit, "Cremonini."

186. ACDFSO:DSO 1632, fo. 30v; not in Spruit, "Cremonini."

187. Francesco Beretta, "La Condamnation de Galilée (1633)" in Francesco Beretta, Michel-Pierre Lerner, et al., *Galilée en procès, Galilée réhabilité* (Saint-Maurice: Éditions Saint-Augustin, 2005), 41–65, quoting ACDFSO, St. st. O 1 a, 16, fo. 104r; Spruit, "Cremonini," 204, prints from "St. st." an excerpt from what must be the same document, dated 17 August.

188. ACDFSO:DSO 1632, fos. 116r and 118v; not in Spruit, "Cremonini."

189. For De Dominis's biography see W. Brown Patterson's article in the *The Oxford*

Dictionary of National Biography (hereafter *ODNB*); his *King James VI and I and the Reunion of Christendom* (Cambridge: Cambridge University Press, 1997), chap. 7; and Noel Malcolm, *De Dominis 1560–1624. Venetian, Anglican, Ecumenist and relapsed Heretic* (London: Strickland & Scott, 1984), and *DSI* 1: 451–52. None have much to say about his trials.

190. *ODNB* and Federico Bonelli and Lucio Russo, "Crisogono, De Dominis and the Origins of the Modern Theory of the Tides," *British Journal for the History of Science* 29 (1996): 385–401.

191. See *ODNB*.

192. Eleonora Belligni, *Auctoritas e potestas: Marcantonio de Dominis fra l'inquisizione e Giacomo I* (Milan: Franco Angeli, 2003), 130–38, stressing De Dominis's agreement with Sarpi, *ODNB* and Patterson, *Reunion of Christendom*, 226–27. Despite her book's promising title, Belligni does not use the decree registers nor handle the Inquisition's proceedings especially carefully even without them. Thus she misses all the Inquisition's attention before De Dominis's flight to England. She did find a number of documents about De Dominis in the ACDFSO, but her principal interest in them was his political ideas. The only other recent treatment of the trial is Pietro Redondi, *Galileo Heretic*, trans. Raymond Rosenthal (Princeton, N.J.: Princeton University Press, 1987; second Italian ed. with unchanged main text, Turin: Einaudi, 2004), 107–18/135–48). Redondi's general thesis that Galileo was condemned as a sacramentarian has come in for almost universal criticism. See, e.g., Vincenzo Ferrone and Massimo Firpo, "Galileo tra inquisitori e microstorici," *Rivista storica italiana* 97 (1985): 177–238. His handling of De Dominis's trial is similarly defective, if dramatic. Its central contention—that De Dominis was incriminated on a trumped-up charge to cover the real reason for his conviction—is both false and designed to serve Redondi's own argument that this is what happened to Galileo. The English translation also causes problems, most seriously by rendering "configurò un'incriminazione di abiura simulata" as "an incrimination for false oath was suggested" (117/146), for which in any case there is no evidence. Nor is there that because of De Dominis's backers the Holy Office moved "with obligatory caution," nor is it entirely true that a recantation meant that any acts previous to it could no longer be matter for investigation (a glance at the sentence will dispel this notion), nor that De Dominis was "officially incriminated for a manuscript on the lawfulness of divorce in the case of adultery," although this was indeed among the points examined (117/146–47).

193. ACDFSO:DSO 1614, p. 54. I have not been able to identify this letter nor to consult Marcantonio De Dominis, *Scritti giurisdizionalistici inediti*, ed. Antonio Russo (Naples: Luigi Loffredo, 1965), but it probably concerned a jurisdictional dispute or disputes, the origins of which appear to go back at least to 1608 and in which Rome took the side of De Dominis's opponents. Sime Ljubić, "Prilozi za zivotopis Markuntuna de Dominisa Rabljanina, spljetskoga nadbiskupa," *Starine na sviet isdaje Jugoslavenska Akademija zanonsti i umjetnosti* 2 (1870): 1–260, 112–26. The only writing De Dominis is known to have been working on about now was probably a version of his magnum opus, *De republica christiana*. Ibid., 132n, entries for 15 and 28 April 1612 and 20 July 1613, and Patterson, *Reunion of Christendom*, 227–29, drawing on Gessi's in-letters to the

cardinal nephew. Andreucci had been De Dominis's rival for the see of Split. Malcolm, *De Dominis*, 21–23. Rome knew all about the hostility between the two. Ljubić, "Prilozi," 132n, entry for 8 March 1614; these are apparently extracts from a summary of Gessi's correspondence, but Ljubić gave no source.

194. ACDFSO:DSO 1614, p. 185. Belligni, *Auctoritas e potestas*, 155 puts Gessi among De Dominis's most dangerous enemies, perhaps rightly, but her evidence is thin.

195. ACDFSO:DSO 1614, pp. 309–10. De Dominis had been trying to resign or at least have a coadjutor appointed since early 1613. Ljubić, "Prilozi," 135–36.

196. Ibid., 132n, entries for 12 and 19 April 1614.

197. ACDFSO:DSO 1614, p. 323. The witness's name is almost impossible to decipher. On his first appearance it seems to be Sleader, later it is once either Slendero, Skendero, or Shendero and another time perhaps Slenda. Ibid., p. 348 and ACDFSO:DSO 1616, p. 244.

198. ACDFSO:DSO 1614, p. 335.

199. Ibid., p. 348.

200. Ibid., p. 409.

201. Ibid., p. 498.

202. Ibid., p. 564.

203. Patterson, *Reunion of Christendom*, 228–30.

204. ACDFSO:DSO 1616, p. 26.

205. Ibid., p. 78. The notary omitted the date of Andreucci's letter.

206. Ibid., p. 119.

207. Ibid., p. 146.

208. Ibid., pp. 225–26.

209. Ibid., 1616, p. 244. For the prohibition of anonymous delations, see a decree of 19 March 1608, "S. Officium in vim litterarum sine nomine non procedit." BC, MS 2631, fo. 119r, printed in Cadène, "Collectio," 4.183, no. 1298.

210. Patterson, *Reunion of Christendom*, 232; ACDFSO:DSO 1616, pp. 460–61.

211. ACDFSO, St. st. L 3-e, fo. 45r.

212. Dispatch from the Venetian ambassador in Rome of 19 November 1616. Ljubić, "Prilozi," 149. Millini reported De Dominis's escape to the Spanish ambassador in Rome before 3 December. Lucienne van Meerbeeck, ed., *Correspondance des nonces Gesualdo, Morra, Sanseverino avec la Secrétairerie d'État pontificale (1615–1621)*, Analecta Vaticano-Belgica 2, Nonciature de Flandre (Brussels: Institut Historique Belge, 1937), 97, no. 285.

213. A copy of the Venetian edition (colophon dated 20 September) is in ACDFSO, St. st. E-6-b, fos. 469r–478v, no title page, many marginalia, endorsed twice with De Dominis's name. De Dominis, calling the book "mio manifesto," sent a copy from Heidelberg on 22 October, where the work must have been printed almost immediately since he had still been in Chur, Switzerland, on 8 October. Ljubić, "Prilozi," 153 and 148. The book sent may have been the Italian translation, called *Manifesto*, also printed at Heidelberg. Once De Dominis reached England it appeared both as *A Manifestation of the Motives, Whereupon [De Dominis] . . . Undertooke his Departure Thence [from Italy]* (London: John Bill, 1616) and in a Latin text also printed by Bill. Patterson, *Reunion of Christendom*,

233 and 376. Bellarmino got a copy of Bill's edition, sent by the general of the Discalced Carmelites. See his note of 4 March 1617 on the printed copy in ACDFSO, St. st. E-6-b, following fo. 1023r. There were at least three other editions of the book, probably all taken from the Venetian editio princeps, including the copy printed by Christoph Kraus (or Krause) at Kempten in Bavaria under the title *Epistola . . . in qua causas discessus a suo episcopatu exponit* found in ACDFSO, St. st. E-6-b, fos. 465r–468v. Another four copies of what is probably this edition are known (OCLC 257028052, Herzog August Bibliothek in Wolfenbüttel, 435.13 Theol. [13], OCLC 311690617 and 186656244), together with a straight reprint at Frankfurt with date "in fine MDCXVI anni" (VD17 23:237501M), and another reprinted at Zerbst on 20 December 1616 (colophon) (VD17 3:608034E with mistaken date of 1626; treated as a reprint by VD17, but one of the two exemplars for the entry has the colophon of Venice [VD17 3:652479F identifed as s. l. and dated 1617, as does VD17 23:249417V]), as well as what may be a variant edition: *Reverendissimi in Christo patris Marci Antonii de Dominis, archiepiscopi Spalatensis, Consilium. Caussas* [*sic*] *dicessus sui ex Italia et e Psychotyrannide Pontificis Romani exponit longe gravissimas. Excusum primo Venetijs 20. Septemb. anno 1616. Iam denuo ad primum exemplar fideliter recusum 12. Januarii anno 1617* (OCLC 257877197 and VD17 14:068313G and VD17 23:246053F). The book was again reprinted in part I of *De republica. The New Schaff-Herzog Encyclopedia of Religious Knowledge*, ed. Philip Schaff et al., 3 (New York: Funk and Wagnalls, 1909), 483. There were also four apparently independent German translations of 1617, all without publication data (VD17 3:311993B, VD17 12:113365U, VD17 14:068317N, and VD17 547:682128K), as well as French and Dutch versions, the second of which the nuncio in Flanders sent to both Rome and Venice. Ljubić, "Prilozi," 131–32. For vague references to other editions and the book's content, see Belligni, *Auctoritas e potestas*, 143–53, where she appears to take her text from another of De Dominis's works, *La pace della religione*, and Patterson, *Reunion of Christendom*, 225. The Venetians instantly accepted Gessi's request that the work be banned, on the strength of Paolo Sarpi's *consulta*. Ljubić, "Prilozi," 132n, entry for 12 November, Sarpi's opinion on 150–51.

214. ACDFSO:DSO 1616, pp. 460–61.

215. Ljubić, "Prilozi," 175. Sfondrato dispatched the ban to Venice a week later with the request that it be endorsed, as it was shortly. Ibid., 179.

216. Ibid., 151–56. This document and others printed in ibid., 151–73 and 183–84 (an extraneous proceeding against Antonio Capogrosso, another of De Dominis's numerous "nephews"; his case was ordered expedited by the Congregation on 20 December 1618, since nothing had been done in Venice or Split [ACDFSO:DSO 1618, p. 445]) as from AsVe, Santo Uffizio, b. 71. The file is probably incomplete; at least, the present gatherings cannot be put in a coherent sequence, and at least one may be missing. The *busta* includes six loose letters: 27 July 1617 from the new archbishop of Split, docketed as exhibited 17 August (173); 14 January 1617 from the bishop of Rab to Gessi, no docket (172); 23 November 1616 De Dominis from s'Gravenhage to his in-law Giovanni Bartoli, turned over to Gessi 10 January 1618 [*anno a natale*] (171–72); 22 October 1616, from Heidelberg, De Dominis to the archbishop of Split, no docket (not in "Prilozi," despite being

mentioned in Sforza Ponzone's deposition printed on 152); 22 October 1616, De Dominis from Heidelberg to Marzio De Dominis in Venice (160); De Dominis to a nephew (address torn off), Brescia, 3 October 1616, no docket (not in "Prilozi," although another such addressed to Bartoli appears in ibid., 160–61); a loose sheet with names of three witnesses, Girolamo Allegretti, archdeacon of Split, Dr. Matteo Alberti of Split, staying in the house of Giovanni Querini, bookseller at San Cassano, and Marino, canon of Split, at San Marcilian (also not in "Prilozi"). The whole *filza* is marked "Pro Urbe." Ljubić's transcriptions are reasonably accurate.

217. The first question to Ponzone called the book "il manifesto o consiglio stampato." Later a copy shown to him was described as "exemplar . . . manifesti sive consilii." Ibid., 152.

218. ACDFSO:DSO 1616, pp. 470–71; ACDFSO, St. st. L 3–e, fo. 47r.

219. Ljubić, "Prilozi," 156.

220. Ibid., 156–58 and 158–60.

221. The archbishop's given name was Pasquale, but I have not found his surname. Ibid., 172.

222. Ibid., letter of 14 January and response of 26 January 1617. Three years later Paul approved Gessi's plan to pursue both the image and De Dominis's correspondence with his relatives who venerated it. ACDFSO:DSO 1620, pp. 395–96.

223. ACDFSO:DSO 1616, pp. 477–78.

224. Ljubić, "Prilozi," 161–65.

225. Ibid., 165–68.

226. ACDFSO:DSO 1616, p. 487. Filonardi's agenda (ACDFSO, St. st. L 3-e, fos. 51r–52r) notes the report from Venice and promised "Resolutiones" on the dorse, but they appear only as a couple of scribbles.

227. Ljubić, "Prilozi," 168–69.

228. Ibid., 170.

229. ACDFSO:DSO 1616, p. 505; cf. ACDFSO, St. st. L 3-e, fo. 55r–v.

230. Ibid., p. 513, and ACDFSO, St. st. L 3-e, fos. 57r–58r.

231. Ascanio Gesualdo–Scipione Borghese, 31 December 1616. van Meerbeeck, ed., *Correspondance des nonces*, 101 and 103, nos. 298 and 301. For the context of events in Louvain and Flanders, see Bruno Boute, "Que ceulx de Flandres se disoijointe tant catholicques, et ce neantmoings les hereticques mesmes ne scauroijent faire pir. The Multiplicity of Catholicism and Roman Attitudes in the Correspondence of the Nunciature of Flanders under Paul V (1598–1621)," in *Die Aussenbeziehungen der römischen Kurie unter Paul V Borghese (1605–1621)*, ed. Alexander Koller (Tübingen: De Gruyter, 2008), 457–92.

232. ACDFSO:DSO 1617, pp. 14–15, 5 January 1617. For the Inquisition's actions via the nunciature in Cologne, see Peter Schmidt, "Inquisition und Zensur in der Kölner Nuntiatur," in Kohler, ed., *Die Aussenbeziehungen*, 409–28.

233. ACDFSO:DSO 1617, p. 32 and ACDFSO, St. st. L 3-e, fo. 65r.

234. Ibid., p. 46.

235. Ibid., pp. 67–68 and 69. Fra Giacinto committed a major blunder in approaching Rome, since it turned out to have a fat file on him for "obscene and dishonest acts of

mortification [of the flesh] done to women penitents" ("obscenis et inhonestis mortificationis factis mulieribus paenitentibus"), and Millini was ordered to summon him. When he arrived it would be decided whether to imprison him or confine him to a convent. ACDFSO:DSO 1617, pp. 157–58 and 207.

236. Unfortunately, none of the numerous texts recording their censures is dated, except that they must post-date Scaglia's promotion to cardinal. There are at least five notes of Bellarmino and Scaglia's collaboration, e.g., "Questo capitolo 12 [of *De republica*] è stato visto dal S. Card.le Bellarmino e da me. Il Card.le de Cremona" (ACDFSO, St. st. E-6-b, fo. 575r), a note that Bellarmino had asked Scaglia for his comments on some of Bellarmino's opinions (ibid., fo. 589r), another that Scaglia asked Bellarmino's views of his opinions with Bellarmino's autograph "subscribo" (ibid., fo. 755r), and a note by Scaglia that Bellarmino had reviewed his censure and added nothing to it, and that it had been exhibited in Congregation before both Paul V and Gregory XV (ibid., fo. 692r, notes on 693r–695v). It is likely that not all the censures between fos. 575r and 719v are by these two, since those on fos. 645r–648r are identified as by Padre Zaccaria, possibly da Saluzzo (see below), who may have been a theologian consultor.

237. ACDFSO:DSO 1617, p. 107 and ACDFSO, St. st. L 3-e, fos. 77r–78r, some of which is written out fair. What works were intended is unclear. It appears that De Dominis had yet to publish anything in English, or indeed anything besides the *Consilium* in 1616. Patterson, *Reunion of Christendom*, 376.

238. ACDFSO, St. st. L 3-e, fo. 79r and ACDFSO:DSO 1617, p. 119.

239. ACDFSO:DSO 1617, p. 128 and ACDFSO, St. st. L 3-e, fo. 81r.

240. ACDFSO, St. st. L 3-e, fo. 83r and ACDFSO:DSO 1617, p. 140.

241. ACDFSO:DSO 1617, pp. 150 and 153; ACDFSO, St. st. L 3-e, fo. 85r. For the equivalence in Roman practice of a *monitorium* to simple citation, see Quintiliano Mandosio, *Tractatus de monitoriis* (Rome: Giorgio Ferrari, 1581), fo. 5r. Mandosio claimed the Roman curia invented the device (fo. 9r). The document itself is now in the same volume as Filonardi's agenda, on fos. 619r–621r, headed "Copia," signed by Millini, countersigned by Notary Adriani, with a note at the foot of fo. 621r dated 2 May 1617 that the citation had been affixed [in the usual places, including the doors of St. Peter's] by Francesco Clerici, cursitor, without explanation of the delay. A few folios later comes an undated fair copy of De Dominis's excommunication for contumacy, which may never have been formally issued (see below). ACDFSO, St. st. L 3-e, fo. 626r.

242. Also noted in his sentence. Eleonora Belligni, "Sentenza e condanna postuma di Marcantonio De Dominis," *Il pensiero politico* 33:2 (2001): 265–94, 274.

243. ACDFSO:DSO 1617, p. 160.

244. Ibid., pp. 200–201. The book was Paul Boudot, *Pythagorica Marci Antonii De Dominis* (Antwerp: Gerard Woenshchate, 1617), of which the nuncio in Brussels forwarded another copy on 1 September 1617; van Meerbeeck, ed., *Correspondance des nonces*, 171, no. 507. The censor was Laurens Beyerlinck, who had also written against De Dominis. Ibid., 194, no. 571.

245. Anthony F. Allison, "The Later Life and Writings of Joseph Cresswell, S.J.

(1556–1623)," *Recusant History* 15 (1979–81): 79–144, 127; according to Allison the order dates from shortly before 30 September 1617, but it may be earlier. Cardinal Borghese acknowledged receipt of "Cresswell's" book against De Dominis already on 29 July 1617. Van Meerbeeck, ed., *Correspondance des nonces*, 156, no. 473.

246. ACDFSO:DSO 1617, p. 239.

247. Ibid., p. 283.

248. Ibid., p. 393. The book, *Profectionis Marci Antonii de Dominis, quondam Archiepiscopi Spalatensis consilium examinat*, had gone through the hands of the nuncio in Brussels. Gesualdo–Borghese, 4 March 1617. Van Meerbeeck, ed., *Correspondance des nonces*, 118, no. 349. See also no. 355, saying Bellarmino had strongly praised the work before Millini sent a long order about its treatment of the Antichrist. Rome had a high opinion of Beyerlinck, so the problem must have been solely the diffusion of an unauthorized work. Ibid., 236, no. 689. A year later the nuncio was to remind Beyerlinck to send his full-scale refutation to Rome before publication. Borghese–nuncio, 30 March 1618. Ibid., 256, no. 745. The nuncio interpreted this explicit order in his own fashion, blandly telling Borghese that he had warned Beyerlinck not to publish without his, the nuncio's, approval. Ibid., 266, no. 773. ACDFSO, St. st. E-6-b, fos. 1023ff. contains a separately bound copy with new foliation of Beyerlinck's book, with a note by Bellarmino of one line to be removed. The Inquisition's archives contain copies of two other printed attacks on De Dominis from radically different perspectives, the bishop of Durham Richard Neile's *Alter Ecebolius* (London: John Bill, 1624) in ACDFSO, St. st. E-6-b, fos. 722r–753r, separately bound, docketed probably in Notary Giovanni Antonio Tommasi's hand, and the Jesuit John Floyd's anonymously published *Hypocrisis Marci Antonii de Dominis detecta* (Antwerp: Morettus and Meursium, 1620), in the same volume following fo. 1024.

249. ACDFSO:DSO 1617, p. 429. The nuncio sent the work to the University of Louvain for censure. On 10 November 1617 Cardinal Borghese ordered him to send another copy, or at least the sections treating the Roman church; it had arrived by 18 November. Van Meerbeeck, ed., *Correspondance des nonces*, 186, 190, 192, and 196, nos. 545, 558, 565, and 577.

250. ACDFSO:DSO 1617, p. 438; added at head of ACDFSO, St. st. L 3-e, fo. 121r.

251. *R. P. Andreae Eudaemon-Ioannis Cydonii e Societate Iesu Admonitio ad lectores librorum M. Antonij de Dominis* (Cologne: Bernhard Gualter, 1619).

252. ACDFSO:DSO 1617, p. 439; ACDFSO, St. st. L 3-e, fo. 121r.

253. ACDFSO:DSO 1617, p. 472.

254. Ibid, p. 482.

255. ACDFSO:DSO 1618, p. 19. For Giudici, see *RI*, 144–45.

256. The censure was dated 15 December 1617 and may already have been in print. See Patterson, *Reunion of Christendom*, 231–32. Apparently about this same time the Index issued yet another decree against De Dominis. Borghese–Nuncio Morra, 17 March 1618, praising his efforts to execute that decree, and perhaps yet another sent to the nuncio by Bellarmino before 23 June. Van Meerbeeck, ed., *Correspondance des nonces*, 250 and 283, nos. 728 and 817.

257. ACDFSO:DSO 1618, p. 32. The notary had trouble with the peculiar entry, having to write "4.0 4.a" above the deleted "3.0 p. 4.a," which he then signed separately, the last act in the session. For the usual three-fold citation in canon law see especially X.3.4.11 and C.5.q.2.c.1 and c.2. The mistake may have arisen from confusion with the practice in some other Roman courts, among them the Camera apostolica and the governor of Rome's court, where four citations were usual. Sebastiano Guazzini, *Tractatus ad defensam inquisitorum carceratorum, reorum et condemnatorum*, 2 vols. (Lyon: Antoine Valançol, 1672), 1, 238.

258. ACDFSO:DSO 1618, p. 37. This may be an instance of the assessor checking the notary's work.

259. Ibid., pp. 97–98.

260. ACDFSO:DSO 1619, p. 236.

261. ACDFSO:DSO 1618, p. 96.

262. Ibid., p. 100.

263. Ibid., pp. 135 and 145. For Fabbri, see pp. XX ab.

264. ACDFSO:DSO 1620, p. 217.

265. Ibid., p. 309.

266. ACDFSO:DSO 1621, p. 153.

267. Ibid., p. 256. This seems not to have been the reply to De Dominis, but rather *Disputationes theologicae complectentes materiam de poenitentia, de peccato, de purgatorio, de suffragijs, de indulgentijs* (Venice: Marco Ginnami, 1623). I have not been able to identify Fabbri's attack on De Dominis. It may perhaps have been included in *Adversus impios atheos disputationes quatuor philosophicae* (Venice: Marco Ginnami, 1627), which I have not been able to read carefully.

268. ACDFSO:DSO 1624, fo. 168v, 29 October 1624.

269. ACDFSO:DSO 1625, fos. 88v, 20 May 1625 and 94v, 30 May 1625.

270. ACDFSO:DSO 1618, pp. 144–45. At that point, Louvain had finished only the first book of *De republica*. Van Meerbeeck, ed., *Correspondance des nonces*, 237, no. 683.

271. ACDFSO:DSO 1618, p. 188.

272. Ibid., p. 223, 30 June 1618, acting on the inquisitor's letter of 15 June.

273. Ibid., p. 279.

274. Ibid., p. 308.

275. Ibid., p. 340.

276. ACDFSO:DSO 1619, pp. 333 and 444 and ACDFSO:DSO 1620, p. 133. Nuncio–Borghese, Brussels, 31 August 1619. Van Meerbeeck, ed., *Correspondance des nonces*, 402, no. 1189. Borghese moved much more slowly than the Inquisition, acknowledging receipt only on 14 December. Ibid., 425, no. 1257. For Bellarmino, see also Belligni, "Sentenza e condanna," 268–69, who makes even more of his involvement, on the strength of documents in ACDFSO, St. st. E-6-b, which I have not seen. These refutations came on top of those acknowledged by Borghese on 29 September 1618 and others sent by the nuncio on 13 October 1618. Van Meerbeeck, ed., *Correspondance des nonces*, 317 and 323, nos. 920 and 936. Neither of these appears in the decree registers.

277. ACDFSO:DSO 1620, p. 400. This latest version of Louvain's refutation had arrived only shortly before this date. Borghese–nuncio, 31 October 1620. Van Meerbeeck, ed., *Correspondance des nonces*, 485, no. 1456. Perhaps in response to the latest censures, the nuncio sent another piece of the refutation on 16 January 1621. Some of them are in ACDFSO, St. st. E-6-b, fos. 238r–242v, 243r–298v (on book 4, chapters 1 and 2, with note of transmission via Borghese on 29 September 1619), 300r–313r (chapter 4), 315r–353v (book 4, chapters 6–7, with note at foot 353v "A S. Card. Millino"), and 354r–419v on chapter 8.

278. Nuncio–Ludovico Ludovisi, Brussels, 20 March 1621. Van Meerbeeck, ed., *Correspondance des nonces*, 497, no. 1494.

279. ACDFSO:DSO 1619, p. 362. http://www.servidimaria.org/en/storia/1500.htm, accessed 5 July 2008. As prior general Baglioni published a revised version of the order's rule, *Regola che diede Papa Martino V e confirmò Innocentio VIII a Fratelli, e le Sorelle della Compagnia de' Servi di Santa Maria* (Florence: Giorgio Marescotti, 1591). A Florentine, he also wrote *Tractatus de praedestinatione*, published by Marescotti in 1577 and again in 1579. More important at the moment, he was among Sarpi's numerous attackers, contributing *Apologia contro le considerationi di fra Paolo da Venezia dell'ordine de Servi* (Perugia: Vincenzo Colombara, 1606), thereby repaying Sarpi for his support when running for general. Fulgenzio Micanzio, *Vita del padre Paolo*, in Paolo Sarpi, *Istoria del Concilio tridentino* (Turin: UTET, 1974), 1294.

280. ACDFSO:DSO 1620, p. 271.

281. ACDFSO:DSO 1621, p. 304, 22 September 1621.

282. Some of the same material may have appeared in Domenico's *Catholicae praescriptiones adversus omnes veteres, et nostri temporis haereticos* (Naples: Secundini Roncalioli, 1625 and 1627), or possibly *Vox turturis seu, deflorenti usq[ue] ad nostra tempora; S.S. Benedicti, Dominici, Francisci, et aliarum sacraru[m] Religionu[m] statu*, published in Naples in 1625 and Cologne two years later, none of which I have been able to see.

283. ACDFSO:DSO 1618, pp. 218–19. The work was De Dominis's *Erste Evangelische Predigt*, a translation of his sermon on 1 Advent 1617 in the Mercers' Chapel in London, published first in the original Italian by Bill. Patterson, *Reunion of Christendom*, 237 and 376.

284. ACDFSO:DSO 1618, p. 260. For the Cologne censures, see Patterson, *Reunion of Christendom*, 232.

285. *Sorex primus Oras Chartarum primi libri De Republica Ecclesiastica* [... *Archiepiscopi Spalatensis corrodens Leonardus Marius Theologaster Coloniensis*] (London: [John Bill], 1618). The supposititious author was Daniel Lohetus, Burgundus Laudonensis, identified further as "eiusdem D. Spalatensis Amanuensi." Its target, Leonardus Marius, was also archpriest of Amsterdam and a major figure in efforts to reconvert the Dutch provinces, who wrote two full-scale confutations of De Dominis. Johann Friedrich von Schulte, *Die Geschichte der Quellen und Literatur der Canonischen Rechts*, 3 vols. (Stuttgart: Ferdinand Enke, 1875), 1, 174n; and Willem Frijhoff and Marijke Spies, *Dutch Culture in a European Perspective: 1650: Hard-Won Unity* (Assen: Van Gorcum, 2004), 384. The Spanish

ambassador, the conde de Gondomar, had a copy of the book. http://avisos.realbiblioteca.es/?p=article&aviso=50&art=947, accessed 5 July 2008.

286. ACDFSO:DSO 1619, pp. 97, 325, 457; ACDFSO:DSO 1620, p. 57.

287. ACDFSO:DSO 1620, pp. 57, 133, and 155–56. The nuncio in Brussels sent word of the book's appearance on 9 November 1619. Van Meerbeeck, ed., *Correspondance des nonces*, 416, no. 1230. De Dominis was involved in preparing it for the press and added a dedication and polemical subtitle to it. Patterson, *Reunion of Christendom*, 247–88.

288. ACDFSO:DSO 1620, p. 159.

289. Cresswell saw the work through the press in Antwerp, but it was written by John Floyd. Allison, "Creswell," 128. It encountered difficulties with the Jesuit general as well, who seems not to have known about either the Inquisition's or Borghese's moves until after the book came out.

290. Allison, "Creswell," 128 and 129.

291. I base this inference on General Vitelleschi's letter to Creswell of 5 December 1620, saying he was glad "to see the copies of the letter of the cardinals" allowing printing of the book. Allison, "Creswell," 129. As Allison well says, "There seems to have been an extraordinary muddle over the whole affair."

292. ACDFSO:DSO 1620, p. 213.

293. Allison, "Creswell," 129 and ACDFSO:DSO 1620, p. 285.

294. ACDFSO:DSO 1621, pp. 260–61.

295. ACDFSO:DSO 1622, pp. 18–19. There is a copy of this breve in "De reditu D. M. Ant. de Dominis Archiepiscopi Spalatensis ex Anglia Romam, Brevis Commentarius cum Notis," Bibliothèque de l'Arsenale, Paris, MS 4111, pp. 30–68 (written on one side of the sheet only), pp. 48–52, (mis?)dated 8 January 1622. It was written by Giovanni Ciampoli. I am grateful to Brown Patterson for lending me his microfilm of this manuscript.

296. ACDFSO:DSO 1621–1622, fo. 213v.

297. Giovanni-Francesco Guidi di Bagno–Millini, Brussels, 14 May 1622. Bernard de Meester, ed., *Correspondance du nonce Giovanni-Francesco Guidi di Bagno*, Analecta Vaticano-Belgica, ser. 2, Nonciature de Flandre (Brussels and Rome: Institut Historique Belge, 1938), 194, no. 365.

298. Bibliothèque de l'Arsenale, Paris, MS 4111, pp. 13–18 for the preliminaries, followed by De Dominis's abjuration on 19–21, Millini's letter on 21–23, and the absolution on 24–25. The whole purports to be a copy of the judicial transcript.

299. ACDFSO:DSO 1621–1622, fo. 231r, 11 August 1622.

300. Guidi di Bagno–Millini, Brussels, 24 September 1622. He had already reported to the secretary of state on 27 August. De Meester, ed., *Correspondance de Guidi di Bagno*, 239, no. 463 and 253, no. 489.

301. ACDFSO:DSO 1621–1622, fo. 257r. Troiano Boccalini has Urban personally conduct De Dominis into the meeting and take part in a long discussion about what penance to assign him. Urban rejected rigorous treatment, saying he did not wish to act as Pius IV did against [Pietro] Carnesecchi. Ljubić, "Prilozi," 249. If we can trust this report, and the

pope's number is not a slip of the pen, either Boccalini's or Urban's history was sadly deficient, since Pius IV ordered the Inquisition to release Carnesecchi, who was executed later on the orders of his successor, Pius V. Massimo Firpo and Dario Marcatto, eds., *I processi inquisitoriali di Pietro Carnesecchi (1557–1567)*, 2 vols. in 4 parts (Vatican City: Archivio Segreto Vaticano, 1998-2000), 1, introduction.

302. ACDFSO:DSO 1621–1622, fo. 258v.

303. Ibid., fo. 261r.

304. Ibid., fo. 269r, 14 December 1622 and ACDFSO:DSO 1623, pp. 146–47, 26 April 1623. The pension turned into the usual long drawn-out affair. See ACDFSO:DSO 1623, fo. 30v. Perhaps especially once De Dominis died, even the pope had trouble getting the arrears. ACDFSO:DSO 1624, fo. 180v, 22 November 1624.

305. E.g., Dillingen: Ulrich Rem, 1623 (VD17 12:118042P) and a German translation (VD17 23:234829P); see also OCLC 36566846 and 311652445, etc. It was also included in Abraham Bzowski, *Annalium ecclesiasticorum post illustriss. et reverendiss. Caesarem Baronium [libri]*, 18 (Cologne: Heir of Anton Boëtzer, 1627), p. 170. See the summaries in Patterson, *Reunion of Christendom*, 251–52 and Malcolm, *De Dominis*, 76–77 who thinks De Dominis tried at first to give the Inquisitors a version of his letter to Hall, but they demanded more.

306. ACDFSO, St. st. E-6-b, fos. 479r–510v, dated Rome, 24 November 1622, with a fair number of corrections and deletions, also marginal headings, perhaps the earliest version; three other copies in ACDFSO, St. st. E-6-b, fos. 515r–524v, 525r–549v and 553r–571r, with autograph (?) corrections; and a fair copy with a few corrections, also dated Rome, 24 November 1622, in ACDFSO, St. st. LL-5-g, fos. 199r–223v.

307. ASV, Sec. Brev. Reg. 667, fos. 30r–33v. The note at the foot "Reg. fol. 109" does not correspond to the decree register in ACDFSO. There is a slightly reworked copy on fo. 30r–v.

308. The breve register contains another such in better shape on fo. 39r.

309. ACDFSO:DSO 1623, p. 84.

310. ACDFSO:DSO 1624, fo. 22v. He was also allowed to dedicate his *Euripus seu de fluxu et refluxu maris* (Rome: Apud Andream Paeum [*sic*; *recte* Fei], 1624) to Francesco Barberini. See Bonelli and Russo, "Crisogono," 392.

311. ACDFSO:DSO 1624, fos. 22v and 55r, added at foot of previous folio with insertion mark as first item of business.

312. Patterson, *Reunion of Christendom*, 256, citing *Newes from Rome, Spalato's Doome* (London: Richard Whitaker, 1624). Ljubić, "Prilozi," 253n gives the same date without a source. For De Dominis's return to Rome and trial, see Malcolm, *De Dominis*, 75–78; he dates the arrest 18 April, citing a Venetian dispatch.

313. Urban "deputavit in commissione huiusmodi causae cum assistentia tum offerabant (?) officii Ill.m Card.em de Cremona [Scaglia], eidemque dedit omnem auctoritatem, et potestatem necessarias et oportunas creandi notarium (?) ad sui placitum examinan. testes, ac eundem Archiep.m, aliosque complices constituendi (?), et in causa seu causis huiusmodi cum illarum dependen. emergen. annexis (?), et connexis (?) tam contra eundem Archep.m, quam contra alios quoscunque processus et (?) informationes usque ad

sentententiam diffinitivam." ACDFSO:DSO 1624, fo. 69v. See also Bzowski, *Annalium*, 18, 172. The bibliography of this volume is tangled, but the two copies I consulted in the Cambridge University Library, Peterborough A.9.18- and 6.8.32-, at least had the same volume number and pagination. The second has an erratum slip not in the first.

314. E.g., Bzowski, *Annalium*, 18, 172. According to Eudaemon-Johannes, "Additum etiam, ut unus e Cardinalibus Sacrae Inquisitionis prepositis reo de more interrogando praeesset." "Epistola, quam de relapsu ac morte poenaque M. Antonii de Dominis Ingolstadium [narrat]" in Georg Stenghel, *Libri duo de duobus apostatis sive duae paraeneses* . . . (Ingolstadt: Gregor Hänlin, 1627), book 2, chapter 36 (556–64), 558. Bzowski's text is virtually identical to the "Relazione" (her title) that Belligni found in and printed from ACDFSO, St. st. LL-5-g, along with another copy in St. st. E-6-b(3) (271–22, cited inaccurately without folio references for either, which for the first should be 180r–181v [tag at foot 181v] and 192r–198r). These two are in Latin. Most of the Dominican Bzowski's account, often word-for-word and with proper credit, was taken over in Philip van Limborch, *Historia inquisitionis* (Amsterdam: Heinrich Wetstenius, 1692), 361–63. Belligni, although noting that his text and the "Relazione" "coincide substantially," appears to doubt that Bzowski authored the account in his volume. "Sentenza," 266n. If he did not, it is possible that the author was Eudaemon-Johannes, although his account does not much resemble Bzowski's, without introducing significant variations in substance. He may well have been a participant in the trial as one of the shadowy theologian consultors. The final source, the only one in Italian, also contains similar content, "Memoriale di quanto s'è passato nella congregatione dell'illustrissimi e reverendissimi cardinali et inquisitori il giorno di san Tomaso nella chiesa della Minerva addi XXI. decembre [*sic*] 1624, secondo che s'è potuto ricordarsene." Bibliothèque de l'Arsenale, Paris, MS 4111, pp. 73–84, printed in Ljubić, "Prilozi," 215–19. There are other descriptions, e.g., the anonymous *A Relation Sent from Rome of the Processe, Sentence and Execution done Upon the Body, Picture and Books of Marcus Antonius de Dominis . . . Published by Command* (London: John Bill, [1624]; I am grateful to Anne Schutte for sending me a copy of this pamphlet), and Troiano Boccalini's long, undated letter to Muzio Pasti (Ljubić, "Prilozi," 219–60). The English pamphlet focuses only on the execution of the sentence and adds nothing significant to the other versions. Boccalini's letter is not of much value. It contains a number of errors, including in dates, as well as undocumented assertions, such as that De Dominis was imprisoned by the Inquisition during Urban's sede vacante in 1623 (253), the list of charges is mostly invented (253–54), Commissary Lanci was not new in his job but had held it for three years (257), Cardinal Leni was never an Inquisitor and therefore could not have defended De Dominis (257), nor was De Dominis's body condemned to be burnt the day after his death (258), etc. The "Lettera di F[rater]. M. [Marcantonio] Cappello . . . ad un religioso amico suo" (ACDFSO, St. st. E-6-b, fos. 421r–463av, "no. 19" separately bound) dated 1 March 1625 is not a narration but a theological attack.

315. ACDFSO:DSO 1624, fo. 91v. It would have been in this period that the charge of "feigned abjuration" would probably have come up, so Redondi's otherwise undocumented assertion cannot be completely disproven. The "Relazione" claimed that Urban sat in on at

least some of De Dominis's interrogations, which would be the only such instance I have come across. Ljubić, "Prilozi," 216–17.

316. ACDFSO:DSO 1624, fo. 73v.

317. Ibid.,, fo. 88r.

318. Malcolm, *De Dominis*, 79 citing a letter of 12 July. According to Belligni, *Auctoritas*, 269, the record of De Dominis's interrogation on 4 June 1624 is in ACDFSO, St. st. C 3-4, fasc. XIII, but there is no codex with that number and I have not been able to determine the correct collocation.

319. ACDFSO:DSO 1624, fo. 94v. Since Micanzio had succeeded Sarpi as theologian consultor, the result of their inquiry was a foregone conclusion.

320. ACDFSO:DSO 1624, fo. 98r. The content of De Dominis's opinion is unknown, but he was accused of believing that the only ground for ecclesiastical dissolution of marriage was adultery. On the other hand, he argued that a secular prince could dissolve a marriage for any reason at all. "Memoriale di quanto s'è passato" printed in Ljubić, "Prilozi," 215–19. De Dominis's letter to Joseph Hall, then dean of Worcester and later bishop of Exeter, contained much the same content as his *Sui reditus* and "Retractationum." It was not published until 1666 as *De pace religionis*. Patterson, *Reunion of Christendom*, 252. De Dominis had tried to issue it in Antwerp during his passage to Rome, but the nuncio had denied a license. Bibliothèque de l'Arsenale, Paris, MS 4111, p. 56. For the Gonzaga annulment, see Paul F. Grendler, *The University of Mantua, the Gonzaga, and the Jesuits, 1584–1630* (Baltimore: Johns Hopkins University Press, 2009), 229–30.

321. Belligni, "Sentenza," 286 and Bzowski, *Annalium*, 18, 172. Redondi, *Heretic/Eretico* (117/147), cited Eudeamon-Johannes rather than Bzowski, but they say almost exactly the same thing.

322. ACDFSO:DSO 1624, fos. 99v–100r.

323. Ibid., fo. 101v.

324. Ibid., fo. 110r.

325. Ibid., fo. 122v. As of 10 October Pianigrani was imprisoned in Rome. Ibid., fo. 159v.

326. Ibid., fos. 124r and 152v (noting payment of 12 *scudi* to him). The first decree but not the second gives the printer's name as Andrea Fui, instead of Fei. For him and his press in Bracciano see "La stamperia di Andrea Fei nella Bracciano del Seicento," *La Voce del Lago* 20 (November 2003), http://www.lavocedellago.it/n20/pag10.htm, accessed 5 July 2008.

327. Mario Guiducci–Galileo, Rome, 6 September 1624. *EN*, 13, no. 1661.

328. ACDFSO:DSO 1624, fo. 133r.

329. Ibid., fo. 141r.

330. Faber–Galileo, 14 September 1624. *EN*, 13, no. 1664. Bzowski, *Annalium*, 18, 174 (cf. the anonymous "Relazione," 291) stressed Urban's solicitude for De Dominis in his last illness. The list in Bibliothèque de l'Arsenale, Paris, MS 4111, p. 70 says the autopsy was conducted by Giovanni Girolamo, surgeon of [the hospital of] Santo Spirito, in the presence of Mancini, Francesco Barberini's physician Taddeo Colliesta, Demetrio Canevari,

"medico di Borgo," Marcantonio Luciani, "medico di S. Spirito," Faber, and the French physician Joseph Truglion, as well as the notary of the Holy Office and others.

331. Bzowski, *Annalium*, 18, 174 and "Relazione," 291.

332. ACDFSO:DSO 1624, fo. 157v. The date is ambiguous, since the arabic numeral appears to be "8," but the day of the week is "feria quarta," Wednesday, which was 9 October.

333. *Dn. Seraphini Olivarii Razzalii . . . Decisiones aureae* (Frankfurt: "e Collegio musarum novenarum Paltheniano," 1615) and *Thedosii Rubei Privernatis I. C. Romani Singularia ex Sacrae Rotae Romanae decisionibus selecta*, 2 vols. (Rome: Ex Typographia Vaticana, 1637), probably reprinted in Sigismondo Scaccia, *Tractatus de appellationibus . . . cum annotationibus omnium singularium eiusdem Rotae Romanae decerptis ex tractatu nouissimo Theodosii Rubei, i.c.r.* (Venice: Torrino, 1642; also Venice: Bertano, 1667). I have not been able to confirm Rossi's theology degree.

334. Ugo Baldini, "The Academy of Mathematics of the Collegio Romano from 1555 to 1612" in Mordechai Feingold, ed., *Jesuit Science and the Republic of Letters* (Cambridge, Mass.: MIT Press, 2003), 47–98, 81n35 and http://www.imss.fi.it/news/emeridborro.html, accessed 7 February 2008. His astronomical and mathematical works include *Tabulae 12. ad elevationem poli graduum 42* (Rome: Luigi Zanetti, 1593); *Diario perpetuo di Theodosio Rossi da Piperno* [*sic*]. *Per il polo elevato gradi 39.42. & 45. qual serve quasi per tutta l'Italia* (Rome: Luigi Zanetti, 1602); and *Horarium universale perpetuum in universo terrarum orbe* (Rome: Ex Typographia Vaticana, 1637). The papal copyright was Rossi's reward for agreeing to defend De Dominis; it was granted on 28 November 1624. Why the book remained unpublished for thirteen years is a mystery. Rossi defended Clavius's views on the Gregorian calendar in *Admonitio pro Christophoro Clavio adversus Francisci Vietae expostulationem* (Rome: n.p., 1603) and referred approvingly to them in *Horarium*, 88.

335. *Soliloquii scritturali, raccolti in piu volte dalla profonda dottrina del revererendissimo padre maestro Filippo Gesualdo de Castrovillari, ministro generale dell'Ordine min. Con. di S. Francesco, da fra Bonaventura Passero di Nola maestro in theologia, & regente nel studio di Milano* (Milan: Pacifico Ponzio, 1595), and *Prediche del molto reverendo padre maestro Bonaventura Passero da Nola minore conventuale* (Naples: Tarquinio Longo, 1605). The books approved by him as regent were *Ufficio della gloriosissima Vergine Maria . . . Rivista dal R.P.M. Buonaventura Passero da Nola* (Rome: Giacomo Mascardi, 1618), and *Pinacotheca selecta praecipuarum conclusionum, ac quaestionum diversas materias continentium. In Collegio seraphico almae Urbis ex doctrina Scoti discussarum sub auspiciis adm. R.P. Mag. Bonaventurae Passeri nolani . . . Tomus primus, De scientia Dei* (Rome: Giacomo Mascardi, 1621).

336. ACDFSO:DSO 1624, fos. 176r, 7 November 1624 and 174v, 6 November. On 22 November, Urban ordered the Inquisador mayor told the man was not De Dominis's accomplice. Ibid., fo. 180r.

337. Ibid., fo. 183v, 21 November 1624. The engraved portrait of De Dominis, ACDFSO, St. st. E-6-b, fo. 654r, does not correspond to the image at the execution described in ACDFSO, St. st. LL-5-g. It may be the missing frontispiece of *De republica* in ACDFSO, St. st. E-6-b, following fo. 1022, not refoliated.

338. ACDFSO:DSO 1624, fo. 198v.

339. Both are fair copies: 1) ACDFSO, St. st. E-6-b, fos. 655r–666v, signed by Tommasi but probably not in his hand, including faked signatures of the cardinals, and 2) ACDFSO, St. st. LL-5-g, fos. 182r–190v, in another hand. The second is printed in Belligni, "Sentenza," 273–81. Most of the substance of the sentence is reproduced in compressed form in "Memoriale" (Ljubić, "Prilozi," 215–19) and reasonably accurately in the anonymous *A Relation Sent from Rome*.

340. Belligni, "Sentenza," 275–76.

341. Belligni, "Sentenza," 291. The Inquisitors feared that De Dominis's abjuration might be simulated, given his past behavior. This fear might have given rise to Redondi's theory that the Congregation considered a charge of "simulated abjuration."

342. Belligni, "Sentenza," 281.

343. ACDFSO:DSO 1625, fos. 7v–8r.

344. "Caeteris vero communicare tamen possint capita quaedam sententiae illis transmittenda, nullo tamen modo copiam sententiae alicui concedant, neque ipsi pro se retineant, sed sub excommunicationis poena teneantur copiam sententiae quae illis transmittitur intra quindecim dies postquam Romam redierint a munere nunciaturae in hoc S. Officio consignare." ACDFSO:DSO 1625, fo. 2r.

345. Ibid., fo. 11r.

346. Guidi di Bagno–Millini, 6 December 1625. De Meester, ed., *Correspondance de Guidi di Bagno*, 684, no. 1441. The nuncio had tried to lay his hands on the baggage in September 1624. Ibid., 535, no. 1121.

CHAPTER 5. FLORENCE I

1. Adriano Prosperi has done the basic work on the Inquisition in Tuscany. *L'Inquisizione romana, letture e ricerche* (Rome: Edizioni di Storia e Letteratura, 2003). See also his *Tribunali della coscienza: inquisitori, confessori, missionari* (Turin: Einaudi, 1996), 75–83 and summary in *DSI* 2: 605–7, and for the nuncio's role 2: 1121, which implicitly underplays the office's importance.

2. John Tedeschi, "The Dispersed Archives of the Roman Inquisition," in *The Prosecution of Heresy: Collected Studies on the Inquisition in Early Modern Italy* (Binghamton, N.Y.: Medieval and Renaissance Texts and Studies, 1991), 23–45, 39–40. Edward L. Goldberg has reconstructed another case on the basis of correspondence in the ASF, Fondo mediceo del principato. *Jews and Magic in Medici Florence: The Secret World of Benedetto Blanis* (Toronto: University of Toronto Press, 2011).

3. Prosperi, *DSI* 2: 605–7.

4. See the list in Pietro Antonio Ribetti, *Giardino serafico istorico* (Venice: Lovisa, 1710), 1, 648. It has two errors, introducing one Francesco Moro da Monte Granario in 1604 in the middle of Lelio Medici's tenure and misdating the beginning of Cornelio Priatoni's to 1606.

5. Giovanni Luisetto, ed., *Archivio Sartori: documenti di storia e arte francescana*, 4 vols. (Padua: Biblioteca Antoniana, Basilica del Santo, 1983–), 2:2, 1650.

6. Euro Puletti, http://www.montecucco.pg.it/Costacciaro_not_corriere_umbria/Costacciaro_art_fr%C3%A0_ dionisio_sammattei.htm, accessed 18 June 2012. Puletti's work is not entirely reliable. For example, he confuses Costacciaro with "Dionisio Fiorentino," a Servite. See the permissions for Silvano Razzi, *Delle vite de' santi e beati Toscani*, 2 (Florence: Cosimo Giunti, 1601). As inquisitor Costacciaro gave the imprimatur 26 September 1580 for Sebastiano Medici, *Summa omnium haeresum et catalogus schismaticorum, haereticorum, et idolatrarum* (Florence: Sermartelli, 1581). But he also gave another license, solely as friar, almost exactly a year later on 27 September 1581, for Andrea Cesalpino, *De plantis* (Florence: Marescotti, 1583). It may be that there is an error in year date for the second of these. There is no entry for Costacciaro in *DSI*.

7. Giovanni Franchini, *Bibliosofia e memorie letterarie di scrittori Francescani conventuali ch'hanno scritto dopo l'anno 1585* (Modena: Soliani, 1693), 385.

8. Franco Cardini, ed., *Goztanza, la strega di San Miniato* (Bari: Laterza, 1989), passim; and see Christopher F. Black, *The Italian Inquisition* (New Haven, Conn.: Yale University Press, 2009), 209 and 239–40.

9. ADCFSO:DSO 1597–1598–1599, p. 715.

10. ADCFSO:DSO 1603 Copia, fo. 226r. Puletti says Matteo was chancellor, which may be a mistake, http://www.montecucco.pg.it/Univ_d_uomini_origi_/Cenni_sulle_ant_fami_condomini.htm, accessed 18 June 2012.

11. Franchini, *Bibliosofia*, 383–86.

12. ACDFSO:DSO 1602, fo. 211v/Copia fo. 213r; and see Franchini, *Bibliosofia*, 385. He was serving in Pisa as of 1582. Franco Paliaga, "Le collezione [*sic*] private e il mercato dei dipinti a Pisa nel Seicento," http://municipalia.sns.it/assets/files/contributi/contributicaricati/ franco_paliaga_pubblicato.pdf, accessed 18 June 2012. According to Luke Wadding et al., eds., *Annales Minorum: seu Trium Ordinum a S. Francisco institutorum . . . Continuatio*, 23 (Ancona: G. S. Cherubini, 1859), 335 he also became inquisitor of Siena in 1599.

13. ASV, Sec. Brev. Reg. 337, fo. 277r–v. Prosperi, "Firenze," *DSI* 2: 606 mistakenly says appointment by breve began in 1639.

14. ACDFSO:DSO Copia 1604–1605, p. 57.

15. Ibid., p. 59.

16. Ibid., pp. 211 and 254.

17. Meetings of 4, 8, 14 and 15 July 1604. Ibid., pp. 269, 275, 282 and 288.

18. Ibid., pp. 764–75.

19. *Discorso dell P. M. Lelio Medici Piacentino Min. Conv. Inquisitore generale di Firenze e suo dominio sopra i fondamenti, e le ragioni delli SS. Veneziani, per le quali pensano di essere scusati della disubbidienza, che fanno alle censure, & interdetto della Santità di Nostro Signor Papa Paolo Quinto* (Bologna: G. B. Bellagamba, 1606), dedicated to the Venetian patrician Antonio Querini on 13 November 1606.

20. ACDFSO:DSO 1609, p. 7 and 1608–1609, fo. 266v.

21. Between 14 January and 7 February 1609. ACDFSO:DSO 1609, pp. 23 and 60 and 1–2.

22. Jean Baptiste de Tillier, *Historique de la Vallée d'Aoste* (1737; 2nd ed. Aoste: Louis Mensio, 1888), 171–72.

23. Franchini, *Bibliosofia*, 598–99. Other than noting Priatoni's service in Florence, Franchini said nothing else about him.

24. BEM:RC, MS 'Y.O.4.26, fo. 10r; and Michele Cioni, *I documenti galileiani del S. Uffizio di Firenze* (Florence: Giampiero Pagnini, 1996; reprint of Florence 1908 ed.), 1 for the degree.

25. ACDFSO:DSO 1607, fo. 179r, garbled as inquisitor of Pisa transferred to Florence 1607 in Luke Wadding, *Annales minorum . . . Continuatio*, ed. Stanislao Melchiorri, 24 (Ancona: Gustavo Sartori Cherubini, 1860), 233.

26. BEM:RC, MS 'Y.O.4.26, fo. 10r. The date is of Priatoni's deputatization transmitted by Secretary Pompeo Arrigoni.

27. Cioni, *Documenti*, 1–3. It is curious that at the same time he also swore "faithfully to exercise the office of inquisitor of this city," an office he certainly already held even though the appointment is not recorded in the decree registers.

28. Christian Wieland, *Fürsten, Freunde, Diplomaten. Die römisch-florentinischen Beziehungen unter Paul V. (1605–1621)* (Cologne: Böhlau, 2004; Norm und Struktur, 20), 365 citing ASF:AMP 3328, 2 and 8 November 1613, unfoliated.

29. ACDFSO:DSO 1614, pp. 34 and 31.

30. Wieland, *Fürsten*, 365.

31. Ibid., 366, citing ASF:AMP, 3329, fos. 596r–v and 620r–v and 3330, unfoliated. The ambassador mistakenly claimed that not even the king of Spain had the right to remove inquisitors. When Cosimo tried to eject the inquisitor of Pisa in 1616, his ambassador to the pope called it "such a new pretension, so unusual, and I believe so dangerous." Ibid., 367, citing his letter of 17 June 1616 in ASF:AMP 3331, unfoliated.

32. After a reading of his letter of 30 December 1614. ACDFSO:DSO 1615, p. 31.

33. Ibid., p. 282. *DV*, XLIIn says his tenure ended in 1614, citing ACDFSO St. st. 2-II-1, fos. 20r and 23r. Wadding's continuator gives the date of Marzari's nomination as 4 July, but that is probably another of his innumerable mistakes. Stanislao Melchiorri de Cerreto, *Annales Minorum, seu Trium Ordinum a S. Francisco institutorum . . . Continuatio*, 25 (Ad Claras Aquas-Quaracchi: Collegio de San Bonaventura, n.d.), 160.

34. Wieland, *Fürsten*, 367, citing ASF:AMP 3331, unfoliated, letter of 10 June 1615.

35. *DV*, no. 10.

36. *DV*, no. 11.

37. Franchini, *Bibliosofia*, 245–46. The rest of Franchini's entry reverses the sequence of Marzari's inquisitorial posts and gets their dates wrong. He also mistakenly says Marzari died in 1618.

38. ACDFSO:DSO 1608–1609, fo. 481r (called Alessandro, name corrected to Lelio but not in ACDFSO:DSO 1609, p. 473) and 1608–1609, fo. 513v.

39. ACDFSO:DSO 1610–1611, fo. 401v, a note at the end of a meeting that Secretary Arrigoni had told "me, the assessor" of the appointment.

40. Ibid., fo. 427v. See also Università di Pisa, Commissione rettorale per la storia dell'Università di Pisa, *Storia dell'Università di Pisa: 1343–1737*, 2 vols. (Pisa: Pacini, 2000), 1:2, 541.

41. ACDFSO:DSO 1612, pp. 463 and 504.

42. ACDFSO:DSO 1615, p. 14, 2 January 1615.

43. The book was *Donellus Enucleatus, sive Commentarii Hugonis Donelli de iure civili in compendium ita redacti* (Jena: Christoph Lippoldt and Heinrich Rauchmaul, 1610–1613; VD 17 23:000125V; and many subsequent editions). *DV*, 47.

44. *DV*, 22.

45. ACDFSO:DSO 1615, p. 444, 5 September 1615. *EN*, 20, p. 477 mistakenly kept Marzari at Pisa until 1617.

46. *EN*, 20, no. 1140bis and Cioni, *Documenti*, no. VIII; *DV*, no. 15, a passage from Marzari's letter of 15 November covering the transcripts which Pagano mistakenly assigned to Priatoni; and ACDFSO:DSO 1615, pp. 542 and 544 (*EN*, 19, 278 and *DV*, no. 122). The depositions are nos. 16 and 17.

47. ACDFSO:DSO 1616, p. 75.

48. Ibid., p. 86.

49. Ibid., p. 197.

50. Ibid., p. 331.

51. ACDFSO:DSO 1617, pp. 55 and 58.

52. Ibid., p. 208.

53. Ibid., pp. 290–91; and Philip van Limborch, *Historia inquisitionis* (Amsterdam: Heinrich Wetstenius, 1692), bk. 3, c. 18, 226–27. The reason may have been that such persons made themselves ipso facto guilty. As Limborch's discussion shows, the Holy Office soon changed its mind. For the ineluctable place of citation in the Roman Inquisition trial process, see *RI*, 177–80.

54. *RI*, 171–77.

55. ACDFSO:DSO 1618, pp. 311 and 328.

56. Ibid., p. 370, 24 October 1618. The permission was repeated on 12 February 1619. ACDFSO:DSO 1619, p. 68. For his name, see Ribetti, *Giardino serafico*, 1, 648.

57. ACDFSO:DSO 1619, p. 355.

58. ACDFSO:DSO 1620, pp. 170, 13 May 1620 (inquisitor), 234 (vicar), and 274 (results).

59. ACDFSO:DSO 1621, pp. 341 (appointment) and 353 (his sobriquet is illegible in the first entry).

60. *Bibliosofia*, 263 and 444 and *HC* 4: 115–16, noting his death before 8 January 1631. Masserotti must not have been pleased by his promotion, since he was not consecrated bishop until 15 March 1629.

61. ACDFSO:DSO 1621, p. 409, 14 December 1621; and ACDFSO:DSO 1621–1622, fo. 248r, 12 October 1622.

62. Ibid., fo. 235r, 18 August 1622.

63. Archivio di Santa Maria Novella, Florence, MS I.B.68 "Copialettere dell'Inquisizione di Firenze ordinato dal R. P. M. Michele Messerotto da Bologna dei Minimi Conventuali della stessa città, Inquisitor Generale di Firenze nel dì 7 dicembre 1621." http://smn.it/polis/guerrini.htm accessed 21 June 2012.

64. ACDFSO:DSO 1627, fo. 1v, 29 December 1626.

65. Sigismondo da Venezia, *Biografia serafica degli uomini illustri che fiorirono nel Francescano istituto* (Venice: G.B. Merlo, 1846), 610; Luke Wadding, ed. José Maria Ribeiro da Fonseca, *Annales Minorum seu trium ordinum a S. Francisco institutorum: 1628–1632* (Quaracchi: [Ad claras aquas], 1934), 350, and Luigi Caratelli, *Manuale dei Novizi e Professi chierici e laici Minori Conventuali sopra la Regola, le Costituzioni, le memorie e le funzioni* (Rome: Tipografia Vaticana, 1897), 297.

66. Germana Ernst, "Cristianesimo e religione naturale. Le censure all'*Atheismus triumphatus* di Tommaso Campanella," *Nouvelles de la République des Lettres* 1–2 (1989): 137–200, 140.

67. Giovanni Giacinto Sbaralea, *Supplementum et castigatio ad scriptores trium ordinum S. Francisci a Waddingo aliisve descriptos; cum adnotationibus ad Syllabum matyrum eorundem ordinum* (Rome: Lino Contedini, 1806), 497.

68. The letter is headed "Al P. Fra Clemente Inquis. di Fiorenza nuovo." BAV, Barb. lat. 6334, fo. 358v. *DV*, p. CXVIII says he became inquisitor in November 1626, without a citation.

69. Egidi came from Montefalco. Filippo Baldinucci, *Notizie de' professori del disegno da Cimabue* (Florence: G. B. Stecchi and Anton Giuseppe Pagani, 1771), 96n.

70. See the imprimaturs dated 15 October 1635 for two books by Jacopo Gaddi, *Adlocutiones et elogia exemplaria, cabalistica, oratoria, mixta sepulcralia* (Florence: Pietro Nesti, 1636) and *Corollarium poeticum scil. poematia, notae, explicationes allegorice olim conscriptae* (Florence: Pietro Nesti, 1636). His successor, "Fr. Io. [Giovanni Mauri dalla Pratta di Perugia]," gave the imprimatur for Jean Comte, *Vita e miracoli del glorioso prencipe San Fiacrio* (Florence: Pietro Nesti, 1636; IT\ICCU\BVEE\073698) which Émile Picot, *Les français italianisants au XVIe siècle* (Paris: H. Champion, 1907), 2, 336 mistakenly assigned to Egidi.

71. Biblioteca Angelica, Rome, MS D. 4. 11, fos. 15–36. Enrico Narducci, *Catalogus codicum manuscriptorum, praeter graecos et orientales, in Bibliotheca Angelica olim coenobii Sancti Augustini de Urbe* (Rome: Ludovico Cecchini, 1892), 200. This MS makes it unlikely that Egidi could have born as late as 1575 as Pagano says. *DV*, CXVIII.

72. Bonaventura Marinangeli, "Descrizione e memorie della chiesa e del convento di San Francesco in Montefalco," *Miscellanea Francescana* 14/15 [1913]: 129–52, 150; and Egidi's imprimatur for Bartholomeus Senensis, *De vita et moribus beati Stephani Maconi Senensis Cartusiani . . . libri quinque* ([Siena]: H. de Goris, 1626).

73. Marinangeli, "Descrizione," 132.

74. Some of his correspondence as inquisitor is supposed to be in "Registro di lettere degli inquisitori generali O.F.M. di Firenze alla Congregatione del S. Uffizio" in the archive of Santa Maria Novella in Florence. *DV*, p. CXVIII, citing Emilio Panella, "Catalogo

dell'archivio di Santa Maria Novella in Firenze," *Archivum Fratrum Praedicatorum* 70 (2000): 191–92. This may be a mistake for Archivio di S.ta Maria Novella, MS I.B.68 (see note 63). For Egidi's involvement in Galileo's trial, see *DV*, passim.

75. ACDFSO:DSO 1632, fo. 118r–v.

76. ACDFSO:DSO 1633, fos. 75v and 82r, 4 and 19 May; ibid., fo. 157r; and Egidi–Antonio Barberini, Sr., 17 September 1633. *DV*, nos. 146 and 72. The reading of this letter does not appear in the decree registers.

77. See *RI*, 210–13 for one of the best examples of success, Girolamo Vecchietti.

78. It may be that his name should be Israele, as it was given in the case of his daughter Ioseffe, but that may be her married name. ACDFSO:DSO, Copia 1604–1605, p. 237. For the problem of Jewish surnames in Florence, see Goldberg, *Jews*, 313–14.

79. For Valori, see Salvino Salvini, *Fasti consolati dell'Accademia Fiorentina* (Florence: Gaetano Tartini and Santi Franchi, [1717]), 169–79, 282–87, and 669, and Mark Jurdjevic, *Guardians of Republicanism: The Valori Family in the Florentine Renaissance* (Oxford: Oxford University Press, 2008), passim.

80. ACDFSO:DSO 1602, pp. 603–4 and 600.

81. ACDFSO:DSO 1603, fos. 13r and 17r.

82. For the pope's appeal, see the nuncio's report of 30 September 1602 in ASV, Seg. Stato, Nunz. Firenze, 14A, fos. 302r–303v. ACDFSO:DSO 1603 Copia, fo. 241v, 23 October 1603.

83. ACDFSO:DSO Copia 1604–1605, p. 127.

84. Ibid., pp. 165 and 171, 27 and 29 April 1604.

85. Ibid., p. 214.

86. Ibid., pp. 237 and 319.

87. Ibid., pp. 237 and 319.

88. Ibid., pp. 482 and 611, 3 March 1605.

89. Ibid., p. 906.

90. Ibid., p. 926 and 1606–1607, fo. 50v, 25 October 1605.

91. ACDFSO:DSO 1603, fos. 1v (?2 January), 40v (21 February), 110v (21 May), 113v (22 May), 215r (24 September) and 219r (25 September).

92. Gaetano Moroni, *Dizionario di erudizione storico–ecclesiastica*, 103 vols. in 53 (Venice: Tipografia Emiliana, 1840–1861), 25, 21. Bernini sculpted his bust. Luigi Salerno, Luigi Spezzaferro, and Manfredo Tafuri, *Via Giulia: Una utopia urbanistica del 500*, 2nd ed. (Rome: A. Staderini, 1975), 238.

93. ACDFSO:DSO 1603, fos. 45v (27 February), 64r (1603 Copia, fo. 68r–v; 20 March), 74r (3 April; ibid., fo. 79v), 135r (Fra Angelo's testimony), 165r (ibid., fo. 172r; 24 July), and 181r (ibid., fo. 189v; 14 August).

94. ACDFSO:DSO 1617, p. 383 (28 September), 1618, pp. 146 (26 April), 313 (6 September) and 318 (sentence.)

95. ACDFSO:DSO 1617, p. 147 (Sebastiano Collesi, 19 April); ACDFSO:DSO 1621–1622, fo. 201r (11 May 1622 Alessandro Venturi); and ACDFSO:DSO 1632, fo. 128v (19 August). His book apparently never appeared.

96. ACDFSO:DSO 1631, fos. 97r and 114v.

97. Ibid., fo. 82r.

98. ACDFSO:DSO 1617, p. 246; and ACDFSO:DSO 1620, p. 255.

99. Jacopo Dionisio Orsini, *Notizie letterarie ed istoriche intorno agli uomini illustri dell'accademia Fiorentina*, 1 (Florence: Piero Matini, 1700), 286–87, http://www.guadagni-family.com/family_tree/images/guadagniplatethree.pdf, accessed 20 March 2010.

100. ACDFSO:DSO 1617, p. 473, 6 December. Gualterotti is almost unstudied, but see Goldberg, *Jews*, 126 and 273–74, and Ferdinando Jacoli, "Intorno a due scritti di Raffaele Gualterotti fiorentino relativi all'apparizione di una nuova stella avvenuta nell'anno 1604," *Bollettino di bibliografia e di storia delle scienze matematiche e fisiche di B. Buoncompagni* 7 (1874): 377–415. He wrote many books in addition to *Discorso sopra l'apparizione della nova stella . . . nell'anno 1605* (Florence: Giunti, 1605).

101. ACDFSO:DSO 1620, p. 332, 10 September. One last Florentine, Francesco Spigliato, was licensed a week after Galileo's trial ended, but I have found no information about him. ACDFSO:DSO 1633, fo. 109r, 28 June.

102. For the general context of Tuscan–Roman relations, see Wieland, *Fürsten*, passim. He does not discuss either the Alidosi case or that of the marchese di Riano (see below).

103. The family's fate has been notorious since at least the early eighteenth century. See P. P. Ginnani, *Memorie storiche dell'antica ed illustre famiglia Alidosia* (Rome: No Publisher, 1714), 108–11. There are three more modern treatments by local historians: G. F. Cortini, *Storia di Castel del Rio* (Imola: Santerno Edizioni, 1985, reprint of Imola: Paolo Galeati, 1933 ed.), especially chap. 5; Cesare Quinto Vivoli and Lorenzo Raspanti, *Gli Alidosi e Castel del Rio: splendore e tramonto di una signoria* (Imola: Santerno, 2001), 63–70, especially valuable for documentation of Rodrigo's legal training; and the detailed study of his case by Paolo Nalli, "Rodrigo Alidosi, Signore di Castel del Rio e il S. Uffizio," *Atti e Memorie de. R. Acc. di scienze, lettere e arti di Modena* s. 5, 3 (1938): 107–40 with many documents in the appendices. For the rendition of the fief forced on Mariano, see Cesare Quinto Vivoli, "Il papa Urbano VIII, il granduca Ferdinando II, Mariano Alidosi, Jacopo Salviati e la crisi di Castel del Rio (1635–1638)," *Pagine di vita e storia imolensi* 3 (1986): 169–91.

104. Nalli, "Alidosi," 110 states the extraction as fact. He also says on unknown evidence that Campori got them from the Machiavelli family. For the possible date of assembly, see a letter of 1731 at the end of the first volume, BEM:RC, MS 'Y.O.4.21, fo. 118r, preceded slightly by a copy dated 30 July 1780 of a sixteenth-century act on fo. 115r–v.

105. ACDFSO:DSO 1608, pp. 439, 446, 485 and 492 and ACDFSO:DSO 1609, pp. 1–2. The *processo* was finished by 25 July 1609. BEM:RC, MS 'Y.O.4.23, fo. 100r–v.

106. The surviving pieces of the "Summarium" are numbered 1, 3, 5, 9, 11, 14, 15, 17, 18, 19, and 20 and each has a descriptive heading repeated throughout each section. These eleven encompass 123 folios, which represents almost exactly half the total of the 255 folios described by the inquisitor of Florence. BEM:RC, MS 'Y.O.4.25, passim and MS 'Y.O.4.23, fo. 100r–v. They are bound in random order: 9 (fos. 21r–8v); 14 (29r–34v); 1 (35r–49r); 20 (49r–54v); 3 (55r–58v); 5 (59r–74r); 15 (75r–80v); 11 (81r–4v); 17 (89r–96v); 18 (97r–106v); and 19 (107r–44v). The first entry is dated 6 June 1608 and the last 13 March

1609. The second reinforces the likelihood that Camillo Giudici drew up the text. I have found no certainly autograph documents for comparison to its hand.

107. The full title on fo. 1r of BEM:RC, MS 'Y.O.4.22 is "1608–1617" "Processo che comprende il To. VII ancora fabbricato dall' S. Uffizio di Faenza contro il Sig. Roderigo Alidosi. . . . Nel Tomo VII vedansi altri Documenti spettanti alla famigila Alidosi, ed al suo dominio di Castell' del Rio. . . . Appariscono pure molti fatti interessanti di Castell' del Rio, e gli Alidosi. Il Sig.r Roderigo era cognato del Sig.r Ciro Pantaleoni, e Suocero del Sig.a [blank; Elena, Rodrigo's daughter] Avogli."

108. Interestingly, Martinelli was the only official involved throughout the formation of the *processo*, no matter in what place. He began by writing the informative process in his home town and then moved to Florence where he wrote, inter alia, the record of Alidosi's examination. ACDFSO:DSO 1608–1609, fo. 325r and 1609, p. 131; and BEM:RC, MS 'Y.O.4.26. His signature appears on many of the acta, e.g., BEM:RC, MSS 'Y.O.4.22, fo. 129r and 'Y.O.4.23, fo. 76r.

109. See the covering letter from Cornelio Marzari to the Inquisitor of Faenza in BEM:RC, MS 'Y.O.4.23, fo. 100r–v/103r–v (wrapper).

110. BEM:RC, MS 'Y.O.4.23, fos. 2r–v and 124r.

111. He was appointed 7 April 1607. ACDFSO:DSO 1607, fo. 87r. See *RI*, 145.

112. Giudici was in Imola, the nearest major Holy Office vicariate to Castel del Rio (also a vicariate but of no use in an investigation of its lord), by 20 December 1608 and left Florence for Rome before 1 April 1609. ACDFSO:DSO 1609, pp. 1–2 and 125–26.

113. Part of his credentials, together with the transcript of two interrogations conducted in Rome that Giudici must have brought with him, are in BEM:RC, MS 'Y.O.4.25, fos. 6v–19v.

114. ACDFSO:DSO 1608, p. 485 and 1609, pp. 1–2 and 80. On 1 January 1609 Rome ordered Giudici to go to Florence and serve a "precept" on Inquisitor Medici about observing secrecy. One of the ringleaders in the opposition had already denounced him as favoring Alidosi, and he was replaced shortly thereafter, only for his successor to be replaced again. 1609, pp. 1–2, 23, and 60.

115. It was sent to Rome, where it was read on 2 September, before later going into Giudici's instructions. ACDFSO:DSO 1608, pp. 373–74.

116. BEM:RC, MS 'Y.O.4.25, fos. 1–20r, "Informatione" on fos. 18r–19r, decretum at top of fo. 19v, misdated 18 September instead of October. The mistake in day (but not of course in month) may arise from the date of the cardinal secretary's letter communicating the order. The rest of that folio and all of fo. 20 are blank.

117. The rest of the "Summarium" is organized as follows: "Quod minatus fuerit eius M.o contra fr.m Albertum et alios" (fos. 29r–34v, gatherings 29r–32v, and 33r–34v, both headed "14"); "Somarium [*sic*] Processus Contra D. Rodericum Alidosium delatum de pluribus," headed "1" (fos. 35r–49r, first sheet blank); "De tractatu de occidendi Andream Thedescum," headed "20" (49r–54v, last two sheets blank); "Quod retinuerit et legerit librum prohibitum," "3" (fos. 55r–58v, last sheet and a half blank); "Quod irridet de censuris," "5" (fos. 59r–74r in gatherings of 59r–62v, 63r–68v, 69r–70v, 71r–74v); "15. De Scriptis"

(75r–80v gathering, 75r–v and 80v blank); "xi. Quod procuraverit fides ipsum esse bonum Catt.cum" (81r–4v, gathering, continued in next gathering 85r–88v with new heading, most of last three leaves blank); "17. Quod carcerari fecerit Sebastianum Burnorum, et Steph.m Morarium de Castro Rivii ex quo subiiecierunt examini in s.to Off.o [???]" (89r–96v [gathering], 89r–v blank, note at foot 90r "Require" with five-pointed star, star again top fo. 93r); "18. De subornatione Testium" (fos. 97r–106v [gathering], 97r–v blank with no heading, heading on fo. 98r, originally numbered 2r–10v (the other gatherings have no original foliation); "19 "Successu ad hostium Civitatis Imolae et trattatu de occidendo And.am Thedescum" (fos. 107r–144v [gathering], continued in gathering of 145r–146v, last sheet blank).

118. BEM:RC, MS 'Y.O.4.23, fos. 34r–49v/105r–120v (original).

119. See *RI*, passim.

120. "Sono unico, et assoluto Sig.re di Cat: del Rio, qual'è stato libero, ne è sottoposto a alcun Principe, e perciò tengo banditi del Gran Duca mio Sig.re, e della Chiesa, e di qualsivoglia altro stato, il che stimo assai, poichè posso giovare agli amici et parenti, quando per qualche homicidio, ò, altro eccesso non potessero stare altrove." BEM:RC, MS 'Y.O.4.24, fo. 90r–93r, a letter without address but probably intended as part of negotiations for one of his sons' marriages, dated 30 October 1620 and signed by Alidosi. Neither of the copies in ASV, Arm. 36:28, fos. 339v–342v (with *constat* at the end) and 345r–346v contains this paragraph, despite the vaguely documented assertion of Cortini, *Storia*, 90.

121. In 1525 it had about 1000 subjects in total, 300 of them in the village itself. The fief was twelve miles in circumference and three miles across. It could raise 250 soldiers, at least some of whom must have been mercenaries. ASV, Arm. 36:28, fo. 37r, dated on fo. 24r.

122. *Avvisi* of 5 and 26 II July in AsMod:AE, 138, fasc. July 1631, unfoliated.

123. This biography is based on the sketch in *DBI*, 1, 377–79 as corrected and amplified. Only the eastern range of the palace was completed. See Cesare Quinto Vivoli, *Il Palazzo Alidosi di Castel del Rio, opera di Francesco da Sangallo* (Imola: Angelini, 2010).

124. G. Gozzadini, "Di alcuni avvenimenti in Bologna e nell'Emilia dal 1506 al 1511 e dei cardinali legati A. Ferrerio e F. Alidosi," *Atti e memorie della Deputazione di storia patria per le Province di Romagna* ser. 3, 4 (1885–86): 67–176 and 7 (1888–89): 161–267, assassination on 224–26.

125. In his first deposition on 29 April 1609 Alidosi gave his age as "about 46." *DBI* gives his birth as ca. 1545.

126. For Alidosi's degree, Vivoli and Raspanti, *Gli Alidosi*, 63 drawing on university records.

127. ASV, Arm. 36:28, fo. 334v gives 1590, *DBI* 1589. In his deposition, he said he had lived there for forty-three of his forty-six years. With his diplomatic missions figured in, there was no time at all left to stay on his fief. His palace in Florence was near the Carmine. BEM:RC, MS 'Y.O.4.24, fo. 38r.

128. Geography is also important to following the action. The town of Castel del Rio lies in the valley of the Santerno twenty-two (or twenty-one; two road signs next to one another in front of Palazzo Alidosi give two different numbers) kilometers north of Firenzuola (the first grand ducal territory south) on the road from Imola, from which it lies

about thirty-six kilometers southwest, two from the even then tiny hamlet of Carseggio, eight from Fontanelice, and twelve from the next major town, Borgo Tossignano. Nine kilometers almost due east across the hills is the next vicariate of the Holy Office, Casola (Valsénio); Sassoleone is six kilometers NNW. Imola and Faenza, headquarters of the Inquisitor of Romagna, of which Imola was a vicariate, are fifteen kilometers apart. Castel del Rio is about seventy-seven kilometers from Florence. All other places mentioned are in Castel del Rio's immediate vicinity.

129. Serafino Gaddoni, *Le chiese d'Imola*, 2: *Casteldelrio, Fontanelice, Tossignano, Casalfiumanese, Dozza* (Imola: Diocesi di Imola, 2007), 10, a work written in the early twentieth century.

130. Gaddoni, *Chiese d'Imola*, 165–66.

131. Alberto Tossani et al.–Mazzoni, Imola, 27 June 1607, endorsed "16. L.ra de' Congiurati a D. Andrea Mazzoni. 17." BEM:RC, MS 'Y.O.4.24, fos. 34r–35v.

132. ASV, Arm. 36:28, fo. 45r–v. Other anonymous and undated complaints are on fos. 40r–v (another copy on 42r–v and in Arm. 36:30, fos. 285r–286v) and one, post-dating Alidosi's abjuration and therefore probably aimed at his son, in ASV, Arm. 36:28, fos. 41r–v and 47r–48r (copy in Arm. 36:30, fos. 294r–295r).

133. ACDFSO:DSO 1608, p. 203. The vicar of the Holy Office of Faenza who took a good deal of testimony was Niccolò da Bologna who held a readership, probably in San Domenico, Bologna (BEM:RC, MS 'Y.O.4.23, fos. 28r and 31). He would serve a second term beginning in 1619 (ACDFSO:DSO 1619, p. 232).

134. 21 May 1608 vicar of Imola–inquisitor general of Romagna. BEM:RC, MS 'Y.O.4.27, fos. 98r–v and 101r–v wrapped around fos. 99r–100v. Da Urgnano occurs in Alidosi's dossier on 4 July and 18 September 1608. BEM:RC, MSS 'Y.O.4.27, fo. 94r and 'Y.O.4.22, fo. 38r. Called Pietro Martire (or Maria) Fatigati (Giulio Cesare Tonduzzi, *Historie di Faenza* [Faenza: G. Zarafagli, 1675], lxvi), he was made inquisitor of Como in 1597 (Francesco Ballarini, *Compendio delle croniche della città di Como* [Como: Giovanni Angelo Turato, 1619], 208), also mistakenly making him inquisitor of Venice). He edited Humbert of Romans's *Commentaria in regulam D. Augustini, . . . et tria vota substantialia religionis* (Como: Girolamo Frova, 1605).

135. Decree of 3 June 1608 in ACDFSO:DSO 1608, pp. 233–34.

136. Decree of 12 June 1608 in ibid., p. 250.

137. Interrogation of 6 June 1608. BEM:RC, MS 'Y.O.4.22, fos. 9r–10v, noted in the "Summarium," fo. 1r (BEM:RC, MS 'Y.O.4.25, fo. 36r).

138. BEM:RC, MS 'Y.O.4.22, fo. 10v. The testimony is signed by a different notary from the one for Schell's first deposition.

139. Deposition of Ippolito Maria d'Alba 22 June 1608. BEM:RC, MS 'Y.O.4.22, fos. 11r–14r, with enclosures, including letters of 21 and 22 May and 6 June 1608, put in the *processo* and marked A, B, and C according to the "Summarium," fo. 4r (BEM:RC, MS 'Y.O.4.25, fo. 36r).

140. ACDFSO:DSO 1608, pp. 281–82.

141. BEM:RC, MS 'Y.O.4.22, fos. 14r–17v.

142. Examinations of 21 July 1608. BEM:RC, MS 'Y.O.4.22, fos. 20v–21v and 18r; cf. the first fascicle of the "Summarium,"originally fo. 10r (25, fo. 37v).

143. See Alidosi's letter to Mazzoni from Florence of 23 July 1608 marked "subito subito." BEM:RC, MS 'Y.O.4.27, fos. 45r–v and 50v (wrapper).

144. The gate survives, isolated on a traffic island, and a line of concrete seats marks the original width of the street leading to it.

145. There is a vast quantity of testimony about this incident. I have drawn mainly on the first interrogation, on the afternoon of 4 July, of Gregorio di Maestro Pietro Biondi, who may have been related to the bargello but still gave a calm description (BEM:RC, MS 'Y.O.4.25, fos. 1r–2r), and his reexamination on 7 August (BEM:RC, MS 'Y.O.4.22, fo. 105r); Tedeschi's deposition of 19 July (BEM:RC, MS 'Y.O.4.22, fo. 64r); Alba's deposition of 20 July (BEM:RC, MS 'Y.O.4.22, fos. 64r–66v) and the exculpatory "Ragguaglio della Causa di Roderico Alidosio in materia di quanto è occorso a me Fra Hippolito Maria d'Alba nel tempo ch'ero Vicario del Santo Off.o in Imola," "Bag.ra" [?Bagnara di Romagna], 9 March 1609, fair copy, signed at end (BEM:RC, MS 'Y.O.4.27, fos. 125r–v and 133r–v wrapped around fos. 126r–132v); the bargello's deposition of 21 August (BEM:RC, MS 'Y.O.4.22, fos. 135r–136r); the deposition of 22 August by Girolamo Rosa, one of Alidosi's toughs, naming thirteen men as in his group (BEM:RC, MS 'Y.O.4.22, fos. 109r–14r); the testimony of one of the *sbirri* (BEM:RC, MS 'Y.O.4.25, fo. 112r–v); and Francesco Filetti's interrogation of 9 January 1609 (BEM:RC, MS 'Y.O.4.25, fos. 137r–139r).

146. See the brief biography in Silvano Giordano, ed., *Istruzioni di Filippo III ai suoi ambasciatori a Roma, 1598–1621*, Pubblicazioni degli Archivi di Stato, Fonti 45 (Rome: Ministero per i Beni e le Attività Culturale, 2006), 167.

147. Irene Fosi, *La giustizia del papa. Sudditi e tribunali nello Stato Pontificio in età moderna* (Rome: Laterza, 2007), 69.

148. Francesco Contarini–doge, 12 July 1608 in ASVe:SDR, f. 59, fos. 342r–343r. The usually less reliable *avvisi* blame Cesi's arrest and condemnation on Prospero Farinacci, allegedly taking revenge on the marchese for gambling debts. Niccolò Del Re, "Prospero Farinacci giureconsulto romano (1544–1618)," *Archivio della Società Romana di Storia Patria* 98 (1975): 135–220, 162, citing *avvisi* of 23 July, 20 August, 22 and 27 September, and 4 October in BAV, Urb. Lat. 1076 II, fos. 694 and 715.

149. Francesco Contarini–doge, 19 July 1608 in ASVe:SDR, f. 59, fos. 328v–329r.

150. Francesco Contarini–doge, 16 August 1608 in ibid., fos. 403r–404r.

151. Francesco Contarini–doge, 23 August 1608 in ibid., fo. 430v. Toschi was a referenday of both *segnature* and, even better for Riano, had been auditor of the Consulta and governor of Rome. Christoph Weber, *Die Päpstlichen Referendare 1566–1809. Chronologie und Prosopographie*, 3 vols. (Stuttgart: Anton Hiersemann, 2003), 3, 946.

152. Francesco Contarini–doge, 30 August 1608 in ASVe:SDR, f. 59, fo. 436v.

153. For the beginning of the investigation, see BEM:RC, MS 'Y.O.4.25, fo. 2r–v and the references in note 145.

154. Decrees of 16 and 17 July 1608 in ACDFSO:DSO 1608, pp. 306 and 310.

155. ACDFSO:DSO 1608, p. 311. He was interrogated in Rome on 30 September (see below).

156. See his undated letter to the inquisitor of Romagna in BEM:RC, MS 'Y.O.4.23, fos. 9r–10v/now 59 and 61.

157. BEM:RC, MS 'Y.O.4.22, fos. 64r–66v.

158. Probably captain of carabine, of Imola, † bef. 2 Jan 1630 (BAV, Barb. Lat. 6273, fo. 17r); Carlo Barberini said he was happy to help him, according to a letter of 9 September 1626. BAV, Barb. lat. 6298, fo. 28v.

159. ACDFSO:DSO 1608, pp. 320–21.

160. *Calendar of State Papers and Manuscripts, relating to English Affairs existing in the Archives and Collections of Venice*, 11 (London: HMSO, 1904), no. 289 from ASVe, Senato, Dispacci Firenze, f. 23, which I was not allowed to consult.

161. Francesco Contarini–doge, 10 September 1608 II; ASVe:SDR, f. 60, fos. 28v–29r.

162. Francesco Contarini–doge, 13 September 1608 II; ibid., fos. 12v–13r.

163. *DBI* 1: 377–79.

164. "Relazione di Fr. Morosini" in Arnaldo Segarizzi, ed., *Relazioni degli ambasciatori veneti al senato*, 6 vols. (Bari: Laterza, 1912, etc.), 3:2, 141.

165. Ibid., no. 296 from the same source; and ACDFSO:DSO 1608, p. 356.

166. BEM:RC, MS 'Y.O.4.23, fos. 15r and 18v.

167. ACDFSO:DSO 1608, pp. 348–49.

168. BEM:RC, MS 'Y.O.4.22, fo. 107r–v. The same day Alba reported Tedeschi's deposition against Alidosi to the inquisitor of Romagna. BEM:RC, MS 'Y.O.4.27, fo. 112r–113v.

169. Camillo Zampieri. BEM:RC, MS 'Y.O.4.22, fos. 75r–77v. For his position, see the testimony of the priest Giovanni Battista Pancheri, who also served in the cathedral; Pancheri claimed Alidosi escaped capture at the Porta dell'Osservanza thanks to Zampieri. BEM:RC, MS 'Y.O.4.22, fo. 72r.

170. ACDFSO:DSO 1610–1611, fo. 326r, letter of the inquisitor of Faenza, 29 May 1611.

171. See his letter of 21 August 1608 to an unknown recipient, possibly the inquisitor of Romagna or Alba, in BEM:RC, MS 'Y.O.4.22, fo. 28v. Lucrezia Concini's irate letter of 18 August is in BEM:RC, MS 'Y.O.4.21, fo. 10r, and another of the 23rd is in BEM:RC, MS 'Y.O.4.27, fo. 23r, wrapper on 28r. Mazzoni entered both into evidence on 5 February 1609.

172. BEM:RC, MS 'Y.O.4.22, fos. 109r–113v; cf. the "Summarium" in BEM:RC, MS 'Y.O.4.25, fos. 112v–114r. Rosa began by saying Alba told him the unnamed inquisitor wished to see him.

173. ACDFSO:DSO 1608, p. 356, 21 August. Caetani's letter was dated the 8th.

174. Ibid., p. 379, 4 September.

175. Ibid., p. 414 and 1607–1609, fos. 201v–202r, 25 September.

176. Ibid., p. 401, 18 September; and the renewal of Baffadi's bond on 1 October 1608 in BEM:RC, MS 'Y.O.4.22, fo. 129r.

177. On 13 October. BEM:RC, MS 'Y.O.4.22, fo. 129v.

178. See the deposition of Giuseppe Rosa of 22 August 1608 in ibid., fo. 109r–v.

179. ACDFSO:DSO 1608, p. 439. Alidosi's petition for release is in BEM:RC, MS 'Y.O.4.22, fos. 129v–30r. The order was executed on 25 October. ACDFSO:DSO 1608, p. 482, 6 November quoting the inquisitor of Florence's letter of that date.

180. Interrogation of Giorgio Paglia 18 September 1608. BEM:RC, MS 'Y.O.4.22, fos. 39v–40r.

181. See Affricano Ravaglia's deposition of 23 October 1608. Ibid., fos. 41r–42r. He had first given his information to Alba in the Chiostri de' Morti in Imola several weeks earlier. Ibid., fo. 40v.

182. BEM:RC, MS 'Y.O.4.25, fo. 6v, the first fascicle of the "Summarium."

183. Ibid., fo. 7r.

184. Ibid., fo. 7v.

185. Ibid., fo. 8r.

186. Ibid., fo. 8v.

187. This section of his testimony may be garbled, since there is no other evidence that either he or the priest had been in Prague and Mordano insisted he had not known Alidosi before he met him in Imola shortly before Alidosi was arrested.

188. Ibid., fo. 9r.

189. "Io non credo, che sia bene, ma male, et mi dispiacer d'haver fatto male, ma all'hora io non considerai piu che tanto, et fui portato cosi inconsideratamente, et imprudentemente." Ibid., fo. 10r.

190. ACDFSO:DSO 1608, pp. 424 and 430.

191. ACDFSO:DSO 1608–1609, fo. 283r; ACDFSO:DSO 1609, p. 43; ACDFSO:DSO 1613, p. 728, 28 December 1612.

192. BEM:RC, MS 'Y.O.4.22, fos. 40r and 98r.

193. Ibid., fo. 46r. Andrea Ferri, ed., *L'inquisizione romana in diocesi di Imola. Inventario del fondo inquisitoriale presso l'Archivio Diocesano di Imola* (Imola: Diocesi di Imola, 2001), 34–35 does not include Vincenzo in his list of vicars and has Virginio in office only from before 19 December.

194. ACDFSO:DSO 1608, p. 436 and 1608–1609, fo. 213r. "De Callio" is the Latin form of his name, which should mean Cagli rather than Caglio (CO). http://www.columbia.edu/acis/ets/Graesse/orblatc.html#Calium accessed 30 March 2010. There is no entry for him in *QE*. Montini had earlier been the vicar of the Holy Office of Modena. M. J. Piozza-Donati, "Procès contre Matteo Gazzotto Modénais soupçonné d'hérésie à la fin du XVIe siècle," *Mélanges de l'école française de Rome* 89 (1977): 945–82, 979.

195. ACDFSO:DSO 1608, pp. 430 and 436, and 1608–1609, fo. 213r. Despite Galamini's intervention, suggesting Montini must have been fairly accomplished, I have found nothing about him.

196. He signed a deposition of 14 November as "fratrem Angelum Dominicum de Callio Not.m Aplicum et S.i Offii Imolae." BEM:RC, MS 'Y.O.4.22, fo. 49r.

197. ACDFSO:DSO 1610–1611, fo. 120v, 7 July 1610.

198. ACDFSO:DSO 1608, pp. 439 and 446.

199. Ibid., pp. 485 and 492, 12 and 19 November.

200. ACDFSO:DSO 1608–1609, fo. 243r; ACDFSO:DSO 1608, pp. 502 and 508, 26 November.

201. ACDFSO:DSO 1609, pp. 1–2, 30 December, quoting his letter of ten days earlier.

202. BEM:RC, MS 'Y.O.4.23, fos. 27r/32v and 28r/31.

203. ACDFSO:DSO 1608, pp. 449 and 453.

204. Undated joint deposition, headed "F" (as was ordered on 17 October) in BEM:RC, MS 'Y.O.4.23, fos. 29r/37 and 30r–v.

205. BEM:RC, MS 'Y.O.4.22, fo. 30v. The "Informatione" is BEM:RC, MS 'Y.O.4.23, fos. 29r/37 and 30r–v.

206. BEM:RC, MS 'Y.O.4.25, fos. 18r–19r, the last text in the first fascicle of the "Summarium."

207. Deposition of 18 October 1608 in BEM:RC, MS 'Y.O.4.22, fos. 31r–33r. Niccolò is explicitly said to have come from Faenza to examine Lorenz.

208. Interrogation of 27 October 1608 in ibid., fos. 33r–36r.

209. Interrogation of 5 November in first fascicle of "Summarium," BEM:RC, MS 'Y.O.4.25, fos. 10v–14r.

210. Ibid., fos. 14r–17v.

211. For Virginio, see BEM:RC, MS 'Y.O.4.22, fo. 46r. He had replaced a man appointed less than a month before, Vincenzo da Cotignola. Ibid., fo. 98r. It is unclear whether Niccolò continued to act in Imola as he had in October or had returned to Faenza. The problem arises from, inter alia, the record of Lorenz's second interrogation. It began with his being brought from prison by Tedeschi, which should mean he was still in Imola, but the notary's notation at the end reads "Acta sunt haec in camera solitae ressidentiae [*sic*] Adm. R. P. Inq.ris per me fratrem Adrianum Ducinellum de Venetiis Not.m S.ti Off. ii Faventiae," which would appear to indicate Faenza. Ibid., fo. 50v.

212. Deposition of 14 November 1608 in ibid., fos. 46r–49r.

213. Interrogations of Francesco Boretti and Tommaso Ferri alias Caroti. Ibid., fos. 50v–53v, both in the "Summarium." BEM:RC, MS 'Y.O.4.25, fos. 117v–118r.

214. Montini may have conducted the interrogations on the previous day, indicated as having been held in "the usual room of [Montini's] residence," but he is not explicitly identified as the interrogator. BEM:RC, MS 'Y.O.4.22, fo. 52r.

215. Ibid., fos. 130r–133r; noted in "Summarium," originally fo. 42v (BEM:RC, MS 'Y.O.4.25, fo. 129r–v).

216. Mazzoni's deposition is in BEM:RC, MS 'Y.O.4.22, fo. 88r–90r, followed by Della Vigna's on fos. 90v–92r. Millini was returning from a legation to the empire (which overlapped Alidosi's mission in Prague) and was en route to Rome from a brief stop in his diocese of Imola, sometime between late July and mid-October. ACDFSO:DSO 1609, p. 291, 21 July and Francesco Contarini–doge, 18 October 1608 in ASVe:SDR, f. 60, fo. 61v. Why he stoppped in Carseggio is unclear; given Alidosi's troubles, the land route via Florence would have seemed an especially poor choice. He could not have been in Imola or its vicinity long, since he was back in Rome on 6 November. Francesco Contarini–doge, 8 November 1608 in ASVe:SDR, f. 60, fo. 78v. Millini reappeared in the Congregation 13

November (ACDFSO:DSO 1608, p. 489). See also Millini's letter to the duke of Modena of 15 November in ASMod, Cancelleria Ducale, Carteggio con principi esteri, b. 1394/134, Millini, unfoliated. I have not seen his correspondence from this period in ASV, Fondo Borghese II 154.

217. The note of the written deposition is undated and lacks any other formalities, including a signature or authentication. Tedeschi apparently confirmed it the next day. BEM:RC, MS 'Y.O.4.22, fos. 115r–v and 116r.

218. BEM:RC, MS 'Y.O.4.22, fos. 116r–118r, deposition of Domenico Gualandi, signed, and fo. 118r, deposition of Ottaviano Codronchi. Gualandi's testimony varied a little in calling Tedeschi a "furbo infame spione" instead of the more usual (and ruder) "becco fotuto," e.g., in Francesco Boreti's deposition of 19 November. Ibid., fo. 50v. Both are in the "Summarium," BEM:RC, MS 'Y.O.4.25, fos. 114rff.

219. Tedeschi–Montini, 25 November 1608, Imola. BEM:RC, MS 'Y.O.4.22, fo. 134r, wrapper on fo. 137r–v.

220. Ibid., fo. 99r–v.

221. Again, it is uncertain whether he was acting in Imola or Faenza. The last of the three interrogations of 27 November involved Montini and was signed by a notary of the Holy Office in Faenza, but it happened in the evening and Fra Niccolò had earlier brought his own notary to Imola, so he might just possibly have returned thence in the interval. Only Beccari was certainly imprisoned at this point. He ended up in the galleys, but whether for his role in Alidosi's case or for blasphemy is not known. ACDFSO:DSO 1612, p. 174.

222. There is a maniculum in the upper left corner of the first page of his testimony in BEM:RC, MS 'Y.O.4.22, fo. 119v; cf. "Summarium," fo. 52. This is the last entry in volume 22.

223. Ibid.; see the "Summarium," BEM:RC, MS 'Y.O.4.25, fos. 115v–116v.

224. BEM:RC, MS 'Y.O.4.22, fo. 123r, signed and authenticated.

225. Ibid., fo. 123v–124v, signed and authenticated.

226. Ibid., fo. 42r, signed "+" and authenticated.

227. Ibid., fos. 125r–126v, signed and authenticated. Noted in "Summarium," BEM:RC, MS 'Y.O.4.25, fos. 116v–117r. Many of the actors in Alidosi's case got in trouble for blasphemy in the vicariate in Imola, including Tedeschi and Mazzoni. See the dossiers listed in Ferri, *L'inquisizione romana*, 45 and 52–53. For Damiano Domenici, see Mazzoni's deposition of 27 October 1608 in BEM:RC, MS 'Y.O.4.22, fo. 35r.

228. 30 November 1608, examination of Lorenzo Valdalba from the district of Tossignano, resident in Castel del Rio. Ibid., fos. 126v–127r, signed and authenticated.

229. Only some of the depositions are excerpted more than briefly in the "Summarium." See, e.g., four depositions summarized on fo. 38r of BEM:RC, MS 'Y.O.4.25. Others are on fos. 51r–v, 91r–92r, 114v–115r, 115r–v, 120r–v, 132v–133r, 133r–v, 134r–135r, etc. Since the "Summarium" is arranged according to the charges, meaning the depositions are dismembered, it is impossible to know who conducted and recorded the interrogations and where, in what sequence the questions were asked, or what else may have been said

that was judged to be irrelevant or exculpatory. Lorenz's *constituti*, for example, of 28–30 December are found on fos. 118v–120r, 40v and 120v. To judge from that volume, a good deal of original testimony has been lost. Thus, Pantaleone's interrogations of 2 and 3 January originally occurred at least eighteen folios apart, but only one deposition by Mazzoni is known to have intervened.

230. ACDFSO:DSO 1608, p. 542.

231. ACDFSO:DSO 1609, pp. 1–2, decree of 30 December 1608, a meeting on Tuesday perhaps because of the feast of the Holy Family on 31 December, although the Congregation met on that day in, e.g., 1630.

232. "faciat praeceptum Inquisitori Florentiae de servando secretum sub poenae excommunicationis latae sententiae, a qua non possit absolui, nisi a S.te Sua, eique non propalet nominas testium." ACDFSO:DSO 1609, p. 7 and 1608–1609, fo. 266v.

233. *Fede* of Alessandro Machiavelli, I.U.D., 3 May 1609 in BEM:RC, MS 'Y.O.4.24, fo. 97r.

234. ACDFSO:DSO 1609, p. 109 and 1608–1609, fo. 314v, Alidosi's wife's surname of Concini illegible.

235. The register says nothing about the letter's content. ACDFSO:DSO 1609, p. 18 and 1608–1609, fo. 271v, 7 January 1609.

236. Andrea Del Col, *L'Inquisizione in Italia* (Milan: Mondadori, 2006), 448–49.

237. The original is missing; the biggest piece of it in the "Summarium" is BEM:RC, MS 'Y.O.4.25, fos. 121r–123r as on fo. 195v.

238. BEM:RC, MS 'Y.O.4.25, fos. 123r–124r and 43r.

239. Ibid., fos. 124r–125v.

240. Ibid., fos. 125v–128r.

241. Ibid., fos. 135r–136v.

242. BEM:RC, MS 'Y.O.4.23, fo. 35v–41r.

243. Ibid., fos. 61r–69v/163r–67r, first four folios blank and originally unnumbered.

244. BEM:RC, MS 'Y.O.4.25, fos. 137r–139r.

245. Ibid., fos. 139v–140v.

246. Letter from Florence of 16 January 1609 in BEM:RC, MS 'Y.O.4.27, fos. 52r–v and 59v.

247. BEM:RC, MS 'Y.O.4.23, fo. 1r, second [*sic*] sheet of 6r.

248. Ibid., fos. 51r–54v/121r–24v fair copy; cf. "Summarium" as on no fo., BEM:RC, MS 'Y.O.4.25, fo. 66v.

249. BEM:RC, MS 'Y.O.4.23, fos. 56r/125r and 59r/126r (blank).

250. Interrogations of 4 February (known from "Summarium" as on fo. 409r; BEM:RC, MS 'Y.O.4.25, fos. 120v–121r); 6 February (known from "Summarium" as on fo. 421ff. [ibid., fo. 42v]); and 19 February (known from "Summarium" as on fos. 433v and 434r, etc.; ibid., fos. 46v–47r).

251. ACDFSO:DSO 1609, p. 56, 7 February 1609.

252. Ibid., p. 80; and ACDFSO:DSO 1608–1609, fo. 304r.

253. ACDFSO:DSO 1608–1609 fo. 302v, 26 February 1609.

254. Interrogation of 18 January 1609. Original missing; known from "Summarium" as on fo. 318v, BEM:RC, MS 'Y.O.4.25, fos. 44r–5r. For the second deposition, ibid., fo. 144r–v.

255. Interrogation of 30 January. Original missing; known from "Summarium" as on fo. 384v, ibid., fos. 44r–45r.

256. Ibid., fo. 46r–v.

257. Ibid., fos. 47v–48r.

258. ACDFSO:DSO 1609, p. 96 and 1608–1609, fo. 308r

259. ACDFSO:DSO 1610–1611, fo. 320r.

260. "Ragguaglio della Causa di Roderico Alidosio," in BEM:RC, MS 'Y.O.4.27, fos. 125r–33v. See the next note for evidence of attention to Alba's actions.

261. In 1607 ("two years ago") according to Battista and Alessandro Suzzi's deposition of 7 and 8 March 1609. BEM:RC, MS 'Y.O.4.25, fos. 144v and 144v–145r.

262. "gli feci un precetto, che non dovesse partirsi di Casa, presente il presente Priore, et sottopriore d'Imola." BEM:RC, MS 'Y.O.4.27, fo. 131v. For this passage about Mordano, see Alba's undated letter in BEM:RC, MS 'Y.O.4.23, fos. 9r–10v.

263. Original missing, known from "Summarium" as on fo. 513v, BEM:RC, MS 'Y.O.4.25, fo. 43v.

264. For Domenici, see Giudici's letter announcing proceedings of 19 March (read 24 March) and the order to Caetani of 26 March to capture the fugitive. ACDFSO:DSO 1608–1609, fos. 320r and 320v.

265. ACDFSO:DSO 1608–1609, fo. 320v and 1609, pp. 122–23, congregation of 26 March when the duke's letter was read. The evidence for the pope and cardinal nephew's action comes from an unsigned letter of 28 March, saying the writer had told Paul that morning about Giudici's arrival there (apparently meaning Florence) to examine Alidosi and his unexpected departure. Paul appeared not to know why Giudici had been sent, but both he and Cardinal Scipione Borghese said expedition had been ordered, the second in a letter to the nuncio, acting after a strong intervention by the French ambassador. The writer may have been the grand duke's ambassador to Rome. BEM:RC, MS 'Y.O.4.27, fo. 110r, glued to blank sheet 115r–v.

266. ACDFSO:DSO 1608–1609, fo. 322r and 1609, pp. 125–26, 1 April. Concini sent the same information.

267. ACDFSO:DSO 1608–1609, fo. 325r and 1609, p. 131, an entry not in the index at the front of the volume.

268. A note "Tenoris ut ibi signatis A annexis in processu" refers to the letter, but it is not now part of the *processo*. BEM:RC, MS 'Y.O.4.26, fo. 10r.

269. ACDFSO:DSO 1608–1609, fo. 332v; ACDFSO:DSO 1609, p. 147, illegible. The name of neither man is clear, but the first was a Carmelite named Alberto whose surname began with "T," perhaps Tossani from the house at Montefune, and the second man's given name was Galeazzo; enough of his surname can be read to suggest that it is Giuntini. For the *expeditio*, see *RI*, 196–200.

270. The *processo* contains a letter from Alidosi to Mazzoni dated 28 April 1609 saying

that Alidosi had an order for the liberation of Domenico Tossani and G. B. Domenici from Montini and expected to come himself to Castel del Rio for a couple of days. There would appear to be something wrong in the date. BEM:RC, MS 'Y.O.4.27, fo. 53r and 58v, no orig. nos.

271. BEM:RC, MS 'Y.O.4.26, fo. 1r–v. Possibly the same Monticelli was later notary of the Florentine Holy Office. Cioni, *Documenti*, 3.

272. ACDFSO:DSO 1632, fo. 118r–v, 29 July.

273. BEM:RC, MS 'Y.O.4.26, fo. 2r.

274. Ibid., fo. 2v. Since Alidosi's interlocutor is rarely identified, his *constituti* lacking the formality of noting in whose presence they had been taken, I have had to resort to anonymous terms like "questioner" and "interrogator."

275. The witnesses's signatures would have been unnecessary according to Roman practice. The notary's signature alone served to authenticate the record. See *RI*, 34.

276. BEM:RC, MS 'Y.O.4.26, fo. 11r. Ravaglia, who lived in either Tossignano or Sassoleone (the notary was unsure), certainly took part in the conspiracy against Alidosi, telling Tedeschi early on that Alidosi wanted to kill him. See Tedeschi's deposition of 19 July 1608. BEM:RC, MS 'Y.O.4.22, fo. 63v. Tedeschi and Mazzoni met at least once in his house to draw up a list of charges against Alidosi. "Informatione per il S. Off.o contra il S. Rodrigo" in ibid., fo. 101r. See further Ravaglia's interrogation of 4 September 1608 and that of his brother of the same date, who could only repeat what Affricano had told him. Ibid., fos. 28v–30r and 38v–39r. Only the first made it into the "Summarium," fo. 92r, BEM:RC, MS 'Y.O.4.25, fo. 37v. Ravaglia was persistent. When the vicar of the inquisition in Imola briefly changed, he immediately showed up with a new denunciation, which did not, however, make much sense and seems not to have been pursued. See his interrogation of 25 October 1608 in BEM:RC, MS 'Y.O.4.22, fo. 98r.

277. BEM:RC, MS 'Y.O.4.26, fos. 11v–13r.

278. The *fede* of Domenico Gambarini, archpriest of Santa Madonna del Ponte Santo d'Imola of 4 February 1609, endorsed, "Fede dell'arciprete della Madonna del Pontesanto de donativo fatto dal S.r a quella santiss. Casa" is BEM:RC, MS 'Y.O.4.24, fo. 136r/141v.

279. BEM:RC, MS 'Y.O.4.26, fo. 57r–v. Alidosi may have been genuinely confused about Caetani's involvement and the bargello at the gate's identity. According to Rosa's deposition, the *bargello di Campagna* (which should have meant Caetani's officer) had set the whole affair in motion by trying to arrest Pantaleone. BEM:RC, MS 'Y.O.4.22, fo. 109r.

280. Possibly Francesco Baffadi, later Mariano's agent, although from 1607 to 1609 he was mainly in Rome in Gonzaga service. Barbara Furlotti, ed., intro by Raffaela Morselli, *Le collezioni Gonzaga: Il carteggio tra Roma e Mantova (1587–1612)* (Milan: Silvana, 2003), docs. 733, 758, 822, 836, 856, 857, and 861. His given name is not in the record. Alidosi's next claim about him suggests that this Baffadi may have been the vicar general of the diocese of Imola.

281. BEM:RC, MS 'Y.O.4.26, fo.

282. For Seculi, see Mazzoni's deposition of 27 October 1608 in BEM:RC, MS 'Y.O.4.22, fo. 34v.

283. Alidosi mentioned an unidentified "he" in response to the inquisitor's question about who had been with him when he left Imola.

284. It is not now in the *processo*.

285. BEM:RC, MS 'Y.O.4.26, fo. 138v. "Io vengo in cognitione da questi essamini che sarebbe necessario che io mi raccordarsi non solo di tutte le mie attioni ma anco di tutte le parole che ho detto in tutto il tempo di vita mia."

286. Annibale Della Vigna's wife Penelope Zuccari, "weeping copiously," appeared spontaneously before the Inquisition's vicar in Faenza on 21 May, complaining that her husband had been imprisoned in Florence on Alidosi's orders, submitting as evidence a letter in his name. BEM:RC, MS 'Y.O.4.24, fos. 85r–86v plus 87r–88v (blank). The letter was marked "R" and put into the *processo*. Her husband's imprisonment is confirmed by a letter from Concini that Mazzoni handed in on 5 February 1609/1610 (BEM:RC, MS 'Y.O.4.27, fo. 19r.

287. *Fede* of 20 May 1609 in BEM:RC, MS 'Y.O.4.23, fo. 107r–v/110r, mounted backward, and Della Vigna's supplication to the Congregation of 28 October. ACDFSO:DSO 1608–1609, fos. 478v–479r, 5 November.

288. BEM:RC, MS 'Y.O.4.24, fo. 109r/108v, mounted backward.

289. The prior's of 4 November 1608 and 22 May 1609 are ibid. fos. 129r/132v and 135r/142v; the sub-prior's of the second date is BEM:RC, MS 'Y.O.4.23, fo. 87r. The Carmelite, Baccio Bandinelli, gave his *fede* on 21 May 1609. BEM:RC, MS 'Y.O.4.23, fo. 79r–v (82r–v, second sheet). The canon's of 22 May is BEM:RC, MS 'Y.O.4.24, fo. 106v/111r, mounted backwards. Caccini's is also one of the new ones, given the day before it was exhibited on 23 May. BEM, Autografoteca Campori, "Caccini, Tommaso."

290. Ambrogio Pratese, the provincial vicar, testified that he had known Alidosi for forty years. BEM:RC, MS 'Y.O.4.24, fos. 126r–127r. The confessor's certificate, handed in by Valentini to Monticelli, is ibid., fo. 137r/140v (blank).

291. Ibid., fo. 123r/128v (blank), dated only 1609 but probably late 1608, the time of the other testimonials from Prague. Unsurprisingly, Priatoni singled this one out in his covering letter for the completed *processo*. BEM:RC, MS 'Y.O.4.23, fo. 100r–v/103r–v.

292. E.g., his servants Giovanni Maria Sacchi (ibid., fo. 88r) and Giovanni di Bastiano Lapi (BEM:RC, MS 'Y.O.4.24, fo. 130r–31v), or his *credenziere* Zanobi Dani (BEM:RC, MS 'Y.O.4.27, fos. 121r–124v, 123r–v attached but blank).

293. BEM:RC, MS 'Y.O.4.23, fo. 94r, second sheet on 97r–v, "Capitoli" on dorse, n.d. Only three witnesses were suggested, and the more specific points mostly concern Mazzoni's testimony, chiefly about eating meat.

294. ACDFSO:DSO 1608–1609, fo. 367r; and ACDFSO:DSO 1609, p. 224, 4 June 1609.

295. ACDFSO:DSO 1608–1609, fos. 352r and 368r–v; and ACDFSO:DSO 1609, p. 403, 20 May, 9 June, and 24 September 1609, the second reporting Martinelli's letter of 1 June saying he was returning to Faenza. The Congregation bent in December and gave him another ten *scudi*. ACDFSO:DSO 1608–1609, fo. 495r–v, 1 December 1609.

296. ACDFSO:DSO 1608–1609, fo. 362r.

297. Ibid., fos. 386v and 384v.

298. Ibid., fos. 391v–392r and 1609, pp. 278–79, 8 July 1609. Luigi Tomassetti, et al., eds., *Magnum Bullarium Romanum*, 24 vols. (Turin: Sebastiano Franco and Enrico Dalmazzo, 1857–1872), 7, 744–46.

299. ACDFSO:DSO 1608–1609, fo. 396r, 16 July.

300. See the document endorsed "9. Penitenza al S.r Rod.go" in the same hand as his "Capitoli." BEM:RC, MS 'Y.O.4.23, fo. 99r–v/104r–v.

301. ACDFSO:DSO 1608–1609, fo. 397r.

302. Ibid., fo. 402v and 1609, p. 301.

303. BEM:RC, MS 'Y.O.4.23, fo. 100r–v/103r–v, Priatoni's covering letter referring to Arrigoni's lost order.

304. ACDFSO:DSO 1609, pp. 318 (Tedeschi's letter of 22 July) and 320 (abjuration). The *DBI* has Alidosi "absolved" by Priatoni on 23 July, on unknown evidence.

305. BEM:RC, MS 'Y.O.4.27, fo. 77v/80r, letter from illegible author and ACDFSO:DSO 1608–1609, fo. 414r and 1609, p. 329.

306. ACDFSO:DSO 1609, p. 343, 20 August. For Hans Christoph, see ibid., pp. 311, 344, 355, 397, and 403–4, decrees of 4, 21, 26 August and two of 24 September.

307. ACDFSO:DSO 1608–1609, fos. 423r (1609, p. 347) and 434r.

308. ACDFSO:DSO 1608–1609, fo. 432v and 1609, pp. 367–68.

309. ACDFSO:DSO 1608–1609, fo. 445r, 24 September.

310. ACDFSO:DSO 1609, p. 413 and 1608–1609, fo. 453v, 1 October, in reply to the grand duke's letter of 26 September.

311. See his letter of 19 November 1609 in BEM:RC, MS 'Y.O.4.23, fos. 101r–102v, marked "copia."

312. ACDFSO:DSO 1609, p. 417 and 1608–1609, fo. 455v, 7 October.

313. ACDFSO:DSO 1608–1609, fo. 458v, 14 October. Priatoni had also written.

314. Ibid., fo. 477r.

315. Ibid., fo. 492r.

316. Ibid., fos. 496v and 503v, 3 and 16 December 1609.

317. ACDFSO:DSO 1610, fo. 16v. Mazzoni, perhaps trying to curry favor, had sent Alidosi news of his liberation before 10 December 1609. See Alidosi's reply of that date in BEM:RC, MS 'Y.O.4.27, fo. 66r–67v. Possibly trying to drive a wedge between two of his three principal antagonists, Alidosi wrote at length about Della Vigna's sins.

318. http://siusa.signum.sns.it/cgi-bin/RSOLSearchSiusa.pl?_op=getsprod&id=ASDD000777&_cobj=yes&_ecclesia=NO&_selectby=SI&curwin=secondNO, accessed 4 July 2010. There are supposed to be family archives in the hands of Lucio Noli in Milan.

319. ACDFSO:DSO 1610–1611, fo. 17r.

320. Horatio F. Brown, Rawdon Brown, et al., eds., *Calendar of State Papers and Manuscripts Relating to English Affairs Existing in the Archives and Collections of Venice and in Other Libraries of Northern Italy*, 32 vols. (London: Longmans, Green, Reader and Dyer [etc.], 1864–1947), 11, *1607–1610*, no. 787.

321. ACDFSO:DSO 1610–1611, fo. 32r, 17 February.

322. Ibid., fo. 35v. See the decree to find out what the Inquisition had against Giovanni Miano di Manfredi Domenici and Domenico Tossani, both of Castel del Rio, and two decrees of 18 March proposing a reconciliation and their release on bond, which was granted on 22 April. ACDFSO:DSO 1610–1611, fos. 35v, 46r, and 69r.

CHAPTER 6. FLORENCE II

1. ACDFSO:DSO 1610–1611, fo. 71r, misdating the commissary's letter 26 April.

2. In the Val d'Elsa, about a mile from Poggibonsi. It probably belonged to the Marzi Medici family. Emanuele Repetti, *Dizionario geografico, fisico, storico della Toscana*, 6 vols. (Florence: Giovanni Mazzoni, 1846), 6, 154.

3. Annibale Giuntini–? (wrapper torn out), 22 April 1610 in BEM:RC, MS 'Y.O.4.27, fo. 116r–v.

4. BEM:RC, MS 'Y.O.4.23, fo. 107r–v/112v.

5. The *DBI* says on unknown evidence that Alidosi was innocent and that Paul V may have quashed the process.

6. BEM, Autografoteca Campori, Millini, Giovanni Garcia.

7. ACDFSO:DSO 1610–1611, fos. 75v–76r.

8. BEM:RC, MS 'Y.O.4.23, fo. 108r/111v.

9. ACDFSO:DSO 1610–1611, fo. 78v.

10. BEM, Autografoteca Campori, Millini, Giovanni Garcia. Most of Millini's letter concerns the case of the canons of Bertinoro.

11. ACDFSO:DSO 1610–1611, fo. 99r, 8 June 1610 and Millini's letter of 11 June 1610 (a Friday) in BEM:RC, MS 'Y.O.4.23, fo. 115r/122v.

12. ACDFSO:DSO 1610–1611, fo. 110r–v, 23 June responding to Montini's letter of 17 June.

13. BEM:RC, MS 'Y.O.4.23, fo. 117r–v/120r (blank), headed "a di 25 di luglio 1610," signed. For Alidosi's surprise visit, see also Mazzoni–Montini, Carseggio (?), 23 July 1610 in BEM:RC, MS 'Y.O.4.27, fos. 105r–106v.

14. BEM:RC, MS 'Y.O.4.23, fos. 118r–119r.

15. ACDFSO:DSO 1610–1611, fo. 138v.

16. ACDFSO:DSO 1608–1609, fo. 431v and 1609, p. 364, 2 September and 1609, pp. 456–57, 30 October. The charges were lodged by one Giovanni Reggiani. For the compensation claim, see 1610–1611, fo. 124r.

17. ACDFSO:DSO 1610–1611, fo. 141r, 5 August 1610.

18. Ibid., fo. 152v.

19. Ibid., fo. 165r.

20. Mazzoni–inquisitor of Romagna, Castel del Rio, 25 October 1610, headed "1610" in BEM:RC, MS 'Y.O.4.23, fo. 125r.

21. ACDFSO:DSO 1610–1611, fo. 212v.

22. Ibid., fos. 249v and 250v.

23. Ibid., fos. 249r and 250v, 26 January. The vicar may have been Lorenzo da Fogliano, O.P., appointed 7 July 1610. Ibid., fo. 120v.

24. Ibid., fos. 242v and 283v, 12 January and 22 March 1611. Montini's vicar in Imola was probably Paolo Maria Vecchi da Bologna, O.P., formerly vicar of the Holy Office in Casola (Valsenio). ACDFSO, Decreta S.O. 1608–1609, fo. 398r, 21 July 1609; and BEM:RC, MS 'Y.O.4.23, fo. 35v. It should be remembered that Millini's vicar may have been Alidosi's nephew Monsignor Baffadi. See Chapter 5.

25. ACDFSO:DSO 1610–1611, fo. 270r–v.

26. Ibid., fo. 285v, 24 March. See Chapter 1 for the trouble blank warrants caused in Naples.

27. Ibid., fo. 280v, 17 March, acting on Priatoni's letter of 8 March.

28. Ibid., fo. 296r.

29. Ibid., fo. 300r.

30. Ibid., fo. 304v.

31. Ibid., fos. 311v and 316v, 12 and 19 May 1611.

32. Ibid., fos. 322r and 325v, 31 May and 3 June 1611.

33. Ibid., fo. 322r, 31 May 1611.

34. Ibid., fo. 326r.

35. Paolo Sarpi, *Discorso dell' origine, forma, leggi, ed uso dell' ufficio dell' Inquisitione nella citta, e dominio di Venetia* (n.p., n.p., 1639), 71; Brian Pullan, *The Jews of Europe and the Inquisition of Venice, 1550–1670* (Oxford: Blackwell, 1983), 86–87; *MOPH* 10: 342–43 for his approval at Cesena by the Dominican general chapter of 1592; and ADCFSO:DSO 1597–1598–1599, p. 820, 20 October 1599.

36. ACDFSO:DSO 1603 Copia, fos. 51r, 81v–82r, 93r, 125r, 139r and 140v, 149r, 156v–157r, 173r–v, 230r, 234r.

37. ACDFSO:DSO 1610, fo. 24r. He may either have moved to Ravenna, or had his position in Forlì confused with the province in which it lay. ACDFSO:DSO 1619, p. 232.

38. ACDFSO:DSO 1610–1611, fo. 334v.

39. *Avviso* of 22 June 1611 in BAV, Urb. lat. 1079, fo. 456v. He had arrived by 18 June. Ibid., fo. 462r.

40. ACDFSO:DSO 1610–1611, fo. 344r, 30 June 1611.

41. Ibid., fo. 347r, 6 July 1611.

42. Alidosi–Emperor Rudolf, Rome, [date in gutter] 1611. BNF, MS Français, 18,006, fo. 272r–v, orig. Alidosi mentioned Mazzoni's removal as vicar and his expectation that he would leave Rome in two days.

43. An *avviso* of 13 July 1611 said he had been "spedito," but there is nothing of this in the decree registers. BAV, Urb. lat. 1079, fo. 499v.

44. ACDFSO:DSO 1610–1611, fo. 351r.

45. Ibid., fo. 368v.

46. *Avviso* of 14 August 1610 in BAV, Barb. lat. 6344, fos 126v–127r, 140r and *HC* 4: 209. Millini kept all the income save a 1000 *scudi* pension to the new holder. Nevertheless,

it was reported that Paul had given him another 1000 *scudi* to make up for the loss of the bishopric. *Avviso* of 13 July 1611 in BAV, Urb. lat. 1079, fo. 499r.

47. ACDFSO:DSO 1610–1611, fo. 368v.

48. Ibid., fo. 372v, 11 August 1611. Arrigoni's letter of 13 August to the bishop is in BEM:RC, MS 'Y.O.4.24, fo. 32r/36r, endorsed "19."

49. ACDFSO:DSO 1610–1611, fo. 381r, 25 August 1611, refusing to reinstate Mazzoni.

50. Ibid., fo. 385r, 1 September 1611.

51. Ibid., fo. 395r, 15 September 1611.

52. The decree reads "exponentis Andream Mazzonum et Annibalem a Vineis ex adita (?), quem pndans [?pendans] apud sacram congregationem velle se vendicare de Roderici Alidosio, ac petentis super hoc provideri, lecto memoriale e contra eiusdem Annibalis supplicantis causam expediri, et provideri eius damnis, et securitati, lectis memorialibus, S.mus ordinavit causam cognosci." ACDFSO:DSO 1611, p. 428.

53. ACDFSO:DSO 1610–1611, fo. 407r, 5 October.

54. Ibid., fo. 414r, 13 October 1611. I have assumed that Montini, last certainly known as in office on 31 May, remained in post for a least a while longer. Ibid., fo. 322r . There is a gap in the list of inquisitors of Romagna before Paolo Delli Franci (de Francis) was appointed in 1615. ACDFSO:DSO 1615, p. 360, and see below.

55. ACDFSO:DSO 1610–1611, fos. 422v (1611, p. 468) and 425v, 26 and 27 October 1611.

56. Ibid., fo. 428r, 2 November 1611.

57. Ibid., fo. 441r, 30 November.

58. Ibid., fo. 449v and BEM:RC, MS 'Y.O.4.23, fos. 135r–138v.

59. ACDFSO:DSO 1612, p. 28, 12 January 1612.

60. Ibid., p. 13, 4 January 1612.

61. Ibid., pp. 33, 52, 63, 85, 17 January, 1, 4 and 22 February 1612; ACDFSO:DSO 1613, p. 189, 24 April 1613.

62. ACDFSO:DSO 1612, p. 74, 15 February and ACDFSO:DSO 1613, pp. 322, 346, and 438, 10 and 18 July and 4 September 1613.

63. ACDFSO:DSO 1612, pp. 150–51, 4 April 1612.

64. Ibid., p. 64, 4 February 1612.

65. Ibid., p. 70, 9 February 1612.

66. Ibid., pp. 242 and 408, 31 May and 30 August 1612.

67. Ibid., p. 419, added at foot.

68. BEM:RC, MS 'Y.O.4.21, fos. 13r–v/18.

69. ACDFSO:DSO 1612, pp. 28–29, 12 January 1612. It took more than a year before a permanent vicar could be found, the rector of Della Vigna's old church of San Miniato. ACDFSO:DSO 1613, p. 189, 24 April 1613.

70. ACDFSO:DSO 1612, p. 191, 10 May.

71. Ibid., p. 461, 27 September.

72. ACDFSO:DSO 1613, p. 57, 30 (?) January. The entry is apparently corrupted. It has something in the middle about restoring process against somebody from Calabria.

73. Dispatch of 28 October 1613. ASV, Seg. Stato, Nunz. Firenze, 15B, fo. 338v.

74. See the nuncio's dispatches of 23 and 30 November 1615. ASV, Seg. Stato, Nunz. Firenze, 15B, fos. 533v and 543v.

75. See the letters from Paolo Delli Franci to Alidosi of 9 September and 13 December 1615. BEM:RC, MS 'Y.O.4.27, fos. 83v/88r and 95r–96v.

76. He held the post from 4 June 1612 until his death in 1621. *HC* 4: 11 and http://www.fiu.edu/~mirandas/bios1611.htm#Rivarola, accessed 6 June 2010.

77. ACDFSO, St. st. L 3-e, fo. 19r, apparently recording a decree from the coram of 14 July. The entry in the register is damaged, but it still seems not to contain this decree. Delli Franci had been inquisitor of Reggio nell'Emilia before his appointment 29 July 1615. He served just less than two years, to 26 July 1617. ACDFSO:DSO 1615, p. 360 and 1617, p. 259.

78. ASV, Arm. 36:29, fo. 77r, Rivarola–Alidosi, 3 August 1616.

79. Grand duke–Rivarola, Pratolino, 17 August 1616 in ibid., fo. 127r–v. Alidosi sent a three-person delegation to the grand duke. 11 Sept 1616 Battista Suzzi–? [probably Rivarola] in ibid., fo. 156r.

80. Letter from the secretary of the Otto di Balì dated 6 September 1616 to the vicar of Firenzuola, reiterating a letter of 1 August 1611 saying that the grand duke's officers should always take prisoners sent from Castel del Rio. BEM:RC, MS 'Y.O.4.24, fos. 27r/30v; the earlier letter is MS 'Y.O.4.24, fos. 70r/73v. There is a note of the grant of the *palio* headed 1616 in BEM:RC, MS 'Y.O.4.21, fo. 45r–v.

81. Della Vigna–[Rivarola], Faenza, 21 August 1616. ASV, Arm. 36:29, fo. 137r.

82. 27 Aug 1616 Cardinal Borghese–legate of Romagna. ASV, Arm. 36:29, fo. 5r–v.

83. ACDFSO:DSO 1616, p. 409, 5 October 1616.

84. 6 Oct 1616 Arduino Suzzi–Rivarola, Caste del Rio. ASV, Arm. 36:29, fo. 167r. See another letter of 8 October on fo. 168r–v.

85. 18 (?) November 1616 (?), Filippo Bartolini–Alidosi in Florence, Rome, marked "subito" and endorsed "Lettera del Canonico [of Florence] Bartolini circa il Santo Officio" in BEM:RC, MS 'Y.O.4.24, fos. 71r–72v.

86. It appears that Alidosi answered with his own proceedings against Luca Del Monte. See the series of interrogations in BEM:RC, MS 'Y.O.4.23, fos. 141r–144v, headed "Adi 17 Febraro 1617" and with later dates in September, no indication of where or by whom conducted, except for one apparent reference to an unidentified commissary reading a letter on fo. 144r. Del Monte's own *fede*, headed only 1617, is BEM:RC, MS 'Y.O.4.23, fos. 154r–155r.

87. ACDFSO:DSO 1617, p. 60.

88. Ibid., p. 284; and ACDFSO, St. st. L 3-e, fo. 69r first entry, 20 July 1617.

89. Ibid., p. 452–53; and ACDFSO, St. st. L 3-e, fo. 129r, 22 November 1617.

90. BEM:RC, MS 'Y.O.4.23, fo. 155v, copy with note of dispatch at foot. Zambeccari was appointed on 26 July 1617. ACDFSO:DSO 1617, p. 259. He owed the post to Scipione Borghese, whose client he had been since at least 1608, when Zambeccari sought Borghese's intercession with the provincial of Bologna after its legate had deprived Zambeccari of office. Borghese several times recommended him to Cardinal Rivarola. S. L. Forte, "I Domenicani nel carteggio del card. Scipione Borghese, protettore dell'ordine (1606–1633)"

Archivum Fratrum Praedicatorum 30 (1960): 351–416, 406 no. 97, 393 no. 19 and nos. 108 (1615) and 217–18 (1618). When the post of inquisitor of Milan came open in 1619, Zambeccari asked Borghese for it. Ibid., 410 no. 115.

91. ACDFSO:DSO 1617, p. 474; ACDFSO, St. st. L 3-e, fo. 129r.

92. ACDFSO:DSO 1618, pp. 99 and 116, 21 March and 4 April 1618.

93. ASV, Arm. 36:28, fos. 336r–337r, dated 23 January 1618, but the following wrapper says 17 August 1616; Rivarola–Borghese, Cesena, 22 February 1618 in ASV, Arm. 36:29, fo. 82r; and 12 May 1618 Annibale Della Vigna, Faenza–? ["Ill.mo et r.mo Sig.re Pron. Coll. mo"] in ASV, Arm. 36:30, fo. 133r–v.

94. Borghese–Rivarola, 19 May 1618. ASV, Arm. 36:29, fo. 13r–v.

95. Rivarola–Borghese, Ravenna, 26 May 1618. ASV, Arm. 36:29, fo. 91r–v.

96. Borghese–Rivarola, 26 May 1618. ASV, Arm. 36:29, fo. 16r–v.

97. Contelori, who was in a sense in charge of the negotiations, gave an account that survives in nine copies, plus a printed version (Rome, 1637) following one of the manuscript texts in ASV, Arm. 36:28, fos. 158r–73r, signed by him at the end. The others are Arm. 36:32, fos. 101r–228r (seven copies) and 37:14, fos. 422r–437r, signed by Contelori. A lawyer, Contelori had moved from prefect of the Vatican Library to the keepership of the Vatican archives, commissary general of the Camera Apostolica, and later secretary of the Consulta, after a stint as secretary of the Congregation *dei Confini*. Andreas Kraus, *Das päpstliche Staatssekretariat unter Urban VIII 1623–1644*, *Römischer Quartalschrift für christliche Altertumskunde and Kirchengeschichte*, Supplementheft 29 (Rome: Herder, 1964), 174–75, calling him "die wichtigste Persönlichkeit bei der Verwaltung des Kirchenstaats." His "Historia cameralis, seu de Dominio et Iurisdictione Sedis Apostolicae" is in BAV, Barb. lat. 2704–8.

98. The second breve to Rivarola ordered him "ut intimaret Roderico. . . .Quapropter Rodericus recessit a tractatu venditionis, & acquievit mandatis Sedis Apostolicae." ASV, Arm. 36:32, fo. 107r. Contelori's "Summarium" makes this "Rodericus Alidosius recessit ab alienatione Castri rivi instantibus Ministris Sedis Apostolicae sub Paulo V" (ASV, Arm. 36:32, fo. 101r) and no. 53 "Castrum non vendidit parendo mandatis Sedis Apostolicae" (36:32, fo. 113r).

99. "Tibi per praesentes iniungimus, ut eidem Roderico auctoritate nostra praecipias, et mandes sub indignatione nostrae, ac S.tae Sedis apostolicae necnon poenis in dictis [of Sixtus V and Clement VIII] constitutionibus contentis ipso facto incurrendis" not to sell without permission . . ."[d]antes tibi plenam et liberam facultatem praefatum Rodericum monendi, ac illi ut praefatur [abbrev.] praecipiendi et propter monitionis, seu praecepti affixionem ad valvas Palatii Curiae Ravennae, sive alterius loci Provinciae Romandiolae tibi benevisi, ita ut affixio monitionis seu praecepti huiusmodi eundem Rodericum arctet et afficiat proinde acsi illi personaliter intimata fuisset," any other laws of whatever kind notwithstanding. ASV, Sec. Brevi 561, fos. 31r–34v. There is a note on fo. 32r of "Un'altro breve simile a quello che fu spedito nel negocio di Castel del Rio ma sub pena ["ammissionis carcere ad favorem Camerae Apostolicae et" del.] indignacionis nostrae ac S.te Sedis Apostolicae." The record of the breves conceding Rivarola the necessary authority is tangled. Neither of those Contelori mentioned has been found, the first of which coincides with

Borghese's first order about the precept. Neither the breve of 16 June (unless the month is a mistake) nor the breve noted on ASV, Sec. Brevi 561, fo. 32r as "similar" to it can be the breve Rivarola had by 2 June. Neither is found under the dates given, but the first is supposed to be in Sec. Brevi 561; nothing was found in Sec. Brev 560, May 1618 nor in ASV, Indice 764, April–July 1618.

100. ASV, Arm. 36:30, fo. 19r.

101. Ibid., fo. 17r.

102. ASV, Arm. 36:29, fo. 22r.

103. It is not in the first edition of the *Vocabulario della Crusca* (Venice: Giovanni Alberti, 1612). There was still discussion in the nineteenth century about what the word meant and whether it belonged in an updated *Vocabulario*. Vincenzo Monti et al., *Proposta di alcune correzioni ed aggiunte al Vocabolario della Crusca*, 3:1 (Milan: Dall'Imp. Regia Stamperia, 1821), 105–6.

104. ASV, Arm. 36:29, fo. 31r. Cf. note on ASV, Sec. Brevi 561, fo. 32v.

105. ASV, Arm. 36:29, fo. 32r. It has not been found.

106. ASV, Arm. 36:30, fo. 34r.

107. ASV, Arm. 36:29, fo. 35r.

108. Della Vigna's letter is in ibid., fo. 136r; the agreements of 24 March 1619, including a resolution of a dispute over chestnuts, are in BEM:RC, MS 'Y.O.4.23, fos. 166r–167v.

109. ASV, Arm. 36:29, fo. 105r–v, copy on 49r.

110. Ibid., fo. 47r.

111. Ibid., fo. 108r, fo. 53r copy.

112. Borghese–legate of Romagna, 20 April 1619. Ibid., fo. 55r.

113. Zambeccari–?, Faenza, 24 Aug 1619, wrapper missing, endorsed "+ 17. L.re dell'Inq.re di Faenza." BEM:RC, MS 'Y.O.4.23, fo. 159r/164v.

114. ACDFSO:DSO 1619, p. 333.

115. ?Alidosi–?Millini ["del Card. Mellini" at foot fo. 171v], Florence, 22 Sept 1619. BEM:RC, MS 'Y.O.4.23, fos. 170r–171v.

116. Zambeccari–Morara, Faenza, 25 Sept 1619. BEM:RC, MS 'Y.O.4.24, fo. 151r/154v docketed as from inquisitor to Fra Ventura [Morara], note at foot of administration. In 1609 Morara had testified to Andrea Mazzoni's "malissima intentione" against Alidosi. BEM:RC, MS 'Y.O.4.24, fo. 150r/155v (blank).

117. ACDFSO:DSO 1619, p. 369.

118. Ibid., p. 394, 30 October.

119. Ibid., p. 445.

120. BEM:RC, MS 'Y.O.4.21, fos. 79r–82v. It encloses lists of eighteen replies, but they may not be related. The document may have been directed to Alidosi.

121. BEM:RC, MS 'Y.O.4.24, fo. 148r–v/143v, mounted backward, headed "+ 43. [53 and 26 del.] and endorsed "Scritto contro alli Mazzoni."

122. ASV, Arm. 36:31, fo. 155r, wrapper prob. on 165v to Rivarola, enclosing Tossani's *constitutus* on fos. 156r–165v.

123. Rivarola–Alidosi, Ravenna, 28 June 1620, endorsed "+ ii. del Card. Rivarola" in BEM:RC, MS Y.O.4.23, fo. 161r/162v.

124. See note 120 ab.

125. Requiem.

126. *DBI* and http://www.archiviodistato.firenze.it/ceramellipapiani2/index.php?page=Famiglia&id=129, accessed 25 June 2012.

127. ASV, Arm. 36:30, fo. 179r–v, 25 August 1629.

128. The inquisitor may still have been Giovanni Michele Pio da Bologna, appointed 19 January 1623. ASV, Sec. Brev. Reg. 667, fo. 2r and ACDFSO: DSO 1623, p. 30.

129. ACDFSO:DSO 1629, fos. 160r and 187r–v, 30 October 1629.

130. Giacomo Suzzi (?)–?, Castel del Rio, 28 Oct 1629 in ASV, Arm. 36:30, fo. 176r.

131. Interrogation of 17 October 1630. BEM:RC, MS Y.O.4.24, fo. 42r/45r; the next, related section says that Suzzi's deposition was sent to the inquisitor of Faenza.

132. ACDFSO:DSO 1631, fo. 52r, index entry also damaged.

133. Ibid., fo. 98r.

134. Ibid., fo. 118r.

135. Ibid., fo. 158r, 10 September.

136. Ibid., fo. 161v, 11 September.

137. Ibid., fo. 190v, 6 November.

138. Ibid., fo. 203r.

139. Ibid., fo. 212r, damaged.

140. Ibid., fo. 216v and ACDFSO:DSO 1632, fo. 2r, 18 and 30 December 1631.

141. Bolognetti had been nuncio since late summer 1630. BAV, Urb. Lat. 1100, fo. 517v.

142. Francesco Barberini–nuncio in Florence, 3 January 1632. BAV, Barb. lat. 6187, fos. 10v–11r.

143. ACDFSO:DSO 1632, fo. 6r.

144. Ibid., fo. 13v.

145. Ibid., fo. 16v. The entry is badly damaged.

146. Ibid., fos. 25v and 26r–v.

147. Ibid., fo. 26r–v. He also ordered the inquisitor of Faenza to use the president of Romagna, but for what is illegible.

148. Ibid., fo. 51v.

149. Ibid., fo. 63v, long entry badly damaged.

150. ASV, Seg. Stato, Nunz. Firenze 20, fo. 23v and BAV, Barb. lat. 7306, fo. 27v.

151. F. Barberini–Bolognetti, 24 April 1632. BAV, Barb. lat. 7310, fo. 16r.

152. ACDFSO:DSO 1632, fo. 72r, badly damaged.

153. Bolognetti–F. Barberini, 8 May 1632. BAV, Barb. lat. 7306, fo. 35r and ASV, Seg. Stato, Nunz. Firenze 20, fo. 30r–v.

154. F. Barberini–Bolognetti, 15 May 1632, cipher; BAV, Barb. lat. 7310, fo. 12r; same content in ASV, Seg. Stato, Nunz. Firenze 20, fo. 31v. The missing letter is not noted in the decree register, either.

155. Bolognetti–F. Barberini, 15 May 1632. BAV, Barb. lat. 7306, fo. 42r–v; same content in ASV, Seg. Stato, Nunz. Firenze 20, fo. 34v.

156. Bolognetti–F. Barberini, 22 May 1632. BAV, Barb. lat. 7306, fo. 45r and ASV, Seg. Stato, Nunz. Firenze 20, fo. 36r–v.

157. F. Barberini–Bolognetti, 29 May 1632. ASV, Seg. Stato, Nunz. Firenze 20, fos. 37v–38r.

158. That letter would have been ordered in the coram of 6 May, which did send instructions to Egidi, but there is nothing about a similar letter to Bolognetti. See above.

159. Bolognetti–F. Barberini, 5 June 1632. BAV, Barb. lat. 7306, fo. 58r–v; ASV, Seg. Stato, Nunz. Firenze 20, fo. 42r–v.

160. F. Barberini–Bolognetti, 12 June 1632. ASV, Seg. Stato, Nunz. Firenze 20, fo. 41v–42r.

161. Martino Tondo–?, Lugo, 12 June 1632. ASV, Arm. 36:28, fos. 50r–55v.

162. 10 July 1632, F. Barberini–Bolognetti, enciphered same day. BAV, Barb. lat. 7310, fos. 18r–19r. The previous undated minute expressed joy that a deal had been completed to get Alidosi to Rome (fo. 17r).

163. Bolognetti– F. Barberini, 17 July 1632. BAV, Barb. lat. 7306, fo. 82r; ASV, Seg. Stato, Nunz. Firenze 20, fo. 49r–v.

164. Bolognetti–F. Barberini, 28 July 1632. BAV, Barb. lat. 7306, fos. 89r–90r.

165. F. Barberini–Bolognetti, 7 August 1632, enciphered same day. BAV, Barb. lat. 7310, fos. 22r–23v.

166. Bolognetti–F. Barberini, 7 August 1632. BAV, Barb. lat. 7307, fo. 6r–v.

167. Bolognetti–F. Barberini, 17 August 1632. Ibid., fo. 9r.

168. ACDFSO:DSO 1632, fo. 128r, 19 August 1632. This man may have become a referendary in 1609, still in 1638. Weber, *Referendare*, 2, 431.

169. F. Barberini–Bolognetti, 21 August 1632. BAV, Barb. lat. 7310, fo. 25r.

170. Bolognetti–F. Barberini, 26 August 1632. BAV, Barb. lat. 7307, fo. 13r–v.

171. F. Barberini–Bolognetti, 11 September 1632. BAV, Barb. lat. 7310, fo. 31r–v.

172. Bolognetti–F. Barberini, 11 September 1632. BAV, Barb. lat. 7307, fos. 23r–24r.

173. Bolognetti–F. Barberini, 18 September 1632. Ibid., fo. 30r–v.

174. ACDFSO:DSO 1632, fo. 149r, 30 September in response to Bolognetti's letter of 21 September.

175. Ibid., fo. 146r.

176. F. Barberini–Bolognetti, 25 September 1632. BAV, Barb. lat. 7310, fo. 36r–v; apparently not enciphered until 28 September (fo. 37v [?]). The letter to Egidi is missing; the order for it may have been incorporated in the decree about Alidosi's bond, even though the register does not explicitly say that.

177. ACDFSO:DSO 1632, fo. 149r, 30 September.

178. Ibid., fo. 177r.

179. F. Barberini–Bolognetti, 4 October 1632. BAV, Barb. lat. 7310, fo. 46r.

180. Bolognetti was a lawyer, making it hard to see why he spoke of *speditione*. Weber, *Referendare*, 2, 460.

181. Bolognetti–F. Barberini, 20 November 1632. BAV, Barb. lat. 7307, fos. 67r–68r. Bolognetti was also keeping an eye on Egidi, who he reported had made "la monitione" to various theologians.

182. ACDFSO:DSO 1632, fo. 185v, 2 December in reply to Baffadi's letter of 20 (?) November.

183. Bolognetti–F. Barberini, 25 December 1632. BAV, Barb. lat. 7307, fo. 94v.

184. ACDFSO:DSO 1633, fos. 5v–6r.

185. Bolognetti–F. Barberini, 8 January 1633. BAV, Barb. lat. 7306, fo. 6r–v.

186. ACDFSO:DSO 1633, fo. 12v.

187. Bolognetti–F. Barberini, 15 January 1633, deciphered 21 January. BAV, Barb. lat. 7308, fo. 12r; short extract printed in *EN*, 15, no. 2386 from "Arch. Vaticano. Cifre di Fiorenza, l'anno 1633; n.° 21, car. 9*t*" without the Alidosi section.

188. F. Barberini–Bolognetti (BAV, Barb. lat. 7310, fo. 57r) and Bolognetti–F. Barberini (BAV, Barb. lat. 7308, fo. 18r–v), both of 22 January 1633. On 5 February Barberini praised Bolognetti's use of Galileo's example. BAV, Barb. lat. 7310, fo. 58r; excerpt printed in *EN*, 15, no. 2406 from "Arch. Vaticano. Cifre di Fiorenza, l'anno 1633; n.° 21, car. 14."

189. ACDFSO:DSO 1633, fo. 25r, 3 February in response to Egidi's of 22 January. The next entry concerns Galileo.

190. Bolognetti–F. Barberini, 5 and 9 February 1633 (BAV, Barb. lat. 7306, fos. 31r and 37r) and ACDFSO:DSO 1633, fo. 29r, 10 February, responding to Bolognetti's first dispatch.

191. ACDFSO:DSO 1633, fo. 32v, 17 February 1633. The pope renewed the decree a week later, but damage obscures his motivation. Ibid., fo. 36v, 24 February 1633.

192. Bolognetti–F. Barberini, 12 February (BAV, Barb. lat. 7306, fo. 41r); exchange with Barberini of 19 February (Bolognetti–F. Barberini and vice versa; BAV, Barb. lat. 7310, fo. 60r); and Bolognetti–F. Barberini, 1 March 1633 (BAV, Barb. lat. 7306, fo. 47r).

193. Bolognetti–F. Barberini, 12 March, 17 March, deciphered 22 March, 19 March, 22 March (BAV, Barb. lat. 7306, fos. 52r, 57r, 58r–v, 6r–v) and 24 March 1633 (BAV, Barb. lat. 7304, fo. 50r).

194. Bolognetti–F. Barberini, 2 April 1633 (BAV, Barb. lat. 7306, fo. 63r–v); ACDFSO:DSO 1633, fo. 60v, 9 April; and F. Barberini–Bolognetti of same date (BAV, Barb. lat. 7310, fo. 62r).

195. F. Barberini–Bolognetti. BAV, Barb. lat. 7310, fo. 61r, 1 April 1633.

196. BEM:RC, MS 'Y.O.4.27, fos. 3r–4r.

197. ACDFSO:DSO 1633, fo. 95r, 8 May 1633. The entry is too badly damaged to allow certainty about most of the details, but they can be reconstructed on the basis of Arduino Suzzi's letter of 29 June (see below). The name of the court in which the *processi* had been formed and by whom is also illegible, but the second may have been Luigi Pala, who appears later in the entry.

198. ACDFSO:DSO 1633, fo. 108r. It is unclear of what Pala was commissary, since it appears from Arduino Suzzi's letter of 29 June that Galeazzo Giuntini still held that office in Castel del Rio.

199. BEM:RC, MS 'Y.O.4.27, fos. 14r–15r.

200. BEM:RC, MS 'Y.O.4.24, fo. 41r/46r, copy.

201. ACDFSO:DSO 1633, fos. 120r and 121v.

202. Ibid., fos. 154r and 162v.

203. Ibid., fo. 165r. Bolognetti was to complain "de gravi praeiudicio quod S. Officium passum est ob dilatam Alidosii carcerationem, et transmissionem ad hoc S. Officio, cum interim mortui sint plures testes, qui reperi non possunt ex quorum depositionibus etiam Alidosius magis gravabatur." For some reason Bolognetti's report of having executed the order on 6 October was not heard in Congregation until 10 November. Ibid., fo. 193r.

204. BAV, Barb. lat. 6468, fo. 54r–v; partially printed in Sante Pieralisi, *Urbano VIII e Galileo Galilei* (Rome: Propaganda Fide, 1875), 185.

205. Cortini, *Castel del Rio*, 91–93. Many of the documents of the case are in ASV, Arm. 36:30.

206. BAV, Vat. lat. 10945, fo. 158v. Secretary Antonio Barberini, Sr. communicated the order the same day. Adriano Prosperi, "L'Inquisizione fiorentina al tempo di Galileo," in P. Galluzzi, ed., *Novità celesti e crisi del sapere* (Florence: Giunti Barbèra, 1984), 315–25), reprinted in Prosperi, *L'Inquisizione romana, letture e ricerche* (Rome: Edizioni di Storia e Letteratura, 2003), 183–98, 319.

207. I am grateful to Chris Black for suggesting this interpretation.

CONCLUSION

1. See Thomas F. Mayer, *Reginald Pole, Prince and Prophet* (Cambridge: Cambridge University Press, 2000), chaps. 6–8, and "The Success of Cardinal Pole's Final Legation," in Eamon Duffy and David Loades, eds., *The Church of Mary Tudor* (Aldershot: Ashgate, 2006), 149–75.

2. Henri Biaudet, *Les nonciatures apostoliques permanentes jusqu'en 1648*, in Annales Academiae Scientiarum Finnicae Ser. B, vol. 2, 1 (Helsinki, 1910).

3. *Vita dell'eminentissimo Signor Cardinale Gio. Garzia Mellino Romano. Scritta dal Sig. Decio Memmoli suo Segretario* (Rome: Giovanni Paolo Rocchetti, 1644), 15.

4. See the article "Nunziature apostoliche" in *DSI* 2: 1119–24, especially 1122 for Naples and 1121 for Venice and Florence. The article underplays the nuncio's importance in all three places, but especially the last, largely because its treatment is almost exclusively confined to the sixteenth century. Adriano Prosperi, *Tribunali della coscienza: inquisitori, confessori, missionari* (Turin: Einaudi, 1996), 103ff. emphasizes the nuncios' prominence, including their role in Florence.

5. Christopher F. Black, *The Trials and Tribulations of a Local Roman Inquisitor: Giacomo Tinti in Modena, 1626–1647* in www.giornaledistoria.net 9 (2012), accessed 15 December 2012.

6. See Prosperi, *Tribunali*, 114–15 and *RI*, 12–14.

7. *RI*, 14.

8. Berlinghiero Gessi–Borghese, 23 May 1609 in ASV:SSV, 40, fo. 162r, and Borghese–Gessi, 23 May 1609 in ASV:SSV, 39, fo. 252r–v.

9. Francesco Beretta, "Galilée devant le Tribunal de l'Inquisition" (Th.D. thesis, Universitè de Fribourg, 1997), 14–17. For examples of the bull added to a sentence, see 16 August 1606, 24 October 1618, and 13 April 1620: ACDFSO:DSO 1606–1607, fo. 144r–v; 1618, p. 384; and 1620, p. 138.

10. Luigi Tomassetti et al., eds., *Magnum Bullarium Romanum*, 24 vols. (Turin: Sebastiano Franco and Enrico Dalmazzo, 1857–1872), 7, 744–46.

11. Biblioteca del Archiginnasio, Bologna, MS B 1863 G., unfoliated, and "Anima del Sant'Offitio spirata dal Sopremo Tribunale della Sacra Congregazione raccolta dal Padre Predicatore F. Giacomo Angarano da Vicenza l'anno del Signore M.DCXLIV," BAV, Vat. lat. 10945, fo. 34r. The inquisitor of Faenza, Girolamo Zambeccari, reported in late 1618 or early 1619 that he had published the bull. ACDFSO:DSO 1619, pp. 22–32. Zambeccari was not then new in office, so it does not appear that the text was among those edicts published by entering inquisitors that had caused such trouble in the Venetian terraferma. See above, 65–66.

12. Paolo Prodi, *Il sovrano pontefice: Un corpo e due anime: la monarchia papale nella prima età moderna* (Bologna: Il Mulino, 1982), 157n61.

ABBREVIATIONS

ACDF Archivum Congregationis Doctrinae Fidei
ACDFSO Archivum Congregationis Doctrinae Fidei Sanctum Officium
ACDFSO:DSO Decreta Sancti Officii

NB In multiple citations to this source in the same note, only the year of subsequent volumes is given after the initial reference. When the year is clear from the volume number, it is not repeated in the citation.

St. st. Stanza storica
AdS Archivio di Stato

Amabile, "L'Andata di Campanella"
Luigi Amabile, "L'Andata di Fra Tommaso Campanella a Roma dopo la lunga priogona a Napoli," *Atti dell'Accademia di Scienze Morali e Politiche di Napoli*, 20, no. 8 (1886), pp. 1–51

Amabile, *Campanella nei Castelli di Napoli*
Luigi Amabile, *Frà Tommaso Campanella nei Castelli di Napoli, in Roma ed in Parigi. Narrazione con molti documenti e 10 opuscoli del Campanella inediti*, 2 vols. (Naples: Morano, 1887–1888)

Amabile, *Congiura*
Luigi Amabile, Frà Tommaso Campanella e la sua congiura, i suoi processi e la sua pazzia. Narrazione con molti documenti inediti politici e giudiziari, con l'intero processo di eresia e 67 poesie di 'Frà Tommaso' fin'oggi ignorate, 3 vols. (Naples: Morano, 1882).

Amabile, *Santo Officio*
Luigi Amabile, *Il santo officio della inquisizione in Napoli*, 2 vols. (Città Castello: S. Lapi, 1892)

Amabile, Spruit, and Preti, *Campanella*

	Luigi Amabile, Leen Spruit, and Cesare Preti, *Fra Tommaso Campanella: la sua congiura, i suoi processi e la sua pazzia*, 3 vols., Theatrum sapientiae. Essais (Paris and Turin: Les Belles lettres and Niccolò Aragno, 2006)
ASF:AMP	Archivio di Stato, Florence, Archivio Mediceo del Principato
ASMod	Archivio di Stato, Modena
ASMod:AE	ASMod, Cancelleria Ducale, Avvisi dall'Estero

NB All volumes are divided into fascicles by month; these are not indicated unless an avviso is misfiled; all are also unfoliated.

ASR	Archivio di Stato, Rome
ASV	Archivio Segreto Vaticano
Seg. Stato, Nunz.	Segretaria di Stato, Nunziatura
ASV:SSV	ASV, Seg. Stato, Venezia
ASVe	Archivio di Stato, Venice
ASVe:SDR	Archivio di Stato, Venice, Senato Dispacci Roma
Baldini and Spruit, eds., *CCMS*	
	Ugo Baldini and Leen Spruit, eds., *Catholic Church and Modern Science: Documents from the Archives of the Roman Congregations of the Holy Office and the Index*, 1, 4 parts, Fontes Archivi Sancti Officii Romani (Rome: Libreria editrice vaticana, 2009); 2 (forthcoming); the four parts of volume 1 are paginated successively
BAV	Biblioteca Apostolica Vaticana
Barb. lat.	MSS Barberiniani latini
Borg. lat.	MSS Borghesiani latini
Urb. lat.	MSS Urbinates latini
Vat. lat.	MSS Vaticani latini
BEM	Biblioteca Estense Universitaria, Modena
BEM:RC	Biblioteca Estense Universitaria, Modena, Raccolta Campori
BC	Biblioteca Casanatense, Rome
BCV	Biblioteca Correr, Venice
Cadène, "Collectio"	
	Félix Cadène, "Collectio decretorum responsorumque S. Officii," *Analecta ecclesiastica. Revue romaine* 2, 3, 4 [1894, 1895, 1896]: 318–21, 360–62, 407–12, 493–5 and 32–33, 79–82, 115–22, 167–69, 262–63, 297–302, 352–54, 457–65,

494–98 and 76–83, 123–28, 179–92, 273–77, 361–66, 421, 462–65

Carusi, "Nuovi documenti"
: E. Carusi, "Nuovi documenti sui processi di Tommaso Campanella," *Giornale critico della filosofia italiana*, 8 (1927), 321–59

DBI
: A. M. Ghisalberti, ed., *Dizionario biografico degli italiani* (Rome: Istituto dell'Enciclopedia italiana, 1960–; the Treccani website (www.trecani.it) does not produce stable URLs for its articles

DSI
: Adriano Prosperi with John Tedeschi and Vincenzo Lavenia, *Dizionario storico dell'Inquisizione*, 5 vols. (Pisa: Edizioni della Nazionale, 2010)

DV
: Sergio M. Pagano, ed., *I documenti vaticani del processo di Galileo Galilei (1611–1741). Nuova edizione accresciuta, rivista e annotata* (Città del Vaticano: Archivio Vaticano, 2009; Collectanea Archivi Vaticani 69)

EN
: Antonio Favaro, ed., *Le Opere di Galileo Galilei*, 20 volumes (Florence: G. Barberà, 1933; reprint of 1890–1909 ed.)

HC
: Patrice Gauchat, ed., *Hierarchia catholica medii et recenti oris aevi*, 4 (Münster: Regensburger Bibliothek, 1935)

ICCU
: Istituto Centrale per il Catalogo Unico, Ministero per i Beni Culturali e Ambientale; numbers refer to catalogue entries

MOPH
: Socii Instituti Historici Fratrum Praedicatorum, ed., *Monumenta Ordinis Praedicatorum Historica*, 30 vols. (Rome: Institutum historicum Ordinis fratrum praedicatorum, 1896–)

Requiem
: The database of cardinals established by Wolfgang Reinhard. The url is usually http://www2.hu-berlin.de/requiem/db/suche.php?function=b_ausgabe&grabmalID=768&PHPSESSID=bebf5bc2ee3fbbe0c54414b3fb5609fc. Searches often do not produce stable URLs. They have been given when they can be verified.

QE
: Jacques Quétif and Jacques Échard, *Scriptores ordinis praedicatorum recensiti, notisque historicis et criticis illustrati*, 2 vols. (Paris: Ballard and Simart, 1721)

RI
: Thomas F. Mayer, *The Roman Inquisition: A Papal*

Bureaucracy and Its Laws in the Age of Galileo (Philadelphia: University of Pennsylvania Press, 2013)

Spruit, "Cremonini"
Leen Spruit, "Cremonini nelle carte del Sant'Uffizio Romano," in Ezio Riondato and Antonino Poppi, eds., *Cesare Cremonini. Aspetti del pensiero e scritti*, 2 vols. (Padua: Academia Galileiana, 2000), 1, 193–204

TCC Trinity College, Cambridge

VD17 Das Verzeichnis der im deutschen Sprachraum erschienenen Drucke des 17. Jahrhunderts (www.vd17.de); this incorporates the similar catalogue for the 16th century, although it still has a portal at the Bayerische Staatsbibliothek site, http://bvba2.bib-bvb.de/V/TRTDIEX34FR2QA5FJKJ45L6XVLD1TPFU4KN3U5NEG7IEGJHBYU?func=file&file_name=search_vd16

NB: References to printed books are assumed to be to pages unless folio/s is given. References to MS sources specify page or folio.

Selected Bibliography

Manuscripts

Cambridge, Trinity College, MS R.3.42

Florence, Archivio di Santa Maria Novella, MS I.B.68

Modena, Archivio di Stato, Cancelleria Ducale

  Ambasciatori Italia Roma, 1629–32

  Avvisi dall'Estero, 134, 137, 138, 139

Modena, Biblioteca Estense e Universitaria, Raccolta Campori, MS Y.O.4.20–27; Autografoteca Campori, Millini, Giovanni Garcia

Paris

  Bibliothèque de l'Arsenale, MS 4111

  Bibliothèque Nationale de France, MS Français, 18,006

Rome, Archivum Congregationis Doctrinae Fidei Sanctum Officium, Decreta Sancti Officii, 1597–1637; Stanza storica, E 6-b, L 3-e, LL-5-g

Vatican City, Archivio Segreto Vaticano

  Arm. 36:28–30, 32, 37:14

  Fondo Borghese III 42b

  Segretaria dei brevi, Reg. 337, 395–96, 446, 560–61, 595, 667, 754, 789, 941, 948

  Segretaria di Stato, Venezia, 38–41; Nunz. Firenze, 14, 14A, 15B, 20

Vatican City, Biblioteca Apostolica Vaticana: MSS

  Barberiniani latini 1369, 6187, 6273, 6298, 6344, 6468, 7304, 7306–8, 7310

  Urbinates latini 1079, 1100

  Vaticani latini 10945

Venice, Archivio di Stato

  Consiglio dei Dieci, Parti Roma, registro 1607

  Collegio, Esposizioni Roma, registro 16

  Sant'Ufficio, b. 82, 153a

  Senato Dispacci Roma, 58–60, 62, 67–72, 74, 87, 96–100, 102–7

Venice, Biblioteca Correr, MS Cicogna 1382; Correr 1051

Primary Sources

Baldini, Ugo, and Leen Spruit, eds. *Catholic Church and Modern Science: Documents from the Archives of the Roman Congregations of the Holy Office and the Index*, 1, 4 parts. Fontes Archivi Sancti Officii Romani. Rome: Libreria Editrice Vaticana, 2009; 2 (forthcoming).

Barozzi, Nicolò, and Guglielmo Berchet. *Relazioni degli stati europei lette al Senato dagli ambasciatori veneti, ser. 3, Italia; Relazioni di Roma*. Venice: Naratovich, 1877, 3:1 and 2.

Cadène, Félix. "Collectio decretorum responsorumque S. Officii." *Analecta ecclesiastica: Revue romaine* 2, 3, 4 [1894, 1895, 1896]: 318–21, 360–62, 407–12, 493–95; 32–33, 79–82, 115–22, 167–69, 262–63, 297–302, 352–54, 457–65, 494–98; 76–83, 123–28, 179–92, 273–77, 361–66, 421, 462–65.

Capello, Marcantonio. *Risposta del P. maestro Marc'Antonio Capello . . . al discorso del P. M. Lelio piacentino . . . & inquisitor di Fiorenza, sopra i fondamenti, & le ragioni delli ss. venitiani intorno all'Interdetto & censure della santita di papa Paolo quinto*. Venice: Alessandro Cavalcalupo, 1606.

Carusi, E. "Nuovi documenti sui processi di Tommaso Campanella." *Giornale critico della filosofia italiana* 8 (1927): 321–59.

Cicogna, Emmanuele Antonio. *Delle inscrizioni veneziane*, 8 vols. Venice: Orlandelli, 1824–53.

Cornet, Enrico, ed. *La repubblica veneta. Giornale dal 22. ottobre 16–9. giugno 1607*. Vienna: Tendler, 1859.

Eudaemon-Johannes, Andreas. "Epistola, quam de relapsu ac morte poenaque M. Antonii de Dominis Ingolstadium [narrat]" in Georg Stenghel, *Libri duo de duobus apostatis sive duae paraeneses . . .* Ingolstadt: Gregor Hänlin, 1627 .

Firpo, Luigi. *Il processo di Giordano Bruno*, ed. Diego Quaglioni. Rome: Salerno, 1993.

Forte, S. L. "I Domenicani nel carteggio del card. Scipione Borghese, protettore dell'ordine (1606–1633)." *Archivum Fratrum Praedicatorum* 30 (1960): 351–416.

Gauchat, Patrice, ed. *Hierarchia catholica medii et recentioris aevi*, 4 vols., 4. Münster: Regensburger Bibliothek, 1935.

Gibbings, Richard. *Were "Heretics" ever burned alive at Rome? A report of the proceedings in the Roman Inquisition against Fulgentio Manfredi. Taken from the original manuscript brought from Italy by a French officer, and edited, with a parallel English version and illustrative additions*. London: Petheram, 1852; Dublin: University Press, 1853.

Goldast, Melchior, ed. *Monarchia S. Romani Imperii*, 3 vols. Frankfurt: Conrad Biermann, 1611–1614.

Ljubich, Sime. "Prilozi za zivotopis Martkantuna de Dominisa Rabljanina spljetskoga nadbiskupa." *Starine na sviet izdaje jugoslavenska akademija znanosti i umjetnosti* 2 (1870): 1–260.

Manfredi, Fulgenzio, et al. *Theologorum Venetorum Joan. Marsilii, Pauli Veneti, Fr. Fulgentii ad excommunicationis, citationis et monitionis Romanae sententiam in ipsos latam Responsio* in Paolo Sarpi, *Opere del padre Paolo*, 1, separately paginated.

Medici, Lelio. *Discorso . . . sopra i fondamenti, e le ragioni delli ss. veneziani, per le quali pensano di essere scusati della disubbidienza, che fanno alle censure, & interdetto della Santita di Nostro Signor Papa Paolo quinto.* Bologna: Giovanni Battista Bellagamba, 1606.

Pagano, Sergio M., ed. *I documenti vaticani del processo di Galileo Galilei (1611–1741).* 2nd ed. Collectanea Archivi Vaticani 69. Vatican City: Archivio Vaticano, 2009.

Poppi, Antonino. *Cremonini, Galilei e gli Inquisitori del Santo a Padova.* Padua: Centro Studi Antoniani, 1993.

Quétif, Jacques, and Jacques Échard. *Scriptores ordinis praedicatorum recensiti, notisque historicis et criticis illustrati.* 2 vols. Paris: Ballard and Simart, 1721.

Sarpi, Paolo. *Discorso dell'origine, forma, leggi, ed uso dell'Ufficio dell'inquisitione nella città, e dominio di venetia.* N.p.: N.p., 1638.

———. *Opere del Padre Paolo dell'ordine de' Servi.* 5 vols. Venice: Roberto Meietti, 1677.

Scaramella, Pierroberto. *Le lettere della Congregazione del Sant'Ufficio ai tribunali di fede di Napoli 1563–1625.* Trieste: Edizioni Università di Trieste, 2001.

Spampanato, Vincenzo. "Nuovi documenti intorno a negozii e processi dell'Inquisizione (1603–1624)." *Giornale critico della filosofia italiana* 5 (1924): 97–137.

Spruit, Leen. "Cremonini nelle carte del Sant'Uffizio romano." In *Cesare Cremonini: Aspetti del pensiero e scritti,* ed. E. Riondato and Antonino Poppi. Padua: Academia Galileiana, 2000. 193–204.

van Meerbeeck, Lucienne, ed. *Correspondance des nonces Gesualdo, Morra, Sanseverino avec la Secrétairerie d'État pontificale (1615–1621),* Analecta Vaticano-Belgica, ser. 2, Nonciature de Flandre. Brussels: Institut Historique Belge, 1937.

Vedova, Giuseppe. *Biografia degli scrittori padovani,* 2 vols. Padua: Minerva, 1831–36.

Secondary Sources

Amabile, Luigi. "L'Andata di Fra Tommaso Campanella a Roma dopo la lunga priogiona a Napoli." *Atti dell'Accademia di Scienze Morali e Politiche di Napoli* 20, 8 (1886): 1–51.

———. *Frà Tommaso Campanella nei Castelli di Napoli, in Roma ed in Parigi. Narrazione con molti documenti e 10 opuscoli del Campanella inediti.* 2 vols. Naples: Morano, 1887–1888.

———. *Frà Tommaso Campanella e la sua congiura, i suoi processi e la sua pazzia. Narrazione con molti documenti inediti politici e giudiziari, con l'intero processo di eresia e 67 poesie di 'Frà Tommaso' fin'oggi ignorate.* 3 vols. Naples: Morano, 1882.

———. *Il santo officio della inquisizione in Napoli,* 2 vols. Città Castello: S. Lapi, 1892.

Amabile, Luigi, Leen Spruit, and Cesare Preti. *Fra Tommaso Campanella: la sua congiura, i suoi processi e la sua pazzia.* 3 vols. Theatrum sapientiae, Essais. Paris and Turin: Belles lettres and Niccolò Aragno, 2006.

Benzoni, Gino. "I 'teologi' minori dell'interdetto." *Archivio Veneto* 101, 5th ser. 126 (1970): 31–108.

Beretta, Francesco. "Galilée devant le Tribunal de l'inquisition." Th.D. thesis, Universitè de Fribourg, 1997.

———. "Giordano Bruno e l'Inquisizione romana: Considerazioni sul processo." *Bruniana & Campanelliana* 7 (2001): 15–49.

Bianchi-Giovini, Aurelio. *Biografia di Frà Paolo Sarpi: teologo e consultore di stato della repubblica Veneta.* 2nd ed. Basel: D.G. Bellini, 1847.

Black, Christopher F. *The Italian Inquisition.* New Haven, Conn.: Yale University Press, 2009.

Bouwsma, William J. *Venice and the Defense of Republican Liberty: Renaissance Values in the Age of the Counter Reformation.* Berkeley: University of California Press, 1968.

Cornet, Enrico. *Paolo V e la Republica Veneta.* Venice: Marco Visentini, 1873.

De Rubertis, Achille. *Ferdinando I de' Medici e la contesa fra Paolo V e la Repubblica veneta.* Reale Deputazione di Storia Patria per le Venezie: Miscellanea di studi e memorie 2. Venice: Reale Deputazione Editrice, 1933.

Del Col, Andrea. *L'inquisizione in Italia.* Milan: Mondadori, 2006.

Ghisalberti, A. M., ed. *Dizionario biografico degli italiani.* Rome: Istituto dell'Enciclopedia Italiana, 1960–.

Kraus, Andreas. *Das päpstliche Staatssekretariat unter Urban VIII 1623–1644.* Römischer Quartalschrift für christliche Altertumskunde and Kirchengeschichte Supplementheft 29. Rome: Herder, 1964.

Mayaud, Pierre-Noël. "Les 'Fuit congregatio sancti officii in . . . coram . . . ' de 1611 à 1642: 32 ans de vie de la Congrégation du Saint Office." *Archivum historiae pontificiae* 30 (1992): 231–89.

Mayer, Thomas F. *Reginald Pole, Prince and Prophet.* Cambridge: Cambridge University Press, 2000.

———. *The Roman Inquisition: A Papal Bureaucracy and Its Laws in the Age of Galileo.* Philadelphia: University of Pennsylvania Press, 2013.

———. "The Success of Cardinal Pole's Final Legation." In *The Church of Mary Tudor*, ed. Eamon Duffy and David Loades. Aldershot: Ashgate, 2006. 149–75.

Müller, Karl. "Einige Aktenstücke und Schriften zur Geschichte der Streitigkeiten unter den Minoriten in der ersten Hälfte des 14. Jahrhunderts." *Zeitschrift für Kirchengeschichte* 6 (1884): 63–112.

Patterson, W. Brown. *King James VI and I and the Reunion of Christendom.* Cambridge: Cambridge University Press, 1997.

Prosperi, Adriano. *Tribunali della coscienza: Inquisitori, confessori, missionari.* Turin: Einaudi, 1996.

Prosperi, Adriano with John Tedeschi and Vincenzo Lavenia, eds. *Dizionario storico dell'Inquisizione.* 5 vols. Pisa: Edizioni della Nazionale, 2010.

Savio, Pietro. "Il nunzio a Venezia dopo l'interdetto." *Archivio veneto* 85 (1955): 55–110.

Spampanato, Vincenzo. *Vita di Giordano Bruno.* Studi filosofici, ed. Giovanni Gentile, 10. Messina: Principato, 1921.

Vezzosi, Antonio Francesco. *I scrittori de' cherici regolari.* Rome: Propaganda Fide, 1780.

INDEX

ACKNOWLEDGMENTS

I have written this book in steadily deteriorating health. The support of an army of friends has greatly lightened the consequences. I would try to name all the names, but I would fear to leave someone out. A generic and heartfelt thanks will have to do, except for a couple of especially supportive people, including Ken Bartlett, Massimo Firpo, Andy Kelly, and Diana Robin together with the members of my department who have chipped in everything from food supply to shoveling sidewalks, as well as several administrators at Augustana, especially Dean Pareena Lawrence and Laura Ford, Director of Human Resources. My wife Jan Popehn and daughter Molly Mayer-Popehn have been absolute rocks.

Since the research for this book was done at the same time as that for *Roman Inquisition* I, I can save a little space by referring to its Acknowledgments and repeating my thanks to the people and institutions named there. I am very glad to be able to acknowledge the then anonymous readers for Penn, Chris Black and Andy Kelly, who gave me enormously helpful commentary, and also with uncommon generosity read the page proofs twice. One other person not named there made a major contribution to this book. Leen Spruit with mind-boggling generosity sent me advance copies of all the documents about Tommaso Campanella he and Ugo Baldini found in the ACDFSO, only a few of which have now appeared in the sixteenth-century volume of *Catholic Church and Modern Science*. Anne Jacobson Schutte helped in a similar way by sending a Xerox of a rare pamphlet about Marcantonio De Dominis.

I dedicate this book to the memory of my parents, Arline E. Knepper Mayer and Herbert T. Mayer.